Hands-On MySQL Administration
Managing MySQL on Premises and in the Cloud

Arunjith Aravindan and Jeyaram Ayyalusamy

Beijing · Boston · Farnham · Sebastopol · Tokyo

Hands-On MySQL Administration

by Arunjith Aravindan and Jeyaram Ayyalusamy

Published by O'Reilly Media, Inc., 1005 Gravenstein Highway North, Sebastopol, CA 95472.

O'Reilly books may be purchased for educational, business, or sales promotional use. Online editions are also available for most titles (*http://oreilly.com*). For more information, contact our corporate/institutional sales department: 800-998-9938 or *corporate@oreilly.com*.

Acquisitions Editor: Andy Kwan
Development Editor: Angela Rufino
Production Editor: Katherine Tozer
Copyeditor: Sharon Wilkey
Proofreader: Dwight Ramsey

Indexer: Judith McConville
Interior Designer: David Futato
Cover Designer: Karen Montgomery
Illustrator: Kate Dullea

July 2024:   First Edition

Revision History for the First Edition
2024-06-28:   First Release

See *http://oreilly.com/catalog/errata.csp?isbn=9781098155896* for release details.

978-1-098-15589-6

[LSI]

Table of Contents

Preface

Why We Wrote This Book

The motivation behind crafting *Hands-On MySQL Administration* stems from recognizing a growing need within the diverse community of individuals involved in database management. MySQL, the second most popular database management system globally and widely adopted by major corporations like Google, Facebook, and LinkedIn, has become an indispensable skill for IT professionals.

As the demand for MySQL continues to rise, a gap has become evident in comprehensive resources tailored to both beginners and intermediate- to advanced-level professionals. This book aims to address this gap by offering valuable insights, practical tips, and in-depth guidance on efficiently managing MySQL databases on premises and in the cloud.

The primary objective is to cater to a wide audience, including database administrators (DBAs), developers, and IT professionals, who aspire to effectively manage, administer, and optimize MySQL databases. The book serves as a resource for individuals looking to enhance their skills in database administration, offering practical solutions for optimizing performance, addressing common issues, and learning new techniques.

Furthermore, we recognize the diverse needs of professionals in the field. *Hands-On MySQL Administration* is not only a comprehensive guide for daily tasks but also a valuable tool for continuous learning and mastery of new concepts. DBAs can leverage this book to fine-tune their databases, while developers can gain insights into designing efficient database schemas and optimizing queries. IT professionals, aiming to stay abreast of the latest trends and best practices in database administration, can rely on this book to enhance their skills and contribute to the success of their organizations in an ever-evolving technological landscape.

Who This Book Is For

Hands-On MySQL Administration is designed for a diverse audience seeking to acquire expertise in efficiently managing MySQL both on premises and in the cloud. The book provides valuable insights and practical tips on how to effectively optimize and manage MySQL databases. The content is tailored to beginners, as well as intermediate- to advanced-level professionals who already have a fundamental knowledge of database administration and aim to enhance their skills in MySQL. The primary audience for this book includes DBAs, developers, and IT professionals looking to manage, administer, and optimize MySQL databases efficiently.

The book can be used as a reference for daily tasks as well as for learning and mastering new concepts. DBAs can use the book to optimize the performance of their databases, identify and solve common issues, and learn new techniques for managing MySQL databases. Developers can also use the book to create efficient and scalable applications by learning how to design database schema and optimize queries. IT professionals can use the book to enhance their skills and keep up with the latest trends and best practices in database administration.

By the End of This Book, You Will Understand

By the end of this book, you will gain a comprehensive understanding of MySQL 8 database administration. This knowledge encompasses fundamental aspects, including the installation and configuration of the software, user account management, and optimization of database performance. The book also delves into advanced topics such as backup and recovery strategies, security measures, and high-availability solutions within the context of MySQL 8 administration. Additionally, you will learn how to design and implement a scalable and reliable database infrastructure using MySQL 8, incorporating best practices for database schema design, indexing strategies, and replication techniques. The exploration extends to the utilization of MySQL in the cloud, covering platforms like Amazon Relational Database Service (RDS), Amazon Aurora, and Microsoft Azure Database for MySQL.

How This Book Is Organized

The book is organized into 13 chapters, each focusing on different aspects of MySQL. We start with an introduction to MySQL 8, discussing its editions and significant updates. Following that, there's a chapter on installing and configuring MySQL server, covering both Windows and Linux platforms. Subsequent chapters delve into topics like the transactional data dictionary (TDD) and InnoDB architecture, backup and recovery, MySQL security, replication, high availability (HA), scalability, performance tuning, monitoring, major upgrades, and deploying MySQL on various cloud platforms such as Amazon RDS, Amazon Aurora, and Microsoft Azure Database for

MySQL. Each chapter provides detailed insights, procedures, and best practices relevant to its topic, aimed at empowering users with a comprehensive understanding of MySQL and its management across various scenarios and environments:

Chapter 1, "Introduction to MySQL 8"

This chapter introduces MySQL 8, offering insights into its Community Edition, Enterprise Edition, and Percona Server for MySQL. It explores the MySQL configuration file and highlights significant updates in version 8. The comprehensive overview covers key aspects, paving the way for a deeper understanding of MySQL 8.

Chapter 2, "Installing and Configuring MySQL Server"

This chapter guides you through installing and configuring MySQL server on both Windows and Linux platforms. It also explores the installation of Percona Server for MySQL 8, emphasizing repository setup and service initialization. Post-installation, you'll delve into server configuration tasks, including character set and collation settings, maximum packet size, and logfile configurations. The removal of the query cache size in MySQL 8 is discussed, and security measures such as changing the default root password and restricting remote access are covered. Monitoring and troubleshooting MySQL server, including scenarios like connection errors and performance issues, are explored. The chapter concludes by addressing system resource checks for MySQL hosts.

Chapter 3, "Transactional Data Dictionary and InnoDB Architecture"

This chapter explores the TDD and InnoDB architecture in MySQL. It begins by explaining the role of the TDD in storing information about database objects and outlines the directory structure of the MySQL data directory. The focus then shifts to optimizing database performance with various InnoDB features such as the buffer pool, change buffer, adaptive hash index, and redo log buffer. The chapter reveals the on-disk structures of InnoDB, covering tables, indexes, tablespaces, doublewrite buffer, redo log, and undo logs. It guides you through the creation of InnoDB tables, importing external tables, and converting MyISAM tables to InnoDB.

The chapter delves into the InnoDB locking and transaction model, addressing topics such as locking reads, hot rows, and configuration settings. It concludes with a guide to InnoDB configuration, covering startup, read-only operation, thread concurrency, I/O threads, and asynchronous I/O on Linux. The concept of persisting global system variables and a summary of MySQL 8 persisted system variables wrap up the chapter.

Chapter 4, "Backup and Recovery"

This chapter delves into the critical aspects of backup and recovery in MySQL. It starts by outlining the factors to consider when selecting a backup strategy and highlights the differences between logical and physical backups. The discussion then unfolds around physical backups, covering the restoration process and how to prepare incremental backups. A thorough exploration of logical backups follows, including setting up backup schedules, selecting options, and monitoring the backup process. The chapter details the setup of the restore environment and introduces point-in-time recovery, instance-level recovery, and table-level recovery.

Managing binary logs is discussed, encompassing enabling, configuring, and purging them. Best practices are emphasized, advocating the use of encryption to safeguard backups. The chapter concludes with insights into XtraBackup encryption, decryption processes, `mysqldump` encryption, and a summary of key considerations for effective backup and recovery strategies.

Chapter 5, "MySQL Security"

This chapter covers MySQL security, addressing various aspects crucial for safeguarding databases. It begins by outlining types of security threats, emphasizing the paramount importance of security. Authentication and authorization mechanisms are explored, covering various authentication types and the creation of secure passwords by using tools like DNF and pwgen. The chapter also covers MySQL authorization, discussing user privileges, permissions, and authentication plug-ins. Ensuring secure communication is highlighted through SSL/TLS encryption, firewall rules, and user account locking. Managing MySQL roles is explained, including their creation, assignment to users, and best practices. The chapter extends its focus to securing MySQL replication, offering suggestions and best practices. MySQL security auditing is also covered, providing insights into monitoring and maintaining a secure MySQL environment.

Chapter 6, "MySQL Replication"

This chapter explores MySQL replication, beginning with an explanation of how it works. It covers the essential steps for setting up MySQL replication, including prerequisites and replication types such as source-replica, group replication, and GTID replication. The configuration process is detailed for each type, using methods like XtraBackup, backup from a replica, and the clone plug-in. The chapter delves into monitoring replication status, offering insights into MySQL commands, third-party tools, and setting up alerts for status changes. Troubleshooting replication issues such as debugging using MySQL logs, resolving conflicts, and managing replication lag is addressed. The chapter concludes by introducing tools for monitoring and managing MySQL replication.

Chapter 7, "High Availability and Scalability"

This chapter explores HA and scalability in MySQL. It begins with an overview of HA and scalability concepts, followed by a discussion on topology management using Orchestrator. The installation and configuration of Orchestrator are detailed, with insights into starting Orchestrator, checking topology, relocating replica nodes, and executing graceful failovers. The chapter then delves into clustering options, including Percona XtraDB Cluster (PXC), MariaDB Galera Cluster, and InnoDB Cluster. The clustering process is explained, along with the configuration of PXC and MariaDB Galera Cluster. The discussion extends to load balancers, ProxySQL installation, monitoring MySQL, health checks, and query performance statistics. Sysbench usage with MySQL 8 is covered, including prerequisites, installation, and performance evaluation. MariaDB Galera Cluster setup is detailed, encompassing package installation, repository addition, server installation, and cluster configuration. The chapter concludes with the installation and deployment of a MySQL 8 InnoDB Cluster, setting up MySQL Router, monitoring cluster status, and troubleshooting issues.

Chapter 8, "MySQL Performance Tuning"

This chapter provides a deep dive into key concepts and strategies of MySQL performance tuning. It begins with the fundamentals, considering hardware resources such as CPU configuration, memory configuration, and disk I/O configuration. The role of database design, including table structure, indexing, and query optimization, is explored in detail. Network latency and workload considerations are discussed, with a spotlight on tools like `pt-query-digest` for query analysis. The chapter further unravels the MySQL query execution process and emphasizes the importance of tuning the InnoDB buffer pool, covering configuration, size adjustments, and monitoring. InnoDB thread concurrency is examined, and the use of MySQL performance schema for identifying and addressing performance issues is detailed.

Chapter 9, "MySQL Monitoring and Management"

This chapter underscores the significance of MySQL monitoring and management for ensuring peak performance and security. It introduces key performance indicators (KPIs) and explores the essential role of monitoring in both performance optimization and security enhancement, along with its contribution to capacity planning. The chapter provides a concise overview of MySQL management tasks, covering the installation and configuration of tools such as Percona Monitoring and Management (PMM) Server, PMM Client, MySQL Enterprise Monitor, and MySQL Workbench. It emphasizes efficient backup and recovery solutions, performance diagnosis tools, and database management within MySQL Workbench. The chapter also introduces basic MySQL command-line tools, their usage, and insights into managing MySQL logs.

Chapter 10, "How to Facilitate Major MySQL Upgrades"

This chapter provides guidance on facilitating major MySQL upgrades, ensuring a smooth transition without compromising data integrity or performance. The process involves server-side testing using the MySQL Shell upgrade checker and application-side query testing using the `pt-upgrade` tool. The chapter outlines the requirements and steps for testing application queries, presenting a high-level plan for `pt-upgrade` testing. It covers both read-only and read/write tests with the `pt-upgrade` tool. The chapter concludes by detailing two major production upgrade strategies: in-place upgrade (async) and standing up a new environment with cutover. The insights provided aim to empower users to execute major MySQL upgrades with confidence and efficiency.

Chapter 11, "MySQL on the Cloud: Amazon RDS"

This chapter covers deploying and managing MySQL on the Amazon Relational Database Service (RDS) platform. It begins with an overview of Amazon RDS MySQL architecture, storage options, and replication, highlighting the benefits such as simplified management, scalability, and enhanced security. The chapter then outlines the steps for creating an RDS MySQL instance, covering instance class and storage type selection, VPC and security group setup, and configuration of advanced settings. It details connecting to RDS MySQL, user management, and optimal performance configurations. The chapter also addresses backup and restore procedures, scaling options, and monitoring using Amazon CloudWatch metrics and alarms. Cost optimization best practices, including right-sizing instances and utilizing reserved capacity, are discussed. The chapter concludes with insights into troubleshooting, performance analysis using Performance Insights, and efficient database backups. The comprehensive guide aims to empower users to effectively leverage MySQL on RDS for optimal performance, security, and cost efficiency.

Chapter 12, "MySQL on the Cloud: Amazon Aurora"

This chapter is a comprehensive guide to deploying and managing MySQL on Aurora, focusing on key features, benefits, and best practices. It covers the storage architecture, use cases, and step-by-step process of creating an Aurora MySQL DB cluster. The chapter details configurations, including Identity and Access Management (IAM) roles, automatic backups, and monitoring setup, along with connecting to the Aurora MySQL database. Performance optimization, query and index optimization, and the use of Amazon RDS Performance Insights are discussed. The chapter explores autoscaling, caching strategies, and monitoring and troubleshooting techniques, including setting up CloudWatch alarms and analyzing slow query logs. HA and failover strategies, backup and recovery processes, and security and compliance best practices are thoroughly examined. The chapter concludes with insights into cost optimization, resource management, and the integration of Amazon Aurora MySQL with other AWS services for enhanced functionality. The comprehensive guide aims to empower users in effectively leveraging MySQL on Aurora while adhering to best practices across various aspects of deployment and management.

Chapter 13, "MySQL on the Cloud: Azure Database for MySQL"

This chapter provides a comprehensive guide to utilizing MySQL on Microsoft Azure, specifically focusing on Azure Database for MySQL. It begins with choosing the right MySQL option, understanding supported versions, and creating an Azure free account. The chapter then delves into securing MySQL instances on Azure's Flexible Server and managing read replicas via the Azure portal. Practical insights are provided on launching Cloud Shell, selecting the shell environment, and registering subscriptions. The chapter also covers server creation using the CLI and explores migrations, including creating and configuring a target Flexible Server and implementing best practices for a successful migration. The migration process is detailed, encompassing source and target settings, database selection, monitoring, and post-migration activities. The chapter concludes with guidelines on migrating large databases to Azure Database for MySQL.

Conventions Used in This Book

The following typographical conventions are used in this book:

Italic

Indicates new terms, URLs, email addresses, filenames, and file extensions.

`Constant width`

Used for program listings, as well as within paragraphs to refer to program elements such as variable or function names, databases, data types, environment variables, statements, and keywords.

`Constant width bold`

Shows commands or other text that should be typed literally by the user.

`Constant width italic`

Shows text that should be replaced with user-supplied values or by values determined by context.

This element signifies a tip or suggestion.

This element signifies a general note.

This element indicates a warning or caution.

O'Reilly Online Learning

 For more than 40 years, *O'Reilly Media* has provided technology and business training, knowledge, and insight to help companies succeed.

Our unique network of experts and innovators share their knowledge and expertise through books, articles, and our online learning platform. O'Reilly's online learning platform gives you on-demand access to live training courses, in-depth learning paths, interactive coding environments, and a vast collection of text and video from O'Reilly and 200+ other publishers. For more information, visit *https://oreilly.com*.

How to Contact Us

Please address comments and questions concerning this book to the publisher:

> O'Reilly Media, Inc.
> 1005 Gravenstein Highway North
> Sebastopol, CA 95472
> 800-889-8969 (in the United States or Canada)
> 707-827-7019 (international or local)
> 707-829-0104 (fax)
> *support@oreilly.com*
> *https://www.oreilly.com/about/contact.html*

We have a web page for this book, where we list errata, examples, and any additional information. You can access this page at *https://oreil.ly/handson-mysql-admin*.

For news and information about our books and courses, visit *https://oreilly.com*.

Find us on LinkedIn: *https://linkedin.com/company/oreilly-media*.

Watch us on YouTube: *https://youtube.com/oreillymedia*.

Acknowledgments

We express our sincere gratitude to all those who played a pivotal role in bringing this project to fruition. A heartfelt thank you extends to everyone who contributed, and we would like to extend a special appreciation to the following individuals.

First and foremost, we want to express our deep appreciation to everyone at O'Reilly. Your support and collaboration throughout the entire life cycle of this book have been nothing short of fantastic. It's been a pleasure working with such a dedicated team.

A special note of gratitude goes to our editors, Katherine Tozer, Angela Rufino, Andy Kwan, and Theresa Jones. Your guidance, attention to detail, and commitment to excellence have truly enhanced the quality of this work. We couldn't have asked for better partners in this endeavor.

We are immensely grateful for the valuable feedback provided by Peter Boros, Frederic Descamps, Colin Charles, Trevoir Williams, Andres Sacco, John David Duncan, Doron Beit-Halahmi, and Marco Ippolito. Your insights, suggestions, and meticulous reviews have significantly enriched the content of this book. Your dedication to ensuring the accuracy and clarity of the material is genuinely appreciated.

A special mention goes to Sveta Smirnova for referring us to O'Reilly for the opportunity to write this book. Your recommendation played a crucial role in making this project a reality, and we are grateful for your support.

Once again, thank you to everyone involved for your unwavering support, valuable contributions, and collaborative spirit. This book would not have been possible without each of you.

Additional Acknowledgments from Arunjith Aravindan

To my dearest wife, Leshma KK, your unwavering support and love have been my anchor through the highs and lows of this creative journey. Thank you for being my inspiration and my sanctuary.

To my beloved son, Ashutosh Arunjith, in your laughter, I find joy, and in your dreams, I see a bright future with possibilities. May you always reach for the stars and know that you are cherished beyond measure.

To my professional family at Percona, the collective passion, dedication, and collaborative spirit within our organization have fueled my ambitions and shaped this narrative. Together, we strive for excellence, and I am grateful for the shared journey. This book is a reflection of the love, support, and teamwork that surrounds me daily. Thank you for being a vital part of my life story.

Additional Acknowledgments from Jeyaram Ayyalusamy

To the guiding light of my life, my mother, Subbulakshmi, your wisdom, strength, and unconditional love have been the pillars upon which my dreams stand. This book is a testament to the values you instilled in me and the endless support you continue to provide.

To my loving wife, Chandra Jeyaram, in the symphony of life, your love is the sweetest melody. Your encouragement and understanding have been the fuel for my creative endeavors. This book is as much yours as it is mine.

To my lovable boy Viswath, my beautiful daughters, Advika Jeyaram and Anvika Jeyaram, in your innocence, I find inspiration. May your futures be filled with endless possibilities, and may this book serve as a reminder of the dreams and aspirations we share as a family.

To my professional family at Doyensys, together we've navigated challenges and celebrated victories. Your dedication and passion have shaped not just the work we do but also the person I am. This book is a collective achievement, and I am grateful for the support and camaraderie within our organization. This journey, both personal and professional, is enriched by the love and support of each one of you.

## CHAPTER 1

Introduction to MySQL 8

MySQL is a highly popular and widely used open source relational database management system. It offers various editions and versions tailored to meet the diverse needs of users. In this book, we extensively discuss the various MySQL editions and versions, providing comprehensive insights into their features and capabilities. Throughout this book, we will enable you to make informed decisions based on your specific project requirements and database management needs.

In this chapter, you will learn about the many versions and editions of MySQL, including the Community Edition, Enterprise Edition, and Percona Server. You'll learn about each edition's features and capabilities, such as platform support, storage engines, performance, scalability, manageability, and security. Furthermore, you'll learn about the MySQL configuration file *my.cnf* and its importance in optimizing server behavior. Ultimately, you will be equipped to make informed decisions about selecting the most suitable MySQL version based on your specific needs, budget, and technical requirements.

Community Edition

The *Community Edition* uses the GNU General Public License (GPL), which allows the user to access and modify the source code. It is the most popular edition of MySQL and is widely used in various applications, including web development, ecommerce, and data analysis. The Community Edition is suitable for small to medium-sized applications that do not require advanced features and support or for large-scale applications with a very skilled database administrator (DBA) team.

Key features of the Community Edition include the following:

- Support is provided for multiple platforms, including Windows, Linux, and macOS. Additionally, you can use it in an agnostic way with Docker.
- Support for multiple storage engines, including InnoDB and memory.
- High performance, scalability, and reliability.
- Easy to use and maintain.
- Support for various programming languages, including Java, PHP, and Python.

Enterprise Edition

The MySQL *Enterprise Edition* encompasses an extensive array of advanced features, management tools, and technical support, enabling the attainment of highest levels of MySQL scalability, security, reliability, and uptime. This edition minimizes the risks, costs, and complexities associated with the development, deployment, and management of business-critical MySQL applications.

Key features of the Enterprise Edition include the following:

- Enterprise-level security, including encryption, firewall, and auditing
- Advanced backup and recovery options
- 24/7 support from MySQL experts
- Thread pool, Active Directory integration, audit
- Advanced monitoring and management tools

To compare editions, visit the MySQL website (*https://oreil.ly/wS1Tp*). Commercial customers enjoy the flexibility of selecting from various editions customized to meet specific business and technical requirements.

Percona Server for MySQL

Percona Server for MySQL is a fork of the popular open source relational database management system (RDBMS), MySQL. It is developed and maintained by Percona (*https://oreil.ly/cgFay*), a leading provider of MySQL, MongoDB, and PostgreSQL solutions, services, and support.

Percona Server for MySQL is a drop-in replacement for MySQL Community Edition and is a production-ready open source solution with enterprise-grade features. Users can harness additional functionalities, including robust security measures, comprehensive monitoring and management tools, efficient backup mechanisms, and reliable high-availability (HA) features. Importantly, opting for Percona Server for MySQL ensures a seamless transition to a more advanced database server without incurring software fees or falling prey to vendor lock-in.

MySQL Configuration File

The *my.cnf* (short for *MySQL Configuration*) file is used by MySQL to define various settings and parameters that affect the behavior of the MySQL server. This configuration file is typically located in the */etc* directory on Linux-based systems or in the installation directory on Windows systems.

You use this file to set various parameters such as the location of the MySQL data directory, the maximum amount of memory that the server can use, the character set to use for data storage, and more. These settings can be crucial for performance and security of your MySQL server.

The file uses a simple text format and consists of various sections and directives that define the MySQL server's behavior. You can edit the *my.cnf* file by using a text editor, such as Vim or GNU nano, to customize the MySQL server settings according to your requirements. However, be careful when editing this file since incorrect changes can cause the MySQL server to malfunction or become insecure.

The following is a sample MySQL configuration file that sets various options for the MySQL client and server. This example shows an overview of the various sections and settings in this file, although it's not an exhaustive list of variables. Depending on the application requirements and server configuration, the variables may need to be adjusted.

> The MySQL 8.0 Reference Manual has a section on server system variables (*https://oreil.ly/JPZfH*) that covers all the variables, including their descriptions and default values.

The `client` section of *my.cnf* contains configuration options for the MySQL client. It sets the port and socket used to connect to the MySQL server:

```
[client]

port = 3306
socket = /var/run/mysqld/mysqld.sock
```

The `mysqld` section of *my.cnf* contains configuration options for the MySQL server. It sets the location of the process identifier (PID) file and socket, as well as the port, base directory, data directory, and temporary directory. It also enables the `skip_external_locking` option, which allows for faster table operations but may result in locking issues (external locking affects only MyISAM table access).

The `bind_address` setting restricts connections to the server to the local machine only, while `server_id` assigns a unique ID to the server:

```
[mysqld]

pid_file = /var/run/mysqld/mysqld.pid
socket = /var/run/mysqld/mysqld.sock
port = 3306
basedir = /usr
datadir = /var/lib/mysql
tmpdir = /tmp
skip_external_locking
bind_address = 127.0.0.1
server_id = 100
```

The next *my.cnf* settings configure the InnoDB storage engine, which is the default engine used by MySQL. The `innodb_buffer_pool_size` option sets the size of the buffer pool, which is used to cache frequently accessed data. The `innodb_flush_log_at_trx_commit` option controls how often data is written to the logfile. The remaining options are used to configure I/O and locking settings for InnoDB:

```
# InnoDB settings

innodb_buffer_pool_size = 512M
innodb_redo_log_capacity = 200M
innodb_flush_log_at_trx_commit = 1
innodb_flush_method = O_DIRECT
innodb_lock_wait_timeout = 60
innodb_read_io_threads = 4
innodb_write_io_threads = 4
innodb_io_capacity = 200
```

The following option enables the performance schema, which provides detailed performance metrics for MySQL operations:

```
# Performance schema

performance_schema = ON
```

The next options set various general configuration settings for MySQL, such as buffer sizes and cache settings. The `key_buffer_size` option sets the size of the key buffer used by the MyISAM storage engine, while `max_allowed_packet` controls the maximum size of packets that can be sent or received by the server. The remaining options are used to configure various buffer sizes used by MySQL:

```
# General settings

key_buffer_size = 128M
max_allowed_packet = 64M
table_open_cache = 1024
```

```
sort_buffer_size = 4M
read_buffer_size = 2M
read_rnd_buffer_size = 8M
```

With MySQL 8, another method to configure the MySQL server is available and preferred: use of SET PERSIST to create a configuration file on the data directory. DBA's very much appreciate this solution when they don't have access to the filesystem. It also allows you to track the changes, as some metadata is stored.

Significant Updates in MySQL 8

Let's explore the latest MySQL enhancements and innovations by delving into the significant updates in MySQL 8, as compared to MySQL 5.7:

Transactional data dictionary (TDD)

The new TDD significantly improves the storage and management of information about database objects. This change enhances data integrity, consistency, and reliability, as InnoDB provides transactions that are ACID compliant (meeting the principles of atomicity, consistency, isolation, and durability). With the TDD, MySQL 8 centralizes object metadata in system tables within InnoDB, ensuring that data dictionary changes are transactional and durable. This transition from MyISAM to InnoDB for the data dictionary contributes to MySQL's overall robustness and scalability, supporting high-performance database operations while ensuring data reliability and consistency.

Atomic data definition language

Atomic data definition language (DDL) statements have been introduced to improve the consistency and reliability of DDL operations. These statements combine data dictionary updates, storage engine operations, and binary log writes associated with a DDL operation into a single, atomic transaction. When you perform a DDL statement, such as creating, altering, or dropping a table, all the related changes are bundled into a single transaction. If any part of the DDL operation fails, the entire transaction is rolled back, ensuring that the database remains in a consistent state. This atomicity of DDL statements enhances the reliability and integrity of schema changes in MySQL 8, making it easier to manage and maintain the database's structure.

utf8mb4 character set

The default character set has indeed been changed from Latin-1 to utf8mb4. This change reflects the shift toward better support for international character sets and the increasing demand for Unicode encoding. UTF-8 is a variable-width encoding that can represent a wide range of characters from various languages and scripts, making it a more suitable default for modern applications with diverse user bases.

Invisible indexes

Support for invisible indexes has been introduced as a feature enhancement. Invisible indexes are indexes that are not used by the query optimizer when generating query execution plans. They allow DBAs to test the impact of removing an index without actually dropping it from the database schema. This feature is particularly useful for performance optimization and testing scenarios.

By making an index invisible, you can observe how query performance is affected without permanently removing the index from the database. This feature provides a way to gather insights into whether an index is beneficial or whether it can be safely removed to reduce storage and maintenance overhead. This capability helps DBAs make more informed decisions about index management and optimization strategies.

Clone plug-in

The clone plug-in is a powerful feature that simplifies the setup of database replication. It creates an exact replica of a MySQL server's data directory, making it an efficient and fast method to establish replication from a donor to a replica server. Instead of traditional and potentially complex backup and restore procedures, this feature allows administrators to easily clone the donor's data onto the replica, significantly reducing the time and effort required to configure a replication environment. This enhancement streamlines replication deployments, minimizes downtime, and improves overall manageability and reliability in MySQL replication setups.

Hot rows with `NOWAIT` *and* `SKIP LOCKED`

The hot rows feature has been enhanced with the `NOWAIT` and `SKIP LOCKED` options, primarily applicable to the `SELECT` statement within concurrent transaction scenarios. When used with `FOR UPDATE` or `FOR SHARE` clauses, `NOWAIT` ensures that if another session already holds a lock on the rows being accessed, MySQL returns an immediate error instead of waiting for the lock to be released, thus reducing contention and potential deadlocks. Conversely, `SKIP LOCKED` enables a `SELECT` statement to skip over rows locked by other transactions, allowing for nonblocking access to rows while excluding those currently locked by other sessions. These features enhance MySQL's concurrency and transaction management capabilities, particularly in scenarios with high contention for data access.

SSL session reuse

SSL session reuse is supported by many Secure Sockets Layer (SSL)/Transaction Layer Security (TLS) implementations, including OpenSSL, which is commonly used in MySQL for securing database connections. This feature allows clients and servers to reuse SSL/TLS session parameters to avoid the overhead of renegotiating a new session for every connection.

In MySQL 8, SSL session reuse is supported by default, so MySQL clients and servers will reuse SSL/TLS sessions when appropriate. The server-side session cache timeout setting (`ssl_session_cache_timeout`) refers to the duration for which SSL/TLS session parameters are cached and considered for reuse. When a client reconnects to the server within this timeout period, it can reuse the existing SSL/TLS session parameters, saving computational resources and potentially improving connection performance.

Persisted system variables

You can now persist global dynamic server variables by using the `SET PERSIST` command, which provides a more streamlined alternative to `SET GLOBAL`. When the `PERSIST` keyword is used, any modifications to server variables are not only applied instantly but also recorded in the *mysqld-auto.cnf* option file located in the data directory. This file stores the variable changes, ensuring they are retained even after server restarts. This feature simplifies the management of server configurations, as it allows for persistent adjustments that remain in effect across sessions and server restarts, promoting better consistency and ease of administration in MySQL deployments.

Resource group management

You can create and manage resource groups as well as assign threads to specific groups. This feature is particularly valuable when you need to allocate server resources efficiently among different workloads or applications. With resource groups, you can define and allocate resources such as CPU and I/O to multiple groups of threads or sessions based on criteria like user accounts, applications, or query patterns. This fine-grained control over resource allocation ensures that critical workloads receive the necessary resources while preventing resource contention and improving overall system performance and stability.

Table encryption

You can manage table encryption globally by defining and enforcing encryption defaults. You can set encryption policies and defaults at the server level, affecting the way tables are encrypted by default across your entire MySQL instance, for tables within the schema, the general tablespace, or the entire MySQL system. This ensures that tables are encrypted consistently, simplifying data security and compliance efforts. This feature allows you to define encryption settings such as encryption algorithms and key management options at the global level, providing a centralized and standardized approach to data encryption within your MySQL database.

Automated MySQL server upgrade tasks

MySQL version 8.0.16 introduced a significant improvement to the upgrade process. The MySQL server now automatically executes all necessary upgrade tasks, including upgrading system tables and objects in other schemas like the `sys` schema and user schemas, during the next server startup. Users no longer need to manually run the mysql_upgrade utility after upgrading their MySQL server. This automation simplifies the upgrade process, reduces the potential for errors, and ensures that the database is properly updated to the new version without manual intervention.

When no option is specified or when using --upgrade=AUTO, the server will automatically upgrade any components it identifies as outdated.

If --upgrade=NONE is specified, the server refrains from upgrading anything. However, it will exit with an error if the data dictionary requires an upgrade. Running the server with an outdated data dictionary is not allowed; the server demands either an upgrade or termination.

When --upgrade=MINIMAL is used, the server upgrades essential components, such as the data dictionary, PERFORMANCE_SCHEMA, and INFORMATION_SCHEMA, if necessary. It's important to note that after upgrading with this option, starting group replication may not be possible. This limitation arises because the system tables crucial for replication internals are not updated, and reduced functionality may be observed in various areas.

With --upgrade=FORCE, the server upgrades crucial components like the data dictionary, PERFORMANCE_SCHEMA, and INFORMATION_SCHEMA as needed. Additionally, it forcefully upgrades all other components. Expect an extended server startup duration with this option, as the server meticulously checks all objects in all schemas.

Custom TCP/IP port configuration for administrative connections
You can configure a separate TCP/IP port specifically for administrative connections, even if the max_connections limit has already been reached on the primary port. This feature provides greater flexibility and control over the way administrative tasks are handled when the primary connection pool is already fully utilized. By allowing a dedicated administrative port, administrators can ensure uninterrupted access to the database server for critical management and troubleshooting tasks, regardless of the concurrent connections on the primary port. This enhancement improves the manageability and robustness of MySQL in high-traffic or resource-constrained scenarios.

Backup lock
A new backup lock type enables data manipulation language (DML) operations during an online backup while simultaneously preventing actions that could lead to an inconsistent snapshot.

Persistent auto-increment counter

The maximum auto-increment counter value is persistent across server restarts. The auto-increment counter, which determines the next value for an auto-incremented column, will retain its value even if the server is restarted. In earlier versions of MySQL, the auto-increment counter was reset to a value that was used and deleted previously upon server restart, which could lead to issues such as duplicate key errors or unexpected data gaps. This enhancement in MySQL 8.0.22 helps ensure data integrity and consistency by preserving the state of the auto-increment counter across server restarts.

Enhanced InnoDB tablespace management

The `innodb_directories` option allows you to specify directories for InnoDB tablespace files. This feature enables you to move or restore tablespace files to a new location while the MySQL server is offline. This capability can be valuable for managing the physical storage of InnoDB tablespace files and ensuring the availability and integrity of your database.

Automated configuration for dedicated MySQL servers

A new system variable called `innodb_dedicated_server` has been introduced. By default, it is disabled. When enabled, this variable instructs InnoDB to automatically configure various options based on the detected memory availability, optimizing the MySQL server's performance for dedicated server environments.

Enabling `innodb_dedicated_server` is beneficial when you have a dedicated MySQL server with ample memory resources available. InnoDB will make certain assumptions and adjustments, such as increasing buffer pool size, to take advantage of the available memory for improved performance. This feature simplifies the configuration process for dedicated MySQL servers, making it more suitable when MySQL has exclusive access to server resources. However, it's essential to review and adjust the automatically configured settings if your server's memory profile changes significantly or if you have specific performance requirements.

Improved temporary table handling

InnoDB temporary tables are created in session temporary tablespaces, which are represented by *.ibt* (InnoDB temporary) files. This change is one of the improvements in temporary table handling and helps enhance the overall performance and manageability of temporary tables in InnoDB.

Enhanced authentication security and performance with `caching_sha2_password`

A new authentication plug-in called `caching_sha2_password` is designed to enhance authentication security while addressing latency issues associated with the previous `sha256_password` plug-in. Both plug-ins implement SHA-256 password hashing for increased security, but `caching_sha2_password` incorporates caching mechanisms to improve performance.

The caching mechanism in `caching_sha2_password` helps reduce the computational overhead of hashing passwords during the authentication process. It does so by caching previously hashed password values, allowing for quicker authentication for users who have recently logged in. This can be especially beneficial in scenarios with high connection rates or where authentication latency is a concern.

Enhanced user account categorization with the SYSTEM_USER *privilege*
A user account categorization system has been introduced, featuring the SYSTEM_USER privilege. This concept allows for a clear distinction between system users and regular users within the MySQL authentication and authorization framework. Users possessing the SYSTEM_USER privilege are classified as system users, typically granted elevated privileges for database management and administration, including access to system-related resources and tables. In contrast, regular users do not hold this privilege and are intended for typical application-level access to the database. This user account categorization enhances security and access control, facilitating a more organized and manageable user structure in MySQL deployments.

Enhanced security with temporary account locking
Administrators can configure user accounts to implement temporary account locking as a security measure. This functionality enables the system to detect and respond to a predefined threshold of consecutive failed login attempts by temporarily locking the user account. By doing so, it adds an extra layer of security against potential unauthorized access attempts, effectively safeguarding the database from brute-force attacks or unauthorized access due to multiple failed login attempts. This feature contributes to improved security and access control in MySQL deployments.

Simplified privilege management with roles
Support for roles has been introduced. *Roles* are named collections of privileges that can simplify and streamline user privilege management. Administrators can create, drop, grant, and revoke roles, and these roles can, in turn, have privileges granted or revoked. Additionally, roles can be granted to or revoked from individual users, making it easier to manage and maintain complex privilege schemes within MySQL. Roles help centralize privilege management, reduce complexity, and improve the maintainability and security of MySQL database systems by allowing administrators to group and assign privileges more efficiently.

Enhanced security with multifactor authentication
As of MySQL 8.0.27, multifactor authentication (MFA) is supported, allowing for enhanced security by enabling up to three authentication methods per user account. Users can be required to provide multiple forms of authentication before gaining access to the database, improving the overall security posture of MySQL deployments. MFA is a crucial feature when strong authentication is essential to protect sensitive data and prevent unauthorized access. By supporting multiple authentication methods, MySQL offers greater flexibility and options for enhancing security based on the specific needs of the application and organization.

Dynamic redo log capacity
Starting with MySQL 8.0.30, the dynamic InnoDB redo log introduces a new capability, enabling users to dynamically resize redo logfiles without requiring a system restart. This marks a substantial enhancement compared to earlier MySQL versions, which required manual resizing and a database restart for such changes to become effective. Insufficient redo log capacity can pose performance challenges, making this dynamic resizing feature a valuable improvement.

Generated invisible primary keys
MySQL 8.0.30 introduces support for generated invisible primary keys (GIPKs) on InnoDB tables created without an explicit primary key. When the `sql_gener ate_invisible_primary_key` server system variable is enabled, the MySQL server will autonomously include a GIPK for any corresponding table.

MySQL as a document store
X Plugin empowers the MySQL server to communicate with clients through X Protocol, a prerequisite for employing MySQL as a document store. It's worth noting that X Plugin is now enabled by default.

Conclusion

MySQL is available on multiple platforms and operating systems, including Windows, Linux, macOS, and various cloud providers. Using MySQL on these platforms offers several benefits, such as easy installation, integration with other applications, scalability, and HA. With the sample configuration settings provided in this chapter, it is easy to set up MySQL on various platforms and start using it for your applications.

## CHAPTER 2

Installing and Configuring MySQL Server

In this chapter, we cover the steps required to install and configure the MySQL server on both Windows and Linux operating systems. Additionally, we will explore best practices for MySQL server configuration, performance tuning, and upgrading.

Installing MySQL Server on Windows

Installing MySQL by using the MySQL Installer Community Edition is a straightforward process, and you can follow these steps to complete the installation successfully:

1. Download the latest MySQL Installer version from the official MySQL website (*https://oreil.ly/5VPE4*). Select the appropriate operating system (Windows or Linux) and architecture (32-bit or 64-bit) of your computer, and download the corresponding installer:

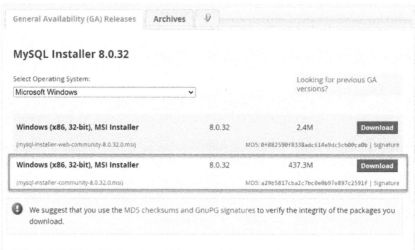

2. Double-click the downloaded file to run the installer:

3. Choose the type of MySQL setup you want to install. You can choose a typical or custom installation, depending on your needs. Click Next to continue:

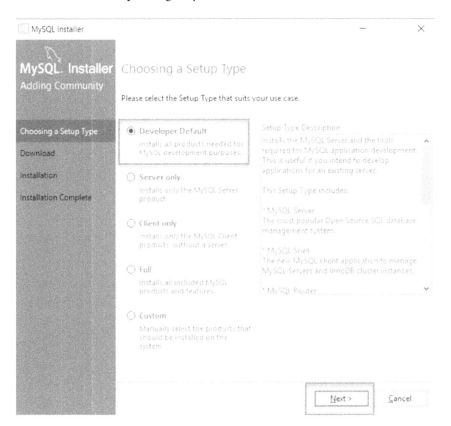

4. The installer checks whether your system meets the minimum requirements for MySQL. If there are any issues, the installer will display them on the next screen:

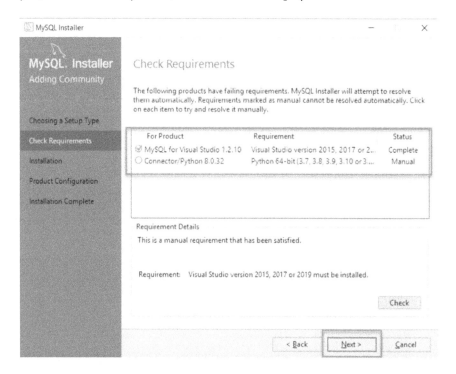

5. Review the list of MySQL products that will be installed. After confirming that you want to proceed with the installation process, click the Execute button:

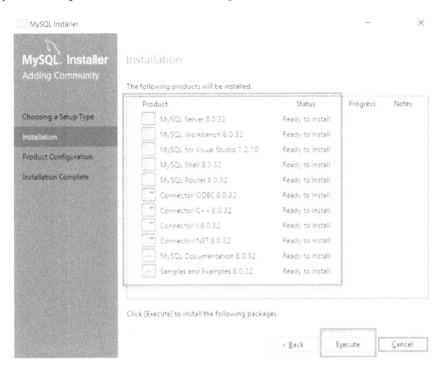

6. The next screen shows the progress of the installation as it takes place. As each product installs, you'll see its status change to Complete. Then you can click Next:

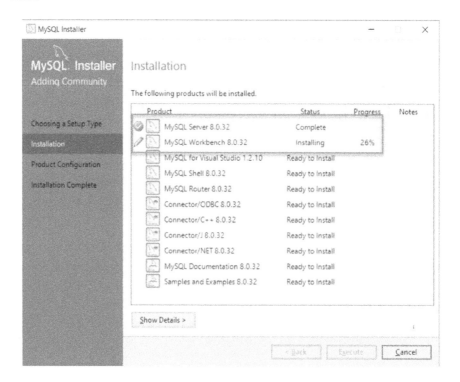

7. The Product Configuration screen will show you the status of the MySQL server 8.0.32 installation; click Next to continue:

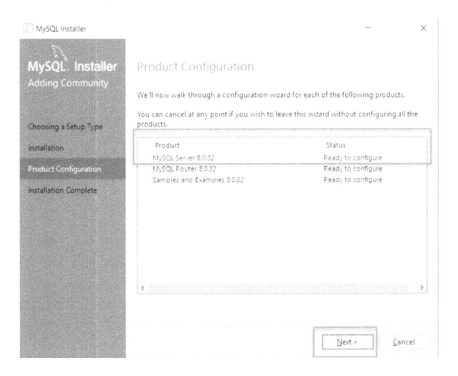

8. Configure the type of MySQL installation (standalone, server only, or client only) as well as network-related settings like the port number; then click Next:

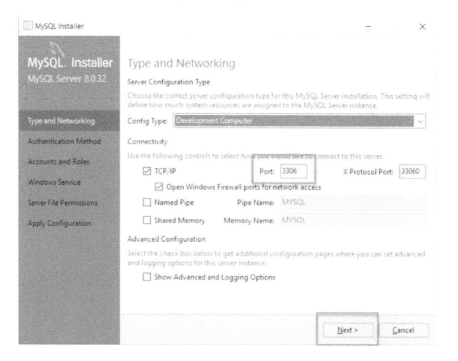

When installing MySQL, it's often recommended to consider changing the default port, particularly in local environments. This precautionary step becomes important if other applications or services are already using the default port on your system. By opting for a different port during installation, you can avoid potential conflicts and ensure smooth coexistence with other local services.

For example, in a development environment, multiple tools may run concurrently on the default port. Changing the MySQL port to a less commonly used one minimizes the risk of interference and ensures seamless operation of both MySQL and other services. This practice is a simple yet effective way to enhance the stability and functionality of your local setup, preventing port conflicts and facilitating a hassle-free development experience.

9. Choose the authentication method for accessing MySQL (we suggest using the strong password encryption option); then click Next:

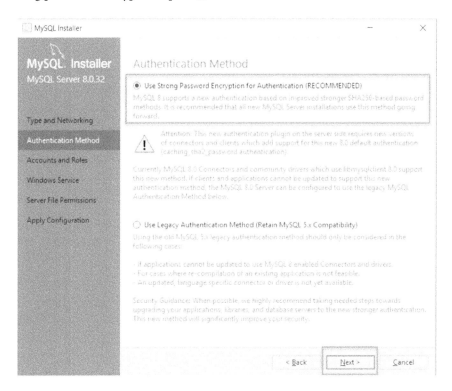

10. On the Accounts and Roles screen, set the root account password and create or modify user accounts and their associated roles; then click Next:

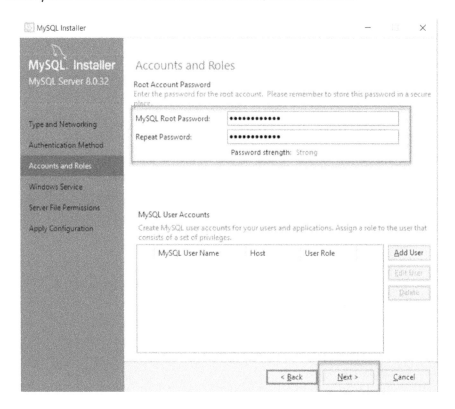

11. On the Windows Service screen, configure the MySQL server as a Windows service, which allows it to start automatically when Windows starts. Then click Next:

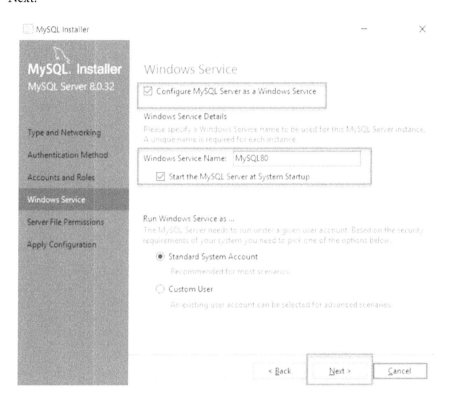

12. On the Server File Permissions screen, configure the file permissions for the MySQL server; then click Next:

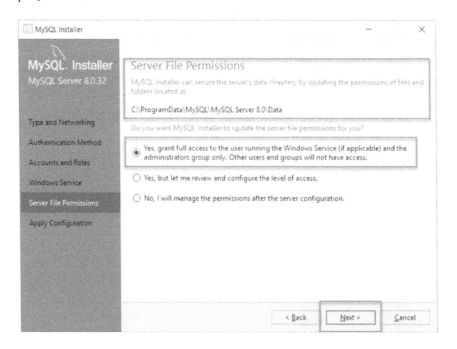

13. On the Apply Configuration screen, confirm that you want to apply the configuration changes you made on the previous screens. These include options for updating firewalls, initiating databases, updating folder permissions, and applying security. Click Execute to continue:

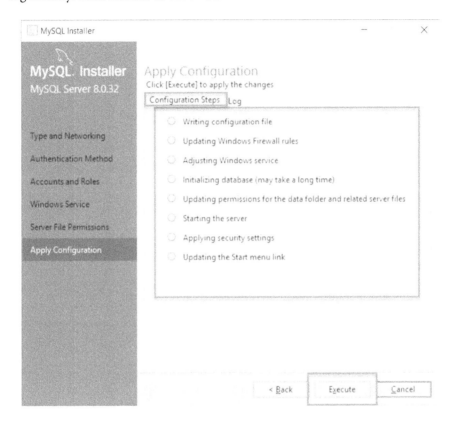

14. The next screen should indicate that the configuration changes have been applied successfully; click the Finish button:

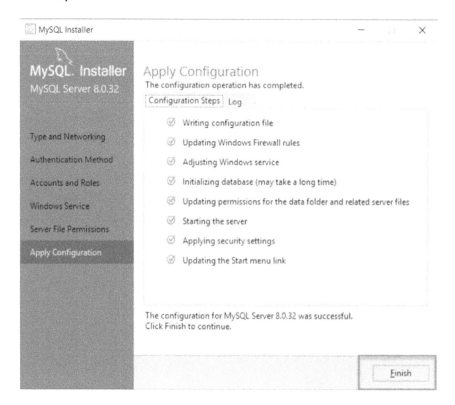

15. On the MySQL Router Configuration screen, configure the MySQL Router, which is a lightweight tool for managing MySQL connections; then click Finish again:

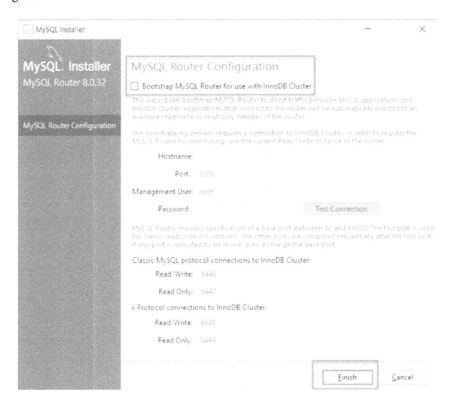

16. The Product Configuration screen shows you the status of the MySQL Router 8.0.32 installation; click Next:

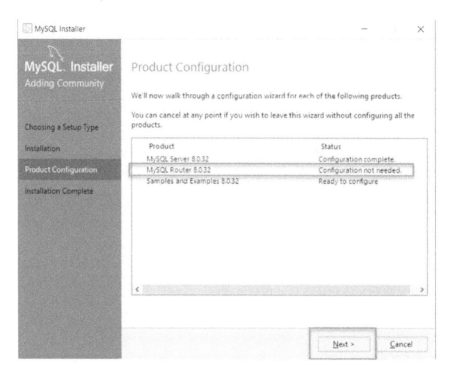

17. The Connect To Server screen allows you to configure your connection to the MySQL server by using root user credentials; then click Next:

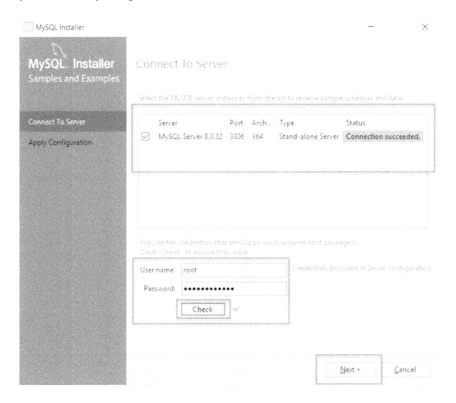

18. The Apply Configuration screen verifies your intention to implement the configuration modifications and enables you to inspect any installed features requiring configuration, as per the changes made on the preceding screens; click Execute to continue:

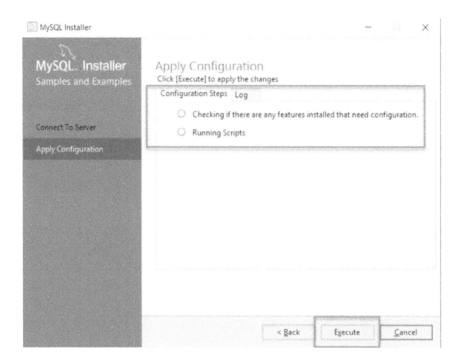

19. The Apply Configuration screen confirms that the all features have been configured successfully; click Finish:

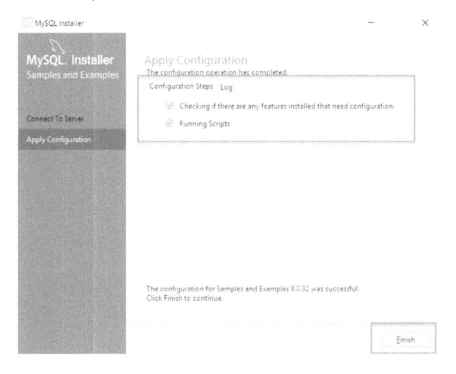

20. The Installation Complete screen confirms that the entire installation process has been completed successfully; click Finish:

Installing MySQL Community Edition on Linux

Installing MySQL on Linux is slightly different from the Windows installation. The package manager yum is used to install MySQL on Linux in this example. However, alternative package managers, like brew (macOS) and apt-get (Debian/Ubuntu), can also be employed based on the system configuration.

To install MySQL 8 Community Edition on your Linux-based system, follow these steps:

1. You'll need to download the MySQL 8 repository package. You can find the exact MySQL version and the required repository based on the Linux distribution online (*https://repo.mysql.com*). Keep in mind that you should always download software from official and trusted sources to ensure its integrity and security. Use the wget command to download the package:

```
[root@mysql80 ~]# wget https://repo.mysql.com/
mysql80-community-release-el9-3.noarch.rpm
--2024-02-16 00:03:40--
https://repo.mysql.com/mysql80-community-release-el9-3.noarch.rpm
Resolving repo.mysql.com (repo.mysql.com)...
mysql80-community-release-el9-3.n
100%[==============================>]
10.46K  --.-KB/s    in 0s
2024-02-16 00:03:40 (148 MB/s) -
'mysql80-community-release-el9-3.noarch.rpm' saved [10715/10715]
[root@mysql80 ~]#
```

2. Install the repository package locally by using the yum command:

```
[root@mysql80 ~]# sudo yum localinstall
mysql80-community-release-el9-3.noarch.rpm
Last metadata expiration check: 0:12:13 ago on
Thu 15 Feb 2024 11:53:10 PM UTC.
Is this ok [y/N]: y
Running transaction
  Preparing  :
  Installing : mysql80-community-release-el9-3.noarch
  Verifying  : mysql80-community-release-el9-3.noarch
Installed products updated.
Installed:
  mysql80-community-release-el9-3.noarch
Complete!
[root@mysql80 ~]#
```

3. To ensure the authenticity of the MySQL 8 packages, you need to import the public key by using the rpm command:

```
[root@mysql80 ~]# sudo rpm --import https://repo.mysql.com/RPM-GPG-KEY-
mysql-2023
[root@mysql80 ~]#
```

4. Once the repository package and public key are installed, you can proceed with the installation of MySQL 8 Community Edition by using the yum command:

```
[root@mysql80 ~]# sudo yum install mysql-community-server -y
MySQL 8.0 Community Server
MySQL Connectors Community
MySQL Tools Community
Dependencies resolved.
...
Downloading Packages:
(1/6): mysql-community-common-8.0.36-1.el9.x86_64.rpm
(2/6): mysql-community-client-plugins-8.0.36-1.el9.x86_64.rpm
(3/6): mysql-community-client-8.0.36-1.el9.x86_64.rpm
(4/6): mysql-community-icu-data-files-8.0.36-1.el9.x86_64.rpm
(5/6): mysql-community-libs-8.0.36-1.el9.x86_64.rpm
(6/6): mysql-community-server-8.0.36-1.el9.x86_64.rpm
Total      16 MB/s |  58 MB     00:03
```

5. To ensure that the MySQL service starts automatically after a system reboot, you need to enable it by using the `systemctl` command:

```
[root@mysql80 ~]# sudo systemctl enable mysqld.service
[root@mysql80 ~]#
```

6. Start the MySQL service by using the `systemctl` command:

```
[root@mysql80 ~]# sudo systemctl start mysqld.service
[root@mysql80 ~]#
```

7. To verify that the MySQL service is up and running, check its status by using the `systemctl` command:

```
[root@mysql80 ~]# systemctl status mysqld
mysqld.service - MySQL Server
    Loaded: loaded (/usr/lib/systemd/system/mysqld.service;
    enabled; preset: disabled)
    Active: active (running) since Fri 2024-02-16 00:07:49 UTC;
    17s ago
      Docs: man:mysqld(8)
            http://dev.mysql.com/doc/refman/en/using-systemd.html
   Process: 35372 ExecStartPre=/usr/bin/mysqld_pre_systemd (
code=exited, status=0/SUCCESS)
  Main PID: 35441 (mysqld)
    Status: "Server is operational"
     Tasks: 38 (limit: 24734)
    Memory: 450.5M
       CPU: 6.534s
    CGroup: /system.slice/mysqld.service
            └─35441 /usr/sbin/mysqld
Feb 16 00:07:40 mysql80 systemd[1]: Starting MySQL Server...
Feb 16 00:07:49 mysql80 systemd[1]: Started MySQL Server.
[root@mysql80 ~]#
```

8. To verify that MySQL 8 Community Edition is installed and running correctly, you can perform a few more checks. First, check whether the MySQL process is running by using the `pidof` command:

```
[root@mysql80 ~]# pidof mysqld
35441
[root@mysql80 ~]#
```

9. Verify that MySQL is listening on the default port (3306) by using the `netstat` command:

```
[root@mysql80 ~]# netstat -ntlp | grep 3306
tcp6       0       0 :::33060     :::*      LISTEN      35441/mysqld
tcp6       0       0 :::3306      :::*      LISTEN      35441/mysqld
[root@mysql80 ~]#
```

10. Verify the MySQL file descriptors by using the `lsof` command:

```
[root@mysql80 ~]# sudo lsof -u mysql
COMMAND   PID USER   FD  TYPE   DEVICE SIZE/OFF
```

```
NODE NAME
mysqld  35441 mysql  cwd  DIR   253,0      4096 151103282 /var/lib/mysql
mysqld  35441 mysql  rtd  DIR   253,0       235       128 /
mysqld  35441 mysql  txt  REG   253,0 56368072 151103276 /usr/sbin/mysqld
mysqld  35441 mysql  mem  REG   253,0     58488 151103253
/usr/lib64/mysql/plugin/component_validate_password.so
```

If the *lsof* package is not installed, you can install it by using the command `yum install lsof -y` via the yum package manager on a Linux system.

Installing Percona Server for MySQL 8

This section will guide you through installing Percona Server for MySQL 8 on a Linux system:

1. The first step in installing Percona Server for MySQL 8 is to download the Percona MySQL 8 repository package. This package contains the necessary files to set up the Percona MySQL 8 repository on your Linux system. Download the repository package with the following command:

   ```
   [root@mysql80 ~]# wget https://repo.percona.com/yum/percona-release-latest
   .noarch.rpm
   --2024-02-16 00:14:38--  https://repo.percona.com/yum/percona-release-latest
   .noarch.rpm                                            -latest.noarch.rpm
   Resolving repo.percona.com (repo.percona.com)...
   147.135.54.159, 2604:2dc0:200:69f::2
   Length: 20096 (20K) [application/x-redhat-package-manager]
   Saving to: 'percona-release-latest.noarch.rpm'
   ...
   2024-02-16 00:14:39 (91.9 KB/s) -
   'percona-release-latest.noarch.rpm' saved [20096/20096]
   [root@mysql80 ~]#
   ```

2. Next, install the Percona MySQL repo locally on your Linux system. This will allow you to access the Percona MySQL 8 packages from the repository. Use the following command:

   ```
   [root@mysql80 ~]# sudo yum localinstall percona-release-latest.noarch.rpm
   yum localinstall percona-release-latest.noarch.rpm2
   Is this ok [y/N]: y
     Preparing   :  1/1
     Installing  : percona-release-1.0-27.noarch  1/1
     Running scriptlet: percona-release-1.0-27.noarch  1/1
   * Enabling the Percona Original repository
   <*> All done!
   * Enabling the Percona Release repository
   <*> All done!
   ```

3. Enable the repository for Percona MySQL 8. Use the following command:

```
[root@mysql80 ~]# sudo percona-release setup -y ps80
* Disabling all Percona Repositories
On Red Hat 8 systems it is needed to disable the following DNF module(s):
mysql  to install Percona-Server
Disabling DNF module...
Percona Release release/noarch YUM repository
1.5 kB/s | 1.8 kB      00:01
Unable to resolve argument mysql
Error: Problems in request:
missing groups or modules: mysql
DNF mysql module was disabled
* Enabling the Percona Server 8.0 repository
* Enabling the Percona Tools repository
<*> All done!
[root@mysql80 ~]#
```

4. You can now install the Percona MySQL Server. This is the actual database management system that you will be using. Here's the command:

```
[root@mysql80 ~]# sudo yum install percona-server-server -y
Percona Server 8.0 release/x86_64 YUM repository
638 kB/s | 2.3 MB      00:03
Percona Tools release/x86_64 YUM repository
396 kB/s | 1.1 MB      00:02
Last metadata expiration check: 0:00:02 ago on Fri 16 Feb 2024
12:20:57 AM UTC.
Dependencies resolved.
===================================================================
 Package        Architecture    Version     Repository      Size
===================================================================
Installing:
 percona-server-server x86_64  8.0.35-27.1.el9 ps-80-release-x86_64 64  M
Installing dependencies:
 percona-icu-data-files x86_64 8.0.35-27.1.el9 ps-80-release-x86_64 2.2 M
 percona-server-client  x86_64 8.0.35-27.1.el9 ps-80-release-x86_64 3.4 M
 percona-server-shared  x86_64 8.0.35-27.1.el9 ps-80-release-x86_64 1.4 M
Transaction Summary
===================================================================
Install  4 Packages
sudo systemctl enable mysqld.service
[root@mysql80 ~]#
```

5. By default, the MySQL service won't start automatically when your Linux system
   boots up. To ensure that the MySQL service is always running, you can enable the
   service to auto-start on reboot by using the following command:

```
[root@mysql80 ~]# sudo systemctl enable mysqld.service
[root@mysql80 ~]#
```

6. Once the MySQL service is installed and enabled to auto-start on reboot, you can
   start the service:

```
[root@mysql80 ~]# sudo systemctl start mysqld.service
[root@mysql80 ~]#
```

7. To verify that the MySQL service is running, check the status of the service:

```
[root@mysql80 ~]# systemctl status mysqld
mysqld.service - MySQL Server
    Loaded: loaded (/usr/lib/systemd/system/mysqld.service; enabled;
     preset: disabled)
    Active: active (running) since Fri 2024-02-16 00:22:19 UTC; 16s ago
      Docs: man:mysqld(8)
            http://dev.mysql.com/doc/refman/en/using-systemd.html
   Process: 5134 ExecStartPre=/usr/bin/mysqld_pre_systemd (code=exited,
    status=0/SUCCESS)
  Main PID: 5210 (mysqld)
    Status: "Server is operational"
     Tasks: 39 (limit: 24734)
    Memory: 462.0M
       CPU: 8.562s
    CGroup: /system.slice/mysqld.service
            └─5210 /usr/sbin/mysqld
Feb 16 00:22:11 mysql80 systemd[1]: Starting MySQL Server...
Feb 16 00:22:19 mysql80 systemd[1]: Started MySQL Server.
[root@mysql80 ~]#
```

8. After installing and configuring the Percona MySQL Server, you can verify that the server is up and running by using the following checks:

a. Check the process ID of the MySQL server:

```
[root@mysql80 ~]# pidof mysqld
5210
[root@mysql80 ~]#
```

b. Check that the MySQL server is listening on port 3306:

```
[root@mysql80 ~]# netstat -ntlp | grep 3306
tcp6       0      0 :::33060    :::*      LISTEN      5210/mysqld
tcp6       0      0 :::3306     :::*      LISTEN      5210/mysqld
[root@mysql80 ~]#
```

c. Check the open files for the MySQL server process:

```
[root@mysql80 ~]# sudo lsof -u mysql
COMMAND  PID  USER    FD      TYPE    DEVICE SIZE/OFF   NODE NAME
mysqld  5210 mysql   cwd      DIR     253,0     4096 204511269 /var/
lib/mysql
mysqld  5210 mysql   rtd      DIR     253,0      235       128 /
mysqld  5210 mysql   txt      REG     253,0 56945904 151103176 /usr/
sbin/mysqld
mysqld  5210 mysql   mem      REG     253,0    58496 204714271 /usr/
lib64/mysql/plugin/component_validate_password.so
mysqld  5210 mysql   mem      REG     253,0  2386976 134350178 /usr/
lib64/libc.so.6
```

By following the steps outlined in this section, you should now have Percona MySQL 8 Community Edition installed and running on your Linux system.

Configuring MySQL Server

Once you have installed MySQL server, the next step is to configure it to meet your specific needs. Proper configuration is essential to ensure that it runs efficiently and securely. This section covers the key configuration options that you should consider when configuring MySQL server.

Configuring the Default Character Set and Collation

In MySQL 8, the default value for the `character_set_server` system variable is `utf8mb4`, supporting a vast array of characters and symbols from various languages and writing systems, including emojis and other symbols that require more than two bytes of storage. The `collation_server` variable determines how characters are compared and sorted within a character set. The default value for `collation_server` is `utf8mb4_0900_ai_ci`, using the `utf8mb4` character set. This collation is tailored to provide linguistic sorting and comparison for a wide range of languages, making it suitable for applications.

Multiple levels of character set and collation definitions exist on the server side. The server-level defaults in cases where the database-level character set and collation are not specified. Similarly, the database level defaults when the table level character set and collation are unspecified. The table level serves as a default when the column level character set and collation are not defined.

Configuring the Maximum Allowed Packet Size

MySQL server has a maximum allowed size for any single communication packet between the server and clients. This setting can affect the performance of large data transfers or bulk inserts. Here's how to change the maximum allowed packet size:

```
max_allowed_packet = 1G
```

The `max_allowed_packet` parameter in MySQL specifies the maximum size of a single packet that can be sent or received by the server.

The value of 1 GB for `max_allowed_packet` is often recommended as a best practice because it provides enough buffer space for handling large queries and data transfer, while still being within reasonable limits for most systems.

Setting a smaller value for `max_allowed_packet` can cause issues when transferring large amounts of data, such as during backups or when importing/exporting large databases. If the packet size is too small, the server will need to split the data into smaller chunks, which can significantly slow the transfer process.

On the other hand, setting a very large value for `max_allowed_packet` can consume more memory on the server and can potentially cause issues with network bandwidth and resource utilization.

Therefore, 1 GB is considered a good balance between performance and resource utilization for most MySQL systems. However, the optimal value for `max_allowed_packet` may vary depending on the specific needs and resources of your system.

What Led to the Removal of the Query Cache Size in MySQL 8?

The removal of the query cache size feature in MySQL 8 was primarily due to scalability issues and performance limitations. The query cache had several drawbacks that made it difficult to maintain and improve over time.

One issue was that the query cache was a global cache, which meant that any changes to a table would cause all cached queries that used that table to be invalidated. This led to frequent cache invalidation and reduced cache hit rates, which in turn led to decreased performance.

The query cache was not well suited for modern application architectures that relied on distributed databases, microservices, and containerized deployments. These architectures required more flexible and scalable caching solutions that could be distributed across multiple nodes and services.

As a result of these issues, the decision was made to remove the query cache feature in MySQL 8 and focus on other performance-optimization techniques, such as better indexing and improved query execution plans.

Configuring MySQL's Logfiles

MySQL server generates several logfiles that record various types of information, such as errors, queries, and connections. The logfiles can be useful for troubleshooting and monitoring the performance of MySQL. Here's how you can configure the logfiles:

1. Open the MySQL configuration file *my.cnf* or *my.ini*.

2. Add the following lines to the `mysqld` section of the configuration file to enable the error log and slow query log:

    ```
    [mysqld]
    log-error = /var/log/mysql/error.log
    slow_query_log = 1
    slow_query_log_file = /var/log/mysql/slow-query.log
    ```

3. Save the configuration file and restart the MySQL server.

Optimizing MySQL Performance

To optimize the performance of a MySQL server, you should consider a few configuration variables:

- include innodb_buffer_pool_size
- innodb_autoinc_lock_mode
- innodb_buffer_pool_instances
- innodb_redo_log_capacity

- innodb_lru_scan_depth
- innodb_sync_array_size
- innodb_thread_concurrency
- binlog_format

Depending on the specific requirements of the application and the hardware on which the server is running, these variables may need to be adjusted to ensure optimal performance.

To update these variables, you can modify them in the *my.cnf* configuration file or set them at runtime by using the SET command for the dynamic variables. However, it's important to carefully consider the impact of any changes and to test the server thoroughly to ensure that the changes have the desired effect. Additionally, keep in mind that some changes may require a server restart to take effect.

Overall, configuring a MySQL server for optimal performance can be a complex task, but by carefully considering the specific needs of the application and tuning the relevant variables, it's possible to achieve excellent performance and reliability.

Securing MySQL Server During Installation

Protecting your instance of MySQL from unauthorized access, manipulation, and theft is of paramount importance to safeguard your data. This section covers the fundamentals of securing MySQL during installation.

Changing the Default Root Password

By default, MySQL server installs with a root user account that has full privileges over all databases and tables. We recommend to change the default root password to a strong, unique password to prevent unauthorized access.

Here are the steps to change the root password in MySQL:

1. Log in to MySQL by using the root account.

2. Retrieve the temporary password from the MySQL error log by using grep:

```
[root@mysql80 ~]# grep -i "A temporary password is generated
" /var/log/mysqld.log
2024-02-16T00:07:45.350062Z 6 [Note] [MY-010454] [Server]
A temporary password is generated for root@localhost: +plQKe&to7oH
```

```
g/mysqld.log
[root@mysql80 ~]#
```

3. Enter the following command to change the password:

```
ALTER USER 'root'@'localhost' IDENTIFIED BY 'new_password';
```

4. Replace *new_password* with your desired password:

```
[root@mysql80 ~]# mysql -uroot -p
Enter password:
Welcome to the MySQL monitor.  Commands end with ; or \g.
Your MySQL connection id is 8
Server version: 8.0.36
Type 'help;' or '\h' for help. Type '\c' to clear
the current input statement.

mysql> ALTER USER 'root'@'localhost' IDENTIFIED BY 'D@#NJU#$@MK28#nM';
Query OK, 0 rows affected (0.01 sec)
mysql>
```

Restricting Remote Access to MySQL

By default, MySQL allows remote connections from any IP address, which can increase the risk of unauthorized access. You should restrict remote access to only trusted IP addresses. This section presents the steps for restricting remote access in MySQL.

The `skip_name_resolve` option is a MySQL configuration variable that can be used to disable hostname resolution during client authentication. When this option is enabled, MySQL will not attempt to resolve the hostname of the client during authentication, which can improve authentication performance and reduce the risk of DNS-related security vulnerabilities.

1. Log in to your MySQL by using the root account.

2. Enter the following command to create a new user account for remote access, but replace *remote_user*, *trusted_ip_address*, and *password* with your desired values:

```
CREATE USER 'remote_user'@'trusted_ip_address' IDENTIFIED BY
'password';
mysql> CREATE USER 'tstappuser'@'192.168.20.73' IDENTIFIED BY
'Mkj#$w@89LKJH#';
Query OK, 0 rows affected (0.03 sec)
mysql>
```

3. Grant the necessary privileges to the remote user account:

```
mysql> GRANT SELECT, INSERT, UPDATE, DELETE ON appdb.* TO 'tstappuser'
@'192.168.20.73';
Query OK, 0 rows affected (0.00 sec)
```

4. Then test the access:

```
[root@ApplicationServer ~]# mysql -h192.168.20.71 -utstappuser -p -e
"show databases";
Enter password:
+--------------------+
| Database           |
+--------------------+
| appdb              |
| information_schema |
| performance_schema |
+--------------------+
[root@ApplicationServer ~]#
```

Creating Separate MySQL Users for Different Applications or Users

Creating separate user accounts for different applications or users can help in enforcing access control and minimizing the risk of data exposure. Here are the steps to create a new user account in MySQL:

1. Log in to your MySQL server by using the root account.

2. Enter the following command to create a new user account, replacing *new_user* and *password* with your desired values:

   ```
   CREATE USER 'new_user'@'localhost' IDENTIFIED BY 'password';
   ```

3. Grant the necessary privileges to the new user account, again, replacing *new_user* with the new username:

   ```
   GRANT SELECT, INSERT, UPDATE, DELETE ON database.* TO 'new_user'@'localhost';
   ```

Monitoring MySQL

Properly monitoring MySQL is crucial to ensure that it is functioning optimally and performing its intended tasks. Monitoring helps identify and resolve issues before they become severe and cause significant disruptions to the system. This section presents tools and techniques you can use to monitor your MySQL server.

Using the Built-in Performance and Information Schema

MySQL server has two built-in schemas, the performance schema and the information schema, that can be used for monitoring the server's performance. The *performance schema* provides data on server performance and activity, while the *information schema* contains metadata about the server's databases and tables:

The performance schema

The performance schema has these key features:

- Provides detailed information about server activity and performance
- Contains tables that provide data on CPU and memory usage, I/O operations, query execution times, and more
- Can be used to identify performance bottlenecks and optimize queries

You can query the performance schema tables to get detailed information on server performance. For example, to get the top 10 queries that take the longest time to execute, you can use the following query:

```
mysql> SELECT * FROM

performance_schema.events_statements_summary_by_digest

ORDER BY SUM_TIMER_WAIT DESC LIMIT 10\G;
*************************** 1. row ***************************
SCHEMA_NAME: appdb
      DIGEST: 8068689efef03df281917f99a32e40d44190227d0bad1f7d7
             dce47a7c0948ae8
DIGEST_TEXT: SELECT `city` . `ID`
AS `CityID` , `city` . `Name` AS `CityName` ,
`city` . `District` AS `CityDistrict` ,
country` . `Code` AS `CountryCode` , `country` . `Name` AS `CountryName` ,
`country` . `Capital` AS `CountryCapital`
, `country` . `Code2` AS `CountryCode2` ,
`countryinfo` . `doc` AS `CountryInfoDoc` , `countryinfo` . `_id`
AS `CountryInfoID` ,
`countrylanguage` . `Language`
AS `CountryLanguage` , `countrylanguage` . `IsOfficial`
AS `IsOfficialLanguage` , `countrylanguage` . `Percentage` AS
`LanguagePercentage` FROM `city` JOIN `country` ON
`city` . `CountryCode` =
`country` . `Code` LEFT JOIN `countryinfo`
ON `country` . `Code` = `countryinfo` . `_json_schema`
 ->> ? JOIN `countrylanguage`
ON `country` . `Code` = `countrylanguage` . `CountryCode`
                COUNT_STAR: 1
            SUM_TIMER_WAIT: 83401227000
            MIN_TIMER_WAIT: 83401227000
            AVG_TIMER_WAIT: 83401227000
            MAX_TIMER_WAIT: 83401227000
             SUM_LOCK_TIME: 11000000
                SUM_ERRORS: 0
              SUM_WARNINGS: 0
         SUM_ROWS_AFFECTED: 0
             SUM_ROWS_SENT: 30670
         SUM_ROWS_EXAMINED: 39067
SUM_CREATED_TMP_DISK_TABLES: 0
     SUM_CREATED_TMP_TABLES: 0
        SUM_SELECT_FULL_JOIN: 1
  SUM_SELECT_FULL_RANGE_JOIN: 0
```

```
         SUM_SELECT_RANGE: 0
   SUM_SELECT_RANGE_CHECK: 0
          SUM_SELECT_SCAN: 1
     SUM_SORT_MERGE_PASSES: 0
           SUM_SORT_RANGE: 0
            SUM_SORT_ROWS: 0
            SUM_SORT_SCAN: 0
        SUM_NO_INDEX_USED: 1
    SUM_NO_GOOD_INDEX_USED: 0
             SUM_CPU_TIME: 0
    MAX_CONTROLLED_MEMORY: 1404736
         MAX_TOTAL_MEMORY: 2332352
          COUNT_SECONDARY: 0
               FIRST_SEEN: 2024-02-16 02:39:54.120086
                LAST_SEEN: 2024-02-16 02:39:54.120086
              QUANTILE_95: 87096358995
              QUANTILE_99: 87096358995
             QUANTILE_999: 87096358995
         QUERY_SAMPLE_TEXT: SELECT
    city.ID AS CityID,
    city.Name AS CityName,
    city.District AS CityDistrict,
    country.Code AS CountryCode,
    country.Name AS CountryName,
    country.Capital AS CountryCapital,
    country.Code2 AS CountryCode2,
    countryinfo.doc AS CountryInfoDoc,
    countryinfo._id AS CountryInfoID,
    countrylanguage.Language AS CountryLanguage,
    countrylanguage.IsOfficial AS IsOfficialLanguage,
    countrylanguage.Percentage AS LanguagePercentage
FROM
    city
JOIN
    country ON city.CountryCode = country.Code
LEFT JOIN
    countryinfo ON country.Code = countryinfo._json_schema->>'$.CountryCode'
JOIN
    countrylanguage ON country.Code = countrylanguage.CountryCode
         QUERY_SAMPLE_SEEN: 2024-02-16 02:39:54.120086
    QUERY_SAMPLE_TIMER_WAIT: 83401227000
```

Information schema

The information schema provides these key features:

- Contains metadata about the server's databases, tables, and columns
- Provides information on indexes, privileges, and other database objects
- Can be used to monitor database usage and identify potential security issues

To query the information schema, you can use standard SQL queries. For example, to get a list of all databases on the server, you can use the following:

```
mysql> SELECT schema_name FROM information_schema.schemata;
+--------------------+
| SCHEMA_NAME        |
+--------------------+
| mysql              |
| information_schema |
| performance_schema |
| sys                |
| world              |
| appdb              |
+--------------------+
6 rows in set (0.00 sec)
mysql>
```

Both schemas can be accessed using SQL queries, which can be run using the MySQL command-line client or a graphical tool like MySQL Workbench.

Using Third-Party Monitoring Tools Like PMM

Percona Monitoring and Management (PMM) is an open source platform for managing and monitoring the performance of databases like MySQL, MongoDB, and PostgreSQL. It provides real-time monitoring and visibility into the database environment, with a user-friendly dashboard that displays critical metrics such as query response time, CPU usage, disk utilization, and memory usage.

PMM uses a client/server architecture: the client runs on the database servers and sends performance data to the PMM server, which stores and visualizes the data. It supports both agent-based and agentless monitoring, allowing administrators to choose the best monitoring approach for their environment.

PMM offers several features to help with database management, including query analytics, which allows administrators to analyze slow queries and optimize query performance. Additionally, PMM is highly scalable, making it suitable for managing large and complex database environments. It is designed to work with both on-premises and cloud-based database environments and is available for download from the Percona website (*https://oreil.ly/D2fDS*).

PMM can be installed on a monitor server, and PMM client can be installed on the MySQL server to collect and send data to the PMM server.

Percona Alerting uses the advanced alerting capabilities of Grafana and adds a layer of alert templates to simplify complex alert rules. Depending on the data sources to be queried and the complexity of the evaluation criteria, the following types of alerts can be created in PMM:

Percona templated alerts

These alerts are based on default templates with common events and expressions for alerting. Custom templates can also be created for customized expressions to base alert rules on.

Grafana managed alerts

These alerts handle complex conditions and can span multiple data sources such as SQL, Prometheus, and InfluxDB. These alerts are stored and executed by Grafana.

Monitoring a MySQL server is a critical task that should be performed regularly to ensure optimal performance and identify and resolve issues before they become severe. Using built-in schemas, working with third-party monitoring tools like PMM, and setting up alerts for critical events are all effective ways to monitor a MySQL server and keep it running smoothly.

Percona Monitoring and Management

PMM offers robust troubleshooting capabilities for MySQL. Users can access a range of metrics for diagnosing performance issues, identifying bottlenecks, and optimizing database performance. PMM provides detailed metrics and visualizations, enabling users to monitor key database parameters in real time. Additionally, PMM includes features like query analytics, allowing users to analyze and optimize SQL queries for improved efficiency. With its comprehensive troubleshooting functionalities, PMM is an essential tool for database administrators aiming to ensure optimal performance and reliability in their MySQL environments.

PMM helps identify performance issues in the following ways:

Real-time monitoring

Real-time monitoring of the database environment includes database performance metrics such as queries per second, database connections, and memory usage. This helps identify performance issues as they occur, allowing for immediate action to be taken.

Query analytics

You can analyze slow queries and identify bottlenecks in your database performance. The query analytics feature enables you to view the slowest queries in real time, allowing you to identify and fix performance issues quickly.

Performance metrics

Various performance metrics can help identify performance issues, such as high network latency affecting database performance; disk I/O bottlenecks from high read/write operations overwhelming the disk; insufficient CPU, memory, or disk

I/O resources; or an insufficient InnoDB buffer pool size. These metrics can be used to pinpoint bottlenecks and optimize performance.

Custom dashboards

You can create custom dashboards that provide an overview of the database environment. This helps identify performance issues quickly by providing a clear overview of system performance.

Alerting

PMM can be configured to send alerts when performance metrics reach specific thresholds. This helps identify performance issues before they become critical.

Overall, PMM is a powerful tool that provides real-time monitoring, query analytics, performance metrics, custom dashboards, and alerting to help identify performance issues and optimize database performance.

Scenario: Troubleshooting Data Corruption

A MySQL server is reporting data corruption errors. The first step in troubleshooting data corruption is to identify which tables are affected. To identify which tables are corrupted using `mysqlcheck`, you can use `mysqlcheck` with the `--check` and `--all-databases` options.

You have a MyISAM table named `mytesttable` containing the following records:

```
mysql> select * from mytesttable;
+----+-------+
| id | name  |
+----+-------+
|  1 | John  |
|  2 | Doe   |
|  3 | Alice |
|  4 | Bob   |
|  5 | John  |
|  6 | Doe   |
|  7 | Alice |
|  8 | Bob   |
+----+-------+
8 rows in set (0.00 sec)
```

The table is currently corrupted. We apologize for not being able to disclose how it became corrupted. Let's run `mysqlcheck` to detect and report the affected table:

```
[root@mysql80 ~]# mysqlcheck --check --all-databases -uroot -p
Enter password:
appdb.city                                    OK
appdb.country                                 OK
appdb.countryinfo                             OK
appdb.countrylanguage                         OK
appdb.mytesttable
```

```
error     : Size of datafile is: 81        Should be: 160
error     : Corrupt
world.city                                  OK
world.country                               OK
world.countryinfo                           OK
world.countrylanguage                       OK
```

Alternatively, you can also check specific tables for corruption as follows:

```
mysqlcheck --check database_name table_name
```

Replace *database_name* and *table_name* with the name of the database and table you want to check for corruption. This command will check the specified table for corruption and report any issues found.

Note that mysqlcheck should be run as the MySQL root user or a user with sufficient privileges to perform repairs. Also, we recommend backing up your databases before running mysqlcheck in case any data is lost during the repair process.

Once you've identified the affected tables, the next step is to determine the cause of the corruption. Some common causes of corruption include the following:

- Hardware issues, such as failing disks or faulty memory
- Software bugs or errors
- Network issues, such as packet loss or corruption

You can use tools like the MySQL error log and system logs to help identify the cause of the corruption. For example, you could check the system logs for any disk or memory errors.

If you're unable to determine the cause, or the corruption is severe, the next step is to restore from a backup. You should always have a backup strategy in place to ensure that you can recover from data loss or corruption.

If the corruption is minor and you have identified the cause, you can try to repair the affected table by using the following command, which will attempt to repair the table and fix any corruption issues:

```
[root@mysql80 ~]# mysqlcheck -r appdb mytesttable -uroot -p
Enter password:
appdb.mytesttable
warning : Number of rows changed from 8 to 4
status  : OK
[root@mysql80 ~]#

mysql> select * from mytesttable;
+----+-------+
| id | name  |
+----+-------+
|  1 | John  |
|  2 | Doe   |
```

```
|  3 | Alice |
|  4 | Bob   |
+----+-------+
4 rows in set (0.00 sec)
```

 REPAIR is practically guaranteed to lose data since it merely deletes corrupt records, and it does not address issues for InnoDB.

The command `mysqlcheck -r -A` is used to repair and optimize all tables in all databases on a MySQL server. Here's a breakdown of the options used in this command:

`mysqlcheck`
This is the command-line utility used to check, repair, and optimize MySQL tables.

`-r`

This option instructs `mysqlcheck` to repair any corrupted tables it finds. This can include fixing index errors, repairing tables that were not closed properly, and resolving other types of corruption.

`-A`

This option tells `mysqlcheck` to check all databases on the server, not just a specific one.

When run, the `mysqlcheck -r -A` command will go through each database on the MySQL server and check each table for errors. If it finds any errors, it will automatically attempt to repair them. Additionally, the command will optimize each table, which can help improve query performance. Running this command can take some time, especially on large servers with many databases and tables. By following these steps, you can quickly identify and address data corruption issues in your MySQL server, helping to ensure that your database remains reliable and consistent.

Starting from MySQL 8, the default storage engine is InnoDB. Dealing with InnoDB corruption presents a distinct set of challenges and requires a completely different approach. To examine database page corruption, consider exporting your tables by using the `SELECT…INTO OUTFILE` method. Typically, data retrieved in this manner remains intact. However, severe corruption might lead to unexpected exits or assertions during statements like `SELECT * FROM tbl_name` or InnoDB background operations. It can even result in crashes during InnoDB roll-forward recovery. In such instances, employing the `innodb_force_recovery` option allows the InnoDB storage engine to start up, preventing background operations and enabling you to export your tables. We advise maintaining at least one replica and comprehensive backups, including logical and physical backups along with binlogs, to mitigate such scenarios.

Troubleshooting MySQL Server Issues

As a MySQL administrator, it's important to have a good understanding of how to troubleshoot common problems that can arise with your database server. Despite having the best configuration and monitoring practices in place, issues can still occur, so it's essential to know how to identify and address them. This section covers some of the most common issues that can affect MySQL and provide you with troubleshooting techniques to help you get your server back up and running in no time.

Connection Errors

Connection errors can happen for a variety of reasons, but the most common ones include incorrect login credentials, network connectivity issues, and server overload. Here are some techniques you can use to troubleshoot connection errors:

Check your login credentials
> Verify that you're using the correct username and password to connect to MySQL.

Check network connectivity
> Make sure that the server is accessible over the network and that no firewall rules are blocking the connection.

Check server load
> Check the server's resource usage to ensure that it's not overloaded.

Scenario: Handling a Connection Error

A user reports that they are unable to connect to MySQL. To help them resolve this issue, you'll first need to verify the MySQL server status. Is MySQL running? You can check this by running the following command:

```
[root@mysql80 ~]# systemctl status mysqld
mysqld.service - MySQL Server
     Loaded: loaded (/usr/lib/systemd/system/mysqld.service;
     enabled; preset: disabled)
     Active: active (running) since Fri 2024-02-16 01:37:57
     UTC; 1h 8min ago
       Docs: man:mysqld(8)
             http://dev.mysql.com/doc/refman/en/using-systemd.html
    Process: 4397 ExecStartPre=/usr/bin/mysqld_pre_systemd
    (code=exited, status=0/SUCCESS)
   Main PID: 4424 (mysqld)
     Status: "Server is operational"
      Tasks: 39 (limit: 24734)
     Memory: 423.5M
        CPU: 25.481s
     CGroup: /system.slice/mysqld.service
```

```
                    └4424 /usr/sbin/mysqld
    Feb 16 01:37:55 mysql80 systemd[1]: Starting MySQL Server...
    Feb 16 01:37:57 mysql80 systemd[1]: Started MySQL Server.
    [root@mysql80 ~]#
```

This command will tell you whether MySQL is running and if there are any errors or warnings. If MySQL is not running, you need to verify why it is down and can start it by running the `service mysql start` command.

Next, check the login credentials. Check the details of the user account such as the host from which it is connecting, whether it has the necessary privileges to connect, and if the user account is locked or expired:

```
mysql> SELECT Host,User,password_expired,account_locked FROM mysql.user
       WHERE
    -> user='tstappuser'\G
*************************** 1. row ***************************
           Host: 192.168.20.73
           User: tstappuser
password_expired: N
  account_locked: Y
1 row in set (0.00 sec)
mysql>
```

In this example, since the user account is locked, the user would encounter the following error:

```
[root@ApplicationServer ~]# mysql -h192.168.20.71
-u'tstappuser'-p -e "show databases;"
Enter password:
ERROR 3118 (HY000): Access denied for user

'tstappuser'@'192.168.20.73'.Account is locked.
[root@ApplicationServer ~]#
```

To resolve this issue, you can unlock the user:

```
mysql> ALTER USER 'tstappuser'@'192.168.20.73' ACCOUNT UNLOCK;
Query OK, 0 rows affected (0.01 sec)
mysql>
```

Running this command will unlock the specified user (appuser in this case) and allow them to access the system again. To verify that the root user can connect, use the following command from the database server itself:

```
[root@mysql80 ~]# mysql -uroot -p
Enter password:
Welcome to the MySQL monitor.  Commands end with ; or \g.
Your MySQL connection id is 15
Server version: 8.0.36 MySQL Community Server - GPL
Type 'help;' or '\h' for help. Type '\c' to clear the current
input statement.
mysql>
```

Running this command will prompt you to enter the root user's password. If you're able to successfully log in to the MySQL server, it indicates that the root user can connect. If everything appears to be in order with the user account, further investigation may be required to check for network connectivity issues, server load, and other factors that could cause MySQL to hang. You can use commands like these to perform network connectivity checks:

Ping test

The command `ping` tests network connectivity to the specified IP address by sending two Internet Control Message Protocol (ICMP) echo request packets:

```
[root@mysql80 ~]# ping 192.168.20.71 -c 2
PING 192.168.20.71 (192.168.20.71) 56(84) bytes of data.
64 bytes from 192.168.20.71: icmp_seq=1 ttl=64 time=0.042 ms
64 bytes from 192.168.20.71: icmp_seq=2 ttl=64 time=0.109 ms

--- 192.168.20.71 ping statistics ---
2 packets transmitted, 2 received, 0% packet loss, time 1009ms
rtt min/avg/max/mdev = 0.042/0.075/0.109/0.033 ms
[root@mysql80 ~]#
```

Telnet test

The command `telnet` checks network connectivity to the MySQL server at IP address 172.31.91.101 on port 3306:

```
[root@mysql80 ~]# telnet 192.168.20.71 3306
Trying 192.168.20.71...
Connected to 192.168.20.71.
Escape character is '^]'.
FHost '192.168.20.71' is not allowed to connect to this MySQL
serverConnection closed by foreign host.
[root@mysql80 ~]#
```

If the server is not accessible, you may need to check the firewall rules and ensure that MySQL is listening on the correct network interface.

Bind address

Verify the bind-address setting. Starting from MySQL 8.0.13, it is possible to configure the server to listen on multiple specific interfaces. For example, if your server has addresses 192.168.1.1 and 10.0.0.1, you can specify the binding as follows:

```
--bind-address=192.168.1.1,10.0.0.1
```

Keep in mind that the port number used for accepting incoming TCP connections remains the same for every IP address listed in the `--bind-address` option. Therefore, this implementation does not alter the way the port number is specified. The configuration for the `mysqld` section of your *my.cnf* file should look like this:

```
[mysqld]
bind-address=192.168.1.1,10.0.1.1
```

Finally, check the server load. If network connectivity is not the issue, the next step would be to check the server's resource usage. You could use the following command to check the server's CPU, memory, and disk usage:

```
[root@mysql80 ~]# top
top - 03:03:17 up  2:38,  2 users,  load average: 0.00, 0.01, 0.00
Tasks: 116 total,   2 running, 114 sleeping,   0 stopped,   0 zombie
%Cpu(s):  0.3 us,  0.3 sy,  0.0 ni, 98.7 id,  0.0 wa,  0.7 hi,  0.0 si,
  0.0 st
MiB Mem :   3904.2 total,   2776.7 free,    893.3 used,
    470.6 buff/cache
MiB Swap:   2084.0 total,   2084.0 free,      0.0 used.
  3010.9 avail Mem
  PID USER      PR  NI    VIRT    RES    SHR S  %CPU  %MEM
      TIME+ COMMAND
 4424 mysql     20   0 1316336 434412  34832 S   0.3  10.9
    0:29.87 mysqld
 4784 vagrant   20   0   19152   7428   5464 S   0.3   0.2
    0:00.02 sshd
    1 root      20   0  172012  16304  10908 S   0.0   0.4
    0:02.23 systemd
    2 root      20   0       0      0      0 S   0.0   0.0
    0:00.00 kthreadd
```

If the server is heavily loaded, you may need to optimize your MySQL configuration or upgrade your server hardware. By following these steps, you can quickly diagnose and troubleshoot the user's connection issue, helping to keep your MySQL server running smoothly and reliably.

Performance Issues

Performance issues can manifest in many ways, including slow query execution times, slow server response times, and high CPU usage. Here are some techniques to help you identify and address performance issues:

Monitor server resources
> Use tools like top, iostat, and vmstat to monitor the server's CPU, memory, and disk usage.

Monitor query performance
> Use the MySQL slow query log and other profiling tools to identify slow-performing queries.

Optimize query performance
> Once you've identified slow-performing queries, you can optimize them by adding indexes, rewriting the queries, or splitting them into smaller queries.

Step 1: Monitor server resources

The first step in troubleshooting a performance issue is to monitor server resources to determine whether the issue is related to resource usage. You can use tools like top, iostat, and vmstat to monitor the server's CPU, memory, and disk usage. For example, you could run the following command to check the server's CPU usage:

```
[root@mysql80 ~]# top
top - 03:03:17 up  2:38,  2 users,  load average: 0.00, 0.01, 0.00
Tasks: 116 total,   2 running, 114 sleeping,   0 stopped,   0 zombie
%Cpu(s):  0.3 us,  0.3 sy,  0.0 ni, 98.7 id,  0.0 wa,  0.7 hi,  0.0 si,  0.0 st
MiB Mem :   3904.2 total,   2776.7 free,    893.3 used,    470.6 buff/cache
MiB Swap:   2084.0 total,   2084.0 free,      0.0 used.   3010.9 avail Mem

    PID USER      PR  NI    VIRT    RES    SHR S  %CPU  %MEM     TIME+ COMMAND
   4424 mysql     20   0 1316336 434412  34832 S   0.3  10.9   0:29.87 mysqld
   4784 vagrant   20   0   19152   7428   5464 S   0.3   0.2   0:00.02 sshd
      1 root      20   0  172012  16304  10908 S   0.0   0.4   0:02.23 systemd
      2 root      20   0       0      0      0 S   0.0   0.0   0:00.00 kthreadd
```

If the CPU usage is consistently high, you may need to investigate what is causing the high usage and optimize accordingly.

Step 2: Monitor query performance

Once you've ruled out resource issues, the next step is to monitor query performance. You can use tools like the MySQL slow query log and other profiling tools to identify slow-performing queries. For example, you could enable the slow query log and set a low threshold for query execution time. Here's an example configuration:

```
slow_query_log = 1
slow_query_log_file = /var/log/mysql/mysql-slow.log
long_query_time = 1
```

This configuration will log any queries that take longer than 1 second to execute.

Step 3: Optimize query performance

Once you've identified slow-performing queries, you can optimize them to improve performance. Some optimization techniques include the following:

- Adding indexes to tables
- Rewriting queries to use more efficient methods
- Splitting large queries into smaller, more manageable ones

For example, you could use the EXPLAIN command to analyze the query execution plan and identify any potential issues. Here's an example:

```
mysql> EXPLAIN SELECT
    ->     city.ID AS CityID,
    ->     city.Name AS CityName,
    ->     city.District AS CityDistrict,
    ->     country.Code AS CountryCode,
    ->     country.Name AS CountryName,
    ->     country.Capital AS CountryCapital,
    ->     country.Code2 AS CountryCode2,
    ->     countryinfo.doc AS CountryInfoDoc,
    ->     countryinfo._id AS CountryInfoID,
    ->     countrylanguage.Language AS CountryLanguage,
    ->     countrylanguage.IsOfficial AS IsOfficialLanguage,
    ->     countrylanguage.Percentage AS LanguagePercentage
    -> FROM
    ->     city
    -> JOIN
    ->     country ON city.CountryCode = country.Code
    -> LEFT JOIN
    ->     countryinfo ON country.Code = countryinfo._json_schema->>'$.
CountryCode'
    -> JOIN
    ->     countrylanguage ON country.Code = countrylanguage.CountryCode\G
*************************** 1. row ***************************
           id: 1
  select_type: SIMPLE
        table: city
   partitions: NULL
         type: ALL
possible_keys: NULL
          key: NULL
      key_len: NULL
          ref: NULL
         rows: 3972
     filtered: 100.00
        Extra: NULL
*************************** 2. row ***************************
           id: 1
  select_type: SIMPLE
        table: country
   partitions: NULL
         type: eq_ref
possible_keys: PRIMARY
          key: PRIMARY
      key_len: 12
          ref: appdb.city.CountryCode
         rows: 1
     filtered: 100.00
        Extra: NULL
*************************** 3. row ***************************
```

```
            id: 1
    select_type: SIMPLE
          table: countrylanguage
     partitions: NULL
           type: ref
  possible_keys: PRIMARY,CountryCode
            key: PRIMARY
        key_len: 12
            ref: appdb.city.CountryCode
           rows: 4
       filtered: 100.00
          Extra: NULL
*************************** 4. row ***************************
            id: 1
    select_type: SIMPLE
          table: countryinfo
     partitions: NULL
           type: ALL
  possible_keys: NULL
            key: NULL
        key_len: NULL
            ref: NULL
           rows: 239
       filtered: 100.00
          Extra: Using where; Using join buffer (hash join)
4 rows in set, 1 warning (0.00 sec)
mysql>
```

This command will show you the query execution plan and highlight any potential performance issues, such as full table scans or inefficient joins. By following these steps, you can quickly identify and address performance issues in your MySQL server, helping to ensure that your database performs optimally and efficiently.

Step 4: Use a third-party tool to gather data and identify issues

In this step, consider employing a third-party tool to gather data or pinpoint performance issues on your MySQL server. The diagnostic tool pt-stalk is included in the Percona Toolkit, a collection of open source tools for MySQL performance analysis, management, and monitoring. The pt-stalk tool is designed to automatically collect diagnostic data when specific conditions are met, such as a high CPU load or slow queries. It periodically checks the server's performance metrics and takes action when the predefined threshold is reached, collecting data and logs for further analysis.

The pt-stalk tool is valuable for troubleshooting intermittent issues or problems that are difficult to reproduce. It can help identify the root cause of performance problems by gathering data at the time the problem occurs, making it easier to diagnose and fix the issue. It can be used in combination with other tools in the Percona Toolkit for a comprehensive diagnostic and analysis solution.

To ensure reliable triggers for MySQL, we recommend considering the number of queries running concurrently. These metrics can be accessed through the SHOW GLOBAL STATUS command as Threads_running, which is pt-stalk's default trigger. As the user of the tool, it is essential to select an appropriate trigger condition to ensure accurate results.

To define a trigger, use the options --function, --variable, --threshold, and --cycles. To collect logs when there is replication delay, a custom script needs to be written and called using the --function=my-custom-plugin.sh option. The default values for these options are generally sufficient, but adjustments may be necessary to meet specific system requirements and needs.

Installing the Percona Toolkit

pt-stalk is a command-line tool part of the Percona Toolkit that can be installed on any MySQL server that meets the system requirements for the Percona Toolkit. It is available for download from the Percona website and is distributed under the open source license.

The package manager yum—for Red Hat Enterprise Linux (RHEL)—is used to install Percona Toolkit on Linux in this section's examples. However, alternative package managers, like apt-get (for Debian or Ubuntu) can also be used, depending on the system configuration. To install the utility, you must first configure the Percona repository. To configure Percona repositories in RHEL, follow these steps:

```
[root@mysql80 mysql]# sudo yum install https://repo.percona.com/yum/
percona-release-latest.noarch.rpm

Updating Subscription Management repositories.
Red Hat Enterprise Linux 9 for x86_64 - AppStream from RHUI (RPMs)
    49 MB/s |  29 MB     00:00
Dependencies resolved.
..
Total size: 20 k
Installed size: 32 k
Is this ok [y/N]: y
```

Confirm the installed repository packages and their versions on the server:

```
Verifying        : percona-release-1.0-27.noarch     1/1
Installed products updated.
Installed:
  percona-release-1.0-27.noarch
Complete!
```

Use the corresponding package manager to install the toolkit:

```
[root@mysql80 mysql]# sudo yum install percona-toolkit
Updating Subscription Management repositories.
Unable to read consumer identity
Last metadata expiration check: 0:01:48 ago on Fri 16
Feb 2024 03:32:09 PM UTC.
Dependencies resolved.
...
Install  14 Packages
Total download size: 20 M
Installed size: 22 M
Is this ok [y/N]: y
```

Verify that the package installed and confirm the version installed on the server:

```
Installed products updated.
Installed:
mariadb-connector-c-3.2.6-1.el9_0.x86_6 percona-toolkit-3.5.7-1.el9.x86_64
perl-DBD-MySQL-4.050-13.el9.x86_64 perl-DBI-1.643-9.el9.x86_64
perl-DynaLoader-1.47-480.el9.x86_64 perl-English-1.11-480.el9.noarch
perl-FindBin-1.51-480.el9.noarch perl-Math-BigInt-1:1.9998.18-460.el9.noarch
perl-Math-Complex-1.59-480.el9.noarch
perl-Sys-Hostname-1.23-480.el9.x86_64
perl-TermReadKey-2.38-11.el9.x86_64
perl-Time-HiRes-4:1.9764-462.el9.x86_64
perl-meta-notation-5.32.1-480.el9.noarch
perl-sigtrap-1.09-480.el9.noarch

Complete!
[root@mysql80 mysql]#
```

For Debian or Ubuntu, use the following command:

```
sudo apt update
sudo apt install curl
curl -O
https://repo.percona.com/apt/percona-release_latest.generic_all.deb
sudo apt install gnupg2 lsb-release
./percona-release_latest.generic_all.deb
sudo apt update
sudo percona-release setup tools
sudo apt-get install percona-toolkit
```

Use the following command to collect the logs with pt-stalk:

```
[root@mysql80 mysql]# /usr/bin/pt-stalk --daemonize --cycles=2
--threshold=30 --sleep=120 --collect
--dest=/home/percona/pt-stalk_logs
[root@mysql80 mysql]#

[root@mysql80 mysql]# ps -ef | grep -i pt-stalk
root       18737       1  0 16:10 pts/1    00:00:00 /usr/bin/bash
/usr/bin/pt-stalk
```

```
--daemonize --cycles=2 --threshold=30 --sleep=120 --collect
--dest=/home/percona/pt-stalk_logs
root       18832    9511  0 16:10 pts/1    00:00:00 grep
--color=auto -i pt-stalk
[root@mysql80 mysql]#
```

This command runs `pt-stalk` in daemon mode, collecting data for two cycles with a threshold of 30, sleeping for 120 seconds between cycles, and storing the collected data in the *home/percona/pt-stalk_logs* directory:[1]

```
[root@mysql80 mysql]# ls /home/percona/pt-stalk_logs/
2024_02_16_16_13_33-df  2024_02_16_16_13_33-meminfo
2024_02_16_16_13_33-prepared-statements  2024_02_16_16_13_33-sysctl
2024_02_16_16_13_33-disk-space  2024_02_16_16_13_33-mutex-status1
2024_02_16_16_13_33-processlist  2024_02_16_16_13_33-top
2024_02_16_16_13_33-diskstats  2024_02_16_16_13_33-mysqladmin
2024_02_16_16_13_33-procstat  2024_02_16_16_13_33-transactions
2024_02_16_16_13_33-dmesg  2024_02_16_16_13_33-netstat
2024_02_16_16_13_33-procvmstat  2024_02_16_16_13_33-trigger
2024_02_16_16_13_33-innodbstatus1  2024_02_16_16_13_33-netstat_s
2024_02_16_16_13_33-ps  2024_02_16_16_13_33-variables
2024_02_16_16_13_33-interrupts  2024_02_16_16_13_33-numastat
2024_02_16_16_13_33-ps-locks-transactions  2024_02_16_16_13_33-vmstat
2024_02_16_16_13_33-lock-waits  2024_02_16_16_13_33-opentables1
2024_02_16_16_13_33-slabinfo 2024_02_16_16_13_33-vmstat-overall
2024_02_16_16_13_33-log_error 2024_02_16_16_13_33-output
2024_02_16_16_13_33-slave-status
[root@mysql80 mysql]#
```

To monitor the usage of swap memory in MySQL, you can create a file called *swap-check* and insert the following trigger code:

```
vi swap_check
function trg_plugin() {
    vmstat 1 2 | awk 'NR==3 {if ($7 > 0 || $8 > 0) print int(($7 + $8)/1024)}'
}
```

This trigger will capture the amount of swap memory that has been used on the server, and if it reaches the threshold of 1,000 MB, it will capture all information about your database and operating system. Note that the trigger will run whenever MySQL starts to swap.

---

1 While MySQL databases historically used the terms *master* and *slave* to describe replication relationships, a shift to more neutral terminology (e.g., *source* and *replica*) is underway. You will likely encounter both sets of terms in your work and in this book.

To run `pt-stalk` with this trigger, use the following command:

```
[root@mysql80 mysql]# pt-stalk --function /home/percona/swap_check
--threshold 1000 --dest=/home/percona/pt-stalk_logs
--daemonize --notify-by-email=YOUR@EMAIL
[root@mysql80 mysql]#

[root@mysql80 mysql]# ps -ef | grep -i pt-stalk
root       25552      1  0 16:18 pts/1    00:00:00 /usr/bin/bash
/bin/pt-stalk --function /home/percona/swap_check
--threshold 1000 --dest=/home/percona/pt-stalk_logs
--daemonize --notify-by-email=YOUR@EMAIL
root       25735  16883  0 16:19 pts/2    00:00:00 grep
--color=auto -i pt-stalk
[root@mysql80 mysql]#
```

The `--function` option specifies the name of the function to be executed as the trigger. The `--threshold` option specifies the threshold value that triggers the function to execute. The `--daemonize` option will run `pt-stalk` in the background, and `--notify-by-email` will send an email notification to the specified email address after the trigger condition has been met.

MySQL Crashes

Server crashes can occur for a variety of reasons, including hardware failures, software bugs, and operating system issues. Here are some techniques to help you identify and address server crashes:

Check error logs
Review the MySQL error logs to identify any issues leading up to the server crash.

Check system logs
Review the system logs to identify any issues with the OS or hardware.

Restore from backups
If the server crash results in data loss, restore the affected databases from backups.

Scenario: Troubleshooting MySQL Crashes

The MySQL server has crashed and is no longer responding. In such situations, troubleshooting steps are crucial to identify the root cause and promptly resolve the issue.

The first step is to check the server logs for error messages or warnings that might indicate the cause of the crash. The MySQL error log is typically located in the */var/log/mysql* directory on Unix-based systems or in the MySQL installation directory on Windows systems. To access it, you must first locate its location on your system. This can typically be found in the *my.cnf* or *my.ini* configuration file. Once you have located the file, you can open it by using a text editor or command-line interface. You can also access the MySQL error log from the console. To view it, follow these steps:

1. Open the MySQL console by typing the following command into your terminal and enter your MySQL password when prompted:

   ```
   [root@mysql80 ~]# mysql -u root -p
   Enter password:
   Welcome to the MySQL monitor.  Commands end with ; or \g.
   Server version: 8.0.36 MySQL Community Server - GPL

   Type 'help;' or '\h' for help. Type '\c' to clear the current input
   statement.
   mysql>
   ```

2. Once you are logged in to the MySQL console, execute the following command to display the location of the error logfile:

   ```
   mysql> SHOW VARIABLES LIKE 'log_error';
   +---------------+---------------------+
   | Variable_name | Value               |
   +---------------+---------------------+
   | log_error     | /var/log/mysqld.log |
   +---------------+---------------------+
   1 row in set (0.02 sec)
   mysql>
   ```

3. Use the less command to view the contents of the error logfile. For example:

   ```
   [root@mysql80 ~]# sudo less /var/log/mysqld.log
   ```

4. This will display the error logfile on your console. You can use the arrow keys to navigate through the log and the Q key to exit the less command.

5. Alternatively, you can select from the table performance_schema.error_log:

```
mysql> mysql>
  select * from performance_schema.error_log
  ORDER BY LOGGED DESC limit 2\G

*************************** 1. row ***************************
    LOGGED: 2024-02-16 05:19:04.192183
 THREAD_ID: 12
      PRIO: Error
ERROR_CODE: MY-011063
 SUBSYSTEM: Server
      DATA: MySQL thread id 12, OS thread handle
      140363899561536, query id 88 localhost root
      Checking table CHECK TABLE `mytesttable`.
*************************** 2. row ***************************
    LOGGED: 2024-02-16 05:19:04.192122
 THREAD_ID: 12
      PRIO: Error
ERROR_CODE: MY-010238
 SUBSYSTEM: Server
      DATA: Got an error from thread_id=12,
      /var/lib/pb2/sb_1-13696040-1702406400.7729394/rpm/
      BUILD/mysql-8.0.36/mysql-8.0.36/storage/myisam/
      ha_myisam.cc:893
2 rows in set (0.00 sec)

mysql>
```

Next, you'll need to check the operating system log. When MySQL crashes, it may generate entries in the operating system log that can provide additional information about the cause of the crash. These entries could include kernel messages, disk I/O errors, and other system events that could have impacted the MySQL service.

To check the system log in Linux, you can use the journalctl command. The exact syntax of the command may vary depending on your Linux distribution, but a common way to search for messages related to MySQL crashes is to use the following command:

```
journalctl -u mysql.service --since "10 minutes ago"
```

This will show all log entries related to the mysql.service unit that have been generated within the last 10 minutes. You can adjust the time window as needed to cover the period when the crash occurred.

Alternatively, you can search for log entries containing specific keywords related to the MySQL service. For example:

```
journalctl -u mysql.service -p err
```

This will show all log entries related to the `mysql.service` unit that have a severity level of `error`. You can adjust the severity level as needed to search for different types of log entries.

In a similar case where MySQL has crashed, `dmesg` can also be helpful in identifying the cause. The `dmesg` command displays the kernel ring buffer, which contains messages generated by the kernel during system startup and operation. When MySQL crashes, the kernel may generate messages related to hardware or software issues that could have caused the crash. These messages could include hardware errors, driver issues, or other system-level problems. To view the `dmesg` output, you can use the following command:

```
dmesg | tail -n 100
```

This will show the last 100 lines of the `dmesg` output. You can adjust the number of lines as needed to show more or fewer messages:

```
dmesg -T
```

The `dmesg` command in Linux is used to display kernel ring buffer messages. The `-T` option displays timestamps in a human-readable format. When you run `dmesg -T` in a terminal, it will show you the kernel messages along with their timestamps.

When reviewing the `dmesg` output, look for any messages related to hardware or system-level issues that could have impacted MySQL. For example, you might see messages related to disk I/O errors, memory issues, or driver problems. These messages can provide valuable clues about the cause of the MySQL crash. The `dmesg` output can be quite verbose, so it may be difficult to identify relevant messages without some knowledge of the system and its hardware components. However, reviewing the `dmesg` output can be a useful step in troubleshooting a MySQL crash.

Finally, check the system resources. Check that there is enough free disk space, memory, and CPU resources available on the server.

How to Check System Resources for the MySQL Host

MySQL server performance can be affected by various factors, including system resources. Therefore, it is important to regularly monitor and check the available system resources on the host machine where MySQL server is running. This section covers several options to monitor system resources on MySQL hosts.

Step 1: Check disk space and status

The first factor to check is the available disk space on the MySQL host. To check the disk space on Linux or Unix-based systems, use the following command:

```
[root@mysql80 ~]# df -h
Filesystem                    Size  Used Avail Use% Mounted on
devtmpfs                      4.0M     0  4.0M   0% /dev
tmpfs                         2.0G     0  2.0G   0% /dev/shm
tmpfs                         781M   17M  765M   3% /run
/dev/mapper/rhel_rhel9-root    70G  2.9G   68G   5% /
/dev/sda1                     960M  177M  784M  19% /boot
MySQL80                       300G  283G   18G  95% /media/sf_MySQL80
tmpfs                         391M     0  391M   0% /run/user/1000
[root@mysql80 ~]#
```

This command displays the disk usage statistics in human-readable format. The output will show the total disk space, used disk space, available disk space, and the percentage of disk space used. If the available disk space is low, it can affect the performance of the MySQL server. In such a case, you may need to delete unnecessary files or add more storage space.

The pt-diskstats tool from Percona Toolkit is used to collect and analyze disk I/O statistics on a Linux system. It gathers information about disk activity, including read and write operations, and presents it in a structured format. DBAs can use pt-diskstats to monitor disk performance, identify potential bottlenecks, and troubleshoot I/O-related issues that might affect the performance of MySQL or other applications running on the server. It is a valuable tool for understanding how disk I/O is affecting the performance of a MySQL database or other processes on a Linux server, helping administrators make informed decisions about optimizing system performance:

```
[root@mysql80 ~]# pt-diskstats --devices-regex 'xvda|xvda1'
  #ts device   rd_s rd_avkb rd_mb_s rd_mrg rd_cnc   rd_rt   wr_s wr_avkb
  wr_mb_s wr_mrg wr_cnc  wr_rt busy in_prg   io_s qtime stime
  0.3 xvda      0.0     0.0     0.0     0%    0.0     0.0   11.7     4.0
  0.0     0%    0.0     0.2    1%      0   11.7    -0.5   0.8
  0.3 xvda1     0.0     0.0     0.0     0%    0.0     0.0   11.7     4.0
  0.0     0%    0.0     0.2    0%      0   11.7     0.0   0.2

  1.0 xvda      0.0     0.0     0.0     0%    0.0     0.0  130.0     7.4
  0.9     0%    0.1     1.0    2%      0  130.0     0.8   0.2
  1.0 xvda1     0.0     0.0     0.0     0%    0.0     0.0   32.0     4.0
  0.1     0%    0.0     0.2    1%      0   32.0     0.0   0.2

  1.0 xvda      0.0     0.0     0.0     0%    0.0     0.0   28.0     4.3
  0.1     0%    0.0     0.1    2%      0   28.0    -0.5   0.7
  1.0 xvda1     0.0     0.0     0.0     0%    0.0     0.0   28.0     4.3
  0.1     0%    0.0     0.1    0%      0   28.0     0.0   0.1
```

Step 2: Check memory usage

The next step is to check the physical memory and swap usage on the MySQL host. To check the memory usage on Linux or Unix-based systems, use the `free -m` command, which displays details on total available memory, used memory, free memory, as well as memory used for cache and buffers, along with swap usage information:

```
[root@mysql80 ~]# free -m
              total  used  free  shared  buff/cache  available
Mem:          3904   929   2634  16      577         2974
Swap:         2083   0     2083
[root@mysql80 ~]#
```

The `ps aux --sort=-%mem` command lists the top three processes in terms of memory usage on a Linux system, sorted by memory usage in descending order. The purpose of the command is to assist in identifying the process that is using the most memory when troubleshooting certain issues:

```
[root@mysql80 ~]# ps aux --sort=-%mem | awk 'NR<=3{print $0}'
USER        PID %CPU %MEM    VSZ    RSS TTY        STAT START
TIME COMMAND
mysql      5910  0.8 11.0 1315192 442360 ?         Ssl  05:13
0:07 /usr/sbin/mysqld
root        677  0.0  1.1 285980 47800 ?           Ssl  00:24
0:01 /usr/bin/python3
-s /usr/sbin/firewalld --nofork --nopid
[root@mysql80 ~]#
```

The output of this command is then piped (|) to the `awk` command, which is a versatile text-processing tool that allows you to perform various operations on text data. In this case, `awk` is used to print the top three processes in terms of memory usage. Here is a breakdown of the command:

NR<=3{print $0}
: An `awk` command that uses a condition (NR<=3) and an action ({print $0}) to filter and print the first three lines of the output from the previous command.

NR
: A built-in `awk` variable that represents the current line number. The NR<=3 condition checks whether the line number is less than or equal to 3.

{print $0}
: The action that is executed if the condition is true. $0 is a special variable that represents the entire line of text, so `print $0` simply prints the entire line.

MySQL server heavily relies on memory, and insufficient memory can severely affect its performance. If the used memory is close to or exceeds the available memory, you may need to add more memory or optimize the MySQL configuration.

Step 3: Check CPU usage

To check the CPU usage on Linux or Unix-based systems, you can use the following command:

top

```
top - 05:29:34 up  5:04,  3 users,  load average: 0.01, 0.04, 0.00
Tasks: 121 total,   1 running, 120 sleeping,   0 stopped,   0 zombie
%Cpu(s):  0.0 us,  6.2 sy,  0.0 ni, 93.8 id,  0.0 wa,  0.0 hi,  0.0 si,  0.0 st
MiB Mem :   3904.2 total,   2705.4 free,    858.2 used,    577.3 buff/cache
MiB Swap:   2084.0 total,   2084.0 free,      0.0 used.   3046.0 avail Mem

    PID USER      PR  NI    VIRT    RES    SHR S  %CPU  %MEM     TIME+ COMMAND
   6295 root      20   0   10592   3980   3372 R   6.2   0.1   0:00.01 top
      1 root      20   0  172012  16312  10908 S   0.0   0.4   0:02.51 systemd
      2 root      20   0       0      0      0 S   0.0   0.0   0:00.00 kthreadd
      3 root       0 -20       0      0      0 I   0.0   0.0   0:00.00 rcu_gp
      4 root       0 -20       0      0      0 I   0.0   0.0   0:00.00 rcu_par_gp
      5 root       0 -20       0      0      0 I   0.0   0.0   0:00.00 slub_flushwq
```

This command displays the real-time CPU usage statistics for all running processes on the system. High CPU usage can indicate that the MySQL server is under heavy load or that other processes are consuming too much CPU resources. In such a case, you may need to optimize the MySQL queries or add more CPU resources to the host machine.

Checking system resources on a regular basis is crucial for ensuring optimal MySQL server performance. By following these best practices, you can ensure that enough free disk space, memory, and CPU resources are available on the MySQL host machine. If any of the resources are running low, it is important to take corrective measures to avoid any potential performance issues.

Step 4: Summarize the status and configuration of a server

The command-line tool `pt-summary` is used for gathering system information on Linux servers. When you run `pt-summary` on a Linux server, it collects data about the system and provides a summary of various components such as CPU usage, memory usage, disk space, and network interfaces. The output is presented in an easy-to-read format and can be useful for monitoring server performance, troubleshooting issues, and identifying potential bottlenecks.

Using `pt-summary` is simple. Percona Toolkit includes this tool, which can be set up or downloaded alone using `wget`. The tool will gather system information and present it in the terminal. You can also use command-line options to customize the output, such as specifying the number of CPU cores to display or showing disk usage in a human-readable format.

Overall, `pt-summary` is a useful tool for system administrators and developers who need to monitor the performance of Linux servers. Here is an example illustrating the appearance of the `pt-summary` report:

```
root@mysql80 ~: ~]pt-summary
# Percona Toolkit System Summary Report ######################
        Date | 2023-11-30 08:01:52 UTC (local TZ: UTC +0000)
    Hostname | ip-195-43-85-227
      Uptime | 2 days, 18:21,  2 users,  load average: 0.36, 0.09, 0.03
      System | Xen; HVM domU; v4.11.amazon (Other)
 Service Tag | ec2********
    Platform | Linux
     Release | Ubuntu 22.04.3 LTS (jammy)
      Kernel | 6.2.0-1012-aws
Architecture | CPU = 64-bit, OS = 64-bit
   Threading | NPTL 2.35
      SELinux | No SELinux detected
 Virtualized | Xen
# Processor #############################################
  Processors | physical = 1, cores = 1, virtual = 1, hyperthreading = no
      Speeds | 1x2399.803
      Models | 1xIntel(R) Xeon(R) CPU E5-2676 v3 @ 2.40GHz
      Caches | 1x30720 KB
# Memory #############################################
       Total | 949.7M
        Free | 150.8M
        Used | physical = 534.9M, swap allocated = 0.0, swap used = 0.0,
               virtual = 534.9M
      Shared | 876.0k
     Buffers | 264.1M
      Caches | 253.6M
       Dirty | 368 kB
     UsedRSS | 580.5M
  Swappiness | 60
 DirtyPolicy | 20, 10
 DirtyStatus | 0, 0
  Locator   Size     Speed              Form Factor    Type          Type Detail
  ========= ======== ================== ============= ============= ===========
  DIMM 0    1 GB     Unknown            DIMM          RAM           None
# Mounted Filesystems ###################################
  Filesystem    Size Used Type  Opts
  /dev/xvda15   105M  6% vfat    rw,relatime,fmask=0077,dmask=0077,codepage=437,
  iocharset=iso8859-1,
  shortname=mixed,errors=remount-ro /boot/efi
  tmpfs          95M  1% tmpfs rw,nosuid,nodev,inode64
  tmpfs          95M  1% tmpfs rw,nosuid,nodev,size=194500k,nr_inodes=819200,
  mode=755,inode64                              /run/user/1000
  tmpfs          95M  1% tmpfs rw,nosuid,nodev,noexec,relatime,size=5120k,
  inode64                                       /run/user/1000
  tmpfs          95M  1% tmpfs rw,nosuid,nodev,size=194500k,nr_inodes=819200,
  mode=755,inode64                              /run/user/1000
  tmpfs          95M  1% tmpfs rw,nosuid,nodev,relatime,size=97248k,
```

```
       nr_inodes=24312,mode=700,
       uid=1000, gid=1000,inode64                    /run/user/1000
       tmpfs       190M   1% tmpfs rw,nosuid,nodev,
       inode64
             /run
       tmpfs       190M   1% tmpfs rw,nosuid,nodev,size=194500k,nr_inodes=819200,
       mode=755,inode64                                           /run
       tmpfs       190M   1% tmpfs rw,nosuid,nodev,noexec,relatime,size=5120k,
       inode64                                                    /run
       tmpfs       190M   1% tmpfs rw,nosuid,nodev,size=194500k,nr_inodes=819200,
       mode=755,inode64                                           /run
       tmpfs       190M   1% tmpfs rw,nosuid,nodev,relatime,size=97248k,
       nr_inodes=24312,mode=700,
       uid=1000, gid=1000,inode64                    /run
       tmpfs       475M   0% tmpfs rw,nosuid,nodev,
       inode64
             /dev/shm
       tmpfs       475M   0% tmpfs rw,nosuid,nodev,size=194500k,nr_inodes=819200,
       mode=755,inode64                                           /dev/shm
       tmpfs       475M   0% tmpfs rw,nosuid,nodev,noexec,relatime,size=5120k,
       inode64                                                    /dev/shm
       tmpfs       475M   0% tmpfs rw,nosuid,nodev,size=194500k,nr_inodes=819200,
       mode=755,inode64                                           /dev/shm
       tmpfs       475M   0% tmpfs rw,nosuid,nodev,relatime,size=97248k,
       nr_inodes=24312,mode=700,
       uid=1000, gid=1000,inode64                    /dev/shm
       tmpfs       5.0M   0% tmpfs rw,nosuid,nodev,
       inode64
             /run/lock
       tmpfs       5.0M   0% tmpfs rw,nosuid,nodev,size=194500k,nr_inodes=819200,
       mode=755,inode64                                           /run/lock
       tmpfs       5.0M   0% tmpfs rw,nosuid,nodev,noexec,relatime,size=5120k,
       inode64                                                    /run/lock
       tmpfs       5.0M   0% tmpfs rw,nosuid,nodev,size=194500k,nr_inodes=819200,
       mode=755,inode64                                           /run/lock
       tmpfs       5.0M   0% tmpfs rw,nosuid,nodev,relatime,size=97248k,
       nr_inodes=24312,mode=700,
       uid=1000, gid=1000,inode64                    /run/lock
       # Disk Schedulers And Queue Size ############################
            xvda | [mq-deadline] 64
       # Disk Partitioning ######################################
       Device       Type    Start       End              Size
       ============ ==== ========== ========== ==================
       /dev/xvda    Disk                               31138512896
       /dev/xvda1   Part    227328   60817374                    0
       /dev/xvda14  Part      2048      10239                    0
       /dev/xvda15  Part     10240     227327                    0
       # Kernel Inode State ####################################
       dentry-state | 32316   14310   45      0       2815    0
            file-nr | 1120     0        9223372036854775807
           inode-nr | 32153   3013
       # LVM Volumes ##########################################
```

```
Unable to collect information
# LVM Volume Groups #######################################
Unable to collect information
# RAID Controller #########################################
  Controller | No RAID controller detected
# Network Config ##########################################
  FIN Timeout | 60
  Port Range | 60999
# Interface Statistics ####################################
  interface  rx_bytes rx_packets  rx_errors   tx_bytes tx_packets  tx_errors
  ========= ========= ========== ========== ========== ========== ==========
  lo           125000       1250          0     125000       1250          0
  eth0      400000000     300000          0    6000000      70000          0
# Network Devices #########################################
  Device     Speed      Duplex
  ========= ========= =========
  eth0
# Top Processes ###########################################
     PID USER      PR  NI    VIRT    RES    SHR S  %CPU  %MEM     TIME+ COMMAND
       1 root      20   0  102000   9600   4992 S   0.0   1.0   0:09.86 systemd
       2 root      20   0       0      0      0 S   0.0   0.0   0:00.00 kthreadd
       3 root       0 -20       0      0      0 I   0.0   0.0   0:00.00 rcu_gp
       4 root       0 -20       0      0      0 I   0.0   0.0   0:00.00 rcu_par+
       5 root       0 -20       0      0      0 I   0.0   0.0   0:00.00 slub_fl+
       6 root       0 -20       0      0      0 I   0.0   0.0   0:00.00 netns
       8 root       0 -20       0      0      0 I   0.0   0.0   0:00.00 kworker+
      10 root       0 -20       0      0      0 I   0.0   0.0   0:00.00 mm_perc+
      11 root      20   0       0      0      0 I   0.0   0.0   0:00.00 rcu_tas+
# Notable Processes #######################################
  PID    OOM    COMMAND
   ?      ?     sshd doesn't appear to be running
# Simplified and fuzzy rounded vmstat (wait please) ##########
  procs  ---swap-- -----io---- ---system---- --------cpu--------
   r  b   si   so    bi    bo    ir     cs  us  sy  il  wa  st
   1  0    0    0    20    25   150    150   0   0 100   0   0
   0  0    0    0   225   125   300   2500   7  12  80   1   0
   0  0    0    0     0     0   150    300   0   0 100   0   0
   0  0    0    0     0     0   150    350   0   0 100   0   0
   0  0    0    0     0     0   150    300   0   0 100   0   0
# Memory management #######################################
Transparent huge pages are enabled.
# The End #################################################
root@mysql80 ~: ~]
```

Step 5: Restore the backups

MySQL crashes can occur for various reasons such as hardware failures, software bugs, or configuration errors. When a crash occurs, it can cause data loss, corruption, or other issues with the MySQL database. To recover from a crash, it's important to have a reliable backup-and-restore process in place.

The first step in restoring from a backup is to identify the cause of the crash and fix the underlying issue. Once the issue has been resolved, the next step is to restore the database from the most recent backup. Depending on the type of backup, this can be done using various tools and methods such as MySQL Enterprise Backup, Percona XtraBackup, mydumper, mysqldump, binlog backups, or replication.

After the backup has been restored, it's important to verify the integrity of the restored data to ensure that it's complete and accurate. This can be done by running various checks and tests on the database to identify any potential issues or inconsistencies.

In addition to restoring from a backup, it's also important to have a plan in place for minimizing the impact of a crash and ensuring a fast recovery. This can include measures such as using redundant hardware, implementing HA and failover solutions, and regularly testing and updating the backup-and-restore process.

Conclusion

In this chapter, you journeyed through the intricate landscape of installing, configuring, monitoring, and troubleshooting MySQL server. You also learned about assessing resources for a MySQL host.

Mastering MySQL server's installation and configuration is foundational for efficient database management. Whether you're on Windows or Linux, understanding the nuances of these processes is key. Optimizing log files, monitoring server performance, and troubleshooting issues will ensure seamless operation. Embracing these essential skills will enable you to maintain a robust MySQL environment.

## CHAPTER 3

Transactional Data Dictionary and InnoDB Architecture

In this chapter, we delve into the intricate details of InnoDB, a powerful storage engine in MySQL. This chapter introduces the transactional data dictionary (TDD) and its role in storing information about database objects. Before MySQL 8, this information was stored in separate system tables that weren't transactional. With TDD, this metadata becomes part of InnoDB, benefiting from the same transaction guarantees and crash recovery mechanisms as user data.

Then we explore the InnoDB storage engine, shedding light on various aspects of optimizing database performance, including the InnoDB buffer pool, change buffer, adaptive hash index, and redo log buffer. The chapter further discusses InnoDB's on-disk structures, such as tables, indexes, tablespaces, doublewrite buffer, redo log, and undo logs, all crucial for ensuring data consistency and efficient storage. Additionally, you'll find insights into InnoDB system tables, locking mechanisms, and valuable configuration tips. This chapter is an essential resource for anyone seeking a comprehensive understanding of InnoDB's architecture and its role in MySQL database management.

Transactional Data Dictionary

MySQL 8 introduced a substantial architectural change by replacing traditional MyISAM-based system tables with the TDD, a more efficient and dependable solution. This improvement has substantially enhanced metadata handling and storage, resulting in improved database object dependability and scalability.

The TDD, which is at the core of MySQL 8's InnoDB storage engine, is critical in maintaining metadata about database objects such as tables, indexes, constraints, triggers, and more. This new architecture replaces the obsolete MyISAM-based system tables, effectively making data dictionary information transactional and ACID compliant. The TDD's primary purpose is to improve the overall performance, reliability, and scalability of MySQL databases. This is accomplished by considerably lowering competition for system table locks and minimizing disk I/O, resulting in increased concurrency and dependability.

The MySQL system database was represented in MySQL 5.7 by a subdirectory named *mysql* in the data directory. However, in MySQL 8, this approach was replaced by the more powerful TDD. The data dictionary tables have been merged into a single InnoDB tablespace called *mysql.ibd*, which is located within the MySQL data directory. The *mysql.ibd* file cannot be updated or utilized by any other tablespace and must remain in its allocated place and preserve its name.

The introduction of the TDD brings several benefits to MySQL users:

Improved data dictionary management
  With a centralized data dictionary, managing and querying metadata becomes more efficient and streamlined.

Atomic data dictionary operations
  The data dictionary operations are now atomic and transactional, ensuring data consistency even during dictionary updates.

Storing Information About Database Objects

Let's dive into how the TDD stores information about various database objects. Here are a few examples:

Tables
  Tables are a fundamental part of any database. The TDD stores information about tables, such as table name, schema, column details, and indexes. This information is used by the query optimizer to generate efficient execution plans. Here's an example query to retrieve table information:

```
mysql> SELECT table_name, column_name, data_type
       FROM information_schema.columns
       WHERE table_schema = 'my_database';
+------------+-------------+-----------+
| TABLE_NAME | COLUMN_NAME | DATA_TYPE |
+------------+-------------+-----------+
| my_table   | id          | int       |
| my_table   | name        | varchar   |
| orders     | order_id    | int       |
| orders     | user_id     | int       |
| orders     | order_date  | timestamp |
| orders     | total_amount| decimal   |
| users      | user_id     | int       |
```

```
| users     | username   | varchar   |
| users     | email      | varchar   |
+-----------+------------+-----------+
9 rows in set (0.00 sec)
```

Indexes

Indexes play a crucial role in speeding up data retrieval. The TDD stores details about indexes, including index name, associated table, and indexed columns. Here's an example query to retrieve index information:

```
mysql> SELECT index_name, table_name, column_name
       FROM information_schema.statistics
       WHERE table_schema = 'my_database';
+--------------+------------+-------------+
| INDEX_NAME   | TABLE_NAME | COLUMN_NAME |
+--------------+------------+-------------+
| PRIMARY      | my_table   | id          |
| PRIMARY      | orders     | order_id    |
| user_id      | orders     | user_id     |
| idx_username | users      | username    |
| PRIMARY      | users      | user_id     |
+--------------+------------+-------------+
5 rows in set (0.00 sec)
```

Foreign keys

Foreign keys maintain referential integrity between tables. The TDD stores foreign-key constraints, including the referencing and referenced tables and columns. Here's an example query to retrieve foreign-key information:

```
mysql> SELECT
       rc.constraint_name,
       rc.table_name,
       kcu.column_name,
       rc.referenced_table_name,
       kcu.referenced_column_name
       FROM
       information_schema.referential_constraints rc
       JOIN
       information_schema.key_column_usage kcu ON rc.constraint_name
       = kcu.constraint_name
       WHERE
       rc.constraint_schema = 'my_database'\G
*************************** 1. row ***************************
        CONSTRAINT_NAME: Orders_ibfk_1
             TABLE_NAME: Orders
            COLUMN_NAME: CustomerID
 REFERENCED_TABLE_NAME: Customers
REFERENCED_COLUMN_NAME: CustomerID
1 row in set (0.04 sec)
```

MySQL includes many data dictionary views that allow users to directly query metadata information.

Understanding the Structure of the Data Directory

The */var/lib/mysql* directory on a MySQL server includes various subdirectories and files essential for MySQL's operation. The structure reveals the organization of MySQL's data, logs, and configuration files within the specified directory:

```
root@mysql80 ~: /var/lib/mysql]#tree -a -L 1 -F
./
├── #ib_16384_0.dblwr
├── #ib_16384_1.dblwr
├── #innodb_redo/
├── #innodb_temp/
├── auto.cnf
├── binlog.000001
├── binlog.index
├── ca-key.pem
├── ca.pem
├── client-cert.pem
├── client-key.pem
├── ib_buffer_pool
├── ibdata1
├── ibtmp1
├── mysql/
├── mysql.ibd
├── mytestdb/
├── performance_schema/
├── private_key.pem
├── public_key.pem
├── server-cert.pem
├── server-key.pem
├── sys/
├── undo_001
└── undo_002

6 directories, 19 files
root@mysql80 ~: /var/lib/mysql]#
```

Notable elements include the *#innodb_redo* directory containing temporary InnoDB redo logfiles, the *#innodb_temp* directory with temporary InnoDB tablespace files, and the *mysql* directory containing logs such as general and slow query logs. The *mytestdb* directory contains InnoDB data files for custom tables in the *mytestdb* database. Additionally, there are directories related to the performance schema, containing various statistical and status information files. Various certificate and key files, as well as MySQL system files like *ibdata1*, *ibtmp1*, and undo logs, are present in the root directory.

The *mysqld-auto.cnf* is a JSON-format file located in the data directory that is created only upon the first execution of the PERSIST or PERSIST_ONLY statement. This file stores persistent system variable configurations generated by the server when executing SET PERSIST or SET PERSIST_ONLY statements. We advise allowing the server to manage *mysqld-auto.cnf* and avoiding manual interventions. In addition, the *auto.cnf* file stores the server's universally unique identifier (UUID), which is used to uniquely identify a server.

The InnoDB Storage Engine

In MySQL 8, InnoDB serves as the default storage engine, utilizing both in-memory and on-disk structures to optimize data storage and boost performance. InnoDB uses these key structures—like the buffer pool, adaptive hash index, and change buffer—to cache frequently accessed data, dynamically adjust hash index size based on workload, and temporarily store changes to secondary indexes in memory, respectively. Additionally, the InnoDB redo log buffer ensures data durability by temporarily storing database changes before writing them to disk, safeguarding against server crashes or unexpected shutdowns. In fact, a very small redo log buffer is used when changes are temporarily written to redo logfiles that are also on disk (and synced by default) before writing the changes as pages on the data files (tablespaces).

This chapter places significant emphasis on configuring and tuning these structures to optimize overall system performance. Key takeaways encompass the recognition of InnoDB's effectiveness in handling large data volumes, comprehension of the importance of both in-memory and on-disk structures in enhancing performance and durability, and acknowledgment of the vital role played by the InnoDB redo log buffer in guaranteeing data persistence.

The InnoDB storage engine architecture, depicted in Figure 3-1, features both in-memory and on-disk structures. The *in-memory structures* include the buffer pool, the adaptive hash index, and the change buffer, which are responsible for caching frequently accessed data and optimizing read and write operations. The *on-disk structures* encompass the system tablespace, responsible for storing metadata, and the doublewrite buffer, which guarantees data consistency during recovery. In versions preceding MySQL 8.0.20, the doublewrite buffer was housed within the InnoDB system tablespace. However, with the advent of MySQL 8.0.20, the doublewrite buffer storage has been shifted to dedicated doublewrite files.

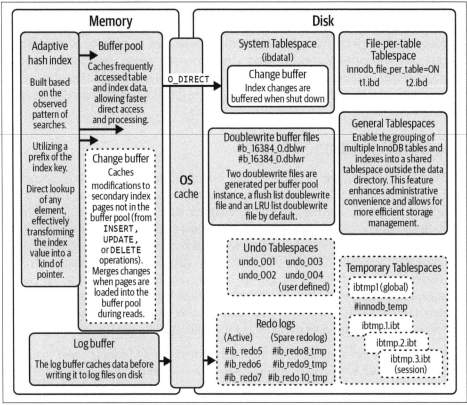

Figure 3-1. InnoDB architecture

Optimizing Database Performance with InnoDB Memory Structures

InnoDB uses several in-memory structures to optimize data access and management. These structures act as a buffer between the database server's memory and the physical storage on disk. The buffer pool caches frequently accessed data, the change buffer caches modifications to secondary index pages not in the buffer pool, the adaptive hash index speeds up searches, and the redo log buffer prepares data for writing to the permanent logs. By keeping frequently used data and operations in memory, InnoDB significantly improves database performance.

The InnoDB Buffer Pool

The *InnoDB buffer pool* is an essential component of the MySQL database. It is responsible for caching frequently accessed data in memory to improve performance.

When a query needs to access data, the InnoDB engine checks whether the data is already in the buffer pool. If it is, the query can be served directly from memory, which is much faster than reading the data from disk. If the data is not in the buffer pool, it needs to be read from disk, which can be much slower.

The amount of memory allocated to the InnoDB buffer pool depends on the size of the database and the available memory on the server. The general rule of thumb is to allocate 70%–80% of available memory to the buffer pool. To allocate 4 GB of memory to the InnoDB buffer pool, add the following line to the MySQL configuration file (*my.cnf*):

```
[mysqld]
innodb_buffer_pool_size=4G
```

Buffer pool size can be also modified online:

```
mysql> set persist innodb_buffer_pool_size=4294967296;
Query OK, 0 rows affected (0.00 sec)
```

MySQL provides several performance metrics that can be used to monitor the InnoDB buffer pool. Some of the most important metrics are as follows:

Innodb_buffer_pool_reads
: The number of times InnoDB had to read a data page from disk because it was not available in the buffer pool

Innodb_buffer_pool_read_requests
: The number of times InnoDB attempted to read a data page from the buffer pool

Innodb_buffer_pool_wait_free
: The number of times a thread had to wait for space to be freed in the buffer pool

Innodb_buffer_pool_pages_free
: The number of free pages in the buffer pool

By monitoring these metrics, DBAs can determine whether the buffer pool is properly sized and identify potential performance bottlenecks.

The InnoDB Change Buffer

The *InnoDB change buffer* plays a crucial role in enhancing the efficiency of database operations within the MySQL InnoDB storage engine. Its primary function is to serve as a specialized data structure tasked with preserving modifications made to secondary index pages. These modifications are tracked and stored in the change buffer when the relevant index pages are not currently residing in the buffer pool.

These buffered modifications encompass a wide range of changes triggered by DML operations, including but not limited to INSERT, UPDATE, and DELETE operations. Instead of immediately committing these changes to the actual index pages stored on disk, the InnoDB change buffer defers their application.

The key benefit of this deferral lies in the optimization of write operations. By holding off on the immediate disk writes for secondary index pages, InnoDB mitigates the write amplification issue that can arise when many individual changes necessitate disk I/O. Instead, these buffered modifications patiently wait in the change buffer. They are subsequently consolidated and efficiently applied to their respective index pages when those pages are loaded into the buffer pool as part of other read operations.

In essence, the InnoDB change buffer serves as a strategic intermediary, postponing the physical application of secondary index modifications until the system's operations necessitate it, thereby contributing to improved database performance and reduced disk I/O overhead. It can be configured using the following parameters:

innodb_change_buffer_max_size
: Determines the maximum size of the change buffer. The default value is 25% of the InnoDB buffer pool size.

innodb_change_buffering
: Enables or disables the change buffer. It has the following options:

inserts
: Only insert operations are buffered.

deletes
: Only delete operations are buffered.

changes
: Both insert and delete operations are buffered.

none
: Change buffering is disabled.

purges
: Background physical deletion operations are cached.

all *(default)*
: Change buffering is used for all operations, including inserts, updates, and deletes.

To enable change buffering for insert and delete operations, add the following configuration to your MySQL configuration file:

```
innodb_change_buffering = changes
```

The InnoDB Adaptive Hash Index

The *InnoDB adaptive hash index* dynamically adjusts its size in response to the workload. This feature is designed to improve performance by avoiding unnecessary I/O operations on frequently accessed data.

The InnoDB adaptive hash index is a hash index of frequently accessed pages in memory, built using the prefix of the index key. When a page is accessed, it's added to the hash index if it's not already there. If the hash index becomes too large, InnoDB removes the least recently used pages until the index size is below a configured limit.

The index's effectiveness can vary depending on the specific use case and workload characteristics. In certain scenarios, especially when dealing with specific data distributions or access patterns, it may be necessary to fine-tune or even disable the adaptive hash index to achieve optimal performance. In general, though, when appropriately configured and utilized, the index is regarded as a valuable tool for enhancing the performance of MySQL databases. The following configuration options are available:

`innodb_adaptive_hash_index`
Enables or disables the adaptive hash index. The default value is ON.

`innodb_adaptive_hash_index_parts`
Sets the number of partitions used by the hash index. The default value is 8.

To enable the adaptive hash index and set the number of partitions to 16, you can use the following configuration code:

```
[mysqld]
innodb_adaptive_hash_index=ON
innodb_adaptive_hash_index_parts=16
```

The adaptive hash index may speed up your SELECT queries only when none of your table data is changed and it's fully cached in buffer pool. As soon as you have writes, are experiencing higher load, or simply cannot cache all the data needed for your SELECTs, the adaptive hash index becomes a massive bottleneck. It's recommended to enable it only if it is absolutely necessary after monitoring the workload or to disable it in production.

The InnoDB Redo Log Buffer

The *InnoDB redo log buffer* plays a crucial role in the storage engine's transaction management. It serves as a dedicated memory area responsible for temporarily storing data that is destined to be written to the logfiles on the disk. The size of this log buffer is adjustable and determined by the `innodb_log_buffer_size` configuration variable, which has a default size of 16 MB.

When it comes to the mechanics of this log buffer, its contents are not immediately written to disk but rather undergo periodic flushing. This controlled flushing process is pivotal in ensuring data durability and recovery capabilities while optimizing performance.

The significance of having a sizable log buffer becomes evident when dealing with large transactions. When transactions involve substantial data modifications, such as updates, inserts, or deletions of numerous rows, a larger log buffer becomes advantageous. It allows these large transactions to execute efficiently without the necessity of immediately persisting all their redo log data to disk before committing. Essentially, this means that increasing the size of the log buffer can result in substantial savings in terms of disk I/O operations, contributing to better database performance.

In addition to the log buffer's size, two other key configuration variables, `innodb_flush_log_at_trx_commit` and `innodb_flush_log_at_timeout`, provide fine-grained control over how the contents of the log buffer are written and flushed to disk and the frequency at which these log-flushing actions occur. These settings allow DBAs to tailor the behavior of the log buffer and disk writes to suit specific performance and durability requirements. To increase the size of the InnoDB redo log buffer to 32 MB, add `innodb_log_buffer_size = 32M` to your MySQL configuration file.

 The `innodb_redo_log_capacity` parameter is much more important than `innodb_log_buffer_size`. The InnoDB redo logfiles play a crucial role in recording changes to the database, ensuring durability and recoverability in the event of a crash or system failure. It is important that you choose an appropriate size for the `innodb_redo_log_capacity` parameter. A decently sized InnoDB logfile is vital for optimizing performance and preventing bottlenecks; it directly influences the efficiency of write operations. A larger value reduces the need for checkpoint flush activity in the buffer pool, thereby decreasing disk I/O. See "Working with the InnoDB Redo Log" on page 121 for more on this parameter.

The redo log buffer provides these benefits for database performance and reliability:

Faster write operations
> By temporarily storing changes in memory, the redo log buffer can improve write performance and reduce the number of disk writes required.

Reduced disk I/O
> Because changes are written to the buffer before they are written to disk, the buffer can reduce the number of disk I/O operations required, which can improve overall database performance.

InnoDB On-Disk Structures

This section of the MySQL documentation covers the on-disk structures (Figure 3-1) used by InnoDB, which is a storage engine for MySQL. Understanding these structures is important for DBAs and developers who want to optimize the performance and reliability of their MySQL databases.

Tables: Unveiling InnoDB's Data Storage Foundation

Tables are the basic structures used to store data in InnoDB. Each table is composed of one or more pages, and each page contains a fixed number of rows. The table structure is stored in the system tablespace, and each table has its own associated index, which is stored in the table's own tablespace.

Indexes: Optimizing Queries with InnoDB's Indexing

Indexes are used to optimize queries by allowing for faster data retrieval. The majority of MySQL indexes, including `PRIMARY KEY`, `UNIQUE`, `INDEX`, and `FULLTEXT`, are stored in B-trees. However, this rule has exceptions. Spatial data type indexes utilize R-trees, `MEMORY` tables support hash indexes, and InnoDB employs inverted lists for `FULLTEXT` indexes.

Clustered and secondary indexes differ only in terms of the data stored in their leaf nodes; structurally, they are the same. When other database engines refer to different index types, they typically mean structurally different indexes, such as hash or B+tree. The term *clustered index* indicates that the leaf nodes of the index contain the full record. In other engines, this concept is often referred to as *index-organized tables*; in InnoDB, all tables are index organized.

With the most common `innodb_file_per_table` setting, the indexes are created in the same tablespace as the table. This can be checked by looking at `SYS_TABLES` and `SYS_INDEXES` and at the table ID and the space ID of each index.

Tablespaces: Efficiently Storing Data and Indexes in InnoDB

InnoDB uses *tablespaces* to store data and indexes separately from the system tablespace. By default, each table and its associated index are stored in their own separate tablespaces. This allows for better performance and easier management of large databases.

Doublewrite Buffer: Ensuring Data Consistency in InnoDB

The *doublewrite buffer* ensures data consistency in the event of a crash or other unexpected shutdown. When data is written to a page, it is first written to the doublewrite buffer before being written to the actual data file. If a crash occurs during the write operation, the data in the doublewrite buffer can be used to restore the database to a consistent state.

Redo Log: Safeguarding Data Changes

The *redo log* is another feature of InnoDB that helps ensure data consistency. This circular buffer contains a record of all changes made to the database. In the event of a crash, the redo log can be used to replay those changes and bring the database back to a consistent state.

Undo Logs: Ensuring Transactional Consistency

The InnoDB storage engine relies heavily on the *undo log*, also known as the *rollback segment*, which plays a vital role in maintaining transactional consistency and enabling the reversal of changes made during transactions. Upon initialization of the MySQL instance, two default undo tablespaces are generated. These tablespaces are created during initialization to serve as the designated location for rollback segments necessary for processing SQL statements. The presence of a minimum of two undo tablespaces is essential to facilitate the automated truncation of undo tablespaces.

For the sake of consistency, the redo log might contain uncommitted changes, and during crash recovery, those changes are rolled back by using the undo log. This example sets some of the important parameters for optimizing the engine's performance:

```
[mysqld]
innodb_buffer_pool_size=50G
SET GLOBAL innodb_redo_log_capacity = 4294967296;
innodb_flush_method=O_DIRECT
innodb_flush_log_at_trx_commit=1
```

In this configuration, the InnoDB buffer pool size is set to 50 GB to cache frequently used data, and the InnoDB redo log capacity is defined as 4 GB for crash recovery. The `innodb_flush_method` parameter is set to O_DIRECT, indicating direct I/O operations for improved I/O performance. The `innodb_flush_log_at_trx_commit` parameter is set to 1, ensuring that changes are written to the redo log at each transaction commit for data durability. When you're unsure of which values to use, it's best to set `innodb_dedicated_server=on`.

Creating InnoDB Tables

To create InnoDB tables in MySQL, follow these steps:

1. Create a new database or select an existing one.

2. Use the `CREATE TABLE` statement to create a new table.

3. Specify the storage engine as InnoDB by using the `ENGINE=InnoDB` option in the `CREATE TABLE` statement.

To create InnoDB tables in MySQL, which offers transaction support, follow these sequential steps for database creation and table definition:

```
mysql> CREATE DATABASE mydatabase;
Query OK, 1 row affected (0.02 sec)
mysql>

mysql> USE mydatabase;
Database changed
mysql>

mysql> CREATE TABLE mytable (
    ->     id INT(11) NOT NULL AUTO_INCREMENT,
    ->     name VARCHAR(50) NOT NULL,
    ->     PRIMARY KEY (id) )
    ->     ENGINE=InnoDB;
Query OK, 0 rows affected, 1 warning (0.04 sec)

mysql>
```

Importing Externally Created Tables into Database

Table data can also be generated externally and subsequently imported into InnoDB tables by using either the `LOAD DATA` command or the MySQL Shell parallel table import utility. Initially, we will detail the steps for using the `LOAD DATA` command, followed by instructions on utilizing the MySQL Shell parallel table import utility.

Using LOAD DATA

When using the `LOAD DATA` statement, certain requirements must be met. Grant the `FILE` privilege to the MySQL server user by executing the following command, replacing *mysqladminuser* with the name of the MySQL user account that you're using to load the data:

```
mysql>  CREATE USER 'mysqladminuser'@'localhost' IDENTIFIED BY 'Mkj#$w@89LKJH#';
Query OK, 0 rows affected (0.01 sec)

mysql>
```

```
mysql> GRANT FILE ON *.* TO 'mysqladminuser'@'localhost';
Query OK, 0 rows affected (0.00 sec)

mysql>

mysql> GRANT SELECT, INSERT, UPDATE, DELETE, CREATE, ALTER  ON
mydatabase.* TO 'mysqladminuser'@'localhost';
Query OK, 0 rows affected (0.02 sec)
```

The MySQL client option local_infile enables the client to read data from a local
file and load it into a MySQL database table by using the LOAD DATA LOCAL INFILE
command. When the local_infile option is enabled, the MySQL client can read
data from a file on the client's local filesystem, rather than on the MySQL server's filesystem. The next query can be used to determine whether local_infile is enabled:

```
mysql> show variables like 'local_infile';
+---------------+-------+
| Variable_name | Value |
+---------------+-------+
| local_infile  | OFF   |
+---------------+-------+
1 row in set (0.00 sec)

mysql>

mysql> SET GLOBAL local_infile=on;
Query OK, 0 rows affected (0.00 sec)

mysql>
```

To verify that the variable is enabled, utilize the following query:

```
mysql> show variables like 'local_infile';
+---------------+-------+
| Variable_name | Value |
+---------------+-------+
| local_infile  | ON    |
+---------------+-------+
1 row in set (0.01 sec)

mysql>
```

If you are using the MySQL client to execute the LOAD DATA LOCAL INFILE command, you can use the --local-infile option to enable local file loading:

```
mysql --local-infile -u user -p dbname
mysql>
```

First, let's see how to load a few records in an existing table with data. Create a table
named **authors** and load data from the *authors.csv* file:

```
CREATE TABLE authors (
    id INT,
```

```
    first_name VARCHAR(50),
    last_name VARCHAR(50),
    age INT
);
```

Transfer the file to a location accessible by MySQL and verify the data in the file:

```
cat /tmp/authors.csv
id,first_name,last_name,age
1,John,Doe,30
2,Jane,\N,25
3,Bob,Johnson,40
```

To handle missing values, such as unknown last names, use null values. To denote null values in the corresponding text file, the \N character sequence can be used.

Connect to the MySQL server as the root user for the mytestdb database, enabling local infile loading:

```
[root@mysql80 ~]# mysql --local-infile -u mysqladminuser -p mydatabase
Enter password:
Reading table information for completion of table and column names
You can turn off this feature to get a quicker startup with -A

Welcome to the MySQL monitor.  Commands end with ; or \g.
Your MySQL connection id is 25
Server version: 8.0.36 MySQL Community Server - GPL

Copyright (c) 2000, 2024, Oracle and/or its affiliates.

Oracle is a registered trademark of Oracle Corporation and/or its
affiliates. Other names may be trademarks of their respective
owners.

Type 'help;' or '\h' for help. Type '\c' to clear the current input statement.

mysql>
```

Retrieve records from the authors table in the mytestdb database, ordering by the id column in descending order, and display it in a detailed format by using \G:

```
mysql> select * from mydatabase.authors order by id desc limit 1\G

mysql>
```

Load data from the local file */tmp/authors.txt* into the authors table of the mydata base database by using the LOAD DATA LOCAL INFILE command:

```
mysql>

mysql> LOAD DATA LOCAL INFILE '/tmp/authors.csv'
    -> INTO TABLE authors
    -> FIELDS TERMINATED BY ','
    -> LINES TERMINATED BY '\n'
```

```
    -> IGNORE 1 ROWS;
Query OK, 3 rows affected (0.02 sec)
Records: 3  Deleted: 0  Skipped: 0  Warnings: 0

mysql>
```

This example assumes that the CSV file is comma-separated (FIELDS TERMINATED BY ',') and each row is terminated by a newline character (LINES TERMINATED BY '\n'). Adjust these options based on the actual format of your CSV file.

Also, note that the IGNORE 1 ROWS option is used to skip the header row in the CSV file, as it typically contains column names and not actual data. Adjust the number of rows to ignore based on your file structure.

To verify the data in the authors table, execute the following select query, which displays all columns from the authors table in the mydatabase database, orders the results by the id column in descending order, and limits the output to three rows. The \G at the end is a MySQL command-line client directive that formats the output vertically for better readability:

```
mysql> select * from mydatabase.authors order by id desc limit 3\G
*************************** 1. row ***************************
        id: 3
first_name: Bob
 last_name: Johnson
       age: 40
*************************** 2. row ***************************
        id: 2
first_name: Jane
 last_name: NULL
       age: 25
*************************** 3. row ***************************
        id: 1
first_name: John
 last_name: Doe
       age: 30
3 rows in set (0.00 sec)

mysql>
```

Using MySQL Shell parallel table import

While traditional data import methods can be slow for large files, MySQL Shell offers a powerful solution. Its parallel table import utility efficiently imports data into MySQL tables, analyzes the data file, splits it into manageable chunks, and then leverages parallel connections to upload those chunks to the target server significantly faster than a single-threaded approach.

Download the MySQL Shell package:

```
[root@mysql80 ~]# wget https://downloads.mysql.com/archives/get/p/43/file/
mysql-shell_8.0.35-1ubuntu22.04_amd64.deb
--2024-01-19 03:28:36--  https://downloads.mysql.com/archives/get/p/43/file/
mysql-shell_8.0.35-1ubuntu22.04_amd64.deb
Resolving downloads.mysql.com (downloads.mysql.com)...
23.208.44.156, 2600:1408:5400:18b::2e31,
2600:1408:5400:19b::2e31
Connecting to downloads.mysql.com (downloads.mysql.com)|23.208.44.156|:443...
connected.
HTTP request sent, awaiting response... 302 Moved Temporarily
Location: https://cdn.mysql.com/archives/mysql-shell/
mysql-shell_8.0.35-1ubuntu22.04_amd64.deb [following]
--2024-01-19 03:28:37--  https://cdn.mysql.com/archives/mysql-shell/
mysql-shell_8.0.35-1ubuntu22.04_amd64.deb
Resolving cdn.mysql.com (cdn.mysql.com)... 104.96.247.58,
2600:1408:5400:1a3::1d68, 2600:1408:5400:186::1d68
Connecting to cdn.mysql.com (cdn.mysql.com)|104.96.247.58|:443... connected.
HTTP request sent, awaiting response... 200 OK
Length: 38432594 (37M) [application/x-debian-package]
Saving to: 'mysql-shell_8.0.35-1ubuntu22.04_amd64.deb'
mysql-shell_8.0.35-1ubuntu22.04_amd6 100%[========================================
=================================>]  36.65M  22.7MB/s    in 1.6s
2024-01-19 03:28:39 (22.7 MB/s) - 'mysql-shell_8.0.35-1ubuntu22.04_amd64.deb'
saved [38432594/38432594]

[root@mysql80 ~]# ls -rlth
total 37M
-rw-r--r-- 1 root root  37M Oct 14 13:48
mysql-shell_8.0.35-1ubuntu22.04_amd64.deb
[root@mysql80 ~]#
```

Install MySQL Shell:

```
[root@mysql80 ~]# dpkg -i  mysql-shell_8.0.35-1ubuntu22.04_amd64.deb
Selecting previously unselected package mysql-shell:amd64.
(Reading database ... 65403 files and directories currently
installed.)
Preparing to unpack mysql-shell_8.0.35-1ubuntu22.04_amd64.deb ...
Unpacking mysql-shell:amd64 (8.0.35-1ubuntu22.04) ...
Setting up mysql-shell:amd64 (8.0.35-1ubuntu22.04) ...
Processing triggers for libc-bin (2.35-0ubuntu3.6) ...
Processing triggers for man-db (2.10.2-1) ...
[root@mysql80 ~]#
```

Log in to MySQL Shell:

```
[root@mysql80 ~]# mysqlsh
MySQL Shell 8.0.35
Copyright (c) 2016, 2023, Oracle and/or its affiliates.
Oracle is a registered trademark of Oracle Corporation and/or its affiliates.
Other names may be trademarks of their respective owners.
Type '\help' or '\?' for help; '\quit' to exit.
```

Connect to the database as a user:

```
MySQL  JS > shell.connect('arun@localhost:3306')
Creating a session to 'arun@localhost:3306'
Please provide the password for 'arun@localhost:3306': ************
Save password for 'arun@localhost:3306'? [Y]es/[N]o/Ne[v]er (default No): Y
Fetching schema names for auto-completion... Press ^C to stop.
Your MySQL connection id is 17
Server version: 8.0.35-0ubuntu0.22.04.1 (Ubuntu)
No default schema selected; type \use <schema> to set one.
<ClassicSession:arun@localhost:3306>
MySQL  localhost:3306 ssl  JS >
```

Set the global local infile. The parallel table import utility employs LOAD DATA LOCAL
INFILE statements for data upload; hence, the local_infile system variable must be
set to ON on the target server. This can be accomplished by executing the following
SQL statement in SQL mode prior to executing the parallel table import utility:

```
MySQL  localhost:3306 ssl  JS > \sql
Switching to SQL mode... Commands end with ;
Fetching global names for auto-completion... Press ^C to stop.
MySQL  localhost:3306 ssl  SQL >

MySQL  localhost:3306 ssl  SQL > SET GLOBAL local_infile = 1;
Query OK, 0 rows affected (0.0003 sec)
MySQL  localhost:3306 ssl  SQL >
```

Create a database and a table to import:

```
MySQL  localhost:3306 ssl  SQL > create database mydatabase;
Query OK, 1 row affected (0.0155 sec)
MySQL  localhost:3306 ssl  SQL >

MySQL  localhost:3306 ssl  SQL > use mydatabase;
Default schema set to `mydatabase`.
Fetching global names, object names from `mydatabase`
for auto-completion... Press ^C to stop.
MySQL  localhost:3306 ssl  mydatabase  SQL >

MySQL  localhost:3306 ssl  mydatabase  SQL > CREATE TABLE authors (
                               ->        id INT,
                               ->        first_name VARCHAR(50),
                               ->        last_name VARCHAR(50),
                               ->        age INT
                               ->        );
Query OK, 0 rows affected (0.0401 sec)
MySQL  localhost:3306 ssl  mydatabase  SQL >
```

Import a CSV file into the table. Utilizing the JavaScript mode of MySQL Shell, the
subsequent examples import data from a single CSV file, located at */tmp/authors.csv*,
into the authors table within the mydatabase database, while excluding the header
row in the file:

```
MySQL  localhost:3306 ssl  JS > util.importTable("/tmp/authors.csv", {schema:
"mydatabase", table: "authors", dialect: "csv-unix",
skipRows: 1, showProgress: true})
Importing from file '/tmp/authors.csv' to table
`mydatabase`.`authors` in MySQL Server at localhost:3306 using
1 thread
[Worker000] authors.csv: Records: 3  Deleted: 0  Skipped:
0  Warnings: 0
61% (44 bytes / 72 bytes), 0.00 B/s
File '/tmp/authors.csv' (44 bytes) was imported in 0.0332
sec at 44.00 B/s
Total rows affected in mydatabase.authors: Records: 3
Deleted: 0  Skipped: 0  Warnings: 0
 MySQL  localhost:3306 ssl  JS >
```

Execute the following query on the table to confirm and validate the data:

```
MySQL  localhost:3306 ssl  SQL > select * from mydatabase.authors\G
*************************** 1. row ***************************
        id: 1
first_name: John
 last_name: Doe
       age: 30
*************************** 2. row ***************************
        id: 2
first_name: Jane
 last_name: NULL
       age: 25
*************************** 3. row ***************************
        id: 3
first_name: Bob
 last_name: Johnson
       age: 40
3 rows in set (0.0006 sec)
 MySQL  localhost:3306 ssl  SQL >
```

You can also move a copy of a table to a different MySQL instance. To do so, follow these steps:

1. Export the table to a file using a format supported by MySQL, such as CSV or SQL.

2. Copy the file to the new MySQL instance.

3. Import the table into the new MySQL instance by using either the LOAD DATA or mysqlimport command.

For example, say you want to copy the mytable table from the mydatabase database on server A to the mydatabase database on server B. On server A:

```
[root@mysql80 ~]# mysqldump -u mysqladminuser -p mydatabase mytable >
mytable.sql
```

```
Enter password:
[root@mysql80 ~]#
```

Then, you would copy *mytable.sql* from server A to server B and import it using the MySQL client:

```
[root@mysql80 ~]# mysql -u mysqladminuser -p mydatabase < mytable.sql
Enter password:
[root@mysql80 ~]#
```

 We encourage utilizing the MySQL Shell Dump & Load Utility. In Chapter 4, we provide details on how to use the utility.

Converting Tables from MyISAM to InnoDB

The SQL command to convert tables from MyISAM to InnoDB is as follows:

```
mysql> show create table Student\G
*************************** 1. row ***************************
       Table: Student
Create Table: CREATE TABLE `Student` (
  `student_id` int NOT NULL,
  `first_name` varchar(50) DEFAULT NULL,
  `last_name` varchar(50) DEFAULT NULL,
  `age` int DEFAULT NULL,
  PRIMARY KEY (`student_id`)
) ENGINE=MyISAM DEFAULT CHARSET=utf8mb4 COLLATE=utf8mb4_0900_ai_ci
1 row in set (0.00 sec)
mysql>

mysql> ALTER TABLE Student ENGINE=InnoDB;
Query OK, 3 rows affected (0.06 sec)
Records: 3  Duplicates: 0  Warnings: 0

mysql>  show create table Student\G
*************************** 1. row ***************************
       Table: Student
Create Table: CREATE TABLE `Student` (
  `student_id` int NOT NULL,
  `first_name` varchar(50) DEFAULT NULL,
  `last_name` varchar(50) DEFAULT NULL,
  `age` int DEFAULT NULL,
  PRIMARY KEY (`student_id`)
) ENGINE=InnoDB DEFAULT CHARSET=utf8mb4 COLLATE=utf8mb4_0900_ai_ci
1 row in set (0.00 sec)
mysql>
```

Note that the conversion process may take some time depending on the size of the tables. Also, it's important to back up your databases before making any changes to the table engines.

An alternative to directly modifying the table with an ALTER query to switch from the MyISAM storage engine to InnoDB is to perform a logical backup and restore the data as an InnoDB table. To convert a table from MyISAM to InnoDB using a logical backup, follow these steps:

1. Export the table to a file using a format supported by MySQL, such as CSV or SQL.

2. Modify the table definition to specify InnoDB as the storage engine.

3. Import the table into the MySQL database.

Say you have a MyISAM table named StudentRecord in the mytestdb database. Let's proceed to dump the data from this table:

```
mysql> CREATE TABLE StudentRecord (
    student_id INT AUTO_INCREMENT PRIMARY KEY,
    student_name VARCHAR(50),
    student_age INT,
    student_grade VARCHAR(10)
);
Query OK, 0 rows affected (0.02 sec)

mysql> INSERT INTO StudentRecord (student_name, student_age, student_grade)
VALUES
    ('Alice', 18, 'A'),
    ('Bob', 19, 'B'),
    ('Charlie', 20, 'C'),
    ('David', 21, 'B'),
    ('Emma', 22, 'A'),
    ('Frank', 20, 'C'),
    ('Grace', 19, 'A'),
    ('Henry', 18, 'B'),
    ('Ivy', 20, 'C'),
    ('Jack', 21, 'A');
Query OK, 10 rows affected (0.01 sec)
Records: 10  Duplicates: 0  Warnings: 0
```

The mydumper command initiates the extraction of data from the MyISAM StudentRe cord table in the mytestdb database. The resulting output is directed to the specified directory */home/percona/backup/*. The extraction includes triggers, routines, and events, utilizing compression, 16 threads, and the compressed protocol. The process is executed with a high verbosity level (3), along with features like killing long queries, excluding locks, and omitting schema information:

```
[root@mysql80 mysql]# mydumper --database=mytestdb --tables-list=StudentRecord
--outputdir=/home/percona/backup/ --rows=500000 --triggers --routines --events
```

```
--compress --threads=16 --compress-protocol --verbose=3 --kill-long-queries
--no-locks --no-schemas
** Message: 17:09:32.823: Server version reported as: 8.0.36-0ubuntu0.22.04.1
** Message: 17:09:32.824: Connected to a MySQL server
** (mydumper:24151): WARNING **: 17:09:32.824: Executing in
no-locks mode, snapshot will notbe consistent
** Message: 17:09:32.825: Started dump at: 2024-02-16 17:09:32
** Message: 17:09:32.825: Written master status
** Message: 17:09:32.826: Thread 1 connected using MySQL
connection ID 16
** Message: 17:09:32.827: Thread 2 connected using MySQL
connection ID 17
```

Upon successful completion of mydumper, you will receive messages in the log similar
to the following:

```
** Message: 17:09:32.914: Thread 15 shutting down
** Message: 17:09:32.914: Thread 16 shutting down
** Message: 17:09:32.917: Thread 2 shutting down
** Message: 17:09:32.917: Finished dump at: 2024-02-16 17:09:32
[root@mysql80 mysql]#
```

You can create a new database and the table with ENGINE=InnoDB, then use myloader
to import data into that table. After that, you can swap the tables by following these
steps:

```
mysql> CREATE TABLE mytestdb_inno.StudentRecord (
    ->      student_id INT AUTO_INCREMENT PRIMARY KEY,
    ->      student_name VARCHAR(50),
    ->      student_age INT,
    ->      student_grade VARCHAR(10)
    -> )ENGINE=InnoDB DEFAULT CHARSET=utf8mb4 COLLATE=utf8mb4_unicode_ci;
Query OK, 0 rows affected (0.04 sec)
```

The myloader command loads data from the directory */home/percona/backup/* into a
new database named mytestdb_inno. It specifies the source database as mytestdb and
employs 16 threads, compressed protocol, and a high verbosity level (3) during the
loading process:

```
[root@mysql80 mysql]# myloader --directory=/home/percona/backup/
--source-db=mytestdb --database=mytestdb_inno --threads=16 --compress-protocol
--verbose=3
** Message: 17:14:21.400: 16 threads created
** Message: 17:14:21.400: Thread 1 restoring `mytestdb`.`StudentRecord` part 0
** Message: 17:14:21.400: Thread 2 shutting down
** Message: 17:14:21.400: Thread 3 shutting down
** Message: 17:14:21.400: Thread 4 shutting down
** Message: 17:14:21.400: Thread 5 shutting down
```

Upon successful completion of myloader, you will receive messages in the log similar
to the following:

```
** Message: 17:14:21.401: Thread 14 shutting down
** Message: 17:14:21.405: Thread 15 shutting down
** Message: 17:14:21.405: Thread 16 shutting down
** Message: 17:14:21.413: Thread 1 shutting down
[root@mysql80 mysql]#
```

Next, swap the table names between mytestdb.StudentRecord and mytestdb.
Student Record_bkp, as well as between mytestdb_inno.StudentRecord and
mytestdb.StudentRecord:

```
mysql>  RENAME TABLE mytestdb.StudentRecord TO
    -> mytestdb.StudentRecord_bkp, mytestdb_inno.StudentRecord TO
    -> mytestdb.StudentRecord;
Query OK, 0 rows affected (0.07 sec)
```

Verify the table structure and retrieve the count of records in the StudentRecord
table of the mytestdb database and display the result in a detailed format by using \G:

```
mysql> show create table mytestdb.StudentRecord\G
*************************** 1. row ***************************
       Table: StudentRecord
Create Table: CREATE TABLE `StudentRecord` (
  `student_id` int NOT NULL AUTO_INCREMENT,
  `student_name` varchar(50) COLLATE utf8mb4_unicode_ci DEFAULT NULL,
  `student_age` int DEFAULT NULL,
  `student_grade` varchar(10) COLLATE utf8mb4_unicode_ci DEFAULT NULL,
  PRIMARY KEY (`student_id`)
) ENGINE=InnoDB AUTO_INCREMENT=11 DEFAULT CHARSET=utf8mb4
COLLATE=utf8mb4_unicode_ci
1 row in set (0.00 sec)

mysql>  select count(*) from mytestdb.StudentRecord\G
*************************** 1. row ***************************
count(*): 10
1 row in set (0.02 sec)
```

Persistence of Auto-Increment Counters

While creating a table, it's important to consider having a primary key with an auto-increment feature. This feature, integral to the database's design, generates unique values for primary key columns. With the launch of MySQL 8, a significant enhancement was introduced to the auto-increment counter. Unlike MySQL 5.7, this enhancement ensures that the maximum auto-increment counter value persists between server restarts, thereby improving consistency and reliability in data management.

In MySQL 5.7, upon inserting a new row into a table featuring an auto-increment column, the counter increments by 1, generating a value employed as the primary key for the inserted row. This counter value remains stored in memory and is not retained across server restarts. Consequently, in the event of a server crash or restart, the counter may revert to a lower value.

In MySQL 8, the maximum value of the auto-increment counter persists through server restarts. Consequently, even after a server restart, the auto-increment counter resumes its counting from the last recorded value, thereby maintaining the sequential nature of auto-increment primary key values.

Let's examine the differences between MySQL 5.7 and MySQL 8 regarding the persistent auto-increment counter with a simple example. We'll create a table called "books" to store book information in MySQL 5.7 with AUTO_INCREMENT PRIMARY KEY:

```
mysql> select version();
+----------------------------+
| version()                  |
+----------------------------+
| 5.7.39-0ubuntu0.18.04.2-log |
+----------------------------+
1 row in set (0.00 sec)


mysql> CREATE TABLE books (
    id INT AUTO_INCREMENT PRIMARY KEY,
    bookname VARCHAR(50) NOT NULL
);
Query OK, 0 rows affected (0.02 sec)
```

Next, we'll insert three records into the "books" table in MySQL 5.7:

```
mysql> INSERT INTO books (bookname) VALUES ('book1');
INSERT INTO books (bookname) VALUES ('book2');
INSERT INTO books (bookname) VALUES ('book3');
Query OK, 1 row affected (0.00 sec)
Query OK, 1 row affected (0.00 sec)
Query OK, 1 row affected (0.01 sec)
```

Afterward, we can retrieve records from the "books" table:

```
mysql> select * from books;
+----+----------+
| id | bookname |
+----+----------+
|  1 | book1    |
|  2 | book2    |
|  3 | book3    |
+----+----------+
3 rows in set (0.00 sec)
```

Next, we'll delete one record and insert a new one:

```
mysql> delete from books where id=3;
Query OK, 1 row affected (0.01 sec)
```

```
mysql> select * from books;
+----+----------+
| id | bookname |
+----+----------+
|  1 | book1    |
|  2 | book2    |
+----+----------+
2 rows in set (0.00 sec)

mysql> INSERT INTO books (bookname) VALUES ('book4');
Query OK, 1 row affected (0.01 sec)
```

Upon deleting the record with ID 3 and inserting a new one, as anticipated, we notice that the new entry is assigned ID 4:

```
mysql> select * from books;
+----+----------+
| id | bookname |
+----+----------+
|  1 | book1    |
|  2 | book2    |
|  4 | book4    |
+----+----------+
3 rows in set (0.00 sec)
```

Following this, we'll delete the last record (ID 4) from the "books" table, proceed with a MySQL restart, and then inspect the table's contents:

```
mysql> delete from books where id=4;
Query OK, 1 row affected (0.01 sec)

mysql> select * from books;
+----+----------+
| id | bookname |
+----+----------+
|  1 | book1    |
|  2 | book2    |
+----+----------+
2 rows in set (0.00 sec)

service mysql restart

mysql> select * from books;
ERROR 2006 (HY000): MySQL server has gone away
No connection. Trying to reconnect...
Connection id:    2
Current database: db1

+----+----------+
| id | bookname |
+----+----------+
|  1 | book1    |
|  2 | book2    |
```

```
+----+----------+
2 rows in set (0.01 sec)
```

With only two records remaining in the table, let's proceed by inserting the fifth record and determining whether it acquires ID 5 or reverts to ID 3 upon insertion:

```
mysql> INSERT INTO books (bookname) VALUES ('book5');
Query OK, 1 row affected (0.00 sec)

mysql> select * from books;
+----+----------+
| id | bookname |
+----+----------+
|  1 | book1    |
|  2 | book2    |
|  3 | book5    |
+----+----------+
3 rows in set (0.00 sec)
```

As a result, in MySQL 5.7, restarting the system resets the auto-increment counter to a lower value, resulting in the insertion of the new record with ID 3.

MySQL 8 offers a solution to the issue of auto-increment counter loss upon server restarts. This enhancement ensures the persistence of the auto-increment counter's value across server restarts, thereby ensuring consistency in primary key generation. Create the table in MySQL 8 with AUTO_INCREMENT PRIMARY KEY:

```
mysql> select version();
+-------------------------+
| version()               |
+-------------------------+
| 8.0.36-0ubuntu0.22.04.1 |
+-------------------------+
1 row in set (0.00 sec)

mysql> CREATE TABLE books (
    ->      id INT AUTO_INCREMENT PRIMARY KEY,
    ->      bookname VARCHAR(50) NOT NULL
    -> );
Query OK, 0 rows affected (0.04 sec)
```

After creating the table, insert three records into the books table in MySQL 8:

```
mysql> INSERT INTO books (bookname) VALUES ('book1');
Query OK, 1 row affected (0.07 sec)

mysql> INSERT INTO books (bookname) VALUES ('book2');
Query OK, 1 row affected (0.02 sec)

mysql> INSERT INTO books (bookname) VALUES ('book3');
Query OK, 1 row affected (0.01 sec)
```

Upon examination, the records in the "books" table appear as follows:

```
mysql> select * from books;
+----+----------+
| id | bookname |
+----+----------+
|  1 | book1    |
|  2 | book2    |
|  3 | book3    |
+----+----------+
3 rows in set (0.00 sec)
```

Following that, we'll delete one record and insert a new entry:

```
mysql> delete from books where id=3;
Query OK, 1 row affected (0.01 sec)

mysql> select * from books;
+----+----------+
| id | bookname |
+----+----------+
|  1 | book1    |
|  2 | book2    |
+----+----------+
2 rows in set (0.00 sec)

mysql> INSERT INTO books (bookname) VALUES ('book4');
Query OK, 1 row affected (0.01 sec)
```

After deleting record ID 3 and inserting a new entry, ID 4 is assigned:

```
mysql>  select * from books;
+----+----------+
| id | bookname |
+----+----------+
|  1 | book1    |
|  2 | book2    |
|  4 | book4    |
+----+----------+
3 rows in set (0.00 sec)
```

After deleting the last record (ID 4), restarting the system, and verifying the table records, we find only two records with IDs 1 and 2:

```
mysql> delete from books where id=4;
Query OK, 1 row affected (0.01 sec)

mysql>  select * from books;
+----+----------+
| id | bookname |
+----+----------+
|  1 | book1    |
|  2 | book2    |
+----+----------+
2 rows in set (0.00 sec)
```

```
service mysql restart

mysql> select * from books;
ERROR 2013 (HY000): Lost connection to MySQL server during query
No connection. Trying to reconnect...
Connection id:    8
Current database: db1
+----+----------+
| id | bookname |
+----+----------+
|  1 | book1    |
|  2 | book2    |
+----+----------+
2 rows in set (0.02 sec)
```

After the restart, the "books" table retains only two records. As anticipated in MySQL 8, upon inserting a new entry, the record is added with the ID 5:

```
mysql> INSERT INTO books (bookname) VALUES ('book5');
Query OK, 1 row affected (0.01 sec)

mysql>  select * from books;
+----+----------+
| id | bookname |
+----+----------+
|  1 | book1    |
|  2 | book2    |
|  5 | book5    |
+----+----------+
3 rows in set (0.00 sec)
```

An Overview of InnoDB Indexes

InnoDB uses indexes to optimize query performance. These indexes can be clustered or secondary and have a physical structure that affects their performance.

Clustered Index

InnoDB tables have a special index known as the *clustered index*, which stores the row data. Typically, the clustered index and the primary key are synonymous, and it is important to understand how InnoDB uses the clustered index to optimize queries, inserts, and other operations for better performance.

To use a primary key as the clustered index, define a primary key for each table. If there is no logical unique and non-null column or set of columns to use as the primary key, add an auto-increment column to the table. This column will automatically assign unique values to new rows as they are inserted.

If no primary key is defined for a table, InnoDB will use the first UNIQUE index with all key columns defined as NOT NULL as the clustered index. If a table has no suitable primary key or UNIQUE index, InnoDB will create a hidden clustered index named GEN_CLUST_INDEX on a synthetic column that contains row ID values. The rows are ordered by the row ID assigned by InnoDB, which is a 6-byte field that increases monotonically as new rows are inserted. As a result, the rows will be physically ordered based on the order of insertion.

Suppose you have a table named users with columns id, name, email, and age. You want to create a clustered index on the id column. To create a clustered index in MySQL, you need to use the CREATE TABLE statement with the ENGINE keyword set to InnoDB. Then, specify the PRIMARY KEY clause with the name of the column you want to use as the clustered index:

```
CREATE TABLE users (
    id int NOT NULL,
    name varchar(50) DEFAULT NULL,
    email varchar(50) DEFAULT NULL,
    age int DEFAULT NULL,
    PRIMARY KEY (id)
) ENGINE=InnoDB DEFAULT CHARSET=utf8mb4 COLLATE=utf8mb4_0900_ai_ci;
```

This example is using the id column as the primary key and the clustered index. The InnoDB storage engine will use the id column's values to physically order the rows in the table.

Secondary Indexes

Secondary indexes in InnoDB are any indexes besides the clustered index. Each record in a secondary index contains the columns specified for the index as well as the primary-key columns for the corresponding row. InnoDB utilizes the primary-key value to locate the row in the clustered index.

If the primary key is lengthy, secondary indexes tend to consume more storage space. Therefore, having a shorter primary key can be advantageous. Suppose you have a table named users with columns id, name, email, and age. You want to create a secondary index on the email column to speed up queries that involve searching for users by email. To create a secondary index in MySQL, you can use the CREATE INDEX statement with the name of the index and the name of the column you want to index:

```
CREATE INDEX email_idx ON users (email);
```

In this example, you're creating a secondary index named email_idx on the email column of the users table. This index will store a copy of the email column's values along with a pointer to the corresponding rows in the table.

MySQL will use the secondary index to quickly locate the rows that match the search criteria and return the results, so you can now run queries that search for users by email more efficiently:

```
SELECT * FROM users WHERE email = 'example@example.com';
```

Creating too many secondary indexes can negatively impact the performance of insert, update, and delete operations. Each index needs to be updated whenever data is added, modified, or deleted from the table. It's important to carefully consider the indexes needed for a table based on the queries that will be run and the trade-offs involved.

Full-Text Indexes

InnoDB full-text indexes are special types of indexes in MySQL that allow for efficient and speedy text-based searches on large amounts of data. They are specifically designed to handle natural language texts, such as articles or books, and provide enhanced functionality to search for specific words or phrases within the text.

These indexes work by breaking the text into individual words or phrases, and then creating an index that maps these words or phrases to their location in the text. This allows for quick and efficient retrieval of the relevant data, even in large data sets.

To use InnoDB full-text indexes, the data must first be indexed using the appropriate syntax, and the search query must be constructed using the MATCH() function. This function allows for various search options, including Boolean searches, natural language searches, and proximity searches.

Suppose you have a table named articles with columns id, title, and content. You want to enable full-text search on the title and content columns by using an InnoDB full-text index. To create a full-text index in MySQL, you first need to ensure that the InnoDB storage engine is being used. You can do this by creating the table with the ENGINE keyword set to InnoDB:

```
CREATE TABLE `articles` (
  `id` int NOT NULL,
  `title` varchar(255) DEFAULT NULL,
  `content` text,
  PRIMARY KEY (`id`)
) ENGINE=InnoDB;
```

Once the table has been created with the InnoDB storage engine, you can add a full-text index to the title and content columns by using the ALTER TABLE statement with the ADD FULLTEXT keyword:

```
ALTER TABLE articles ADD FULLTEXT(title, content);
```

This creates a full-text index on the `title` and `content` columns, allowing you to perform full-text search queries on the table. For example, you can search for articles containing the word `database` by using the `MATCH AGAINST` keyword:

```
SELECT * FROM articles WHERE MATCH(title, content) AGAINST('database');
```

MySQL will use the full-text index to quickly locate the rows that contain the search term `database` in either the `title` or `content` columns and return the results.

Full-text indexes can consume a lot of disk space, especially for large data sets, and can slow the performance of insert and update operations. It's important to carefully consider the trade-offs involved and use full-text indexes only when necessary.

A Table Without a Primary

A *table without a primary* key will cause InnoDB to create a hidden primary key of 6 bytes. However, this key is not controllable and is shared globally among all tables without primary keys. As a result, it can cause contention issues when multiple simultaneous writes are performed on such tables. InnoDB is optimized for primary-key lookups, so having a primary key can greatly benefit query performance.

Adding a primary key to a table in MySQL can indeed improve query performance, especially when dealing with secondary index lookups. This optimization is related to the way the MySQL query optimizer utilizes primary keys to efficiently access data in secondary indexes.

When a table has a primary key defined, the MySQL query optimizer can use it as a reference to locate the corresponding rows in secondary indexes more efficiently. Primary keys can enhance queries in the following ways:

- The primary key uniquely identifies each row in the table. Secondary indexes, on the other hand, contain references (pointers) to the primary-key values associated with the rows they index.

- When you execute a query that involves searching for specific values in a secondary index, MySQL can take advantage of the primary key's uniqueness to optimize the search. It uses the secondary index to quickly find the relevant primary-key values.

- Once the primary-key values are retrieved from the secondary index, MySQL can perform a direct lookup in the table based on the primary key. Since primary keys are typically implemented as clustered indexes in InnoDB, this direct lookup is highly efficient and ensures fast access to the required rows.

- Reduced I/O and improved performance: By leveraging the primary key in this way, MySQL minimizes the number of I/O operations required to fetch the desired rows. This results in improved query performance, especially when dealing with tables with large data sets and complex queries.

- For replication, not having a primary key can lead in full table scans on the replica. Several HA solutions like InnoDB Cluster (group replication) will require a primary key.

To find tables without a primary key in MySQL, you can execute the following SQL query:

```
mysql>    SELECT
    ->          t.TABLE_NAME
    ->    FROM
    ->          INFORMATION_SCHEMA.TABLES AS t
    ->    LEFT JOIN
    ->          INFORMATION_SCHEMA.KEY_COLUMN_USAGE AS k
    ->    ON
    ->          t.TABLE_NAME = k.TABLE_NAME
    ->          AND k.CONSTRAINT_SCHEMA = t.TABLE_SCHEMA
    ->          AND k.constraint_name = 'PRIMARY'
    ->    WHERE
    ->          t.TABLE_SCHEMA NOT IN ('information_schema',
    'performance_schema', 'mysql', 'sys')
    ->          AND k.constraint_name IS NULL;
+------------+
| TABLE_NAME |
+------------+
| authors    |
+------------+
1 row in set (0.01 sec)
mysql>
```

Another option to identify tables without a primary key is to use GEN_CLUST_INDEX. If a table lacks a PRIMARY KEY or a fitting UNIQUE index, InnoDB automatically creates a hidden clustered index known as GEN_CLUST_INDEX. This index is applied to a synthetic column housing row ID values:

```
mysql> SELECT i.table_id, t.NAME
    -> FROM    information_schema.innodb_indexes i
    -> JOIN information_schema.innodb_tables t using (table_id)
    -> WHERE   i.NAME = 'GEN_CLUST_INDEX';
+----------+--------------------+
| table_id | NAME               |
+----------+--------------------+
|     1109 | mydatabase/authors |
+----------+--------------------+
1 row in set (0.00 sec)
```

Generated Invisible Primary Keys

Generated invisible primary keys (GIPKs), introduced in MySQL 8.0.30, enable the automatic generation of primary-key values for tables without explicit user input, as long as the sql_generate_invisible_primary_key variable is set to ON.

The sql_generate_invisible_primary_key variable controls whether GIPKs are automatically added to tables. By default, it's set to OFF, meaning manual primary-key definition is still required:

```
mysql> SELECT @@sql_generate_invisible_primary_key;
+--------------------------------------+
| @@sql_generate_invisible_primary_key |
+--------------------------------------+
|                                    0 |
+--------------------------------------+
1 row in set (0.00 sec)

mysql> CREATE TABLE my_table (
    ->    c1 INT,
    ->    c2 VARCHAR(255)
    -> );
Query OK, 0 rows affected (0.07 sec)
```

The SHOW CREATE TABLE command result indicates that the table does not have a primary key added, and a manual primary key is needed, as the variable sql_generate_invisible_primary_key is set to OFF:

```
mysql> show create table my_table\G
*************************** 1. row ***************************
       Table: my_table
Create Table: CREATE TABLE `my_table` (
  `c1` int DEFAULT NULL,
  `c2` varchar(255) DEFAULT NULL
) ENGINE=InnoDB DEFAULT CHARSET=utf8mb4 COLLATE=utf8mb4_0900_ai_ci
1 row in set (0.00 sec)
```

However, you can set it to ON to enable automatic GIPK generation:

```
mysql> SET sql_generate_invisible_primary_key=ON;
Query OK, 0 rows affected (0.00 sec)

mysql> SELECT @@sql_generate_invisible_primary_key;
+--------------------------------------+
| @@sql_generate_invisible_primary_key |
+--------------------------------------+
|                                    1 |
+--------------------------------------+
1 row in set (0.00 sec)

mysql> CREATE TABLE my_GIPKs_table (
    ->    c1 INT,
```

```
     ->    c2 VARCHAR(255)
     -> );
Query OK, 0 rows affected (0.03 sec)

mysql> show create table my_GIPKs_table\G
*************************** 1. row ***************************
       Table: my_GIPKs_table
Create Table: CREATE TABLE `my_GIPKs_table` (
  `my_row_id` bigint unsigned NOT NULL AUTO_INCREMENT /**!80023 INVISIBLE **/,
  `c1` int DEFAULT NULL,
  `c2` varchar(255) DEFAULT NULL,
  PRIMARY KEY (`my_row_id`)
) ENGINE=InnoDB DEFAULT CHARSET=utf8mb4 COLLATE=utf8mb4_0900_ai_ci
1 row in set (0.00 sec)
```

The output of the last CREATE TABLE command will show that a my_row_id column has been automatically added to the table along with the specified columns (c1 and c2). This invisible column, named my_row_id by default, acts as a hidden primary key, ensuring data integrity without requiring users to define one themselves.

While my_row_id is invisible by default, you can make it visible by using the ALTER TABLE statement. Since my_row_id is designated as an invisible column, it remains absent in the output of SELECT * or TABLE. To include this column in the output, it must be explicitly selected by name, or alternatively, you can use ALTER to make my_row_id visible:

```
mysql> INSERT INTO my_GIPKs_table (c1, c2) VALUES (123, 'Sample Data');
Query OK, 1 row affected (0.01 sec)

mysql> select * from my_GIPKs_table; TABLE my_GIPKs_table\G
+------+-------------+
| c1   | c2          |
+------+-------------+
|  123 | Sample Data |
+------+-------------+
1 row in set (0.00 sec)


*************************** 1. row ***************************
c1: 123
c2: Sample Data
1 row in set (0.00 sec)

mysql> ALTER TABLE my_GIPKs_table ALTER COLUMN my_row_id SET VISIBLE;
Query OK, 0 rows affected (0.01 sec)
Records: 0  Duplicates: 0  Warnings: 0

mysql> select * from my_GIPKs_table; TABLE my_GIPKs_table\G
+-----------+------+-------------+
| my_row_id | c1   | c2          |
+-----------+------+-------------+
|         1 |  123 | Sample Data |
```

```
+----------+------+-------------+
1 row in set (0.00 sec)

*************************** 1. row ***************************
my_row_id: 1
       c1: 123
       c2: Sample Data
1 row in set (0.00 sec)
```

What About Duplicate, Redundant, and Invisible Indexes?

The MySQL index is a data structure designed to enhance database query performance by adding additional writes and storage space to maintain up-to-date index data. It enables quick data location without searching every row in a table. Indexes can be created by using one or more columns of a table and given a unique name. They are particularly beneficial for filtering results based on columns with many distinct values.

However, redundant, unused, or duplicate indexes can decrease performance by confusing the optimizer with query plans, requiring additional storage engine maintenance, calculation, and update of index statistics, as well as increasing disk space usage.

Since MySQL 8, indexes can be made invisible, allowing for better index management. This option allows administrators to ensure that the index is not in use before dropping it. If it turns out to be in use, it can be restored quickly.

Identifying Duplicate Indexes in MySQL

Percona Toolkit provides a command-line tool called `pt-duplicate-key-checker`, which scans MySQL databases and detects tables with duplicate primary keys or indexes. The tool is useful for identifying potential issues with the database schema and provides recommendations on how to resolve them.

By default, `pt-duplicate-key-checker` generates a `DROP INDEX` statement for each duplicate key that it identifies. You can copy and paste the statement into MySQL to remove the duplicate key from the table. For instance, consider the following:

```
$ pt-duplicate-key-checker --host=localhost --user=root --ask-pass
```

Duplicate indexes can also be identified directly by using the `sys schema` table:

```
mysql> select * from sys.schema_redundant_indexes\G
*************************** 1. row ***************************
            table_schema: appdb
              table_name: countrylanguage
      redundant_index_name: CountryCode
   redundant_index_columns: CountryCode
redundant_index_non_unique: 1
```

```
           dominant_index_name: PRIMARY
        dominant_index_columns: CountryCode,Language
     dominant_index_non_unique: 0
                 subpart_exists: 0
                 sql_drop_index: ALTER TABLE `appdb`.`countrylanguage`
                                 DROP INDEX `CountryCode`
*************************** 2. row ***************************
                  table_schema: world
                    table_name: countrylanguage
           redundant_index_name: CountryCode
        redundant_index_columns: CountryCode
     redundant_index_non_unique: 1
            dominant_index_name: PRIMARY
         dominant_index_columns: CountryCode,Language
      dominant_index_non_unique: 0
                  subpart_exists: 0
                  sql_drop_index: ALTER TABLE `world`.`countrylanguage`
                                  DROP INDEX `CountryCode`
2 rows in set (0.01 sec)
mysql>
```

What About Unused MySQL Indexes?

Indexes that are created but not used in any queries are known as *unused indexes*. These indexes can occupy significant space in the database and may slow query performance if they are not maintained. Therefore, it is crucial to identify and remove unused indexes to improve the database's overall performance. The sys.schema unused indexes view can be used to display the indexes that have not been used since the last MySQL server restart:

```
mysql> select * from sys.schema_unused_indexes
where index_name not like
  ->       'fk_%' and
object_schema='sakila' and object_name='payment';
+---------------+-------------+--------------------+
| object_schema | object_name | index_name         |
+---------------+-------------+--------------------+
| sakila        | payment     | idx_fk_staff_id    |
| sakila        | payment     | idx_fk_customer_id |
+---------------+-------------+--------------------+
2 rows in set (0.01 sec)
mysql>
```

We recommend setting indexes to be invisible in MySQL before deleting them. By marking an index as invisible, it is still maintained by the database system but is not used by the optimizer during query execution. This allows you to test the performance impact of removing the index without actually deleting it, as well as giving you the option to easily enable it again if necessary.

To use invisible indexes, you can set the variable `optimizer_switch` to `use_invisi` `ble_indexes=on`. This allows the index to be used for specific application activities or modules during a single query, while preventing it from being used across the entire application. This feature can be useful when you want to test the performance of a query with or without an index, or when you want to temporarily disable an index for a particular query without actually removing it.

By default, MySQL indexes are visible. However, we can use the `ALTER TABLE` statement with the `ALTER INDEX` option to make them invisible or visible. To view the details of the indexes, you can use the `SHOW INDEXES FROM table;` command or query the `INFORMATION_SCHEMA.STATISTICS` table:

```
mysql> SELECT TABLE_SCHEMA, INDEX_NAME, TABLE_NAME , IS_VISIBLE
    ->     FROM INFORMATION_SCHEMA.STATISTICS
    ->     WHERE TABLE_SCHEMA = 'sakila' AND TABLE_NAME = 'customer';
+--------------+------------------+------------+------------+
| TABLE_SCHEMA | INDEX_NAME       | TABLE_NAME | IS_VISIBLE |
+--------------+------------------+------------+------------+
| sakila       | idx_fk_address_id | customer  | YES        |
| sakila       | idx_fk_store_id  | customer   | YES        |
| sakila       | idx_last_name    | customer   | YES        |
| sakila       | PRIMARY          | customer   | YES        |
+--------------+------------------+------------+------------+
4 rows in set (0.00 sec)
mysql>
```

This SQL statement alters the `customer` table by making the `idx_last_name` index invisible:

```
mysql> ALTER TABLE customer ALTER INDEX idx_last_name  INVISIBLE;
Query OK, 0 rows affected (0.02 sec)
Records: 0  Duplicates: 0  Warnings: 0
mysql>
```

This query will return the index name and whether the index is visible for the `customer` table in the `sakila` database:

```
mysql> SELECT TABLE_SCHEMA, INDEX_NAME, TABLE_NAME , IS_VISIBLE
    ->     FROM INFORMATION_SCHEMA.STATISTICS
    ->     WHERE TABLE_SCHEMA = 'sakila' AND TABLE_NAME = 'customer';
+--------------+------------------+------------+------------+
| TABLE_SCHEMA | INDEX_NAME       | TABLE_NAME | IS_VISIBLE |
+--------------+------------------+------------+------------+
| sakila       | idx_fk_address_id | customer  | YES        |
| sakila       | idx_fk_store_id  | customer   | YES        |
| sakila       | idx_last_name    | customer   | NO         |
| sakila       | PRIMARY          | customer   | YES        |
+--------------+------------------+------------+------------+
4 rows in set (0.00 sec)
mysql>
```

The query cannot utilize the index on the last_name column since it is invisible:

```
mysql> explain select last_name from customer WHERE last_name ='BROWN'\G
*************************** 1. row ***************************
           id: 1
  select_type: SIMPLE
        table: customer
   partitions: NULL
         type: ALL
possible_keys: NULL
          key: NULL
      key_len: NULL
          ref: NULL
         rows: 599
     filtered: 0.17
        Extra: Using where
1 row in set, 1 warning (0.00 sec)
mysql>
```

You can use the SET VAR optimizer hint to modify the value of an optimizer switch on a temporary basis, enabling the use of invisible indexes for a particular query. Here is an example of how it can be used:

```
mysql> explain select /*+ SET_VAR(optimizer_switch ='use_invisible_indexes=on')
*/ last_name from customer WHERE last_name ='BROWN'\G
*************************** 1. row ***************************
           id: 1
  select_type: SIMPLE
        table: customer
   partitions: NULL
         type: ref
possible_keys: idx_last_name
          key: idx_last_name
      key_len: 182
          ref: const
         rows: 1
     filtered: 100.00
        Extra: Using index
1 row in set, 1 warning (0.00 sec)
mysql>
```

In high concurrent workloads with suboptimal data distribution on a table, we advise removing duplicate and unnecessary indexes to avoid performance degradation. These redundant indexes occupy unnecessary disk space, leading to overhead on DML and read queries. However, before completely removing an index, it can be made invisible to test the impact of its removal. This way, the effects of removing the index can be evaluated without the time-consuming process of fully deleting and reading it to a larger table.

InnoDB Tablespaces

InnoDB uses tablespaces to store data, indexes, and undo logs. The *system tablespace* functions as the storage location for the change buffer. Additionally, it can hold table and index data, especially if tables are generated within the system tablespace instead of utilizing file-per-table or general tablespaces. In earlier MySQL versions, the system tablespace accommodated the InnoDB data dictionary. However, with the introduction of MySQL 8, InnoDB now stores metadata within the MySQL data dictionary.

File-per-table tablespaces allow you to store each InnoDB table and its indexes in a separate file. This provides greater flexibility, as you can move, back up, or restore individual tables without affecting other tables. By default, `innodb_file_per_table` is enabled, leading InnoDB to create tables in tablespaces following the file-per-table approach.

General tablespaces allow you to create a single shared tablespace that can be used by multiple tables. This provides greater flexibility in managing disk space, as you can add or remove tables from the shared tablespace as needed. General tablespaces are created by using the `CREATE TABLESPACE` statement:

```
mysql> CREATE TABLESPACE `my_tablespace` ADD DATAFILE 'my_tablespace.ibd';
Query OK, 0 rows affected (0.01 sec)
mysql>
```

Undo tablespaces are used to store undo logs. The undo log, recognized as the rollback segment, holds significant importance within the InnoDB storage engine. Its principal function revolves around upholding transactional consistency and enabling the capacity to reverse modifications performed during a transaction, making it a vital component for the multiversion concurrency control (MVCC) mechanism. In MySQL 8, the undo logs find their place within two undo tablespaces, which are generated during the initialization of the MySQL instance; undo logs are no longer created in the system tablespace.

Because of the potential for undo logs to grow considerably during extended transactions, generating extra undo tablespaces can mitigate the risk of individual undo tablespaces becoming overly large. Starting from MySQL 8.0.14, it is feasible to craft additional undo tablespaces while the system is operational, employing the `CREATE UNDO TABLESPACE` syntax:

```
mysql> CREATE UNDO TABLESPACE `my_undo_tablespace` ADD DATAFILE
    -> 'my_undo_tablespace.ibu';
Query OK, 0 rows affected (0.26 sec)
mysql>
```

Temporary tablespaces are used to store temporary data. Complex queries employ temporary tables to store intermediate results. Temporary tables were created in the system tablespace in prior versions (MySQL 5.7), which could potentially lead to performance bottlenecks when working with many concurrent sessions. The temporary tablespaces in MySQL 8 alleviate this limitation by introducing session-level temporary tablespaces. Temporary tables are now kept in separate *.ibt* (InnoDB temporary) files rather than in the system tablespace.

Moving InnoDB System Tablespace Files While the Server Is Offline

The InnoDB system tablespace is a crucial component of the MySQL server that stores internal data dictionary information and undo logs. We recommend configuring the system tablespace properly to ensure the proper functioning of the server. In this section, we discuss the best practices for configuring the InnoDB system tablespace.

To relocate the InnoDB tablespace file, you must shut down MySQL. Before shutting down the MySQL server, ensure a clean shutdown by setting the innodb_fast_shut down variable to 0. This performs a sharp checkpoint and an insert buffer merge, which means that there will be no table data in the shared areas. Even in case of a kill -9, and with properly configured innodb_flush_log_at_trx_commit, everything is properly written to disk too.

Here's how you can set the variable. Before setting a new value, use the following query to verify the current value:

```
mysql> show global variables like 'innodb_fast_shutdown';
+----------------------+-------+
| Variable_name        | Value |
+----------------------+-------+
| innodb_fast_shutdown | 1     |
+----------------------+-------+
1 row in set (0.01 sec)
mysql>

mysql> SET GLOBAL innodb_fast_shutdown = 0;
Query OK, 0 rows affected (0.00 sec)
mysql>
```

After setting the innodb_fast_shutdown variable, you can shut down the MySQL server by using the following command:

```
[root@mysql80 ~]# systemctl stop mysqld.service
[root@mysql80 ~]#
```

You could also shut down MySQL directly from the MySQL client:

```
MySQL> shutdown;
```

To configure the InnoDB system tablespace, you need to create a directory to store the system data files. You can create the directory by using the following command:

```
[root@mysql80 ~]# sudo mkdir /var/lib/mysql/datafile
[root@mysql80 ~]#
```

Next you can move the existing system data file (*ibdata1*) to the newly created directory:

```
[root@mysql80 ~]# sudo mv /var/lib/mysql/ibdata1 /var/lib/mysql/datafile
[root@mysql80 ~]#
```

Then, you need to set the ownership of the directory to the mysql user:

```
[root@mysql80 ~]# sudo chown -R mysql:mysql /var/lib/mysql
[root@mysql80 ~]#
```

After creating the directory and moving the system data file, you need to reconfigure the *innodb.cnf* file to point to the new directory.

Modify the *my.cnf* file and add the following line for includedir:

```
[root@mysql80 ~]# vi /etc/my.cnf
[root@mysql80 ~]# cat /etc/my.cnf | grep includedir
!includedir /etc/mysql/percona/
[root@mysql80 ~]#
```

Create the includedir directory path mentioned in the */etc/my.cnf* if it does not exist:

```
[root@mysql80 ~]# mkdir -p /etc/mysql/percona/
[root@mysql80 ~]#
```

Grant ownership of the directory to the mysql user:

```
[root@mysql80 ~]# sudo chown -R mysql:mysql /etc/mysql/percona/
[root@mysql80 ~]#
```

Copy the file located at */etc/my.cnf* to */etc/mysql/percona/*:

```
[root@mysql80 ~]# cp /etc/my.cnf /etc/mysql/percona/innodb.cnf
[root@mysql80 ~]#
```

In the *innodb.cnf* file, you need to set the innodb-data-home-dir variable to point to the new directory and set the innodb-data-file-path variable to specify the size and number of system data files. Here's an example configuration:

```
[root@mysql80 ~]# sudo vi /etc/mysql/percona/innodb.cnf
[root@mysql80 ~]#

[root@mysql80 ~]# cat /etc/mysql/percona/innodb.cnf | grep innodb
innodb-data-home-dir = /var/lib/mysql/datafile/
innodb-data-file-path = ibdata1:12M;ibdata2:10M:autoextend
[root@mysql80 ~]#
```

After reconfiguring the *innodb.cnf* file, you can start the MySQL server:

```
[root@mysql80 ~]# sudo systemctl start mysqld.service
[root@mysql80 ~]#
```

To verify that the system data files are properly configured, you can list the files in the new directory:

```
[root@mysql80 ~]# sudo ls -ltr /var/lib/mysql/datafile/
total 34816
-rw-r-----. 1 mysql mysql 10485760 Feb 16 09:04 ibdata2
-rw-r-----. 1 mysql mysql 12582912 Feb 16 09:04 ibtmp1
-rw-r-----. 1 mysql mysql 12582912 Feb 16 09:04 ibdata1
[root@mysql80 ~]#
```

To verify that the system tablespace is properly configured, run the following SQL commands:

```
mysql> SHOW GLOBAL VARIABLES LIKE 'innodb_data%';
+----------------------+------------------------------------+
| Variable_name        | Value                              |
+----------------------+------------------------------------+
| innodb_data_file_path | ibdata1:12M;ibdata2:10M:autoextend |
| innodb_data_home_dir  | /var/lib/mysql/datafile/           |
+----------------------+------------------------------------+
2 rows in set (0.00 sec)
mysql>
```

The query retrieves information about files associated with the InnoDB system tablespace from the INFORMATION_SCHEMA.FILES table:

```
mysql> SELECT * FROM INFORMATION_SCHEMA.FILES WHERE TABLESPACE_NAME LIKE
'innodb_system'\G
*************************** 1. row ***************************
             FILE_ID: 0
           FILE_NAME: ./ibdata1
           FILE_TYPE: TABLESPACE
     TABLESPACE_NAME: innodb_system
       TABLE_CATALOG:
        TABLE_SCHEMA: NULL
          TABLE_NAME: NULL
  LOGFILE_GROUP_NAME: NULL
LOGFILE_GROUP_NUMBER: NULL
              ENGINE: InnoDB
       FULLTEXT_KEYS: NULL
        DELETED_ROWS: NULL
        UPDATE_COUNT: NULL
         FREE_EXTENTS: 2
        TOTAL_EXTENTS: 22
         EXTENT_SIZE: 1048576
        INITIAL_SIZE: 12582912
        MAXIMUM_SIZE: 12582912
     AUTOEXTEND_SIZE: 67108864
       CREATION_TIME: NULL
    LAST_UPDATE_TIME: NULL
    LAST_ACCESS_TIME: NULL
        RECOVER_TIME: NULL
 TRANSACTION_COUNTER: NULL
```

```
             VERSION: NULL
          ROW_FORMAT: NULL
          TABLE_ROWS: NULL
      AVG_ROW_LENGTH: NULL
         DATA_LENGTH: NULL
     MAX_DATA_LENGTH: NULL
        INDEX_LENGTH: NULL
           DATA_FREE: 16777216
         CREATE_TIME: NULL
         UPDATE_TIME: NULL
          CHECK_TIME: NULL
            CHECKSUM: NULL
              STATUS: NORMAL
               EXTRA: NULL
*************************** 2. row ***************************
             FILE_ID: 0
           FILE_NAME: ./ibdata2
           FILE_TYPE: TABLESPACE
     TABLESPACE_NAME: innodb_system
       TABLE_CATALOG:
        TABLE_SCHEMA: NULL
          TABLE_NAME: NULL
  LOGFILE_GROUP_NAME: NULL
LOGFILE_GROUP_NUMBER: NULL
              ENGINE: InnoDB
       FULLTEXT_KEYS: NULL
        DELETED_ROWS: NULL
        UPDATE_COUNT: NULL
         FREE_EXTENTS: 2
        TOTAL_EXTENTS: 22
          EXTENT_SIZE: 1048576
         INITIAL_SIZE: 10485760
         MAXIMUM_SIZE: NULL
      AUTOEXTEND_SIZE: 67108864
        CREATION_TIME: NULL
     LAST_UPDATE_TIME: NULL
     LAST_ACCESS_TIME: NULL
         RECOVER_TIME: NULL
 TRANSACTION_COUNTER: NULL
              VERSION: NULL
           ROW_FORMAT: NULL
           TABLE_ROWS: NULL
       AVG_ROW_LENGTH: NULL
          DATA_LENGTH: NULL
      MAX_DATA_LENGTH: NULL
         INDEX_LENGTH: NULL
            DATA_FREE: 16777216
          CREATE_TIME: NULL
          UPDATE_TIME: NULL
           CHECK_TIME: NULL
             CHECKSUM: NULL
               STATUS: NORMAL
```

```
                    EXTRA: NULL
2 rows in set (0.01 sec)
mysql>
```

These commands will display the configuration parameters related to the system tablespace and the list of files associated with the tablespace, respectively. By following these best practices, you can ensure that the InnoDB system tablespace is properly configured and the MySQL server is functioning optimally.

Disabling Tablespace Path Validation

By default, InnoDB validates the filepath when creating or opening a tablespace file. However, in some cases, you may want to disable this validation, such as when using network filesystems or storage area networks. To disable tablespace path validation, set the `innodb_validate_tablespace_paths` option to `OFF` in the MySQL configuration file:

```
[mysqld]
innodb_validate_tablespace_paths=OFF
```

Optimizing Tablespace Space Allocation on Linux

Starting with MySQL 8.0.22, InnoDB offers a way to optimize the allocation of space to file-per-table and general tablespaces on Linux systems. By default, when additional space is required, InnoDB allocates pages to the tablespace and writes null values to those pages, a behavior that can negatively impact performance when new pages are allocated frequently. With the introduction of `innodb_extend_and_initial ize` in MySQL 8.0.22, Linux users can now disable the writing of null values to newly allocated tablespace pages, which is accomplished by using `posix_fallocate()` calls to allocate space. This function reserves space without writing nulls, improving performance.

However, `posix_fallocate()` calls by default allocate only a few pages at a time with a small extension size, which can result in fragmentation and increased random I/O. To mitigate this issue, we recommend increasing the tablespace extension size by using the `AUTOEXTEND_SIZE` option, allowing for an extension size up to 4 GB.

Before allocating a new tablespace page, InnoDB writes a redo log record to ensure that page allocation operations can be replayed from the redo log record during recovery in the event of an interruption. Regardless of the `innodb_extend_and_initi alize` setting, a redo log record is always written before allocating a page.

On non-Linux systems and Windows, the default behavior for InnoDB is to allocate new pages to the tablespace and write NULL values to those pages. Attempting to disable `innodb_extend_and_initialize` on these systems results in an error message stating that changing the setting is not supported on the platform and that the default behavior will be used instead.

Configuring Tablespaces with AUTOEXTEND_SIZE

The tablespaces serve as logical containers for database objects, offering flexibility in data organization and storage management. InnoDB, the default storage engine, actively utilizes tablespaces to house tables and indexes. As data grows, tablespaces often need to expand to accommodate this growth. The AUTOEXTEND_SIZE configuration plays a crucial role in automating this expansion process, ensuring uninterrupted database operations.

You can configure the maximum size of a tablespace file by using the innodb_data_file_path option in the MySQL configuration file. You can also configure the autoextend size of a system tablespace file by using the innodb_autoex tend_increment option. This option specifies the amount by which a tablespace file should be extended when it becomes full.

Understanding AUTOEXTEND_SIZE

The purpose of the AUTOEXTEND_SIZE configuration parameter is to determine the size increment by which a tablespace extends when it reaches its maximum size. By default, tablespaces expand in one-page increments (typically 16 KB) until reaching 32 extents (usually 4 MB). Beyond that, they extend in four-extent increments (16 MB). However, you have the option to customize this behavior according to your storage needs and workload patterns by setting a specific AUTOEXTEND_SIZE value for each tablespace.

Key considerations

Keep in mind that frequent, small extensions can introduce I/O overhead. Larger extensions reduce this overhead but can lead to more significant disk space usage spikes.

You also should carefully consider available disk space and growth patterns to avoid unexpected disk capacity issues. The following configuration sets up InnoDB data files (*ibdata1* and *ibdata2*) initially sized at 10 MB and 20 MB respectively, with autoextension enabled and set to increase by 50 MB increments:

```
[mysqld]
innodb_data_file_path=ibdata1:10M;ibdata2:20M:autoextend
innodb_autoextend_increment=50M
```

Starting from MySQL 8.0.23, it is possible to configure the amount by which a file-per-table or general tablespace is extended using the AUTOEXTEND_SIZE option. By setting a larger extension size, fragmentation can be avoided, and data ingestion can be facilitated.

To configure the extension size for a file-per-table tablespace, specify the AUTOEXTEND_SIZE in a CREATE TABLE or ALTER TABLE statement:

```
mysql> CREATE TABLE your_table_name (c1 INT) AUTOEXTEND_SIZE = 4M;
Query OK, 0 rows affected (0.08 sec)

mysql> ALTER TABLE your_table_name AUTOEXTEND_SIZE = 8M;
Query OK, 0 rows affected (0.02 sec)
Records: 0  Duplicates: 0  Warnings: 0
```

To configure the extension size for a general tablespace, specify the AUTOEXTEND_SIZE in a CREATE TABLESPACE or ALTER TABLESPACE statement:

```
mysql> CREATE TABLESPACE your_tablespace_name AUTOEXTEND_SIZE = 4M;
Query OK, 0 rows affected (0.04 sec)

mysql> ALTER TABLESPACE your_tablespace_name AUTOEXTEND_SIZE = 8M;
Query OK, 0 rows affected (0.00 sec)
```

Note that the AUTOEXTEND_SIZE setting must be a multiple of 4 MB, and specifying a value that is not a multiple of 4 MB will result in an error. The default AUTOEXTEND_SIZE setting is 0, which causes the tablespace to be extended according to the default behavior. The maximum AUTOEXTEND_SIZE setting is 64 MB in MySQL 8.0.23 and 4 GB from MySQL 8.0.24 onward.

The minimum AUTOEXTEND_SIZE setting depends on the InnoDB page size. To determine the InnoDB page size for your MySQL instance, query the innodb_page_size setting. The minimum AUTOEXTEND_SIZE setting for each page size is shown in Table 3-1.

Table 3-1. Minimum AUTOEXTEND_SIZE settings

InnoDB page size	Minimum AUTOEXTEND_SIZE
4K	4M
8K	4M
16K	4M
32K	8M
64K	16M

When the AUTOEXTEND_SIZE setting for a tablespace is altered, the first extension that occurs afterward increases the tablespace size to a multiple of the AUTOEXTEND_SIZE setting. Subsequent extensions are of the configured size. If you specify a nonzero AUTOEXTEND_SIZE setting when creating a file-per-table or general tablespace, the tablespace is initialized at the specified AUTOEXTEND_SIZE size.

It isn't possible to use ALTER TABLESPACE to configure the AUTOEXTEND_SIZE of a file-per-table tablespace. ALTER TABLE must be used instead. If tables are created in file-per-table tablespaces, SHOW CREATE TABLE displays the AUTOEXTEND_SIZE option only when it is set to a nonzero value.

To determine the AUTOEXTEND_SIZE for any InnoDB tablespace, query the information schema INNODB_TABLESPACES table, as shown in the following examples:

```
mysql> SELECT NAME, AUTOEXTEND_SIZE FROM INFORMATION_SCHEMA.INNODB_TABLESPACES
    -> WHERE NAME LIKE 'yourdb/your_table_name';
+------------------------+-----------------+
| NAME                   | AUTOEXTEND_SIZE |
+------------------------+-----------------+
| yourdb/your_table_name |         8388608 |
+------------------------+-----------------+
1 row in set (0.01 sec)

mysql> SELECT NAME, AUTOEXTEND_SIZE FROM INFORMATION_SCHEMA.INNODB_TABLESPACES
    -> WHERE NAME LIKE 'your_tablespace_name';
+----------------------+-----------------+
| NAME                 | AUTOEXTEND_SIZE |
+----------------------+-----------------+
| your_tablespace_name |         8388608 |
+----------------------+-----------------+
1 row in set (0.00 sec)
```

InnoDB tablespaces are an important aspect of MySQL performance and reliability. By understanding the types of tablespaces and their configuration options, you can optimize your MySQL server for your specific needs.

Understanding the InnoDB Doublewrite Buffer

As you learned earlier in this chapter, InnoDB doublewrite buffer is a crucial component in the InnoDB storage engine, designed to enhance data integrity and reliability during write operations. It plays a significant role in preventing data corruption and improving recovery mechanisms.

This buffer is essentially a storage area within the InnoDB storage engine. Its primary purpose is to act as a temporary buffer for write operations, specifically for data pages that are being modified. When data changes are to be written to disk, these changes are initially recorded in the doublewrite buffer before being written to the actual data files.

This two-step write process is essential for maintaining data consistency. It prevents partial writes or torn pages from occurring, which can happen for various reasons such as power failures or hardware issues. By first writing the changes to the doublewrite buffer, InnoDB ensures that either both the data page and its corresponding change record in the doublewrite buffer are written successfully, or none of them are. This atomic write operation helps maintain the integrity of the data.

Another crucial aspect of the doublewrite buffer is its role in crash recovery. In the event of a system crash or an unexpected shutdown, the doublewrite buffer comes into play during the recovery process. During MySQL's crash recovery, it checks the doublewrite buffer to identify any unapplied changes that were buffered before the crash occurred. These changes are then applied to the actual data files, ensuring that the database is brought back to a consistent state, free from any incomplete or corrupted write operations.

Here are the related variables, which are essential to understand and manage:

innodb_doublewrite
> Enables or disables the doublewrite buffer. The default value is 1, which means the buffer is enabled.

innodb_doublewrite_batch_size
> Controls the size of each batch of pages written to the doublewrite buffer. The default value is 0, which means the buffer writes pages one by one.

innodb_doublewrite_files
> Controls the number of doublewrite buffer files used. By default, for each buffer pool instance, two doublewrite files are generated: one for the flush list and another for the least recently used (LRU) list.

The flush list doublewrite file is designated for pages that have been flushed from the buffer pool's flush list, while the LRU list doublewrite file is intended for pages that have been flushed from the buffer pool's LRU list.

The LRU list comes into play when InnoDB attempts to retrieve data from disk, but no available pages are free. In such a scenario, InnoDB must free up space by flushing some data. It does so by employing the LRU list and ejecting the least recently used page, as denoted by the acronym LRU.

On the other hand, the flush list is utilized under two circumstances: when the proportion of dirty pages reaches innodb_max_dirty_pages_pct or when flushing is needed to carry out checkpoint operations.

Setting innodb_doublewrite to to 1 ensures enhanced data integrity by writing data pages to the doublewrite buffer before updating the database:

```
innodb_doublewrite=1
```

In versions of MySQL prior to 8.0.30, the innodb_doublewrite setting could be configured as either ON or OFF during server startup to control doublewrite buffering. However, MySQL 8.0.30 expanded this setting to include options such as DETECT_AND_RECOVER and DETECT_ONLY. Furthermore, MySQL 8.0.30 and later versions support dynamic changes to the `innodb_doublewrite` setting, allowing transitions between `ON`, `DETECT_AND_RECOVER`, and `DETECT_ONLY` modes.

InnoDB `doublewrite_batch_size` set to 2 MB optimizes I/O performance by specifying the size of the doublewrite buffer batch:

```
innodb_doublewrite_batch_size=2M
```

The `innodb_doublewrite_batch_size` variable was introduced in MySQL 8.0.20 and allows for batch writing of doublewrite pages. While it can provide advanced performance-tuning options, the default value should suffice for most users.

By default, if no location is specified, the InnoDB doublewrite buffer directory will be located in the data directory. The buffer directory contains at least two doublewrite files, and the maximum number is twice the number of buffer pool instances. The number of buffer pool instances is determined by the value of the `innodb_buffer_pool_instances` variable:

```
mysql> show global variables like 'innodb_doublewrite%';
+------------------------------+-------+
| Variable_name                | Value |
+------------------------------+-------+
| innodb_doublewrite           | ON    |
| innodb_doublewrite_batch_size| 0     |
| innodb_doublewrite_dir       |       |
| innodb_doublewrite_files     | 2     |
| innodb_doublewrite_pages     | 4     |
+------------------------------+-------+
5 rows in set (0.00 sec)
mysql>
```

The InnoDB doublewrite buffer has a default value of four doublewrite pages per thread. This default value is suitable for most cases. The filename of the InnoDB doublewrite buffer contains a number, such as 16384, which represents the InnoDB page size (16 KB by default):

```
# ls -ltr *ib_16384*
-rw-r----- 1 mysql mysql 8585216 Nov 30 06:07 '#ib_16384_1.dblwr'
-rw-r----- 1 mysql mysql  196608 Jan  1 11:00 '#ib_16384_0.dblwr'

mysql> show global variables like 'innodb_page%';
+----------------------+-------+
| Variable_name        | Value |
+----------------------+-------+
| innodb_page_cleaners | 1     |
| innodb_page_size     | 16384 |
+----------------------+-------+
2 rows in set (0.02 sec)
mysql>
```

This setting enables the doublewrite buffer and ensures that data is written to it before being written to the database file. By default, the doublewrite buffer is enabled in InnoDB.

To disable the InnoDB doublewrite buffer, add `skip-innodb-doublewrite` in the configuration file and restart the `mysql` instance. If you want to enable it and put the files in a specific location, create a directory and set the location in the InnoDB configuration file. Remember to stop and start the MySQL service after making changes. Disabling the doublewrite buffer is not recommended. When it is located on a Fusion-io device that supports atomic write, it is automatically disabled, and data file writes are performed utilizing Fusion-io's atomic write capabilities instead.

The following command extracts information about the MySQL server's options related to the doublewrite buffer. It runs the MySQL server in verbose mode and retrieves help information, then filters the output by using `grep` to display lines containing `doublewrite`. This helps identify and review settings or options related to the doublewrite buffer configuration:

```
[root@mysql80 ~]# mysqld --verbose --help | grep -i doublewrite
 --innodb-doublewrite[=name]
 Enable InnoDB doublewrite buffer (enabled by default).
 Disable with --skip-innodb-doublewrite.
 --innodb-doublewrite-batch-size=#
 --innodb-doublewrite-dir=name
 Use a separate directory for the doublewrite buffer
 --innodb-doublewrite-files=#
 --innodb-doublewrite-pages=#
innodb-doublewrite               ON
innodb-doublewrite-batch-size    0
innodb-doublewrite-dir           (No default value)
innodb-doublewrite-files         0
innodb-doublewrite-pages         0
[root@mysql80 ~]#
```

The `skip-innodb-doublewrite` option, when enabled in the *my.cnf* file and MySQL is restarted, disables InnoDB's doublewrite mechanism.

To deactivate the InnoDB doublewrite buffer, add `skip-innodb-doublewrite` into the *my.cnf* configuration file and then restart MySQL:

```
[root@mysql80 ~]# cat /etc/my.cnf | grep skip-innodb-doublewrite
skip-innodb-doublewrite
[root@mysql80 ~]#

[root@mysql80 ~]# systemctl restart mysqld
[root@mysql80 ~]#
```

This can provide information about the current configuration and status of InnoDB doublewrite settings:

```
mysql> show global variables like 'innodb_doublewrite%';
+------------------------------+-------+
| Variable_name                | Value |
+------------------------------+-------+
| innodb_doublewrite           | OFF   |
| innodb_doublewrite_batch_size | 0    |
| innodb_doublewrite_dir       |       |
| innodb_doublewrite_files     | 0     |
| innodb_doublewrite_pages     | 0     |
+------------------------------+-------+
5 rows in set (0.01 sec)
mysql>
```

Working with the InnoDB Redo Log

As you learned earlier in this chapter, the redo log is a data structure stored on disk, utilized for crash recovery to rectify data written by incomplete transactions. In regular operations, the redo log records requests to modify table data resulting from SQL statements or low-level API calls. Any modifications that were not fully applied to data files before an unexpected shutdown are automatically replayed during initialization, prior to accepting any connections.

The redo logfiles on disk physically represent the redo log. The redo log stores data in the form of records affected, known as redo. As data modifications occur, the redo log data is encoded and appended to the redo logfiles. The progression of data through the redo logfiles is tracked by an increasing log sequence number (LSN). As the checkpoint progresses, the oldest redo log data is truncated to make room for new modifications. The innodb_redo_log_capacity variable indicates the total capacity of the redo log in bytes. It combines the functionalities of both innodb_log_file_size and innodb_log_files_in_group by providing a unified approach to specify the redo log capacity.

We recommend updating your MySQL configurations and migrating to using innodb_redo_log_capacity when setting the redo log capacity to align with the latest best practices and ensure compatibility with future MySQL versions. This variable can be set either at startup in an option file or at runtime by using a SET GLOBAL statement. For instance, to set the redo log capacity to 4 GB, the following command can be used:

```
mysql> SET GLOBAL innodb_redo_log_capacity = 4294967296;
Query OK, 0 rows affected (0.01 sec)
mysql>
```

If the value is set at runtime, the configuration change takes effect immediately, but it may take some time to fully implement the new limit. If the redo logfiles occupy less space than the specified value, dirty pages are flushed from the buffer pool to tablespace data files less frequently, eventually increasing the disk space occupied by the redo logfiles. Conversely, if the redo logfiles occupy more space than the specified value, dirty pages are flushed more often, eventually reducing the disk space occupied by redo logfiles.

If none of these variables are set, the default value for innodb_redo_log_capacity is 104,857,600 bytes (100 MB), and the maximum capacity is 128 GB.

The following queries fetch information related to InnoDB redo logfiles from the performance schema:

```
mysql> SELECT FILE_NAME, START_LSN, END_LSN FROM
performance_schema.innodb_redo_log_files;
+------------------------------+-----------+----------+
| FILE_NAME                    | START_LSN | END_LSN  |
+------------------------------+-----------+----------+
| ./#innodb_redo/#ib_redo11    |  36030464 | 39305216 |
+------------------------------+-----------+----------+
1 row in set (0.00 sec)

mysql> select @@innodb_redo_log_capacity;
+----------------------------+
| @@innodb_redo_log_capacity |
+----------------------------+
|                 4294967296 |
+----------------------------+
1 row in set (0.00 sec)
```

You can query the innodb_redo_log_files table in the performance schema to obtain details about active redo logfiles. The query here retrieves data from all columns of the table:

```
mysql> SELECT FILE_ID, START_LSN, END_LSN, SIZE_IN_BYTES, IS_FULL,
CONSUMER_LEVEL FROM performance_schema.innodb_redo_log_files\G
********* 1. row *********
       FILE_ID: 11
     START_LSN: 36030464
       END_LSN: 39305216
 SIZE_IN_BYTES: 3276800
       IS_FULL: 0
CONSUMER_LEVEL: 0
1 row in set (0.00 sec)
mysql>
```

Redo logfiles are stored in the *#innodb_redo* directory within the data directory, unless a different directory is specified via the innodb_log_group_home_dir variable. If innodb_log_group_home_dir is defined, the redo logfiles reside in the *#innodb_redo* subdirectory within that directory.

There are two types of redo logfiles: ordinary and spare. *Ordinary* redo logfiles are actively used, while *spare* redo logfiles are waiting to be utilized. InnoDB aims to maintain a total of 32 redo logfiles, with each file size equal to 1/32 of the innodb_redo_log_capacity. However, file sizes may temporarily differ after modifying the innodb_redo_log_capacity setting.

In an inactive instance, even after we set the innodb_redo_log_capacity to 4G (4,294,967,296 bytes), the output from the SELECT statement on innodb_redo_log_files indicates only one redo logfile present. It is possible that only one redo logfile is currently active, and the remaining files are not shown in the output. You can monitor the redo logfiles over time to observe any changes in their number and sizes:

```
mysql> SELECT FILE_ID, START_LSN, END_LSN, SIZE_IN_BYTES, IS_FULL,
CONSUMER_LEVEL
FROM performance_schema.innodb_redo_log_files;
+---------+-----------+-----------+---------------+---------+---------------+
| FILE_ID | START_LSN | END_LSN   | SIZE_IN_BYTES | IS_FULL | CONSUMER_LEVEL |
+---------+-----------+-----------+---------------+---------+---------------+
|       7 |  22931456 |  26206208 |       3276800 |       1 |             0 |
|       8 |  26206208 |  29480960 |       3276800 |       1 |             0 |
|       9 |  29480960 |  32755712 |       3276800 |       1 |             0 |
|      10 |  32755712 |  36030464 |       3276800 |       1 |             0 |
|      11 |  36030464 |  39305216 |       3276800 |       1 |             0 |
|      12 |  39305216 |  42579968 |       3276800 |       1 |             0 |
|      13 |  42579968 |  45854720 |       3276800 |       1 |             0 |
|      14 |  45854720 |  49129472 |       3276800 |       1 |             0 |
|      15 |  49129472 |  52404224 |       3276800 |       1 |             0 |
|      16 |  52404224 |  55678976 |       3276800 |       1 |             0 |
|      17 |  55678976 |  58953728 |       3276800 |       1 |             0 |
|      18 |  58953728 |  62228480 |       3276800 |       1 |             0 |
|      19 |  62228480 |  65503232 |       3276800 |       1 |             0 |
|      20 |  65503232 |  68777984 |       3276800 |       1 |             0 |
|      21 |  68777984 |  72052736 |       3276800 |       1 |             0 |
|      22 |  72052736 |  75327488 |       3276800 |       1 |             0 |
|      23 |  75327488 |  78602240 |       3276800 |       1 |             0 |
|      24 |  78602240 |  81876992 |       3276800 |       1 |             0 |
|      25 |  81876992 |  85151744 |       3276800 |       1 |             0 |
|      26 |  85151744 |  88426496 |       3276800 |       1 |             0 |
|      27 |  88426496 |  91701248 |       3276800 |       1 |             0 |
|      28 |  91701248 |  94976000 |       3276800 |       1 |             0 |
|      29 |  94976000 |  98250752 |       3276800 |       1 |             0 |
|      30 |  98250752 | 101525504 |       3276800 |       1 |             0 |
|      31 | 101525504 | 104800256 |       3276800 |       1 |             0 |
|      32 | 104800256 | 108075008 |       3276800 |       1 |             0 |
|      33 | 108075008 | 111349760 |       3276800 |       1 |             0 |
|      34 | 111349760 | 114624512 |       3276800 |       1 |             0 |
|      35 | 114624512 | 117899264 |       3276800 |       1 |             0 |
|      36 | 117899264 | 121174016 |       3276800 |       1 |             0 |
|      37 | 121174016 | 124448768 |       3276800 |       0 |             0 |
+---------+-----------+-----------+---------------+---------+---------------+
31 rows in set (0.01 sec)

mysql> SELECT FILE_ID, START_LSN, END_LSN, SIZE_IN_BYTES, IS_FULL, CONSUMER_LEVEL
```

```
FROM performance_schema.innodb_redo_log_files;
+---------+-------------+-------------+---------------+---------+---------------+
| FILE_ID | START_LSN   | END_LSN     | SIZE_IN_BYTES | IS_FULL | CONSUMER_LEVEL |
+---------+-------------+-------------+---------------+---------+---------------+
|      34 | 111349760   | 114624512   |     3276800   |     1   |           0   |
|      35 | 114624512   | 117899264   |     3276800   |     1   |           0   |
|      36 | 117899264   | 121174016   |     3276800   |     1   |           0   |
|      37 | 121174016   | 124448768   |     3276800   |     1   |           0   |
|      38 | 124448768   | 127723520   |     3276800   |     0   |           0   |
+---------+-------------+-------------+---------------+---------+---------------+
5 rows in set (0.01 sec)
```

innodb_fast_shutdown is a configuration parameter that determines how InnoDB performs a fast shutdown of the database engine during a server shutdown or restart. This setting is related to InnoDB's transaction log—specifically, the InnoDB redo log.

When shutting down MySQL, it is essential to ensure that the shutdown is clean. A clean shutdown ensures that all data is safely written to the redo logfiles. The system variable innodb_fast_shutdown controls how MySQL shuts down when it is shut down using the mysqladmin shutdown command or the shutdown statement. The default value for innodb_fast_shutdown is 1, which means that MySQL will perform a fast shutdown.

InnoDB goes through a clean shutdown when the value is set to 0 (change buffer merge), flushing the logfiles and performing other necessary cleanup tasks. For fully intact *.ibd* files, this is necessary because it ensures that no valid data will be present in the redo logs, and no valid data will be in the change buffer. This ensures that the database will be in a consistent state when it's brought back online.

When set to 1, InnoDB performs a faster shutdown. It skips some of the usual cleanup steps and flushes only the necessary information to the redo log, which speeds up the shutdown process. It does a sharp checkpoint (no dirty data will be in the redo log), but no change buffer merge. However, this method can lead to a slightly longer startup time when the server is restarted because some recovery steps might be required.

The 2 setting is similar to the previous one (1), but it's even faster. InnoDB tries to shut down as quickly as possible without flushing the redo log or performing crash recovery when the server starts up again. This is the same as kill -9; the redo logs will have uncheckpointed data in this case, and the server will need to go through crash recovery. This option is the fastest way to shut down, but it carries a higher risk of potential data loss or corruption if the server crashes or loses power.

Choosing an appropriate value for innodb_fast_shutdown depends on your specific use case and the balance you want to strike between shutdown speed and startup recovery time. While faster shutdown modes can save time, they also increase the likelihood of data inconsistencies or the need for longer recovery processes during server startup. It's important to carefully weigh these factors and choose the option that aligns best with your system's reliability and recovery requirements.

To verify the value of `innodb_fast_shutdown`, run the following SQL query:

```
mysql> show global variables like 'innodb_fast_shutdown';
+----------------------+-------+
| Variable_name        | Value |
+----------------------+-------+
| innodb_fast_shutdown | 1     |
+----------------------+-------+
1 row in set (0.00 sec)
mysql>
```

To set `innodb_fast_shutdown` to 0, which ensures a clean shutdown, run the following SQL query:

```
mysql> SET GLOBAL innodb_fast_shutdown = 0;
Query OK, 0 rows affected (0.00 sec)
mysql>
```

After setting `innodb_fast_shutdown` to 0, you can shut down MySQL by using the following command:

```
[root@mysql80 ~]# sudo systemctl stop mysqld.service
[root@mysql80 ~]#
```

InnoDB Locking and Transaction Model

InnoDB supports ACID transactions. The storage engine provides locking mechanisms that ensure data consistency and transaction isolation in a multiuser environment. Shared and exclusive locks are the most common types of InnoDB locks, but InnoDB has several others as well:

Shared lock

Allows multiple transactions to read the same data simultaneously but does not allow them to modify it.

Exclusive lock

Prevents other transactions from reading or modifying the same data. To set a shared or exclusive lock, use the SELECT…FOR SHARE or SELECT…FOR UPDATE syntax in a transaction. For example:

```
BEGIN; SELECT * FROM table_name WHERE id = 1 FOR UPDATE;
-- Perform some operations
COMMIT;
```

Intention lock

Indicates the type of lock that a transaction intends to set on a row. There are two types of intention locks:

Intent shared (IS) lock
> Indicates that a transaction intends to set a shared lock on a row.

Intent exclusive (IX) lock
> Indicates that a transaction intends to set an exclusive lock on a row.

Record locks
> Protects individual rows from being modified or read by other transactions. When a transaction modifies a row, it sets an exclusive lock on that row. When a transaction reads a row, it sets a shared lock on that row. For example:
>
> ```
> BEGIN; SELECT * FROM table_name WHERE id = 1 FOR UPDATE;
> UPDATE table_name SET column1 = 'new_value' WHERE id = 1;
> COMMIT;
> ```

Gap locks
> Prevents other transactions from inserting new rows that might match the search condition of a SELECT statement. Gap locks are set on a range of index records, not on the actual rows. For example:
>
> ```
> BEGIN; SELECT * FROM table_name WHERE id > 1 AND id < 10 FOR UPDATE;
> -- Other transactions cannot insert a new row with id between 1 and 10
> COMMIT;
> ```

Next-key locks
> A combination of a record lock and a gap lock used to prevent phantom reads in an MVCC environment. A phantom read occurs when a transaction reads a set of rows that satisfy a certain condition, and another transaction inserts a new row that also satisfies that condition before the first transaction finishes. For example:
>
> ```
> BEGIN; SELECT * FROM table_name WHERE id > 1 AND id < 10 FOR UPDATE;
> -- Other transactions cannot insert a new row with id between 1 and 10
> INSERT INTO table_name (id, column1) VALUES (5, 'new_value');
> -- The above statement will wait until the lock is released
> COMMIT;
> ```

Insert intention locks
> Indicate that a transaction intends to insert a new row into a table. There are two types of insert intention locks:

Insert intention shared (IS) lock
> Indicates that a transaction intends to insert a new row without setting an exclusive lock on the table.

Insert intention exclusive (IX) lock
> Indicates that a transaction intends to insert a new row and set an exclusive lock on the table.

AUTO-INC locks

Ensures that concurrent transactions do not insert rows with the same AUTO_INCREMENT value. For example:

```
BEGIN; INSERT INTO table_name (column1) VALUES ('new_value');
-- The above statement will wait until the AUTO-INC lock is released
COMMIT
```

Predicate locks

Protects spatial index searches. When a transaction searches a spatial index, it sets a predicate lock on the index. The predicate lock prevents other transactions from inserting or deleting rows that match the search condition. For example:

```
BEGIN; SELECT * FROM table_name WHERE ST_Intersects(column1,
ST_GeomFromText('POINT(1 1)')) FOR UPDATE;

-- Other transactions cannot insert or delete rows that intersect
-- with the preceding point until the commit is executed.

COMMIT;
```

Transaction Isolation Levels

InnoDB uses a multiversioning model to achieve high concurrency without sacrificing consistency.

InnoDB supports multiple transaction isolation levels to allow for different levels of concurrency and consistency. The following are the supported transaction isolation levels:

- Read Uncommitted
- Read Committed
- Repeatable Read
- Serializable

Each isolation level provides a different level of transaction visibility and concurrency control. For example, the higher the isolation level, the lower the concurrency and the higher the consistency:

```
SET TRANSACTION ISOLATION LEVEL READ COMMITTED;
```

InnoDB uses the concepts of *autocommit*, *commit*, and *rollback* to manage transactions. Autocommit is enabled by default, which means that each statement is treated as a separate transaction:

```
SET autocommit=0;
START TRANSACTION;
UPDATE table1 SET col1='value1' WHERE id=1;
```

```
UPDATE table2 SET col2='value2' WHERE id=2;
COMMIT;
```

In this example, the two UPDATE statements are grouped into a transaction via START TRANSACTION and COMMIT. If any of the statements fail, the transaction can be rolled back with ROLLBACK.

InnoDB provides *consistent nonlocking reads*, which means that concurrent transactions can read the same data without blocking one another. This is achieved by using multiversioning, which allows each transaction to see a consistent snapshot of the database at the time it started:

```
SELECT col1 FROM table1 WHERE id=1;
```

In this example, the SELECT statement reads the value of col1 from table1 without locking the row.

Locking Reads

InnoDB also provides *locking reads*, which can be used to prevent concurrent transactions from modifying the same data. Locks can be placed on individual rows or on ranges of rows:

```
SELECT col1 FROM table1 WHERE id=1 FOR UPDATE;
```

In this example, the SELECT statement places an exclusive lock on the row with id=1. If another transaction tries to modify the same row, it will be blocked until the lock is released.

Locks can also be placed on ranges of rows by using the SELECT...FOR UPDATE and SELECT...FOR SHARE syntax. SELECT...FOR SHARE serves as a replacement for SELECT... LOCK IN SHARE MODE; the latter remains accessible for backward compatibility purposes. The following are examples of locking reads:

- Locking the next available row:

  ```
  SELECT col1 FROM table1 WHERE col1 IS
  NULL LIMIT 1 FOR UPDATE;
  ```

- Locking a range of rows:

  ```
  SELECT col1 FROM table1 WHERE col1 BETWEEN
  10 AND 20 FOR UPDATE;
  ```

InnoDB also supports nonblocking locking reads with NOWAIT and SKIP LOCKED. These options can be used to avoid blocking when a lock cannot be acquired immediately:

```
SELECT col1 FROM table1 WHERE id=1 FOR UPDATE NOWAIT;
```

In this example, the SELECT statement tries to place a lock on the row with id=1 without blocking. If the lock cannot be acquired immediately because another transaction is holding the lock, an error will be returned instead of blocking.

Similarly, the SKIP LOCKED option can be used to skip over rows that are already locked:

```
SELECT col1 FROM table1 WHERE col1 IS NULL LIMIT 1 FOR UPDATE SKIP
LOCKED;
```

The SELECT statement tries to lock the next available row where col1 is NULL. If the row is already locked, it will be skipped over and the next available row will be locked instead.

By using these options, concurrent transactions can access the same data without blocking one another, improving the overall system throughout. By understanding these features and using them appropriately, you can design high-performance applications that can scale to meet the needs of your users.

Locks Set by Different SQL Statements in InnoDB

When multiple SQL statements are executed concurrently, they may set locks on the same rows in the same table. InnoDB uses lock modes to determine how the locks are acquired and released. Table 3-2 shows lock modes set by different SQL statements.

Table 3-2. Lock modes and SQL statements

SQL statement	Lock mode
SELECT ... FROM ... WHERE ...	Shared (S) lock
SELECT ... FROM ... WHERE ... FOR UPDATE	Exclusive (X) lock
INSERT INTO ...	Exclusive (X) lock
UPDATE ... SET ... WHERE ...	Exclusive (X) lock
DELETE FROM ... WHERE ...	Exclusive (X) lock

For example, say transaction T1 executes the following SQL statement:

```
SELECT * FROM table WHERE id = 1 FOR UPDATE;
```

And transaction T2 executes the following SQL statement:

```
SELECT * FROM table WHERE id = 2 FOR UPDATE;
```

Then InnoDB will set exclusive locks on the rows with ID 1 and 2, respectively, to prevent conflicts between the transactions. InnoDB has a *configurable lock wait timeout* that determines how long a transaction waits for a lock to be released by another transaction. If a lock is not released within the timeout period, the waiting transaction rolls back. The default value of lock wait timeout is 50 seconds.

To configure the lock wait timeout, set the `innodb_lock_wait_timeout` system variable to a value in seconds. For example, to set the lock wait timeout to 30 seconds, run the following SQL statement:

```
SET GLOBAL innodb_lock_wait_timeout = 30;
```

Setting the lock wait timeout too low may cause transactions to roll back frequently, while setting it too high may cause transactions to wait for too long and affect system performance. Therefore, we recommend setting the lock wait timeout to a value that is appropriate for the workload of the system.

Hot Rows with NOWAIT and SKIP LOCKED

MySQL 8 introduced two new features, NOWAIT and SKIP LOCKED, which are specifically designed to support lock handling. These features are useful for managing *hot rows*, frequently accessed rows that may be subject to locks by other concurrent transactions.

Traditionally, when encountering locks that are part of an active transaction or hot rows, the application attempts to access the data, and if there is a lock on the requested rows, it incurs a timeout and has to retry the transaction. This can be a time-consuming and inefficient process, especially when multiple transactions are involved. However, with the NOWAIT and SKIP LOCKED features, users can implement sophisticated lock-handling scenarios to improve application performance and manage timeouts more efficiently.

NOWAIT allows the application to attempt to acquire a lock on a row without waiting for the lock to be released. If the row is already locked, the application receives an immediate response indicating that the lock cannot be acquired. This feature is useful when the application needs to access a particular row quickly and cannot wait for a lock to be released.

SKIP LOCKED allows the application to skip over locked rows when performing an operation, rather than waiting for the lock to be released. This feature is useful when the application can tolerate skipping over certain rows and still achieve the desired result, rather than waiting for a lock to be released.

Table 3-3 shows the Goods table with five items, including their costs and availability.

Table 3-3. Goods

Pro ProductID	ProductName	Cost $	Availability
1	Item1	10.0000	Yes
2	Item2	20.0000	Yes
3	Item3	30.0000	Yes
5	Item5	50.0000	Yes

Pro ProductID	ProductName	Cost $	Availability
6	Item6	60.0000	Yes

The following queries will generate Table 3-3 and insert some sample data into it:

```
mysql> CREATE TABLE `goods` (
    ->    `p_id` int NOT NULL AUTO_INCREMENT,
    ->    `p_name` varchar(255) DEFAULT NULL,
    ->    `p_cost` decimal(19,4) NOT NULL,
    ->    `p_availability` enum('YES','NO') DEFAULT 'NO',
    ->    PRIMARY KEY (`p_id`),
    ->    KEY `p_cost` (`p_cost`),
    ->    KEY `p_name` (`p_name`)
    -> ) ENGINE=InnoDB AUTO_INCREMENT=0 DEFAULT CHARSET=utf8mb4
    COLLATE=utf8mb4_0900_ai_ci ;
Query OK, 0 rows affected (0.03 sec)

mysql> INSERT INTO goods (p_id, p_name, p_cost, p_availability) VALUES
    -> (1,'Item1', 10.0000, 'Yes'),
    -> (2,'Item2', 20.0000, 'Yes'),
    -> (3,'Item3', 30.0000, 'Yes'),
    -> (5,'Item5', 50.0000, 'Yes'),
    -> (6,'Item6', 60.0000, 'Yes');
Query OK, 5 rows affected (0.00 sec)
Records: 5  Duplicates: 0  Warnings: 0
```

If rows 2 and 3 are not already locked, the next transaction will lock them. Once the transaction is committed or rolled back, the lock on these rows will be released. Autocommit is enabled by default for any transaction, but it can be disabled by setting autocommit to 0 or by using the START TRANSACTION clause.

A MySQL *session* denotes the duration in which a user connects to and engages with the MySQL server, encompassing query execution, transactional activities, and database resource management. To explore the new features NOWAIT and SKIP LOCKED, we will use two sessions (session 1 and session 2) in this section.

In session 1, initiate a transaction with START TRANSACTION, followed by a SELECT query with a range condition and FOR UPDATE locking:

```
mysql> START TRANSACTION; SELECT * FROM mytestdb.goods WHERE p_cost >=20 and
p_cost <=30 FOR UPDATE\G
Query OK, 0 rows affected (0.00 sec)

********* 1. row *********
         p_id: 2
       p_name: Item2
       p_cost: 20.0000
p_availability: YES
********* 2. row *********
         p_id: 3
       p_name: Item3
```

```
        p_cost: 30.0000
p_availability: YES
2 rows in set (0.00 sec)

mysql>
```

InnoDB implements row-level locking by setting shared or exclusive locks on the index records it encounters when searching or scanning a table index. Consequently, the row-level locks are essentially index-record locks.

To obtain transaction details, such as the transaction ID and row lock count, the InnoDB engine status command (SHOW ENGINE INNODB STATUS;) or the perfor mance_schema.data_locks table can be queried. However, the output from the InnoDB engine status command can be perplexing. The following engine status snippet reveals that, because of the previous query, it can result in the locking of all rows within the table:

```
SHOW ENGINE INNODB STATUS;

Trx id counter 7270
Purge done for trx's n:o < 7269 undo n:o < 0 state: running but idle
History list length 0
LIST OF TRANSACTIONS FOR EACH SESSION:
---TRANSACTION 421693843570688, not started
0 lock struct(s), heap size 1128, 0 row lock(s)
---TRANSACTION 421693843569072, not started
0 lock struct(s), heap size 1128, 0 row lock(s)
---TRANSACTION 421693843568264, not started
0 lock struct(s), heap size 1128, 0 row lock(s)
---TRANSACTION 7269, ACTIVE 96 sec
3 lock struct(s), heap size 1128, 5 row lock(s)
MySQL thread id 7, OS thread handle 140218335434304, query id 33 localhost root
```

Even though our query locked only rows 3 and 4, the output reports that five rows are locked (which includes the count of the locked primary, locked selected column secondary index, and supremum pseudo-record). As a result of our query, we can see that the row directly adjacent to the selected rows is also listed as locked. This behavior is anticipated and documented since a full scan of the table, rather than an index search, is much faster for small tables with only five rows.

Alternatively, we can use the performance_schema.data_locks, introduced in MySQL 8.0.1, to get the locked row details. The following query displays the locks grouped by ENGINE_TRANSACTION_ID, INDEX_NAME, OBJECT_NAME, and OBJECT_SCHEMA, revealing locks on the mydb.product table's p_cost index and primary key:

```
mysql> SELECT engine_transaction_id,
    -> Concat(object_schema, '.', object_name)TBL,
    -> index_name,
    -> Count(*) LOCK_DATA
    -> FROM performance_schema.data_locks
```

```
    -> WHERE lock_data != 'supremum pseudo-record'
    -> GROUP BY engine_transaction_id,
    -> index_name,
    -> object_name,
    -> object_schema\G
********* 1. row *********
engine_transaction_id: 7269
                  TBL: mytestdb.goods
           index_name: p_cost
            LOCK_DATA: 3
********* 2. row *********
engine_transaction_id: 7269
                  TBL: mytestdb.goods
           index_name: PRIMARY
            LOCK_DATA: 2
2 rows in set (0.00 sec)
mysql>
```

The results show that transaction ID 7269 holds an intention exclusive lock on the table itself, while also maintaining exclusive locks on specific records within the p_cost and PRIMARY indexes. These locks indicate ongoing activity related to updating or accessing data within the goods table, with specific records being exclusively locked for modification or access:

```
mysql> SELECT engine_transaction_id AS ENG_TRX_ID,
    ->        object_name,
    ->        index_name,
    ->        lock_type,
    ->        lock_mode,
    ->        lock_data
    -> FROM   performance_schema.data_locks
    -> WHERE  object_name = 'goods'\G
********* 1. row *********
 ENG_TRX_ID: 7269
object_name: goods
 index_name: NULL
  lock_type: TABLE
  lock_mode: IX
  lock_data: NULL
********* 2. row *********
 ENG_TRX_ID: 7269
object_name: goods
 index_name: p_cost
  lock_type: RECORD
  lock_mode: X
  lock_data: 0x800000000000140000, 2
********* 3. row *********
 ENG_TRX_ID: 7269
object_name: goods
 index_name: p_cost
  lock_type: RECORD
  lock_mode: X
```

```
  lock_data: 0x8000000000001E0000, 3
********* 4. row *********
 ENG_TRX_ID: 7269
object_name: goods
 index_name: p_cost
  lock_type: RECORD
  lock_mode: X
  lock_data: 0x800000000000320000, 5
********* 5. row *********
 FNG_TRX_ID: 7269
object_name: goods
 index_name: PRIMARY
  lock_type: RECORD
  lock_mode: X,REC_NOT_GAP
  lock_data: 2
********* 6. row *********
 ENG_TRX_ID: 7269
object_name: goods
 index_name: PRIMARY
  lock_type: RECORD
  lock_mode: X,REC_NOT_GAP
  lock_data: 3
6 rows in set (0.00 sec)

mysql>
```

Now let's commit the transaction in session 1:

```
mysql> COMMIT;
Query OK, 0 rows affected (0.00 sec)
mysql>
```

innodb_lock_wait_timeout and SELECT FOR UPDATE

The innodb_lock_wait_timeout feature is used to manage lock conflicts in MySQL's InnoDB storage engine. By default, this variable is set to 50 seconds, meaning that any transaction waiting for a lock for longer than 50 seconds will be terminated and a timeout message will be returned to the user. This timeout value can be configured to meet the specific requirements of an application.

To illustrate how this feature works, let's consider an example involving a SELECT FOR UPDATE query:

```
mysql> select @@innodb_lock_wait_timeout;
+----------------------------+
| @@innodb_lock_wait_timeout |
+----------------------------+
|                         50 |
+----------------------------+
1 row in set (0.00 sec)

mysql>
```

In session 1, a transaction is initiated and a query is executed to select all items from the database `mytestdb.goods`, where the cost falls between $20 and $30 (inclusive) and locks the selected rows for update. The results show two items, `Item2` with a cost of $20 and `Item3` with a cost of $30:

```
mysql> START TRANSACTION;SELECT * FROM mytestdb.goods WHERE p_cost >=20 and
p_cost <=30 FOR UPDATE\G
Query OK, 0 rows affected (0.01 sec)

********* 1. row *********
         p_id: 2
       p_name: Item2
       p_cost: 20.0000
p_availability: YES
********* 2. row *********
         p_id: 3
       p_name: Item3
       p_cost: 30.0000
p_availability: YES
2 rows in set (0.00 sec)
mysql>
```

Back in session 2, let's execute a query to retrieve the current timestamp using `now()` and then select the item from `mytestdb.goods`, where the product ID is 3 and locks the corresponding row for update:

```
mysql> select now(); SELECT * FROM mytestdb.goods WHERE p_id=3 FOR UPDATE;
select now()\G
+---------------------+
| now()               |
+---------------------+
| 2024-02-16 11:26:51 |
+---------------------+
1 row in set (0.00 sec)

ERROR 1205 (HY000): Lock wait timeout exceeded; try restarting transaction
********* 1. row *********
now(): 2024-02-16 11:27:41
1 row in set (0.00 sec)
mysql>
```

A lock wait timeout error occurs because the record was locked by the session 1 transaction. Remember to `COMMIT` the transaction in session 1 to complete it.

In MySQL, the `NOWAIT` clause can be used in a query to terminate it immediately if any candidate rows are already locked. If an application requires that it does not wait for locks to be released or for a timeout, the `NOWAIT` clause is a useful solution. Alternatively, setting the `innodb_lock_wait_timeout` variable to a value of 1 in the current session will also have a similar effect.

The following query in session 1 initiates a transaction with START TRANSACTION and then selects rows from the mytestdb.goods table where the p_cost column is from 20 to 30 (inclusive) with the FOR UPDATE clause. FOR UPDATE indicates that the selected rows are locked for update within the transaction, preventing other transactions from modifying them until the current transaction is committed or rolled back:

```
mysql> START TRANSACTION;SELECT * FROM mytestdb.goods WHERE p_cost >=20 and
p_cost <=30 FOR UPDATE\G
Query OK, 0 rows affected (0.00 sec)

********* 1. row *********
        p_id: 2
      p_name: Item2
      p_cost: 20.0000
p_availability: YES
********* 2. row *********
        p_id: 3
      p_name: Item3
      p_cost: 30.0000
p_availability: YES
2 rows in set (0.00 sec)
```

In session 2, if you attempt to select data from the mystestdb.goods table where p_id equals 3 and apply FOR UPDATE NOWAIT, the following error will occur:

```
mysql> SELECT * FROM mytestdb.goods WHERE p_id = 3 FOR UPDATE NOWAIT\G
ERROR 3572 (HY000): Statement aborted because lock(s) could not be acquired
immediately and NOWAIT is set.
mysql>
```

As usual, COMMIT the transaction in session 1.

When the SKIP LOCKED clause is used in a MySQL query, it instructs the engine to skip any locked rows and process only the remaining rows based on the WHERE clause in a nondeterministic order. To illustrate how this works, consider the following examples.

The next sequence of SQL statements in session 1 starts a transaction with START TRANSACTION and then selects rows from the mytestdb.goods table where the p_cost column is from 20 to 30 (inclusive) with the FOR UPDATE clause. The FOR UPDATE clause is used to lock the selected rows, ensuring exclusive access for the transaction until it is either committed or rolled back:

```
mysql> START TRANSACTION;SELECT * FROM mytestdb.goods WHERE p_cost >=20 and
p_cost <=30 FOR UPDATE\G
Query OK, 0 rows affected (0.00 sec)

********* 1. row *********
        p_id: 2
      p_name: Item2
      p_cost: 20.0000
```

```
p_availability: YES
********* 2. row *********
        p_id: 3
      p_name: Item3
      p_cost: 30.0000
p_availability: YES
2 rows in set (0.00 sec)
mysql>
```

In session 2, a query was executed to select data from the `mytestdb.goods` table where `p_cost` equals 30. However, the result returned an empty set, as `SKIP LOCKED` is used without erroring out:

```
mysql>
mysql> SELECT * FROM mytestdb.goods WHERE p_cost = 30
FOR UPDATE SKIP LOCKED\G
Empty set (0.00 sec)
mysql>
```

The query includes a `WHERE` clause on the `p_id`, querying records `IN(1,2,3,4,5)`. The results display records 1 and 5, as records 2 and 3 are currently locked in session 1, preventing them from being retrieved by the query:

```
mysql> SELECT * from mytestdb.goods where p_id IN (1,2,3,4,5) FOR UPDATE
SKIP LOCKED\G
********* 1. row *********
        p_id: 1
      p_name: Item1
      p_cost: 10.0000
p_availability: YES
********* 2. row *********
        p_id: 5
      p_name: Item5
      p_cost: 50.0000
p_availability: YES
2 rows in set (0.00 sec)

mysql>
```

Now, to complete the transaction in session 1, let's proceed with committing it:

```
mysql> COMMIT;
```

Suppose that in a scenario with two concurrent transactions, the first transaction selects rows 2 and 3 and locks them for update. In this case, when the `SKIP LOCKED` clause is used in the second transaction, it will skip these locked rows and return the remaining rows.

The `SELECT…FOR UPDATE` clause can have a significant impact on concurrency in MySQL, and should be used only when necessary. If used improperly, it can lead to table locks and other performance issues. To avoid this, it's important to index the column specified in the `WHERE` clause to ensure that only the candidate rows are locked. Without proper indexes, the entire table may be locked.

Therefore, use this clause with caution and only when necessary, and ensure that the relevant columns are properly indexed to avoid unnecessary table locks and improve performance.

Important InnoDB Configuration Variables

This section provides detailed information for configuring various InnoDB variables. To optimize its functionality and meet specific requirements, it is essential to understand and configure its variables appropriately.

Configuring innodb_buffer_pool_size

As you learned earlier in this chapter, the `innodb_buffer_pool_size` system variable in MySQL 8 is used to set the size of the InnoDB buffer pool, the in-memory cache that stores frequently accessed data and index information for InnoDB tables. The buffer pool is not only used for frequently accessed data but also for the write path. It can contain pages that have been written but never accessed.

```
innodb_buffer_pool_size=50G
```

When a query needs to access data from an InnoDB table, the InnoDB buffer pool is the first place that MySQL looks for the data. If the data is already in the buffer pool, MySQL can access it quickly without having to read it from disk. If the data is not in the buffer pool, MySQL must read it from disk and load it into the buffer pool.

Setting an appropriate value for `innodb_buffer_pool_size` is important because it affects the performance of queries that access InnoDB tables. If the buffer pool is too small, queries may need to read data from disk more frequently, which can lead to slower query performance. If the buffer pool is too large, system memory may be wasted on a cache that is not being fully utilized.

The optimal value for `innodb_buffer_pool_size` depends on several factors, including the amount of available memory on the server, the size of the InnoDB tables being accessed, and the workload on the server. It is generally recommended to allocate a significant portion of available memory to the buffer pool, but not to allocate so much that other system processes are starved for memory.

The default value of `innodb_buffer_pool_size` in MySQL 8 is 134,217,728 (128 MB), but we recommend adjusting this value based on the specific requirements of the application and the server hardware.

Configuring innodb_buffer_pool_instances

The innodb_buffer_pool_instances system variable in MySQL 8 specifies the number of buffer pool instances to create. The InnoDB buffer pool is divided into buffer pool instances to minimize contention among threads accessing the buffer pool.

Each buffer pool instance has its own set of LRU lists, flush list, and buffer pool mutex, which helps reduce contention on these resources. When a thread needs to access a page in the buffer pool, it selects the buffer pool instance based on the page number and then acquires the buffer pool mutex for that instance.

By default, your innodb_buffer_pool_instances will be set to 8 (or 1 if innodb_buffer_pool_size < 1GB), which means that the InnoDB buffer pool is not divided into multiple instances. However, on systems with many CPUs or large buffer pools, we recommend setting innodb_buffer_pool_instances to a value equal to or greater than the number of CPU cores.

The optimal value for innodb_buffer_pool_instances depends on the number of CPU cores, the amount of available memory, and the workload on the server. In general, increasing the number of buffer pool instances can help reduce contention and improve performance, but it also requires additional memory overhead. Changing the value of innodb_buffer_pool_instances requires a server restart to take effect.

Configuring Thread Concurrency

InnoDB uses multiple threads to manage concurrent access to the database. Configuration of thread concurrency includes setting the number of threads that can access the database simultaneously.

innodb_thread_concurrency is a configuration option in MySQL 8 that controls the number of threads that InnoDB uses for processing queries concurrently. InnoDB uses multiple threads to process different operations, such as flushing dirty pages to disk, handling connections, and performing I/O operations. The innodb_thread_con currency option limits the number of threads that InnoDB will use for processing queries, which can help prevent contention and improve performance.

By default, innodb_thread_concurrency is set to 0, which means that InnoDB will automatically determine the number of threads to use based on the number of available CPUs and other factors. In this case, InnoDB may use multiple threads for processing queries concurrently:

```
innodb_thread_concurrency=0
```

If `innodb_thread_concurrency` is set to a non-zero value, InnoDB will limit the number of threads that it uses for processing queries to the specified value. This can be useful in cases where there are limited system resources or when there is contention for resources such as CPU or disk I/O.

It is important to note that setting `innodb_thread_concurrency` too low can result in poor query performance, while setting it too high can result in contention and poor performance due to context switching and other factors. Therefore, it is important to monitor the performance of the system and adjust the value of `innodb_thread_con currency` based on the available resources and workload characteristics.

In addition to `innodb_thread_concurrency`, there are other related configuration options such as `innodb_read_io_threads` and `innodb_write_io_threads` that control the number of threads used for performing read and write operations respectively. These options can also affect the concurrency of queries in InnoDB.

As per best practices, it is recommended to set the value of `innodb_thread_concur rency` to 2 times the number of available CPUs (nproc) on the system. This is because InnoDB requires CPU resources to process queries, and setting the value to `2*nproc` can help ensure that there are enough threads available to handle concurrent queries efficiently without causing excessive context switching or other performance issues.

Configuring the Number of Background I/O Threads

InnoDB uses background I/O threads to improve performance when handling I/O-intensive workloads. Configuration of the number of background InnoDB I/O threads includes setting their count:

```
innodb_read_io_threads=8
innodb_write_io_threads=8
```

The `innodb_read_io_threads` and `innodb_write_io_threads` system variables in MySQL 8 are used to configure the number of background I/O threads used by InnoDB for read and write operations, respectively.

By default, both variables are set to 4. This default value is based on the assumption that most systems have multiple CPU cores and that setting the number of I/O threads to a low value can help avoid contention for CPU and I/O resources. However, the optimal number of I/O threads can vary depending on the specific workload and system characteristics. For example, increasing the number of I/O threads may be beneficial for systems with a high volume of concurrent read or write operations.

It's important to monitor the performance of your system and adjust the values of `innodb_read_io_threads` and `innodb_write_io_threads` as needed to achieve optimal performance for your specific workload and system characteristics.

Using Asynchronous I/O on Linux

Asynchronous I/O can improve InnoDB performance on Linux systems by allowing I/O operations to occur in parallel with other processing. Configuration of asynchronous I/O includes setting appropriate parameters, like `innodb_use_native_aio`, in the configuration file.

The `innodb_use_native_aio` configuration option controls whether InnoDB uses native asynchronous I/O (AIO) on supported platforms. AIO is a technique for performing I/O operations without blocking the calling thread, which can improve I/O performance and scalability in certain situations.

By default, `innodb_use_native_aio` is set to `ON` on platforms where it is supported. When enabled, InnoDB will use the native AIO implementation provided by the operating system for asynchronous I/O operations. This can improve I/O performance on systems with high I/O loads by allowing InnoDB to perform I/O operations without blocking the calling thread.

If native AIO is not supported on the platform or if there are issues with the native implementation, `innodb_use_native_aio` can be set to `OFF` to disable it. In this case, InnoDB will use a fallback implementation of AIO that is provided by the MySQL server.

Note that enabling `innodb_use_native_aio` can have performance implications and may require tuning of other configuration options such as `innodb_io_capacity` and `innodb_io_capacity_max` to achieve optimal performance. Additionally, it may not be beneficial in all cases, so we recommend you perform testing and analysis to determine the best configuration for a particular workload and platform.

Configuring I/O Capacity

The `innodb_io_capacity` and `innodb_io_capacity_max` configuration options in MySQL are used to control the I/O capacity that InnoDB will use for flushing dirty pages from the buffer pool to disk. InnoDB maintains a pool of pages in memory to improve query performance, but periodically it must write these pages to disk to ensure durability and consistency of the data.

When InnoDB flushes dirty pages to disk, it uses a certain amount of I/O capacity. The `innodb_io_capacity` option sets the minimum I/O capacity that InnoDB will use for these operations, while the `innodb_io_capacity_max` option sets the maximum I/O capacity that InnoDB will use when it is performing the most intensive I/O operations.

By default, the `innodb_io_capacity` option is set to 200 I/O operations per second (IOPS), and the `innodb_io_capacity_max` option is also set to 200 IOPS. This means that InnoDB will use up to 200 IOPS for flushing dirty pages to disk under normal load conditions. If the load becomes more intense, InnoDB will use the value of innodb_io_capacity_max to determine the maximum IOPS that it can use.

Increasing the value of innodb_io_capacity can improve the performance of the system on I/O-bound workloads by allowing InnoDB to use more I/O capacity to flush dirty pages from the buffer pool to disk. However, increasing this value can also increase the risk of I/O overload on the system; with more pages flushed, pages are also flushed that could otherwise wait. Not delaying the background I/O will cause more background I/O, which can cause other applications to slow down or crash.

The innodb_io_capacity_max option can be increased to allow InnoDB to use more I/O capacity when it is performing the most intensive I/O operations. This can improve performance on systems with high I/O capacity by allowing InnoDB to use more of the available resources to flush dirty pages from the buffer pool to disk.

It is important to carefully monitor the I/O usage of the system and adjust the values of innodb_io_capacity and innodb_io_capacity_max based on the available resources and workload characteristics to ensure optimal performance without overloading the system. Additionally, other related configuration options such as innodb_flush_neighbors may also need to be adjusted to achieve optimal performance.

innodb_spin_wait_pause_multiplier

The innodb_spin_wait_pause_multiplier variable, introduced in MySQL 8.0.16, is used to control the length of time that InnoDB waits before retrying a spin lock acquisition. InnoDB uses spin locks to protect its internal data structures, and when contention for these locks is high, a thread may have to wait to acquire a lock. During this wait, the thread will spin in a loop, repeatedly attempting to acquire the lock.

To avoid consuming too much CPU time, InnoDB uses a technique called *adaptive spin loop pausing*, which gradually increases the length of time that a thread waits before retrying a spin lock acquisition. The innodb_spin_wait_pause_multiplier option controls the rate at which this pause time increases.

By default, innodb_spin_wait_pause_multiplier is set to 50, which means that the pause time will increase by 50% each time a thread fails to acquire a spin lock. If you set this to a higher value, the spin loop will pause for longer periods, which can help reduce CPU usage when there is high contention for spin locks. Conversely, if you set this to a lower value, the spin loop will pause for shorter periods, which can help reduce latency when there is low contention for spin locks.

Overall, the innodb_spin_wait_pause_multiplier option can help balance the trade-off between CPU usage and latency in InnoDB's spin lock implementation.

innodb_lru_scan_depth

The innodb_lru_scan_depth system variable in MySQL specifies the number of pages that the background LRU page cleaner thread scans each time it runs. The purpose of the LRU page cleaner thread is to free up space in the InnoDB buffer pool by removing pages that are least recently used.

When the LRU page cleaner thread runs, it selects a batch of dirty pages that are least recently used and writes them to disk to free up space in the buffer pool. The innodb_lru_scan_depth variable determines the number of pages selected in each batch. By default, innodb_lru_scan_depth is set to 1,024 pages.

Setting a higher value for innodb_lru_scan_depth can increase the efficiency of the LRU page cleaner thread by scanning more pages in each batch. However, this also increases the amount of CPU and I/O resources used by the thread and can cause more contention on the buffer pool mutex. On the other hand, setting a lower value for innodb_lru_scan_depth can reduce the CPU and I/O resources used by the LRU page cleaner thread, but may also reduce its efficiency in freeing up space in the buffer pool.

Purge Configuration

The innodb_max_purge_lag and innodb_purge_threads configuration parameters affect the performance of the InnoDB storage engine in MySQL 8.

The innodb_max_purge_lag parameter sets the maximum number of logfile writes (in other words, the number of transactions) that can be pending in the InnoDB purge queue at any given time. The purge thread is responsible for deleting old versions of records and making space available in the undo tablespace. If the purge thread is unable to keep up with the rate of writes to the logfiles, the number of pending transactions in the purge queue can grow, leading to an increase in disk usage and potentially to performance issues. By setting a limit on the number of pending transactions, you can prevent the purge queue from growing too large and potentially causing issues.

The default value of innodb_max_purge_lag in MySQL 8 is 0, which means that there is no maximum purge lag by default.

The innodb_purge_threads parameter sets the number of background threads used to execute the purge operation in InnoDB. By default, this value is set to 4, but you can increase it to improve performance on systems with high write loads. However, increasing this value can also increase CPU usage and I/O activity, so it's important to monitor the system's performance and adjust the value accordingly.

The `innodb_max_purge_lag` and `innodb_purge_threads` parameters both affect the performance of InnoDB's purge process, which is responsible for deleting old versions of records and freeing up space in the undo tablespace. By adjusting these parameters, you can improve the performance and reliability of your MySQL server.

Enabling Automatic Configuration for a Dedicated MySQL Server

If the MySQL instance is hosted on a shared server with other applications, we do not recommended enabling `innodb_dedicated_server`. This feature should be considered only for a dedicated server, where the MySQL instance can utilize all system resources available.

However, by explicitly configuring the parameters (`innodb_buffer_pool_size`, `innodb_redo_log_capacity`, and `innodb_flush_method`), users can optimize InnoDB's performance for their specific workload. It is important to carefully consider the impact of each parameter and to test thoroughly before making changes in a production environment.

Additionally, it's worth noting that InnoDB configuration is not a one-size-fits-all solution. Optimal configuration parameters depend on various factors, such as workload, hardware, and database schema. Therefore, we recommend monitoring the performance of the database regularly and adjusting the configuration parameters accordingly.

Furthermore, some of these configuration parameters are interdependent, so changing one parameter may affect the behavior of others. For example, changing the buffer pool size may also require adjusting the number of buffer pool instances to maintain optimal performance.

In summary, the InnoDB storage engine offers many configuration options to optimize its performance. By understanding the impact of each configuration parameter and their interdependencies, users can fine-tune their database to achieve the best performance for their workload.

Configuring Read-Only Operation

In MySQL 8, the `innodb_read_only` system variable not only starts InnoDB in read-only mode, but also prevents table creation, dropping, and modification operations for all storage engines. This feature is useful for distributing database applications or data sets on read-only media, and for data warehouses to share the same data directory among multiple instances.

However, enabling `innodb_read_only` can also cause certain operations to fail, such as ANALYZE TABLE, ALTER TABLE, CREATE USER, GRANT, INSTALL PLUGIN, UNINSTALL PLUGIN, CREATE FUNCTION, and DROP FUNCTION. This is because these operations require modifying data dictionary tables that use the InnoDB storage engine, which cannot be modified when `innodb_read_only` is enabled. To enable the variable, you need to add it to the *my.cnf* and restart `mysql` as shown here:

```
[mysqld]
innodb_read_only=1
```

MySQL 8 Persisted System Variables

The MySQL server utilizes system variables to govern its operations. However, dynamic variables used prior to MySQL 8 were not persistent and were reset upon server restart. Although these variables could be modified at runtime by using the `SET` statement to influence the current server instance, making them persistent required manual updates to the *my.cnf* configuration file. Updating the configuration file from the server side is often inconvenient, and leaving dynamically updated variables unreferenced on subsequent restarts does not retain any history.

Persisted system variables, a notable feature introduced in MySQL 8, allows DBAs to update variables dynamically and register them without needing to modify the configuration files on the server side.

Persist the Global System Variables

One way to make global system variables persistent is to utilize the feature of persisted system variables introduced in MySQL 8. *Persisted system variables* allow you to dynamically update and register variables without having to modify configuration files on the server side. This ensures that changes made to global system variables are retained even after server restarts. By using persisted system variables, you can avoid the inconvenience of manually updating configuration files from the server side and prevent any loss of historical data due to dynamically updated variables not being referenced upon subsequent server restarts.

Similar to `SET GLOBAL`, `SET PERSIST` can be used to modify system variables during runtime and keep those changes persistent across restarts. The `PERSIST` keyword is used to save the variable modifications to the *mysqld-auto.cnf* option file, which is located in the data directory. This file is in JSON format and is created only when the `PERSIST` or `PERSIST_ONLY` statement is executed for the first time.

To illustrate how persisted system variables work, let's consider an example of updating the maximum connections:

```
mysql> SET PERSIST max_connections = 1000;
Query OK, 0 rows affected (0.01 sec)
mysql>
```

This SQL query retrieves the current value of the `max_connections` system variable:

```
mysql> select @@max_connections\G
*************************** 1. row ***************************
@@max_connections: 1000
1 row in set (0.01 sec)
mysql>
```

Here is an example of what the resulting *mysqld-auto.cnf* might look like:

```
[root@mysql80 ~]# cat /var/lib/mysql/mysqld-auto.cnf
{"Version": 2, "mysql_dynamic_parse_early_variables"
: {"max_connections": {"Value": "1000", "Metadata":
{"Host": "localhost", "User": "root", "Timestamp":
1708079737306147}}}}
[root@mysql80 ~]#
```

When it is necessary to modify read-only variables, the PERSIST_ONLY keyword can be used. This clause updates the change in the *mysqld-auto.cnf* file but does not apply it in MySQL, making the change persist only after the next MySQL restart. PER SIST_ONLY is useful for configuring read-only system variables that can be set only during server startup:

```
mysql> SET PERSIST back_log=200;
ERROR 1238 (HY000): Variable 'back_log' is a read only variable
mysql>
```

```
mysql> SET persist_only  back_log=200;
Query OK, 0 rows affected (0.01 sec)
mysql>
```

To clear persisted system variable settings in MySQL, you can use RESET PERSIST. This command removes all persisted settings and reverts to the default values specified in the configuration files. This can be useful when reverting to a previous configuration or when starting with a clean slate for new settings.

Removing persisted settings from *mysqld-auto.cnf* is possible by using the RESET PER SIST command. However, it is essential to exercise caution while running the command without a specific variable name as it will remove all settings from the configuration file. Although the command removes persisted settings from *mysqld-auto.cnf*, it does not impact MySQL:

```
mysql> RESET PERSIST;
Query OK, 0 rows affected (0.00 sec)
mysql>
```

```
[root@mysql80 ~]# cat /var/lib/mysql/mysqld-auto.cnf
{"Version": 2}[root@mysql80 ~]#
[root@mysql80 ~]#
```

```
mysql> select @@max_connections;
+-------------------+
| @@max_connections |
+-------------------+
|              1000 |
```

```
+--------------------+
1 row in set (0.00 sec)
```

Suppose you want to remove a specific variable instead of clearing all settings from the configuration file. The following example demonstrates how to achieve this. If you attempt to remove a variable that does not exist in *mysqld-auto.cnf*, an error will occur. In such cases, the IF EXISTS clause can be used to suppress the error:

```
mysql> RESET PERSIST innodb_max_dirty_pages_pct;
ERROR 3615 (HY000): Variable innodb_max_dirty_pages_pct
does not exist in persisted config file
mysql>

mysql> RESET PERSIST IF EXISTS innodb_max_dirty_pages_pct;
Query OK, 0 rows affected, 1 warning (0.00 sec)
mysql>
```

The SHOW WARNINGS statement is used to display the warning messages generated during the execution of the previous SQL statement within the current session:

```
mysql> show warnings\G
********* 1. row *********
  Level: Warning
   Code: 3615
Message: Variable innodb_max_dirty_pages_pct does not exist
in persisted config file
1 row in set (0.00 sec)
mysql>
```

To disable persistence, you can use the persisted_globals_load parameter, which controls whether persisted system variables are loaded during server startup. If this parameter is disabled (persisted_globals_load=no), the server will ignore the *mysqld-auto.cnf* file, and any changes made to it manually will result in a parse error at startup. If this happens, the server will report an error and exit. To resolve the issue, you can start the server with the persisted_globals_load parameter disabled or use the --no-defaults option, as shown in this example:

```
mysql> select @@persisted_globals_load ;
+--------------------------+
| @@persisted_globals_load |
+--------------------------+
|                        1 |
+--------------------------+
1 row in set (0.00 sec)
mysql>

[root@mysql80 ~]# grep -i persisted_globals_load /etc/my.cnf
persisted_globals_load=no
[root@mysql80 ~]#

mysql> restart;
Query OK, 0 rows affected (0.00 sec)
mysql>
```

```
mysql> select @@persisted_globals_load ;
+--------------------------+
| @@persisted_globals_load |
+--------------------------+
|                        0 |
+--------------------------+
1 row in set (0.00 sec)

mysql> select @@max_connections;
+-------------------+
| @@max_connections |
+-------------------+
|               151 |
+-------------------+
1 row in set (0.00 sec)
```

In terms of security, assigning the appropriate permissions to users is essential. To use the SET PERSIST_ONLY command to persist global system variables to *mysqld-auto.cnf*, a user must have the SYSTEM_VARIABLES_ADMIN and PERSIST_RO_VARI ABLES_ADMIN privileges. Additionally, the user must possess the SHUTDOWN privilege to use the RESTART command. This command allows the restart of MySQL from the client session without requiring command-line access on the server host.

This SQL statement is used to create a new user admin_persist:

```
mysql>  CREATE USER 'admin_persist'@'localhost'
IDENTIFIED BY 'Welcome@123';
Query OK, 0 rows affected (0.03 sec)

mysql> GRANT SYSTEM_VARIABLES_ADMIN, PERSIST_RO_VARIABLES_ADMIN,
    -> SHUTDOWN on *.* to 'admin_persist'@'localhost';
Query OK, 0 rows affected (0.00 sec)
mysql>
```

Monitor the Variables

To retrieve a list of variables updated via the PERSIST option, you can execute a query that joins the performance_schema.persisted_variables table with a couple of other tables, as demonstrated here. This serves as a straightforward illustration of how to monitor MySQL variables, and you have the flexibility to adapt the query to suit your specific requirements:

```
mysql> select v.VARIABLE_NAME,g.VARIABLE_VALUE
current_value,p.VARIABLE_VALUE as
persist_value,SET_TIME,SET_USER,VARIABLE_SOURCE,VARIABLE_PATH from
performance_schema.variables_info v JOIN
performance_schema.persisted_variables p USING(VARIABLE_NAME) JOIN
performance_schema.global_variables g USING(VARIABLE_NAME)\G

*************************** 1. row ***************************
VARIABLE_NAME: innodb_log_file_size
```

```
current_value: 50331648
persist_value: 100663296
SET_TIME: 2023-02-01 18:54:35.725177
SET_USER: arun
VARIABLE_SOURCE: COMPILED
VARIABLE_PATH:
*************************** 2. row ***************************
VARIABLE_NAME: max_connections
current_value: 1000
persist_value: 1000
SET_TIME: 2013-02-01 18:53:19.336115
SET_USER: root
VARIABLE_SOURCE: DYNAMIC
VARIABLE_PATH:
2 rows in set (0.06 sec)

mysql> restart;
Query OK, 0 rows affected (0.01 sec)

select v.VARIABLE_NAME,g.VARIABLE_VALUE current_value,p.VARIABLE_VALUE
as persist_value,SET_TIME,SET_USER,VARIABLE_SOURCE,VARIABLE_PATH from
performance_schema.variables_info v JOIN
performance_schema.persisted_variables p USING(VARIABLE_NAME) JOIN
performance_schema.global_variables g USING(VARIABLE_NAME)\G

*************************** 1. row ***************************
VARIABLE_NAME: innodb_log_file_size
current_value: 100663296
persist_value: 100663296
SET_TIME: 2013-02-01 18:54:35.725177
SET_USER: arun
VARIABLE_SOURCE: PERSISTED
VARIABLE_PATH: /var/lib/mysql/mysqld-auto.cnf
*************************** 2. row ***************************
VARIABLE_NAME: max_connections
current_value: 1000
persist_value: 1000
SET_TIME: 2013-02-01 18:53:19.335909
SET_USER: root
VARIABLE_SOURCE: PERSISTED
VARIABLE_PATH: /var/lib/mysql/mysqld-auto.cnf
2 rows in set (0.16 sec)
```

Conclusion

This chapter provided a comprehensive review of the TDD and InnoDB architecture
and its various components. You should now be equipped with valuable insights into
configuring, optimizing, and managing InnoDB-based databases effectively.

## CHAPTER 4

Backup and Recovery

Backup and recovery are two distinct but related concepts in data protection. *Backup* is the process of making a copy of data and storing it in a safe location. *Recovery*, on the other hand, is the process of restoring data from a backup in the event of a data loss. The goal of backup and recovery is to ensure that data is available and usable when needed.

In this chapter, we discuss the fundamental concepts of backup and recovery and then explore the various types available. We also provide guidance on taking a backup, restoring a backup, and managing binary logs. Finally, you will learn how to manage your backup and recovery in order to ensure that your data is safe and easy to retrieve in the event of a disaster.

Before we dive into the specifics, it is essential to understand the basic concepts that underpin these critical activities. As a DBA, ensuring that your data is protected and recoverable in the event of a disaster is crucial. Data loss can occur for a variety of reasons, including hardware failure, human error, natural disasters, or malicious attacks. Without proper backup and recovery mechanisms in place, a significant amount of time, money, and effort may be required to restore lost data or even re-create it from scratch.

Factors to Consider When Choosing a Backup Strategy

Choosing a backup strategy that meets your business requirements can be challenging. Here are some factors to consider:

Recovery point objective (RPO)
    The RPO is the maximum amount of data loss that can be tolerated in the event of a disaster. A shorter RPO requires more frequent backups or point-in-time

recovery with streaming capabilities. An RPO of a few seconds or 0 typically can be achieved only with frequent backups or points-in-time recovery.

Recovery time objective (RTO)
The RTO is the maximum amount of time it takes to recover from a disaster. A shorter RTO requires a faster recovery mechanism, such as a warm or hot standby system.

Backup type
MySQL supports several backup types, including physical backup, logical backup, incremental backup, and differential backup. Each backup type has its advantages and disadvantages, and the choice of backup type depends on the business requirements.

Backup storage location
Backups should be stored in a secure location that is separate from the production system to avoid the risk of data loss due to a disaster affecting both the production system and the backup storage location.

In summary, we need to back up the entire data directory as a physical backup, including with binary logs. This backup will be essential for critical situations requiring the need to restore the instance or environment.

Difference Between Physical and Logical Backups

Logical backups and physical backups serve distinct purposes and are implemented differently.

A *logical backup* is a backup of the logical structure and contents of a database, such as tables, views, stored procedures, triggers, and data. It is created by dumping the data to a file by using utilities like mydumper or MySQL Shell's instance dump utility, schema dump utility, and table dump utility. Logical backups are portable and can be used to migrate a database from one server to another, or to restore specific tables or data to a database. However, they can be slower to create and restore than physical backups.

A physical backup, on the other hand, is a binary copy of the MySQL database files, including the data, indexes, and table structures. It is created by copying the physical files directly from the server to a backup storage device or server. Therefore, they are faster to create and restore than logical backups.

Both types of backups are important for ensuring the availability and integrity of a MySQL database. Logical backups are useful for migrating data between servers, restoring specific tables or data, and for long-term archival purposes. Physical backups are useful for disaster recovery, system-level backups, and for HA solutions such as database replication.

Physical Backups

The two most popular physical backups are MySQL Enterprise Backup and Percona XtraBackup.

MySQL Enterprise Backup

To back up and restore a MySQL database, you can use the MySQL Enterprise Backup tool. Backing up a MySQL instance is crucial for ensuring data recovery in case of any disaster or loss. It is essential to have a backup strategy in place that enables the restoration of data with minimal downtime.

For example, to configure this backup, create a new directory named `backupdir`:

```
[root@mysql80 ~]# mkdir /backupdir
[root@mysql80 ~]#
```

This backup command instructs the MySQL backup utility (`mysqlbackup`) to perform a backup operation using the following options:

```
root@mysql80 ~]# mysqlbackup --user=root --password --backup-image=/backupdir/
my.mbi --backup-dir=/backupdir/backup-tmp backup-to-image
MySQL Enterprise Backup  Ver 8.0.36-commercial for Linux on x86_64
(MySQL Enterprise - Commercial)
Copyright (c) 2003, 2024, Oracle and/or its affiliates.

Oracle is a registered trademark of Oracle Corporation and/or its
affiliates. Other names may be trademarks of their respective owners.

Starting with following command line ...
mysqlbackup
--user=root
--password
--backup-image=/backupdir/my.mbi
--backup-dir=/backupdir/backup-tmp
backup-to-image

IMPORTANT: Please check that mysqlbackup run completes successfully.
At the end of a successful 'backup-to-image' run mysqlbackup
prints "mysqlbackup completed OK!"

Enter password:
240216 11:42:48 MAIN     INFO: Establishing connection to server.
WARNING: MYSQL_OPT_RECONNECT is deprecated and will be removed in a
future version.
240216 11:42:48 MAIN     INFO: No SSL options specified.
240216 11:42:48 MAIN     INFO: MySQL server version is '8.0.36'
240216 11:42:48 MAIN     INFO: MySQL server compile os version is 'Linux'
240216 11:42:48 MAIN     INFO: Got some server configuration information from
running server.
```

From the log, you can validate the server repository and backup configuration options:

```
240216 11:42:48 MAIN  INFO: The MySQL server has no active keyring.
-----------------------------------------------------------------
                    Server Repository Options:
-----------------------------------------------------------------
  datadir                        = /var/lib/mysql/
  innodb_data_home_dir           = /var/lib/mysql/datafile/
  innodb_data_file_path          = ibdata1:12M;ibdata2:10M:autoextend
  innodb_log_group_home_dir      = /var/lib/mysql/
  innodb_undo_directory          = /var/lib/mysql/
  innodb_undo_tablespaces        = 2
  innodb_buffer_pool_filename    = ib_buffer_pool
  innodb_page_size               = 16384
  innodb_checksum_algorithm      = crc32


-----------------------------------------------------------------
                    Backup Config Options:
-----------------------------------------------------------------
  datadir                        = /backupdir/backup-tmp/datadir
  innodb_data_home_dir           = /backupdir/backup-tmp/datadir
  innodb_data_file_path          = ibdata1:12M;ibdata2:10M:autoextend
  innodb_log_group_home_dir      = /backupdir/backup-tmp/datadir
  innodb_undo_directory          = /backupdir/backup-tmp/datadir
  innodb_undo_tablespaces        = 2
  innodb_buffer_pool_filename    = ib_buffer_pool
  innodb_page_size               = 16384
  innodb_checksum_algorithm      = crc32

Backup Image Path = /backupdir/my.mbi
240216 11:42:48 MAIN     INFO: Unique generated backup id for
this is 17080837682941805
```

Upon the completion of the backup, you receive the status of completion as indicated in the log:

```
240216 11:42:49 RDR1    INFO: Copying /var/lib/mysql/binlog.000012.
240216 11:42:49 RDR1    INFO: Completed the copy of binlog files...
240216 11:42:49 RDR1    INFO: The server instance is unlocked after
0.236 seconds.
240216 11:42:49 RDR1    INFO: Reading all global variables from the server.
240216 11:42:49 RDR1    INFO: Completed reading of all 640 global variables
from the server.
240216 11:42:49 RDR1    INFO: Writing server defaults files 'server-my.cnf'
and 'server-all.cnf' for server '8.0.36' in '/backupdir/backup-tmp'.
240216 11:42:49 RDR1    INFO: Copying meta file /backupdir/backup-tmp/
meta/backup_variables.txt.
240216 11:42:49 RDR1    INFO: Copying meta file /backupdir/backup-tmp/
datadir/ibbackup_logfile.
240216 11:42:49 RDR1    INFO: Copying meta file /backupdir/backup-tmp/
server-all.cnf.
240216 11:42:49 RDR1    INFO: Copying meta file /backupdir/backup-tmp/
```

```
server-my.cnf.
240216 11:42:49 RDR1    INFO:  Copying meta file /backupdir/backup-tmp/
meta/backup_content.xml.
240216 11:42:49 RDR1    INFO:  Copying meta file /backupdir/backup-tmp/
meta/image_files.xml.
240216 11:42:49 MAIN    INFO: Full Image Backup operation completed
successfully.
240216 11:42:49 MAIN    INFO:  Backup image created successfully.
240216 11:42:49 MAIN    INFO: Image Path = /backupdir/my.mbi
240216 11:42:49 MAIN    INFO: MySQL binlog position: filename binlog.000012,
position 4131.

-------------------------------------------------------------
    Parameters Summary
-------------------------------------------------------------
    Start LSN                  : 37130752
    Last Checkpoint LSN        : 37130784
    End LSN                    : 37204275
-------------------------------------------------------------

mysqlbackup completed OK!
[root@mysql80 ~]#
```

Here are the details of the various options used in the command:

--user

Specifies the MySQL user with sufficient privileges to access and back up the database.

--password

Provides the password for the MySQL user specified in the --user option.

--backup-image

Specifies the name and location of the backup file that will be created. This file will contain the entire MySQL instance.

--backup-dir

Specifies the temporary backup directory where the backup files will be stored during the backup process.

backup-to-image

Specifies the backup type.

Once the command is executed, the backup process will start, and the backup files will be stored in the specified backup directory. Upon completion of the backup process, the message mysqlbackup completed OK! will be displayed.

Upon completing a backup, it's essential to verify the backup's integrity and ensure that all data is correctly backed up. This can help avoid data loss due to corrupted backups.

The following command can be used to validate a backup image:

```
[root@mysql80 ~]# mysqlbackup --backup-image=/backupdir/my.mbi validate
MySQL Enterprise Backup  Ver 8.0.36-commercial for Linux on x86_64
(MySQL Enterprise - Commercial)
Copyright (c) 2003, 2024, Oracle and/or its affiliates.
Oracle is a registered trademark of Oracle Corporation and/or its
affiliates. Other names may be trademarks of their respective owners.
Starting with following command line ...
mysqlbackup
--backup-image=/backupdir/my.mbi
validate

IMPORTANT: Please check that mysqlbackup run completes successfully.
           At the end of a successful 'validate' run mysqlbackup
           prints "mysqlbackup completed OK!".

240216 11:49:26 MAIN    INFO: Backup Image MEB version string: 8.0.36
240216 11:49:26 MAIN    INFO: MySQL server version is '8.0.36'
240216 11:49:26 MAIN    INFO: The backup image has no keyring.
240216 11:49:26 MAIN    INFO: Creating 14 buffers each of size 16777216.
240216 11:49:26 MAIN    INFO: Validate operation starts with
following threads

                          1 read-threads    6 process-threads
240216 11:49:26 MAIN    INFO: Validating image ... /backupdir/my.mbi
240216 11:49:26 PCR6    INFO: Validate: [Dir]: meta
240216 11:49:26 PCR5    INFO: Validate: [Dir]: datadir/appdb
240216 11:49:26 PCR5    INFO: Validate: [Dir]: datadir/datafile
240216 11:49:26 PCR6    INFO: Validate: [Dir]: datadir/mydatabase
240216 11:49:26 PCR4    INFO: Validate: [Dir]: datadir/mysql
240216 11:49:26 PCR3    INFO: Validate: [Dir]: datadir/mytestdb
```

Upon the completion of the validation, you will receive the backup completion status as displayed in the log:

```
240216 11:49:26 MAIN    INFO: datadir/sakila/
fts_0000000000000442_being_deleted.ibd validated.
240216 11:49:26 MAIN    INFO: Validate operation completed successfully.
240216 11:49:26 MAIN    INFO: Backup Image validation successful.
240216 11:49:26 MAIN    INFO: Source Image Path = /backupdir/my.mbi

mysqlbackup completed OK!
[root@mysql80 ~]#
```

Let's break this down further:

mysqlbackup
> Validates the backup image

--backup-image
> Specifies the path to the backup image

```
--validate
```
Specifies the validation operation

If the validation is successful, the following message will be displayed:

```
mysqlbackup completed OK!
```

It's also essential to check the backup logs to ensure that no errors occurred during the backup process. For example:

```
[root@mysql80 meta]# cat MEB_2024-02-16.11-42-48_backup-to-image.log |
grep "error"
[root@mysql80 meta]#
```

These commands will display the backup-related entries in the backup logfiles.

Depending on the situation, such as a crash, human mistake and data loss, or disaster recovery, restoring a database can be a crucial activity. Before restoring a backup, you need to shut down the MySQL instance. This is essential to avoid any data inconsistency issues. You can use the following command to stop the MySQL server:

```
[root@mysql80 meta]# systemctl stop mysqld
[root@mysql80 meta]#
```

After you shut down the MySQL server, delete all the files located in the data directory. Delete all the files that you can find under the directory specified by the restoration options `--innodb_data_home_dir`, `--innodb_log_group_home_dir`, and `--innodb_undo_directory` as well if the directories are different from the data directory.

Prior to executing the `rm -rf *` command, ensure that you are in the correct current directory and confirm that it is the data directory:

```
[root@mysql80 mysql]# pwd
/var/lib/mysql
[root@mysql80 mysql]# rm -rf *
[root@mysql80 mysql]#
```

Once you have deleted all the necessary files, use the `copy-back-and-apply-log` option with the `mysqlbackup` command to restore the backup. This option is used to apply all the incremental changes from the backup to the target server. Here is a sample command for your reference:

```
[root@mysql80 backup-tmp]# mysqlbackup --datadir=/var/lib/mysql
--backup-image=/backupdir/my.mbi --backup-dir=/backupdir/backup-tmp1
copy-back-and-apply-log
MySQL Enterprise Backup  Ver 8.0.36-commercial for Linux on x86_64
(MySQL Enterprise - Commercial)
Copyright (c) 2003, 2024, Oracle and/or its affiliates.
Oracle is a registered trademark of Oracle Corporation and/or its
affiliates. Other names may be trademarks of their respective owners.
Starting with following command line ...
```

```
mysqlbackup
--datadir=/var/lib/mysql
--backup-image=/backupdir/my.mbi
--backup-dir=/backupdir/backup-tmp1
copy-back-and-apply-log
...
240216 12:10:24 PCR1     INFO: Last MySQL binlog file position 0
4131, file name binlog.000012
240216 12:10:24 PCR1     INFO: The first data file is
'/var/lib/mysql/datafile/ibdata1'
 and the new created log files are at '/var/lib/mysql'
240216 12:10:24 MAIN     INFO: Apply-log operation completed successfully.
240216 12:10:24 MAIN     INFO: Full Backup has been restored successfully.
mysqlbackup completed OK!
[root@mysql80 backup-tmp]#
```

The restored files currently have ownership set to the root user:

```
[root@mysql80 mysql]# cd /var/lib/mysql
[root@mysql80 mysql]#
[root@mysql80 mysql]# ls -ltr
total 80104
-rw-r-----. 1 root root        56 Feb 16 12:10  backup-auto.cnf
-rw-r-----. 1 root root        14 Feb 16 12:10  backup-mysqld-auto.cnf
drwxr-x---. 2 root root        28 Feb 16 12:10  sys
drwxr-x---. 2 root root        91 Feb 16 12:10  world
drwxr-x---. 2 root root      4096 Feb 16 12:10  sakila
drwxr-x---. 2 root root        44 Feb 16 12:10  mydatabase
-rw-r-----. 1 root root    114688 Feb 16 12:10  my_tablespace.ibd
drwxr-x---. 2 root root       164 Feb 16 12:10  appdb
drwxr-x---. 2 root root        72 Feb 16 12:10  datafile
-rw-r-----. 1 root root       180 Feb 16 12:10  binlog.000011
-rw-r-----. 1 root root      1102 Feb 16 12:10  binlog.000010
drwxr-x---. 2 root root       140 Feb 16 12:10  mytestdb
drwxr-x---. 2 root root       170 Feb 16 12:10  mysql
drwxr-x---. 2 root root      8192 Feb 16 12:10  performance_schema
-rw-r-----. 1 root root      4131 Feb 16 12:10  binlog.000012
-rw-r-----. 1 root root       192 Feb 16 12:10  binlog.index
-rw-r-----. 1 root root       660 Feb 16 12:10  server-my.cnf
-rw-r-----. 1 root root     19983 Feb 16 12:10  server-all.cnf
-rw-r-----. 1 root root  16777216 Feb 16 12:10  undo_002
-rw-r-----. 1 root root  16777216 Feb 16 12:10  undo_001
-rw-r-----. 1 root root  16777216 Feb 16 12:10  my_undo_tablespace.ibu
-rw-r-----. 1 root root  27262976 Feb 16 12:10  mysql.ibd
drwxr-x---. 2 root root        23 Feb 16 12:10  '
innodb_redo'
-rw-r--r--. 1 root root       723 Feb 16 12:10  backup_variables.txt
[root@mysql80 mysql]
```

After restoring the backup, change the ownership of the restored files to the mysql
user. You can use the following command to change the ownership:

```
[root@mysql80 mysql]# chown -R mysql.mysql /var/lib/mysql
[root@mysql80 mysql]#

[root@mysql80 mysql]# ls -ltr
total 80104
-rw-r-----. 1 mysql mysql       56 Feb 16 12:10  backup-auto.cnf
-rw-r-----. 1 mysql mysql       14 Feb 16 12:10  backup-mysqld-auto.cnf
drwxr-x---. 2 mysql mysql       28 Feb 16 12:10  sys
drwxr-x---. 2 mysql mysql       91 Feb 16 12:10  world
drwxr-x---. 2 mysql mysql     4096 Feb 16 12:10  sakila
drwxr-x---. 2 mysql mysql       44 Feb 16 12:10  mydatabase
-rw-r-----. 1 mysql mysql   114688 Feb 16 12:10  my_tablespace.ibd
drwxr-x---. 2 mysql mysql      164 Feb 16 12:10  appdb
drwxr-x---. 2 mysql mysql       72 Feb 16 12:10  datafile
-rw-r-----. 1 mysql mysql      180 Feb 16 12:10  binlog.000011
-rw-r-----. 1 mysql mysql     1102 Feb 16 12:10  binlog.000010
drwxr-x---. 2 mysql mysql      140 Feb 16 12:10  mytestdb
drwxr-x---. 2 mysql mysql      170 Feb 16 12:10  mysql
drwxr-x---. 2 mysql mysql     8192 Feb 16 12:10  performance_schema
-rw-r-----. 1 mysql mysql     4131 Feb 16 12:10  binlog.000012
-rw-r-----. 1 mysql mysql      192 Feb 16 12:10  binlog.index
-rw-r-----. 1 mysql mysql      660 Feb 16 12:10  server-my.cnf
-rw-r-----. 1 mysql mysql    19983 Feb 16 12:10  server-all.cnf
-rw-r-----. 1 mysql mysql 16777216 Feb 16 12:10  undo_002
-rw-r-----. 1 mysql mysql 16777216 Feb 16 12:10  undo_001
-rw-r-----. 1 mysql mysql 16777216 Feb 16 12:10  my_undo_tablespace.ibu
-rw-r-----. 1 mysql mysql 27262976 Feb 16 12:10  mysql.ibd
drwxr-x---. 2 mysql mysql       23 Feb 16 12:10  '
innodb_redo'
-rw-r--r--. 1 mysql mysql      723 Feb 16 12:10  backup_variables.txt
[root@mysql80 mysql]
```

Once you have changed the ownership, start the MySQL server by using the following command:

```
[root@mysql80 mysql]# systemctl start mysqld
[root@mysql80 mysql]#
```

If you're restoring a backup on a replication instance, you'll need the binary logfile name and position from which replication should commence. You can find these details in the *backup_variables.txt* file located in a *meta* directory within the backup directory. Open the file and retrieve the most recent binary log position along with the corresponding logfile number, which are both stored within the file. This information will be necessary for configuring the replica server to begin replication from the correct position in the binary log:

```
[root@mysql80 meta]# pwd
/backupdir/backup-tmp/meta
[root@mysql80 meta]# cat backup_variables.txt | grep binlog_position
binlog_position=binlog.000012:4131
[root@mysql80 meta]#
```

Using --replica-info

Introduced in MySQL Enterprise Backup 8.0.32, `--replica-info` captures the necessary information for setting up an identical replica server when backing up a replica server. This option generates a file named *ibbackup_replica_info* in the backup directory's *meta* folder. The file contains a `CHANGE REPLICATION SOURCE TO` statement that includes the binary logfile name and position of the source server. This information is also displayed in the output of the `mysqlbackup` command. To create a new replica for the source server, restore the backup data to a new server, start a replica server using the backup data, and execute the `CHANGE REPLICATION SOURCE TO` command with the binary log position specified in *ibbackup_replica_info*.

The option `--slave-info` has been deprecated since MySQL Enterprise Backup version 8.0.32 and should now be replaced with `--replica-info`. In versions 8.0.31 and earlier, `--slave-info` captured information necessary for setting up an identical replica server when backing up a replica server. This option would create a file called *meta/ibbackup_slave_info* within the backup directory that contained a `CHANGE MASTER` statement with the binary log position and name of the binary logfile from the source server. This information would also be displayed in the `mysqlbackup` output. To set up a new replica using this information, you would restore the backup data on another server, start a replica server with the backup data, and issue a `CHANGE MASTER` command using the binary log position saved in the *ibbackup_slave_info* file.

Percona XtraBackup

Percona XtraBackup is an open source tool used for backing up and restoring MySQL databases. Before you start performing backups using Percona XtraBackup, certain prerequisites must be met:

- Percona XtraBackup must be installed on the server.
- The MySQL instance being backed up must be running and accessible.
- Sufficient disk space must be available to store the backup in a local share or in a remote server.

Backing up from a replication server

Completing a full backup from a replica server using Percona XtraBackup is recommended as it reduces impact on the primary server. Initiating a backup on the primary server can impair performance, which can affect the applications that rely on it. By taking the backup from a replica server, you can minimize the impact on the primary server, allowing it to continue serving the applications without interruption.

A full backup, which backs up the entire database, is the most comprehensive type of backup. The backup includes all the data, indexes, tables, views, triggers, and stored procedures. Here's an example:

```
[root@mysql80 ~]# xtrabackup --backup --target-dir=/root/backupdir -u root -p

2024-02-20T07:27:13.279554-00:00 0 [Note] [MY-011825] [Xtrabackup] recognized
server arguments: --datadir=/var/lib/mysql
2024-02-20T07:27:13.279897-00:00 0 [Note] [MY-011825] [Xtrabackup] recognized
client arguments: --user=root --password=* --backup=1 --target-dir=/root/
backupdir --user=root --password
Enter password:
xtrabackup version 8.0.35-30 based on MySQL server 8.0.35 Linux (x86_64)
(revision id: 6beb4b49)
240220 07:27:14  version_check Connecting to MySQL server with DSN
'dbi:mysql:;mysql_read_default_group=xtrabackup' as 'root'  (using password:
YES).
240220 07:27:14  version_check Connected to MySQL server
240220 07:27:14  version_check Executing a version check against the server...

# A software update is available:
240220 07:27:15  version_check Done.
2024-02-20T07:27:15.257381-00:00 0 [Note] [MY-011825] [Xtrabackup]
Connecting to MySQL server host: localhost, user: root, password: set,
port: not set, socket: not set
2024-02-20T07:27:15.269103-00:00 0 [Note] [MY-011825] [Xtrabackup]
Using server version 8.0.36
..
2024-02-20T07:27:19.627144-00:00 0 [Note] [MY-011825] [Xtrabackup]
Writing /root/backupdir/backup-my.cnf
2024-02-20T07:27:19.627324-00:00 0 [Note] [MY-011825] [Xtrabackup]
Done: Writing file /root/backupdir/backup-my.cnf
2024-02-20T07:27:19.736769-00:00 0 [Note] [MY-011825] [Xtrabackup]
Writing /root/backupdir/xtrabackup_info
2024-02-20T07:27:19.736961-00:00 0 [Note] [MY-011825] [Xtrabackup]
Done: Writing file /root/backupdir/xtrabackup_info
2024-02-20T07:27:19.768177-00:00 0 [Note] [MY-011825] [Xtrabackup]
Transaction log of lsn (20366453) to (20366463) was copied.
2024-02-20T07:27:19.998055-00:00 0 [Note] [MY-011825] [Xtrabackup] completed OK!
[root@mysql80 ~]#
```

See the Percona docs (*https://oreil.ly/jLTs_*) for a complete list of variable options available with the tool.

Here are the details of the two options used in the command. To initiate a backup, execute XtraBackup with the --backup option. The option --target-dir=DIRECTORY designates the backup's destination directory. If the specified directory doesn't exist, XtraBackup will create it. When the directory exists and is empty, the backup will proceed successfully. However, if the directory contains existing files, XtraBackup won't overwrite them, resulting in a failure with operating system error 17 (file exists).

The --slave-info option is particularly beneficial when creating a backup of a replication slave server. It not only displays the name and binary log position of the master server but also records this information in the *xtrabackup_slave_info* file as a CHANGE MASTER command. This allows you to conveniently set up a new slave server for the same master by starting a slave server on the backup and running the CHANGE MASTER command using the binary log position saved in the *xtrabackup_slave_info* file.

Restoring a database

This section explains how to restore a backup taken with Percona XtraBackup. However, before restoring the backup, you need to prepare the backup files by using the xtrabackup --prepare command. This step applies the pending changes to the backup data so that it is in a consistent state:

```
[root@mysql80 ~]# xtrabackup --prepare --target-dir=/root/backupdir

2024-02-20T07:29:48.539204-00:00 0 [Note] [MY-011825] [Xtrabackup] recognized
server arguments: --innodb_checksum_algorithm=crc32 --innodb_log_checksums=1
--innodb_data_file_path=ibdata1:12M:autoextend --innodb_log_file_size=50331648
--innodb_page_size=16384 --innodb_undo_directory=./ --innodb_undo_tablespaces=2
--server-id=0 --innodb_log_checksums=ON --innodb_redo_log_encrypt=0
--innodb_undo_log_encrypt=0
2024-02-20T07:29:48.539575-00:00 0 [Note] [MY-011825] [Xtrabackup] recognized
client arguments: --prepare=1 --target-dir=/root/backupdir
xtrabackup version 8.0.35-30 based on MySQL server 8.0.35 Linux (x86_64)
(revision id: 6beb4b49)
2024-02-20T07:29:48.539839-00:00 0 [Note] [MY-011825] [Xtrabackup]
cd to /root/backupdir/
2024-02-20T07:29:48.543518-00:00 0 [Note] [MY-011825] [Xtrabackup]
This target seems to be not prepared yet.
2024-02-20T07:29:48.562638-00:00 0 [Note] [MY-011825] [Xtrabackup]
xtrabackup_logfile detected: size=8388608, start_lsn=(20366453)
..
2024-02-20T07:29:49.169641-00:00 0 [Note] [MY-011825] [Xtrabackup]
Completed loading of 2 tablespaces into cache in 0.00413599 seconds
2024-02-20T07:29:49.221375-00:00 0 [Note] [MY-011825] [Xtrabackup]
Time taken to build dictionary: 0.0515769 seconds
2024-02-20T07:29:49.239865-00:00 0 [Note] [MY-011825] [Xtrabackup]
starting shutdown with innodb_fast_shutdown = 1
2024-02-20T07:29:49.240024-00:00 0 [Note] [MY-012330] [InnoDB]
FTS optimize thread exiting.
2024-02-20T07:29:50.232093-00:00 0 [Note] [MY-013072] [InnoDB]
Starting shutdown...
2024-02-20T07:29:50.240493-00:00 0 [Note] [MY-013084] [InnoDB]
Log background threads are being closed...
2024-02-20T07:29:50.260550-00:00 0 [Note] [MY-012980] [InnoDB]
Shutdown completed; log sequence number 20366870
```

```
2024-02-20T07:29:50.266082-00:00 0 [Note] [MY-011825] [Xtrabackup] completed OK!
[root@mysql80 ~]#
```

Stop the MySQL server on the machine where you want to restore the backup:

```
[root@mysql80 ~]# sudo systemctl stop mysqld
[root@mysql80 ~]#
```

Copy the backup files from their original backup location to the destination where you intend to perform the restoration. You can use a tool like rsync or scp to do this efficiently.

Copy the MySQL configuration files from the backup location to the MySQL configuration directory on the machine where you want to restore the backup. The location of the configuration directory may vary depending on your operating system. If the backup wasn't copied to the data directory, you can use the xtrabackup --copy-back command to copy the files from the backup directory to the MySQL data directory:

```
[root@mysql80 ~]# sudo xtrabackup --copy-back --target-dir=/root/backupdir

2024-02-20T07:34:03.208252-00:00 0 [Note] [MY-011825] [Xtrabackup] recognized
server arguments: --datadir=/var/lib/mysql
2024-02-20T07:34:03.208429-00:00 0 [Note] [MY-011825] [Xtrabackup] recognized
client arguments: --user=root --password=* --copy-back=1 --target-dir=/root/
backupdir
xtrabackup version 8.0.35-30 based on MySQL server 8.0.35 Linux (x86_64)
(revision id: 6beb4b49)
2024-02-20T07:34:03.208499-00:00 0 [Note] [MY-011825] [Xtrabackup]
cd to /root/backupdir/
2024-02-20T07:34:03.212994-00:00 0 [Note] [MY-011825] [Xtrabackup]
Copying undo_001 to /var/lib/mysql/undo_001
2024-02-20T07:34:03.372784-00:00 0 [Note] [MY-011825] [Xtrabackup]
Done: Copying undo_001 to /var/lib/mysql/undo_001
2024-02-20T07:34:03.379912-00:00 0 [Note] [MY-011825] [Xtrabackup]
Copying undo_002 to /var/lib/mysql/undo_002
2024-02-20T07:34:03.481821-00:00 0 [Note] [MY-011825] [Xtrabackup]
Done: Copying undo_002 to /var/lib/mysql/undo_002
2024-02-20T07:34:03.488697-00:00 0 [Note] [MY-011825] [Xtrabackup]
Copying ibdata1 to /var/lib/mysql/ibdata1
2024-02-20T07:34:03.557571-00:00 0 [Note] [MY-011825] [Xtrabackup]
Done: Copying ibdata1 to /var/lib/mysql/ibdata1
...
2024-02-20T07:34:04.081817-00:00 1 [Note] [MY-011825] [Xtrabackup]
Copying ./ib_buffer_pool to /var/lib/mysql/ib_buffer_pool
2024-02-20T07:34:04.082713-00:00 1 [Note] [MY-011825] [Xtrabackup]
Done: Copying ./ib_buffer_pool to /var/lib/mysql/ib_buffer_pool
2024-02-20T07:34:04.084413-00:00 1 [Note] [MY-011825] [Xtrabackup]
Copying ./xtrabackup_info to /var/lib/mysql/xtrabackup_info
2024-02-20T07:34:04.084548-00:00 1 [Note] [MY-011825] [Xtrabackup]
Done: Copying ./xtrabackup_info to /var/lib/mysql/xtrabackup_info
2024-02-20T07:34:04.086055-00:00 1 [Note] [MY-011825] [Xtrabackup]
Creating directory ./#innodb_redo
```

```
2024-02-20T07:34:04.086133-00:00 1 [Note] [MY-011825] [Xtrabackup]
Done: creating directory ./#innodb_redo
2024-02-20T07:34:04.086241-00:00 1 [Note] [MY-011825] [Xtrabackup]
Copying ./ibtmp1 to /var/lib/mysql/ibtmp1
2024-02-20T07:34:04.131401-00:00 1 [Note] [MY-011825] [Xtrabackup]
Done: Copying ./ibtmp1 to /var/lib/mysql/ibtmp1
2024-02-20T07:34:04.177825-00:00 0 [Note] [MY-011825] [Xtrabackup] completed OK!
[root@mysql80 ~]#
```

After copying the files, you need to set the ownership and permissions of the data directory to the `mysql` user:

```
[root@mysql80 ~]# sudo chown -R mysql:mysql /var/lib/mysql
[root@mysql80 ~]#
```

Start the MySQL server with the following command:

```
[root@mysql80 ~]# sudo systemctl start mysqld
[root@mysql80 ~]#
```

After starting MySQL, you need to verify the log and confirm that the MySQL instance is ready for connection. If you `tail` the `mysqld` error log, you should get a similar result:

```
[root@mysql80 ~]# tail -2 /var/log/mysqld.log

2024-02-20T07:37:48.624988Z 0 [System] [MY-011323] [Server] X Plugin ready for
connections. Bind-address: '::' port: 33060, socket: /var/run/mysqld/mysqlx.sock
2024-02-20T07:37:48.625234Z 0 [System] [MY-010931] [Server] /usr/sbin/mysqld:
ready for connections. Version: '8.0.36'  socket: '/var/lib/mysql/mysql.sock'
port: 3306  MySQL Community Server - GPL.
[root@mysql80 ~]#
```

Using incremental backups

Percona XtraBackup provides support for incremental backups, allowing it to copy only the data that has changed since the previous backup. You can perform multiple incremental backups. This allows you to establish a backup schedule, such as performing a full backup once a week and incremental backups every day, or full backups every day with incremental backups every hour.

The incremental backup process works by leveraging the LSN that is associated with each InnoDB page. The LSN serves as a system version number for the entire database and indicates when a page was last modified. During an incremental backup, only pages that have an LSN that is newer than the previous incremental or full backup's LSN are copied. An algorithm is used to identify the pages that meet this criteria by reading the data pages and checking their respective LSN values.

To create an incremental backup by using Percona XtraBackup, start with a regular full backup. After taking the full backup, the `xtrabackup` utility writes a file called *xtrabackup_checkpoints* to the backup's target directory. This file contains a line showing to_lsn, which represents the database's LSN at the end of the backup process. You can take a full backup by running the following command:

```
[root@mysql8 ~]# mkdir -p /data/backups/base

[root@mysql8 ~]# xtrabackup --backup --target-dir=/data/backups/base

2024-02-23T11:50:13.697883-00:00 0 [Note] [MY-011825] [Xtrabackup] recognized
server arguments: --datadir=/var/lib/mysql
2024-02-23T11:50:13.698792-00:00 0 [Note] [MY-011825] [Xtrabackup] recognized
client arguments: --user=root --password=* --backup=1 --target-dir=/data/
backups/base
xtrabackup version 8.0.35-30 based on MySQL server 8.0.35 Linux (x86_64)
(revision id: 6beb4b49)
Can't locate English.pm in @INC (you may need to install the English module)
(@INC contains: /usr/local/lib64/perl5/5.32 /usr/local/share/perl5/5.32 /usr/
lib64/perl5/vendor_perl /usr/share/perl5/vendor_perl /usr/lib64/perl5 /usr/
share/perl5) at - line 3.
BEGIN failed--compilation aborted at - line 3.
2024-02-23T11:50:13.728094-00:00 0 [Note] [MY-011825] [Xtrabackup] Connecting
to MySQL server host: localhost, user: root, password: set, port: not set,
socket: not set
2024-02-23T11:50:14.135079-00:00 0 [Note] [MY-011825] [Xtrabackup] Using server
version 8.0.36
2024-02-23T11:50:14.149822-00:00 0 [Note] [MY-011825] [Xtrabackup] Executing
LOCK INSTANCE FOR BACKUP ...
2024-02-23T11:50:14.151389-00:00 0 [Note] [MY-011825] [Xtrabackup] uses
posix_fadvise().
2024-02-23T11:50:14.151443-00:00 0 [Note] [MY-011825] [Xtrabackup] cd to /var/
lib/mysql
2024-02-23T11:50:14.151460-00:00 0 [Note] [MY-011825] [Xtrabackup] open files
limit requested 0, set to 1024
2024-02-23T11:50:14.174389-00:00 0 [Note] [MY-011825] [Xtrabackup] using the
following InnoDB configuration:
2024-02-23T11:50:14.174418-00:00 0 [Note] [MY-011825] [Xtrabackup]
innodb_data_home_dir = .
2024-02-23T11:50:14.174429-00:00 0 [Note] [MY-011825] [Xtrabackup]
innodb_data_file_path = ibdata1:12M:autoextend
2024-02-23T11:50:14.174470-00:00 0 [Note] [MY-011825] [Xtrabackup]
innodb_log_group_home_dir = ./
2024-02-23T11:50:14.174482-00:00 0 [Note] [MY-011825] [Xtrabackup]
innodb_log_files_in_group = 2
....
2024-02-23T11:50:32.554338-00:00 0 [Note] [MY-011825] [Xtrabackup] Done:
Writing file /data/backups/base/backup-my.cnf
2024-02-23T11:50:33.071966-00:00 0 [Note] [MY-011825] [Xtrabackup] Writing /
data/backups/base/xtrabackup_info
2024-02-23T11:50:33.072211-00:00 0 [Note] [MY-011825] [Xtrabackup] Done:
Writing file /data/backups/base/xtrabackup_info
2024-02-23T11:50:33.188617-00:00 0 [Note] [MY-011825] [Xtrabackup] Transaction
log of lsn (20289655) to (20289665) was copied.
```

```
2024-02-23T11:50:33.405903-00:00 0 [Note] [MY-011825] [Xtrabackup] completed OK!
[root@mysql8 ~]#
```

After completing the full backup, you can view the *xtrabackup_checkpoints* file to check the LSN value. The file will contain information similar to the following, depending on the LSN number:

```
[root@mysql8 ~]# cat /data/backups/base/xtrabackup_checkpoints
backup_type = full-backuped
from_lsn = 0
to_lsn = 20289655
last_lsn = 20289655
flushed_lsn = 20289655
redo_memory = 0
redo_frames = 0
[root@mysql8 ~]#
```

This output confirms that the full backup was successful and shows the to_lsn value that will be used as a reference point for the next incremental backup.

Once you have taken a full backup, you can create an incremental backup based on it by using the xtrabackup command. The following command can be used to create an incremental backup:

```
[root@mysql8 ~]# xtrabackup --backup --target-dir=/data/backups/inc1 \
--incremental-basedir=/data/backups/base -u root -p
2024-02-23T12:07:38.147005-00:00 0 [Note] [MY-011825] [Xtrabackup] recognized
server arguments: --datadir=/var/lib/mysql
2024-02-23T12:07:38.147368-00:00 0 [Note] [MY-011825] [Xtrabackup] recognized
client arguments: --user=root --password=* --backup=1 --target-dir=/data/
backups/inc1 --incremental-basedir=/data/backups/base --user=root --password
Enter password:
xtrabackup version 8.0.35-30 based on MySQL server 8.0.35 Linux (x86_64)
(revision id: 6beb4b49)
Can't locate English.pm in @INC (you may need to install the English module)
(@INC contains: /usr/local/lib64/perl5/5.32 /usr/local/share/perl5/5.32 /usr/
lib64/perl5/vendor_perl /usr/share/perl5/vendor_perl /usr/lib64/perl5 /usr/
share/perl5) at - line 3.
BEGIN failed--compilation aborted at - line 3.
2024-02-23T12:07:39.895793-00:00 0 [Note] [MY-011825] [Xtrabackup] Connecting
to MySQL server host: localhost, user: root, password: set, port: not set,
socket: not set
2024-02-23T12:07:39.918181-00:00 0 [Note] [MY-011825] [Xtrabackup] Using server
version 8.0.36
2024-02-23T12:07:39.935737-00:00 0 [Note] [MY-011825] [Xtrabackup]
innodb_log_group_home_dir = ./
2024-02-23T12:07:52.016205-00:00 0 [Note] [MY-011825] [Xtrabackup] MySQL binlog
position: filename 'binlog.000006', position '157'
2024-02-23T12:07:52.016406-00:00 0 [Note] [MY-011825] [Xtrabackup] Writing /
data/backups/inc1/backup-my.cnf
2024-02-23T12:07:52.016580-00:00 0 [Note] [MY-011825] [Xtrabackup] Done:
Writing file /data/backups/inc1/backup-my.cnf
```

```
2024-02-23T12:07:52.185241-00:00 0 [Note] [MY-011825] [Xtrabackup] Writing /
data/backups/inc1/xtrabackup_info
2024-02-23T12:07:52.185445-00:00 0 [Note] [MY-011825] [Xtrabackup] Done:
Writing file /data/backups/inc1/xtrabackup_info
2024-02-23T12:07:53.188689-00:00 0 [Note] [MY-011825] [Xtrabackup] Transaction
log of lsn (20784993) to (20784993) was copied.
2024-02-23T12:07:53.414360-00:00 0 [Note] [MY-011825] [Xtrabackup] completed OK!
[root@mysql8 ~]#
```

This command creates an incremental backup in the *data/backups/inc1/* directory, based on the previous full backup taken in */data/backups/base/*. The delta files generated by this command represent the changes made to the database since the LSN value of the previous backup. For example, you may see files such as *ibdata1.delta* and *test/table1.ibd.delta* in the incremental backup directory.

After completing the incremental backup, you can check the *xtrabackup_checkpoints* file in the */data/backups/inc1/* directory. This file should show the new LSN value, as well as the incremental-basedir value that was used as the reference point for the backup process. The content of the *xtrabackup_checkpoints* file may look similar to the following:

```
[root@mysql8 ~]# cat /data/backups/inc1/xtrabackup_checkpoints
backup_type = incremental
from_lsn = 20289655
to_lsn = 20784993
last_lsn = 20784993
flushed_lsn = 20784993
redo_memory = 0
redo_frames = 0
[root@mysql8 ~]#
```

The from_lsn value in the *xtrabackup_checkpoints* file represents the starting LSN of the incremental backup, and it should be the same as the to_lsn value of the previous or base backup's checkpoint file.

After creating the first incremental backup, you can use it as the base for creating another incremental backup. You can use the following command to create an incremental backup based on the previous incremental backup:

```
[root@mysql8 ~]# xtrabackup --backup --target-dir=/data/backups/inc2 \
--incremental-basedir=/data/backups/inc1
2024-02-23T13:10:43.005350-00:00 0 [Note] [MY-011825] [Xtrabackup] recognized
server arguments: --datadir=/var/lib/mysql
2024-02-23T13:10:43.008358-00:00 0 [Note] [MY-011825] [Xtrabackup] recognized
client arguments: --user=root --password=* --backup=1 --target-dir=/data/
backups/inc2 --incremental-basedir=/data/backups/inc1
xtrabackup version 8.0.35-30 based on MySQL server 8.0.35 Linux (x86_64)
(revision id: 6beb4b49)
Can't locate English.pm in @INC (you may need to install the English module)
(@INC contains: /usr/local/lib64/perl5/5.32 /usr/local/share/perl5/5.32 /usr/
lib64/perl5/vendor_perl /usr/share/perl5/vendor_perl /usr/lib64/perl5 /usr/
```

```
share/perl5) at - line 3.
BEGIN failed--compilation aborted at - line 3.
2024-02-23T13:10:43.044764-00:00 0 [Note] [MY-011825] [Xtrabackup] Connecting
to MySQL server host: localhost, user: root, password: set, port: not set,
socket: not set
2024-02-23T13:10:43.053579-00:00 0 [Note] [MY-011825] [Xtrabackup] Using server
version 8.0.36
2024-02-23T13:10:43.056222-00:00 0 [Note] [MY-011825] [Xtrabackup] Executing
LOCK INSTANCE FOR BACKUP ...
2024-02-23T13:10:43.057492-00:00 0 [Note] [MY-011825] [Xtrabackup] incremental
backup from 20784993 is enabled.
2024-02-23T13:10:43.057721-00:00 0 [Note] [MY-011825] [Xtrabackup] uses
posix_fadvise().
2024-02-23T13:10:43.057745-00:00 0 [Note] [MY-011825] [Xtrabackup] cd to /var/
lib/mysql
2024-02-23T13:10:43.057757-00:00 0 [Note] [MY-011825] [Xtrabackup] open files
limit requested 0, set to 1024
2024-02-23T13:10:43.060579-00:00 0 [Note] [MY-011825] [Xtrabackup] using the
following InnoDB configuration:
2024-02-23T13:10:43.060604-00:00 0 [Note] [MY-011825] [Xtrabackup]
innodb_data_home_dir = .
2024-02-23T13:10:43.060613-00:00 0 [Note] [MY-011825] [Xtrabackup]
innodb_data_file_path = ibdata1:12M:autoextend
2024-02-23T13:10:43.060650-00:00 0 [Note] [MY-011825] [Xtrabackup]
innodb_log_group_home_dir = ./
2024-02-23T13:10:43.060662-00:00 0 [Note] [MY-011825] [Xtrabackup]
innodb_log_files_in_group = 2
2024-02-23T13:10:43.060672-00:00 0 [Note] [MY-011825] [Xtrabackup]
innodb_log_file_size = 50331648
....
2024-02-23T13:10:50.751443-00:00 0 [Note] [MY-011825] [Xtrabackup] MySQL binlog
position: filename 'binlog.000011', position '157'
2024-02-23T13:10:50.814250-00:00 0 [Note] [MY-011825] [Xtrabackup] Writing /
data/backups/inc2/backup-my.cnf
2024-02-23T13:10:50.814471-00:00 0 [Note] [MY-011825] [Xtrabackup] Done:
Writing file /data/backups/inc2/backup-my.cnf
2024-02-23T13:10:51.014542-00:00 0 [Note] [MY-011825] [Xtrabackup] Writing /
data/backups/inc2/xtrabackup_info
2024-02-23T13:10:51.014890-00:00 0 [Note] [MY-011825] [Xtrabackup] Done:
Writing file /data/backups/inc2/xtrabackup_info
2024-02-23T13:10:51.018154-00:00 0 [Note] [MY-011825] [Xtrabackup] Transaction
log of lsn (21291941) to (21291941) was copied.
2024-02-23T13:10:51.140104-00:00 0 [Note] [MY-011825] [Xtrabackup] completed OK!
[root@mysql8 ~]#
```

This command creates a new incremental backup in the */data/backups/inc2/* directory, based on the previous incremental backup in */data/backups/inc1/*. The *xtra-
backup_checkpoints* file in this directory should show the new LSN value, which
represents the endpoint of the new incremental backup.

You can continue creating multiple incremental backups in this way, with each new
incremental backup based on the previous one. Each incremental backup will contain

only the changes made since the previous backup, which helps reduce the amount of time and space needed for backup and restore operations:

```
[root@mysql8 ~]# cat /data/backups/inc2/xtrabackup_checkpoints
backup_type = incremental
from_lsn = 20784993
to_lsn = 21291941
last_lsn = 21291941
flushed_lsn = 21291941
redo_memory = 0
redo_frames = 0
[root@mysql8 ~]#
```

You've now taken a full backup along with two incremental backups, all stored within the backup directory. Each backup is stored in its respective directory within this backup directory. Upon listing the contents of the backup directory by using the `ls -ltr` command, you'll find the following:

```
[root@mysql8 backups]# ls -ltr
total 12
drwxr-xr-x. 5 root root 4096 Feb 23 11:50 base
drwxr-x---. 6 root root 4096 Feb 23 12:07 inc1
drwxr-x---. 6 root root 4096 Feb 23 13:10 inc2
[root@mysql8 backups]#
```

Preparing incremental backups

The `--prepare` step for incremental backups is different from that for full backups. In full backups, the `--prepare` step performs two types of operations to make the database consistent: it replays committed transactions from the logfile against the data files, and it rolls back uncommitted transactions. However, when preparing an incremental backup, you need to skip the rollback of uncommitted transactions. This is because transactions that were uncommitted at the time of your backup may still be in progress and are likely to be committed in the next incremental backup.

To prevent the rollback phase during the `--prepare` step for incremental backups, use the `--apply-log-only` option. This option only applies the logfiles to the backup to update its pages and does not roll back any transactions. After applying the logfiles, the backup will be ready to be restored to the point in time when the backup was taken:

```
[root@mysql8 backups]# xtrabackup --prepare --apply-log-only \
--target-dir=/data/backups/base
2024-02-23T13:28:08.266142-00:00 0 [Note] [MY-011825] [Xtrabackup] recognized
server arguments: --innodb_checksum_algorithm=crc32 --innodb_log_checksums=1
--innodb_data_file_path=ibdata1:12M:autoextend --innodb_log_file_size=50331648
--innodb_page_size=16384 --innodb_undo_directory=./ --innodb_undo_tablespaces=2
--server-id=0 --innodb_log_checksums=ON --innodb_redo_log_encrypt=0
--innodb_undo_log_encrypt=0
2024-02-23T13:28:08.266501-00:00 0 [Note] [MY-011825] [Xtrabackup] recognized
```

```
client arguments: --prepare=1 --apply-log-only=1 --target-dir=/data/backups/base
xtrabackup version 8.0.35-30 based on MySQL server 8.0.35 Linux (x86_64)
(revision id: 6beb4b49)
2024-02-23T13:28:08.266735-00:00 0 [Note] [MY-011825] [Xtrabackup] cd to /data/
backups/base/
2024-02-23T13:28:08.268271-00:00 0 [Note] [MY-011825] [Xtrabackup] This target
seems to be not prepared yet.
2024-02-23T13:28:08.290071-00:00 0 [Note] [MY-011825] [Xtrabackup]
inititialize_service_handles suceeded
2024-02-23T13:28:08.290782-00:00 0 [Note] [MY-011825] [Xtrabackup] using the
following InnoDB configuration for recovery:
2024-02-23T13:28:08.290856-00:00 0 [Note] [MY-011825] [Xtrabackup]
innodb_data_home_dir = .
2024-02-23T13:28:08.290906-00:00 0 [Note] [MY-011825] [Xtrabackup]
innodb_data_file_path = ibdata1:12M:autoextend
```

After this command completes, the output should end with text similar to this:

```
2024-02-23T13:28:09.840970-00:00 0 [Note] [MY-013072] [InnoDB]
Starting shutdown...
2024-02-23T13:28:09.848432-00:00 0 [Note] [MY-013084] [InnoDB]
Log background threads are being closed...
2024-02-23T13:28:09.868724-00:00 0 [Note] [MY-012980] [InnoDB]
Shutdown completed; log sequence number 20289665
2024-02-23T13:28:09.876150-00:00 0 [Note] [MY-011825] [Xtrabackup] completed OK!
[root@mysql8 backups]#
```

To apply the first incremental backup to the full backup, you can run the following
command:

```
[root@mysql8 backups]# xtrabackup --prepare --apply-log-only --target-dir=/data/
backups/base \
    --incremental-dir=/data/backups/inc1
2024-02-23T13:30:43.873233-00:00 0 [Note] [MY-011825] [Xtrabackup] recognized
server arguments: --innodb_checksum_algorithm=crc32 --innodb_log_checksums=1
--innodb_data_file_path=ibdata1:12M:autoextend --innodb_log_file_size=50331648
--innodb_page_size=16384 --innodb_undo_directory=./ --innodb_undo_tablespaces=2
--server-id=0 --innodb_log_checksums=ON --innodb_redo_log_encrypt=0
--innodb_undo_log_encrypt=0
2024-02-23T13:30:43.874162-00:00 0 [Note] [MY-011825] [Xtrabackup] recognized
client arguments: --prepare=1 --apply-log-only=1 --target-dir=/data/backups/base
--incremental-dir=/data/backups/inc1
xtrabackup version 8.0.35-30 based on MySQL server 8.0.35 Linux (x86_64)
(revision id: 6beb4b49)
2024-02-23T13:30:43.877184-00:00 0 [Note] [MY-011825] [Xtrabackup] incremental
backup from 20289655 is enabled.
2024-02-23T13:30:43.877299-00:00 0 [Note] [MY-011825] [Xtrabackup] cd to /data/
backups/base/
2024-02-23T13:30:43.878200-00:00 0 [Note] [MY-011825] [Xtrabackup] This target
seems to be already prepared with --apply-log-only.
2024-02-23T13:30:43.888050-00:00 0 [Note] [MY-011825] [Xtrabackup]
xtrabackup_logfile detected: size=8388608, start_lsn=(20784993)
2024-02-23T13:30:43.888535-00:00 0 [Note] [MY-011825] [Xtrabackup] using the
```

```
following InnoDB configuration for recovery:
2024-02-23T13:30:43.888643-00:00 0 [Note] [MY-011825] [Xtrabackup]
innodb_data_home_dir = .
2024-02-23T13:30:43.888699-00:00 0 [Note] [MY-011825] [Xtrabackup]
innodb_data_file_path = ibdata1:12M:autoextend
2024-02-23T13:30:43.888796-00:00 0 [Note] [MY-011825] [Xtrabackup]
innodb_log_group_home_dir = /data/backups/inc1/
2024-02-23T13:30:46.424279-00:00 0 [Note] [MY-011825] [Xtrabackup] Done:
Copying /data/backups/inc1/binlog.000006 to ./binlog.000006
2024-02-23T13:30:46.425801-00:00 0 [Note] [MY-011825] [Xtrabackup] Copying /
data/backups/inc1/binlog.index to ./binlog.index
2024-02-23T13:30:46.425940-00:00 0 [Note] [MY-011825] [Xtrabackup] Done:
Copying /data/backups/inc1/binlog.index to ./binlog.index
2024-02-23T13:30:46.427799-00:00 0 [Note] [MY-011825] [Xtrabackup] completed OK!
[root@mysql8 backups]#
```

This command applies the delta files in */data/backups/inc1* to the files in */data/backups/base*, which rolls them forward to the time of the incremental backup. It then applies the redo log as usual to the result. The final data is in */data/backups/base*, not in the incremental directory.

When merging incremental backups, the --apply-log-only option should be used for all the intermediate incremental backups except the last one. This is because the --apply-log-only option skips the rollback phase and prepares the backup only for applying the next incremental backup.

Therefore, for merging the last incremental backup, you should run the following command:

```
[root@mysql8 backups]# xtrabackup --prepare --target-dir=/data/backups/base \
--incremental-dir=/data/backups/inc2
2024-02-23T13:32:54.413264-00:00 0 [Note] [MY-011825] [Xtrabackup] recognized
server arguments: --innodb_checksum_algorithm=crc32 --innodb_log_checksums=1
--innodb_data_file_path=ibdata1:12M:autoextend --innodb_log_file_size=50331648
--innodb_page_size=16384 --innodb_undo_directory=./ --innodb_undo_tablespaces=2
--server-id=0 --innodb_log_checksums=ON --innodb_redo_log_encrypt=0
--innodb_undo_log_encrypt=0
2024-02-23T13:32:54.414978-00:00 0 [Note] [MY-011825] [Xtrabackup] recognized
client arguments: --prepare=1 --target-dir=/data/backups/base
--incremental-dir=/data/backups/inc2
xtrabackup version 8.0.35-30 based on MySQL server 8.0.35 Linux (x86_64)
(revision id: 6beb4b49)
2024-02-23T13:32:54.415995-00:00 0 [Note] [MY-011825] [Xtrabackup] incremental
backup from 20784993 is enabled.
2024-02-23T13:32:54.416111-00:00 0 [Note] [MY-011825] [Xtrabackup] cd to /data/
backups/base/
2024-02-23T13:32:54.416290-00:00 0 [Note] [MY-011825] [Xtrabackup] This target
seems to be already prepared with --apply-log-only.
2024-02-23T13:32:54.426669-00:00 0 [Note] [MY-011825] [Xtrabackup]
xtrabackup_logfile detected: size=8388608, start_lsn=(21291941)
2024-02-23T13:32:54.427121-00:00 0 [Note] [MY-011825] [Xtrabackup] using the
following InnoDB configuration for recovery:
```

```
2024-02-23T13:32:54.427198-00:00 0 [Note] [MY-011825] [Xtrabackup]
innodb_data_home_dir = .
2024-02-23T13:32:54.427266-00:00 0 [Note] [MY-011825] [Xtrabackup]
innodb_data_file_path = ibdata1:12M:autoextend
2024-02-23T13:32:54.427333-00:00 0 [Note] [MY-011825] [Xtrabackup]
innodb_log_group_home_dir = /data/backups/inc2/
2024-02-23T13:32:57.169249-00:00 0 [Note] [MY-011825] [Xtrabackup] Done:
Copying /data/backups/inc2/binlog.000011 to ./binlog.000011
2024-02-23T13:32:57.170686-00:00 0 [Note] [MY-011825] [Xtrabackup] Copying /
data/backups/inc2/binlog.index to ./binlog.index
2024-02-23T13:32:57.170819-00:00 0 [Note] [MY-011825] [Xtrabackup] Done:
Copying /data/backups/inc2/binlog.index to ./binlog.index
2024-02-23T13:32:57.173092-00:00 0 [Note] [MY-011825] [Xtrabackup] completed OK!
[root@mysql8 backups]#
```

Since this is the last incremental backup, you can run `--prepare` without the `--apply-log-only` option. The backup will still be consistent, but the server will perform the rollback phase. After the preparation, the backup is ready to be used.

Logical Backups

The most popular logical backup tools are the MySQL shell dump utility, `mydumper`, and `mysqldump`. In this section, we cover the MySQL Shell dump utility and for `mysql dump`, explaining how to perform a full backup and restore.

We cover `mydumper` and `myloader` in "Migrate Large Databases to Azure Database for MySQL" on page 573. Return to "Converting Tables from MyISAM to InnoDB" on page 90 to find more on table-level migration.

The MySQL Shell Dump Utility

MySQL Shell is an advanced command-line client and scripting interface for MySQL. It provides a powerful set of utilities for database management and administration, including the dump utility, which is used for backing up and restoring databases.

The dump utility is a feature-rich tool provided by MySQL Shell for backing up MySQL databases. It enables you to perform full instance backups or partial backups of selected schemas or tables. You can also customize the backup process by using various options available in the utility.

After you have logged in, you can use the dump utility to perform backups, as shown in this example:

```
[root@mysql80 ~]# mysqlsh --uri root@localhost:3306
MySQL Shell 8.0.36

Copyright (c) 2016, 2023, Oracle and/or its affiliates.
Oracle is a registered trademark of Oracle Corporation and/or its
Server version: 8.0.36 MySQL Community Server - GPL
```

```
No default schema selected; type \use <schema> to set one.
 MySQL  localhost:3306 ssl  JS >
```

Before running the actual backup, perform a dry-run procedure to validate the backup process. The following command, util.dumpInstance, can be used for the dry run:

```
MySQL  localhost:3306 ssl  JS > util.dumpInstance("/mysqlsh/backuputildump/",
 {dryRun:"true"})

dryRun enabled, no locks will be acquired and no files will be created.
Acquiring global read lock
Global read lock acquired
Initializing - done
1 out of 5 schemas will be dumped and within them 1 table, 0 views.
1 out of 4 users will be dumped.
Gathering information - done
All transactions have been started
Locking instance for backup
Global read lock has been released
Writing global DDL files
Writing users DDL
Writing DDL - done
Starting data dump
0% (0 rows / ~20 rows), 0.00 rows/s, 0.00 B/s uncompressed, 0.00 B/s compressed
 MySQL  localhost:3306 ssl  JS >
```

A full instance backup ensures that you have a backup of the entire database instance in case of any unforeseen circumstances. You can use the following command to perform a full instance backup:

```
MySQL  localhost:3306 ssl  JS > util.dumpInstance("/backuputildump")
Acquiring global read lock
Global read lock acquired
Initializing - done
1 out of 5 schemas will be dumped and within them 1 table, 0 views.
1 out of 4 users will be dumped.
Gathering information - done
All transactions have been started
Locking instance for backup
Global read lock has been released
Writing global DDL files
Writing users DDL
Running data dump using 4 threads.
NOTE: Progress information uses estimated values and may not be accurate.
Writing schema metadata - done
Writing DDL - done
Writing table metadata - done
Starting data dump
100% (20 rows / ~20 rows), 0.00 rows/s, 0.00 B/s uncompressed,
0.00 B/s compressed
Dump duration: 00:00:00s
Total duration: 00:00:00s
```

```
Schemas dumped: 1
Tables dumped: 1
Uncompressed data size: 727 bytes
Compressed data size: 258 bytes
Compression ratio: 2.8
Rows written: 20
Bytes written: 258 bytes
Average uncompressed throughput: 727.00 B/s
Average compressed throughput: 258.00 B/s
 MySQL  localhost:3306 ssl  JS >
```

The backup is stored in the following directory:

```
[root@mysql80 ~]# ls -ltr /backuputildump
total 44
-rw-r-----. 1 root root  240 Feb 20 10:37 @.sql
-rw-r-----. 1 root root  240 Feb 20 10:37 @.post.sql
-rw-r-----. 1 root root  774 Feb 20 10:37 @.json
-rw-r-----. 1 root root 1965 Feb 20 10:37 @.users.sql
-rw-r-----. 1 root root  301 Feb 20 10:37 mytestdb.json
-rw-r-----. 1 root root  575 Feb 20 10:37 mytestdb.sql
-rw-r-----. 1 root root  784 Feb 20 10:37 mytestdb@test_table.sql
-rw-r-----. 1 root root  649 Feb 20 10:37 mytestdb@test_table.json
-rw-r-----. 1 root root    8 Feb 20 10:37 mytestdb@test_table@@0.tsv.zst.idx
-rw-r-----. 1 root root  258 Feb 20 10:37 mytestdb@test_table@@0.tsv.zst
-rw-r-----. 1 root root  228 Feb 20 10:37 @.done.json
[root@mysql80 ~]#
```

To run the instance dump with more advanced options, use the following command:

```
MySQL  localhost:3306 ssl  JS > util.dumpInstance(\"/backuputildump/
mysqlinstance", {threads:8,maxRate:\"100M",consistent:true,chunking:true,
bytesPerchunk:\"64M",compression:\"zstd"})

Acquiring global read lock
Global read lock acquired
Initializing - done
1 out of 5 schemas will be dumped and within them 1 table, 0 views.
1 out of 4 users will be dumped.
Gathering information - done
All transactions have been started
Locking instance for backup
Global read lock has been released
Writing global DDL files
Writing users DDL
Running data dump using 8 threads.
NOTE: Progress information uses estimated values and may not be accurate.
Writing schema metadata - done
Writing DDL - done
Writing table metadata - done
Starting data dump
100% (20 rows / ~20 rows), 0.00 rows/s, 0.00 B/s uncompressed,
0.00 B/s compressed
Dump duration: 00:00:00s
```

```
Total duration: 00:00:00s
Schemas dumped: 1
Tables dumped: 1
Uncompressed data size: 727 bytes
Compressed data size: 258 bytes
Compression ratio: 2.8
Rows written: 20
Bytes written: 258 bytes
Average uncompressed throughput: 727.00 B/s
Average compressed throughput: 258.00 B/s
 MySQL  localhost:3306 ssl  JS >
```

In this command, you can specify various options to control and enhance the dump process. For example, you can specify the number of threads to be used, the maximum rate at which the backup should be written, whether to perform a consistent backup, whether to perform chunking of the backup data, the size of each chunk, and the compression algorithm to be used.

Use the schema dump utility to perform partial backups of chosen schemas. You can use the following command, util.dumpSchemas, to back up specified schemas:

```
MySQL  localhost:3306 ssl  JS > util.dumpSchemas([\"employees"],
 \"/backupdir/employees",{threads :2})
Acquiring global read lock
Global read lock acquired
Initializing - done
1 schemas will be dumped and within them 2 tables, 0 views.
Gathering information - done
All transactions have been started
Locking instance for backup
Global read lock has been released
Writing global DDL files
Running data dump using 2 threads.
NOTE: Progress information uses estimated values and may not be accurate.
Writing schema metadata - done
Writing DDL - done
Writing table metadata - done
Starting data dump
100% (8 rows / ~8 rows), 0.00 rows/s, 0.00 B/s uncompressed, 0.00 B/s compressed
Dump duration: 00:00:00s
Total duration: 00:00:00s
Schemas dumped: 1
Tables dumped: 2
Uncompressed data size: 224 bytes
Compressed data size: 182 bytes
Compression ratio: 1.2
Rows written: 8
Bytes written: 182 bytes
Average uncompressed throughput: 224.00 B/s
Average compressed throughput: 182.00 B/s
 MySQL  localhost:3306 ssl  JS >
```

In this command, you can specify the backup location and the names of the schemas to be backed up. The backup is stored in the following directory, which is only for the employees database:

```
[root@mysql80 ~]# ls -ltr /backupdir/employees
total 64
-rw-r-----. 1 root root 240 Feb 20 10:51 @.sql
-rw-r-----. 1 root root 240 Feb 20 10:51 @.post.sql
-rw-r-----. 1 root root 771 Feb 20 10:51 @.json
-rw-r-----. 1 root root 362 Feb 20 10:51 employees.json
-rw-r-----. 1 root root 716 Feb 20 10:51 employees@salaries.sql
-rw-r-----. 1 root root 631 Feb 20 10:51 employees@salaries.json
-rw-r-----. 1 root root 798 Feb 20 10:51 employees@employees.sql
-rw-r-----. 1 root root 657 Feb 20 10:51 employees@employees.json
-rw-r-----. 1 root root 581 Feb 20 10:51 employees.sql
-rw-r-----. 1 root root   8 Feb 20 10:51 employees@salaries@0.tsv.zst.idx
-rw-r-----. 1 root root   8 Feb 20 10:51 employees@employees@@0.tsv.zst.idx
-rw-r-----. 1 root root  52 Feb 20 10:51 employees@salaries@0.tsv.zst
-rw-r-----. 1 root root   8 Feb 20 10:51 employees@salaries@@1.tsv.zst.idx
-rw-r-----. 1 root root 121 Feb 20 10:51 employees@employees@@0.tsv.zst
-rw-r-----. 1 root root   9 Feb 20 10:51 employees@salaries@@1.tsv.zst
-rw-r-----. 1 root root 344 Feb 20 10:51 @.done.json
[root@mysql80 ~]#
```

You can use the table dump utility to perform partial backups of chosen tables. Use the following command, util.dumpTables, to back up individual tables:

```
MySQL  localhost:3306 ssl  JS > util.dumpTables(\"employees",[\"salaries"],
\"/backupdir/employees/salaries",{threads:2})
Acquiring global read lock
Global read lock acquired
Initializing - done
1 tables and 0 views will be dumped.
Gathering information - done
All transactions have been started
Locking instance for backup
Global read lock has been released
Writing global DDL files
Running data dump using 2 threads.
NOTE: Progress information uses estimated values and may not be accurate.
Writing schema metadata - done
Writing DDL - done
Writing table metadata - done
Starting data dump
100% (4 rows / ~4 rows), 0.00 rows/s, 0.00 B/s uncompressed, 0.00 B/s compressed
Dump duration: 00:00:00s
Total duration: 00:00:00s
Schemas dumped: 1
Tables dumped: 1
Uncompressed data size: 88 bytes
Compressed data size: 61 bytes
Compression ratio: 1.4
```

```
Rows written: 4
Bytes written: 61 bytes
Average uncompressed throughput: 88.00 B/s
Average compressed throughput: 61.00 B/s
 MySQL  localhost:3306 ssl  JS >
```

The backup is stored in the following directory, which is only for the employees
.salaries table:

```
[root@mysql80 ~]# ls -ltr /backupdir/employees/salaries
total 48
-rw-r-----. 1 root root 240 Feb 20 11:05 @.sql
-rw-r-----. 1 root root 240 Feb 20 11:05 @.post.sql
-rw-r-----. 1 root root 770 Feb 20 11:05 @.json
-rw-r-----. 1 root root 236 Feb 20 11:05 employees.json
-rw-r-----. 1 root root 478 Feb 20 11:05 employees.sql
-rw-r-----. 1 root root 631 Feb 20 11:05 employees@salaries.json
-rw-r-----. 1 root root 716 Feb 20 11:05 employees@salaries.sql
-rw-r-----. 1 root root   8 Feb 20 11:05 employees@salaries@0.tsv.zst.idx
-rw-r-----. 1 root root   8 Feb 20 11:05 employees@salaries@@1.tsv.zst.idx
-rw-r-----. 1 root root  52 Feb 20 11:05 employees@salaries@0.tsv.zst
-rw-r-----. 1 root root   9 Feb 20 11:05 employees@salaries@@1.tsv.zst
-rw-r-----. 1 root root 266 Feb 20 11:05 @.done.json
[root@mysql80 ~]#
```

In this command, you can specify the backup location and the names of the tables to
be backed up, along with their respective schema names.

After backing up the database, you'll want to restore the data to another or the same
database. MySQL Shell includes a data load utility for this purpose. This utility helps
you import data from a backup file into a database.

Before restoring the data, we recommend performing a dry-run process to validate
the backup file. Use this simple loadDump command to perform a dry run:

```
 MySQL  localhost:3306 ssl  JS > util.loadDump(\"/backuputildump/",{dryRun:true})
Loading DDL and Data from '/backuputildump/' using 4 threads.
Opening dump...
dryRun enabled, no changes will be made.
Target is MySQL 8.0.36. Dump was produced from MySQL 8.0.36
Scanning metadata - done
Checking for pre-existing objects...
Executing common preamble SQL
Executing DDL - done
Executing view DDL - done
Starting data load
Executing common postamble SQL
0% (0 bytes / 727 bytes), 0.00 B/s, 1 / 1 tables done
Recreating indexes - done
No data loaded.
0 warnings were reported during the load.
 MySQL  localhost:3306 ssl  JS >
```

Similarly, you can test the command (depending on the requirement) before loading the data to ensure that it works properly. The following example shows how to use this utility for backup restoration:

```
MySQL  localhost:3306 ssl  JS > util.loadDump(\"/backuputildump/",
{progressFile:
\"/backuputildump/backuplog.json",threads:4,backgroundThreads:4,
maxBytesPerTransaction:"4096"})
Loading DDL and Data from '/backuputildump/' using 4 threads.
Opening dump...
Target is MySQL 8.0.36. Dump was produced from MySQL 8.0.36
Scanning metadata - done
Checking for pre-existing objects...
Executing common preamble SQL
Executing DDL - done
Executing view DDL - done
Starting data load
Executing common postamble SQL
100% (727 bytes / 727 bytes), 0.00 B/s, 1 / 1 tables done
Recreating indexes - done
1 chunks (20 rows, 727 bytes) for 1 tables in 1 schemas were loaded in 0 sec
(avg throughput 727.00 B/s)
0 warnings were reported during the load.
 MySQL  localhost:3306 ssl  JS >
```

The preceding command will restore the data from the */backuputildump/* directory backup and use four threads and four background threads during the restore process. It will also create a progress file at */backuputildump/backuplog.json* and set the maximum bytes per transaction to 4,096.

mysqldump

MySQL provides the mysqldump command-line utility for creating logical database backups. In this section, we will explore how to use mysqldump effectively. But before we dive into the backup process, it's important to understand the mysqldump command and its options. The easiest way to access the mysqldump documentation is through the command-line help:

```
[root@mysql80 ~]# man mysqldump
```

This command will bring up the mysqldump manual, which provides detailed information on the command's syntax, options, and usage.

Backing up individual tables

Backing up individual tables is useful when you need to restore only specific data sets. To use the mysqldump command to create backups of individual tables in a database, use the following syntax:

```
mysqldump database_name table_name > backup_file.sql
```

For example, to create a backup of the city table in the world database, use the following command:

```
[root@mysql80 backup]# mysqldump -uroot -p world city > city.sql
Enter password:
[root@mysql80 backup]# ls -ltr
total 176
-rw-r--r--. 1 root root 179263 Feb 20 12:59 city.sql
[root@mysql80 backup]#
```

Use the --where option to back up only a subset of data from a table. For example, to back up only the rows in the city table where CountryCode is 5, execute the following command:

```
[root@mysql80 backup]# mysqldump world -u root -p city
--where=\"CountryCode='USA'" > city_USA.sql
Enter password:
[root@mysql80 backup]# ls -ltr
-rw-r--r--. 1 root root  14060 Feb 20 13:01 city_USA.sql
[root@mysql80 backup]#
```

Use the --ignore-table option to exclude specific tables from your backup. For example, you can use the following command to back up all tables in the world database except the city table:

```
[root@mysql80 backup]# mysqldump -u root -p world
--ignore-table=world.city > ignore_city_world.sql
Enter password:
[root@mysql80 backup]# ls -ltr
-rw-r--r--. 1 root root  66071 Feb 20 13:08 ignore_city_world.sql
[root@mysql80 backup]#
```

To create a whole database backup, use the mysqldump command with the database name as an argument:

```
mysqldump database_name > backup_file.sql
```

For example, to back up the world database, use the following command:

```
[root@mysql80 backup]# mysqldump -u root -p world > world.sql
Enter password:
[root@mysql80 backup]# ls -ltr
-rw-r--r--. 1 root root 244085 Feb 20 13:05 world.sql
[root@mysql80 backup]#
```

Backing up multiple databases

To back up several databases, specify them as a comma-separated list:

```
mysqldump --databases database1,database2 > backup_file.sql
```

To back up the mytestdb sakila world_x and example_db1 databases, for example, execute the following command:

```
[root@mysql80 backup]# mysqldump -u root -p --databases mytestdb employees
sakila> all_db_backup.sql
Enter password:
[root@mysql80 backup]# ls -ltr
-rw-r--r--. 1 root root 3390832 Feb 20 13:27 all_db_backup.sql
[root@mysql80 backup]#
```

Backing up all databases

To back up all databases on the MySQL server, use the --all-databases option:

```
[root@mysql80 backup]# mysqldump -u root -p --all-databases
> all_databases_backup.sql
Enter password:
[root@mysql80 backup]# ls -ltr
-rw-r--r--. 1 root root 4937167 Feb 20 13:29 all_databases_backup.sql
[root@mysql80 backup]#
```

This will create a single backup file containing all databases on the server.

The mysqldump command-line tool creates a logical backup of a database by generating a set of SQL statements that can be used to re-create the database objects and data. The following example creates a backup of the sakila database with several options for a more efficient and consistent backup:

```
[root@mysql80 backup]# mysqldump -u root -p --single-transaction --quick
--lock-tables=false --routines --events --triggers
--default-character-set=utf8mb4 sakila >backup.sql
Enter password:
[root@mysql80 backup]# ls -ltr
-rw-r--r--. 1 root root 3397023 Feb 20 13:31 backup.sql
[root@mysql80 backup]#
```

Let's break down each option in the command. This command tells mysqldump to create a backup of the specified database (dbname) and save it to a file called *backup.sql*:

--single-transaction
Ensures that the backup is consistent, even if other transactions are occurring on the database at the same time.

--quick
Tells mysqldump to retrieve rows one at a time instead of retrieving the entire result set at once, which can help to reduce memory usage.

--lock-tables=false
Ensures that the tables are not locked during the backup process, which allows the database to continue functioning normally.

`--routines`, `--events`, *and* `--triggers`

Tells `mysqldump` to include stored routines, events, and triggers in the backup, respectively.

`--default-character-set=utf8mb4`

Allows you to enforce the use of the utf8mb4 character set in the generated SQL script. This can be useful when you need to ensure that the backup will support all the characters used in your database, especially if it includes emojis or other special characters that are outside the scope of the standard UTF-8 character set.

Once you've created a logical backup using `mysqldump`, you can use it to re-create the database on another server or to restore the database if it becomes corrupted. To restore a logical backup, you would simply use the MySQL client to run the SQL statements contained in the backup file.

To back up and restore a replica node, you can utilize either the `--source-data` or `--master-data` option. Use `--source-data` for MySQL 8.0.26 and newer, or use `--master-data` for prior versions. Both options have the same purpose, which is to generate a dump file that can be used to set up another server as a replica of the source server during replication.

When these options are used, the resulting dump output includes a CHANGE REPLICA TION SOURCE TO statement (introduced in MySQL 8.0.23) or CHANGE MASTER TO statement (used before MySQL 8.0.23). This statement specifies the binary log coordinates (filename and position) of the dumped server, indicating where the replication source server should start replicating from after loading the dump file into the replica.

If the `--source-data` or `--master-data` options are set to 2, the CHANGE REPLICA TION SOURCE TO or CHANGE MASTER TO statement in the dump file is commented out, preventing it from taking effect when the dump file is reloaded. The option value 1 will write the statement uncommented and take effect when the dump file is reloaded. If no option value is explicitly supplied, the default value of 1 is used.

Setting up a backup schedule

Create a shell script that will take the MySQL backup using Percona XtraBackup. You can create a new file by using any text editor (for example, nano or Vim), and save it with the *.sh* extension. In this script, you need to include the following commands:

```
[root@mysql80 backup]# cat backup_script.sh
#!/bin/bash
# Set the MySQL username and password
MYSQL_USER="root"
MYSQL_PASSWORD='D@#NJU#$@MK28#nM'
# Set the backup directory
BACKUP_DIR="/root/backupdir/newbackup"
```

```
# Take a full backup using Percona XtraBackup
xtrabackup --backup --user=$MYSQL_USER --password=$MYSQL_PASSWORD
--target-dir=$BACKUP_DIR/full_backup_$(date +%Y-%m-%d_%H-%M-%S)
[root@mysql80 backup]#
```

In this script, you need to replace the values for MYSQL_USER, MYSQL_PASSWORD, and
BACKUP_DIR with the appropriate values for your system. Also, make sure to give execute permissions to this script by using the command:

```
[root@mysql80 backup]#  chmod +x backup_script.sh
[root@mysql80 backup]# ls -ltr
total 4
-rwxr-xr-x. 1 root root 344 Feb 20 13:35 backup_script.sh
[root@mysql80 backup]#
```

The command ./backup_script.sh executes a shell script named *backup_script.sh*
that is located in the current directory:

```
[root@mysql80 backup]# ./backup_script.sh

2024-02-20T13:42:56.095800-00:00 0 [Note] [MY-011825] [Xtrabackup] recognized
server arguments: --datadir=/var/lib/mysql
2024-02-20T13:42:56.096132-00:00 0 [Note] [MY-011825] [Xtrabackup] recognized
client arguments: --user=root --password=* --socket=/var/lib/mysql/mysql.sock
--backup=1 --user=root --password=*
--target-dir=/root/backupdir/newbackup/full_backup_2024-02-20_13-42-55
xtrabackup version 8.0.35-30 based on MySQL server 8.0.35 Linux (x86_64)
(revision id: 6beb4b49)
240220 13:42:56  version_check Connecting to MySQL server with DSN 'dbi:mysql:;
mysql_read_default_group=xtrabackup;mysql_socket=/var/lib/mysql/mysql.sock'
as 'root'  (using password: YES).
240220 13:42:56  version_check Connected to MySQL server
240220 13:42:56  version_check Executing a version check against the server...
240220 13:42:56  version_check Done.
2024-02-20T13:42:56.369830-00:00 0 [Note] [MY-011825] [Xtrabackup]
Connecting to MySQL server host: localhost, user: root, password: set,
port: not set, socket: /var/lib/mysql/mysql.sock
2024-02-20T13:42:59.708031-00:00 0 [Note] [MY-011825] [Xtrabackup]
Done: Writing file /root/backupdir/newbackup/full_backup_2024-02-20_13-42-55/
xtrabackup_info
2024-02-20T13:43:00.711702-00:00 0 [Note] [MY-011825] [Xtrabackup]
Transaction log of lsn (32549485) to (32549485) was copied.
2024-02-20T13:43:00.831082-00:00 0 [Note] [MY-011825] [Xtrabackup] completed OK!
[root@mysql80 backup]#
```

Setting up a backup schedule is crucial to ensure that your database is backed up regularly. To set up a backup schedule, use cron jobs or other scheduling tools. Here is
an example of a cron job that runs a backup every day at 2 A.M.:

```
crontab -e
0 2 * * * /root/backupdir/newbackup/backup_script.sh
```

To set up a backup schedule, you can use a combination of crontab and your chosen backup method. Here's an example configuration for setting up a daily backup schedule using `mysqldump`:

1. Create a backup directory to store the backup files:

    ```
    [root@mysql80 ~]# sudo mkdir -p /mnt/backups/mysql/
    [root@mysql80 ~]#
    ```

2. Grant the necessary permissions to the backup directory:

    ```
    [root@mysql80 ~]# sudo chown -R mysql:mysql /mnt/backups/mysql/
    [root@mysql80 ~]#
    ```

3. Use `sudo chmod -R 700 /mnt/backups/mysql/` to modify the permissions of the directory */mnt/backups/mysql/* and all its subdirectories and files:

    ```
    [root@mysql80 ~]# sudo chmod -R 700 /mnt/backups/mysql/
    [root@mysql80 ~]#
    ```

4. Create a shell script:

    ```
    [root@mysql80 mysql]# cat /mnt/backups/mysql/backup_mysqldump.sh

    #!/bin/bash
    # Set the backup directory
    backup_dir="/mnt/backups/mysql"
    # Set the MySQL credentials
    mysql_user="root"
    mysql_password='D@#NJU#$@MK28#nM'
    # Create the backup filename with date stamp
    backup_filename="$backup_dir/daily_backup_$(date +%Y%m%d).sql"
    # Execute the mysqldump command and save output to file
    mysqldump --all-databases --user="$mysql_user" --password="$mysql_password"
    > "$backup_filename"
    [root@mysql80 mysql]#
    ```

5. Test the script by executing it:

    ```
    [root@mysql80 mysql]# /mnt/backups/mysql/backup_mysqldump.sh
    /mnt/backups/mysql/daily_backup_20240220.sql
    [root@mysql80 mysql]# ls -ltr
    total 4828
    -rwxr-xr-x. 1 root root     472 Feb 20 14:18 backup_mysqldump.sh
    -rw-r--r--. 1 root root 4937167 Feb 20 14:18 daily_backup_20240220.sql
    [root@mysql80 mysql]#
    ```

6. Open the crontab configuration:

    ```
    crontab -e
    ```

7. Add the following line to the crontab file to schedule a daily backup at 2 A.M.:

    ```
    0 2 * * * /mnt/backups/mysql/backup_mysqldump.sh
    ```

8. Save and close the crontab file.

By following this example configuration, you can use `mysqldump` to set up a daily backup schedule for a MySQL database and ensure that the backup files are stored securely and can be restored when needed. The provided backup scripts are basic examples. Depending on your requirements, you may need to write scripts using scripting languages such as Python or a shell script.

Selecting backup options

When taking a backup, select various backup options to customize the backup process. Here are some essential backup options:

Backup type
> Select either a full backup or an incremental backup. Full backups create a complete backup of the database, while incremental backups back up only changes made since the last backup.

Compression
> Compress the backup file to save disk space. XtraBackup, `mydumper`, and `mysql dump` support compression.

Encryption
> Encrypt the backup file to protect sensitive data. XtraBackup supports encryption via the `--encrypt` option.

Monitoring the backup process

It is essential to monitor the backup process to ensure that it completes successfully. Here are some ways to monitor this process:

- Check the backup logfile for any errors or warnings.
- Check the backup file size to ensure that it is not too small or too large.
- To ensure the backup file's validity, periodically perform restores by using the production backup on the testing system.

Setting up the restore environment

After selecting a restore method, set up the environment for the restore process. Ensure that the server configuration is compatible with the backup files, including the version of MySQL and the location of the data directory. If necessary, create a new MySQL instance with the same configuration as the original instance.

Assuming that the backup was taken from a MySQL 8.0.23 instance and you want to restore it to a new MySQL 8.0.25 instance, you can set up the environment for the restore process by using the following steps:

- Install MySQL 8.0.25 on the server where you want to restore the database.
- Stop the MySQL service by using the command `systemctl stop mysqld`.
- Copy the configuration file from the original instance to the new instance by using a command like `scp`.
- Edit the configuration file */etc/my.cnf* to match the configuration of the original instance, including the location of the data directory.
- Depending on the backup, the restore process will vary.
- Start the MySQL service by using the command `systemctl start mysqld`.

When choosing a backup method, consider the size of your database, the amount of data changes, and the RTO and RPO of your organization. For example, XtraBackup is an efficient backup method for large databases that require quick recovery time, while `mydumper` takes more time compared to XtraBackup, and the `mysqldump` is suitable for smaller databases that can afford longer recovery times.

Point-in-Time Recovery

Point-in-time recovery (PITR) is a technique used to restore a database to a specific point in time, typically to recover from accidental deletion, data corruption, or other types of data loss. It involves restoring a database to a previous state by replaying transaction logs that were captured at specific points in time.

PITR is necessary when you need to recover your database to a specific point in time. For example, if you accidentally deleted important data from the database and realized it only a few hours later, you could use PITR to recover the database to a point in time just before the data was deleted. Similarly, if the database becomes corrupted, you can use PITR to restore it to a point in time before the corruption occurred.

PITR is necessary in the following situations:

Disaster recovery
　　If you experience data loss due to a disaster such as hardware failure, power outages, or a natural calamity, PITR helps you restore the data to a specific point in time before the disaster occurred.

Human error
　　If you accidentally delete or modify data, PITR allows you to restore the data to the point in time before the error occurred.

Compliance
　　PITR is often required to meet compliance regulations such as the Health Insurance Portability and Accountability Act (HIPAA), Sarbanes-Oxley Act (SOX), and General Data Protection Regulation (GDPR). These regulations may require

that you keep backups of data and that you are able to restore the data to a specific point in time.

Instance-Level Recovery

This recovery method allows you to recover the entire MySQL instance, including databases, tables, schemas, and configurations, to a consistent state. Here's a straightforward example of how to execute PITR. However, the steps may differ based on the backup tool used (such as XtraBackup, MySQL Shell dump utility, or mydumper), and the backup and scenario of the production environment, so it's essential to take appropriate actions accordingly.

Let's say you have a database for an online store and accidentally deleted a customer's order. You want to recover that order but don't want to lose any data that has been added since the order was deleted.

Here's how you could use PITR to recover the order up to the moment before it was deleted:

1. To ensure regular backups of the database, it is important to schedule them at specific intervals. One way to perform a full backup of the database is by utilizing the `xtrabackup` command, which was already detailed in "Percona XtraBackup" on page 160.

2. Create a binary log backup of the database by using the `mysqlbinlog` command. To ensure regular backups, it is important to create a script and schedule them at specific intervals.

   When backing up a server's binary logfiles with `mysqlbinlog`, you need to provide the actual filenames that exist on the server. You can use the SHOW BINARY LOGS statement to see the current names if you are not sure what they are:

   ```
   mysql> SHOW BINARY LOGS;
   +----------------+-----------+-----------+
   | Log_name       | File_size | Encrypted |
   +----------------+-----------+-----------+
   | binlog.000001  |     35421 |        No |
   | binlog.000002  |     12416 |        No |
   | binlog.000003  |     52273 |        No |
   +----------------+-----------+-----------+
   ```

   To create a static backup of *binlog.000001* through *binlog.000003*, you can use either of these commands:

   ```
   mysqlbinlog --read-from-remote-server --host=host_name --raw
   binlog.000001 binlog.000002 binlog.000003

   mysqlbinlog --read-from-remote-server --host=host_name --raw
   --to-last-log binlog.000001
   ```

The first command explicitly lists every filename, while the second names only the first file and uses `--to-last-log` to read through the last. One difference between these commands is that if the server opens *binlog.000133* before `mysql binlog` reaches the end of *binlog.000003*, the first command does not read it, but the second command does.

To create a live backup, where `mysqlbinlog` starts with *binlog.000001* to copy existing logfiles and then stays connected to copy new events as the server generates them, you can use the following:

```
mysqlbinlog --read-from-remote-server --host=host_name --raw
--stop-never binlog.000001
```

With `--stop-never`, it is not necessary to specify all the binary logfiles that already exist.

3. Restore the full backup. (See "Percona XtraBackup" on page 160 for the steps required to restore the full backup made by XtraBackup.)

4. Apply incremental backups to restore the database up to the desired point in time:

```
mysqlbinlog --start-datetime='2023-03-01 12:00:00'
--stop-datetime='2023-03-01 13:00:00' /var/log/mysql/binlog.000001 |
mysql -u root -p mydatabase
```

 This example demonstrates the use of XtraBackup. Depending on the backup system employed in production, you have the option to utilize either MySQL Shell dump utility, `mydumper`, XtraBackup, or MySQL Enterprise Backup.

In this example, we are restoring the database up to a specific hour on March 1, 2023, which is the hour before the order was deleted.

By following these steps, you can recover the deleted order without losing any data that has been added since the deletion. PITR gives you greater control over your data recovery process and can be a valuable tool in disaster recovery scenarios.

Table-Level Recovery

To restore the table alone to a new instance, ensure that you have a valid backup of the table's tablespace files. Once you've done that, you're ready to follow these steps to create a table-level recovery:

1. Connect to the MySQL instance where you want to restore the table and create the table structure:

```
mysql> use adddb;
Database changed
mysql> CREATE TABLE `authors` (
    ->        `id` int NOT NULL AUTO_INCREMENT,
    ->        `first_name` varchar(50) COLLATE utf8mb3_unicode_ci NOT NULL,
    ->        `last_name` varchar(50) COLLATE utf8mb3_unicode_ci NOT NULL,
    ->        `email` varchar(100) COLLATE utf8mb3_unicode_ci NOT NULL,
    ->        `birthdate` date NOT NULL,
    ->        `added` timestamp NOT NULL DEFAULT CURRENT_TIMESTAMP,
    ->        PRIMARY KEY (`id`)
    ->        ) ENGINE=InnoDB AUTO_INCREMENT=72639469 DEFAULT CHARSET=utf8mb4
    COLLATE=utf8mb4_0900_ai_ci;
Query OK, 0 rows affected, 3 warnings (0.03 sec)
```

2. Discard the tablespace of the authors table:

```
mysql> select count(*) from authors;
+----------+
| count(*) |
+----------+
|        0 |
+----------+
1 row in set (0.01 sec)
mysql> ALTER TABLE authors DISCARD TABLESPACE;
Query OK, 0 rows affected (0.01 sec)
mysql>
```

When a tablespace is discarded, the association between the table and its under-lying tablespace is removed. The table structure and metadata remain intact, but the tablespace files are no longer associated with the table. This operation is typi-cally performed when you want to replace the tablespace files with a different set of files or when you want to restore the table from a backup.

3. Copy the tablespace from the backup:

```
root@UbuntuMysql8:~# scp /var/lib/mysql/adddb/authors.ibd 172.31.84.219:/var/
lib/mysql/adddb/
authors.
ibd
100%  544KB  49.3MB/s    00:00
root@MyUbuntuMysql8:~#
```

4. Change the ownership of the file *authors.ibd* located in the */var/lib/mysql/adddb* directory. The following command assigns the user and group mysql as the new owners of the file:

```
[root@mysql80 ~]# chown mysql.mysql /var/lib/mysql/adddb/authors.ibd
[root@mysql80 ~]#
```

5. Import the tablespace. The statement ALTER TABLE authors IMPORT TABLE SPACE; is used in MySQL to import a tablespace for the authors table within the adddb database. This command allows you to restore or replace the tablespace of the authors table by using a previously exported or backup tablespace file

(typically with an *.ibd* extension). By executing this statement, you instruct MySQL to associate the imported tablespace file with the `authors` table in the specified database.

Importing the tablespace enables you to recover or migrate a table along with its data and index structures. It establishes the link between the table definition and the underlying tablespace file, allowing the table to be fully accessible and operational within the MySQL database instance:

```
[root@mysql80 mysql]# mysql
Welcome to the MySQL monitor.  Commands end with ; or \g.
mysql>

mysql> ALTER TABLE adddb.authors IMPORT TABLESPACE;
Query OK, 0 rows affected, 1 warning (0.05 sec)
mysql>
```

6. Following the import of the tablespace for the `authors` table, verify the data in the table:

```
select count(id) from adddb.authors;mysql> select count(id) from
adddb.authors;
+-----------+
| count(id) |
+-----------+
|      6000 |
+-----------+
1 row in set (0.03 sec)
```

After importing the table as part of the PITR process, you'll need to use the binlog backups to restore the remaining data from the time of the initial backup to the current time. To accomplish this, follow the steps outlined here:

1. Copy the required binlog and create the index:

```
sudo cp or scp mysql-bin.* /data/
sudo chown mysql.mysql /data/mysql-bin.*
```

2. Update the *my.cnf* file:

```
relay-log = mysql-bin
```

3. Prepare the index by using the copied binlogs:

```
ls ./mysql-bin.0* >mysql-bin.index
```

With `IMPORT TABLESPACE`, you have already imported the table from the existing backup.

4. Configure this table as a dummy replica:

```
mysql> CHANGE REPLICATION SOURCE TO
RELAY_LOG_FILE='mysql-bin.000001',RELAY_LOG_POS=4, SOURCE_HOST='dummy';
Query OK, 0 rows affected (0.08 sec)
```

```
mysql> CHANGE REPLICATION FILTER REPLICATE_DO_TABLE = (adddb.authors);
Query OK, 0 rows affected (0.00 sec)
```

5. Validate the output and start the replication thread (only the SQL thread is needed):

```
mysql> START REPLICA SQL_THREAD;
Query OK, 0 rows affected (0.01 sec)
```

PITR is a crucial process that requires expertise from a DBA. In MySQL, it empowers you to restore your database to a precise point in time during critical situations, including accidental data deletion, data corruption, human errors, and disaster recovery. The skillful implementation of PITR ensures data integrity and minimizes potential data loss in these critical scenarios.

By enabling binary logging, taking a full backup, restoring the backup to a new location, determining the point in time to recover to, and recovering the database to that time, you can ensure data integrity and protect against data loss.

Management of Binary Logs

MySQL provides a robust and reliable logging mechanism for tracking changes made to the database, known as *binary logging*. In this section, we discuss the significance of binary logs and provide a comprehensive guide on managing them.

Binary logs are a type of logfile generated by MySQL to record all changes made to the database. These changes include any data modifications, schema alterations, and administrative operations such as user management. Binary logs are stored in a binary format, which makes them platform independent and allows for easy replication of changes across multiple servers.

Binary logs are a critical component of MySQL's HA and disaster-recovery mechanisms. They are used to restore the database in the event of a server crash, data corruption, or user error. Binary logs are also required for replication, to synchronize data changes between source and replica servers.

Enabling Binary Logging

In previous versions of MySQL, binary logging had to be manually enabled by specifying the --log-bin option since it was disabled by default. However, as of MySQL 8, binary logging is enabled by default regardless of whether the --log-bin option is specified.

The only exception occurs when initializing the data directory manually by using mysqld and the --initialize or --initialize-insecure option, which disables binary logging by default. To enable binary logging in this case, the --log-bin option must be specified. Enabling binary logging sets the `log_bin` system variable to `ON`, indicating the status of binary logging on the server.

To enable binary logging, add the following line to the MySQL configuration file (*my.cnf* or *my.ini*):

```
[mysqld]
log-bin=mysql-bin
```

This configuration will create a binary logfile named *mysql-bin* in the data directory specified in the MySQL configuration file.

Configuring Binary Logging

MySQL provides a range of configuration options for binary logging. These options can be set in the MySQL configuration file or dynamically by using the `SET GLOBAL` command. Some of the key configuration options for binary logging include the following:

`binlog_format`
> Specifies the format used for binary logging. MySQL supports three formats: `ROW`, `STATEMENT`, and `MIXED`. The default format is `ROW`.

`expire_logs_days`
> Sets the number of days after which binary logs will be automatically purged. The default value is `0`, which means that binary logs will not be automatically deleted.

`max_binlog_size`
> Specifies the maximum size of a binary logfile before a new file is created. The default value is 1,073,741,824 bytes (1 GB).

`binlog_row_image`
> Specifies the format used for binary logging of row-based events. MySQL supports three formats: `FULL`, `MINIMAL` and `NOBLOB`. The default format is `FULL`.

For example, to set the `binlog_format` option to `ROW`, add the following line to the MySQL configuration file:

```
[mysqld]
binlog_format=ROW
```

Purging Binary Logs

Over time, binary logs can consume a significant amount of disk space. To prevent this, MySQL provides the option to purge old binary logs. You can purge binary logs in two ways: manually or automatically.

To *manually* purge binary logs, use the PURGE BINARY LOGS command, which will purge all binary logs up to and including the file *mysql-bin.000003*:

```
PURGE BINARY LOGS TO 'mysql-bin.000003';
```

To *automatically* purge binary logs, set the expire_logs_days option in the MySQL configuration file.

Here, 604,800 seconds are equivalent to seven days (60 seconds/minute × 60 minutes/hour × 24 hours/day × 7 days). This configuration will automatically purge binary logs that are older than seven days:

```
[mysqld]
binlog_expire_logs_seconds=604800;
```

Here's an example of how to use the PURGE BINARY LOGS command to delete old binary logfiles in MySQL:

1. Use the MySQL client to connect to the MySQL server:

   ```
   mysql -u root -p
   ```

2. List the binary logfiles currently in use:

   ```
   mysql> SHOW BINARY LOGS;
   +----------------+-----------+-----------+
   | Log_name       | File_size | Encrypted |
   +----------------+-----------+-----------+
   | binlog.000003  |       157 | No        |
   | binlog.000004  |       201 | No        |
   | binlog.000005  |       157 | No        |
   | binlog.000006  |       201 | No        |
   | binlog.000007  |      1357 | No        |
   | binlog.000008  |       201 | No        |
   | binlog.000009  |       157 | No        |
   | binlog.000010  |       905 | No        |
   | binlog.000011  |      1743 | No        |
   | binlog.000012  |   2097859 | No        |
   | binlog.000013  |       201 | No        |
   | binlog.000014  |      1402 | No        |
   +----------------+-----------+-----------+
   12 rows in set (0.01 sec)
   mysql>
   ```

   Along with the binary logfiles currently in use, this command will display their sizes and creation timestamps.

3. Use the PURGE BINARY LOGS command to delete old binary logfiles. For example, to delete all binary logfiles older than seven days, use the following command:

   ```
   mysql> PURGE BINARY LOGS BEFORE DATE_SUB(NOW(), INTERVAL 7 DAY);
   Query OK, 0 rows affected (0.02 sec)
   ```

You can adjust the interval as needed to delete files older or newer than a certain number of days.

4. Verify that the old binary logfiles have been deleted by running the SHOW BINARY LOGS command again:

```
mysql> SHOW BINARY LOGS;
+----------------+-----------+-----------+
| Log_name       | File_size | Encrypted |
+----------------+-----------+-----------+
| binlog.000013  |       201 | No        |
| binlog.000014  |      1402 | No        |
+----------------+-----------+-----------+
2 rows in set (0.00 sec)
```

Now you'll see the binary logfiles currently in use, excluding any files that were deleted by the PURGE BINARY LOGS command.

By using the PURGE BINARY LOGS command, you can keep your binary logfiles under control and prevent them from consuming too much disk space over time. Binary logs are a critical component of MySQL's HA and disaster-recovery mechanisms. They provide a reliable way to track changes made to the database and allow for easy replication of changes across multiple servers. By following the guidelines outlined in this section, you can ensure that your binary logs are properly configured and managed.

Best Practices for Backup and Recovery

In the world of databases, backup and recovery are essential to ensure the integrity of data. A single database failure can lead to loss of important data, which can impair business operations. Therefore, it is important to implement best practices for backup and recovery in MySQL.

Regular backups are critical to ensure that your data is safe and recoverable. A regular backup schedule depends on the size of your data and the rate of change in the data. A general rule of thumb is to perform backups daily for high-volume transactional databases, and weekly or monthly for databases with lower data-change rates. Here are some other backup best practices:

Create a backup strategy
Define a backup strategy that meets your recovery requirements, such as backup frequency, backup types (full or incremental), and retention periods.

Back up from a replica node
Taking a MySQL backup from a replica node is recommended because it reduces the load on the primary node and ensures a consistent backup. By taking a backup from a replica node, the primary node is not burdened with additional

workload, which can impact the live system's performance. Additionally, since the replica node is in sync with the primary node, taking a backup from it guarantees consistency and reduces the risk of data corruption or loss. Overall, taking backups from a replica node is a best practice for MySQL DBAs to ensure the availability and integrity of their data.

Confirming the integrity of the data in the replica is also very important and is not necessarily guaranteed solely by having replication running. It is the DBA's job to ensure that it is an exact copy by running tools such as `pt-table-checksum`.

Back up the MySQL binlog, or binary log
A binary log is a logfile that records all modifications made to a database, including insertions, updates, and deletions. Backing up the MySQL binlog is essential because it can help recover data from a specific point in time, which can be useful in several scenarios, such as disaster recovery, replication, and auditing. In the case of a disaster, such as a hardware failure or data corruption, the binlog can be used to restore the database to a specific point in time before the disaster occurred, minimizing data loss. Additionally, backing up the binlog is critical for replication, as it enables replica databases to synchronize with the primary database. Finally, the binlog can be used for auditing purposes, providing a detailed record of all modifications made to the database, which can be useful for compliance and security. Overall, backing up the MySQL binlog is an essential practice for ensuring data availability, integrity, and security.

Use MySQL Enterprise Backup
MySQL Enterprise Backup is a commercial backup solution that provides enterprise-grade backup and recovery features for MySQL databases. It offers fast, reliable, and scalable backups, along with support for PITR and partial backups.

Use Percona XtraBackup
XtraBackup is a popular open source tool used for backing up and restoring MySQL databases. One of the primary reasons to use XtraBackup is that it performs hot backups of InnoDB and XtraDB storage engines, which means it can take backups without locking the database or causing any downtime. XtraBackup also offers several other useful features, such as parallel compression and incremental backups, which can further improve backup performance and efficiency. Additionally, XtraBackup is highly customizable, allowing DBAs to tailor backups to their specific needs. Overall, XtraBackup is a reliable and flexible tool that simplifies the backup and recovery process for MySQL databases.

MySQL Shell dump utility

MySQL Shell dump is a command-line tool used to back up and restore MySQL databases. One of the key benefits of using the MySQL Shell dump utility is that it provides a more comprehensive backup solution than traditional backup methods. With MySQL Shell dump, it is possible to back up not only the database schema and data but also stored routines, triggers, and user accounts. MySQL Shell dump also offers support for parallel backups, enabling faster and more efficient backups of large databases. Additionally, MySQL Shell dump is highly customizable, allowing DBAs to specify backup options such as compression and selective backups. Overall, MySQL Shell dump is a powerful and flexible tool that simplifies the backup and recovery process for MySQL databases.

Use `mysqldump` for small databases

For small databases, `mysqldump` is a reliable and cost-effective backup solution. It can back up MySQL databases in SQL format, making it easy to restore them in case of data loss.

Test your backups

Backing up data is not sufficient if you haven't verified that the backups are restorable. Therefore, it is important to test your backups regularly to ensure that they can be restored in the event of a disaster. You can test your backups by restoring them to a test environment and checking the data for accuracy and consistency.

Store your backups offsite

Storing backups offsite is important in the event of a disaster like fire, theft, or natural calamities that may affect your primary data center. Keeping backups in a different location ensures that they are safe and recoverable. You can store backups in different cloud storage solutions such as Amazon Simple Storage Service (S3), Google Cloud Storage, or Microsoft Azure, or use physical storage devices such as tapes or external hard drives.

Use cloud storage

Cloud storage providers like Amazon S3, Google Cloud Storage, and Microsoft Azure offer reliable and secure offsite storage options for your backups. When using S3, you can use the Amazon Web Services (AWS) CLI to automate the backup and restore process. For example, you can use the following command to upload your backup to the S3 bucket named *mybucket/backups*:

```
aws s3 cp /backup/full/backup-to-image s3://mybucket/backups/
```

Use secure transport protocols

Use secure transport protocols like SSL or Secure Shell (SSH) to protect your backups from unauthorized access. The AWS CLI employs SSL as its default communication protocol, and for every SSL connection, SSL certificates are verified by the AWS CLI. The following command will transfer your backup image to S3 via SSL:

```
aws s3 cp /backup/full/backup-to-image s3://mybucket/backups/ --sse
```

The `--sse` parameter specifies server-side encryption for an object in S3 and can accept the values `AES256` or `aws:kms`. If no value is provided for the parameter, the default `AES256` encryption is used.

Encryption to Protect Your Backups

Encrypting backups ensures that they are secure and protected from unauthorized access. You can use various encryption methods, such as symmetric or asymmetric encryption, to encrypt your backups. MySQL provides encryption options such as the `--ssl*` option for `mysqldump` or the `--encrypt` option for MySQL Enterprise Backup. Here are some best practices for encrypting your backups:

Use MySQL Enterprise Backup
  MySQL Enterprise Backup offers encryption features that allow you to encrypt your backups with AES-256 encryption. It also supports using key management systems like Oracle Key Vault.

Use third-party encryption tools
  You can use third-party encryption tools like GNU Privacy Guard (GnuPG) or OpenSSL to encrypt your backups before storing them offsite.

Use encryption plug-ins
  MySQL Enterprise Backup provides encryption plug-ins that you can use to encrypt your backups. For example, you can use the AES-256 encryption plug-in to encrypt your backups via the following command:

```
mysqlbackup --backup-dir=/backup/full
--backup-image=/backup/full/backup-to-image \
--encrypt=AES256 --key-file=/path/to/keyfile --host=mydb.example.com \
--port=3306 --user=admin --password backup-to-image
```

This command encrypts your backup image using AES-256 encryption and the key file located at */path/to/key*.

XtraBackup Encryption

Since MySQL 8 and Percona Server 8.0 are not supported by Percona XtraBackup 2.4.*x*, you'll need to use Percona XtraBackup 8.0.*x* for backups and restores. This section provides the updated steps to install Percona XtraBackup 8.0.*x*.

As mentioned before, you'll need to add the Percona repository to your package manager's list of available repositories. Open a terminal or command prompt and run the commands in this section.

For Debian/Ubuntu, download the Debian package file by using wget:

```
root@MyUbuntuMysql8:~# wget https://repo.percona.com/apt/p
ercona-release_latest.generic_all.deb
--2024-02-20 14:57:01--  https://repo.percona.com/apt/
percona-release_latest.generic_all.deb
Resolving repo.percona.com (repo.percona.com)... 147.135.54.159,
Length: 11804 (12K) [application/x-debian-package]
Saving to: 'percona-release_latest.generic_all.deb'
percona-release_latest.generic_all.deb        100%
[==============================================>]  11.53K  --.-KB/s    in 0s
2024-02-20 14:57:01 (196 MB/s) - 'percona-release_latest.generic_all.deb'
saved [11804/11804]
root@MyUbuntuMysql8:~#
```

The command sudo dpkg is used to install the Debian package:

```
root@MyUbuntuMysql8:~# sudo dpkg -i percona-release_latest.generic_all.deb
Selecting previously unselected package percona-release.
<*> All done!
* Enabling the Percona Release repository
<*> All done!
For example, to enable the Percona Server 8.0 repository use:
  percona-release setup ps80
Note: To avoid conflicts with older product versions, the percona-release
root@MyUbuntuMysql8:~#
```

Update the package lists for available software repositories:

```
root@MyUbuntuMysql8:~# sudo apt-get update
Hit:1 http://us-east-1.ec2.archive.ubuntu.com/ubuntu jammy InRelease
Get:2 http://us-east-1.ec2.archive.ubuntu.com/ubuntu jammy-updates
InRelease [119 kB]
Hit:3 http://us-east-1.ec2.archive.ubuntu.com/ubuntu jammy-backports InRelease
Get:11 http://repo.percona.com/prel/apt jammy/main amd64 Packages [415 B]
Fetched 3088 kB in 2s (1713 kB/s)
Reading package lists... Done
root@MyUbuntuMysql8:~#
```

To install version 80 of the Percona XtraBackup tool on a system, execute the following command:

```
root@MyUbuntuMysql8:~# sudo apt-get install percona-xtrabackup-80
Reading package lists... Done
Building dependency tree... Done
Reading state information... Done
The following additional packages will be installed:
  libcurl4-openssl-dev libev4
Suggested packages:
  libcurl4-doc libidn11-dev libkrb5-dev libldap2-dev librtmp-dev libssh2-1-dev
```

```
  libssl-dev pkg-config zlib1g-dev
The following NEW packages will be installed:
  libcurl4-openssl-dev libev4 percona-xtrabackup-80
Processing triggers for libc-bin (2.35-0ubuntu3.6) ...
Scanning processes...
Running kernel seems to be up-to-date.
Restarting services...
Service restarts being deferred:
 systemctl restart systemd-logind.service
No containers need to be restarted.
No user sessions are running outdated binaries.
No VM guests are running outdated hypervisor (qemu) binaries on this host.
root@MyUbuntuMysql8:~#
```

Verify the version of the installed XtraBackup:

```
root@MyUbuntuMysql8:~# xtrabackup --version
2024-02-20T15:02:37.633932-00:00 0 [Note] [MY-011825] [Xtrabackup] recognized
server arguments: --innodb_directories=/var/lib/user_defined_general_tablespace
xtrabackup version 8.0.35-30 based on MySQL server 8.0.35 Linux (x86_64)
(revision id: 6beb4b49)
root@MyUbuntuMysql8:~#
```

To create an encrypted backup using Percona XtraBackup, you can follow these steps:

1. Determine the encryption algorithm. Percona XtraBackup supports three encryption algorithms: AES-128, AES-192, and AES-256. Choose the algorithm you want to use for encryption.

2. Generate an encryption key. You have two options to specify the encryption key when creating encrypted backups: xtrabackup --encrypt-key and xtrabackup --encrypt-key-file. Here's an example command to generate an encryption key:

```
root@MyUbuntuMysql8:~# openssl rand -base64 24
P/Fu9cZo9gzkzpmtvUKFku3u4ONTrj5Z
root@MyUbuntuMysql8:~#
```

Here's an example of the XtraBackup command utilizing the xtrabackup --encrypt-key option:

```
root@MyUbuntuMysql8:~# mkdir /root/backups/
root@MyUbuntuMysql8:~# xtrabackup --backup --target-dir=/root/backups/
--encrypt=AES256 --encrypt-key=""P/Fu9cZo9gzkzpmtvUKFku3u4ONTrj5Z""
2024-02-20T15:04:59.723781-00:00 0 [Note] [MY-011825] [Xtrabackup]
recognized server arguments: --innodb_directories=/var/lib/
user_defined_general_tablespace
2024-02-20T15:04:59.724228-00:00 0 [Note] [MY-011825] [Xtrabackup]
recognized client arguments: --ssl-mode=REQUIRED --ssl-cert=/var/lib/mysql/
client-cert.pem --ssl-key=/var/lib/mysql/client-key.pem --backup=1
--target-dir=/root/backups/ --encrypt=AES256 --encrypt-key=*
xtrabackup version 8.0.35-30 based on MySQL server 8.0.35 Linux (x86_64)
(revision id: 6beb4b49)
```

```
240220 15:04:59  version_check Connecting to MySQL server with DSN
'dbi:mysql:; mysql_read_default_group=xtrabackup' (using password: NO).
240220 15:05:00  version_check Connected to MySQL server
240220 15:05:00  version_check Executing a version check against
the server...
```

3. After completing the backup, check the log to confirm its successful completion. You should get a log similar to this:

```
2024-02-20T15:05:03.706837-00:00 0 [Note] [MY-011825] [Xtrabackup]
Encrypting /root/backups/xtrabackup_info.xbcrypt
2024-02-20T15:05:03.707047-00:00 0 [Note] [MY-011825] [Xtrabackup]
Done: Encrypting file /root/backups/xtrabackup_info.xbcrypt
2024-02-20T15:05:04.717140-00:00 0 [Note] [MY-011825] [Xtrabackup]
Transaction log of lsn (42914523) to (42914533) was copied.
2024-02-20T15:05:04.826343-00:00 0 [Note] [MY-010733] [Server]
Shutting down plugin 'keyring_file'
2024-02-20T15:05:04.828326-00:00 0 [Note] [MY-010733] [Server]
Shutting down plugin 'daemon_keyring_proxy_plugin'
2024-02-20T15:05:04.831369-00:00 0 [Note] [MY-011825] [Xtrabackup]
completed OK!
root@MyUbuntuMysql8:~#
```

In the backup directory, all files are in *.xbcrypt* format, representing encrypted versions of MySQL database files:

```
root@MyUbuntuMysql8:~# ls -ltr /root/backups/
total 76232
-rw-r----- 1 root root 12600576 Feb 20 15:05 ibdata1.xbcrypt
drwxr-x--- 2 root root     4096 Feb 20 15:05 sys
drwxr-x--- 2 root root     4096 Feb 20 15:05 mydatabase
drwxr-x--- 2 root root     4096 Feb 20 15:05 mytestschema
drwxr-x--- 2 root root     4096 Feb 20 15:05 unencryptedschema
-rw-r----- 1 root root   114872 Feb 20 15:05
  user_defined_general_tablespace.ibd.xbcrypt
-rw-r----- 1 root root   114872 Feb 20 15:05
  user_defined_general_tablespace_1.ibd.xbcrypt
drwxr-x--- 2 root root     4096 Feb 20 15:05 encryptedschema
drwxr-x--- 2 root root     4096 Feb 20 15:05 mytest
drwxr-x--- 2 root root     4096 Feb 20 15:05 mytestdb
drwxr-x--- 2 root root     4096 Feb 20 15:05 adddb
-rw-r----- 1 root root 31501440 Feb 20 15:05 mysql.ibd.xbcrypt
-rw-r----- 1 root root 16800768 Feb 20 15:05 undo_002.xbcrypt
-rw-r----- 1 root root 16800768 Feb 20 15:05 undo_001.xbcrypt
drwxr-x--- 2 root root    12288 Feb 20 15:05 performance_schema
drwxr-x--- 2 root root     4096 Feb 20 15:05 test
drwxr-x--- 2 root root     4096 Feb 20 15:05 mytestdb_inno
drwxr-x--- 2 root root     4096 Feb 20 15:05 mysql
drwxr-x--- 2 root root     4096 Feb 20 15:05 d1
-rw-r----- 1 root root      249 Feb 20 15:05 binlog.000076.xbcrypt
-rw-r----- 1 root root      108 Feb 20 15:05 binlog.index.xbcrypt
-rw-r----- 1 root root      110 Feb 20 15:05 xtrabackup_binlog_info.xbcrypt
-rw-r----- 1 root root     2744 Feb 20 15:05 xtrabackup_logfile.xbcrypt
```

```
-rw-r----- 1 root root        134 Feb 20 15:05 xtrabackup_checkpoints
-rw-r----- 1 root root       4600 Feb 20 15:05 ib_buffer_pool.xbcrypt
-rw-r----- 1 root root        567 Feb 20 15:05 backup-my.cnf.xbcrypt
-rw-r----- 1 root root        597 Feb 20 15:05 xtrabackup_info.xbcrypt
-rw-r----- 1 root root        131 Feb 20 15:05 xtrabackup_tablespaces.xbcrypt
root@MyUbuntuMysql8:~#
```

How to Decrypt Encrypted Backups

The `--decrypt` option in Percona XtraBackup allows for the decryption of backups:

```
root@MyUbuntuMysql8:~/backups/mysql# xtrabackup --decrypt=AES256
--encrypt-key="P/Fu9cZo9gzkzpmtvUKFku3u4ONTrj5Z" --target-dir=/root/backups/
--remove-original
2024-02-20T15:12:08.321590-00:00 0 [Note] [MY-011825] [Xtrabackup] recognized
server arguments: --innodb_directories=/var/lib/user_defined_general_tablespace
2024-02-20T15:12:08.322065-00:00 0 [Note] [MY-011825] [Xtrabackup] recognized
client arguments: --ssl-mode=REQUIRED --ssl-cert=/var/lib/mysql/client-cert.pem
--ssl-key=/var/lib/mysql/client-key.pem --decrypt=AES256 --encrypt-key=*
--target-dir=/root/backups/ --remove-original=1
xtrabackup version 8.0.35-30 based on MySQL server 8.0.35 Linux (x86_64)
(revision id: 6beb4b49)
2024-02-20T15:12:08.354574-00:00 0 [Note] [MY-011825] [Xtrabackup] decrypting ./
performance_schema/replication_conn_162.sdi.xbcrypt
```

After the decryption process, examine the log to ensure that it has been successfully completed. You should observe a log resembling this:

```
2024-02-20T15:12:09.727703-00:00 0 [Note] [MY-011825] [Xtrabackup] decrypting
./xtrabackup_binlog_info.xbcrypt
2024-02-20T15:12:09.731566-00:00 0 [Note] [MY-011825] [Xtrabackup] removing
./xtrabackup_binlog_info.xbcrypt
2024-02-20T15:12:09.733903-00:00 0 [Note] [MY-011825] [Xtrabackup] completed OK!
root@MyUbuntuMysql8:~/backups/mysql#
```

Use a secure key-management solution to store and manage your encryption keys. For example, you can use the AWS Key Management Service (KMS) to generate and manage your encryption keys.

How to Prepare the Decrypted Backups

The command `xtrabackup --prepare` is used to prepare the backup files in the specified directory:

```
root@MyUbuntuMysql8:~# xtrabackup --prepare --target-dir=/root/backups/
2024-02-20T15:15:10.126368-00:00 0 [Note] [MY-011825] [Xtrabackup] recognized
server arguments: --innodb_checksum_algorithm=crc32 --innodb_log_checksums=1
--innodb_data_file_path=ibdata1:12M:autoextend --innodb_log_file_size=50331648
--innodb_page_size=16384 --innodb_undo_directory=./ --innodb_undo_tablespaces=2
--server-id=0 --innodb_log_checksums=ON --innodb_redo_log_encrypt=0
--innodb_undo_log_encrypt=0
2024-02-20T15:15:10.126706-00:00 0 [Note] [MY-011825] [Xtrabackup] recognized
```

```
client arguments: --prepare=1 --target-dir=/root/backups/
xtrabackup version 8.0.35-30 based on MySQL server 8.0.35 Linux (x86_64)
(revision id: 6beb4b49)
2024-02-20T15:15:10.127029-00:00 0 [Note] [MY-011825] [Xtrabackup] cd to
/root/backups/
2024-02-20T15:15:10.127237-00:00 0 [Note] [MY-011825] [Xtrabackup]
This target seems to be not prepared yet.
```

After completing the preparation process, review the log to confirm its successful
execution:

```
2024-02-20T15:15:12.162295-00:00 0 [Note] [MY-012980] [InnoDB]
Shutdown completed; log sequence number 42914838
2024-02-20T15:15:12.166062-00:00 0 [Note] [MY-010733] [Server]
Shutting down plugin 'keyring_file'
2024-02-20T15:15:12.166261-00:00 0 [Note] [MY-010733] [Server]
Shutting down plugin 'daemon_keyring_proxy_plugin'
2024-02-20T15:15:12.166814-00:00 0 [Note] [MY-011825] [Xtrabackup] completed OK!
root@MyUbuntuMysql8:~#
```

mysqldump Encryption

mysqldump encryption secures database backups by converting data into unreadable
ciphertext, preventing unauthorized access. A decryption key is needed to revert the
ciphertext back to its original, readable form.

You can use the command mysqldump to create a backup of a MySQL database named
mytestdb and save it to a file named *backup.sql*:

```
root@MyUbuntuMysql8:~/backups# mysqldump -u root -p mytestdb > backup.sql
Enter password:
root@MyUbuntuMysql8:~/backups# ls -ltr
total 8
-rw-r--r-- 1 root root 5714 Feb 20 15:22 backup.sql
root@MyUbuntuMysql8:~/backups#
```

After taking the backup, use the openssl command to encrypt a file named
backup.sql with the AES-256-CBC encryption algorithm:

```
root@MyUbuntuMysql8:~/backups# openssl aes-256-cbc -salt -in backup.sql -out
backup.sql.enc
enter AES-256-CBC encryption password:
Verifying - enter AES-256-CBC encryption password:
root@MyUbuntuMysql8:~/backups#
```

This code will create a backup of the mydatabase database by using the mysqldump
command and encrypt it using OpenSSL with the AES-256-CBC algorithm.

To decrypt the backup, you can use the following command:

```
root@MyUbuntuMysql8:~/backups# openssl aes-256-cbc -d -in backup.sql.enc -out
backup.sql
```

```
enter AES-256-CBC decryption password:
root@MyUbuntuMysql8:~/backups#
```

This code will decrypt the backup file *backup.sql.enc* by using the AES-256-CBC algorithm and output the decrypted file to *backup.sql*.

Conclusion

Backup and recovery are critical activities in any MySQL environment. By following the guidelines in this chapter, you can help ensure that your data is protected and easily recoverable in the event of a disaster.

## CHAPTER 5

MySQL Security

The security of a MySQL database is critical to ensure that unauthorized access and manipulation of data do not occur. This chapter covers important topics such as user management, network security, encryption, and other security suggestions. We will discuss the recommended best practices for managing users, including using strong passwords that are difficult to guess. Additionally, we'll cover various ways to secure network connections, such as configuring SSL/TLS encryption.

A robust security strategy helps organizations maintain the confidentiality, integrity, and availability of their databases. MySQL provides several built-in security features to ensure that only authorized users can access and modify data. In this chapter, we will explore the various MySQL security concepts, types of security threats, and the importance of MySQL security.

Exploring Types of Security Threats

Databases are vulnerable to several types of security threats that can compromise the security of sensitive data. Attacks occur when a malicious user injects SQL commands into a query to gain unauthorized access to the database. Here are some common types of attacks:

SQL injection attacks
    Lead to data breaches, data loss, and data corruption.

Password attacks
    Involve brute-forcing or guessing passwords to gain access to the database. Weak passwords, password reuse, and password storage issues can make databases vulnerable to password attacks.

Denial-of-service (DoS) attacks
Aim to disrupt the normal operation of a database by overwhelming it with traffic or requests. DoS attacks can cause downtime, data loss, and data corruption.

Man-in-the-middle attacks
Compromise the confidentiality and integrity of data. Attacks occur when a third-party intercepts the communication between a client and a server to steal sensitive data.

Understanding the Importance of MySQL Security

MySQL security is crucial to protect sensitive data from unauthorized access, theft, and modification. A robust security strategy helps organizations comply with regulatory requirements and maintain the trust of their customers. Some of the benefits of MySQL security include the following:

Protection of sensitive data
MySQL security ensures that only authorized users can access and modify sensitive data. This helps protect against data breaches and data loss.

Compliance with regulatory requirements
Many industries have regulatory requirements that mandate the protection of sensitive data. MySQL security helps organizations comply with these requirements and avoid costly penalties.

Customer trust
Customers expect their data to be protected from unauthorized access and theft. A robust MySQL security strategy helps organizations maintain the trust of their customers.

Brute-force attacks involve guessing a user's username and password by trying combinations until the correct one is found. To prevent brute-force attacks, you can implement a password policy that requires users to choose strong passwords and limits the number of login attempts.

Performing Authentication and Authorization in MySQL

The MySQL database management system provides a variety of authentication and authorization mechanisms to secure data access. This section covers the fundamentals of MySQL authentication and authorization and provides detailed information on various types of authentication, creation of secure passwords, user privileges and permissions, and authentication plug-ins.

MySQL uses a pluggable authentication system that supports various authentication methods, including the following:

Caching SHA-2 pluggable authentication

The authentication plug-in `sha256_password` implements basic SHA-256 authentication for MySQL server connections. It securely hashes passwords by using the SHA-256 algorithm, providing a level of security against unauthorized access.

The `caching_sha2_password` authentication plug-in also utilizes SHA-256 for authentication. However, it enhances performance by implementing caching on the server side, leading to improved efficiency, especially in scenarios with high connection rates or multiple authentications.

Native authentication

This is based on the password stored in the MySQL user table. MySQL authenticates users by comparing their password with the one stored in the user table.

LDAP authentication

Allows MySQL to use an external Lightweight Directory Access Protocol (LDAP) server for authentication. This method can simplify authentication management by centralizing user accounts.

PAM authentication

Allows MySQL to use the pluggable authentication modules (PAM) provided by the operating system. This authentication method is highly flexible and can support various authentication mechanisms, such as two-factor authentication. Kerberos authentication provides a highly secure authentication mechanism that uses tickets to authenticate users. This method is commonly used in enterprise environments.

Windows native authentication

Allows MySQL to use Windows authentication for users. This method can simplify authentication management by using existing Windows user accounts.

Here are some example configurations for MySQL authentication and authorization with `caching_sha2_password`. To configure native authentication in MySQL, follow these steps:

1. Create a new MySQL user:

```
mysql> CREATE USER 'arun'@localhost IDENTIFIED WITH caching_sha2_password
BY 'ARU#G*12#T#HLpA';
Query OK, 0 rows affected (0.01 sec)

mysql>
```

2. Grant privileges to the user:

```
mysql> GRANT SELECT, INSERT, UPDATE ON sakila.* TO 'arun'@'localhost';
Query OK, 0 rows affected (0.00 sec)

mysql>
```

3. Verify the user's credentials:

```
[root@mysql80 ~]# mysql -u arun -p
Enter password:
Welcome to the MySQL monitor.  Commands end with ; or \g.
Your MySQL connection id is 33
Server version: 8.0.36 MySQL Community Server - GPL

Type help; or \h for help. Type \c to clear the current input
statement.

mysql>
```

4. Display a list of databases:

```
mysql> show databases;
+--------------------+
| Database           |
+--------------------+
| information_schema |
| performance_schema |
| sakila             |
+--------------------+
3 rows in set (0.01 sec)
```

This is just a simple example of the authentication and authorization mechanisms available in MySQL. By choosing the appropriate authentication and authorization methods and configuring them correctly, you can ensure that your MySQL server is secure and your data is protected.

Implementing a Password Policy

Implementing a password policy in MySQL is crucial for maintaining the security of your database system. A password policy defines rules and requirements that govern the creation and usage of passwords by users accessing the MySQL database. By enforcing a password policy, you can mitigate the risk of unauthorized access and enhance the overall security posture of your database environment.

Creating Secure Passwords

Creating secure passwords is an essential part of securing a MySQL server. MySQL provides a password policy that can help enforce password complexity requirements. A strong password policy can help prevent password cracking attacks. Here are some tips for creating secure passwords:

- Use a combination of upper- and lowercase letters, numbers, and special characters.
- Use long passwords (at least 8 characters).

- Avoid using easily guessable information, such as your name or birth date, in your password.

- Avoid using common passwords, such as password, 123456, admin, or qwerty.

- MySQL provides several password policies that can be used to enforce password strength requirements.

- Use a strong-password generator. This tool can help you generate a random combination of characters that meet the security criteria.

Create a user with limited login attempts

Configurable options, such as `FAILED_LOGIN_ATTEMPTS` and `PASSWORD_LOCK_TIME`, can be used with the `CREATE USER` and `ALTER USER` statements to enhance security. Here is an example that uses these options:

```
mysql> CREATE USER 'jey'@'localhost' IDENTIFIED BY 'ARU#G*12#T#HLpA'
FAILED_LOGIN_ATTEMPTS 5 PASSWORD_LOCK_TIME 4;
Query OK, 0 rows affected (0.01 sec)
mysql>
```

In this example, the user *jey@localhost* is created with a password, and the option `FAILED_LOGIN_ATTEMPTS` is set to 5 and `PASSWORD_LOCK_TIME` is set to 4, which means that if this user fails to log in four times consecutively, the account will be locked for three days.

In the following example, the option `FAILED_LOGIN_ATTEMPTS` is set to 3 and `PASS WORD_LOCK_TIME` is set to `UNBOUNDED` for the user *username@localhost*. This means that if this user fails to log in three times consecutively, the account will be locked indefinitely until an administrator unlocks it:

```
mysql> ALTER USER 'jey'@'localhost' FAILED_LOGIN_ATTEMPTS 3 PASSWORD_LOCK_TIME
UNBOUNDED;
Query OK, 0 rows affected (0.01 sec)

mysql>
```

Once a user has been set up with these options, an error message will be displayed if too many consecutive failed logins occur:

```
ERROR 3957 (HY000) : Access denied for user username.
```

The account is blocked for *D* day(s) (*R* day(s) remaining) due to *N* consecutive failed logins:

```
[root@mysql80 ~]# mysql -u jey -p
Enter password:
ERROR 1045 (28000): Access denied for user 'jey'@'localhost' (using password: NO)
[root@mysql80 ~]# mysql -u jey -p
Enter password:
ERROR 1045 (28000): Access denied for user 'jey'@'localhost' (using password: NO)
```

```
[root@mysql80 ~]# mysql -u jey -p
Enter password:
ERROR 3955 (HY000): Access denied for user 'jey'@'localhost'. Account is blocked
for unlimited day(s) (unlimited day(s) remaining) due to 3 consecutive
failed logins.
[root@mysql80 ~]#
```

This error message indicates that the account has been blocked for a certain number of days because of a certain number of consecutive failed logins. The remaining days are also displayed in the error message.

Create a password policy that requires strong passwords

Creating a password policy that requires strong passwords is essential for enhancing the security of your MySQL database. Strong passwords help protect against unauthorized access and various forms of cyber threats such as brute-force attacks and password guessing.

Use these queries to check whether the validate_password plug-in is installed:

```
mysql> pager grep -i validate_password;
PAGER set to 'grep -i validate_password'
mysql> SHOW PLUGINS;
48 rows in set (0.00 sec)

mysql>
```

Since the validate_password_policy plug-in is not installed or activated, as the preceding result shows, you can install it by running the following queries:

```
mysql> INSTALL PLUGIN validate_password SONAME 'validate_password.so';
Query OK, 0 rows affected, 1 warning (0.00 sec)

mysql>

mysql> pager grep -i validate_password;
PAGER set to 'grep -i validate_password'
mysql> show plugins;
| validate_password                | ACTIVE   | VALIDATE PASSWORD  |
validate_password.so | GPL       |
49 rows in set (0.00 sec)

mysql>
```

Then, activate the plug-in by setting the validate_password.policy system variable:

```
mysql> SET GLOBAL validate_password.policy=STRONG;
Query OK, 0 rows affected (0.00 sec)

mysql>
```

Set the global variable validate_password_length to 8. This variable determines the minimum length required for passwords:

```
mysql> SET GLOBAL validate_password_length=8;
Query OK, 0 rows affected (0.00 sec)

mysql>
```

Set the global variable validate_password.mixed_case_count to 1. This variable determines the minimum number of mixed-case (both uppercase and lowercase) characters required in a password:

```
mysql> SET GLOBAL validate_password.mixed_case_count=1;
Query OK, 0 rows affected (0.00 sec)

mysql>
```

Set the global variable validate_password.number_count to 1. This variable determines the minimum number of numeric (digit) characters required in a password:

```
mysql> SET GLOBAL validate_password.number_count=1;
Query OK, 0 rows affected (0.00 sec)

mysql>
```

To view global variables related to password validation, you can use the following SQL query. This query will display a list of global variables whose names match the pattern %validate_password%. It provides information about the current configuration of the MySQL server's password validation settings:

```
mysql> show global variables like '%validate_password%';
+-------------------------------------------------+--------+
| Variable_name                                   | Value  |
+-------------------------------------------------+--------+
| validate_password.changed_characters_percentage | 0      |
| validate_password.check_user_name               | ON     |
| validate_password.dictionary_file               |        |
| validate_password.length                        | 8      |
| validate_password.mixed_case_count              | 1      |
| validate_password.number_count                  | 1      |
| validate_password.policy                        | STRONG |
| validate_password.special_char_count            | 1      |
| validate_password_check_user_name               | ON     |
| validate_password_dictionary_file               |        |
| validate_password_length                        | 8      |
| validate_password_mixed_case_count              | 1      |
| validate_password_number_count                  | 1      |
| validate_password_policy                        | MEDIUM |
| validate_password_special_char_count            | 1      |
+-------------------------------------------------+--------+
15 rows in set (0.00 sec)

mysql>
```

In this example, you set the `validate_password_policy` option to `STRONG`, which requires passwords to contain at least one uppercase letter, one lowercase letter, one number, and one special character. You also set the `validate_password_length` option to 8, which requires passwords to be at least eight characters long.

By implementing these security measures, you can protect your MySQL database from brute-force attacks and ensure that your users are using strong passwords. Additionally, you can limit the number of login attempts for users to prevent attackers from guessing their passwords.

Installing DNF

The `yum install dnf -y` command is used in CentOS or RHEL operating systems to install the DNF package manager. CentOS and RHEL versions up to 7 used the yum package manager, but starting with CentOS/RHEL 8, DNF is the default package manager. However, if you are using an older version and want to switch to DNF, you can use the `yum install dnf -y` command to install DNF.

The `-y` option is used to automatically answer yes to any prompt that may appear during the installation process, without the need for user confirmation:

```
[root@mysql80 ~]# yum install dnf -y
Updating Subscription Management repositories.
Unable to read consumer identity

This system is not registered with an entitlement server.
You can use subscription-manager to register.
Last metadata expiration check: 1:44:38 ago on Wed 21 Feb 2024 09:37:07 AM UTC.
Dependencies resolved.
  Verifying        : dnf-4.14.0-8.el9.noarch
  1/1
Installed products updated.
Installed:
  dnf-4.14.0-8.el9.noarch
Complete!
[root@mysql80 ~]#
```

Installing pwgen

The pwgen package is a utility that generates random, pronounceable passwords. It can be used to generate passwords with different lengths, character sets, and complexity. The command `sudo dnf install pwgen` installs the pwgen package on a Linux system, using the DNF package manager with root privileges:

```
# sudo dnf install pwgen
Extra Packages for Enterprise Linux 7 - x86_64 54 MB/s | 17 MB 00:00
Percona Release Packages - Alternative Access 25 kB/s | 7.5 kB 00:00
…..
Installed:
```

```
pwgen-2.08-1.el7.x86_64
Complete!
```

The command `pwgen -s 12` generates a random password: `-s` specifies that the generated password should be completely random and not based on a pattern or algorithm, and `12` specifies the length of the password to be generated (in this case, 12 characters).

So this command will output a 12-character password consisting of random characters, symbols, and numbers:

```
# pwgen -s 12
9wPJJCXUE4N8 f2uFou6GXpNz uZks71qAyr0d dOHqxy1w1UKm PuqBF0Bhq8MK
l22xOzWp7mkf
Y0j6RkK807J6 ZI2jTugSfs4H EiOtlE40uMQs ie9OfpHLP032 AJVK5pWQxMJr
XGeT1lpcNvIu
…
I7aCHiqEyBR8 DhaphZR9hFC4 xCs1wvaWHgqy 7naYmOtw3ai4 D9UvCb0Z2O4H
YvbFK4NxwbxR
oNhdYLPTKD13 xehUDn53JUwg vzmt0qJubxs1 E1OQMZlgwoVR lZNIeZlNyr6K
IRcwIlDNVsR0
```

To configure password policies in MySQL, you can modify the MySQL configuration file (*my.cnf*). Here is an example configuration that sets the password policy to STRONG and enforces a minimum password length of 8 characters:

```
[mysqld]
validate_password.policy=STRONG
validate_password.length=8
```

Creating strong and secure passwords is an important aspect of securing your MySQL server. By using a strong password generator, avoiding common passwords, and enforcing password policies, you can ensure that your MySQL server is protected from unauthorized access.

A recently introduced system variable for password validation now allows users to set and implement a minimum requirement for the number of characters that need to be altered when they try to update their MySQL account passwords. This new verification option is based on a percentage of the total characters in the existing password. For instance, if the value of `validate_password.changed_characters_percentage` is set to 50, then at least half of the characters in the new password must differ from those in the current password; otherwise, the password change will be declined.

Using MySQL Authorization

MySQL authorization is the process of determining which operations a user can perform on a MySQL server. MySQL provides a robust authorization system that allows administrators to manage user privileges and permissions. *User privileges* control the operations that a user can perform, such as creating or deleting databases, while *user permissions* control the specific objects that a user can access, such as tables or columns.

To better illustrate the concept of MySQL authorization, let's consider an example scenario. Suppose you have a MySQL database that contains sensitive customer data, such as names, addresses, and credit card information. You want to ensure that only authorized users have access to this data and that they can perform only specific operations on it.

First, you would set up authentication rules for your users, using a secure authentication method such as SSL/TLS-based authentication. This would ensure that only users with valid credentials and a secure connection can access your database.

Next, you would set up authorization rules for your users based on their roles and responsibilities. For example, you might create three types of users:

Administrators
> These users have full access to the database and can perform any operation on it, including creating tables, modifying data, and dropping the database.

Analysts
> These users have read-only access to the database and can perform only operations such as querying data and generating reports.

Developers
> These users have read/write access to specific tables within the database and can modify data only in those tables.

To grant privileges to these users, you would use the GRANT statement to specify the type of privilege, object, and user/host combination. For example, to grant the user admin full access to all tables within the mydatabase database, you would use the following statement:

```
GRANT ALL PRIVILEGES ON mytestdb.* TO 'admin'@'localhost' IDENTIFIED BY
'password';
```

Similarly, to grant the user analyst only the ability to select data from all tables within the mydatabase database, you would use the following statement:

```
GRANT SELECT ON mydatabase.* TO 'analyst'@'localhost' IDENTIFIED BY
'password';
```

Finally, to grant the user developer the ability to insert and update data in the customers table within the mydatabase database, you would use the following statement:

```
GRANT INSERT, UPDATE ON mydatabase.customers TO 'developer'@'localhost'
IDENTIFIED BY 'password';
```

By setting up authentication and authorization rules for your users, and granting them specific privileges based on their roles and responsibilities, you can ensure that your MySQL database is secure and accessible by only authorized users.

Understanding User Privileges and Permissions

MySQL provides a wide range of user privileges that can be used to control user access to the server. These are some of the most commonly used user privileges:

SELECT
> Allows a user to select data from a table

INSERT
> Allows a user to insert data into a table

UPDATE
> Allows a user to update data in a table

DELETE
> Allows a user to delete data from a table

CREATE
> Allows a user to create new databases and tables

DROP
> Allows a user to delete databases and tables

MySQL also allows for a granular level of control over user privileges and permissions. This allows you to control who can access and manipulate specific databases, tables, and even individual columns.

Global privileges, for example, are applied to the entire MySQL server, including all databases and tables. Examples of global privileges include the following:

CREATE USER
> Allows the user to create new MySQL users

RELOAD
> Allows the user to reload server settings and flush caches

SHUTDOWN
> Allows the user to shut down the MySQL server

Database privileges are applied to specific databases within the MySQL server. Here are some examples of database privileges:

CREATE
> Allows the user to create new tables within the specified database

ALTER

Allows the user to modify the structure of existing tables within the specified database

DROP

Allows the user to delete tables within the specified database

Table privileges are applied to specific tables within a database. Examples of table privileges include the following:

SELECT

Allows the user to retrieve data from the specified table

INSERT

Allows the user to add new data to the specified table

UPDATE

Allows the user to modify existing data within the specified table

Column privileges are applied to specific columns within a table. Here are some examples of column privileges:

SELECT

Allows the user to retrieve data from the specified column

INSERT

Allows the user to add new data to the specified column

UPDATE

Allows the user to modify existing data within the specified column

MySQL version 8.2.0 has a total of 72 privileges. You can view and enumerate all these privileges by executing the SHOW PRIVILEGES statement:

```
mysql> SHOW PRIVILEGES\G
********* 1. row *********
Privilege: Alter
  Context: Tables
  Comment: To alter the table
********* 2. row *********
Privilege: Alter routine
  Context: Functions,Procedures
  Comment: To alter or drop stored functions/procedures
********* 3. row *********
Privilege: Create
  Context: Databases,Tables,Indexes
  Comment: To create new databases and tables
********* 4. row *********
Privilege: Create routine
  Context: Databases
```

```
   Comment: To use CREATE FUNCTION/PROCEDURE
********* 5. row *********
Privilege: Create role
  Context: Server Admin
  Comment: To create new roles
********* 6. row *********
Privilege: Create temporary tables
  Context: Databases
  Comment: To use CREATE TEMPORARY TABLE
********* 7. row *********
```

To grant privileges to a MySQL user, use the GRANT command. Here is an example:

```
GRANT SELECT, INSERT, UPDATE ON mydatabase.* TO 'myuser'@'localhost';
```

This command grants the user *myuser@localhost* the SELECT, INSERT, and UPDATE privileges on all tables within the mydatabase database. Note that the * character is used to apply the privileges to all tables within the specified database.

User privileges and permissions are an important aspect of securing your MySQL server. By granting appropriate privileges to specific users and limiting their access to specific databases, tables, and columns, you can ensure that your data is protected and your MySQL server is secure.

Using MySQL Authentication Plug-ins

MySQL authentication plug-ins provide additional authentication mechanisms that can be used to enhance the security of a MySQL server. The following are some commonly used authentication plug-ins:

SHA256 Password Authentication
    Uses the SHA-256 hashing algorithm to store passwords securely

PAM Authentication plug-in
    Allows MySQL to use the authentication modules provided by the OS

LDAP Authentication plug-in
    Allows MySQL to use an external LDAP server for authentication

Kerberos Authentication plug-in
    Provides a highly secure authentication mechanism using tickets

Windows Native Authentication plug-in
    Allows MySQL to use Windows authentication for user authentication

---

Securing MySQL Communication

It is essential to secure the communication channel between the MySQL server and client to protect sensitive data from unauthorized access. Following are the various measures that can be taken to ensure the security of MySQL communication.

SSL/TLS Encryption

Secure Sockets Layer (SSL) and Transport Layer Security (TLS) are cryptographic protocols that ensure the secure communication of data over the internet. SSL and TLS encryption provide a secure connection between the MySQL server and client, protecting against eavesdropping and data theft. SSL and TLS encryption can be enabled on both the MySQL server and client to ensure secure communication.

SSL certificates (self-signed) are generated automatically in MySQL, eliminating the default necessity of using `mysql_ssl_rsa_setup` (though you can still use it if desired). To configure SSL/TLS on the MySQL server, take the following steps:

1. Using the `ls` command, list all files with a *.pem* extension in the data directory. If the `auto_generate_certs` system variable is enabled upon startup, SSL options (other than `--ssl`) are not specified, the server-side SSL files are absent from the data directory, and the server automatically generates server-side and client-side SSL certificate and key files in the data directory:

   ```
   [root@mysql80 ~]# ls -ltr /var/lib/mysql/*.pem)
   -rw-------. 1 mysql mysql 1705 Feb 20 07:37 /var/lib/mysql/ca-key.pem
   -rw-r--r--. 1 mysql mysql 1112 Feb 20 07:37 /var/lib/mysql/ca.pem
   -rw-------. 1 mysql mysql 1705 Feb 20 07:37 /var/lib/mysql/server-key.pem
   -rw-r--r--. 1 mysql mysql 1112 Feb 20 07:37 /var/lib/mysql/server-cert.pem
   -rw-------. 1 mysql mysql 1705 Feb 20 07:37 /var/lib/mysql/client-key.pem
   -rw-r--r--. 1 mysql mysql 1112 Feb 20 07:37 /var/lib/mysql/client-cert.pem
   -rw-------. 1 mysql mysql 1705 Feb 20 07:37 /var/lib/mysql/private_key.pem
   -rw-r--r--. 1 mysql mysql  452 Feb 20 07:37 /var/lib/mysql/public_key.pem
   [root@mysql80 ~]#
   ```

2. Edit the MySQL configuration file located at */etc/mysql/my.cnf*. Open the file in a text editor and add the following lines to the `mysqld section`:

   ```
   [client]
   ssl-mode=REQUIRED
   ssl-cert=/var/lib/mysql/client-cert.pem
   ssl-key=/var/lib/mysql/client-key.pem

   [mysqld]
   ssl-ca=/var/lib/mysql/ca.pem
   ssl-cert=/var/lib/mysql/server-cert.pem
   ssl-key=/var/lib/mysql/server-key.pem
   ssl-cipher=AES256-SHA
   ```

3. Verify the *my.cnf* and the SSL configurations:

```
[root@mysql80 ~]# grep -i ssl /etc/my.cnf
ssl-ca=/var/lib/mysql/ca.pem
ssl-cert=/var/lib/mysql/server-cert.pem
ssl-key=/var/lib/mysql/server-key.pem
ssl-cipher=AES256-SHA
ssl-mode=REQUIRED
ssl-cert=/var/lib/mysql/client-cert.pem
ssl-key=/var/lib/mysql/client-key.pem
[root@mysql80 ~]#
```

4. Restart MySQL:

```
[root@mysql80 ~]# sudo systemctl restart mysqld
[root@mysql80 ~]#
```

5. Log in and ensure that SSL is activated:

```
mysql> \s
--------------
mysql  Ver 8.0.36 for Linux on x86_64 (MySQL Community Server - GPL)

Connection id:          8
Current user:           root@localhost
SSL:                    Cipher in use is TLS_AES_256_GCM_SHA384
Server version:         8.0.36 MySQL Community Server - GPL
Uptime:                 1 min 14 sec
--------------

mysql>
```

In addition to SSL/TLS encryption, other measures can be taken to secure MySQL connections. These measures include the following:

- Using strong passwords and changing them regularly
- Limiting access to the MySQL server by configuring firewall rules
- Disabling unnecessary MySQL services and features
- Using secure authentication mechanisms, such as SHA-256 password authentication

Creating a new MySQL user account with restricted privileges

If SSL encryption is enabled in MySQL, before proceeding with the code to create a new MySQL user account with SSL, let's first understand how to create a new MySQL user account with limited privileges. The first user account will permit connection without SSL encryption, while users created with the requirement for SSL will establish connections with SSL encryption. Therefore, ensure you create users with the required SSL for enhanced security.

The following CREATE USER query will create user1 and allow connections without SSL encryption:

```
mysql> CREATE USER 'user1'@'localhost' IDENTIFIED BY 'QH1f9ulmHAOv#';
Query OK, 0 rows affected (0.03 sec)

mysql>
```

When creating a user, you can also include REQUIRE SSL to ensure the use of an encrypted connection:

```
mysql> CREATE USER 'user1'@'\localhost' IDENTIFIED BY 'QH1f9ulmHAOv#'
REQUIRE SSL;
Query OK, 0 rows affected (0.01 sec)

mysql> GRANT SELECT, INSERT, UPDATE, DELETE ON mytestdb.* TO 'user1'@'localhost';
Query OK, 0 rows affected (0.01 sec)

mysql>
```

This command creates a new user account named user1 with a password of *QH1f9ulm HAOv#* and grants it only the minimum privileges needed for its intended use. In this example, the user account is granted SELECT, INSERT, UPDATE, and DELETE privileges on a database named mydatabase.

Using strong passwords for all MySQL user accounts

Passwords should be at least eight characters long and include a combination of letters, numbers, and symbols:

```
mysql> ALTER USER 'user1'@'localhost' IDENTIFIED BY 'KDU#G*12#T#HLpoA$
5&*0Qws';
Query OK, 0 rows affected (0.01 sec)

mysql>
```

This command changes the password for the user account named user1 to a new strong password.

Disabling plain-text passwords when connecting to the MySQL server

This configuration option requires all connections to use SSL/TLS encryption and prevents the use of plain-text passwords:

```
[mysqld]
require_secure_transport = on
```

Configure the MySQL server to log all connection attempts and activity:

```
[mysqld]
general_log = on
```

This option logs all SQL queries executed on the MySQL server, including connection attempts and user authentication. Enabling the general log can negatively impact performance, especially under heavy workloads. Consider using an audit plug-in as an alternative, which may be more suitable.

Firewall Rules

Firewall rules can be used to control access to the MySQL server and limit incoming connections to authorized IP addresses or network ranges. For example:

```
iptables -A INPUT -p tcp --dport 3306 -s 192.168.1.0/24 -j ACCEPT
iptables -A INPUT -p tcp --dport 3306 -j DROP
```

These commands allow incoming connections to the MySQL server only from the IP address range 192.168.1.0/24 and block all other incoming connections. Note that these commands use iptables, which is a commonly used firewall program on Linux systems. The specific commands may vary depending on the firewall program being used.

By following these suggestions for securing MySQL connections, sensitive data can be protected from unauthorized access or interception, ensuring the integrity and confidentiality of the data transmitted over the network.

A firewall isn't really related to MySQL. It can be done anywhere on the network, not necessarily from the packet filter of the operating system. Here's an example of how to configure firewall rules for a MySQL server running in an Ubuntu operating system:

1. Identify the firewall software running on the server. For example, if using the UFW firewall on an Ubuntu server, the following command can be used to check its status:

   ```
   root@MyUbuntuMysql8:~# sudo ufw status
   Status: inactive
   root@MyUbuntuMysql8:~#
   ```

2. Add rules to the firewall to allow incoming MySQL connections from authorized IP addresses or network ranges. For example, to allow incoming connections to the MySQL server from IP address 192.168.13.71, the following command can be used:

   ```
   root@MyUbuntuMysql8:~# sudo ufw allow from 192.168.13.71 to any port 3306
   Rules updated
   root@MyUbuntuMysql8:~#
   ```

   This command allows incoming connections to port 3306 (the default port for MySQL) from IP address 192.168.13.71.

3. Deny all other incoming MySQL connections to the server. For example, to deny all incoming connections to port 3306 except those allowed in step 2, the following command can be used:

```
root@MyUbuntuMysql8:~# sudo ufw deny 3306/tcp
Rules updated
Rules updated (v6)
root@MyUbuntuMysql8:~#
```

This command denies all incoming connections to port 3306 (the default port for MySQL) that are not explicitly allowed in step 2.

After these steps, only authorized IP addresses or network ranges are allowed to connect to the MySQL server, and all other incoming connections are blocked.

SSL/TLS encryption, secure authentication mechanisms, and firewall rules can all be used to ensure the security of MySQL communication. By following these steps, you can ensure that your MySQL server is secure and protected against unauthorized access and data theft.

User Account Locking

MySQL allows you to lock and unlock user accounts to prevent unauthorized access to the database. The following commands demonstrate how to lock and unlock user accounts, respectively:

```
mysql> ALTER USER 'newuser'@'localhost' ACCOUNT LOCK;
Query OK, 0 rows affected (0.01 sec)

mysql>

mysql> ALTER USER 'newuser'@'localhost' ACCOUNT UNLOCK;
Query OK, 0 rows affected (0.00 sec)

mysql>
```

Managing MySQL Roles

One of the key features of MySQL is its support for role-based access control (RBAC), which allows DBAs to assign permissions to roles instead of individual users. This provides an efficient way to manage user access and simplify database administration.

MySQL roles are collections of privileges that can be assigned to users. They allow administrators to define sets of permissions and apply them to multiple users, simplifying database management. Roles can also be granted to other roles, allowing for hierarchical role structures.

Creating and Managing MySQL Roles

Creating a role in MySQL is a straightforward process. You can use the following SQL statement to create a new role:

```
mysql> CREATE ROLE sales;
Query OK, 0 rows affected (0.01 sec)

mysql>
```

Once the role is created, privileges can be assigned to it by using the GRANT statement. For example, the following statement grants SELECT and INSERT privileges on the employees table to the sales role:

```
mysql> GRANT SELECT, INSERT ON employees TO sales;
Query OK, 0 rows affected (0.01 sec)

mysql>
```

Roles can also be altered or dropped by using the ALTER ROLE and DROP ROLE statements, respectively.

Assigning Roles to Users

Once roles have been created and privileges assigned to them, they can be assigned to users. This is done using the SET ROLE statement. For example, the following statement assigns the sales role to the user jdoe:

```
SET ROLE sales TO 'jdoe'@'localhost';
```

It's also possible to grant a role to a user at the same time the user is created. For example, the following statement creates a new user jsmith and grants them the sales role:

```
mysql> CREATE USER 'jsmith'@localhost IDENTIFIED BY 'DE13gllmHAOv%';
Query OK, 0 rows affected (0.01 sec)

mysql> GRANT sales TO 'jsmith'@'localhost';
Query OK, 0 rows affected (0.01 sec)

mysql>
```

This SQL query retrieves information related to roles in MySQL:

```
mysql> SELECT any_value(User) 'Role Name',
    ->        IF(any_value(from_user) is NULL,'No', 'Yes') Active,
    ->        count(to_user) 'Assigned #times'
    -> FROM mysql.user
    -> LEFT JOIN mysql.role_edges ON from_user=user
    -> WHERE account_locked='Y' AND password_expired='Y'
    -> AND authentication_string='' GROUP BY(user);
+-----------+--------+-----------------+
| Role Name | Active | Assigned #times |
+-----------+--------+-----------------+
| sales     | Yes    |               1 |
+-----------+--------+-----------------+
1 row in set (0.00 sec)
```

Using InnoDB Data-at-Rest Encryption

Data security is a top priority in today's digital world, and protecting sensitive information stored in databases is crucial. InnoDB offers comprehensive data-at-rest encryption for various components, including file-per-table tablespaces, general tablespaces, the MySQL system tablespace, redo logs, and undo logs.

Data-at-rest encryption ensures that the data stored on disk is encrypted, providing an additional layer of security for sensitive information. It scrambles data stored in InnoDB tablespaces and individual tables by using powerful algorithms like Advanced Encryption Standard (AES). This renders the data unreadable to anyone without the decryption key, even if they gain physical access to the storage device.

InnoDB's two-tier encryption key architecture involves a master encryption key and tablespace keys. Tablespace keys are encrypted and stored in the tablespace header, providing security for the actual data. Access to encrypted data involves decrypting the tablespace key by using the master encryption key. While the decrypted tablespace key remains consistent, the master encryption key can be changed through the master-key rotation process for security maintenance.

MySQL 8 introduces a comprehensive encryption architecture to enhance data security. Here's an overview of the key encryption elements and their functionalities:

Two-tier encryption key architecture
> The first tier is the master encryption key. The second tier consists of tablespace keys.

Tablespace encryption
> When a tablespace is designated for encryption, a specific tablespace key is generated. This tablespace key is then encrypted and securely stored in the header of the corresponding tablespace. The encryption of the tablespace key ensures that the actual data within the tablespace remains protected.

Access to encrypted tablespace data
> When an application or an authenticated user needs to access data within an encrypted tablespace, InnoDB comes into play. InnoDB utilizes the master encryption key to decrypt the stored tablespace key. The tablespace key, once decrypted using the master encryption key, provides access to the encrypted data within the tablespace.

Decrypted tablespace key consistency
> It's important to note that the decrypted version of the tablespace key remains constant. Even though the tablespace key is encrypted when stored, once decrypted, its form does not change. This consistency ensures reliable and predictable access to the encrypted data.

Master-key rotation

The master encryption key, being the higher-level key in the two-tier architecture, can be changed as needed. When there is a requirement to modify the master encryption key, the process is known as *master-key rotation*. Master-key rotation enhances security by updating the primary key used for decrypting tablespace keys.

Installing Keyring Components for Encryption

To enable the functionality of a keyring component or plug-in, it is imperative to install and configure it during the startup phase of the system. The early loading of this component or plug-in is crucial as it ensures availability before the initiation of the InnoDB storage engine. This preemptive measure guarantees that the necessary tools for managing encryption keys are in place and ready for use when the InnoDB storage engine initializes. Examples of keyring plug-ins include `keyring_file` or `keyring_encrypted_file`. These plug-ins handle the storage and retrieval of encryption keys. To confirm the status of the keyring component or plug-in, you can execute the following SQL query:

```
mysql> pager grep -i keyring_file;
PAGER set to 'grep -i keyring_file'
mysql> SHOW PLUGINS;
46 rows in set (0.00 sec)
mysql>
```

The `pager` command is used to pipe the output of `SHOW PLUGINS` through the `grep` command, specifically looking for lines that contain the case-insensitive string `keyring_file`. Look for the entry related to the keyring component or plug-in in the result set. Ensure that the status is marked as `ACTIVE` to verify that it has been successfully installed and is ready for operation.

In this example, the result shows that the keyring plug-in is not installed and therefore needs to be installed. The installation is typically done using the `INSTALL PLUGIN` statement, specifying the plug-in's name and the shared object (*.so*) file as given:

```
mysql> INSTALL PLUGIN keyring_file SONAME 'keyring_file.so';
Query OK, 0 rows affected (0.08 sec)
mysql>

mysql> pager grep -i keyring_file; SHOW PLUGINS;
PAGER set to 'grep -i keyring_file'
| keyring_file                  | ACTIVE   | KEYRING
| keyring_file.so | GPL     |
47 rows in set (0.00 sec)
```

The `keyring_file` plug-in is configured to use a file named *keyring* located in the directory */var/lib/mysql-keyring/* to store the keys. The default value of the variable is

platform-specific. For DEB, RPM, and Unix System V Release 4 (SVR4) systems, the
default path is set to */var/lib/mysql-keyring/keyring*:

```
mysql> select @@keyring_file_data;
+------------------------------+
| @@keyring_file_data          |
+------------------------------+
| /var/lib/mysql-keyring/keyring |
+------------------------------+
1 row in set (0.00 sec)
root@mysql8:/var/lib/mysql-keyring# ls
keyring
root@mysql8:/var/lib/mysql-keyring#
```

Setting the Default Table Encryption

The default_table_encryption system variable sets the default encryption behavior
for newly created schemas or general tablespaces. This variable is set to OFF by
default. This variable controls whether tables are encrypted by default or not.

Let's examine the behavior of the variable when it's set to both ON and OFF, considering both session and global levels to understand its behavior comprehensively. This
next query results in the value 0 for the default_table_encryption variable, indicating that default table encryption is disabled:

```
mysql> select @@default_table_encryption;
+---------------------------+
| @@default_table_encryption |
+---------------------------+
|                         0 |
+---------------------------+
1 row in set (0.00 sec)
```

Set default_table_encryption globally:

```
-- Set the global default to create tables with encryption
SET GLOBAL default_table_encryption = 'ON';
```

Now, any new tables created in the MySQL instance will be encrypted by default. You
can also set the default table encryption for a particular session, as shown here:

```
-- Set the session default to create tables without encryption
SET SESSION default_table_encryption = 'OFF';
```

For the current session, any new tables created will not be encrypted by default. You
can then check the current global or session setting, respectively, as follows:

```
mysql> SHOW VARIABLES LIKE 'default_table_encryption';
+---------------------------+-------+
| Variable_name             | Value |
+---------------------------+-------+
| default_table_encryption  | ON    |
```

```
+---------------------------+-------+
1 row in set (0.00 sec)

mysql> SHOW SESSION VARIABLES LIKE 'default_table_encryption';
+---------------------------+-------+
| Variable_name             | Value |
+---------------------------+-------+
| default_table_encryption  | ON    |
+---------------------------+-------+
1 row in set (0.00 sec)
```

When the `default_table_encryption` is enabled, all tables in the subsequently created database are encrypted by default:

```
mysql> create database encryptedschema;
Query OK, 1 row affected (0.00 sec)

mysql> use encryptedschema;
Database changed

mysql> CREATE TABLE encrypted_table (
    ->     id INT PRIMARY KEY,
    ->     data VARCHAR(255)
    -> );
Query OK, 0 rows affected (0.06 sec)

mysql> show create table encrypted_table\G
*************************** 1. row ***************************
       Table: encrypted_table
Create Table: CREATE TABLE `encrypted_table` (
  `id` int NOT NULL,
  `data` varchar(255) DEFAULT NULL,
  PRIMARY KEY (`id`)
) ENGINE=InnoDB DEFAULT CHARSET=utf8mb4 COLLATE=utf8mb4_0900_ai_ci ENCRYPTION='Y'
1 row in set (0.00 sec)
```

The table `encrypted_table` has been successfully created within the `encrypted schema` database. The ENCRYPTION=Y in the output indicates that the table is encrypted, which aligns with the enabled `default_table_encryption` setting.

Turn off `default_table_encryption` for the current session. You can now proceed to create a database and a table and check whether the table is encrypted within the schema after disabling the `default_table_encryption` variable:

```
mysql> SET SESSION default_table_encryption = 'OFF';
Query OK, 0 rows affected (0.00 sec)

mysql> SHOW SESSION VARIABLES LIKE 'default_table_encryption';
+---------------------------+-------+
| Variable_name             | Value |
+---------------------------+-------+
| default_table_encryption  | OFF   |
```

```
+---------------------------+-------+
1 row in set (0.00 sec)
```

The `default_table_encryption` for the current session has been successfully set to OFF. Create an unencrypted schema:

```
mysql> create database unencryptedschema;
Query OK, 1 row affected (0.01 sec)

mysql> use unencryptedschema;
Database changed

mysql> CREATE TABLE unencrypted_table (
    ->      id INT PRIMARY KEY,
    ->      data VARCHAR(255)
    -> );
Query OK, 0 rows affected (0.03 sec)

mysql> show create table unencrypted_table\G
*************************** 1. row ***************************
       Table: unencrypted_table
Create Table: CREATE TABLE `unencrypted_table` (
  `id` int NOT NULL,
  `data` varchar(255) DEFAULT NULL,
  PRIMARY KEY (`id`)
) ENGINE=InnoDB DEFAULT CHARSET=utf8mb4 COLLATE=utf8mb4_0900_ai_ci
1 row in set (0.00 sec)
mysql>
```

The table creation details confirm that the table is using the InnoDB engine and is not encrypted, in line with the disabled default encryption setting for the session.

Checking Encryption Status

Now that you've set up your default table encryption, it's time to check its status. You can use the following select query to check the table's status in the 'encrypted schema' or 'unencryptedschema' databases.

This query retrieves information about tables in the specified databases. Focus on the `CREATE_OPTIONS` column to check if encryption is enabled for each table. The output shows that `encrypted_table` has encryption enabled (`ENCRYPTION=Y`), while `unencrypted_table` does not have specific encryption options set:

```
mysql> SELECT TABLE_SCHEMA, TABLE_NAME, CREATE_OPTIONS FROM
INFORMATION_SCHEMA.TABLES WHERE TABLE_SCHEMA IN ('encryptedschema',
'unencryptedschema');
+-------------------+-------------------+----------------+
| TABLE_SCHEMA      | TABLE_NAME        | CREATE_OPTIONS |
+-------------------+-------------------+----------------+
| unencryptedschema | unencrypted_table |                |
| encryptedschema   | encrypted_table   | ENCRYPTION='Y' |
```

```
+-------------------+-------------------+----------------+
2 rows in set (0.00 sec)
mysql>
```

Alternatively, you can use INFORMATION_SCHEMA.INNODB_TABLESPACES to retrieve details about encrypted tables. This query will also display information about whether any general tablespace is encrypted:

```
mysql> select NAME,ENCRYPTION from INFORMATION_SCHEMA.INNODB_TABLESPACES
where ENCRYPTION='Y';
+-----------------------------------+------------+
| NAME                              | ENCRYPTION |
+-----------------------------------+------------+
| encryptedschemac/encrypted_table  | Y          |
+-----------------------------------+------------+
2 rows in set (0.00 sec)
```

To identify encrypted schemas, you can utilize the following query:

```
mysql> select SCHEMA_NAME,DEFAULT_ENCRYPTION from INFORMATION_SCHEMA.SCHEMATA
WHERE DEFAULT_ENCRYPTION='YES';
+-----------------+--------------------+
| SCHEMA_NAME     | DEFAULT_ENCRYPTION |
+-----------------+--------------------+
| encryptedschema | YES                |
+-----------------+--------------------+
1 row in set (0.00 sec)
```

Performing General Tablespaces Encryption

A general tablespace within MySQL serves as a versatile storage area capable of housing multiple databases and tables. Using general tablespaces enhances storage management flexibility and streamlines database operations. This section illustrates the creation and encryption of a general tablespace:

1. A directory named *user_defined_general_tablespace* is created in the */var/lib/* directory:

   ```
   root@mysql8:/var/lib# mkdir user_defined_general_tablespace
   ```

2. Change the ownership of the directory to the MySQL user (*mysql.mysql*):

   ```
   root@mysql8:/var/lib# chown -R mysql.mysql user_defined_general_tablespace
   root@mysql8:/var/lib#
   ```

3. Verify the innodb_directories variable is set to empty:

   ```
   mysql> SHOW VARIABLES LIKE 'innodb_directories';
   +--------------------+-------+
   | Variable_name      | Value |
   +--------------------+-------+
   | innodb_directories |       |
   ```

```
+--------------------+-------+
1 row in set (0.00 sec)
```

4. Add the `innodb_directories` variable in the configuration file (*mysqld.cnf*) to point to the previously created directory:

```
root@mysql8:/etc/mysql/mysql.conf.d# vi /etc/mysql/mysql.conf.d/mysqld.cnf
root@mysql8:/etc/mysql/mysql.conf.d# cat /etc/mysql/mysql.conf.d/mysqld.cnf
| grep -i innodb_directories
innodb_directories=/var/lib/user_defined_general_tablespace
root@mysql8:/etc/mysql/mysql.conf.d#
```

5. Restart MySQL to apply the configuration changes:

```
mysql> RESTART;
Query OK, 0 rows affected (0.00 sec)

mysql>

mysql> SHOW VARIABLES LIKE 'innodb_directories';
+--------------------+-----------------------------------------+
| Variable_name      | Value                                   |
+--------------------+-----------------------------------------+
| innodb_directories | /var/lib/user_defined_general_tablespace |
+--------------------+-----------------------------------------+
1 row in set (0.00 sec)
mysql>
```

6. Enable the variable:

```
mysql> SET GLOBAL default_table_encryption = 'ON';
Query OK, 0 rows affected (0.00 sec)
mysql>

mysql> SHOW VARIABLES LIKE 'default_table_encryption';
+--------------------------+-------+
| Variable_name            | Value |
+--------------------------+-------+
| default_table_encryption | ON    |
+--------------------------+-------+
1 row in set (0.00 sec)
```

7. Create a general tablespace in the specified directory:

```
mysql> CREATE TABLESPACE user_defined_general_tablespace
    -> ADD DATAFILE 'user_defined_general_tablespace.ibd'
    -> ENGINE=InnoDB;
Query OK, 0 rows affected (0.04 sec)
The provided query will create the user_defined_general_tablespace,
automatically designating it as an 'encrypted' tablespace due to the
'default_table_encryption' being set to ON. Alternatively,
you have the option to explicitly indicate encryption for the
tablespace by using the ENCRYPTION = 'Y' parameter.
mysql> CREATE TABLESPACE user_defined_general_tablespace_1
    -> ADD DATAFILE 'user_defined_general_tablespace_1.ibd'
```

```
-> ENCRYPTION = 'Y'
-> ENGINE=InnoDB;
Query OK, 0 rows affected (0.05 sec)
```

8. Try to create an unencrypted table within an encrypted tablespace. You can create an encrypted table within the encrypted general tablespace with the attribute ENCRYPTION=Y. This CREATE TABLE is an example:

```
mysql> use unencryptedschema;
Database changed
mysql>

mysql> CREATE TABLE encrypted_table_in_general_tablespace(
    ->      id INT PRIMARY KEY,
    ->      data VARCHAR(255)
    -> ) TABLESPACE user_defined_general_tablespace;
ERROR 3825 (HY000): Request to create 'unencrypted' table while using
an 'encrypted' tablespace.
mysql>
```

9. Try to create an encrypted table in an encrypted tablespace. An encrypted table named encrypted_table_in_general_tablespace with the attribute ENCRYPTION='Y' can be created within the designated general tablespace while having encryption enabled:

```
mysql> CREATE TABLE encrypted_table_in_general_tablespace(
    ->      id INT PRIMARY KEY,
    ->      data VARCHAR(255)
    -> ) TABLESPACE user_defined_general_tablespace ENCRYPTION='Y';
Query OK, 0 rows affected (0.02 sec)
```

The show create table shows that the table encryption is enabled (ENCRYPTION=Y):

```
mysql> show create table encrypted_table_in_general_tablespace\G
*************************** 1. row ***************************
       Table: encrypted_table_in_general_tablespace
Create Table: CREATE TABLE `encrypted_table_in_general_tablespace` (
  `id` int NOT NULL,
  `data` varchar(255) DEFAULT NULL,
  PRIMARY KEY (`id`)
) /*!50100 TABLESPACE `user_defined_general_tablespace` */ ENGINE=InnoDB DEFAULT
CHARSET=utf8mb4 COLLATE=utf8mb4_0900_ai_ci /*!80016 ENCRYPTION='Y' */
1 row in set (0.00 sec)
```

An exclusively encrypted tablespace contains encrypted tables, just as an encrypted schema exclusively consists of encrypted tables.

Encrypting Doublewrites

Starting from MySQL 8.0.23, InnoDB offers encryption for doublewrite files. Automatic encryption is applied to doublewrite file pages in encrypted tablespaces, requiring no additional steps. These pages use the encryption key from the associated tablespace. Encrypted doublewrite file pages are decrypted and checked for corruption during recovery. Pages from an unencrypted tablespace in the doublewrite file remain unencrypted.

Encrypting the MySQL System Tablespace

MySQL 8.0.16 introduced encryption support for the `mysql` system tablespace, which houses the `mysql` system database and MySQL data dictionary tables. By default, the system tablespace is unencrypted. To enable or disable encryption, use `ALTER TABLE SPACE` statements, as shown in the following examples.

To enable encryption:

```
mysql> ALTER TABLESPACE mysql ENCRYPTION = 'Y';
Query OK, 0 rows affected (3.78 sec)
```

To disable encryption:

```
mysql> ALTER TABLESPACE mysql ENCRYPTION = 'N';
Query OK, 0 rows affected (3.43 sec)
```

Encryption requires the `CREATE TABLESPACE` privilege on all tables in the instance.

Encrypting Redo Logs

Redo log data encryption, controlled by the `innodb_redo_log_encrypt` option, is disabled by default. Encryption occurs when writing to disk and is decrypted during read operations. The encryption key is used for both encryption and decryption. Metadata storage changed in MySQL 8.0.30; earlier versions stored metadata in the first redo logfile. Removal of the file with encryption metadata disables redo log encryption.

> Once redo log encryption is enabled, normal restart without the encryption key or keyring component is not possible.

Encrypting Undo Logs

Undo log data encryption, governed by `innodb_undo_log_encrypt`, is disabled by default. Similar to redo log encryption, it occurs during write and read operations. The encryption key handles both encryption and decryption. Metadata, including the encryption key, is stored in the undo logfile header.

Rotating the Master Key

Rotate the master encryption key periodically or when compromised. This instance-level operation re-encrypts all tablespace keys. The operation is atomic, and if interrupted by a server failure, InnoDB rolls it forward on restart. Rotation requires the ENCRYPTION_KEY_ADMIN privilege. To rotate, use the following:

```
root@mysql8:~# ls -ltr /var/lib/mysql-keyring/
total 4
-rw-r----- 1 mysql mysql 187 Jan 27 19:02 keyring
root@mysql8:

mysql> ALTER INSTANCE ROTATE INNODB MASTER KEY;
Query OK, 0 rows affected (0.01 sec)

mysql>
root@mysql8: ls -ltr /var/lib/mysql-keyring/
total 4
-rw-r----- 1 mysql mysql 315 Jan 28 07:31 keyring
root@mysql8:~#
```

Rotation cannot run concurrently with tablespace encryption operations; locks prevent conflicts. The operation changes only the master encryption key and re-encrypts tablespace keys; it does not affect tablespace data.

Safeguarding the Encryption Key

When encrypting production data, safeguard the master encryption key to prevent irreversible data loss. For components like component_keyring_file or component_keyring_encrypted_file, and plug-ins like keyring_file or keyring_encrypted_file, immediately back up the keyring data file after creating the first encrypted tablespace, before and after master-key rotation. Check each component's configuration file for the data file location. Configure the keyring_file_data and keyring_encrypted_file_data options for their respective plug-ins. For keyring_okv or keyring_aws plug-ins, ensure proper configuration has been performed:

```
mysql> show variables like 'keyring_file_data';
+-------------------+-------------------------------+
| Variable_name     | Value                         |
+-------------------+-------------------------------+
| keyring_file_data | /var/lib/mysql-keyring/keyring |
+-------------------+-------------------------------+
1 row in set (0.00 sec)
root@mysql8:/var/lib# ls -ltr /var/lib/mysql-keyring/
total 4
-rw-r----- 1 mysql mysql 187 Jan 27 19:02 keyring
root@mysql8:/var/lib#
root@mysql8:/var/lib/mysql-keyring# service mysql stop
root@mysql8:/var/lib/mysql-keyring#
```

```
root@mysql8:/var/lib/mysql-keyring# mv keyring /root/
root@mysql8:/var/lib/mysql-keyring# ls -ltr
total 0
root@mysql8:/var/lib/mysql-keyring# service mysql start
root@mysql8:/var/lib/mysql-keyring#
```

Because of the absence of the keyring, querying encrypted tables results in the following error:

```
mysql> select * from encrypted_table;
ERROR 3185 (HY000): Can't find master key from keyring, please check in the
server log if a keyring is loaded and initialized successfully.
mysql>
```

The corresponding errors are logged in the MySQL error log:

```
2024-01-28T06:52:55.029550Z 1 [ERROR] [MY-012657] [InnoDB] Encryption
can't find master key, please check the keyring is loaded.
2024-01-28T06:52:55.029768Z 1 [ERROR] [MY-012226] [InnoDB] Encryption
information in datafile: ./encryptedschema/encrypted_table.ibd can't be
decrypted, please confirm that keyring is loaded.
2024-01-28T06:52:55.031342Z 1 [ERROR] [MY-012657] [InnoDB] Encryption
can't find master key, please check the keyring is loaded.
2024-01-28T06:52:55.031475Z 1 [ERROR] [MY-012226] [InnoDB] Encryption
information in datafile: user_defined_general_tablespace.ibd can't be
decrypted, please confirm that keyring is loaded.
```

Securing MySQL Replication

MySQL replication is a powerful feature that allows data to be replicated across multiple MySQL servers. While it provides significant benefits, it also introduces security risks that must be addressed to ensure the safety and integrity of your data. In this section, we cover securing MySQL replication.

Replication Security Best Practices

To ensure the security of your MySQL replication setup, do the following:

Use secure connections
Use SSL/TLS to encrypt replication traffic between the source and replica servers. This will prevent network sniffing attacks.

Limit access
Restrict access to the replication environment to authorized personnel only. Use strong passwords and implement two-factor authentication.

Monitor replication traffic
Set up alerts to notify you of any unusual replication activity, such as an increase in replication traffic or an unexpected source or destination.

Validate replication data

Use checksums or other validation techniques to ensure that the data being replicated is consistent and has not been modified.

Here are some additional best practices for securing your MySQL replication setup:

- Use a firewall to restrict access to the replication environment. Allow only traffic from authorized IP addresses.
- If possible, *use separate networks* for the replication traffic and other network traffic.
- Use encrypted storage for your MySQL data to prevent data theft in the event of physical access to the server.

MySQL Security Auditing

MySQL security auditing assesses the security of a MySQL database to identify vulnerabilities and potential risks. The following steps can help in conducting a MySQL security audit:

1. Identify security risks and vulnerabilities that could impact the MySQL database.
2. Review access controls to ensure that users have the appropriate roles and privileges.
3. Review authentication mechanisms to ensure that strong passwords are used.
4. Review network security to ensure that firewalls and SSL/TLS encryption are used.
5. Review backup and recovery plans to ensure that data can be recovered in case of data loss or corruption.
6. Review logging and monitoring to ensure that logs are regularly monitored for unusual activity.

Conclusion

This chapter provided an array of strategies and practices to fortify your databases against security threats, underscoring the significance of robust authentication, authorization, encryption, role management, and proactive monitoring. This knowledge will enable you to cultivate a secure and resilient MySQL environment in the face of evolving security challenges.

## CHAPTER 6

MySQL Replication

MySQL replication is a process in which one MySQL server, referred to as the *source*, copies its data to one or more MySQL servers, called the *replicas*. The replicas then replicate the data changes from the source, allowing multiple instances of MySQL servers to contain the same data. This replication enables better scalability and reliability.

In this chapter, you'll gain a comprehensive understanding of MySQL replication.

Understanding How MySQL Replication Works

The replication process in MySQL involves three key components: the source server, the replica server(s), and the replication process itself. The source server is responsible for recording all the changes made to its data. It writes these changes to a binary logfile, which contains all the SQL statements that have been executed on the database.

The replica servers connect to the source server and retrieve a copy of the binary logfile. The replicas then parse this file and execute the same SQL statements on their copies of the data, thereby ensuring that all data changes are synchronized across all databases.

Replication operates by using three threads:

I/O thread on the replica server

> The process commences by initiating an I/O thread on the replica server, which establishes a connection with the source server to begin receiving replication events.

Source connection handler thread

In its role as a connection handler, the source server initiates a thread whenever a replica server establishes a connection. The source server dispatches events from its binary logfile to the replica I/O thread, informing the replica about recently generated events in its binary log. Subsequently, the replica I/O thread logs these events in the replica's relay logfile.

Replica SQL thread

Upon initiation, SQL thread promptly reads events from the relay log and applies them on the replica DB. After completing the processing of each relay log, if the I/O thread is currently recording events to a fresh relay logfile, the processed one is removed. If the I/O thread is writing events to a relay logfile that the SQL thread is simultaneously reading from, the SQL thread halts until additional events become accessible in the relay log.

MySQL replication enhances scalability through load distribution and increases availability via failover mechanisms, making it a robust solution for database management. Here are some details about the advantages of replication:

Improved scalability

Distributing the load of reading and writing data across multiple servers can improve the performance of your database.

Increased availability

If the source server goes down, you can promote one of the replicas to become the new source, providing high availability for your application.

Better disaster recovery

Maintaining multiple copies of your data can help in disaster recovery scenarios.

Geographic distribution

Copying your data to different locations can improve the performance of your application for users in different regions.

Next, we'll look at the high-level details of how to configure replication. First, you'll need to modify the configuration files on both the source and the replicas. On the *source server*, add the following lines to the *my.cnf* file:

```
[mysqld]
log-bin=mysql-bin
server-id=1
```

On the *replica servers*, add the following lines to the *my.cnf* file:

```
[mysqld]
server-id=2
```

Then, on the *replica servers*, execute the following command to start the replication process:

```
CHANGE MASTER TO MASTER_HOST='master_host_name',
MASTER_USER='replication_user', MASTER_PASSWORD='replication_password',
MASTER_LOG_FILE='mysql-bin.000001', MASTER_LOG_POS=0;
```

MySQL 8.0.23 introduces CHANGE REPLICATION SOURCE TO as the preferred method for setting the replication sources (the older syntax, CHANGE MASTER TO, is now deprecated):

```
mysql> CHANGE REPLICATION SOURCE TO
    -> SOURCE_HOST='_source_host_name_',
    -> SOURCE_USER='_replication_user_name_',
    -> SOURCE_PASSWORD='_replication_password_',
    -> SOURCE_LOG_FILE='_recorded_log_file_name_',
    -> SOURCE_LOG_POS=__recorded_log_position__;
```

The command CHANGE REPLICATION SOURCE TO is used in MySQL to change the replication source for a particular replica server.

The CHANGE REPLICATION SOURCE TO command requires the following parameters:

SOURCE_HOST
: The hostname or IP address of the replication source server.

SOURCE_USER
: The username of a replication user that has the privileges required to replicate data from the source server.

SOURCE_PASSWORD
: The password for the replication user specified in SOURCE_USER.

SOURCE_LOG_FILE
: The name of the binary logfile on the source server that contains the events to be replicated.

SOURCE_LOG_POS
: The position within the binary logfile specified in SOURCE_LOG_FILE where replication should start.

Enabling read_only and super_read_only in replication instances is important for several reasons:

- By setting read_only and super_read_only to ON, you can prevent accidental modifications of data on a replica. This can be particularly important when using replicas for reporting or backup purposes. If a user inadvertently modifies data on a replica, it can cause data inconsistencies and may lead to the need for data recovery.

- In a replication setup, it's important to ensure that all replicas have the same data as the source server. By setting read_only and super_read_only to ON, you can prevent any data modifications on the replicas that could lead to inconsistencies in the data.

- Enabling the `read_only` system variable on a MySQL server prevents clients, except those with the `CONNECTION_ADMIN` privilege or the deprecated `SUPER` privilege, from making updates to the server. If the `super_read_only` system variable is also enabled, even clients with `CONNECTION_ADMIN` or `SUPER` privileges are prohibited from making updates.

- Enabling `super_read_only` prevents certain operations, including `CREATE FUNCTION`, `INSTALL PLUGIN`, and `INSTALL COMPONENT`, which make changes to tables in the `mysql` system schema. Additionally, if the Event Scheduler is enabled, `super_read_only` prevents it from updating event "last executed" timestamps in the events data dictionary table, which can cause the Event Scheduler to stop working. Enabling `super_read_only` does not change the status of the `event_scheduler` system variable.

- Changes to `super_read_only` on a replication source server are not replicated to replica servers, and the value can be set independently on replicas. If `super_read_only` is subsequently disabled after being enabled, the server automatically restarts the Event Scheduler as needed in MySQL 8.0.26 or later. Prior to MySQL 8.0.26, the Event Scheduler must be manually restarted by enabling it again.

Overall, enabling `read_only` and `super_read_only` in replication instances can help ensure the integrity and consistency of data and enforce security.

Reviewing Prerequisites for Replication

Before setting up MySQL replication, you must ensure that the following prerequisites are met:

- MySQL server installed and running on all instances involved in replication, comprising at least two instances: one serving as the source and the other as the replica
- Network connectivity between the source and replica instances
- Proper firewall rules allowing for communication between source and replica instances
- MySQL users with appropriate permissions to replicate data

Types of Replication in MySQL

MySQL provides various replication options, including standard asynchronous replication and global transaction identifier (GTID) replication, which are implemented within the broader framework of source-replica replication, along with group replication. In this section, we'll delve into each type, highlighting the drawbacks of master-master replication. Additionally, we'll explore diverse approaches to configuring replication, such as employing XtraBackup and the clone plug-in.

Configure MySQL Source-Replica Replication

MySQL *source-replica replication* is a powerful feature that allows data from a single MySQL database to be replicated to one or more replica databases, enabling scalable, HA systems. This architecture uses two MySQL instances: a source and a replica.

The source server is responsible for receiving all updates and modifications to the database, and it writes these changes to a binary logfile. The binary logfile contains all the changes to the database, such as inserts, updates, and deletes, in a binary format that can be easily read by other servers. Figure 6-1 illustrates the MySQL source-replica replication architecture.

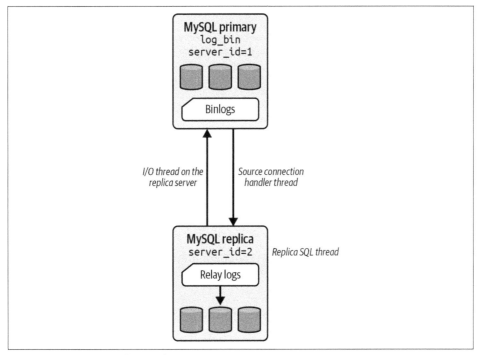

Figure 6-1. Source-replica architecture

On the replica server, a MySQL process called the *I/O thread* is responsible for connecting to the source server and downloading the events from the binary logfiles. Once the I/O thread has downloaded the events from the binary logfiles, it writes them to a relay logfile on the replica server.

Another process on the replica server, called the *SQL thread*, reads the relay logfile and applies the changes to the database on the replica server. This way, the data on the replica server is always synchronized with the data on the primary server.

MySQL source-replica replication is a popular and reliable technique to maintain a backup or to scale read operations. In this technique, changes made on the primary instance are propagated to one or more replica instances, which then apply the same changes to their own data.

Configuring the source

Follow these steps to configure the source instance:

1. Edit the MySQL configuration, which is usually located at */etc/my.cnf* or */etc/mysql/my.cnf*, by adding the following lines in the `mysqld` section:

   ```
   [root@mysql1 ~]# cat /etc/my.cnf
   # Percona Server template configuration
   #
   # For advice on how to change settings please see
   # http://dev.mysql.com/doc/refman/8.0/en/server-configuration-defaults.html

   [mysqld]

   datadir=/var/lib/mysql
   socket=/var/lib/mysql/mysql.sock

   server-id = 1
   log-bin = /var/log/mysql/mysql-bin.log

   log-error=/var/log/mysqld.log
   pid-file=/var/run/mysqld/mysqld.pid
   [root@mysql1 ~]#
   ```

   In this example, you're replicating all the databases in the instance to the replica.

2. Restart the MySQL service to apply the configuration changes.

Configuring the replica

Follow these steps to configure the replica instance:

1. Edit MySQL configuration by adding the following lines in the `mysqld` section:

   ```
   [root@mysql2 ~]# cat /etc/my.cnf
   # Percona Server template configuration
   ```

```
#
# For advice on how to change settings please see
# http://dev.mysql.com/doc/refman/8.0/en/server-configuration-defaults.html

[mysqld]

datadir=/var/lib/mysql
socket=/var/lib/mysql/mysql.sock

server-id = 2
relay-log = /var/log/mysql/mysql-relay-bin.log

log-error=/var/log/mysqld.log
pid-file=/var/run/mysqld/mysqld.pid
[root@mysql2 ~]#
```

2. Restart the MySQL service to apply the configuration changes to the source and replication instances. Here's the source instance:

```
[root@mysql1 ~]# systemctl restart mysqld
[root@mysql1 ~]#
```

Followed by the replication instance:

```
[root@mysql2 ~]# systemctl restart mysqld
[root@mysql2 ~]#
```

After adding the configurations and restarting the replica instance to initiate replication, you need to create a user in the source instance, grant the REPLICATION privilege, and execute the "change replication source" query to specify the source. Then, we need to start the replica using the following steps:

1. Log in to the source instance by using the root account and then use the following command to create a replication user with the privilege indicated:

```
mysql> CREATE USER 'repl_user'@'%' IDENTIFIED WITH
caching_sha2_password BY 'Mkj#$w@89LKJH#';
Query OK, 0 rows affected (0.02 sec)
mysql>

mysql> GRANT REPLICATION SLAVE ON *.* TO 'repl_user'@'%';
Query OK, 0 rows affected (0.01 sec)
mysql>
```

Make sure to replace 'repl_user' and password 'Mkj#$w@89LKJH#' with the username and password of your choice.

2. Get the binary logfile name and position from the source instance, which will be used for configuring replication, and note the values of File and Position:

```
mysql> SHOW MASTER STATUS\G
*************************** 1. row ***************************
            File: mysql-bin.000001
        Position: 670
```

```
        Binlog_Do_DB:
     Binlog_Ignore_DB:
    Executed_Gtid_Set:
1 row in set (0.00 sec)
mysql>
```

 In this example, we are configuring replication by using a fresh installation of MySQL. If you want to configure replication from a source server that is already in production, you need to use tools like XtraBackup or the clone plug-in to take a backup of the source, restore it in the replica, and then configure the replication.

3. To configure the replica instance to replicate from the source instance, log in to the replica instance using the root account and use the CHANGE REPLICATION query to specify the source. Binlog coordinates where to start along with replication user credentials:

```
mysql> CHANGE REPLICATION SOURCE TO
    -> SOURCE_HOST='192.168.60.51',
    -> SOURCE_USER='repl_user',
    -> SOURCE_PASSWORD='Mkj#$w@89LKJH#',
    -> SOURCE_LOG_FILE='mysql-bin.000001',
    -> SOURCE_LOG_POS=670;
Query OK, 0 rows affected, 2 warnings (0.01 sec)
mysql>
```

4. Start replication on the replica instance:

```
mysql> START REPLICA;
Query OK, 0 rows affected (0.02 sec)
mysql>
```

Starting from MySQL 8.0.22, the use of START SLAVE command is deprecated, and MySQL recommends using its alias START REPLICA instead.

5. Verify that replication is working by executing the following command in the replica instance:

```
mysql> SHOW REPLICA STATUS\G
*************************** 1. row ***************************
             Replica_IO_State: Waiting for source to send event
                  Source_Host: 192.168.60.51
                  Source_User: repl_user
                  Source_Port: 3306
                Connect_Retry: 60
              Source_Log_File: mysql-bin.000001
          Read_Source_Log_Pos: 157
               Relay_Log_File: mysql-relay-bin.000002
                Relay_Log_Pos: 326
        Relay_Source_Log_File: mysql-bin.000001
```

```
            Replica_IO_Running: Yes
           Replica_SQL_Running: Yes
              Replicate_Do_DB:
          Replicate_Ignore_DB:
           Replicate_Do_Table:
       Replicate_Ignore_Table:
      Replicate_Wild_Do_Table:
  Replicate_Wild_Ignore_Table:
                    Last_Errno: 0
                    Last_Error:
                  Skip_Counter: 0
           Exec_Source_Log_Pos: 670
                Relay_Log_Space: 752
              Until_Condition: None
                Until_Log_File:
                 Until_Log_Pos: 0
             Source_SSL_Allowed: No
             Source_SSL_CA_File:
             Source_SSL_CA_Path:
               Source_SSL_Cert:
             Source_SSL_Cipher:
               Source_SSL_Key:
          Seconds_Behind_Source: 0
 Source_SSL_Verify_Server_Cert: No
                 Last_IO_Errno: 0
                 Last_IO_Error:
                Last_SQL_Errno: 0
                Last_SQL_Error:
     Replicate_Ignore_Server_Ids:
              Source_Server_Id: 1
                   Source_UUID: 7f1f5e78-cd52-11ee-b8de-080027b3a29c
               Source_Info_File: mysql.slave_master_info
                     SQL_Delay: 0
           SQL_Remaining_Delay: NULL
     Replica_SQL_Running_State: Replica has read all relay log;
                                 waiting for more updates
             Source_Retry_Count: 86400
                   Source_Bind:
        Last_IO_Error_Timestamp:
       Last_SQL_Error_Timestamp:
                 Source_SSL_Crl:
             Source_SSL_Crlpath:
              Retrieved_Gtid_Set:
               Executed_Gtid_Set:
                 Auto_Position: 0
            Replicate_Rewrite_DB:
                  Channel_Name:
             Source_TLS_Version:
          Source_public_key_path:
         Get_Source_public_key: 0
              Network_Namespace:
```

```
1 row in set (0.00 sec)
mysql>
```

Beginning with MySQL 8.0.22, the use of the SHOW SLAVE STATUS command is deprecated and MySQL recommends using its alias SHOW REPLICA STATUS instead. Look
for the values of Replica_IO_Running and Replica_SQL_Running in the output. If
both have the value Yes, replication is working properly.

Using the log_replica_updates Option

The log_replica_updates option in MySQL 8 is used to control the binary logging
behavior of the MySQL replication process. When this option is enabled on a MySQL
replica server, any updates made on the replica will also be written to the binary log,
along with the replication events received from the source. This means that any
changes made to the data on the replica will be propagated back to the source and any
other replicas that are connected downstream from the current replica.

Starting from MySQL 8.0.26, using log_slave_updates is no longer recommended.
Instead, MySQL advises using the alternative, log_replica_updates. For versions
preceding MySQL 8.0.26, MySQL recommends sticking with log_slave_updates
(see Figure 6-2).

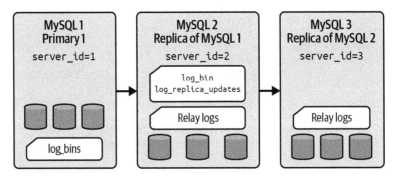

Figure 6-2. log_replica_updates

XtraBackup for Source-Replica Replication

Configuring replication in a production environment running with a single source
node can be challenging, especially when it comes to taking consistent backups and
determining the correct binlog position to start replication after restoring the backup
on the replica server.

Data is undoubtedly the most valuable component of any system, and having a systematic backup process in place is essential for rapid recovery in the event of a failure. However, this is often not practiced because of the associated costs, infrastructure requirements, or simply the monotony of the task.

Fortunately, Percona XtraBackup is designed to address this issue by providing almost real-time backups through a simple replication setup. This tool performs hot backups on MySQL, as well as Percona Server for MySQL, without causing any interruptions. It is completely free and open source.

Make a backup on the source

To perform a backup using Percona XtraBackup, execute the following command on the source server's shell:

```
[root@mysql1 ~]# xtrabackup --backup --user=root --password --target-dir=
/data/backups/mysql

2024-02-18T03:03:38.938140-00:00 0 [Note] [MY-011825] [Xtrabackup] recognized
server arguments: --server-id=1 --log_bin=/var/log/mysql/mysql-bin.log
--datadir=/var/lib/mysql
2024-02-18T03:03:38.938444-00:00 0 [Note] [MY-011825] [Xtrabackup] recognized
client arguments: --user=root --password=* --backup=1 --user=root --password
--target-dir=/data/backups/mysql
Enter password:
xtrabackup version 8.0.35-30 based on MySQL server 8.0.35 Linux (x86_64)
(revision id: 6beb4b49)
...
2024-02-18T03:03:57.663879-00:00 0 [Note] [MY-011825] [Xtrabackup]
Done: Writing file /data/backups/mysql/backup-my.cnf
2024-02-18T03:03:57.677576-00:00 0 [Note] [MY-011825] [Xtrabackup]
Writing /data/backups/mysql/xtrabackup_info
2024-02-18T03:03:57.677769-00:00 0 [Note] [MY-011825] [Xtrabackup]
Done: Writing file /data/backups/mysql/xtrabackup_info
2024-02-18T03:03:58.681368-00:00 0 [Note] [MY-011825] [Xtrabackup]
Transaction log of lsn
(88011308) to (88011308) was copied.
2024-02-18T03:03:58.806133-00:00 0 [Note] [MY-011825] [Xtrabackup] completed OK!
[root@mysql1 ~]#
```

Let's break down the individual components of the command:

`xtrabackup`
  The name of the command-line tool used for backup and restore operations by Percona XtraBackup.

`--backup`
  Specifies that we want to perform a backup operation.

```
--user=root
```
Specifies the MySQL user account that the backup process will use to connect to the database. You can use either the root user or replace it with the username of a MySQL user who has appropriate privileges.

```
--password=XYZ%$KG
```
Specifies the password for the MySQL user account specified by the `--user` option. Replace *XYZ%$KG* with the actual password for the MySQL user.

```
--target-dir=/data/backups/mysql
```
Specifies the directory where the backup files will be stored. Replace */data/back ups/mysql* with the actual path to the directory where you want to store the backup files.

By executing this command, Percona XtraBackup will connect to the MySQL database with the specified user account and password, and will take a backup of all the databases and tables in the server, storing the resulting files in the specified directory.

Prepare the backup

After creating a backup of your MySQL data on the source, you need to prepare the data to ensure the consistency of the snapshot. Use the `xtrabackup` command with with the `--prepare` option to apply the necessary changes to the backup directory specified by `--target-dir`. Additionally, the `--user` and `--password` options specify the MySQL database user and password, respectively:

```
[root@mysql1 ~]# xtrabackup --user=DBuser --password --prepare --target-dir=
/data/backups/mysql

2024-02-18T03:05:41.388629-00:00 0 [Note] [MY-011825] [Xtrabackup] recognized
server arguments: --innodb_checksum_algorithm=crc32 --innodb_log_checksums=1
--innodb_data_file_path=ibdata1:12M:autoextend --innodb_log_file_size=50331648
--innodb_page_size=16384 --innodb_undo_directory=./ --innodb_undo_tablespaces=2
--server-id=1 --innodb_log_checksums=ON --innodb_redo_log_encrypt=0
--innodb_undo_log_encrypt=0
2024-02-18T03:05:41.390846-00:00 0 [Note] [MY-011825] [Xtrabackup] recognized
client arguments: --user=DBuser --password --prepare=1 --target-dir=/data/
backups/mysql
Enter password:
xtrabackup version 8.0.35-30 based on MySQL server 8.0.35 Linux (x86_64)
(revision id: 6beb4b49)
...
2024-02-18T03:05:54.816234-00:00 0 [Note] [MY-012980] [InnoDB] Shutdown
completed; log sequence number 88011798
2024-02-18T03:05:54.821459-00:00 0 [Note] [MY-011825] [Xtrabackup] completed OK!
[root@mysql1 ~]#
```

Transfer the backed-up data to the replica

To copy the backed-up data from the source to the replica server, you first need to install MySQL on the replica server. After installation, you should stop the MySQL service if it autostarts. Then, you can use either rsync or scp to transfer the data from the source to the replica. Make sure to clear or move the default installed files from the data directory:

```
[root@mysql2 lib]# systemctl stop mysqld
[root@mysql2 lib]# rm -rf mysql
[root@mysql2 lib]#
```

To transfer the backup to the replica server using the rsync operation, you can either use the OS user and password to connect to the replication server or establish pass-wordless SSH by configuring public-private key pairs. Generate RSA key pair by using the ssh-keygen -t rsa command:

```
[root@mysql1 ~]# ssh-keygen -t rsa

Generating public/private rsa key pair.
Enter file in which to save the key (/root/.ssh/id_rsa):
Enter passphrase (empty for no passphrase):
Enter same passphrase again:
Your identification has been saved in /root/.ssh/id_rsa
Your public key has been saved in /root/.ssh/id_rsa.pub
The key fingerprint is:
SHA256:rZ93Q2MHGPnfY1JjMCrU3fPUdAQDMedR5t7dQPxBz24 root@mysql1
The key's randomart image is:
+---[RSA 3072]----+
|          . ==O*B|
|         . .oO.X=|
|        .   .+=oB|
|         o .. oB*|
|        S o   ooE|
|         .   .+++|
|         .   ooo.|
|          . .. o |
|           o. . .|
+----[SHA256]-----+
[root@mysql1 ~]#
```

Check the contents of the *.ssh* directory by using the ll .ssh/ command:

```
[root@mysql1 ~]# ll .ssh/

total 20
-rw-------. 1 root root  560 Feb 18 02:02 authorized_keys
-rw-------. 1 root root 2590 Feb 18 03:11 id_rsa
-rw-r--r--. 1 root root  565 Feb 18 03:11 id_rsa.pub
-rw-------. 1 root root  834 Feb 18 03:15 known_hosts
-rw-r--r--. 1 root root   94 Feb 18 03:10 known_hosts.old
[root@mysql1 .ssh]#
```

Copy contents of the *id_rsa.pub* file and update it in the replica server:

```
[root@mysql1 ~]# cat .ssh/id_rsa.pub

ssh-rsa AAAAB3NzaC1yc2EAAAADAQABAAABgQDVg6uw4EInwThzm+/
u*******iv7fUcrn0XXqte3nr3uw*******pfJ31BKM= root@mysql1
[root@mysql1 ~]#
```

Edit the *authorized_keys* file by using the vi .ssh/authorized_keys command and append the key from the source server:

```
[root@mysql2 ~]# vi  .ssh/authorized_keys
[root@mysql2 ~]#
```

Set appropriate permissions for the *authorized_keys* file using chmod 640 .ssh/ authorized_keys command.

Check the PermitRootLogin configuration in the *sshd_config* file by using the following command:

```
[root@mysql2 ~]#  grep -i PermitRootLogin /etc/ssh/sshd_config

#PermitRootLogin prohibit-password
# the setting of "PermitRootLogin without-password".
[root@mysql2 ~]
```

Connect to the remote server (mysql2) by using the ssh command and confirm it is working fine:

```
[root@mysql1 ~]# ssh 172.31.23.78

Register this system with Red Hat Insights: insights-client --register
Create an account or view all your systems at https://red.ht/insights-dashboard
Last login: Sun Feb 18 02:56:10 2024
[root@mysql2 ~]#
```

Transfer the prepared backup from the source server to the replica server:

```
[root@mysql1 ~]# rsync -avpP -e ssh /data/backups/mysql 172.31.23.78:/var/lib/

sending incremental file list
mysql/
mysql/backup-my.cnf
            447 100%    0.00kB/s    0:00:00 (xfr#1, to-chk=141/143)
mysql/ib_buffer_pool
          3,454 100%    3.29MB/s    0:00:00 (xfr#2, to-chk=140/143)
mysql/ibdata1
     12,582,912 100%  109.09MB/s    0:00:00 (xfr#3, to-chk=139/143)
mysql/ibtmp1
     12,582,912 100%   54.79MB/s    0:00:00 (xfr#4, to-chk=138/143)
...
     7,960 100%   13.93kB/s    0:00:00 (xfr#136, to-chk=1/143)
mysql/sys/
mysql/sys/sys_config.ibd
```

```
       114,688 100%  200.00kB/s    0:00:00 (xfr#137, to-chk=0/143)

sent 169,930,538 bytes  received 2,663 bytes  113,288,800.67 bytes/sec
total size is 169,879,763  speedup is 1.00
[root@mysql1 ~]#
```

This command uses the rsync utility with various options to synchronize the backup directory on the source with the MySQL data directory on the replica.

In the replica instance, ensure that the mysql user on the replica has the appropriate permissions for the data directory by executing the following command:

```
[root@mysql2 mysql]# chown -R mysql:mysql /var/lib/mysql
[root@mysql2 mysql]#

[root@mysql2 mysql]# ll
total 115756
-rw-r-----. 1 mysql mysql      447 Feb 18 03:03  backup-my.cnf
drwxr-x---. 2 mysql mysql      132 Feb 18 03:03  employees
-rw-r-----. 1 mysql mysql     3454 Feb 18 03:03  ib_buffer_pool
-rw-r-----. 1 mysql mysql 12582912 Feb 18 03:05  ibdata1
-rw-r-----. 1 mysql mysql 12582912 Feb 18 03:05  ibtmp1
drwxr-x---. 2 mysql mysql        6 Feb 18 03:05  '#innodb_redo'
drwxr-x---. 2 mysql mysql      143 Feb 18 03:03  mysql
-rw-r-----. 1 mysql mysql      157 Feb 18 03:03  mysql-bin.000003
-rw-r-----. 1 mysql mysql       32 Feb 18 03:03  mysql-bin.index
-rw-r-----. 1 mysql mysql 26214400 Feb 18 03:03  mysql.ibd
drwxr-x---. 2 mysql mysql     8192 Feb 18 03:03  performance_schema
drwxr-x---. 2 mysql mysql       28 Feb 18 03:03  sys
-rw-r-----. 1 mysql mysql 16777216 Feb 18 03:03  undo_001
-rw-r-----. 1 mysql mysql 16777216 Feb 18 03:03  undo_002
-rw-r-----. 1 mysql mysql       21 Feb 18 03:03  xtrabackup_binlog_info
-rw-r-----. 1 mysql mysql      134 Feb 18 03:05  xtrabackup_checkpoints
-rw-r-----. 1 mysql mysql      488 Feb 18 03:03  xtrabackup_info
-rw-r-----. 1 mysql mysql 33554432 Feb 18 03:05  xtrabackup_logfile
-rw-r-----. 1 mysql mysql       39 Feb 18 03:05  xtrabackup_tablespaces
[root@mysql2 mysql]#
```

To configure the *my.cnf* file for the replica, copy it from the source server configuration and adjust the settings according to the resources of the replica server. It's important to update the server_id setting with a unique value for the replica.

In the source instance, create a user and grant the necessary permissions for the replica to connect by executing the following commands:

```
mysql> CREATE USER 'repl_user'@'%' IDENTIFIED WITH mysql_native_password BY
'Pass21word$$';
Query OK, 0 rows affected (0.03 sec)
mysql>

mysql> GRANT REPLICATION SLAVE ON *.* TO 'repl_user'@'%';
Query OK, 0 rows affected (0.02 sec)
mysql>
```

This command grants the replication slave permission to the `repl_user` with the specified IP address and password.

Configure replication in the replica instance

Start the MySQL server on the replica and check the MySQL error log to ensure that no issues need to be addressed:

```
[root@mysql2 lib]# systemctl start mysqld.service
[root@mysql2 lib]#
```

To configure replication on the replica server, execute the following CHANGE REPLICA TION SOURCE statement on the MySQL console, using the username and password set up in the previous steps. You can obtain the SOURCE_LOG_FILE and SOURCE_LOG_POS values from the *xtrabackup_binlog_info* file in the data directory (as you copied all backup):

```
[root@mysql2 mysql]# ll /var/lib/mysql/xtrabackup_binlog_info
-rw-r-----. 1 mysql mysql 21 Feb 18 03:03 xtrabackup_binlog_info
[root@mysql2 mysql]#

[root@mysql2 mysql]# cat /var/lib/mysql/xtrabackup_binlog_info
mysql-bin.000003        157
[root@mysql2 mysql]#

mysql> CHANGE REPLICATION SOURCE TO
    -> SOURCE_HOST='172.31.24.0',
    -> SOURCE_USER='repl_user',
    -> SOURCE_PASSWORD='Pass21word$$',
    -> SOURCE_LOG_FILE='mysql-bin.000003',
    -> SOURCE_LOG_POS=157;
Query OK, 0 rows affected, 2 warnings (0.03 sec)

mysql>
```

Then, start the replica by running the following command:

```
mysql> START REPLICA;
Query OK, 0 rows affected (0.01 sec)

mysql>
```

From MySQL 8.0.22 onward, START SLAVE is deprecated, and START REPLICA should be used instead.

To confirm that everything has been set up correctly, check the replication status on the replica server by running the following command on the MySQL console:

```
[root@mysql2 mysql]# mysql -e "SHOW REPLICA STATUS \G" |egrep
'Running|Source' | egrep -v 'SSL|TLS'
                Source_Host: 172.31.24.0
                Source_User: repl_user
                Source_Port: 3306
```

```
             Source_Log_File: mysql-bin.000003
         Read_Source_Log_Pos: 670
      Relay_Source_Log_File: mysql-bin.000003
          Replica_IO_Running: Yes
         Replica_SQL_Running: Yes
        Exec_Source_Log_Pos: 670
      Seconds_Behind_Source: 0
            Source_Server_Id: 1
               Source_UUID: db570a5b-ce02-11ee-9bda-02d7862349a7
           Source_Info_File: mysql.slave_master_info
    Replica_SQL_Running_State: Replica has read all relay log;
                              waiting for more updates
          Source_Retry_Count: 86400
                 Source_Bind:
       Source_public_key_path:
[root@mysql2 mysql]
```

Check that both I/O and SQL threads are running, and confirm that the Sec
onds_Behind_Source value is not too high. This value indicates the lag between the
source and the replica, and it may initially be high because the replica needs to catch
up with the source.

Stream the backup to replication server

The previous example demonstrated using XtraBackup for replication by backing up
to the source server's local backup share. However, you also could directly stream the
backup to the replication server. For instance, you can employ the following command for this purpose. Once the backup is streamed to the target server, you'll need
to proceed with the same steps for preparing the backup and initiating replication, as
discussed in the earlier example:

```
[root@mysql1 ~]# xtrabackup --backup   --stream=xbstream --target-dir=./ |
ssh 172.31.23.78 "xbstream -x -C /var/lib/mysql"

2024-02-18T03:53:54.737304-00:00 0 [Note] [MY-011825] [Xtrabackup] recognized
server arguments: --server-id=1 --log_bin=/var/log/mysql/mysql-bin.log
--datadir=/var/lib/mysql
2024-02-18T03:53:54.737702-00:00 0 [Note] [MY-011825] [Xtrabackup] recognized
client arguments: --user=root --password=* --backup=1 --stream=xbstream
--target-dir=./
xtrabackup version 8.0.35-30 based on MySQL server 8.0.35 Linux (x86_64)
(revision id: 6beb4b49)
...
2024-02-18T04:00:35.151746-00:00 0 [Note] [MY-011825] [Xtrabackup] Streaming
<STDOUT>
2024-02-18T04:00:35.371895-00:00 0 [Note] [MY-011825] [Xtrabackup] Done:
Streaming file <STDOUT>
2024-02-18T04:00:35.610130-00:00 0 [Note] [MY-011825] [Xtrabackup] Transaction
log of lsn (88013651) to (88013661) was copied.
2024-02-18T04:00:36.137983-00:00 0 [Note] [MY-011825] [Xtrabackup] completed OK!
[root@mysql1 ~]#
```

Configure replication using backup from a replica

To set up replication using a backup from an existing replica, you can follow a similar procedure to the one described earlier with some adjustments for adding new replicas to the source. To clone an already configured replica, you can use Percona Xtra-Backup. In this scenario, assume that you have a source database and a replica, and you want to add a new replica to the setup (Figure 6-3).

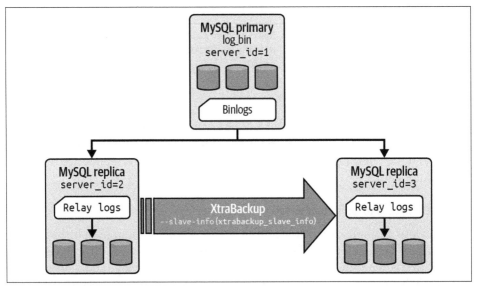

Figure 6-3. Set up replication from an existing replica

When performing a backup on a replication slave server, the `--slave-info` option comes in handy. It displays the name and binary log position of the master server, and writes this information as a `CHANGE MASTER` command to a file called *xtra-backup_slave_info*. This file can be used to configure a new slave for the same master by launching a slave server on the backup and executing a `CHANGE MASTER` command with the binary log position stored in the *xtrabackup_slave_info* file.

To start, perform a full backup on the replica by using the following command:

```
$ xtrabackup -backup --slave-info --user=DBuser --password=XYZ%$KG
--target-dir=/path/to/backupdir/
```

By including the `--slave-info` option, Percona XtraBackup will create an additional file called *xtrabackup_slave_info*. This file contains important replication metadata for the source database at the time of the backup. With the binlog filename and coordinates within this file, we can initiate the new replica by connecting it to the primary instance.

Once you have prepared (`--prepare`) and copied the backup to the new replica, and after starting MySQL, you can use the `CHANGE REPLICATION TO` statement to configure the replication to connect to the primary instance:

```
mysql> CHANGE REPLICATION SOURCE TO
SOURCE_HOST='source_host_name',
SOURCE_USER='replication_user_name',
SOURCE_PASSWORD='replication_password',
SOURCE_LOG_FILE='Binlog file name from xtrabackup_slave_info',
SOURCE_LOG_POS=Binlog position from xtrabackup_slave_info;
```

Master-Master Replication

Master-master replication allows two MySQL instances to act as both a master and replica to each other, enabling changes to be made on either instance and then propagated to the other. In this book, we exclude the configuration steps because this approach is not recommended for production use and we don't want to promote it.

Master-master replication in MySQL can present several drawbacks:

Data conflicts
Concurrent modifications to the same data on both servers can result in conflicts, leading to data inconsistencies and integrity issues.

Increased complexity
Compared to other replication methods like source-replica replication, setting up and maintaining master-master replication is more intricate. It requires meticulous configuration to ensure constant synchronization and proper handling of failover scenarios.

Elevated network traffic
Master-master replication generates substantial network traffic as both servers continuously exchange information to maintain data consistency.

Higher risk of data corruption
If one server experiences a failure while the other server continues writing data to it, the risk of data corruption is heightened.

Limited scalability
Master-master replication may not be ideal for large databases or high-traffic applications as scaling beyond a certain point becomes challenging.

Considering these disadvantages, we recommend switching from the master-master topology to either the source-replica topology or the Percona XtraDB cluster-like solutions.

Group Replication

Group replication enables a group of MySQL instances to act as a single entity, providing automatic failover and load balancing. In this section, we will discuss how to configure MySQL group replication.

Before we begin, it's important to note that group replication requires MySQL 5.7 or later, and MySQL 8 is recommended. In addition, group replication requires a dedicated multicast IP address and port for communication between instances.

Configure group replication components

To configure group replication, you need to install and configure the following components on each instance:

MySQL server
> Install MySQL 8 or later on each instance. Make sure that each instance has a unique server ID and a unique port number.

Group replication plug-in
> Install the group replication plug-in on each instance. You can do this by using the following command:
>
> ```
> mysql> INSTALL PLUGIN group_replication SONAME 'group_replication.so';
> ```

Configuration file
> Create a configuration file for each instance, specifying the group replication settings. Here is an example configuration file:
>
> ```
> # group_replication.cnf
> [mysqld]
> server-id=1
> port=3306
> log-bin
> enforce-gtid-consistency
> gtid-mode=ON
> plugin-load=group_replication.so
> group_replication_group_name="mygroup"
> group_replication_local_address="127.0.0.1:6606"
> group_replication_group_seeds="127.0.0.1:6606,127.0.0.1:6607,127.0.0.1:6608"
> ```

The preceding example specifies the following group replication settings:

`server-id`
> Sets the unique server ID for each instance

`port`
> Sets the unique port number for each instance

log-bin
    Enables binary logging

enforce-gtid-consistency
    Enforces GTID consistency

gtid-mode
    Sets the GTID mode to ON

plugin-load
    Loads the Group Replication plug-in

group_replication_group_name
    Sets a unique name for the Group Replication group

group_replication_local_address
    Indicates the IP address and port number for the

local instance group_replication_group_seeds
    Indicates IP addresses and port numbers for the other instances in the group

Firewall rules
    Configures the firewall to allow communication between instances on the multi-cast IP address and port.

Start group replication

Once you have installed and configured the group replication components on each instance, you can start group replication. Follow these steps:

1. Start the first instance by using the following command:

    ```
    mysql> SET GLOBAL group_replication_bootstrap_group=ON;
    mysql> START GROUP_REPLICATION;
    ```

    This will initialize the Group Replication group and create a new group on the first instance.

2. Start the other instances:

    ```
    mysql> START GROUP_REPLICATION;
    ```

    This will join the other instances to the Group Replication group.

3. Verify the status of the Group Replication group:

    ```
    mysql> SELECT * FROM performance_schema.replication_group_members;
    ```

    This will display the status of each instance in the group.

To enable read/write splitting, you can use a load balancer such as MySQL Router or ProxySQL. Configure the load balancer to distribute read and write requests to the appropriate instances based on the workload.

Here is an example configuration file for MySQL Router:

```
[routing:group_replication_rwsplit]

bind_address = 0.0.0.0
bind_port = 6446
destinations = localhost:6606,localhost:6607,localhost:6608
routing_strategy = round-robin
mode = read-write
```

This example specifies the following settings:

bind_address
: IP address for the router

bind_port
: Port number for the router

destinations
: IP addresses and port numbers for the instances in the Group Replication group

routing_strategy
: Routing strategy for read and write requests (round-robin in this case)

mode
: Routing mode (read/write in this case)

Group replication is a powerful feature that provides automatic failover and load balancing for MySQL instances. By following the steps outlined in this section, you can configure group replication on your own MySQL instances and achieve high availability in your environment. Remember to test your configuration thoroughly before deploying it to production.

GTID Replication

MySQL global transaction identifier (GTID) replication using Percona XtraBackup is a powerful and efficient way to track transactions in a MySQL database, allowing for easier failover and recovery. This technology is used by many organizations to ensure that their databases remain highly available and can withstand a variety of failures. In this section, we'll walk through the steps required to configure MySQL GTID replication using Percona XtraBackup, including the necessary configuration code and example configurations.

GTID replication is a method of tracking transactions in a MySQL database using a unique identifier, called a GTID. The GTID is a global, unique identifier assigned to each transaction in the database, regardless of which server it originates from. This allows for more efficient and reliable replication of data across multiple servers, as each transaction can be tracked and replicated with precision.

Using Percona XtraBackup GTID replication can simplify the process of setting up and maintaining a replication topology, while also reducing the risk of data loss or corruption. Here's how:

1. Install Percona XtraBackup on all servers that will participate in the replication topology. This can typically be done using the package manager for your operating system, or by downloading the package from the Percona website.

2. Enable GTID replication in MySQL on all servers. This can be done by adding the following lines to the MySQL configuration file on both nodes:

   ```
   gtid_mode=ON
   enforce_gtid_consistency=ON
   ```

   a. On node1, modify the MySQL configuration file by updating gtid_mode and enforce_gtid_consistency. You can open the file and add or update the variables with the vi /etc/my.cnf command.

   b. Now open your *my.cnf* file on node2 with the vi /etc/my.cnf command. Then modify the MySQL configuration file by updating gtid_mode and enforce_gtid_consistency.

3. Restart the MySQL instance on both nodes with systemctl restart mysqld.

4. Before setting up replication, you need to take a backup of the source server by using Percona XtraBackup. Use this command to create the */data/backups/mysql* directory structure:

   ```
   [root@node1 ~]# mkdir -p /data/backups/mysql
   [root@node1 ~]#

   [root@node1 ~]# xtrabackup --backup --target-dir=/data/backups/mysql
   2024-02-18T06:51:19.431483-00:00 0 [Note] [MY-011825] [Xtrabackup] recognized
   server arguments: --datadir=/var/lib/mysql --server-id=1
   2024-02-18T06:51:19.432341-00:00 0 [Note] [MY-011825] [Xtrabackup] recognized
   client arguments: --user=root --password=* --backup=1 --target-dir=/data/
   backups/mysql
   xtrabackup version 8.0.35-30 based on MySQL server 8.0.35 Linux (x86_64)
   (revision id: 6beb4b49)
   ...

   2024-02-18T06:51:47.978628-00:00 0 [Note] [MY-011825] [Xtrabackup]
   Done: Writing
   file /data/backups/mysql/xtrabackup_info
   2024-02-18T06:51:48.126671-00:00 0 [Note] [MY-011825] [Xtrabackup]
   Transaction
   log of lsn (21348764) to (21351102) was copied.
   ```

```
2024-02-18T06:51:48.291397-00:00 0 [Note] [MY-011825] [Xtrabackup]
completed OK!
[root@node1 ~]#
```

5. On node2, remove all files under the */var/lib/mysql* directory:

```
[root@node2 ~]# cd /var/lib/mysql
[root@node2 mysql]# ls -ltr
total 91596
-rw-r-----. 1 mysql mysql         56 Feb 18 06:34  auto.cnf
-rw-r-----. 1 mysql mysql    8585216 Feb 18 06:34  '#ib_16384_1.dblwr'
drwxr-x---. 2 mysql mysql       8192 Feb 18 06:34  performance_schema
-rw-------. 1 mysql mysql       1705 Feb 18 06:34  ca-key.pem
-rw-r--r--. 1 mysql mysql       1112 Feb 18 06:34  ca.pem
-rw-------. 1 mysql mysql       1705 Feb 18 06:34  server-key.pem
-rw-r--r--. 1 mysql mysql       1112 Feb 18 06:34  server-cert.pem
-rw-------. 1 mysql mysql       1705 Feb 18 06:34  client-key.pem
-rw-r--r--. 1 mysql mysql       1112 Feb 18 06:34  client-cert.pem
-rw-------. 1 mysql mysql       1705 Feb 18 06:34  private_key.pem
-rw-r--r--. 1 mysql mysql        452 Feb 18 06:34  public_key.pem
drwxr-x---. 2 mysql mysql        143 Feb 18 06:34  mysql
drwxr-x---. 2 mysql mysql         28 Feb 18 06:34  sys
-rw-r-----. 1 mysql mysql        180 Feb 18 06:40  binlog.000001
-rw-r-----. 1 mysql mysql       3554 Feb 18 06:40  ib_buffer_pool
drwxr-x---. 2 mysql mysql        187 Feb 18 06:40  '#innodb_temp'
drwxr-x---. 2 mysql mysql       4096 Feb 18 06:40  '#innodb_redo'
-rw-r-----. 1 mysql mysql         32 Feb 18 06:40  binlog.index
-rw-------. 1 mysql mysql          6 Feb 18 06:40  mysql.sock.lock
srwxrwxrwx. 1 mysql mysql          0 Feb 18 06:40  mysql.sock
-rw-r-----. 1 mysql mysql   12582912 Feb 18 06:40  ibtmp1
-rw-r-----. 1 mysql mysql        476 Feb 18 06:46  binlog.000002
-rw-r-----. 1 mysql mysql   16777216 Feb 18 06:46  undo_002
-rw-r-----. 1 mysql mysql   26214400 Feb 18 06:46  mysql.ibd
-rw-r-----. 1 mysql mysql   12582912 Feb 18 06:46  ibdata1
-rw-r-----. 1 mysql mysql     196608 Feb 18 06:48  '#ib_16384_0.dblwr'
-rw-r-----. 1 mysql mysql   16777216 Feb 18 06:48  undo_001
[root@node2 mysql]#
[root@node2 mysql]# rm -rf *
[root@node2 mysql]#
```

6. Once the backup is complete, you need to copy it to the replica server by using a
   secure file-transfer protocol such as scp or rsync on node1:

```
[root@node1 ~]# rsync -avpP -e ssh /data/backups/mysql 172.31.21.21:/var/lib/
sending incremental file list
mysql/
mysql/backup-my.cnf
            447 100%    0.00kB/s    0:00:00 (xfr#1, to-chk=141/143)
mysql/binlog.000003
            197 100%  192.38kB/s    0:00:00 (xfr#2, to-chk=140/143)
mysql/binlog.index
             16 100%   15.62kB/s    0:00:00 (xfr#3, to-chk=139/143)
mysql/ib_buffer_pool
          3,558 100%    1.70MB/s    0:00:00 (xfr#4, to-chk=138/143)
```

```
mysql/ibdata1
...
mysql/sys/sys_config.ibd
        114,688 100%  140.70kB/s    0:00:00 (xfr#138, to-chk=0/143)

sent 75,278,806 bytes  received 2,674 bytes  50,187,653.33 bytes/sec
total size is 75,251,106  speedup is 1.00
[root@node1 ~]#
```

7. On the replica server, you need to prepare the backup by using Percona Xtra-Backup. To do this, change the owner from `root` to `mysql` for the directory */var/lib/mysql* on node2:

```
[root@node2 mysql]# chown -R mysql.mysql /var/lib/mysql
[root@node2 mysql]# ls -ltr
total 70708
-rw-r-----. 1 mysql mysql 12582912 Feb 18 06:51 ibdata1
drwxr-x---. 2 mysql mysql       28 Feb 18 06:51 sys
drwxr-x---. 2 mysql mysql      173 Feb 18 06:51 classicmodels
-rw-r-----. 1 mysql mysql 26214400 Feb 18 06:51 mysql.ibd
-rw-r-----. 1 mysql mysql 16777216 Feb 18 06:51 undo_002
-rw-r-----. 1 mysql mysql 16777216 Feb 18 06:51 undo_001
drwxr-x---. 2 mysql mysql      143 Feb 18 06:51 mysql
drwxr-x---. 2 mysql mysql     8192 Feb 18 06:51 performance_schema
-rw-r-----. 1 mysql mysql      197 Feb 18 06:51 binlog.000003
-rw-r-----. 1 mysql mysql       16 Feb 18 06:51 binlog.index
-rw-r-----. 1 mysql mysql       60 Feb 18 06:51 xtrabackup_binlog_info
-rw-r-----. 1 mysql mysql     5120 Feb 18 06:51 xtrabackup_logfile
-rw-r-----. 1 mysql mysql      134 Feb 18 06:51 xtrabackup_checkpoints
-rw-r-----. 1 mysql mysql     3558 Feb 18 06:51 ib_buffer_pool
-rw-r-----. 1 mysql mysql      447 Feb 18 06:51 backup-my.cnf
-rw-r-----. 1 mysql mysql      528 Feb 18 06:51 xtrabackup_info
-rw-r-----. 1 mysql mysql       39 Feb 18 06:51 xtrabackup_tablespaces
[root@node2 mysql]#

[root@node2 mysql]# xtrabackup  --prepare --target-dir=/var/lib/mysql
2024-02-18T07:00:03.237516-00:00 0 [Note] [MY-011825] [Xtrabackup]
recognized server arguments: --innodb_checksum_algorithm=crc32
--innodb_log_checksums=1 --innodb_data_file_path=ibdata1:12M:autoextend
--innodb_log_file_size=50331648 --innodb_page_size=16384
--innodb_undo_directory=./ --innodb_undo_tablespaces=2
--server-id=1 --innodb_log_checksums=ON --innodb_redo_log_encrypt=0
--innodb_undo_log_encrypt=0
2024-02-18T07:00:03.237807-00:00 0 [Note] [MY-011825] [Xtrabackup]
recognized client arguments: --prepare=1 --target-dir=/var/lib/mysql..
2024-02-18T07:00:04.773801-00:00 0 [Note] [MY-012980] [InnoDB] Shutdown
completed; log sequence number 21351446
2024-02-18T07:00:04.776778-00:00 0 [Note] [MY-011825] [Xtrabackup]
completed OK!
[root@node2 mysql]#
```

8. Start the MySQL instance on the replica server:

```
[root@node2 mysql]# systemctl start mysqld.service
[root@node2 mysql]#
```

9. In the source instance on node1, create a user and grant the necessary permissions for the replica to connect:

```
mysql> CREATE USER 'repl_user'@'%' IDENTIFIED WITH caching_sha2_password BY
'Pass21word$$';
Query OK, 0 rows affected (0.04 sec)
mysql>

mysql> GRANT REPLICATION SLAVE ON *.* TO 'repl_user'@'%';
Query OK, 0 rows affected (0.01 sec)
mysql>
```

This command grants the replication replica permission to the repl_user with the specified IP address and password.

10. The destination directory will contain a file named *xtrabackup_binlog_info*, which includes both binary log coordinates and GTID information:

```
[root@node2 mysql]# cat xtrabackup_binlog_info
binlog.000003    197    c3b09097-ce27-11ee-9f1a-026bd47bfb91:1-26
[root@node2 mysql]#
```

11. Update the gtid_purged variable with the GTID obtained from xtrabackup_bin log_info. Next, refresh the details regarding the source node, and ultimately, initiate the replication process:

```
mysql> RESET MASTER;
Query OK, 0 rows affected (0.01 sec)

mysql> SET GLOBAL gtid_purged='c3b09097-ce27-11ee-9f1a-026bd47bfb91:1-26';
Query OK, 0 rows affected (0.01 sec)

mysql>
mysql> CHANGE REPLICATION SOURCE TO
    -> SOURCE_HOST='172.31.16.119',
    -> SOURCE_USER='repl_user',
    -> SOURCE_PASSWORD='Pass21word$$',
    -> SOURCE_AUTO_POSITION=1,
    -> MASTER_SSL = 1 ;
Query OK, 0 rows affected, 3 warnings (0.02 sec)
mysql>
```

12. Start the replication:

```
mysql> START REPLICA;
Query OK, 0 rows affected (0.01 sec)
mysql>
```

13. Check the status of the replication by executing the following SQL command:

```
mysql> show replica status\G
*************************** 1. row ***************************
             Replica_IO_State: Waiting for source to send event
                  Source_Host: 172.31.16.119
                  Source_User: repl_user
                  Source_Port: 3306
                Connect_Retry: 60
              Source_Log_File: binlog.000003
          Read_Source_Log_Pos: 739
               Relay_Log_File: node2-relay-bin.000002
                Relay_Log_Pos: 909
        Relay_Source_Log_File: binlog.000003
            Replica_IO_Running: Yes
           Replica_SQL_Running: Yes
…..
                    Last_Errno: 0
                    Last_Error:
                 Skip_Counter: 0
           Exec_Source_Log_Pos: 739
               Relay_Log_Space: 1119
               Until_Condition: None
                Until_Log_File:
                 Until_Log_Pos: 0
             Source_SSL_Allowed: Yes
….
           Seconds_Behind_Source: 0
 Source_SSL_Verify_Server_Cert: No
                 Last_IO_Errno: 0
                 Last_IO_Error:
                Last_SQL_Errno: 0
                Last_SQL_Error:
   Replicate_Ignore_Server_Ids:
              Source_Server_Id: 1
                   Source_UUID: c3b09097-ce27-11ee-9f1a-026bd47bfb91
               Source_Info_File: mysql.slave_master_info
                     SQL_Delay: 0
           SQL_Remaining_Delay: NULL
     Replica_SQL_Running_State: Replica has read all relay log;
                                waiting for more updates
             Source_Retry_Count: 86400
…
            Retrieved_Gtid_Set: c3b09097-ce27-11ee-9f1a-026bd47bfb91:27-28
             Executed_Gtid_Set: c3b09097-ce27-11ee-9f1a-026bd47bfb91:1-28
                 Auto_Position: 1
…
          Get_Source_public_key: 0
              Network_Namespace:
1 row in set (0.00 sec)
mysql>
```

Once this command is executed, replication should begin automatically, and any changes made to the source server will be replicated to the replica server in real time.

Here's an example configuration file for MySQL that enables GTID replication and sets up replication between two servers:

```
# Configuration for replica Server
[mysqld]
gtid_mode=ON
enforce_gtid_consistency=ON
server-id=2
log-bin=mysql-bin
binlog_format=row

[client]
port=3306
socket=/var/run/mysqld/mysqld.sock

[mysql]
default-character-set=utf8mb4

[mysqldump]
default-character-set=utf8mb4

[mysqladmin]
default-character-set=utf8mb4

[mysqld_safe]
pid-file=/var/run/mysqld/mysqld.pid
```

In this example configuration file, GTID replication is enabled through the settings `gtid_mode=ON` and `enforce_gtid_consistency=ON`. This code also sets a unique server-ID for each server, and enables binary logging via the `log-bin` and `bin log_format` parameters.

Replication Using the Clone Plug-in

The *clone plug-in*, which was introduced in MySQL 8.0.17, allows for the cloning of data either locally or from a remote MySQL server instance. The cloned data represents a physical snapshot of the data stored in InnoDB, including schemas, tables, tablespaces, and data dictionary metadata. This cloned data forms a fully functional data directory, enabling the use of the clone plug-in for MySQL server provisioning.

To load the plug-in during server startup, you can utilize the `--plugin-load-add` option and specify the library file that contains it. Note that this option needs to be provided each time the server starts when using this plug-in-loading method. You can add the following lines to your *my.cnf* file, adjusting the plug-in library filename extension according to your platform:

```
[mysqld]
plugin-load-add=mysql_clone.so
```

The plug-in library filename extension may vary—*.so* for Unix and Unix-like systems or *.dll* for Windows, for example. To apply the changes made to *my.cnf*, restart the server to ensure that the new settings come into effect.

Alternatively, you can load the plug-in at runtime by using the following statements, adjusting the *.so* suffix to match your platform if needed. Before loading the plug-in, confirm that the plug-in is not already present by executing the following SQL command:

```
source mysql> select version();
+-----------+
| version() |
+-----------+
| 8.0.36    |
+-----------+
1 row in set (0.00 sec)
source mysql>
source mysql> SELECT PLUGIN_NAME, PLUGIN_STATUS
    -> FROM INFORMATION_SCHEMA.PLUGINS
    -> WHERE PLUGIN_NAME = 'clone';
Empty set (0.00 sec)
source mysql>

source mysql> INSTALL PLUGIN clone SONAME 'mysql_clone.so';
Query OK, 0 rows affected (0.03 sec)
source mysql>
source mysql> SELECT PLUGIN_NAME, PLUGIN_STATUS
    -> FROM INFORMATION_SCHEMA.PLUGINS
    -> WHERE PLUGIN_NAME = 'clone';
+-------------+---------------+
| PLUGIN_NAME | PLUGIN_STATUS |
+-------------+---------------+
| clone       | ACTIVE        |
+-------------+---------------+
1 row in set (0.00 sec)
source mysql>
```

If the plug-in has been registered previously using INSTALL PLUGIN or loaded with --plugin-load-add, you can use the --clone option during server startup to control the activation state of the plug-in. For example, to load the plug-in at startup and ensure it remains active without being removed at runtime, you can use the following options in your configuration file:

```
[mysqld]
plugin-load-add=mysql_clone.so
clone=FORCE_PLUS_PERMANENT
```

If you intend to prevent the server from starting if the clone plug-in fails to initialize, you can use the --clone option with a value of FORCE or FORCE_PLUS_PERMANENT.

This will force the server startup to fail if the plug-in does not initialize successfully, ensuring that the clone plug-in is essential for running the server.

Now you need to create a new user to execute the clone operation. So, create a user called 'arn_clone_user' with the password "Xjuh4##8jkL". The user must have BACKUP_ADMIN privilege on *.*. The @'%' notation indicates that this user is allowed to connect from any host. The second command, grant backup_admin on to arn_clone_user'@'%', grants the arn_clone_user user the backup_admin privilege on all databases and tables. This privilege enables the user to perform backup-related operations across the entire MySQL server. Together, these commands establish a new user with the necessary privileges to execute backup and administrative tasks within the MySQL environment:

```
source mysql> create user 'arn_clone_user'@'%' identified by 'Xjuh4##8jkL';
Query OK, 0 rows affected (0.01 sec)
source mysql> grant backup_admin on *.* to 'arn_clone_user'@'%';
Query OK, 0 rows affected (0.00 sec)
source mysql>
```

Verify the privileges for the user *arn_clone_user*:

```
source mysql> show grants for 'arn_clone_user'@'%';
+---------------------------------------------------+
| Grants for arn_clone_user@%                       |
+---------------------------------------------------+
| GRANT USAGE ON *.* TO `arn_clone_user`@`%`        |
| GRANT BACKUP_ADMIN ON *.* TO `arn_clone_user`@`%` |
+---------------------------------------------------+
2 rows in set (0.00 sec)
source mysql>
```

To clone the instance from a donor (i.e., a source), you need to install the mysql_clone component in the receiver instance:

```
replica mysql> install plugin clone soname 'mysql_clone.so';
Query OK, 0 rows affected (0.03 sec)
replica mysql>
```

Check that the status of the plug-in is active:

```
replica mysql> SELECT PLUGIN_NAME, PLUGIN_STATUS
    -> FROM INFORMATION_SCHEMA.PLUGINS
    -> WHERE PLUGIN_NAME = 'clone';
+-------------+---------------+
| PLUGIN_NAME | PLUGIN_STATUS |
+-------------+---------------+
| clone       | ACTIVE        |
+-------------+---------------+
1 row in set (0.00 sec)

replica mysql>
```

As the receiver instance is new and expected to be restored from the donor instance, the following databases were available in the receiver before the cloning process:

```
replica mysql> SHOW DATABASES;
+--------------------+
| Database           |
+--------------------+
| information_schema |
| mysql              |
| performance_schema |
| sys                |
+--------------------+
4 rows in set (0.00 sec)

replica mysql>
```

To ensure successful cloning, the recipient's clone_valid_donor_list setting must include the host address of the donor MySQL server instance. It is essential to have the donor host listed as a valid donor in order to clone data. Configuring this variable requires a MySQL user with the SYSTEM_VARIABLES_ADMIN privilege.

You can use the SHOW VARIABLES syntax to check the current value of the clone_valid_donor_list setting. This dynamic variable can assign the donor using set global query or make it permanent by updating it in *my.cnf*. If the donor isn't specified, you'll encounter the following error:

```
replica mysql> clone instance from arn_clone_user@172.31.16.119:3306 identified
by 'Xjuh4##8jkL';
ERROR 3869 (HY000): Clone system configuration: 172.31.16.119:3306 is not found
in clone_valid_donor_list:
replica mysql>
```

The following command sets the global variable clone_valid_donor_list to the IP address and port 172.31.16.119:3306:

```
replica mysql> set global clone_valid_donor_list='172.31.16.119:3306';
Query OK, 0 rows affected (0.00 sec)
replica mysql>
```

To clone an instance from a donor server, you can use the following command, which initiates the cloning process by connecting to the donor server specified by the IP address 172.31.16.119 on port 3306. The arn_clone_user is the username used to authenticate with the donor server, and Xjuh4##8jkL is the corresponding password for that user. Replace *arn_clone_user*, *172.31.16.119*, and *Xjuh4##8jkL* with the actual values specific to your environment:

```
replica mysql> clone instance from arn_clone_user@172.31.16.119:3306 identified
by 'Xjuh4##8jkL';
Query OK, 0 rows affected (1.06 sec)
replica mysql>
replica mysql> show databases;
```

```
+-------------------+
| Database          |
+-------------------+
| classicmodels     |
| information_schema |
| mysql             |
| performance_schema |
| sys               |
+-------------------+
5 rows in set (0.00 sec)

replica mysql>

clone instance from arn_clone_user@52.90.85.120:3306 identified by 'Xjuh4##8jkL'
data directory='/mysql_backup/mysql';
```

 During a remote cloning operation, the default behavior is to remove the data in the recipient's data directory and replace it with the cloned data. However, an alternative option is available. By utilizing the DATA DIRECTORY option, you can clone the data to a different directory on the recipient. This approach allows you to avoid removing any existing data in the original data directory.

To monitor the progress of the cloning process, you can query the perfor mance_schema.clone_progress table. When the cloning is in progress, you can execute the following command to retrieve the relevant information:

```
SELECT * FROM performance_schema.clone_progress;
```

This query will provide details about the current status and progress of the cloning operation, allowing you to track the ongoing process. Here are the completed clone statuses:

```
replica mysql> SELECT * FROM performance_schema.clone_progress\G
*************************** 1. row ***************************
           ID: 1
        STAGE: DROP DATA
        STATE: Completed
   BEGIN_TIME: 2024-02-18 08:27:47.814773
     END_TIME: 2024-02-18 08:27:47.964751
      THREADS: 1
     ESTIMATE: 0
         DATA: 0
      NETWORK: 0
   DATA_SPEED: 0
NETWORK_SPEED: 0
*************************** 2. row ***************************
           ID: 1
        STAGE: FILE COPY
        STATE: Completed
   BEGIN_TIME: 2024-02-18 08:27:47.964856
```

```
          END_TIME: 2024-02-18 08:27:48.495403
           THREADS: 1
          ESTIMATE: 74911206
              DATA: 74911206
           NETWORK: 74924986
        DATA_SPEED: 0
     NETWORK_SPEED: 0
*************************** 3. row ***************************
                ID: 1
             STAGE: PAGE COPY
             STATE: Completed
        BEGIN_TIME: 2024-02-18 08:27:48.495555
          END_TIME: 2024-02-18 08:27:48.531297
           THREADS: 1
          ESTIMATE: 0
              DATA: 0
           NETWORK: 99
        DATA_SPEED: 0
     NETWORK_SPEED: 0
*************************** 4. row ***************************
                ID: 1
             STAGE: REDO COPY
             STATE: Completed
        BEGIN_TIME: 2024-02-18 08:27:48.531437
          END_TIME: 2024-02-18 08:27:48.538850
           THREADS: 1
          ESTIMATE: 4608
              DATA: 4608
           NETWORK: 5005
        DATA_SPEED: 0
     NETWORK_SPEED: 0
*************************** 5. row ***************************
                ID: 1
             STAGE: FILE SYNC
             STATE: Completed
        BEGIN_TIME: 2024-02-18 08:27:48.539002
          END_TIME: 2024-02-18 08:27:48.598758
           THREADS: 1
          ESTIMATE: 0
              DATA: 0
           NETWORK: 0
        DATA_SPEED: 0
     NETWORK_SPEED: 0
*************************** 6. row ***************************
                ID: 1
             STAGE: RESTART
             STATE: Completed
        BEGIN_TIME: 2024-02-18 08:27:48.598758
          END_TIME: 2024-02-18 08:27:54.487234
           THREADS: 0
          ESTIMATE: 0
              DATA: 0
```

```
          NETWORK: 0
       DATA_SPEED: 0
    NETWORK_SPEED: 0
    *************************** 7. row ***************************
               ID: 1
            STAGE: RECOVERY
            STATE: Completed
       BEGIN_TIME: 2024-02-18 08:27:54.487234
         END_TIME: 2024-02-18 08:27:54.984392
          THREADS: 0
         ESTIMATE: 0
             DATA: 0
          NETWORK: 0
       DATA_SPEED: 0
    NETWORK_SPEED: 0
    7 rows in set (0.00 sec)

    replica mysql>
```

By querying the performance_schema.clone_status table, you can obtain the binlog coordinates needed to initiate replication:

```
    replica mysql> select binlog_file,binlog_position from performance_schema
    .clone_status\G
    *************************** 1. row ***************************
        binlog_file: binlog.000003
    binlog_position: 1584
    1 row in set (0.00 sec)
    replica mysql>
```

For every replica to successfully connect with the source in MySQL, it's essential to create a user account on the source. For instance, to create a new user named repl_user with replication privileges, permitting connections from any host within the domain *example.com*, execute these statements on the source server:

```
    CREATE USER 'repl_user'@'%.example.com' IDENTIFIED BY 'password';
    GRANT REPLICATION SLAVE ON *.* TO 'repl_user'@'%.example.com';
```

Furthermore, to establish replication, you can use these statements:

```
    CHANGE REPLICATION SOURCE TO
    SOURCE_HOST='Donor host_name or IP',
    SOURCE_USER='repl_user',
    SOURCE_PASSWORD='Password',
    SOURCE_LOG_FILE='source_log_name',
    SOURCE_LOG_POS=source_log_pos;

    START REPLICA;
```

During a local cloning operation, data is cloned from the MySQL server instance where the operation is initiated to a directory located on the same server or node where the MySQL server instance is running.

For successful execution, the MySQL server must possess the required write access to create the specified directory:

```
[root@node1 ~]# mkdir -p /var/lib/mysql_clone/
[root@node1 ~]# chown -R mysql.mysql /var/lib/mysql_clone/
[root@node1 ~]# ls -ltr /var/lib/mysql_clone/
total 0
[root@node1 ~]#
```

The command clone local data directory='/var/lib/mysql_clone/backup/'; initiates the cloning process with a local data directory specified for the recipient server. In this case, the */var/lib/mysql_clone/backup/* directory is designated as the location where the cloned data will be stored. The command instructs the cloning operation to use the specified directory as the destination for the replicated data. It is essential to ensure that the MySQL server has the necessary write permissions to create and access the specified directory:

```
source mysql> clone local data directory='/var/lib/mysql_clone/backup/';
Query OK, 0 rows affected (0.33 sec)
source mysql>
```

After completing the backup, you can find the backup directory in the specified location provided during the execution of the clone local data command:

```
[root@node1 ~]# ls -ltr /var/lib/mysql_clone/
total 0
drwxr-x---. 7 mysql mysql 171 Feb 18 08:35 backup
[root@node1 ~]#
```

You can use ls to display the files and directories in the backup directory:

```
[root@node1 ~]# ls -ltr /var/lib/mysql_clone/backup/
total 71688
drwxr-x---. 2 mysql mysql        6 Feb 18 08:35  mysql
drwxr-x---. 2 mysql mysql       28 Feb 18 08:35  sys
drwxr-x---. 2 mysql mysql     4096 Feb 18 08:35  classicmodels
-rw-r-----. 1 mysql mysql     3558 Feb 18 08:35  ib_buffer_pool
-rw-r-----. 1 mysql mysql 12582912 Feb 18 08:35  ibdata1
-rw-r-----. 1 mysql mysql 27262976 Feb 18 08:35  mysql.ibd
-rw-r-----. 1 mysql mysql 16777216 Feb 18 08:35  undo_002
-rw-r-----. 1 mysql mysql 16777216 Feb 18 08:35  undo_001
drwxr-x---. 2 mysql mysql       23 Feb 18 08:35  '#innodb_redo'
drwxr-x---. 2 mysql mysql       89 Feb 18 08:35  '#clone'
[root@node1 ~]#
```

To verify that replication is working correctly, you can check the Replica_IO_Run ning and Replica_SQL_Running columns of the SHOW REPLICA STATUS command output. If both values are Yes, replication is working. The clone plug-in offers the fastest and most efficient approach to establishing replication in MySQL 8.

Monitoring Replication Status

Monitoring replication status is an essential task for database administrators, as it helps ensure that data is being replicated correctly across multiple MySQL servers. This section presents various ways of monitoring replication status, including using MySQL commands, third-party tools, and setting up alerts for replication status changes.

Using MySQL Commands for Monitoring Replication

MySQL provides several commands that can be used to monitor replication status. These commands can be executed on either the source or the replica server. The `SHOW REPLICA STATUS\G` command shows the replication status on the replica server. It provides information such as the replication status, the position of the replica in the replication stream, and the last error that occurred during replication. The output of this command is quite detailed and provides useful information for troubleshooting replication issues.

The `SHOW MASTER STATUS;` command shows the current position of the source server in the replication stream. It provides information such as the binlog filename and position. This command is useful when setting up a new replica server or when troubleshooting replication issues.

In addition to `SHOW REPLICA STATUS\G`, you can use the `performance_schema.repli cation%` tables to get more information. These tables are part of the MySQL 8 performance schema and are related to replication. They can be queried to monitor and manage the replication process:

```
mysql> show tables like 'replication%';
+----------------------------------------------------------+
| Tables_in_performance_schema (replication%)              |
+----------------------------------------------------------+
| replication_applier_configuration                        |
| replication_applier_filters                              |
| replication_applier_global_filters                       |
| replication_applier_status                               |
| replication_applier_status_by_coordinator                |
| replication_applier_status_by_worker                     |
| replication_asynchronous_connection_failover             |
| replication_asynchronous_connection_failover_managed     |
| replication_connection_configuration                     |
| replication_connection_status                            |
| replication_group_member_stats                           |
| replication_group_members                                |
+----------------------------------------------------------+
12 rows in set (0.00 sec)
```

Tables containing information regarding the connection of the replica to the source encompass several key aspects. The `replication_connection_configuration` table stores crucial configuration parameters necessary for establishing a connection with the source. Meanwhile, the `replication_connection_status` table tracks the real-time status of the connection established with the source, providing valuable insights into its stability and functionality. Additionally, the `replication_asynchronous_con nection_failover` table lists sources designated for asynchronous connection fail-over mechanisms, enhancing the resilience of the replication setup.

In parallel, tables containing general information about the transaction applier shed light on the functionality and status of this crucial component on the replica. The `replication_applier_configuration` table houses configuration parameters rele-vant to the transaction applier's operation, ensuring its alignment with specific requirements and performance objectives. Complementing this, the `replica tion_applier_status` table provides ongoing updates on the current status of the transaction applier, facilitating monitoring and troubleshooting efforts.

Further details about threads responsible for applying transactions are encapsulated in specialized tables. The `replication_applier_status_by_coordinator` table specifically displays the status of the coordinator thread, particularly pertinent in the context of multithreaded replicas where coordination among threads is essential for efficient transaction processing. Correspondingly, the `replication_applier_sta tus_by_worker` table offers insights into the status of applier or worker threads in multithreaded replicas, allowing for granular monitoring and optimization of resource utilization.

Channel-based replication filters, pivotal for controlling the flow of replicated data, are documented in dedicated tables. The `replication_applier_filters` table con-tains pertinent data regarding replication filters configured for specific replication channels, facilitating targeted data manipulation and synchronization strategies. Con-versely, the `replication_applier_global_filters` table stores information about global replication filters applicable across all replication channels, streamlining man-agement and ensuring consistent data replication policies.

Finally, tables pertaining to Group Replication members provide comprehensive insights into the composition and performance of replication groups. The `replica tion_group_members` table furnishes network and status details for individual mem-bers within the replication group, enabling administrators to assess their connectivity and health. Complementing this, the `replication_group_member_stats` table offers statistical information regarding group members' participation in transactions, aiding in performance analysis and capacity planning endeavors.

Using Third-Party Tools for Monitoring Replication

In addition to MySQL commands, several third-party tools are available for monitoring replication status. These tools provide a more graphical and user-friendly interface for monitoring replication:

Two popular tools are MySQL Enterprise Monitor, a commercial monitoring tool from Oracle; and Percona Monitoring and Management (PMM), an open source option. Both provide real-time monitoring and alerting for MySQL servers, including replication status. They also provide a range of other features, including performance monitoring, query analysis, and backup management.

Setting Up Alerts for Replication Status Changes

Setting up alerts for replication status changes is an important part of monitoring replication. Alerts can be configured to notify the database administrator when replication status changes occur. This allows the administrator to take immediate action to address any replication issues. Here are some tips for setting up alerts:

Use a monitoring tool that provides alerting capabilities
As mentioned earlier, both MySQL Enterprise Monitor and PMM provide alerting capabilities for replication status changes.

Define appropriate thresholds for alerts
When setting up alerts, it is important to define appropriate thresholds for replication lag and other replication-related metrics. For example, if replication lag exceeds a certain threshold, an alert should be generated.

Configure alert notifications
Alert notifications should be configured to notify the database administrator when replication status changes occur. This can be done through email, text messages, or other methods.

In conclusion, monitoring replication status is an important task for DBAs. By using MySQL commands, third-party tools, and setting up alerts for replication status changes, database administrators can ensure that data is being replicated correctly across multiple MySQL servers.

Troubleshooting Replication Issues

Replication is a critical component of a MySQL database architecture, allowing for data to be duplicated across multiple servers. However, replication issues commonly occur, causing inconsistencies in the data between servers. This section discusses common replication issues and how to troubleshoot them.

Identifying Common Issues

Replication lag is a delay that occurs between the time that changes are made to the source server and the time that those changes are applied to the replica server. Here are some steps you can take to troubleshoot replication lag:

- Check the network connection between the source and replica servers to ensure it is stable and fast enough to handle the replication traffic.
- Check the replica server's configuration and resources to ensure that the server has enough memory and CPU to handle the replication workload.
- Use the MySQL performance schema to identify slow queries or long-running transactions that could be causing the replication lag.

Duplicate-key errors occur when a primary key or unique index value already exists on the replica server, preventing the replication of the data from the source server. To troubleshoot duplicate-key errors, try the following:

- Check the replication configuration to ensure that the primary key or unique index value is being replicated correctly.
- Identify and resolve any conflicts in the data between the source and replica servers.

Schema mismatches occur when the schema on the replica server is different from the source server, preventing the replication of data. Use these steps to troubleshoot:

- Compare the schema on the source and replica servers to identify differences.
- Modify the schema on the replica server to match the source server's schema.

Replication conflicts occur when the same data is modified on both the source and replica servers. This can result in data inconsistencies and requires resolution. You can take the following steps to resolve replication conflicts:

Identify the conflict
  Use the MySQL logs to identify the conflicting data and the cause of the conflict.

Resolve the conflict
  Choose which version of the conflicting data to keep and then modify the other server's data to match the chosen version.

Restart replication
  After resolving the conflict, restart the replication to ensure that the data is consistent between the source and replica servers.

Using Logs to Troubleshoot

MySQL logs can provide valuable information when troubleshooting replication issues. The following logs are particularly useful:

Error log
> Contains information about errors that occur during replication.

Binary log
> Contains a record of all changes made to the database, allowing for the replication of data from the source server to the replica server.

Slow query log
> Contains information about queries that take longer than a specific threshold to execute, allowing for the identification of slow queries that could be causing replication lag.

Here's an example configuration file for a replica server:

```
[mysqld]

server-id = 2
relay-log = /var/lib/mysql/mysql-relay-bin
relay-log-index = /var/lib/mysql/mysql-relay-bin.index
log-error = /var/log/mysql/mysql-error.log
log-bin = /var/log/mysql/mysql-bin.log
binlog-format = ROW
read-only = 1
super-read-only=1
```

In this example, the replica server has a server ID of 2, and the relay log and error log are stored in the */var/lib/mysql/* directory. The binlog format is set to row-based replication, and the server is set to read-only and super-read-only modes to prevent any accidental modifications to the data.

Managing Replication Lag

In a MySQL replication environment, replication lag occurs when the replica server falls behind the source server in applying updates. As we stated previously, replication lag can be a common issue and can lead to data inconsistencies and poor performance. To address this problem, it's important to understand the causes of replication lag and the techniques for reducing it.

As noted previously in this chapter, replication lag is the time delay between when a transaction is committed on the source server and when it is applied on the replica server. It is measured in seconds or milliseconds, and it can be caused by various factors, including these:

High network latency

When the network between the source and replica servers is slow, it can cause delays in replication.

Heavy write activity

If there is a lot of write activity on the source server, the replica server may fall behind in processing updates.

Slow I/O operations

If the replica server is unable to keep up with the rate of updates being sent by the source server because of slow I/O operations, it can result in replication lag.

Inefficient SQL statements

Inefficient SQL statements can lead to replication lag, especially when large data sets are being transferred.

Several techniques can be used to reduce replication lag:

Improving network connectivity

To reduce replication lag caused by network latency, you can improve the network connectivity between the source and replica servers. This can be done by using a faster network connection or by reducing the distance between the two servers.

Optimizing write activity

To reduce replication lag caused by heavy write activity on the source server, you can optimize the write activity by batching updates in small chunks and reducing the frequency of updates.

Improving I/O performance

To reduce replication lag caused by slow I/O operations, you can improve the I/O performance of the replica server. This can be done by adding more disks or by using faster disks.

Optimizing SQL statements

To reduce replication lag caused by inefficient SQL statements, you can optimize the SQL statements by using indexes, reducing the amount of data being transferred, or using more-efficient SQL statements.

Managing replication lag is critical to ensuring a stable and high-performing MySQL replication environment. By understanding the causes of replication lag and using the techniques outlined in this section, you can reduce replication lag and improve the overall performance of your MySQL replication setup.

It's crucial to have a replication monitoring system in place to ensure that replication is functioning correctly and that lag is current. Traditionally, we use `SHOW REPLICA STATUS` to obtain information such as `Replica_IO_Running: Yes`, `Replica_SQL_Running: Yes`, and `Seconds_Behind_Master: 0`. However, this method can be unreliable as `Seconds_Behind_Master` shows the difference between the last timestamp read in the binlogs and the current time. Many factors, such as slow networks, lengthy queries, blocking operations, or a hierarchy of second-level replicas (source > replica 1> replica 2), can result in an irrelevant value for the variable.

Valuable tools from Percona Toolkit can assist you in monitoring and managing MySQL replication. Percona Toolkit's `pt-heartbeat` tool monitors replication lag on a MySQL database in real time.

Therefore, we suggest using `pt-heartbeat`, which relies solely on the heartbeat record being replicated to the replica instead of the aforementioned unreliable method of determining lag. The `pt-heartbeat` tool will insert/update a row in the source, and the time delay is calculated based on when the data was inserted and when it became available to read in the replica. It operates at any depth in the replication hierarchy, providing reliable reporting on how long a replica lags its original source (the source's source), for instance.

Run these commands to set up heartbeat monitoring between the primary and replica. On the source:

```
[root@Primary ~]#pt-heartbeat --daemonize -D test --update -h<IP
address> --create-table
```

On the replica:

```
[root@Replica ~]#pt-heartbeat -D test --monitor --master-server-id 1

0.00s [ 0.00s, 0.00s, 0.00s ]
0.00s [ 0.00s, 0.00s, 0.00s ]
0.00s [ 0.00s, 0.00s, 0.00s ]
0.00s [ 0.00s, 0.00s, 0.00s ]
```

To reduce the load on the source server, we typically schedule backups from the replica. However, it is critical to ensure that the replica is up-to-date with the source to guarantee that the backup contains the most recent data. To accomplish this, you can use a straightforward script to check the replication status periodically (through cron) and verify the status just before the backup is scheduled.

This bash script monitors MySQL replication delay and sends email notifications based on predefined thresholds. It categorizes delays as Good, Warning, or Critical, and triggers alerts accordingly:

```bash
#!/bin/bash

# <300 - [Good]
# 300> <600 - [Warning]
# > 600 - [Critical]

MAIL_FROM="root@`hostname`"
MAIL_TO="mailid@mail.com"
Warningthreshold=300
Criticalthreshold=600
backup=$1
CMD=$(/root/bin/pt-heartbeat -D test --master-server-id 1 --check | cut
-d. -f1)

# Pass the parameter "test.sh backup" to denote the call is from the
backup script.

if [ $CMD -lt $Warningthreshold ]
then
MESSAGE=`date +'%m:%d:%Y %H:%M:%S'`" [Good] current delay: "$CMD;
elif [ $CMD -gt $Warningthreshold ] && [ $CMD -lt $Criticalthreshold ]
then
MESSAGE=`date +'%m:%d:%Y %H:%M:%S'`" [Warning] current delay: "$CMD;
elif [ $CMD -gt $Criticalthreshold ]
then
MESSAGE=`date +'%m:%d:%Y %H:%M:%S'`" [Critical] current delay: $CMD
Check the replication"
else
MESSAGE=`date +'%m:%d:%Y %H:%M:%S'`" [Error] Replication status check
failed need to investigate."
fi

#No arguments supplied"

if [ -z "$1" ] && [ $CMD -gt $Warningthreshold ]
then
(echo "Subject: Replication status on `hostname`";
echo "Replication status : "
echo $MESSAGE
) | /usr/sbin/sendmail -O NoRecipientAction=add-to -f$\{MAIL_FROM}
$\{MAIL_TO}

elif [ $# -eq 1 ]
then
(echo "Subject: Replication status check prior to backup on `hostname`";
echo "Replication status prior to backup:"
echo $MESSAGE
) | /usr/sbin/sendmail -O NoRecipientAction=add-to -f$\{MAIL_FROM}
$\{MAIL_TO}

fi
```

Percona Toolkit's pt-slave-find tool is designed to locate and display the replication hierarchy of your MySQL replica servers. By displaying the topology and replication hierarchy of your replication instances, it enables you to gain a clear understanding of your system's structure and dependencies:

```
[root@Tst1Master ~]# ./pt-slave-find --host=192.168.56.10
192.168.56.10
Version 5.6.22-72.0-log
Server ID 1
Uptime 42:09 (started 2023-03-03T01:40:42)
Replication Is not a slave, has 1 slaves connected, is not read_only
Filters
Binary logging STATEMENT
Slave status
Slave mode STRICT
Auto-increment increment 1, offset 1
InnoDB version 5.6.22-72.0
+- 192.168.56.11
Version 5.6.22-72.0
Server ID 2
Uptime 41:48 (started 2023-03-03T01:41:03)
Replication Is a slave, has 0 slaves connected, is not read_only
Filters
Binary logging STATEMENT
Slave status 0 seconds behind, running, no errors
Slave mode STRICT
Auto-increment increment 1, offset 1
InnoDB version 5.6.22-72.0

[root@Tst1Master ~]# ./pt-slave-find --host=192.168.56.10
--report-format=hostname
192.168.56.10
+- 192.168.56.11
InnoDB version 5.6.22-72.0
```

The pt-slave-restart tool is designed to monitor your MySQL replication replicas for any errors and attempt to restart replication if any errors occur. This tool is particularly helpful for skipping statements that cause errors and resuming replication, but it must be used with caution to ensure that data consistency is maintained between the source and replica servers. We recommended to confirm the consistency of data between the source and replica by using the pt-table-checksum tool after using pt-slave-restart. For example, you can use pt-slave-restart to restart the replica if it encounters error 1062 (which indicates a duplicate entry in a primary-key column):

```
#pt-slave-restart --socket=/var/lib/mysql/custom-feeds/mysql.sock
--ask-pass --error-numbers=1062
```

The pt-table-checksum tool is used to perform an online replication consistency check by running checksum queries on the source database. This will produce different results on replicas that are inconsistent with the source, thus helping to identify inconsistencies in the replication process. Here is an example of how to use pt-table-checksum:

```
[root@Primary ~]# ./pt-table-checksum -dD
TS ERRORS DIFFS ROWS CHUNKS SKIPPED TIME TABLE
03-03T02:34:44 0 1 2 1 0 0.011 d.t
```

Running the pt-table-checksum tool is crucial to ensure that the data on the replica side is identical to that of the source, even if you have never skipped an event using the pt-slave-restart tool. It helps to perform an online replication consistency check by executing checksum queries on the source, which produces different results on replicas that are inconsistent with the source.

The pt-table-sync tool helps synchronize the data between MySQL tables efficiently. It can be used to identify and resolve discrepancies between the source and replica, ensuring that the data is consistent. This tool can help save a lot of time and effort by automating the synchronization process.

This command executes pt-table-sync with specific options to print the synchronization actions needed to align a MySQL replica with its primary server:

```
[root@Replica ~]# ./pt-table-sync -dD --print --sync-to-master
192.168.56.11

REPLACE INTO `d`.`t`(`id`, `data`) VALUES ('1', 'Test1')
/*percona-toolkit src_db:d src_tbl:t src_dsn:P=3306,h=192.168.56.10
dst_db:d dst_tbl:t dst_dsn:h=192.168.56.11 lock:1 transaction:1
changing_src:1 replicate:0 bidirectional:0 pid:6435 user:root
host:Tst1Slave.mysql*/;

REPLACE INTO `d`.`t`(`id`, `data`) VALUES ('2', 'Test2')
/*percona-toolkit src_db:d src_tbl:t src_dsn:P=3306,h=192.168.56.10
dst_db:d dst_tbl:t dst_dsn:h=192.168.56.11 lock:1 transaction:1
changing_src:1 replicate:0 bidirectional:0 pid:6435 user:root
host:Tst1Slave.mysql*/;

[root@Tst1Slave ~]#

[root@Replica ~]# ./pt-table-sync -dD --verbose --execute
--sync-to-master 192.168.56.11
# Syncing h=192.168.56.11
# DELETE REPLACE INSERT UPDATE ALGORITHM START END EXIT DATABASE.TABLE
# 0 2 0 0 Chunk 03:38:09 03:38:09 2 d.t
```

Let's perform the checksum again to confirm that the tables are now in sync after using pt-table-sync:

```
[root@Tst1Master ~]# ./pt-table-checksum -dD
TS ERRORS DIFFS ROWS CHUNKS SKIPPED TIME TABLE
03-03T03:03:40 0 0 2 1 0 0.111 d.t
```

Conclusion

This chapter guided you through the intricate terrain of MySQL replication, enabling you to grasp its complexities, set up various replication types, monitor their status, troubleshoot challenges, and ultimately harness replication to achieve robust and reliable database architectures.

## CHAPTER 7

High Availability and Scalability

In this chapter, we'll explore the concepts of high availability (HA) and scalability in MySQL, and how they can be achieved using various techniques such as load balancing, replication, and MySQL clustering.

Understanding High Availability and Scalability Concepts

High availability refers to the capability of a system to remain operational continuously, even in the event of hardware or software failures. In MySQL, HA ensures that the database system is always accessible to users and has no single point of failure that could lead to downtime.

To achieve HA in MySQL, it is essential to have redundant hardware and software components. In a distributed system, this means having multiple nodes that can perform the same functions. In the event of a failure, these nodes should be able to take over the workload and ensure no disruption in service.

One common way to achieve HA in MySQL is through source-replica replication, which we covered in Chapter 6. In this setup, the source node handles all write requests, and the replica nodes handle read requests. Each replica node contains a copy of the source database and can take over as the new source in the event of a failure. This setup ensures that the database system has no single point of failure and can remain available even if one node fails.

Scalability refers to the capability of a system to handle increased workloads without experiencing performance degradation. In MySQL, scalability ensures that the database system can handle a growing number of users, requests, and data volumes without affecting the response times.

To achieve scalability in MySQL, it is essential to ensure that the database system can distribute the workload across multiple nodes. This requires a load-balancing mechanism that can distribute requests evenly across nodes based on their capacity and availability.

One common way to achieve scalability in MySQL is through *horizontal scaling*. This adds more nodes to the system to distribute the workload. In a distributed system, this requires configuring the nodes to work together and synchronize their data. It also requires a load balancer that can distribute requests across the nodes based on their capacity and availability.

High availability and scalability are crucial in MySQL for the following reasons:

- Downtime can result in significant financial losses for businesses, and HA ensures that the database system remains accessible to users, even in the event of failures.

- Scalability ensures that the database system can handle a growing number of users and requests, which is critical in businesses with rapidly expanding data volumes and user bases.

- High availability and scalability ensure that the database system can handle mission-critical applications that require constant access and high performance levels.

Achieving HA and scalability in MySQL presents several challenges:

- Ensuring that the database system is always accessible to users, even in the event of hardware or software failures, requires redundant hardware and software components. This can be expensive and may require specialized skills and expertise to configure and maintain.

- Balancing workloads across multiple nodes in a distributed system can be challenging, particularly when dealing with write-intensive workloads. In a source-replica replication setup, this requires ensuring that write requests are directed only to the source node and that the replica nodes are kept up-to-date with the latest changes.

- Managing the complexity of configuration and maintenance of a distributed system, including data synchronization, load balancing, and failover, requires specialized skills and expertise. This can be time-consuming and may require additional resources and personnel.

Using Orchestrator for Topology Management

Orchestrator is a MySQL replication topology manager. It's a tool designed to simplify and automate the management of MySQL replication clusters. Orchestrator helps monitor, detect, and recover from replication topology issues, making it easier to maintain the HA and reliability of MySQL database clusters. Figure 7-1 illustrates the fundamental architecture of an Orchestrator-managed configuration consisting of one primary server and two replicas.

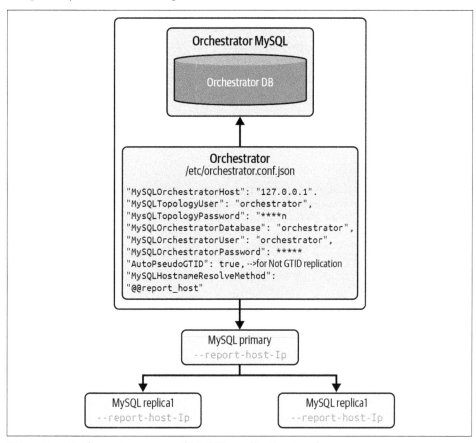

Figure 7-1. Orchestrator-managed MySQL replication topology

MySQL Orchestrator uses the backend MySQL database to store information about the replication topology, server state, failover information, and configuration settings. This allows for centralized management and monitoring of the replication setup, enabling automated failover and recovery and providing a consistent view of the topology.

In MySQL replication setups, GTID Global Transaction ID is used to uniquely identify each transaction, which helps ensure data consistency and facilitate failover and recovery operations. AutoPseudoGTID is a feature in MySQL Orchestrator that generates unique GTID-like identifiers for MySQL servers that don't support GTID. When AutoPseudoGTID is set to true, MySQL Orchestrator will automatically generate a pseudo-GTID for any server in the topology that does not support GTID. This allows MySQL Orchestrator to manage these servers in the same way as servers with native GTID support. Using AutoPseudoGTID helps in simplifying the configuration and management of MySQL replication setups, as it allows MySQL Orchestrator to treat all servers in the topology as if they support GTID. This makes it easier to automate failover and recovery operations, and provides a consistent way to identify transactions across all servers in the topology.

Installing Orchestrator

Before you can use Orchestrator to manage your topology, you need to install it. Follow these steps:

1. Download the Orchestrator package:

    ```
    [root@node3 ~]# wget https://github.com/openark/orchestrator/releases/
    download/v3.2.6/orchestrator-3.2.6-1.x86_64.rpm
    --2024-02-18 10:44:24--  https://github.com/openark/orchestrator/releases/
    download/v3.2.6/orchestrator-3.2.6-1.x86_64.rpm
    Resolving github.com (github.com)... 192.30.255.112
    Connecting to github.com (github.com)|192.30.255.112|:443... connected.
    ...

    HTTP request sent, awaiting response... 200 OK
    Length: 10561207 (10M) [application/octet-stream]
    Saving to: 'orchestrator-3.2.6-1.x86_64.rpm'
    orchestrator-3.2.6-1.x86_64.r 100%[===========================================>]
    10.07M  65.4MB/s    in 0.2s
    2024-02-18 10:44:25 (65.4 MB/s) - 'orchestrator-3.2.6-1.x86_64.rpm'
    saved [10561207/10561207]
    [root@node3 ~]#
    ```

2. Install the necessary dependencies as follows:

    ```
    yum install epel-release -y
    ```

    The jq package is another dependency you'll need to install by using the yum package manager. jq is a command-line JSON processor that enables parsing, filtering, and manipulation of JSON data on Linux systems. The -y flag is used to automatically confirm and proceed with the installation without manual confirmation:

    ```
    [root@node3 ~]# yum install jq -y
    Updating Subscription Management repositories.
    Unable to read consumer identity
    ```

```
...
1/1
  Installing       : oniguruma-6.9.6-1.el9.5.x86_64
  1/2
  Installing       : jq-1.6-15.el9.x86_64
  2/2
  Running scriptlet: jq-1.6-15.el9.x86_64
  2/2
  Verifying        : oniguruma-6.9.6-1.el9.5.x86_64
  1/2
  Verifying        : jq-1.6-15.el9.x86_64
  2/2
Installed products updated.
Installed:
  jq-1.6-15.el9.x86_64
  oniguruma-6.9.6-1.el9.5.x86_64
Complete!
[root@node3 ~]#
```

3. Install the Orchestrator package by using the RPM package manager:

```
[root@node3 ~]#  sudo rpm -i orchestrator-3.2.6-1.x86_64.rpm
[root@node3 ~]#
```

4. Download and install the Orchestrator client:

```
wget https://github.com/openark/orchestrator/releases/download/v3.2.6/
orchestrator-client-3.2.6-1.x86_64.rpm

sudo rpm -i orchestrator-client-3.2.6-1.x86_64.rpm
```

Configuring Orchestrator

Once Orchestrator is installed, you need to configure it for HA deployment. Follow these steps:

1. Create a new database named orchestrator by running the following command:

```
mysql> CREATE DATABASE orchestrator;
Query OK, 1 row affected (0.01 sec)
mysql>
```

2. Create a user named orchestrator with the password GdKG*12#ULmE and grant it all privileges on the orchestrator database:

```
mysql> CREATE USER 'orchestrator'@'127.0.0.1' IDENTIFIED BY 'GdKG*12#ULmE';
Query OK, 0 rows affected (0.01 sec)
mysql> GRANT ALL PRIVILEGES ON `orchestrator`.* TO
'orchestrator'@'127.0.0.1';
Query OK, 0 rows affected (0.01 sec)
mysql>
```

3. Copy the sample configuration file to the appropriate location:

```
[root@node3 ~]# cp /usr/local/orchestrator/orchestrator-sample.conf.json
/etc/orchestrator.conf.json
[root@node3 ~]#
```

4. Edit the *orchestrator.conf.json* file and update the MySQL orchestrator database, username, and password with the correct values:

```
[root@node3 etc]# cat orchestrator.conf.json
{
  "Debug": true,
  "EnableSyslog": false,
  "ListenAddress": ":3000",
  "MySQLTopologyUser": "orc_client_user",
  "MySQLTopologyPassword": "orc_client_password",
  "MySQLTopologyCredentialsConfigFile": "",
  "MySQLTopologySSLPrivateKeyFile": "",
  "MySQLTopologySSLCertFile": "",
  "MySQLTopologySSLCAFile": "",
  "MySQLTopologySSLSkipVerify": true,
  "MySQLTopologyUseMutualTLS": false,
  "MySQLOrchestratorHost": "127.0.0.1",
  "MySQLOrchestratorPort": 3306,
  "MySQLOrchestratorDatabase": "orchestrator",
  "MySQLOrchestratorUser": "orchestrator",
  "MySQLOrchestratorPassword": "GdKG*12#ULmE",
  "MySQLOrchestratorCredentialsConfigFile": "",
  "MySQLOrchestratorSSLPrivateKeyFile": "",
  "MySQLOrchestratorSSLCertFile": "",
  "MySQLOrchestratorSSLCAFile": "",
  "MySQLOrchestratorSSLSkipVerify": true,
  "MySQLOrchestratorUseMutualTLS": false,
  "MySQLConnectTimeoutSeconds": 1,
  "DefaultInstancePort": 3306,
  "DiscoverByShowSlaveHosts": true,
  "InstancePollSeconds": 5,
  "DiscoveryIgnoreReplicaHostnameFilters": [
    "a_host_i_want_to_ignore[.]example[.]com",
    ".*[.]ignore_all_hosts_from_this_domain[.]example[.]com",
    "a_host_with_extra_port_i_want_to_ignore[.]example[.]com:3307"
  ],
```

5. Create a user named topologyuser with the password TsKG*12#ULVMS on the primary MySQL instance and replicate it to all replica instances. Grant the necessary privileges to the user:

```
source mysql> CREATE USER 'topologyuser'@'%' IDENTIFIED BY 'TsKG*12#ULVMS';
Query OK, 0 rows affected (0.01 sec)

source mysql> GRANT SUPER, PROCESS, REPLICATION SLAVE, RELOAD ON *.*
TO \'topologyuser'@\'%';
Query OK, 0 rows affected, 1 warning (0.01 sec)
```

```
source mysql> GRANT ALL PRIVILEGES ON *.* TO 'topologyuser'@'%';
Query OK, 0 rows affected (0.01 sec)
source mysql>
```

6. Update the *orchestrator.conf.json* file again and replace the MySQL topology user's username and password with the correct values:

```
{
  "Debug": true,
  "EnableSyslog": false,
  "ListenAddress": ":3000",
  "MySQLTopologyUser": "topologyuser",
  "MySQLTopologyPassword": "TsKG*12#ULVMS",
  "MySQLTopologyCredentialsConfigFile": "",
  "MySQLTopologySSLPrivateKeyFile": "",
  "MySQLTopologySSLCertFile": "",
  "MySQLTopologySSLCAFile": "",
  "MySQLTopologySSLSkipVerify": true,
```

Starting Orchestrator and Checking Topology

Now that Orchestrator is properly configured, you can start the service and check the topology. Follow these steps:

1. Start the Orchestrator service:

   ```
   systemctl start orchestrator
   ```

2. Verify the status of the Orchestrator service:

   ```
   [root@node3 ~]# systemctl start orchestrator

   [root@node3 ~]# systemctl status orchestrator
   orchestrator.service - orchestrator: MySQL replication management
   and visualization
        Loaded: loaded (/etc/systemd/system/orchestrator.service; disabled;
                preset: disabled)
        Active: active (running) since Sun 2024-02-18 11:01:53 UTC; 10s ago
          Docs: https://github.com/openark/orchestrator
      Main PID: 16155 (orchestrator)
         Tasks: 6 (limit: 4329)
        Memory: 20.6M
           CPU: 70ms
        CGroup: /system.slice/orchestrator.service
                └─16155 /usr/local/orchestrator/orchestrator http

   Feb 18 11:01:58 node3 orchestrator[16155]: 2024-02-18 11:01:58
   INFO Connecting to backend 127.0.0.1:3306: maxConnecti>
   Feb 18 11:01:59 node3 orchestrator[16155]: 2024-02-18 11:01:59
   INFO Starting Discovery
   Feb 18 11:01:59 node3 orchestrator[16155]: 2024-02-18 11:01:59
   INFO Registering endpoints
   ```

```
Feb 18 11:01:59 node3 orchestrator[16155]: 2024-02-18 11:01:59
INFO Starting HTTP listener on :3000
Feb 18 11:01:59 node3 orchestrator[16155]: 2024-02-18 11:01:59
INFO continuous discovery: setting up
Feb 18 11:01:59 node3 orchestrator[16155]: 2024-02-18 11:01:59
INFO continuous discovery: starting
Feb 18 11:01:59 node3 orchestrator[16155]: 2024-02-18 11:01:59
DEBUG Queue.startMonitoring(DEFAULT)
Feb 18 11:02:01 node3 orchestrator[16155]: 2024-02-18 11:02:01
DEBUG Waiting for 15 seconds to pass before running fa>>
Feb 18 11:02:02 node3 orchestrator[16155]: 2024-02-18 11:02:02
DEBUG Waiting for 15 seconds to pass before running fa>
Feb 18 11:02:03 node3 orchestrator[16155]: 2024-02-18 11:02:03
DEBUG Waiting for 15 seconds to pass before running fa>
[root@node3 ~]#
```

3. Access the Orchestrator web interface at *http://192.168.20.71:3000/web/discover*. The default port number is 3000:

4. Use this interface to discover the nodes topology using the primary node IP and the MySQL port number. In this example, the IP is 192.168.20.72, and the default MySQL port 3306 is entered into the input box and submitted:

5. Check the topology status on the interface to ensure that it's functioning correctly:

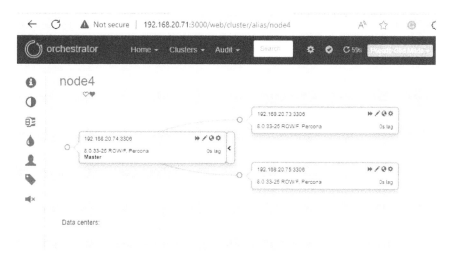

The instance running on 192.168.20.74:3306 is the primary server, running version 8.0.33-25. The first replica, 192.168.20.73:3306, is running version 8.0.33-25. The second replica, 192.168.20.75:3306, is running version 8.0.33-25.

You also have the option of using the command-line interface to find the cluster alias. On the command prompt of the Orchestrator-installed server, run the following command, which will list the cluster alias you can then use in the next step:

```
[root@node3 ~]# sudo orchestrator-client -c clusters-alias
node1:3306,node1
[root@node3 ~]#
```

6. To retrieve the topology details, execute the following command:

```
[root@node3 ~]# sudo orchestrator-client -c topology -a node1:3306
node1:3306    [0s,ok,8.0.36,rw,ROW,>>]
+ node2:3306  [0s,ok,8.0.36,rw,ROW,>>]
+ node3:3306  [0s,ok,8.0.36,rw,ROW,>>]
[root@node3 ~]#
```

Relocating Replica Nodes

In case you need to relocate a replica node, follow these steps:

1. To relocate a replica node from one location to another, use this command:

```
[root@node3 ~]# sudo orchestrator-client -c relocate -i node3 -d node2
node3:3306<node2:3306
[root@node3 ~]#
```

```
[root@node3 ~]# sudo orchestrator-client -c topology -a node1:3306
node1:3306     [0s,ok,8.0.36,rw,ROW,>>]
+ node2:3306   [0s,ok,8.0.36,rw,ROW,>>]
  + node3:3306 [0s,ok,8.0.36,rw,ROW,>>]
[root@node3 ~]#
```

2. Verify the relocation process by checking the Orchestrator web interface and ensuring that the replica node has been successfully relocated.

Performing Graceful Failover

To perform a graceful failover from one MySQL server to another, follow these steps:

1. Initiate the graceful failover process by executing the following command:

```
[root@node3 ~]# orchestrator-client -c graceful-master-takeover -a node1 -d
node2:3306
node2:3306
[root@node3 ~]#

[root@node3 ~]# sudo orchestrator-client -c topology -a node1:3306]
node2:3306     [0s,ok,8.0.36,rw,ROW,>>
- node1:3306 [null,nonreplicating,8.0.36,ro,ROW,>>,downtimed]]
+ node3:3306 [0s,ok,8.0.36,rw,ROW,>>
[root@node3 ~]#
```

2. Check the Orchestrator web interface to confirm that the old primary replica has stopped as expected after the failover:

Currently the instance running on 192.168.20.75:3306 is the primary server running version 8.0.33-25. The first replica, 192.168.20.73:3306, is running version 8.0.33-25 and replicating from 192.168.20.75:3306. The previous primary—currently the second replica, 192.168.20.74:3306—is running version 8.0.33-25 and connected to the primary 192.168.20.75:3306.

3. To start the replica, use the following command:

```
[root@node3 ~]#
[root@node3 ~]# orchestrator-client -c start-replica -i  node1:3306
node1:3306
[root@node3 ~]#
[root@node3 ~]# sudo orchestrator-client -c topology -a node1:3306
node2:3306   [0s,ok,8.0.36,rw,ROW,>>]
+ node1:3306 [0s,ok,8.0.36,ro,ROW,>>,downtimed]
+ node3:3306 [0s,ok,8.0.36,rw,ROW,>>]
[root@node3 ~]#
```

4. Confirm the status of the replicas by checking the Orchestrator web interface:

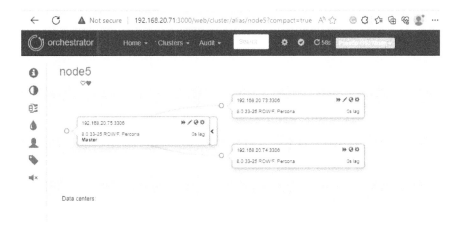

You should see the same results as in the previous image, except now the second replica is connected and replicating from the primary.

By following these steps, you can effectively install, deploy, and manage topology by using Orchestrator. Ensure that you execute the commands accurately and monitor the Orchestrator web interface for any changes or issues.

Clustering

Clustering is a technique used to provide HA and scalability in MySQL by replicating data across multiple servers. Clustering in MySQL groups multiple nodes or servers to work as a single unit. The types of clustering in MySQL include the following:

Percona XtraDB Cluster (PXC)
> Built on top of Percona Server, an enhanced version of MySQL, this solution uses Galera Cluster technology for synchronous replication.

MariaDB Galera Cluster

Built on top of MariaDB, a community-driven version of MySQL, this option uses Galera Cluster technology for synchronous replication. It's important to note that MariaDB is not equivalent to MySQL 8.

InnoDB Cluster

Built on top of MySQL, this option uses group replication technology for synchronous replication.

Each of these options replicates data across multiple nodes in real time, ensuring that all nodes have an identical copy of the data. All three allow for automatic node recovery and failover, making them ideal for HA systems. Understanding the clustering process is crucial to ensure optimal performance and high availability.

Understanding the Clustering Process

To understand the clustering process in MySQL, you need to grasp several key components. First and foremost is the clustering architecture, which determines how nodes or servers are organized within a cluster. A well-structured architecture is vital for maintaining HA and optimizing performance.

Second, we have synchronous versus asynchronous replication, which delineates how data is duplicated across nodes. Synchronous replication ensures real-time data replication, ideal for HA systems, while asynchronous replication introduces a delay in data replication, suitable for read-intensive applications.

Finally, load balancing comes into play, distributing incoming traffic across multiple nodes to maintain optimal performance and availability. This step is crucial in preventing nodes from becoming overwhelmed with traffic, an essential aspect of effective clustering.

Here is an example configuration code for PXC clustering:

```
[mysqld]
wsrep_provider=/usr/lib64/galera4/libgalera_smm.so
wsrep_provider_options="gcache.size=2G"
wsrep_cluster_address="gcomm://node1,node2,node3"
binlog_format=row
default_storage_engine=InnoDB
innodb_autoinc_lock_mode=2
```

Configuring Percona XtraDB Cluster

Percona XtraDB Cluster (PXC) is a high-performing and cost-effective clustering solution designed for critical data applications. It incorporates all the enhancements and features of MySQL 8 alongside Percona Server for MySQL's enterprise capabilities and an updated Galera library from Percona. This type of environment is well-suited for applications with high read workloads that demand five-9s uptime, particularly in industries like finance or healthcare that require dedicated or in-house database resources.

The basic architecture of a three-node PXC is shown in Figure 7-2.

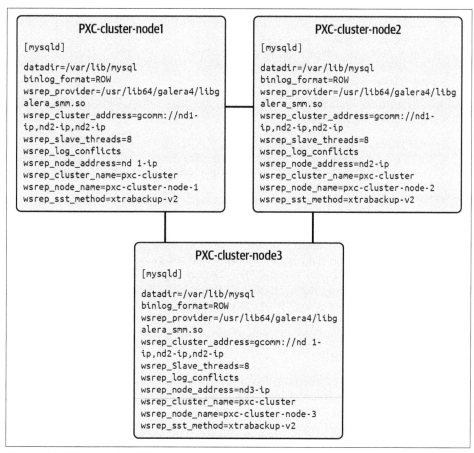

Figure 7-2. Three-node PXC architecture

The first step in configuring PXC is to configure the hostnames of all servers. This can be done by editing the */etc/hosts* file on each server. Replace the IP addresses with the ones that match your local network configuration. Then save and exit.

Check the IP address by using the following command:

```
[root@PXCNode1 ~]# ip a
1: lo: <LOOPBACK,UP,LOWER_UP> mtu 65536 qdisc noqueue state UNKNOWN
group default qlen 1000
    link/loopback 00:00:00:00:00:00 brd 00:00:00:00:00:00
    inet 127.0.0.1/8 scope host lo
```

```
        valid_lft forever preferred_lft forever
    inet6 ::1/128 scope host
        valid_lft forever preferred_lft forever
2: eth0: <BROADCAST,MULTICAST,UP,LOWER_UP> mtu 9001 qdisc mq state UP
group default qlen 1000
    link/ether 02:46:2a:e7:87:01 brd ff:ff:ff:ff:ff:ff
    inet 172.31.25.32/20 brd 172.31.31.255 scope global dynamic
    noprefixroute eth0
        valid_lft 3595sec preferred_lft 3595sec
    inet6 fe80::46:2aff:fee7:8701/64 scope link
        valid_lft forever preferred_lft forever
[root@PXCNode1 ~]#
```

Include the entries in */etc/hosts* file for each of the three nodes. This is needed only if DNS is otherwise not required:

```
[root@PXCNode1 ~]# cat /etc/hosts
127.0.0.1    localhost localhost.localdomain localhost4 localhost4.localdomain4
::1          localhost localhost.localdomain localhost6 localhost6.localdomain6
172.31.29.221 PXCNode1
172.31.30.140 PXCNode2
172.31.30.239 PXCNode3
[root@PXCNode1 ~]#
```

You have the option to utilize either a cloud-based infrastructure or an on-premises solution. This chapter explains the fundamental settings required to establish and deploy PXC 8.0 on Amazon Elastic Compute Cloud (EC2), as well as the updates made to the setup compared to PXC 8.0.

Setting up a three-node cluster

To demonstrate this process, we will use three on-premises instances to create the environment. However, different infrastructures can also be used to build the cluster environment, depending on specific business needs.

To set up a PXC 8.0 environment with three nodes, the initial step involves configuring three servers. Red Hat, CentOS, Ubuntu, or any of the operating systems supported by Percona can also be used. All nodes within a cluster should possess identical configurations:

```
PXCNode1 IP Address: 172.31.29.221
PXCNode2 IP Address: 172.31.30.140
PXCNode3 IP Address: 172.31.30.239
```

Use the following command to install the Percona repository on all three nodes:

```
[root@PXCNode1 ~]# sudo yum install https://repo.percona.com/yum/
percona-release-latest.noarch.rpm
Updating Subscription Management repositories.
Unable to read consumer identity
```

```
...
Last metadata expiration check: 0:12:10 ago on Sun 18 Feb 2024 02:38:47 PM UTC.
percona-release-latest.noarch.rpm
294 kB/s |  20 kB     00:00
Dependencies resolved.
<*> All done!
The percona-release package now contains a percona-release script that can
enable additional repositories for our newer products.
For example, to enable the Percona Server 8.0 repository use:
  percona-release setup ps80
Note: To avoid conflicts with older product versions, the percona-release setup
command may disable our original repository for some products.
For more information, please visit:
  https://www.percona.com/doc/percona-repo-config/percona-release.html
  Verifying        : percona-release-1.0-27.noarch
  1/1
Installed products updated.
Installed:
  percona-release-1.0-27.noarch
Complete!
[root@PXCNode1 ~]#
```

Enable the Percona Server for the MySQL 8 repository on all three nodes:

```
[root@PXCNode1 ~]# sudo percona-release setup pxc-80 -y
* Disabling all Percona Repositories
On Red Hat 8 systems it is needed to disable the following DNF module(s):
mysql  to install Percona XtraDB Cluster
* Enabling the Percona XtraDB Cluster 8.0 repository
* Enabling the Percona Tools repository
<*> All done!
[root@PXCNode1 ~]#
```

Install the PXC packages and software on all three nodes:

```
[root@PXCNode1 ~]#  sudo yum install percona-xtradb-cluster -y
Updating Subscription Management repositories.
Percona XtraDB Cluster 8.0 release/x86_64 YUM repository
             10 MB/s | 2.1 MB     00:00
Percona Tools release/x86_64 YUM repository
             14 MB/s | 1.1 MB     00:00
Dependencies resolved.
Installing:
percona-xtradb-cluster                    x86_64      8.0.35-27.1.el9
    pxc-80-release-x86_64     8.1 k
...
percona-xtradb-cluster-client             x86_64      8.0.35-27.1.el9
    pxc-80-release-x86_64     3.0 M
percona-xtradb-cluster-icu-data-files     x86_64      8.0.35-27.1.el9
    pxc-80-release-x86_64     2.2 M
percona-xtradb-cluster-server             x86_64      8.0.35-27.1.el9
    pxc-80-release-x86_64     101 M
percona-xtradb-cluster-shared             x86_64      8.0.35-27.1.el9
    pxc-80-release-x86_64
```

```
...
  perl-subs-1.03-480.el9.noarch              perl-vars-1.05-480.el9.noarch
  qpress-11-3.el9.x86_64                      socat-1.7.4.1-5.el9.x86_64
Complete!
[root@PXCNode1 ~]#
```

Before commencing with the node startup, you need to update the essential variables for each node. When performing initial installations, it's important to modify the following default variables. Users who are migrating from PXC 5.7 might notice that the wsrep_sst_auth variable is missing in PXC 8.0. This is because the wsrep_sst_auth variable was removed in PXC 8.0 because of security concerns. Storing the user and password in the configuration file could potentially make them visible to OS users, which is not ideal for security reasons.

PXC 8.0 incorporates a security improvement: the addition of a new node to an established cluster triggers the automatic creation of a temporary user. This security enhancement is designed to prevent unauthorized access to the cluster. After installing the latest percona-xtradb-cluster-8.0.31-23, the autogenerated *my.cnf* file will appear as shown here, and modifications can be made as necessary:

```
# cat my.cnf
# Template my.cnf for PXC
# Edit to your requirements.

[client]
socket=/var/lib/mysql/mysql.sock

[mysqld]
server-id=1
datadir=/var/lib/mysql
socket=/var/lib/mysql/mysql.sock
log-error=/var/log/mysqld.log
pid-file=/var/run/mysqld/mysqld.pid
# Binary log expiration period is 604800 seconds, which equals 7 days
binlog_expire_logs_seconds=604800

######## wsrep ##############
# Path to Galera library
wsrep_provider=/usr/lib64/galera4/libgalera_smm.so

# Cluster connection URL contains IPs of nodes
#If no IP is found, this implies that a new cluster needs to be created,
#in order to do that you need to bootstrap this node
wsrep_cluster_address=gcomm://

# In order for Galera to work correctly binlog format should be ROW
binlog_format=ROW

# Slave thread to use
wsrep_slave_threads=8
wsrep_log_conflicts
```

```
# This changes how InnoDB autoincrement locks are managed and is a
requirement for Galera
innodb_autoinc_lock_mode=2

# Node IP address
#wsrep_node_address=192.168.70.63
# Cluster name
wsrep_cluster_name=pxc-cluster

#If wsrep_node_name is not specified, then system hostname will be used
wsrep_node_name=pxc-cluster-node-1

#pxc_strict_mode allowed values: DISABLED,PERMISSIVE,ENFORCING,MASTER
pxc_strict_mode=ENFORCING

# SST method
wsrep_sst_method=xtrabackup-v2
```

Adjust the configuration variables to meet the cluster's demands, as demonstrated in the next example.

Configuring PXC node 1

You must adjust the configuration variables to meet the cluster's requirements on node 1. Customize the wsrep_cluster_address, wsrep_node_address, and wsrep_node_name according to your specific setup:

```
[root@PXCNode1 ~]# cat /etc/my.cnf
# Template my.cnf for PXC
# Edit to your requirements.
[client]
socket=/var/lib/mysql/mysql.sock
[mysqld]
server-id=1
datadir=/var/lib/mysql
socket=/var/lib/mysql/mysql.sock
log-error=/var/log/mysqld.log
pid-file=/var/run/mysqld/mysqld.pid
# Binary log expiration period is 604800 seconds, which equals 7 days
binlog_expire_logs_seconds=604800
######## wsrep ##############
# Path to Galera library
wsrep_provider=/usr/lib64/galera4/libgalera_smm.so
# Cluster connection URL contains IPs of nodes
#If no IP is found, this implies that a new cluster needs to be created,
#in order to do that you need to bootstrap this node
wsrep_cluster_address=gcomm://172.31.29.221,172.31.30.140,172.31.30.239
# In order for Galera to work correctly binlog format should be ROW
binlog_format=ROW
# Slave thread to use
wsrep_slave_threads=8
```

```
wsrep_log_conflicts
# This changes how InnoDB autoincrement locks are managed and is a
requirement for Galera
innodb_autoinc_lock_mode=2
# Node IP address
wsrep_node_address=172.31.29.221
# Cluster name
wsrep_cluster_name=pxc-cluster
#If wsrep_node_name is not specified,  then system hostname will be used
wsrep_node_name=PXCNode1
#pxc_strict_mode allowed values: DISABLED,PERMISSIVE,ENFORCING,MASTER
pxc_strict_mode=ENFORCING
# SST method
wsrep_sst_method=xtrabackup-v2

[root@PXCNode1 ~]#
```

Configuring PXC node 2

The configuration of node 2 will mirror that of node 1, with the exception of variables such as wsrep_node_address and wsrep_node_name. Adjust the configuration variables to align with the cluster's requirements:

```
[root@PXCNode2 ~]# cat /etc/my.cnf
# Template my.cnf for PXC
# Edit to your requirements.
[client]
socket=/var/lib/mysql/mysql.sock
[mysqld]
server-id=1
datadir=/var/lib/mysql
socket=/var/lib/mysql/mysql.sock
log-error=/var/log/mysqld.log
pid-file=/var/run/mysqld/mysqld.pid
# Binary log expiration period is 604800 seconds, which equals 7 days
binlog_expire_logs_seconds=604800
######## wsrep ##############
# Path to Galera library
wsrep_provider=/usr/lib64/galera4/libgalera_smm.so
# Cluster connection URL contains IPs of nodes
# If no IP is found, this implies that a new cluster needs to be created,
# in order to do that you need to bootstrap this node
wsrep_cluster_address=gcomm://172.31.29.221,172.31.30.140,172.31.30.239
# In order for Galera to work correctly binlog format should be ROW
binlog_format=ROW
# Slave thread to use
wsrep_slave_threads=8
wsrep_log_conflicts
# This changes how InnoDB autoincrement locks are managed
# and is a requirement for Galera
innodb_autoinc_lock_mode=2
# Node IP address
```

```
wsrep_node_address=172.31.30.140
# Cluster name
wsrep_cluster_name=pxc-cluster
#If wsrep_node_name is not specified,  then system hostname will be used
wsrep_node_name=PXCNode2
#pxc_strict_mode allowed values: DISABLED,PERMISSIVE,ENFORCING,MASTER
pxc_strict_mode=ENFORCING
# SST method
wsrep_sst_method=xtrabackup-v2

[root@PXCNode2 ~]#
```

PXC nodes use designated ports for communication as a default setting. It's crucial to confirm the accessibility of these ports and verify seamless communication between the nodes.

 PXC nodes use the following port settings: 3306 for MySQL client connections and State Snapshot Transfer (SST) via `mysqldump`, 4444 for SST via Percona XtraBackup, 4567 for write-set replication traffic (over TCP) and multicast replication (over TCP and UDP), and 4568 for Incremental State Transfer (IST).

For instance, to verify access port, you can use the `socat` network utility. Use the following command to listen on TCP port 4444:

```
[root@PXCNode1 ~]# socat - TCP-LISTEN:4444
hello
[root@PXCNode1 ~]#
```

The following command sends the string "hello" through a TCP connection to the specified IP address (172.21.18.119) and port (4444) using `socat`:

```
[root@PXCNode2 ~]# echo "hello" | socat - TCP:172.31.29.221:4444
[root@PXCNode2 ~]#
```

Bootstrapping the first node in PXC

After setting up configuration for every node within the PXC, the next step involves bootstrapping the cluster, starting with the initial node. It is vital to ensure that all the data intended for replication to other nodes is already available on this first node.

To initiate the bootstrap process for the first node, run the following command:

```
[root@PXCNode1 ~]# systemctl start mysql@bootstrap.service
[root@PXCNode1 ~]#
```

Since this is a new installation, a temporary password is created for the MySQL root user, and it's retrievable from the *mysqld.log* file:

```
[root@PXCNode1 ~]# grep -i "A temporary password is generated "
/var/log/mysqld.log
```

```
2024-02-18T15:01:26.515854Z 6 [Note] [MY-010454] [Server]
A temporary password is generated for root@localhost: rQeg6ny/iCm9
[root@PXCNode1 ~]#
```

To change the temporary password, log in to MySQL and execute the following ALTER
statement:

```
[root@PXCNode1 ~]# mysql -uroot -p
Enter password:
Welcome to the MySQL monitor.  Commands end with ; or \g.
Type 'help;' or '\h' for help. Type '\c' to clear the current input statement.
mysql>

mysql> SET PASSWORD = 'Pass21word$$';
Query OK, 0 rows affected (0.02 sec)
mysql>
```

Add the remaining nodes to the PXC

Before starting node 2, it is necessary to copy the SSL certificates from node 1 to node
2 (and also to node3). PXC 8.0 encrypts all replication communication by default, so
this step is critical. Failure to perform this step can result in cluster startup failures:

```
[root@PXCNode1 ~]# scp /var/lib/mysql/*.pem 172.31.30.140:/var/lib/mysql/
ca-key.pem
100% 1705      1.6MB/s    00:00
ca.pem
100% 1120      1.5MB/s    00:00
client-cert.pem
100% 1120      1.1MB/s    00:00
client-key.pem
100% 1705      2.3MB/s    00:00
private_key.pem
100% 1705      2.3MB/s    00:00
public_key.pem
100% 452     668.8KB/s    00:00
server-cert.pem
100% 1120      1.5MB/s    00:00
server-key.pem
100% 1705      2.5MB/s    00:00
[root@PXCNode1 ~]#
```

Change the ownership of all *.pem* files in */var/lib/mysql/* to the mysql user and mysql
group:

```
[root@PXCNode2 ~]# chown -R mysql.mysql /var/lib/mysql/*.pem
[root@PXCNode2 ~]#
```

Start the node:

```
[root@PXCNode2 ~]# systemctl start mysql
[root@PXCNode2 ~]#
```

After adding a node to the cluster, it's important to verify the following status variables:

wsrep_cluster_size
> Should be set to the expected value. In this case, as it is the second node added to the cluster, the value should be 2.

wsrep_cluster_status
> Ensure it is Primary.

wsrep_local_state_comment
> Ensure it's Synced to confirm that the node has successfully joined the cluster.

Using the following query, you can verify the cluster status of PXC node 1 after adding the second node to the cluster:

```
[root@PXCNode1 ~]# mysql -uroot -p -e " show global status where
variable_name IN ('wsrep_local_state','wsrep_local_state_comment',
 'wsrep_cluster_size','wsrep_cluster_status','wsrep_connected',
 'wsrep_ready');"
Enter password:
+---------------------------+---------+
| Variable_name             | Value   |
+---------------------------+---------+
| wsrep_cluster_size        | 2       |
| wsrep_cluster_status      | Primary |
| wsrep_connected           | ON      |
| wsrep_local_state         | 4       |
| wsrep_local_state_comment | Synced  |
| wsrep_ready               | ON      |
+---------------------------+---------+
[root@PXCNode1 ~]#
```

The status remains consistent across all three nodes:

```
[root@PXCNode2 ~]# mysql -uroot -p -e " show global status
where variable_name IN ('wsrep_local_state','wsrep_local_state_comment',
 'wsrep_cluster_size','wsrep_cluster_status', 'wsrep_connected',
 'wsrep_ready');"
Enter password:
+---------------------------+---------+
| Variable_name             | Value   |
+---------------------------+---------+
| wsrep_cluster_size        | 2       |
| wsrep_cluster_status      | Primary |
| wsrep_connected           | ON      |
| wsrep_local_state         | 4       |
| wsrep_local_state_comment | Synced  |
| wsrep_ready               | ON      |
+---------------------------+---------+
[root@PXCNode2 ~]#
```

Use the same procedures that you used for adding the second node to add the third node. Once the third node is started, the `wsrep_cluster_size` should be 3, the `wsrep_cluster_status` should be Primary, and `wsrep_local_state_comment` should be set to Synced to confirm that the node has successfully joined the cluster:

```
[root@PXCNode3 ~]# systemctl start mysql
[root@PXCNode3 ~]#
[root@PXCNode3 ~]# mysql -uroot -p -e " show global status
where variable_name IN ('wsrep_local_state','wsrep_local_state_comment',
 'wsrep_cluster_size','wsrep_cluster_status', 'wsrep_connected',
 'wsrep_ready');"
Enter password:
+----------------------------+----------+
| Variable_name              | Value    |
+----------------------------+----------+
| wsrep_cluster_size         | 3        |
| wsrep_cluster_status       | Primary  |
| wsrep_connected            | ON       |
| wsrep_local_state          | 4        |
| wsrep_local_state_comment  | Synced   |
| wsrep_ready                | ON       |
+----------------------------+----------+
[root@PXCNode3 ~]#
```

Consider additional support

Using failover technologies like ProxySQL is also advisable. These technologies can assist in eliminating unresponsive nodes from the operational read pool and facilitate the necessary transitions of the primary node.

Strongly consider establishing a backup plan for the PXC, employing tools like the open source XtraBackup. This utility is capable of creating physical data-set duplicates, enabling expedited recovery times. Furthermore, ensure the backup of binary logs through `mysqlbinlog` to facilitate PITR options.

To effectively monitor query analytics and gain performance insights over time, it's strongly advised to leverage PMM. This tool can be set up on a distinct host through the Amazon Marketplace. It effectively tracks both operating system and MySQL metrics while delivering advanced query analytics capabilities.

Configuring Load Balancing with ProxySQL for PXC

ProxySQL stands as a high-performance open source MySQL proxy, empowering users to scale and enhance the security of their MySQL infrastructure. In this section, we will outline the steps to installing ProxySQL2 on distributions that use RPM packaging:

1. Retrieve and install the Percona repository by executing this command:

```
[root@proxysql ~]# sudo yum install https://repo.percona.com/yum/
percona-release-latest.noarch.rpm
Updating Subscription Management repositories.
Last metadata expiration check: 0:08:31 ago on Sun 18 Feb 2024
04:19:41 PM UTC.
percona-release-latest.noarch.rpm                      270 kB/s |   20 kB
00:00
Dependencies resolved.
...
  Verifying         : percona-release-1.0-27.noarch
  1/1
Installed products updated.
Installed:
  percona-release-1.0-27.noarch
Complete!
[root@proxysql ~]#
```

2. Verify the availability of the ProxySQL package:

```
[root@proxysql ~]# yum list all | grep "proxysql"
proxysql2.x86_64
2.5.5-1.1.el9                           percona-release-x86_64
[root@proxysql ~]#
```

3. Install ProxySQL2 by executing the subsequent command:

```
[root@proxysql ~]# yum install proxysql2
Updating Subscription Management repositories.
Last metadata expiration check: 0:00:52 ago on Sun 18 Feb 2024
04:21:21 PM UTC.
Dependencies resolved.
...
  perl-libnet-3.13-4.el9.noarch
    perl-libs-4:5.32.1-480.el9.x86_64
  perl-mro-1.23-480.el9.x86_64
    perl-overload-1.31-480.el9.noarch
  perl-overloading-0.02-480.el9.noarch
    perl-parent-1:0.238-460.el9.noarch
  perl-podlators-1:4.14-460.el9.noarch
    perl-subs-1.03-480.el9.noarch
  perl-vars-1.05-480.el9.noarch
    proxysql2-2.5.5-1.1.el9.x86_64

Complete!
[root@proxysql ~]#
```

4. Verify the availability of the PXC client package:

```
[root@proxysql ~]# yum list all | grep percona | grep client
Percona-Server-client-57.x86_64
  5.7.44-48.1.el9                       percona-release-x86_64
Percona-Server-client-57-debuginfo.x86_64
  5.7.44-48.1.el9                       percona-release-x86_64
Percona-XtraDB-Cluster-client-57.x86_64
  5.7.44-31.65.1.el9                    percona-release-x86_64
```

```
Percona-XtraDB-Cluster-client-57-debuginfo.x86_64
   5.7.44-31.65.1.el9            percona-release-x86_64
pmm2-client.x86_64
   2.41.1-6.el9                  percona-release-x86_64
[root@proxysql ~]#
```

5. Install the PXC client by executing the following command:

```
[root@proxysql ~]# yum install -y percona-xtradb-cluster-client
Updating Subscription Management repositories.
Unable to read consumer identity
Last metadata expiration check: 0:00:16 ago on Sun 18 Feb 2024
04:34:28 PM UTC.
Dependencies resolved.
...
Installed:
  percona-xtradb-cluster-client-8.0.35-27.1.el9.x86_64
  perl-DBI-1.643-9.el9.x86_64
  perl-DynaLoader-1.47-480.el9.x86_64
  perl-Math-BigInt-1:1.9998.18-460.el9.noarch
  perl-Math-Complex-1.59-480.el9.noarch

Complete!
[root@proxysql ~]#
```

6. Confirm the installation by examining the configuration file:

```
[root@proxysql ~]# cat /etc/proxysql.cnf
#file proxysql.cfg

datadir="/var/lib/proxysql"
errorlog="/var/lib/proxysql/proxysql.log"

admin_variables=
{
        admin_credentials="admin:admin"
#       mysql_ifaces="127.0.0.1:6032;/tmp/proxysql_admin.sock"
        mysql_ifaces="0.0.0.0:6032"
#       refresh_interval=2000
#       debug=true
}
```

7. Determine the version of ProxySQL:

```
[root@proxysql ~]# proxysql --version
ProxySQL version 2.5.5-percona-1.1, codename Truls
[root@proxysql ~]#
```

8. Initiate the ProxySQL service:

```
[root@proxysql ~]# service proxysql start
Redirecting to /bin/systemctl start proxysql.service
[root@proxysql ~]#
```

9. Stop the ProxySQL service:

```
[root@proxysql ~]# service proxysql stop
Redirecting to /bin/systemctl stop proxysql.service
[root@proxysql ~]#
```

10. Inspect the current status of the ProxySQL service and proceed to restart it once more:

```
[root@proxysql ~]# service proxysql status
Redirecting to /bin/systemctl status proxysql.service
proxysql.service - High Performance Advanced Proxy for MySQL
    Loaded: loaded (/usr/lib/systemd/system/proxysql.service; enabled;
    preset: disabled)
    Active: inactive (dead) since Sun 2024-02-18 16:38:02 UTC; 39s ago
  Duration: 26.797s
   Process: 16095 ExecStart=/usr/bin/proxysql --idle-threads -c
   /etc/proxysql.cnf $PROXYSQL_OPTS (code=exited, statu>
  Main PID: 16097 (code=exited, status=0/SUCCESS)
       CPU: 406ms
...
Feb 18 16:38:02 ip-172-31-26-35.us-west-2.compute.internal systemd[1]:
proxysql.service: Deactivated successfully.
Feb 18 16:38:02 ip-172-31-26-35.us-west-2.compute.internal systemd[1]:
Stopped High Performance Advanced Proxy for My>
[root@proxysql ~]#

[root@proxysql ~]# service proxysql start
Redirecting to /bin/systemctl start proxysql.service
[root@proxysql ~]#
```

11. After starting, check the status of the ProxySQL service:

```
[root@proxysql ~]# service proxysql status
Redirecting to /bin/systemctl status proxysql.service
proxysql.service - High Performance Advanced Proxy for MySQL
    Loaded: loaded (/usr/lib/systemd/system/proxysql.service; enabled;
    preset: disabled)
    Active: active (running) since Sun 2024-02-18 16:39:40 UTC; 17s ago
   Process: 16139 ExecStart=/usr/bin/proxysql --idle-threads -c
   /etc/proxysql.cnf $PROXYSQL_OPTS (code=exited, statu>
  Main PID: 16141 (proxysql)
     Tasks: 25 (limit: 22830)
    Memory: 62.9M
       CPU: 284ms
    CGroup: /system.slice/proxysql.service
            ├─16141 /usr/bin/proxysql --idle-threads -c
              /etc/proxysql.cnf
            └─16142 /usr/bin/proxysql --idle-threads -c
              /etc/proxysql.cnf

Feb 18 16:39:40 ip-172-31-26-35.us-west-2.compute.internal systemd[1]:
Starting High Performance Advanced Proxy for M>
Feb 18 16:39:40 ip-172-31-26-35.us-west-2.compute.internal systemd[1]:
Started High Performance Advanced Proxy for My>
[root@proxysql ~]#
```

12. Monitor the ProxySQL logs:

```
[root@proxysql ~]# tail -100f /var/lib/proxysql/proxysql.log
2024-02-18 16:37:35 [INFO] Angel process started ProxySQL process 16098
2024-02-18 16:37:35 [INFO] SSL keys/certificates found in datadir
 (/var/lib/proxysql): loading them.
2024-02-18 16:37:35 [INFO] Loaded built-in SQLite3
Standard ProxySQL MySQL Logger rev. 2.5.0421 -- MySQL_Logger.cpp
 -- Mon Aug 21 10:45:19 2023
Standard ProxySQL Cluster rev. 0.4.0906 -- ProxySQL_Cluster.cpp
 -- Mon Aug 21 10:45:19 2023
Standard ProxySQL Statistics rev. 1.4.1027 -- ProxySQL_Statistics.cpp
 -- Mon Aug 21 10:45:19 2023
Standard ProxySQL HTTP Server Handler rev. 1.4.1031 --
2024-02-18 16:37:35 [INFO] Computed checksum for
 'LOAD ADMIN VARIABLES TO RUNTIME' was '0x8D4A330CBF0FE4EC',
 with epoch '1708274255'
…
2024-02-18 16:37:35 [INFO] Computed checksum for
 'LOAD MYSQL USERS TO RUNTIME' was '0x0000000000000000',
 with epoch '1708274255'
2024-02-18 16:37:35 [INFO] Dumping mysql_servers_incoming
+--------------+----------+------+-----------+--------+--------+------------
+-----------------+--------------------+---------+----------------+--------+
| hostgroup_id | hostname | port | gtid_port | weight | status | compression
| max_connections | max_replication_lag | use_ssl | max_latency_ms | comment|
+--------------+----------+------+-----------+--------+--------+------------
+-----------------+--------------------+---------+----------------+--------+
+--------------+----------+------+-----------+--------+--------+------------
+-----------------+--------------------+---------+----------------+--------+
2024-02-18 16:37:35 [INFO] Dumping mysql_servers LEFT JOIN
mysql_servers_incoming
+-------------+--------------+----------+------+
| mem_pointer | hostgroup_id | hostname | port |
+-------------+--------------+----------+------+
+-------------+--------------+----------+------+
```

Configuring the ProxySQL administrator password

To configure ProxySQL, you'll establish a connection to the ProxySQL administration interface by using the MySQL command-line tool. Follow these steps:

1. Enter the ProxySQL administration interface by using the default password admin:

```
[root@proxysql ~]# mysql -u admin -padmin -h 127.0.0.1 -P6032
--prompt=\'ProxySQLAdmin> '
mysql: [Warning] Using a password on the command line interface can be
insecure.
Welcome to the MySQL monitor.  Commands end with ; or \g.
Oracle is a registered trademark of Oracle Corporation and/or its
```

affiliates. Other names may be trademarks of their respective owners.

Type 'help;' or '\h' for help. Type '\c' to clear the current input statement.

ProxySQLAdmin>

2. Modify the ProxySQL administration password:

```
ProxySQLAdmin> UPDATE global_variables SET variable_value='admin:password'
WHERE variable_name='admin-admin_credentials';
```

3. Load the administrative variables configuration into the runtime configuration:

```
ProxySQLAdmin> LOAD ADMIN VARIABLES TO RUNTIME;
Query OK, 0 rows affected (0.00 sec)
ProxySQLAdmin>
```

4. Use the command SAVE ADMIN VARIABLES TO DISK to save the administrative variables configuration to disk. This ensures that the changes made to administrative variables are saved and will survive a ProxySQL service restart:

```
ProxySQLAdmin> SAVE ADMIN VARIABLES TO DISK;
Query OK, 49 rows affected (0.01 sec)
ProxySQLAdmin>;
```

Checking for existing rules and server configuration

Ensure that the configuration is empty of content by verifying that there are no entries within the tables for mysql_servers, mysql_users, mysql_replica tion_hostgroups, and mysql_query_rules:

```
ProxySQLAdmin> SELECT  FROM mysql_servers;
Empty set (0.00 sec)
ProxySQLAdmin>

ProxySQLAdmin> SELECT  FROM mysql_users;
Empty set (0.00 sec)
ProxySQLAdmin>

ProxySQLAdmin> SELECT  FROM mysql_replication_hostgroups;
Empty set (0.00 sec)
ProxySQLAdmin>

ProxySQLAdmin> SELECT  FROM mysql_query_rules;
Empty set (0.00 sec)
ProxySQLAdmin>
```

The mysql_query_rules table in ProxySQL is a configuration table that allows you to define rules for routing and manipulating SQL queries. These rules determine how ProxySQL handles incoming SQL queries, including which MySQL server or server group to route queries to, query rewriting, and access control based on various criteria such as SQL patterns, user identities, and client IP addresses. This table is essential for optimizing query routing, enhancing query security, and implementing query rewriting in ProxySQL.

Adding database nodes as backend servers in ProxySQL server list

Following the installation of ProxySQL, the next task is to set up the backend MySQL servers within the `mysql_servers` table. For this example, we'll illustrate the configuration of three PXC/MySQL servers by integrating them into the `mysql_servers` table. Follow these steps:

1. You'll add the three servers to the pool. First, add the server with the IP address 192.168.10.51 in the pool:

   ```
   ProxySQLAdmin> INSERT INTO mysql_servers (hostname, hostgroup_id, port,
   weight) VALUES ('172.31.29.221', 10, 3306, 1000);
   Query OK, 1 row affected (0.00 sec)
   ProxySQLAdmin>
   ```

   Then add the server with the IP address 192.168.10.52 in the pool:

   ```
   ProxySQLAdmin> INSERT INTO mysql_servers (hostname, hostgroup_id, port,
   weight) VALUES ('172.31.30.140', 10, 3306, 1000);
   Query OK, 1 row affected (0.00 sec)
   ProxySQLAdmin>
   ```

   Finally, add the server with the IP address 192.168.10.53 in the pool:

   ```
   ProxySQLAdmin> INSERT INTO mysql_servers (hostname, hostgroup_id, port,
   weight)
   VALUES ('172.31.30.239', 10, 3306, 1000);
   Query OK, 1 row affected (0.00 sec)
   ProxySQLAdmin>
   ```

2. Set up the host groups for the PXC cluster:

   ```
   INSERT INTO mysql_galera_hostgroups
   (writer_hostgroup,
   backup_writer_hostgroup, reader_hostgroup,
   offline_hostgroup,active,max_writers,
   writer_is_also_reader, max_transactions_behind)
   VALUES (10,12, 11, 13, 1, 1, 2, 100);
   ```

   Alternatively, in scenarios where multiple primary nodes are present, you can adjust the `max_writers` option to guarantee ProxySQL's capability to manage multiple write operations:

   ```
   ProxySQLAdmin> INSERT INTO mysql_galera_hostgroups
   (writer_hostgroup,backup_writer_hostgroup,
   reader_hostgroup, offline_hostgroup, active,
   max_writers, writer_is_also_reader, max_transactions_behind)
   VALUES (10,12, 11, 13, 1, 3, 2, 100);
   Query OK, 1 row affected (0.00 sec)
   ProxySQLAdmin>
   ```

3. Once the host groups have been configured, apply the modifications to the run-time configuration and then preserve these changes on disk as follows:

```
ProxySQLAdmin> LOAD MYSQL SERVERS TO RUNTIME;
Query OK, 0 rows affected (0.00 sec)
ProxySQLAdmin>
```

4. Persist these changes to disk:

```
ProxySQLAdmin> SAVE MYSQL SERVERS TO DISK;
Query OK, 0 rows affected (0.04 sec)
ProxySQLAdmin>
```

Keep in mind that modifications made to the configuration will remain inactive until they are loaded into the runtime. Additionally, any alterations not saved to disk will be lost following a ProxySQL restart.

Confirm the changes applied to the mysql_servers:

```
ProxySQLAdmin> SELECT hostgroup_id, hostname, status FROM
runtime_mysql_servers;
+--------------+---------------+---------+
| hostgroup_id | hostname      | status  |
+--------------+---------------+---------+
| 13           | 172.31.29.221 | SHUNNED |
| 13           | 172.31.30.140 | SHUNNED |
| 13           | 172.31.30.239 | SHUNNED |
+--------------+---------------+---------+
3 rows in set (0.00 sec)
>ProxySQLAdmin>
```

Be aware that ProxySQL identifies backend instances with a read_only value of 0 as WRITER instances. As a result, this configuration should be applied to only primary MySQL servers or to all primary servers in situations involving PXC or group (multi-primary) replication. The backend MySQL servers used as replicas should have their read_only value set to 1.

MySQL users

Once you've set up the MySQL server backends in the mysql_servers section, the subsequent task is to configure MySQL users:

1. To introduce a new user, run this query:

```
ProxySQLAdmin> INSERT INTO mysql_users (username, password,default_hostgroup)
VALUES ('sbuser', 'sbpass', 10);
Query OK, 1 row affected (0.00 sec)
ProxySQLAdmin>
```

2. Activate the current in-memory MySQL user configuration as follows:

```
ProxySQLAdmin> LOAD MYSQL USERS TO RUNTIME;
Query OK, 0 rows affected (0.00 sec)
ProxySQLAdmin>
```

3. Save the current in-memory MySQL user configuration:

```
ProxySQLAdmin> SAVE MYSQL USERS TO DISK;
Query OK, 0 rows affected (0.02 sec)
ProxySQLAdmin>
```

Set up monitoring for MySQL

ProxySQL serves as a high-performance MySQL proxy, offering features such as load balancing and query routing. By implementing ProxySQL monitors, we can effectively monitor the status of our MySQL backend nodes, enhancing their overall health and reducing potential downtime.

For MySQL monitoring configuration, it's essential to establish a user equipped with the required privileges, enabling ProxySQL to access and monitor the backend database servers. Connect to the primary node and execute this within the ProxySQL administration prompt to create a MySQL user with the essential privileges, enabling ProxySQL to access and monitor the backend database servers:

```
ProxySQLAdmin> UPDATE global_variables SET
variable_value='monitor'
WHERE variable_name in
('mysql-monitor_username','mysql-monitor_password');
```

On the PXC nodes, create the monitoring user:

```
mysql> CREATE USER 'monitor'@'%' IDENTIFIED BY 'monitor';
Query OK, 0 rows affected (0.01 sec)
mysql>

mysql> GRANT USAGE ON *.* TO 'monitor'@'%';
Query OK, 0 rows affected (0.01 sec)
mysql>
```

The first command establishes the monitoring user with the username monitor and password monitor. The second command provides the user with the essential privileges for monitoring the backend database servers.

Enabling ProxySQL's access to the MySQL database requires creating a user within the MySQL database, using the identical credentials as the monitoring user established on the ProxySQL server. On the PXC nodes or MySQL cluster servers, produce the ProxySQL client user by executing these commands:

```
mysql> CREATE DATABASE sbtest;
Query OK, 1 row affected (0.01 sec)
mysql>

mysql> CREATE USER 'sbuser'@'172.31.26.35'
IDENTIFIED WITH
mysql_native_password BY 'sbpass';
Query OK, 0 rows affected (0.02 sec)
mysql>

mysql> GRANT ALL ON *.* TO 'sbuser'@'172.31.26.35';
Query OK, 0 rows affected (0.01 sec)
mysql>
```

The initial command creates a database sbtest. The subsequent command creates the ProxySQL client user with the username sbuser, password sbpass, and host 172.31.26.35. The third command grants the user all privileges on all databases and tables.

Configuring monitoring in ProxySQL

To proficiently monitor MySQL backends using ProxySQL, specific configurations need to be established. Follow these steps to set up monitoring:

1. Update the MySQL server version. Within the ProxySQL administration prompt, modify the MySQL server version to 8.0 as follows:

   ```
   ProxySQLAdmin> UPDATE GLOBAL_VARIABLES
   SET variable_value='8.0'
   WHERE variable_name='mysql-server_version';
   Query OK, 1 row affected (0.00 sec)
   ProxySQLAdmin>
   ```

2. Set monitor intervals. Update the monitor connect, ping, and read-only intervals to 2000 with the following command:

   ```
   ProxySQLAdmin> UPDATE global_variables
   SET variable_value='2000'
   WHERE variable_name IN
   ('mysql-monitor_connect_interval','mysql-monitor_ping_interval',
   'mysql-monitor_read_only_interval');
   Query OK, 3 rows affected (0.00 sec)
   ProxySQLAdmin>
   ```

3. Enable the admin web interface by setting the variable_value to true:

   ```
   ProxySQLAdmin> UPDATE GLOBAL_VARIABLES
   SET variable_value='true' WHERE variable_name='admin-web_enabled';
   Query OK, 1 row affected (0.00 sec)
   ProxySQLAdmin>
   ```

4. Verify whether the monitor module has been appropriately configured by using this command:

```
ProxySQLAdmin> SELECT * FROM global_variables
WHERE variable_name LIKE 'mysql-monitor_%';
+------------------------------------------------------------------------+
----------------+
| variable_name                                                          |

 variable_value |
+------------------------------------------------------------------------+
----------------+
| mysql-monitor_enabled                                                  |

 true           |
| mysql-monitor_connect_timeout                                          |

 600            |
| mysql-monitor_ping_max_failures                                        |

 3              |
| mysql-monitor_ping_timeout                                             |
 1000           |
| mysql-monitor_read_only_max_timeout_count                              |
 3              |
| mysql-monitor_replication_lag_group_by_host                           |
 false          |
| mysql-monitor_replication_lag_interval                                |
 10000          |
| mysql-monitor_replication_lag_timeout                                 |
 1000           |
| mysql-monitor_replication_lag_count                                   |
 1              |
| mysql-monitor_groupreplication_healthcheck_interval                   |
 5000           |
| mysql-monitor_groupreplication_healthcheck_timeout                    |
 800            |
| mysql-monitor_groupreplication_healthcheck_max_timeout_count          |
 3              |
| mysql-monitor_groupreplication_max_transactions_behind_count          |
 3              |
| mysql-monitor_groupreplication_max_transactions_behind_for_read_only  |
 1              |
| mysql-monitor_galera_healthcheck_interval                             |
 5000           |
| mysql-monitor_galera_healthcheck_timeout                              |
 800            |
| mysql-monitor_galera_healthcheck_max_timeout_count                    |
 3              |
| mysql-monitor_replication_lag_use_percona_heartbeat                   |
                |
| mysql-monitor_query_interval                                          |
```

```
  60000           |
| mysql-monitor_query_timeout                              |
  100             |
| mysql-monitor_slave_lag_when_null                        |
  60              |
| mysql-monitor_threads_min                                |
  8               |
| mysql-monitor_threads_max                                |
  128             |
| mysql-monitor_threads_queue_maxsize                      |
  128             |
| mysql-monitor_local_dns_cache_ttl                        |
  300000          |
| mysql-monitor_local_dns_cache_refresh_interval           |
  60000           |
| mysql-monitor_local_dns_resolver_queue_maxsize           |
  128             |
| mysql-monitor_wait_timeout                               |
  true            |
| mysql-monitor_writer_is_also_reader                      |
  true            |
| mysql-monitor_username                                   |
  monitor         |
| mysql-monitor_password                                   |
  monitor         |
| mysql-monitor_history                                    |
  600000          |
| mysql-monitor_connect_interval                           |
  2000            |
| mysql-monitor_ping_interval                              |
  2000            |
| mysql-monitor_read_only_interval                         |
  2000            |
| mysql-monitor_read_only_timeout                          |
  500             |
+----------------------------------------------------------------------+
----------------+
36 rows in set (0.00 sec)
ProxySQLAdmin>
```

5. Apply the configuration changes. Run the statement LOAD MYSQL VARIABLES TO
   RUNTIME to implement the modifications made to mysql-monitor in the
   global_variables table:

```
ProxySQLAdmin> LOAD MYSQL VARIABLES TO RUNTIME;
Query OK, 0 rows affected (0.00 sec)
ProxySQLAdmin>
```

6. Save the configuration changes. To ensure that the configuration changes remain in effect after restarts, run `SAVE MYSQL VARIABLES TO DISK`. This command saves the current MySQL variable configuration from memory to disk:

```
ProxySQLAdmin> SAVE MYSQL VARIABLES TO DISK;
Query OK, 158 rows affected (0.01 sec)
ProxySQLAdmin>
```

Health check for backend servers

Once the monitoring configuration is active, it's crucial to confirm the status of the MySQL backends. Use the following steps to examine the monitor database tables within the ProxySQL administration prompt:

1. Check the connection logs:

```
ProxySQLAdmin> SELECT * FROM monitor.mysql_server_connect_log
ORDER BY time_start_us DESC limit 10;
+---------------+------+-------------------+------------------------
+---------------+
| hostname      | port | time_start_us     | connect_success_time_us |
connect_error |
+---------------+------+-------------------+------------------------
+---------------+
| 172.31.29.221 | 3306 | 1708276477204033  | 1803                    |
NULL          |
| 172.31.30.140 | 3306 | 1708276477184546  | 1818                    |
NULL          |
| 172.31.30.239 | 3306 | 1708276477165028  | 1867                    |
NULL          |
| 172.31.30.239 | 3306 | 1708276475216662  | 1902                    |
NULL          |
| 172.31.30.140 | 3306 | 1708276475190625  | 1762                    |
NULL          |
| 172.31.29.221 | 3306 | 1708276475164654  | 1958                    |
NULL          |
| 172.31.29.221 | 3306 | 1708276473192674  | 1676                    |
NULL          |
| 172.31.30.239 | 3306 | 1708276473178436  | 1796                    |
NULL          |
| 172.31.30.140 | 3306 | 1708276473164255  | 1799                    |
NULL          |
| 172.31.30.239 | 3306 | 1708276471194548  | 1811                    |
NULL          |
+---------------+------+-------------------+------------------------
+---------------+
10 rows in set (0.00 sec)

ProxySQLAdmin>
```

2. Check the ping logs:

```
ProxySQLAdmin> SELECT * FROM monitor.mysql_server_ping_log
ORDER BY time_start_us DESC limit 10;
+---------------+------+------------------+---------------------+-----------+
| hostname      | port | time_start_us    | ping_success_time_us| ping_error|
+---------------+------+------------------+---------------------+-----------+
| 172.31.30.140 | 3306 | 1708276535013146 | 669                 | NULL      |
| 172.31.30.239 | 3306 | 1708276535013143 | 655                 | NULL      |
| 172.31.29.221 | 3306 | 1708276535013030 | 716                 | NULL      |
| 172.31.30.239 | 3306 | 1708276533012747 | 687                 | NULL      |
| 172.31.30.140 | 3306 | 1708276533012746 | 673                 | NULL      |
| 172.31.29.221 | 3306 | 1708276533012644 | 745                 | NULL      |
| 172.31.29.221 | 3306 | 1708276531012540 | 652                 | NULL      |
| 172.31.30.239 | 3306 | 1708276531012435 | 804                 | NULL      |
| 172.31.30.140 | 3306 | 1708276531012433 | 707                 | NULL      |
| 172.31.29.221 | 3306 | 1708276529011992 | 599                 | NULL      |
+---------------+------+------------------+---------------------+-----------+
10 rows in set (0.00 sec)
ProxySQLAdmin>
```

3. ProxySQL is now prepared to handle traffic on port 6033 (as the default). Use the following command to establish a connection to ProxySQL through the client prompt:

```
[root@proxysql ~]# mysql -usbuser -psbpass -h 127.0.0.1 -P6033
--prompt='ProxySQLClient> '
mysql: [Warning] Using a password on the command line interface can be
insecure.
Welcome to the MySQL monitor.  Commands end with ; or \g.
Your MySQL connection id is 3
Type 'help;' or '\h' for help. Type '\c' to clear the current input
statement.

ProxySQLClient>
```

4. Assess the connection and cluster status.

   a. Fetch details regarding the hostname and port of the MySQL server, connecting through ProxySQL:

   ```
   ProxySQLClient> select @@hostname, @@port;
   +------------+--------+
   | @@hostname | @@port |
   +------------+--------+
   | PXCNode1   |   3306 |
   +------------+--------+
   1 row in set (0.00 sec)
   ProxySQLClient&gt;
   ```

   b. Retrieve information about the Galera Cluster size connecting through ProxySQL:

```
ProxySQLClient> show status like 'wsrep_cluster_size';
+---------------------+-------+
| Variable_name       | Value |
+---------------------+-------+
| wsrep_cluster_size  | 3     |
+---------------------+-------+
1 row in set (0.01 sec)
ProxySQLClient>
```

c. Retrieve information about the status of the Galera Cluster connecting through ProxySQL:

```
ProxySQLClient> show status like 'wsrep_cluster_status';
+----------------------+---------+
| Variable_name        | Value   |
+----------------------+---------+
| wsrep_cluster_status | Primary |
+----------------------+---------+
1 row in set (0.01 sec)
ProxySQLClient>
```

d. Retrieve information about the connection status of a node in a Galera Cluster connecting through ProxySQL:

```
ProxySQLClient> show status like 'wsrep_connected';
+-----------------+-------+
| Variable_name   | Value |
+-----------------+-------+
| wsrep_connected | ON    |
+-----------------+-------+
1 row in set (0.00 sec)
ProxySQLClient>
```

5. To examine data replication, create a table and insert data:

```
mysql> create table t1(id int not null auto_increment primary key,
f1 int) engine=innodb;
Query OK, 0 rows affected (0.03 sec)
mysql>

mysql> insert into t1(f1) values(1),(2),(3);
Query OK, 3 rows affected (0.01 sec)
Records: 3  Duplicates: 0  Warnings: 0
mysql>
```

6. Connect to a MySQL server by using ProxySQL and execute a SELECT query on the table t1 in the sbtest database:

```
[root@proxysql ~]# mysql -usbuser -psbpass -h 127.0.0.1 -P6033
--prompt='ProxySQLClient >' -e "select * from sbtest.t1";
mysql: [Warning] Using a password on the command line interface can be
insecure.
+----+------+
| id | f1   |
+----+------+
```

```
|  3 |    1 |
|  6 |    2 |
|  9 |    3 |
+----+------+
[root@proxysql ~]#
```

Validating the ProxySQL configuration and automatic failover

Following the configuration of ProxySQL and the establishment of automated fail-over, it's crucial to confirm the configuration's proper functionality. The following steps outline the process:

1. Stop the MySQL process on one of the MySQL servers to simulate a failure by executing the following on the server's command line.

   a. Connect to a MySQL server using ProxySQL and execute a SELECT query to retrieve the values of the @@hostname and @@port system variables:

      ```
      [root@proxysql ~]# mysql -usbuser -psbpass -h 127.0.0.1 -P6033
      --prompt='ProxySQLClient >' -e "SELECT @@hostname,@@port";
      mysql: [Warning] Using a password on the command line interface can be
      insecure.
      +------------+--------+
      | @@hostname | @@port |
      +------------+--------+
      | PXCNode1   |   3306 |
      +------------+--------+
      [root@proxysql ~]#
      ```

   b. Query runtime_mysql_servers to verify the status of the MySQL servers, and confirm that all three servers are ONLINE:

      ```
      ProxySQLAdmin> SELECT hostgroup_id, hostname, status FROM
      runtime_mysql_servers;
      +--------------+---------------+--------+
      | hostgroup_id | hostname      | status |
      +--------------+---------------+--------+
      | 10           | 172.31.29.221 | ONLINE |
      | 10           | 172.31.30.140 | ONLINE |
      | 10           | 172.31.30.239 | ONLINE |
      +--------------+---------------+--------+
      3 rows in set (0.00 sec)
      ```

   c. This command *stops* the MySQL service and mimics a server failure:

      ```
      [root@PXCNode3 ~]# systemctl stop mysql
      [root@PXCNode3 ~]#
      ```

2. Execute a query on the runtime_mysql_servers table within the ProxySQL administration prompt to verify whether the shunning of the unsuccessful node has been applied successfully.

   a. Connect to a ProxySQL admin interface:

```
[root@proxysql ~]# mysql -u admin -padmin -h 127.0.0.1 -P6032
--prompt=\'ProxySQLAdmin> '
mysql: [Warning] Using a password on the command line interface can be
insecure.
Welcome to the MySQL monitor.  Commands end with ; or \g.
Your MySQL connection id is 8
Server version: 8.0 (ProxySQL Admin Module)

Copyright (c) 2009-2023 Percona LLC and/or its affiliates
Copyright (c) 2000, 2023, Oracle and/or its affiliates.

Type 'help;' or '\h' for help. Type '\c' to clear the current input
statement.

ProxySQLAdmin>
```

b. Query `runtime_mysql_servers` to verify the status of the MySQL servers and confirm that the *stopped* MySQL instance is set to SHUNNED, while all the remaining servers are marked as ONLINE:

```
ProxySQLAdmin> SELECT hostgroup_id, hostname, status FROM
runtime_mysql_servers;
+--------------+----------------+---------+
| hostgroup_id | hostname       | status  |
+--------------+----------------+---------+
| 10           | 172.31.29.221  | ONLINE  |
| 10           | 172.31.30.140  | ONLINE  |
| 10           | 172.31.30.239  | SHUNNED |
| 13           | 172.31.30.239  | SHUNNED |
+--------------+----------------+---------+
4 rows in set (0.01 sec)
ProxySQLAdmin>
```

Running this command will show the host-group ID, hostname, and status of every MySQL server, including the one that has experienced a failure.

3. Start the failed node by executing the following command on the MySQL server:

```
[root@PXCNode3 ~]# systemctl start mysql
[root@PXCNode3 ~]#
```

4. Run the following query from the ProxySQL administration prompt again to check whether the failed node is back online:

```
ProxySQLAdmin> SELECT hostgroup_id, hostname, status
FROM runtime_mysql_servers;
+--------------+----------------+--------+
| hostgroup_id | hostname       | status |
+--------------+----------------+--------+
| 10           | 172.31.29.221  | ONLINE |
| 10           | 172.31.30.140  | ONLINE |
| 10           | 172.31.30.239  | ONLINE |
+--------------+----------------+--------+
```

```
3 rows in set (0.00 sec)
ProxySQLAdmin>
```

Running this command will show the host-group ID, hostname, and status of every MySQL server, including the one that has experienced a failure.

If the previously excluded node is no longer being shunned and has returned to an online state, the automatic failover setup is functioning properly.

Query performance statistics

In the realm of ProxySQL administration, gaining insight into query performance statistics is paramount. Real-time statistics tracking ProxySQL's behavior and workload processing are meticulously recorded, offering a wealth of information to monitor and fine-tune your database environment. The stats schema boasts a collection of tables that serve as windows into various statistical aspects. Within this framework, you can execute tailored queries to extract valuable information. Whether you seek a global overview, connection pool insights, process list details, query digest breakdowns, or command counter data, ProxySQL provides the means to scrutinize and optimize your database operations.

Let's delve into some commonly used queries to harness these statistics effectively:

1. To display global statistics of ProxySQL, run the following command:

```
ProxySQLAdmin> SELECT * FROM stats_mysql_global;
+--------------------------------------------+----------------+
| Variable_Name                              | Variable_Value |
+--------------------------------------------+----------------+
| ProxySQL_Uptime                            | 3112           |
| Active_Transactions                        | 0              |
| Client_Connections_aborted                 | 0              |
| Client_Connections_connected               | 0              |
| Client_Connections_created                 | 4              |
| Server_Connections_aborted                 | 0              |
| Server_Connections_connected               | 2              |
| Questions                                  | 17             |
| Slow_queries                               | 0              |
| Queries_backends_bytes_recv                | 267            |
| Queries_backends_bytes_sent                | 357            |
| Queries_frontends_bytes_recv               | 934            |
| Queries_frontends_bytes_sent               | 2347           |
| ConnPool_get_conn_success                  | 3              |
| mysql_killed_backend_connections           | 0              |
| Servers_table_version                      | 13             |
| MySQL_Thread_Workers                       | 4              |
| MySQL_Monitor_Workers                      | 8              |
| MySQL_Monitor_Workers_Started              | 8              |
| MySQL_Monitor_connect_check_OK             | 1675           |
| MySQL_Monitor_connect_check_ERR            | 2              |
```

```
| MySQL_Monitor_ping_check_OK               | 1897        |
| MySQL_Monitor_ping_check_ERR              | 152         |
| MyHGM_myconnpoll_get                      | 3           |
| MyHGM_myconnpoll_get_ok                   | 3           |
| MyHGM_myconnpoll_push                     | 7           |
| MyHGM_myconnpoll_reset                    | 2           |
| SQLite3_memory_bytes                      | 2830992     |
| ConnPool_memory_bytes                     | 145120      |
| Stmt_Server_Active_Unique                 | 0           |
| Stmt_Max_Stmt_id                          | 1           |
| new_req_conns_count                       | 0           |
+-------------------------------------------+-------------+
107 rows in set (0.00 sec)
ProxySQLAdmin>
```

2. Run the following command to see the host group and server host-specific connection pool statistics:

```
ProxySQLAdmin> SELECT * FROM stats_mysql_connection_pool order by
hostgroup,srv_host\G
*************************** 1. row ***************************
        hostgroup: 10
         srv_host: 172.31.29.221
         srv_port: 3306
           status: ONLINE
         ConnUsed: 0
         ConnFree: 1
           ConnOK: 1
          ConnERR: 0
      MaxConnUsed: 1
          Queries: 12
 Queries_GTID_sync: 0
  Bytes_data_sent: 334
  Bytes_data_recv: 243
       Latency_us: 656
*************************** 2. row ***************************
        hostgroup: 10
         srv_host: 172.31.30.140
         srv_port: 3306
           status: ONLINE
         ConnUsed: 0
         ConnFree: 1
           ConnOK: 1
          ConnERR: 0
      MaxConnUsed: 1
          Queries: 1
 Queries_GTID_sync: 0
  Bytes_data_sent: 23
  Bytes_data_recv: 24
       Latency_us: 667
*************************** 3. row ***************************
        hostgroup: 10
         srv_host: 172.31.30.239
```

```
        srv_port: 3306
          status: ONLINE
        ConnUsed: 0
        ConnFree: 0
          ConnOK: 0
         ConnERR: 0
     MaxConnUsed: 0
         Queries: 0
Queries_GTID_sync: 0
  Bytes_data_sent: 0
  Bytes_data_recv: 0
       Latency_us: 675
3 rows in set (0.01 sec)

ProxySQLAdmin>
```

3. To display the process list statistics, run the following command:

```
ProxySQLAdmin> SELECT * FROM stats_mysql_processlist;
Empty set (0.00 sec)
ProxySQLAdmin>
```

4. Run the following command to view the query digest statistics:

```
ProxySQLAdmin> SELECT * FROM stats_mysql_query_digest\G
*************************** 1. row ***************************
          hostgroup: 10
         schemaname: information_schema
           username: sbuser
     client_address:
             digest: 0xa56346186f5c59df
        digest_text: SELECT @@hostname,@@port
         count_star: 1
         first_seen: 1708277105
          last_seen: 1708277105
           sum_time: 1308
           min_time: 1308
           max_time: 1308
  sum_rows_affected: 0
      sum_rows_sent: 1
*************************** 2. row ***************************
          hostgroup: 10
         schemaname: information_schema
           username: sbuser
     client_address:
             digest: 0x51ed00ab4c0ba539
        digest_text: select * from sbtest.t1
         count_star: 1
         first_seen: 1708277063
          last_seen: 1708277063
           sum_time: 2904
           min_time: 2904
           max_time: 2904
  sum_rows_affected: 0
```

```
        sum_rows_sent: 3
*************************** 3. row ***************************
          hostgroup: 10
         schemaname: information_schema
           username: sbuser
     client_address:
             digest: 0x143f317f0738a953
        digest_text: show status like ?
         count_star: 3
         first_seen: 1708276762
          last_seen: 1708276824
           sum_time: 7352
           min_time: 1912
           max_time: 3200
  sum_rows_affected: 0
      sum_rows_sent: 3
*************************** 4. row ***************************
          hostgroup: 10
         schemaname: information_schema
           username: sbuser
     client_address:
             digest: 0x268cb88676b0e27c
        digest_text: select @@hostname,@@port
         count_star: 8
         first_seen: 1708276703
          last_seen: 1708276731
           sum_time: 12921
           min_time: 728
           max_time: 4255
  sum_rows_affected: 0
      sum_rows_sent: 8
*************************** 5. row ***************************
          hostgroup: 10
         schemaname: information_schema
           username: sbuser
     client_address:
             digest: 0x226cd90d52a2ba0b
        digest_text: select @@version_comment limit ?
         count_star: 4
         first_seen: 1708276583
          last_seen: 1708277105
           sum_time: 0
           min_time: 0
           max_time: 0
  sum_rows_affected: 0
      sum_rows_sent: 0
5 rows in set (0.00 sec)
ProxySQLAdmin>
```

Load Testing ProxySQL with Sysbench for PXC

The open source sysbench stands as a well-recognized, script-driven, multithreaded benchmarking utility designed to assess the performance of MySQL databases. This tool holds significant importance in conducting load tests, benchmarks, and outcome analyses for database systems. Sysbench has a variety of predesigned benchmarking tests capable of emulating diverse behaviors of online transaction processing (OLTP) applications. These tests were constructed using the user-friendly Lua scripting language. Some of the predefined scripts are as follows:

oltp_read_write
Simulates the workload of a typical OLTP application, which includes both database reads and writes.

oltp_point_select
Simulates the workload of a typical OLTP application with a lot of point selects.

tpcc
Imitates the functionality of a sophisticated OLTP application.

oltp_insert
Simulates the workload of an ordinary OLTP application, which involves entering data into a database.

Customizing sysbench scripts

If your application doesn't follow the typical OLTP framework, you can write a unique custom Lua script. You can use this custom script to test the functionality of your database under particular circumstances—for instance, to evaluate how well your database performs under demanding write loads or sophisticated read patterns.

You must be familiar with Lua scripting in order to write a custom script, but the process is fairly simple. You should define the following in your script:

Initialization function
Initializes any required data structures as well as the test environment.

Event function
Defines the behavior of the test workload. It should produce multiple queries that replicate the actions of your application.

Cleanup function
Clears any resources allotted throughout the test.

After crafting your personalized script, you can initiate its execution through sysbench. The following command will execute a custom script called *mytest.lua* for a duration of 60 seconds, utilizing 10 threads:

```
sysbench --test=mytest.lua --mysql-host=localhost --mysql-port=3306
--mysql-user=root --mysql-password=password --mysql-db=mydatabase
--time=60 --threads=10 run
```

Using ProxySQL with sysbench

To use ProxySQL with sysbench, you need to configure ProxySQL so that traffic is distributed equally among numerous MySQL servers. You'll create a ProxySQL configuration file specifying the MySQL servers and traffic distribution rules to do this. The following configuration file example creates two MySQL servers and mandates a fair traffic split between them:

```
mysql_servers =
\{
\{ address = '192.168.1.1', port = 3306, max_connections = 100 },
\{ address = '192.168.1.2', port = 3306, max_connections = 100 },
}

mysql_query_rules =
\{
\{ rule = 'SELECT * FROM mytable', destination_servers = \{ 1, 2 } },
\{ rule = 'INSERT INTO mytable', destination_servers = \{ 1 } },
\{ rule = 'UPDATE mytable', destination_servers = \{ 2 } },
\{ rule = 'DELETE FROM mytable', destination_servers = \{ 1 } },
}
```

Sysbench is unique as a flexible and widely used tool for running server benchmarks. It is equipped to run a variety of benchmarks on various server components, including OLTP transactions, filesystems, CPU, RAM, threads, and mutex. This section explores the wide range of benchmarks that sysbench provides together with accompanying characteristics.

The `oltp*` prefix designates OLTP benchmarks, which can be run on MySQL and PostgreSQL databases. The OLTP benchmarks that sysbench can run are listed in the following table:

Benchmark	Description
oltp_common.lua	A set of common OLTP benchmarks for both MySQL and PostgreSQL
oltp_delete.lua	Measures the performance of deleting records from a database
oltp_insert.lua	Measures the performance of inserting new records into a database
oltp_point_select.lua	Measures the performance of point queries in a database
oltp_read_only.lua	Measures the performance of read-only transactions in a database
oltp_read_write.lua	Measures the performance of read/write transactions in a database
oltp_update_index.lua	Measures the performance of updating indexed records in a database
oltp_update_non_index.lua	Measures the performance of updating nonindexed records in a database

The oltp_*.lua scripts' implementation of OLTP-like database benchmarks serves as the foundation for the OLTP benchmarks, which simulate a typical OLTP workload and assess a database system's performance under those circumstances. Sysbench can run benchmarks for file I/O, CPU, memory, threads, and mutex in addition to OLTP workloads. This table presents these benchmarks and their associated features:

Benchmark	Description
fileio	Measures the performance of file I/O operations on a filesystem
cpu	Measures the performance of CPU-intensive operations such as arithmetic and logic
memory	Measures the performance of memory access operations
threads	Measures the performance of a thread-based scheduler
mutex	Measures the performance of a POSIX mutex

Using MySQL with sysbench

Let's discuss how to benchmark MySQL 8 databases by using sysbench. Before running sysbench, ensure that you have the following:

- A running MySQL 8 instance
- A database named sbtest
- An authorized user possessing complete privileges for the sbtest database, enabling remote connections or socket-based connections based on the location of sysbench installation

Installing sysbench

You must install sysbench before you can use it to assess the performance of your MySQL 8 installation. Perform the following on a ProxySQL node:

1. Use this command to see whether sysbench is already installed:

```
[root@sysbench ~]# yum list all | grep sysbench
sysbench.x86_64
1.0.20-6.el8                                    percona-release-x86_64
sysbench-debuginfo.x86_64
1.0.20-6.el8                                    percona-release-x86_64
sysbench-debugsource.x86_64
1.0.20-6.el8                                    percona-release-x86_64
sysbench-tpcc.x86_64
1.0.20-6.el8                                    percona-release-x86_64
[root@sysbench ~]#
```

2. Install sysbench if it isn't already installed:

```
[root@sysbench ~]# yum install sysbench -y
Last metadata expiration check: 0:02:34 ago on Mon 19 Feb 2024
08:19:47 AM UTC.
```

```
Dependencies resolved.
...
Total download size: 898 k
Installed size: 1.7 M
Downloading Packages:
(1/5): mariadb-connector-c-config-3.1.11-2.el8_3.noarch.rpm
130 kB/s | 15 kB    00:00
(2/5): mariadb-connector-c-3.1.11-2.el8_3.x86_64.rpm
1.6 MB/s | 200 kB    00:00
(3/5): libaio-0.3.112-1.el8.x86_64.rpm
2.8 MB/s | 33 kB    00:00
(4/5): sysbench-1.0.20-6.el8.x86_64.rpm
3.1 MB/s | 454 kB    00:00
(5/5): libpq-13.5-1.el8.x86_64.rpm
737 kB/s | 198 kB    00:00
--------------------------------------------------------------------
Total                                        1.4 MB/s | 898 kB
00:00
Percona Original release/x86_64 YUM repository    4.5 MB/s | 4.7 kB
00:00
Importing GPG key 0x8507EFA5:
 Userid      : "Percona Development Team (Packaging key) <info@percona.com>"
 Fingerprint: 4D1B B29D 63D9 8E42 2B21 13B1 9334 A25F 8507 EFA5
 From        : /etc/pki/rpm-gpg/PERCONA-PACKAGING-KEY
Key imported successfully
Running transaction check
Transaction check succeeded.
Running transaction test
Transaction test succeeded.
```

Using sysbench to evaluate MySQL 8 performance

You can assess the performance of your MySQL 8.0 installation by using sysbench after it has been installed. Test the connection from the sysbench-installed server to the PXC node via ProxySQL:

```
[root@sysbench ~]# mysql -usbuser -psbpass -h 172.31.26.35 -P6033 -e"SELECT
@@hostname,@@port"
mysql: [Warning] Using a password on the command line interface can be insecure.
+------------+--------+
| @@hostname | @@port |
+------------+--------+
| PXCNode1   |   3306 |
+------------+--------+
[root@sysbench ~]#
```

This time, the query is being redirected to PXCNode2:

```
[root@sysbench ~]# mysql -usbuser -psbpass -h 172.31.26.35 -P6033 -e"SELECT
@@hostname,@@port"
mysql: [Warning] Using a password on the command line interface can be insecure.
+------------+--------+
| @@hostname | @@port |
```

```
+-------------+--------+
| PXCNode2    |  3306  |
+-------------+--------+
[root@sysbench ~]#
```

Sysbench commands

The general command-line syntax for sysbench is as follows:

```
sysbench [options] <testname> [command]
```

When running tests, sysbench has three types of options: log options, database options, and general options. The specific test being run is identified by *testname*. Additionally, commands like `Prepare`, `Run`, `Clean`, and `Help` are examples of actions that can be taken during the testing process.

Sysbench tests

Sysbench can execute the following types of tests:

- Insert-only
- Read/write
- Point select
- Update index

- Update non-index
- Select random points
- Select random ranges

To guarantee the optimal functionality of a MySQL cluster, comprehensive testing is essential.

Insert-only test. The *insert-only test* inserts data into the database. Before running the OLTP insert test, check the tables available in the `sbtest` database:

```
mysql> use sbtest;
Reading table information for completion of table and column names
You can turn off this feature to get a quicker startup with -A

Database changed
mysql> show tables;
+------------------+
| Tables_in_sbtest |
+------------------+
| t1               |
+------------------+
1 row in set (0.00 sec)
mysql>

[root@sysbench ~]# sysbench /usr/share/sysbench/oltp_insert.lua \
--mysql-db=sbtest \
> --mysql-host=172.31.26.35 --mysql-port=6033 --mysql-user='sbuser' \
> --mysql-password='sbpass' --db-driver=mysql --threads=4 --tables=20 \
> --report-interval=20 --table-size=15 prepare
```

```
sysbench 1.0.20 (using bundled LuaJIT 2.1.0-beta2)

Initializing worker threads...

Creating table 'sbtest2'...
Creating table 'sbtest1'...
Creating table 'sbtest3'...
Creating table 'sbtest4'...
Inserting 15 records into 'sbtest2'
Inserting 15 records into 'sbtest3'
Inserting 15 records into 'sbtest4'
Creating a secondary index on 'sbtest2'...
Creating a secondary index on 'sbtest3'...
Creating a secondary index on 'sbtest4'...
Inserting 15 records into 'sbtest1'
Creating table 'sbtest6'...
Creating table 'sbtest7'...
Creating table 'sbtest8'...
Creating a secondary index on 'sbtest1'...
Inserting 15 records into 'sbtest6'
Inserting 15 records into 'sbtest7'
Inserting 15 records into 'sbtest8'
Creating a secondary index on 'sbtest10'...
....
Creating table 'sbtest17'...
Creating a secondary index on 'sbtest18'...
Inserting 15 records into 'sbtest20'
Creating a secondary index on 'sbtest19'...
Inserting 15 records into 'sbtest17'
Creating a secondary index on 'sbtest20'...
Creating a secondary index on 'sbtest17'...
[root@sysbench ~]#
```

After completing the sysbench process, switch to the database named `sbtest` and display the list of tables in the current database:

```
mysql> use sbtest;
Database changed
mysql>
mysql> show tables;
+------------------+
| Tables_in_sbtest |
+------------------+
| sbtest1          |
| sbtest10         |
| sbtest11         |
| sbtest12         |
| sbtest13         |
| sbtest14         |
| sbtest15         |
| sbtest16         |
| sbtest17         |
| sbtest18         |
```

```
| sbtest19           |
| sbtest2            |
| sbtest20           |
| sbtest3            |
| sbtest4            |
| sbtest5            |
| sbtest6            |
| sbtest7            |
| sbtest8            |
| sbtest9            |
| t1                 |
+--------------------+
21 rows in set (0.00 sec)
mysql>
```

The test file in this instance is called *oltp_insert.lua*, and the database is called sbtest.
The --table-size and --threads options specify the number of rows in each table
and the number of threads to be used, respectively.

Read/write test. The database's reading and writing processes are also covered by this
investigation. Start the sysbench *read/write test* by using the following command:

```
[root@sysbench ~]# sysbench /usr/share/sysbench/oltp_read_write.lua
--mysql-db=sbtest \
> --mysql-host=172.31.26.35 --mysql-port=6033 --mysql-user='sbuser' \
> --mysql-password='sbpass' --db-driver=mysql --threads=4 --tables=20 \
> --table-size=15000 --time=200 --report-interval=20 --rate=10 --events=0 run
sysbench 1.0.20 (using bundled LuaJIT 2.1.0-beta2)

Running the test with following options:
Number of threads: 4
Target transaction rate: 10/sec
Report intermediate results every 20 second(s)
Initializing random number generator from current time
Initializing worker threads...
Threads started!
[ 20s ] thds: 4 tps: 8.60 qps: 171.98 (r/w/o: 120.39/9.05/42.54) lat (ms,95%):
 34.33 err/s: 0.00 reconn/s: 0.00
[ 20s ] queue length: 0, concurrency: 0
[ 40s ] thds: 4 tps: 10.05 qps: 201.00 (r/w/o: 140.70/12.60/47.70) lat (ms,95%):
 38.94 err/s: 0.00 reconn/s: 0.00
[ 40s ] queue length: 0, concurrency: 0
[ 60s ] thds: 4 tps: 8.85 qps: 177.00 (r/w/o: 123.90/11.90/41.20) lat (ms,95%):
 32.53 err/s: 0.00 reconn/s: 0.00
[ 60s ] queue length: 0, concurrency: 0
[ 80s ] thds: 4 tps: 10.20 qps: 204.00 (r/w/o: 142.80/14.85/46.35) lat (ms,95%):
 32.53 err/s: 0.00 reconn/s: 0.00
...
[ 200s ] queue length: 0, concurrency: 0
SQL statistics:
    queries performed:
        read:                         27272
```

```
            write:                    3194
            other:                    8494
            total:                    38960
        transactions:                 1948    (9.73 per sec.)
        queries:                      38960   (194.62 per sec.)
        ignored errors:               0       (0.00 per sec.)
        reconnects:                   0       (0.00 per sec.)
    General statistics:
        total time:                   200.1788s
        total number of events:       1948
    Latency (ms):
            min:                              24.29
            avg:                              30.61
            max:                              125.70
            95th percentile:                  36.89
            sum:                              59623.92
    Threads fairness:
        events (avg/stddev):          487.0000/0.71
        execution time (avg/stddev):  14.9060/0.08
    [root@sysbench ~]#
```

In this context, *oltp_read_write.lua* refers to the test file, and sbtest represents the database's name. The --time parameter designates the test's duration in seconds, while the --rate parameter indicates the quantity of queries to be executed per second.

Point select test.   Each transaction in this evaluation involves a single point-select operation. Execute the following command to start the sysbench test:

```
[root@sysbench ~]# sysbench /usr/share/sysbench/oltp_point_select.lua
--mysql-db=sbtest \
> --mysql-host=172.31.26.35 --mysql-port=6033 --mysql-user='sbuser' \
> --mysql-password='sbpass' --db-driver=mysql --threads=4 --tables=20 \
> --table-size=15000 --time=200 --report-interval=20 run
sysbench 1.0.20 (using bundled LuaJIT 2.1.0-beta2)
Running the test with following options:
Number of threads: 4
Report intermediate results every 20 second(s)
Initializing random number generator from current time
Initializing worker threads...
Threads started!
[ 20s ] thds: 4 tps: 3308.01 qps: 3308.01 (r/w/o: 3308.01/0.00/0.00) lat
(ms,95%):
 1.89 err/s: 0.00 reconn/s: 0.00
[ 200s ] thds: 4 tps: 3421.64 qps: 3421.64 (r/w/o: 3421.64/0.00/0.00) lat
(ms,95%):
 1.70 err/s: 0.00 reconn/s: 0.00
SQL statistics:
    queries performed:
        read:                         688594
        write:                        0
```

```
        other:                        0
        total:                        688594
     transactions:                    688594 (3442.88 per sec.)
     queries:                         688594 (3442.88 per sec.)
     ignored errors:                  0       (0.00 per sec.)
     reconnects:                      0       (0.00 per sec.)
General statistics:
     total time:                      200.0031s
     total number of events:          688594
Latency (ms):
          min:                              0.76
          avg:                              1.16
          max:                             20.88
          95th percentile:                  1.58
          sum:                         798349.51
Threads fairness:
     events (avg/stddev):        172148.5000/391.12
     execution time (avg/stddev):   199.5874/0.00
[root@sysbench ~]#
```

In this case, *oltp_point_select.lua* stands as the test file, and sbtest is designated as the database name.

Update index. This benchmark evaluates the efficiency of updating rows within an indexed table. Each transaction modifies either a single row or a designated number of rows. By default, the benchmark's runtime is 10 seconds, and each statement functions as an individual transaction. Utilize the following command to execute this benchmark:

```
[root@sysbench ~]#
[root@sysbench ~]# sysbench /usr/share/sysbench/oltp_update_index.lua
--mysql-db=sbtest \
> --mysql-host=172.31.26.35 --mysql-port=6033 --mysql-user='sbuser' \
> --mysql-password='sbpass' --db-driver=mysql --threads=4 --tables=20 \
> --table-size=15 --time=200 --report-interval=20 run
sysbench 1.0.20 (using bundled LuaJIT 2.1.0-beta2)
Running the test with following options:
Number of threads: 4
Report intermediate results every 20 second(s)
Initializing random number generator from current time
Initializing worker threads...
Threads started!
[ 20s ] thds: 4 tps: 1826.62 qps: 1826.62 (r/w/o: 0.00/251.48/1575.15) lat
(ms,95%):
 7.84 err/s: 1.65 reconn/s: 0.00
[ 200s ] thds: 4 tps: 1775.93 qps: 1775.93 (r/w/o: 0.00/244.50/1531.44) lat
(ms,95%):
 8.13 err/s: 1.90 reconn/s: 0.00
SQL statistics:
    queries performed:
        read:                         0
```

```
        write:                        50922
        other:                        319333
        total:                        370255
    transactions:                     370255 (1851.20 per sec.)
    queries:                          370255 (1851.20 per sec.)
    ignored errors:                   401    (2.00 per sec.)
    reconnects:                       0      (0.00 per sec.)
General statistics:
    total time:                       200.0059s
    total number of events:           370255
Latency (ms):
         min:                                 0.78
         avg:                                 2.16
         max:                                43.31
         95th percentile:                     7.84
         sum:                            799092.81
Threads fairness:
    events (avg/stddev):           92563.7500/206.24
    execution time (avg/stddev):   199.7732/0.00
[root@sysbench ~]#
```

Update non-index. This benchmark evaluates how effectively rows in a table can be updated without using an index. Either a single row or a specified number of rows are changed by each transaction. Each statement in the benchmark serves as a transaction, and by default it runs for 10 seconds. To run this benchmark, use the following command:

```
[root@sysbench ~]# sysbench /usr/share/sysbench/oltp_update_non_index.lua
--mysql-db=sbtest \
> --mysql-host=172.31.26.35 --mysql-port=6033 --mysql-user='sbuser' \
> --mysql-password='sbpass' --db-driver=mysql --report-interval=20 \
> --tables=20 --table-size=1500 --threads=8 --time=60 run
sysbench 1.0.20 (using bundled LuaJIT 2.1.0-beta2)

Running the test with following options:
Number of threads: 8
Report intermediate results every 20 second(s)
Initializing random number generator from current time


Initializing worker threads...

Threads started!

[ 20s ] thds: 8 tps: 6391.43 qps: 6391.43 (r/w/o: 0.00/0.00/6391.43) lat
(ms,95%): 1.82 err/s: 0.00 reconn/s: 0.00
[ 40s ] thds: 8 tps: 6011.79 qps: 6011.79 (r/w/o: 0.00/0.00/6011.79) lat
(ms,95%): 2.30 err/s: 0.00 reconn/s: 0.00
[ 60s ] thds: 8 tps: 6764.20 qps: 6764.20 (r/w/o: 0.00/0.00/6764.20) lat
(ms,95%): 1.55 err/s: 0.00 reconn/s: 0.00
SQL statistics:
```

```
          queries performed:
               read:                       0
               write:                      0
               other:                      383369
               total:                      383369
          transactions:                    383369 (6388.84 per sec.)
          queries:                         383369 (6388.84 per sec.)
          ignored errors:                  0        (0.00 per sec.)
          reconnects:                      0        (0.00 per sec.)

     General statistics:
          total time:                      60.0041s
          total number of events:          383369

     Latency (ms):
               min:                              0.77
               avg:                              1.25
               max:                             21.30
               95th percentile:                  1.86
               sum:                         479136.40

     Threads fairness:
          events (avg/stddev):        47921.1250/291.07
          execution time (avg/stddev):  59.8920/0.00

     [root@sysbench ~]#
```

Select random points. This benchmark evaluates how well random point selection from a table performs. Each statement has 10 or a predetermined number of random points in the IN clause of the select query, and it functions with only one table at a time. A transaction is a statement. This benchmark can be run with the following command:

```
[root@sysbench ~]# sysbench /usr/share/sysbench/select_random_points.lua
--mysql-db=sbtest \
> --mysql-host=172.31.26.35 --mysql-port=6033 --mysql-user='sbuser' \
> --mysql-password='sbpass' --db-driver=mysql --report-interval=2 \
> --tables=1 --threads=8 --time=60 run
sysbench 1.0.20 (using bundled LuaJIT 2.1.0-beta2)

Running the test with following options:
Number of threads: 8
Report intermediate results every 2 second(s)
Initializing random number generator from current time


Initializing worker threads...

Threads started!

[ 2s ] thds: 8 tps: 6231.59 qps: 6231.59 (r/w/o: 6231.59/0.00/0.00) lat
```

```
(ms,95%): 1.64 err/s: 0.00 reconn/s: 0.00
[ 4s ] thds: 8 tps: 6211.16 qps: 6211.16 (r/w/o: 6211.16/0.00/0.00) lat
(ms,95%): 1.70 err/s: 0.00 reconn/s: 0.00
[ 6s ] thds: 8 tps: 5788.05 qps: 5788.05 (r/w/o: 5788.05/0.00/0.00) lat
(ms,95%): 1.79 err/s: 0.00 reconn/s: 0.00
[ 8s ] thds: 8 tps: 4631.47 qps: 4631.47 (r/w/o: 4631.47/0.00/0.00) lat
(ms,95%): 3.25 err/s: 0.00 reconn/s: 0.00
...
[ 60s ] thds: 8 tps: 5929.81 qps: 5929.81 (r/w/o: 5929.81/0.00/0.00) lat
(ms,95%): 1.67 err/s: 0.00 reconn/s: 0.00
SQL statistics:
    queries performed:
        read:                      342722
        write:                     0
        other:                     0
        total:                     342722
    transactions:                  342722 (5711.37 per sec.)
    queries:                       342722 (5711.37 per sec.)
    ignored errors:                0      (0.00 per sec.)
    reconnects:                    0      (0.00 per sec.)

General statistics:
    total time:                    60.0051s
    total number of events:        342722

Latency (ms):
        min:                              0.81
        avg:                              1.40
        max:                             21.09
        95th percentile:                  2.18
        sum:                         478967.08

Threads fairness:
    events (avg/stddev):       42840.2500/137.06
    execution time (avg/stddev):   59.8709/0.00

[root@sysbench ~]#
```

You can make sure that your cluster is operating at peak efficiency and satisfying your organization's needs by following these best practices for testing a MySQL 8 cluster with sysbench using ProxySQL.

Select random ranges.   Executing a SELECT statement using random range values to obtain data from a table is one of the most typical performance-testing criteria. Just that is accomplished by the SELECT random ranges benchmark in sysbench. There is currently no support for multiple tables, and this benchmark works with only the sbtest1 table. The benchmark conducts a series of transactions, each of which has 10 or a predetermined number of BETWEEN clauses, with a size of 5 or the predetermined delta for each BETWEEN operation.

To run the benchmark, use the following command:

```
[root@sysbench ~]# sysbench /usr/share/sysbench/select_random_ranges.lua
--mysql-db=sbtest \
> --mysql-host=172.31.26.35 --mysql-port=6033 --mysql-user='sbuser' \
> --mysql-password='sbpass' --db-driver=mysql --report-interval=2 \
> --tables=1 --threads=8 --time=60 run
sysbench 1.0.20 (using bundled LuaJIT 2.1.0-beta2)

Running the test with following options:
Number of threads: 8
Report intermediate results every 2 second(s)
Initializing random number generator from current time
Initializing worker threads...
Threads started!
[ 2s ] thds: 8 tps: 6087.45 qps: 6087.45 (r/w/o: 6087.45/0.00/0.00) lat
(ms,95%): 1.61 err/s: 0.00 reconn/s: 0.00
....
[ 60s ] thds: 8 tps: 6031.43 qps: 6031.43 (r/w/o: 6031.43/0.00/0.00) lat
(ms,95%): 2.03 err/s: 0.00 reconn/s: 0.00
SQL statistics:
    queries performed:
        read:                            352000
        write:                           0
        other:                           0
        total:                           352000
    transactions:                        352000 (5866.03 per sec.)
    queries:                             352000 (5866.03 per sec.)
    ignored errors:                      0      (0.00 per sec.)
    reconnects:                          0      (0.00 per sec.)

General statistics:
    total time:                          60.0047s
    total number of events:              352000

Latency (ms):
        min:                                    0.85
        avg:                                    1.36
        max:                                   35.42
        95th percentile:                        1.96
        sum:                               478942.77

Threads fairness:
    events (avg/stddev):          44000.0000/184.54
    execution time (avg/stddev):     59.8678/0.00

[root@sysbench ~]#
```

Using eight threads, this command performs the benchmark for 60 seconds and outputs the results every 2 seconds. It is essential to provide the correct hostname, port number, and user credentials for the MySQL server.

Clean up. Cleaning up the sysbench-generated data is essential after carrying out the required performance tests. This cleanup can be done manually or with the help of the sysbench command.

For manual cleanup, enter the DB server by using a valid login and drop the sbtest database to manually clean up the data. Alternatively, you can purge the data by using the sysbench command:

```
[root@sysbench ~]# sysbench /usr/share/sysbench/oltp_read_write.lua
--mysql-db=sbtest \
> --mysql-host=172.31.26.35 --mysql-port=6033 --mysql-user='sbuser' \
> --mysql-password='sbpass' --db-driver=mysql --tables=8 \
> --table-size=1000000 --threads=8 cleanup
sysbench 1.0.20 (using bundled LuaJIT 2.1.0-beta2)

Dropping table 'sbtest1'...
Dropping table 'sbtest2'...
Dropping table 'sbtest3'...
Dropping table 'sbtest4'...
Dropping table 'sbtest5'...
Dropping table 'sbtest6'...
Dropping table 'sbtest7'...
Dropping table 'sbtest8'...
[root@sysbench ~]#
```

The OLTP read/write benchmark generates eight tables with a total of one million rows each. This command cleans away the data generated by that benchmark. It is crucial to provide the correct hostname, port number, and user credentials for the MySQL server.

MariaDB Galera Cluster Setup

MariaDB Galera Cluster is based on the Galera replication library, which provides a reliable and scalable replication mechanism designed to work in high-traffic environments. Galera Cluster ensures that all nodes in the cluster have the same data at all times, which means that in the event of a node failure, failover can be achieved without data loss or corruption.

This section covers installing MariaDB Galera 4 on Ubuntu.

Installing required packages

To set up MariaDB on your Ubuntu system using the MariaDB repository, begin by installing the necessary packages. Install the *apt-transport-https* package and curl:

```
root@galeranode1:~# curl -LsS https://downloads.mariadb.com/MariaDB/
mariadb_repo_setup | sudo bash -s --
# [info] Checking for script prerequisites.
# [info] MariaDB Server version 11.3 is valid
```

```
# [info] Repository file successfully written to /etc/apt/sources.list.d/
mariadb.list
# [info] Adding trusted package signing keys...
# [info] Running apt-get update...
# [info] Done adding trusted package signing keys
root@galeranode1:~#
```

Installing MariaDB on all servers

At this point, you are prepared to initiate the installation of MariaDB 11.3 on your Ubuntu system. Use the following steps to update the repository and execute the installation of the MariaDB server:

1. Update the package list and upgrade all installed packages on a Debian-based Linux system in one go:

```
root@galeranode1:~# sudo apt update
Hit:1 http://us-west-2.ec2.archive.ubuntu.com/ubuntu jammy InRelease
Get:2 http://us-west-2.ec2.archive.ubuntu.com/ubuntu jammy-updates
  InRelease [119 kB]
Get:5 http://security.ubuntu.com/ubuntu jammy-security InRelease [110 kB]
Get:6 http://us-west-2.ec2.archive.ubuntu.com/ubuntu jammy/universe
  Translation-en [5652 kB]
Get:38 http://security.ubuntu.com/ubuntu jammy-security/multiverse
  amd64 c-n-f Metadata [260 B]
Fetched 29.5 MB in 4s (6610 kB/s)
Reading package lists... Done
Building dependency tree... Done
Reading state information... Done
74 packages can be upgraded. Run 'apt list --upgradable' to see them.
root@galeranode1:~#
```

2. Install the MariaDB database server on a Debian-based Linux system with automatic confirmation of prompts (-y):

```
root@galeranode1:~# sudo apt install vim mariadb-server mariadb-client -y
Reading package lists... Done
Building dependency tree... Done
Reading state information... Done
The following additional packages will be installed:
  galera-4 libcgi-fast-perl libcgi-pm-perl libclone-perl
  libconfig-inifiles-perl libdaxctl1 libdbd-mysql-perl
```

3. Starting from MariaDB version 11.3 and beyond, the root user of MariaDB doesn't come with a predefined password. To establish a password for the root user, access MariaDB by executing this command:

```
root@galeranode1:~# mariadb -uroot -p
Enter password:
Welcome to the MariaDB monitor.  Commands end with ; or \g.
Your MariaDB connection id is 31
Server version: 11.3.2-MariaDB-1:11.3.2+maria~ubu2204 mariadb.org
binary distribution
```

```
Copyright (c) 2000, 2018, Oracle, MariaDB Corporation Ab and others.
Type 'help;' or '\h' for help. Type '\c' to clear the current input
statement.
MariaDB [(none)]>
```

4. Once you've entered the MariaDB shell, modify the password as follows:

```
MariaDB [(none)]> set password = password("Pass21word$$");
Query OK, 0 rows affected (0.001 sec)
MariaDB [(none)]>
```

Substitute *Pass21word$$* with a robust password. The preceding command establishes the password for the root user. Upon executing the command, you should observe the subsequent output confirming the successful setting of the password.

5. Rsync is necessary for Galera Cluster's file synchronization between nodes. To install rsync, run the following command on each of the three servers:

```
root@galeranode1:~# sudo apt install rsync
Reading package lists... Done
Building dependency tree... Done
Reading state information... Done
rsync is already the newest version (3.2.7-0ubuntu0.22.04.2).
rsync set to manually installed.
0 upgraded, 0 newly installed, 0 to remove and 70 not upgraded.
root@galeranode1:~#
```

This command verifies the presence of the latest rsync version or prompts you to upgrade or install it if needed.

6. After you've successfully installed MariaDB and configured the root password on the initial server, proceed to repeat the installation process on the remaining two servers. With the successful installation of MariaDB on all three servers, you're now ready to move on to the configuration.

Configuring the first node

In this section, we will guide you through setting up the configuration for your initial Galera cluster node. Every node within the cluster should possess a closely matching configuration. As a result, all configuration adjustments will be applied to the first machine and subsequently copied to the other nodes.

The */etc/mysql/conf.d* directory contains files that end in *.cnf*, and MariaDB by default looks for further configuration instructions within these files. Let's create an entirely new file in this directory that has all the cluster-specific commands to get started:

```
/etc/mysql/mariadb.conf.d/galera.cnf
```

Once you have created the file, copy and paste the following configuration into it. This configuration specifies cluster options, details about the current server and the other servers in the cluster, and replication-related settings. Be sure to replace the bolded IP addresses with the appropriate private IP addresses for your respective servers:

```
root@galeranode1:~# cat /etc/mysql/mariadb.conf.d/galera.cnf
[mysqld]
bind-address=0.0.0.0
default_storage_engine=InnoDB
binlog_format=row
innodb_autoinc_lock_mode=2

# Galera cluster configuration
wsrep_on=ON
wsrep_provider=/usr/lib/galera/libgalera_smm.so
wsrep_cluster_address="gcomm://172.31.25.186,172.31.21.17,172.31.17.75"
wsrep_cluster_name="mariadb-galera-cluster"
wsrep_sst_method=rsync

# Cluster node configuration
wsrep_node_address="172.31.25.186"
wsrep_node_name="galeranode1"
root@galeranode1:~#
```

Rsync, mysqldump, xtrabackup, xtrabackup-v2, and mariabackup are methods utilized as `wsrep_sst_method` options for conducting State Snapshot Transfer (SST) in databases. Each of these methods has its own advantages and considerations regarding performance, resource usage, and reliability. The choice of which method to use depends on factors such as the size of the database, the available resources, and the specific requirements of the deployment.

The `mysqld` section of the configuration file specifies the default settings for MySQL/MariaDB that the cluster will use. The following options must be set to ensure that Galera works correctly:

`binlog_format=ROW`

Specifies the binary logging format for transactions. Galera uses the row-based format to ensure that data is replicated correctly across all nodes in the cluster.

`default-storage-engine=innodb`

Specifies the default storage engine to use for new tables. InnoDB is the recommended engine for Galera, as it provides better concurrency control and row-level locking.

`innodb_autoinc_lock_mode=2`

Specifies the InnoDB auto-increment lock mode. A value of 2 allows multiple transactions to insert rows into a table with auto-increment columns without locking each other out.

The Galera Provider Configuration section configures the MariaDB components that provide a WriteSet replication API. This section includes the following options:

```
wsrep_on=ON
```
Enables the Galera replication provider.

```
wsrep_provider*=/usr/lib/galera/libgalera_smm.so
```
Specifies the location of the Galera provider library.

The Galera Cluster Configuration section of the file defines the cluster, identifying the cluster members by IP address or resolvable domain name and creating a name for the cluster to ensure that members join the correct group. This section includes the following options:

```
wsrep_cluster_name*="test_cluster"
```
Specifies the name of the cluster. All nodes in the cluster must have the same cluster name.

```
wsrep_cluster_address*="gcomm://
First_Node_IP,Second_Node_IP,Third_Node_IP"
```
Specifies the IP addresses of the nodes in the cluster. Replace the highlighted lines with the private IP addresses of the other nodes in the cluster.

```
wsrep_sst_method=rsync
```
Specifies the method used to synchronize the data between nodes. Rsync is a reliable and fast synchronization method, but may not be suitable for very large databases.

In the Galera Node Configuration section, you'll define two essential parameters: `wsrep_node_address`, which designates the IP address of the current node, and `wsrep_node_name`, which assigns a name to the node. After configuring these settings, save the file and exit the text editor to complete the setup.

```
wsrep_node_address*="This_Node_IP"
```
Specifies the IP address of the current node.

```
wsrep_node_name*="This_Node_Name"
```
Sets the name of the current node.

Once you have added all the necessary configurations, save the file and exit the text editor.

Configuring the remaining nodes

In this section, you'll configure the remaining nodes in the Galera Cluster with MariaDB on Ubuntu servers:

1. Open the configuration file on the second node:

   ```
   sudo nano /etc/mysql/conf.d/galera.cnf
   ```

2. Paste the configuration copied from the first node and update the Galera Node Configuration section with the IP address or resolvable domain name for the specific node you're setting up, as shown here:

```
# Galera Node Configuration
wsrep_node_address="This_Node_IP"
wsrep_node_name="This_Node_Name"
```

3. Save and exit the file.

4. Repeat these steps on the third node.

The output will indicate that only SSH traffic is allowed through. Since only SSH traffic is permitted, you need to add rules for MySQL and Galera traffic.

> Galera can make use of four ports: 3306 for MySQL client connections and SST that use the mysqldump method, 4567 for Galera Cluster replication traffic (multicast replication uses both UDP transport and TCP on this port), 4568 for IST, and 4444 for all other SST.

Starting the cluster

After completing the necessary configurations, it's time to start your Galera cluster with MariaDB on Ubuntu servers. In this section, we walk you through starting the cluster, bringing up each node, and verifying the cluster size.

Before bringing up the cluster, you need to stop the running MariaDB service on all three servers to avoid conflicts during startup. You can use the following command on each server to stop MariaDB:

```
root@galeranode1:~# sudo systemctl stop mysql
root@galeranode1:~#
```

To confirm that the MariaDB service has been stopped, run the following command:

```
root@galeranode1:~# sudo systemctl status mysql
mariadb.service - MariaDB 11.3.2 database server
    Loaded: loaded (/lib/systemd/system/mariadb.service; enabled;
    vendor preset: enabled)
    Drop-In: /etc/systemd/system/mariadb.service.d
            └─migrated-from-my.cnf-settings.conf
    Active: inactive (dead) since Mon 2024-02-19 12:41:46 UTC; 32s ago

Feb 19 12:41:46 galeranode1 systemd[1]: mariadb.service: Deactivated
successfully.
Feb 19 12:41:46 galeranode1 systemd[1]: Stopped MariaDB 11.3.2 database server.
root@galeranode1:~#
```

If the last line of the output shows that the service is inactive and stopped, you have successfully stopped the MariaDB service on that server.

To bring up the first node in the cluster, you need to use a special startup script called *galera_new_cluster*. This script allows systemd to pass the `--wsrep-new-cluster` parameter, which is required for the first node to connect with other nodes in the cluster. Executing this command will initiate the first node without displaying any output upon successful completion:

```
root@galeranode1:~# galera_new_cluster
root@galeranode1:~#
```

Running the following command verifies that the cluster first node has been successfully bootstrapped; the cluster size is 1:

```
root@galeranode1:~# mariadb -u root -p -e "SHOW STATUS LIKE
'wsrep_cluster_size'"
Enter password:
+--------------------+-------+
| Variable_name      | Value |
+--------------------+-------+
| wsrep_cluster_size | 1     |
+--------------------+-------+
root@galeranode1:~#
```

With the first node up and running, you can now bring up the second node in the cluster. You can start MariaDB on the second server as follows:

```
root@galeranode2:~# sudo systemctl start mysql
root@galeranode2:~#
```

Then verify that the second node has joined the cluster:

```
mysql -u root -p -e "SHOW STATUS LIKE 'wsrep_cluster_size'"
```

You should see the following output indicating that the second node has joined the cluster and that there are now two nodes in total:

```
root@galeranode2:~# mariadb -u root -p -e "SHOW STATUS LIKE
'wsrep_cluster_size'"
Enter password:
+--------------------+-------+
| Variable_name      | Value |
+--------------------+-------+
| wsrep_cluster_size | 2     |
+--------------------+-------+
root@galeranode2:~#
```

Now it's time to bring up the third and final node in the cluster. You can start MariaDB on the third server:

```
root@galeranode3:~# sudo systemctl start mysql
root@galeranode3:~#
```

To verify that the third node has joined the cluster, run this command:

```
mysql -u root -p -e "SHOW STATUS LIKE 'wsrep_cluster_size'"
```

You should see the following output indicating that the third node has joined the cluster and that the total number of nodes in the cluster is now three:

```
root@galeranode3:~# mariadb -u root -p -e "SHOW STATUS LIKE
'wsrep_cluster_size'"
Enter password:
+---------------------+-------+
| Variable_name       | Value |
+---------------------+-------+
| wsrep_cluster_size  | 3     |
+---------------------+-------+
root@galeranode3:~#
```

Now, your entire Galera cluster with MariaDB on Ubuntu servers is online and communicating successfully; you can test replication to ensure that the cluster is working properly. To test the Galera replication process, make changes to the database on the first node and see whether they're changes reflected in the other nodes.

Install and Deploy MySQL 8 InnoDB Cluster with Three Nodes

InnoDB Cluster is a HA solution provided by MySQL, the popular open source relational database management system. It allows users to create a fault-tolerant cluster of MySQL instances with built-in replication and automatic failover capabilities. By following the steps in this section, you can ensure that your database is highly available and can handle any failures without any downtime (Figure 7-3).

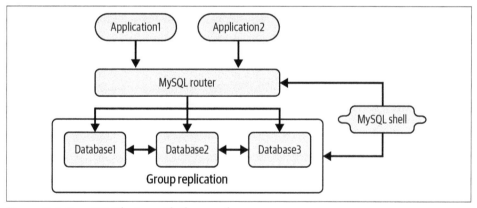

Figure 7-3. InnoDB Cluster with three nodes

Follow these steps to install the mysql community server in the first node using the *mysql80-community-release-el9* repo:

1. Open a terminal and run the following command to download the RPM repository file from the MySQL website:

```
[root@INNODBNode1 ~]# wget https://repo.mysql.com/
mysql80-community-release-el9-3.noarch.rpm
--2024-02-19 15:20:52--  https://repo.mysql.com/
mysql80-community-release-el9-3.noarch.rpm
Resolving repo.mysql.com (repo.mysql.com)... 2.19.137.210,
2600:1409:9800:f8c::1d68, 2600:1409:9800:f91::1d68
Connecting to repo.mysql.com (repo.mysql.com)|2.19.137.210|:443... connected.
HTTP request sent, awaiting response... 200 OK
Length: 10715 (10K) [application/x-redhat-package-manager]
Saving to: 'mysql80-community-release-el9-3.noarch.rpm'

mysql80-community-release-el9 100%
[=================================================>]  10.46K  --.-KB/s    in 0s
2024-02-19 15:20:52 (218 MB/s) - 'mysql80-community-release-el9-3.noarch.rpm'
saved [10715/10715]
[root@INNODBNode1 ~]#
```

2. Once the download is complete, install the RPM repository file with the following command:

```
[root@INNODBNode1 ~]# dnf install -y
./mysql80-community-release-el9-3.noarch.rpm
Updating Subscription Management repositories.
Unable to read consumer identity
This system is not registered with an entitlement server.
You can use subscription-manager to register.
Last metadata expiration check: 0:07:57 ago on Mon 19 Feb 2024
03:14:11 PM UTC.
Install  1 Package
Total size: 10 k
Installed size: 7.8 k
Downloading Packages:
Running transaction check
Transaction check succeeded.
Running transaction test
Transaction test succeeded.
Running transaction
  Preparing        :
  1/1
  Installing       : mysql80-community-release-el9-3.noarch
  1/1
  Verifying        : mysql80-community-release-el9-3.noarch
  1/1
Installed products updated.
Installed:
  mysql80-community-release-el9-3.noarch
Complete!
[root@INNODBNode1 ~]#
```

3. To use the official MySQL repository, disable the mysql module:

```
[root@INNODBNode1 ~]# dnf module disable mysql
Updating Subscription Management repositories.
Unable to read consumer identity
```

```
This system is not registered with an entitlement server.
You can use subscription-manager to register.
MySQL 8.0 Community Server
8.7 MB/s | 1.4 MB     00:00
MySQL Connectors Community
888 kB/s |  45 kB     00:00
MySQL Tools Community
6.0 MB/s | 536 kB     00:00
Unable to resolve argument mysql
Error: Problems in request:
missing groups or modules: mysql
[root@INNODBNode1 ~]#

[root@INNODBNode1 ~]# sudo rpm --import https://repo.mysql.com/
RPM-GPG-KEY-mysql-2023
[root@INNODBNode1 ~]#
```

4. Run the following command to install the MySQL 8 server:

```
[root@INNODBNode1 ~]# dnf install -y mysql-community-server
Updating Subscription Management repositories.
Unable to read consumer identity
This system is not registered with an entitlement server.
You can use subscription-manager to register.
Last metadata expiration check: 0:00:46 ago on Mon 19 Feb 2024
03:22:56 PM UTC.
Dependencies resolved.
```

Package	Arch	Version	Repository Size
Installing:			
mysql-community-server mysql80-community	x86_64 49 M	8.0.36-1.el9	
Installing dependencies:			
libaio rhel-9-baseos-rhui-rpms	x86_64 26 k	0.3.111-13.el9	
libtirpc rhel-9-baseos-rhui-rpms	x86_64 96 k	1.3.3-2.el9	
mysql-community-client mysql80-community	x86_64 3.4 M	8.0.36-1.el9	
mysql-community-client-plugins mysql80-community	x86_64 1.4 M	8.0.36-1.el9	
mysql-community-common mysql80-community	x86_64 556 k	8.0.36-1.el9	
mysql-community-icu-data-files mysql80-community	x86_64 2.3 M	8.0.36-1.el9	
mysql-community-libs mysql80-community	x86_64 1.4 M	8.0.36-1.el9	
perl-Exporter rhel-9-appstream-rhui-rpms	noarch 34 k	5.74-461.el9	
perl-interpreter-4:5.32.1-480.el9.x86_64			
perl-libnet-3.13-4.el9.noarch			

```
perl-libs-4:5.32.1-480.el9.x86_64
perl-mro-1.23-480.el9.x86_64
perl-overload-1.31-480.el9.noarch
perl-overloading-0.02-480.el9.noarch
perl-parent-1:0.238-460.el9.noarch
perl-podlators-1:4.14-460.el9.noarch
perl-subs-1.03-480.el9.noarch
perl-vars-1.05-480.el9.noarch
Complete!
[root@INNODBNode1 ~]#
```

5. Once the installation is complete, start the MySQL server with the following command:

```
[root@INNODBNode1 ~]# systemctl start mysqld
[root@INNODBNode1 ~]#
```

6. Enable the MySQL server to start automatically on boot:

```
[root@INNODBNode1 ~]# systemctl enable mysqld
[root@INNODBNode1 ~]#
```

7. Verify the status of the MySQL server:

```
[root@INNODBNode1 ~]# systemctl status mysqld
mysqld.service - MySQL Server
     Loaded: loaded (/usr/lib/systemd/system/mysqld.service; enabled;
     preset: disabled)
     Active: active (running) since Mon 2024-02-19 15:27:22 UTC; 4min 29s ago
       Docs: man:mysqld(8)
             http://dev.mysql.com/doc/refman/en/using-systemd.html
   Main PID: 16037 (mysqld)
     Status: "Server is operational"
      Tasks: 37 (limit: 22829)
     Memory: 481.0M
        CPU: 6.644s
     CGroup: /system.slice/mysqld.service
             └─16037 /usr/sbin/mysqld

Feb 19 15:27:12 INNODBNode1 systemd[1]: Starting MySQL Server...
Feb 19 15:27:22 INNODBNode1 systemd[1]: Started MySQL Server.
[root@INNODBNode1 ~]#
```

The output of the command will show the status of the MySQL server, including whether it is running.

Basic configurations for InnoDB Cluster

The process of setting up MySQL 8 InnoDB Cluster involves several steps, including installing MySQL Shell, configuring the system's hosts file, and adjusting SELinux settings. MySQL Shell 8 is a versatile command-line client that facilitates interaction with the cluster, supporting SQL and Python scripting. Begin by ensuring you have MySQL Shell installed:

---

1. Install MySQL Shell to create and manage the MySQL 8 InnoDB Cluster:

```
[root@INNODBNode1 ~]# dnf install -y mysql-shell
Updating Subscription Management repositories.
Unable to read consumer identity
This system is not registered with an entitlement server.
You can use subscription-manager to register.
Last metadata expiration check: 0:10:24 ago on Mon 19 Feb 2024
03:22:56 PM UTC.
Dependencies resolved.
Total download size: 24 M
Installed size: 214 M
Downloading Packages:
mysql-shell-8.0.36-1.el9.x86_64.rpm              46 MB/s |  24 MB    00:00
--------------------
Total                                            46 MB/s |  24 MB    00:00
Running transaction check
Transaction check succeeded.
Running transaction test
Transaction test succeeded.
Figure 7-162. Edit hosts file
[root@INNODBNode1 ~]#
```

2. While not obligatory, it is advisable to include the domains and IPs in the */etc/hosts* file. This practice facilitates quicker local resolution of domain names within the system. To append the domains and IPs to the */etc/hosts* file, open the hosts file using vi:

```
[root@INNODBNode1 ~]# sudo vi /etc/hosts
[root@INNODBNode1 ~]#
```

3. Add the following lines to the file, replacing the IPs and domains with your own, then save the file, press Esc, type :w, and hit Enter:

```
172.31.18.95 INNODBNode1
172.31.31.63 INNODBNode2
172.31.25.69 INNODBNode3
```

4. After adding the IP and node details, verify the *hosts* file:

```
[root@INNODBNode1 ~]# cat /etc/hosts
127.0.0.1 localhost localhost.localdomain localhost4 localhost4.localdomain4
::1 localhost localhost.localdomain localhost6 localhost6.localdomain6
172.31.18.95 INNODBNode1
172.31.31.63 INNODBNode2
172.31.25.69 INNODBNode3
[root@INNODBNode1 ~]#
```

SELinux configuration

SELinux offers three modes: enforcing, permissive, and disabled. The default mode is enforcing. In permissive mode, actions that aren't allowed in enforcing mode are permitted, and these actions are recorded in the SELinux audit log. Permissive mode is commonly employed for policy development or diagnostics. Conversely, disabled mode doesn't enforce policies or apply contexts to system objects, making it challenging to enable SELinux at a later time. In our scenario, we're configuring SELinux to function in permissive mode. Here are the steps:

1. Check the SELinux status:

    ```
    [root@INNODBNode1 ~]# getenforce
    Enforcing
    [root@INNODBNode1 ~]#
    ```

2. If SELinux is currently in enforcing mode, switch it to permissive mode:

    ```
    [root@INNODBNode1 ~]# setenforce 0
    [root@INNODBNode1 ~]#
    ```

3. To edit the SELinux configuration file, open the file using vi, update the *SELI-NUX=permissive*, and save the file:

    ```
    [root@INNODBNode1 ~]# sudo vi /etc/selinux/config
    ```

4. Verify the SELinux configuration:

    ```
    [root@INNODBNode1 ~]# cat  /etc/selinux/config | grep SELINUX
    # SELINUX= can take one of these three values:
    # NOTE: Up to RHEL 8 release included, SELINUX=disabled would also
    SELINUX=permissive
    # SELINUXTYPE= can take one of these three values:
    SELINUXTYPE=targeted
    [root@INNODBNode1 ~]#
    ```

Set up MySQL access for a Linux user

Modify the MySQL client configuration file in the root user's home directory, *my.cnf*, to automatically supply the MySQL root password when entering the MySQL console by adding the following configuration to the client section:

```
[root@INNODBNode1 ~]# cat .my.cnf
[client]
user=root
password="D@#NJU#$@MK28#nM"
[root@INNODBNode1 ~]#
```

Configure MySQL 8 InnoDB Cluster and create an admin account

Before establishing the MySQL 8 InnoDB Cluster, it's crucial to verify that the existing MySQL configuration aligns with the cluster arrangement. To engage with MySQL InnoDB Cluster features, users make use of the dba object via the mysqlsh interface.

1. To check the MySQL readiness for the MySQL 8 InnoDB Cluster, enter the MySQL Shell and execute the following command:

```
[root@INNODBNode1 ~]# mysqlsh

MySQL Shell 8.0.36
Copyright (c) 2016, 2023, Oracle and/or its affiliates.
Oracle is a registered trademark of Oracle Corporation and/or its affiliates.
Other names may be trademarks of their respective owners.
Type '\help' or '\?' for help; '\quit' to exit.
Creating a Classic session to 'root@localhost'
Fetching schema names for auto-completion... Press ^C to stop.
Your MySQL connection id is 25
Server version: 8.0.36 MySQL Community Server - GPL
No default schema selected; type \use <schema> to set one.
 MySQL  localhost  JS >

 MySQL  localhost  JS > dba.checkInstanceConfiguration("root@localhost")

Please provide the password for 'root@localhost': ****************
Save password for 'root@localhost'? [Y]es/[N]o/Ne[v]er (default No): No
Validating local MySQL instance listening at port 3306 for use in an InnoDB
cluster...

 MySQL  localhost  JS >
```

2. Create a cluster administrative account capable of network connections. To establish this account, employ the local root administrative account and execute the following command:

```
 MySQL  localhost  JS > dba.configureInstance("root@localhost")

Please provide the password for 'root@localhost': ****************
Save password for 'root@localhost'? [Y]es/[N]o/Ne[v]er (default No): N
Configuring local MySQL instance listening at port 3306 for use in an InnoDB
cluster...
This instance reports its own address as INNODBNode1:3306
1) Create remotely usable account for 'root' with same grants and password
2) Create a new admin account for InnoDB cluster with minimal required grants
3) Ignore and continue
4) Cancel
Please select an option [1]: 2
Please provide an account name (e.g: icroot@%) to have it created with the
necessary privileges or leave empty and press Enter to cancel.
Account Name: adminuser@%
Password for new account: ************
Confirm password: ************
applierWorkerThreads will be set to the default value of 4.

NOTE: Some configuration options need to be fixed:
+-------------------------------------------+---------------+----------------
+-------------------------------------------------+
| Variable                                  | Current Value | Required Value |
Note                                        |
+-------------------------------------------+---------------+----------------
+-------------------------------------------------+
```

```
| binlog_transaction_dependency_tracking | COMMIT_ORDER  | WRITESET      |
Update the server variable               |
| enforce_gtid_consistency               | OFF           | ON            |
Update read-only variable and restart the server |
| gtid_mode                              | OFF           | ON            |
Update read-only variable and restart the server |
| server_id                              | 1             | <unique ID>   |
Update read-only variable and restart the server |
+----------------------------------------+---------------+----------------
+------------------------------------------------+
```

```
Some variables need to be changed, but cannot be done dynamically
on the server.
Do you want to perform the required configuration changes? [y/n]: y
Do you want to restart the instance after configuring it? [y/n]: y

Creating user adminuser@%.
Account adminuser@% was successfully created.

Configuring instance...

WARNING: '@@binlog_transaction_dependency_tracking' is deprecated and
will be removed in a future release. (Code 1287).
The instance 'INNODBNode1:3306' was configured to be used in an
InnoDB cluster.
Restarting MySQL...
NOTE: MySQL server at INNODBNode1:3306 was restarted.
 MySQL  localhost  JS >
```

The preceding command creates an admin account, specifically an administrative cluster account, for InnoDB cluster. This account is provided with essential permissions and verifies that the MySQL configuration aligns with MySQL Cluster InnoDB standards. Should any noncompliant configurations be identified, the command rectifies them and initiates a restart of the MySQL server.

Once the cluster administrative account has been created, it becomes simple to verify whether the issues previously mentioned have been resolved by the dba.configure Instance. This can be achieved by using the recently created admin user:

```
MySQL  localhost  JS > dba.checkInstanceConfiguration("adminuser@INNODBNode1")

Please provide the password for 'adminuser@INNODBNode1': ************
Instance configuration is compatible with InnoDB cluster
The instance 'INNODBNode1:3306' is valid to be used in an InnoDB cluster.

{
    "status": "ok"
}
 MySQL  localhost  JS >
```

The server is now prepared to form the MySQL InnoDB Cluster. It's advisable to retain the password for *clusteradmin@INNODBNode1* for future reference when using mysqlsh.

Create the MySQL cluster

Creating a MySQL cluster is a straightforward process that creates a group replication with the initial server acting as the primary within the group. To initiate the cluster creation, begin by connecting to MySQL by using the cluster administrator account; follow these steps:

1. Execute a creation command with the designated logical name of the cluster. Connect to the database node named INNODBNode1 using the username adminuser:

   ```
   MySQL  localhost  JS > \connect adminuser@INNODBNode1

   Creating a session to 'adminuser@INNODBNode1'
   Please provide the password for 'adminuser@INNODBNode1': ************
   Save password for 'adminuser@INNODBNode1'? [Y]es/[N]o/Ne[v]er (default No): N
   Fetching schema names for auto-completion... Press ^C to stop.
   Closing old connection...
   Your MySQL connection id is 10 (X protocol)
   Server version: 8.0.36 MySQL Community Server - GPL
   No default schema selected; type \use <schema> to set one.
    MySQL  INNODBNode1:33060+ ssl  JS >
   ```

2. Create a cluster named myinnocluster in a database environment:

   ```
   MySQL  INNODBNode1:33060+ ssl  JS > dba.createCluster("myinnodbcluster")

   A new InnoDB Cluster will be created on instance 'INNODBNode1:3306'.
   Validating instance configuration at INNODBNode1:3306...
   This instance reports its own address as INNODBNode1:3306
   Instance configuration is suitable.
   NOTE: Group Replication will communicate with other members using
     'INNODBNode1:3306'. Use the localAddress option to override.
   * Checking connectivity and SSL configuration...
   Creating InnoDB Cluster 'myinnodbcluster' on 'INNODBNode1:3306'...
   Adding Seed Instance...
   Cluster successfully created. Use Cluster.addInstance() to add MySQL
   instances. At least 3 instances are needed for the cluster to be
   able to withstand up to one server failure.

   <Cluster:myinnodbcluster>
    MySQL  INNODBNode1:33060+ ssl  JS >
   ```

3. After creating the cluster, use this command to obtain its status:

   ```
   MySQL  INNODBNode1:33060+ ssl  JS > var cluster = dba.getCluster()
   MySQL  INNODBNode1:33060+ ssl  JS >
   ```

4. Then, verify the current status and information about a cluster in a database environment:

```
MySQL  INNODBNode1:33060+ ssl  JS > cluster.status()

{
    "clusterName": "myinnodbcluster",
    "defaultReplicaSet": {
        "name": "default",
        "primary": "INNODBNode1:3306",
        "ssl": "REQUIRED",
        "status": "OK_NO_TOLERANCE",
        "statusText": "Cluster is NOT tolerant to any failures.",
        "topology": {
            "INNODBNode1:3306": {
                "address": "INNODBNode1:3306",
                "memberRole": "PRIMARY",
                "mode": "R/W",
                "readReplicas": {},
                "replicationLag": "applier_queue_applied",
                "role": "HA",
                "status": "ONLINE",
                "version": "8.0.36"
            }
        },
        "topologyMode": "Single-Primary"
    },
    "groupInformationSourceMember": "INNODBNode1:3306"
}
MySQL  INNODBNode1:33060+ ssl  JS >
```

Install and configure the remaining two cluster nodes

In the preceding stages, we effectively installed and set up a primary MySQL node for the InnoDB cluster. To add two more nodes to the cluster, follow the steps for installing MySQL (specifically the same MySQL Community version installed on the first node) onto the two additional nodes. After installing MySQL, along with MySQL Shell, you can proceed to include the two nodes in the InnoDB cluster using the MySQL Shell. Here are the steps:

1. Download MySQL 8 Community Release RPM with wget:

```
[root@INNODBNode2 ~]# wget https://repo.mysql.com/
mysql80-community-release-el9-3.noarch.rpm

--2024-02-19 16:28:00--  https://repo.mysql.com/
mysql80-community-release-el9-3.noarch.rpm
Resolving repo.mysql.com (repo.mysql.com)... 2.19.137.210,
2600:1409:9800:f91::1d68, 2600:1409:9800:f8c::1d68
mysql80-community-release-el9 100%[==============>]  10.46K  --.-KB/s  in 0s
```

```
2024-02-19 16:28:00 (206 MB/s) - 'mysql80-community-release-el9-3.noarch.rpm'
saved [10715/10715]
[root@INNODBNode2 ~]#
```

2. Install MySQL 8 Community Release:

```
[root@INNODBNode2 ~]# dnf install -y
./mysql80-community-release-el9-3.noarch.rpm

Updating Subscription Management repositories.
Total size: 10 k
Transaction test succeeded.
Running transaction
  Preparing        :                                          1/1
  Installing       : mysql80-community-release-el9-3.noarch   1/1
  Verifying        : mysql80-community-release-el9-3.noarch   1/1
Installed products updated.

Installed:
  mysql80-community-release-el9-3.noarch
Complete!
[root@INNODBNode2 ~]#
```

3. Disable the MySQL module with DNF:

```
[root@INNODBNode2 ~]# dnf module disable mysql

Updating Subscription Management repositories.
MySQL 8.0 Community Server        12 MB/s | 1.4 MB     00:00
MySQL Connectors Community        969 kB/s |  45 kB     00:00
MySQL Tools Community             2.8 MB/s | 536 kB     00:00
Unable to resolve argument mysql
Error: Problems in request:
missing groups or modules: mysql
[root@INNODBNode2 ~]#

[root@INNODBNode2 ~]# sudo rpm --import https://repo.mysql.com/
RPM-GPG-KEY-mysql-2023
[root@INNODBNode2 ~]#
```

4. Install MySQL Community Server with DNF:

```
[root@INNODBNode2 ~]# dnf install -y mysql-community-server

Updating Subscription Management repositories.
Installing:
 mysql-community-server      x86_64      8.0.36-1.el9
mysql80-community            49 M
Installing dependencies:
 libaio                      x86_64      0.3.111-13.el9
rhel-9-baseos-rhui-rpms      26 k
 libtirpc                    x86_64      1.3.3-2.el9
rhel-9-baseos-rhui-rpms      96 k
 mysql-community-client      x86_64      8.0.36-1.el9
mysql80-community            3.4 M
```

```
  mysql-community-client-plugins  x86_64      8.0.36-1.el9
mysql80-community               1.4 M
 mysql-community-common          x86_64      8.0.36-1.el9
mysql80-community               556 k
 mysql-community-icu-data-files  x86_64      8.0.36-1.el9
mysql80-community               2.3 M
 mysql-community-libs            x86_64      8.0.36-1.el9
mysql80-community               1.4 M
 net-tools                       x86_64      2.0-0.62.20160912git.el9
rhel-9-baseos-rhui-rpms         309 k
Complete!
[root@INNODBNode2 ~]#
```

5. Start MySQL Service with `systemctl`:

```
[root@INNODBNode2 ~]# systemctl start mysqld
[root@INNODBNode2 ~]#
```

Install MySQL Shell

MySQL Shell is an advanced command-line tool provided by MySQL for DBAs, developers, and database users. It offers a comprehensive set of features and capabilities for working with MySQL and compatible database systems.

You must also install the MySQL Shell on both nodes by using this command:

```
[root@INNODBNode2 ~]# dnf install -y mysql-shell
Updating Subscription Management repositories.
Installing:
 mysql-shell   x86_64    8.0.36-1.el9    mysql-tools-community    24 M\
Transaction Summary
mysql-shell-8.0.36-1.el9.x86_64.rpm
39 MB/s |  24 MB    00:00
--------------------------------------------------------------------
Total
39 MB/s |  24 MB    00:00
Running transaction check
Transaction check succeeded.
Running transaction test
Transaction test succeeded.                           1/1
Installed products updated.
Installed:
  mysql-shell-8.0.36-1.el9.x86_64
Complete!
[root@INNODBNode2 ~]#
```

Set up the hosts file

Subsequently, it's essential to configure the hosts file on both nodes by adding the IP addresses and hostnames of all cluster nodes. This can be accomplished by appending these lines to the */etc/hosts* file:

```
[root@INNODBNode2 ~]# cat /etc/hosts
127.0.0.1    localhost localhost.localdomain localhost4 localhost4.localdomain4
::1          localhost localhost.localdomain localhost6 localhost6.localdomain6
172.31.18.95 INNODBNode1
172.31.31.63 INNODBNode2
172.31.25.69 INNODBNode3
[root@INNODBNode2 ~]#
```

Optimize the MySQL configuration

You must fine-tune the MySQL configuration on both nodes. This involves editing the */etc/my.cnf* file and introducing generic variables to enhance the performance of the MySQL server.

Establish the root password

You are required to define the root password for the MySQL server on both nodes, using the same procedure employed for the initial node:

1. Search for password entries in the MySQL log:

   ```
   [root@INNODBNode2 ~]# cat /var/log/mysqld.log | grep password
   2024-02-19T16:35:59.641449Z 6 [Note] [MY-010454] [Server] A temporary
   password is generated for root@localhost: qtOiDo1aBD-j
   [root@INNODBNode2 ~]#
   ```

2. Log into MySQL as the root user:

   ```
   [root@INNODBNode2 ~]# mysql -uroot -p
   Enter password:
   Server version: 8.0.36
   mysql>
   ```

3. Set a new password:

   ```
   mysql>  SET PASSWORD = 'D@#NJU#$@MK28#nM';
   Query OK, 0 rows affected (0.01 sec)
   mysql>
   ```

Furthermore, you must append the recently set root password to the */root/.my.cnf* file on both nodes.

Configure the MySQL instance

Ultimately, configuring the MySQL instance on both nodes requires using the MySQL Shell.

1. Log in to MySQL Shell:

   ```
   [root@INNODBNode2 ~]# mysqlsh
   MySQL Shell 8.0.36

   Copyright (c) 2016, 2023, Oracle and/or its affiliates.
   ```

```
Oracle is a registered trademark of Oracle Corporation and/or its affiliates.
Other names may be trademarks of their respective owners.

Type '\help' or '\?' for help; '\quit' to exit.
Creating a Classic session to 'root@localhost'
Fetching schema names for auto-completion... Press ^C to stop.
Your MySQL connection id is 11
Server version: 8.0.36 MySQL Community Server - GPL
No default schema selected; type \use <schema> to set one.
 MySQL  localhost  JS >
```

2. Connect to INNODBNode1 as an admin user:

```
[root@INNODBNode2 ~]# mysqlsh

MySQL Shell 8.0.36
Type '\help' or '\?' for help; '\quit' to exit.
Creating a Classic session to 'root@localhost'
Server version: 8.0.36 MySQL Community Server - GPL
No default schema selected; type \use <schema> to set one.
 MySQL  localhost  JS > \connect adminuser@INNODBNode1
Creating a session to 'adminuser@INNODBNode1'
Please provide the password for 'adminuser@INNODBNode1': ************
Save password for 'adminuser@INNODBNode1'? [Y]es/[N]o/Ne[v]er (default No): N
Fetching schema names for auto-completion... Press ^C to stop.
Closing old connection...
Your MySQL connection id is 37 (X protocol)
Server version: 8.0.36 MySQL Community Server - GPL
No default schema selected; type \use <schema> to set one.
 MySQL  INNODBNode1:33060+ ssl  JS >
```

Add the nodes to the cluster

After successfully installing and configuring the MySQL server on both nodes, proceed to include them in the InnoDB cluster by using the MySQL Shell:

1. Initialize the cluster variable with dba.getCluster():

```
MySQL  INNODBNode1:33060+ ssl  JS > var cluster = dba.getCluster()
MySQL  INNODBNode1:33060+ ssl  JS >
```

2. Check the cluster status:

```
MySQL  INNODBNode1:33060+ ssl  JS > cluster.status()

{
    "clusterName": "myinnodbcluster",
    "defaultReplicaSet": {
        "name": "default",
        "primary": "INNODBNode1:3306",
        "ssl": "REQUIRED",
        "status": "OK_NO_TOLERANCE",
        "statusText": "Cluster is NOT tolerant to any failures.",
        "topology": {
```

```
            "INNODBNode1:3306": {
                "address": "INNODBNode1:3306",
                "memberRole": "PRIMARY",
                "mode": "R/W",
                "readReplicas": {},
                "replicationLag": "applier_queue_applied",
                "role": "HA",
                "status": "ONLINE",
                "version": "8.0.36"
            }
        },
        "topologyMode": "Single-Primary"
    },
    "groupInformationSourceMember": "INNODBNode1:3306"
}
 MySQL  INNODBNode1:33060+ ssl  JS >
```

3. Configure an instance with dba.configureInstance():

```
MySQL  INNODBNode1:33060+ ssl  JS > dba.configureInstance("root@localhost")

Please provide the password for 'root@localhost': ****************
Save password for 'root@localhost'? [Y]es/[N]o/Ne[v]er (default No): N
Configuring local MySQL instance listening at port 3306 for use in an InnoDB
cluster...

This instance reports its own address as INNODBNode2:3306

Account Name: adminuser@%
Password for new account: ************
Confirm password: ************

applierWorkerThreads will be set to the default value of 4.

NOTE: Some configuration options need to be fixed:
+-----------------------------------------+---------------+----------------
+------------------------------------------------+
| Variable                                | Current Value | Required Value |
Note                                      |
+-----------------------------------------+---------------+----------------
+------------------------------------------------+
| binlog_transaction_dependency_tracking | COMMIT_ORDER  | WRITESET       |
Update the server variable                |
| enforce_gtid_consistency                | OFF           | ON             |
Update read-only variable and restart the server |
| gtid_mode                               | OFF           | ON             |
Update read-only variable and restart the server |
| server_id                               | 1             | <unique ID>    |
Update read-only variable and restart the server |
+-----------------------------------------+---------------+----------------
+------------------------------------------------+

Some variables need to be changed, but cannot be done dynamically
```

```
on the server.
Do you want to perform the required configuration changes? [y/n]: y
Do you want to restart the instance after configuring it? [y/n]: y

Creating user adminuser@%.
Account adminuser@% was successfully created.

Configuring instance...

WARNING: '@@binlog_transaction_dependency_tracking' is deprecated and will be
  removed in a future release. (Code 1287).
The instance 'INNODBNode2:3306' was configured to be used in an InnoDB cluster.
Restarting MySQL...
NOTE: MySQL server at INNODBNode2:3306 was restarted.
 MySQL  INNODBNode1:33060+ ssl  JS >
```

4. Add an instance to the cluster:

```
MySQL  INNODBNode1:33060+ ssl  JS > cluster.addInstance(
  'adminuser@INNODBNode2:3306')

NOTE: The target instance 'INNODBNode2:3306' has not been pre-provisioned
(GTID set is empty). The Shell is unable to decide whether incremental
state recovery can correctly provision it.
NOTE: INNODBNode2:3306 is being cloned from innodbnode1:3306
** Stage DROP DATA: Completed
** Clone Transfer
    FILE COPY  ##########################################################
    100%  Completed
    PAGE COPY  ##########################################################
    100%  Completed
    REDO COPY  ##########################################################
    100%  Completed
NOTE: INNODBNode2:3306 is shutting down...

* Clone process has finished: 75.39 MB transferred in about 1 second
(~75.39 MB/s)

State recovery already finished for 'INNODBNode2:3306'

The instance 'INNODBNode2:3306' was successfully added to the cluster.

 MySQL  INNODBNode1:33060+ ssl  JS >
```

5. Check the cluster status:

```
MySQL  INNODBNode1:33060+ ssl  JS > cluster.status()

{
    "clusterName": "myinnodbcluster",
    "defaultReplicaSet": {
        "name": "default",
        "primary": "INNODBNode1:3306",
        "ssl": "REQUIRED",
```

```
            "status": "OK_NO_TOLERANCE",
            "statusText": "Cluster is NOT tolerant to any failures.",
            "topology": {
                "INNODBNode1:3306": {
                    "address": "INNODBNode1:3306",
                    "memberRole": "PRIMARY",
                    "mode": "R/W",
                    "readReplicas": {},
                    "replicationLag": "applier_queue_applied",
                    "role": "HA",
                    "status": "ONLINE",
                    "version": "8.0.36"
                },
                "INNODBNode2:3306": {
                    "address": "INNODBNode2:3306",
                    "memberRole": "SECONDARY",
                    "mode": "R/O",
                    "readReplicas": {},
                    "replicationLag": "applier_queue_applied",
                    "role": "HA",
                    "status": "ONLINE",
                    "version": "8.0.36"
                }
            },
            "topologyMode": "Single-Primary"
        },
        "groupInformationSourceMember": "INNODBNode1:3306"
    }
     MySQL  INNODBNode1:33060+ ssl  JS >
```

6. Add another instance to the cluster:

```
MySQL  INNODBNode1:33060+ ssl  JS > cluster.addInstance
('adminuser@INNODBNode3:3306')

This instance reports its own address as INNODBNode3:3306
Instance configuration is suitable.
NOTE: Group Replication will communicate with other members using
'INNODBNode3:3306'. Use the localAddress option to override.
* Checking connectivity and SSL configuration...
A new instance will be added to the InnoDB Cluster. Depending on the amount
of data on the cluster this might take from a few seconds to several hours.
MySQL  INNODBNode1:33060+ ssl  JS >
```

7. Set the root password with the root password you've assigned to all nodes. Initiating this will begin the process of including the two nodes within the cluster. The duration of this procedure may vary based on your data set's size. To oversee the progress of the operation, execute this command:

```
MySQL  INNODBNode1:33060+ ssl  JS > cluster.status()
{
    "clusterName": "myinnodbcluster",
    "defaultReplicaSet": {
```

```
        "name": "default",
        "primary": "INNODBNode1:3306",
        "ssl": "REQUIRED",
        "status": "OK",
        "statusText": "Cluster is ONLINE and can tolerate up to ONE
        failure.",
        "topology": {
            "INNODBNode1:3306": {
                "address": "INNODBNode1:3306",
                "memberRole": "PRIMARY",
                "mode": "R/W",
                "readReplicas": {},
                "replicationLag": "applier_queue_applied",
                "role": "HA",
                "status": "ONLINE",
                "version": "8.0.36"
            },
            "INNODBNode2:3306": {
                "address": "INNODBNode2:3306",
                "memberRole": "SECONDARY",
                "mode": "R/O",
                "readReplicas": {},
                "replicationLag": "applier_queue_applied",
                "role": "HA",
                "status": "ONLINE",
                "version": "8.0.36"
            },
            "INNODBNode3:3306": {
                "address": "INNODBNode3:3306",
                "memberRole": "SECONDARY",
                "mode": "R/O",
                "readReplicas": {},
                "replicationLag": "applier_queue_applied",
                "role": "HA",
                "status": "ONLINE",
                "version": "8.0.36"
            }
        },
        "topologyMode": "Single-Primary"
    },
    "groupInformationSourceMember": "INNODBNode1:3306"
}
MySQL  INNODBNode1:33060+ ssl  JS >
```

After finishing the process, you'll see that the output of the command lists all three nodes.

Consider that when you're in the process of adding a node to the cluster, you have the option to choose between two recovery modes: the Clone and Incremental modes. The Clone mode is used when adding a completely new node to the cluster, while the

Incremental mode is employed when incorporating a node with data akin to the other nodes in the cluster.

As a general guideline, we advise using the Clone mode when introducing a new node, as it offers a more secure choice. Nevertheless, if you're adding a node with a substantial volume of data, you might want to consider using the Incremental mode instead.

Setting up and executing MySQL Router

MySQL Router serves as lightweight middleware offering enhanced availability and scalability for your MySQL database. The following steps outline the process of installing and running MySQL Router:

1. Proceed with the installation of MySQL Router by executing this command:

```
[root@INNODBNode1 ~]# dnf install -y mysql-router-community
Red Hat Enterprise Linux 9 for x86_64 - AppStream from RHUI (RPMs)
                    68 kB/s | 4.5 kB     00:00
Red Hat Enterprise Linux 9 for x86_64 - BaseOS from RHUI (RPMs)
                    65 kB/s | 4.1 kB     00:00
Red Hat Enterprise Linux 9 Client Configuration
                              27 kB/s | 1.5 kB     00:00
Dependencies resolved.
========================================================================
 Package                      Architecture      Version
              Repository                       Size
========================================================================
Installing:
 mysql-router-community          x86_64           8.0.36-1.el9
            mysql-tools-community           3.7 M

Transaction Summary
========================================================================
Install  1 Package
Total download size: 3.7 M
Installed size: 14 M
Downloading Packages:
mysql-router-community-8.0.36-1.el9.x86_64.rpm
                              4.8 MB/s | 3.7 MB      00:00
------------------------------------------------------------------------
Total                         4.8 MB/s | 3.7 MB      00:00
Running transaction check
Transaction check succeeded.
Running transaction test
Transaction test succeeded.
Running transaction
  Preparing        :
                    1/1
  Running scriptlet: mysql-router-community-8.0.36-1.el9.x86_64
                    1/1
```

```
Installing       : mysql-router-community-8.0.36-1.el9.x86_64
                   1/1
Running scriptlet: mysql-router-community-8.0.36-1.el9.x86_64
                   1/1
Verifying        : mysql-router-community-8.0.36-1.el9.x86_64
                   1/1
Installed products updated.
Installed:
  mysql-router-community-8.0.36-1.el9.x86_64
Complete!
[root@INNODBNode1 ~]#
```

2. Initiate the configuration bootstrap to establish the initial configuration and required user(s):

```
[root@INNODBNode1 ~]# mysqlrouter --bootstrap adminuser@localhost:3306 --user
mysqlrouter \
--conf-use-sockets --account adminrouter --account-create if-not-exists
Please enter MySQL password for adminuser:
# Bootstrapping system MySQL Router 8.0.36 (MySQL Community - GPL)
instance...
- Creating configuration /etc/mysqlrouter/mysqlrouter.conf
Existing configuration backed up to '/etc/mysqlrouter/mysqlrouter.conf.bak'
# MySQL Router configured for the InnoDB Cluster 'myinnodbcluster'
After this MySQL Router has been started with the generated configuration
    $ /etc/init.d/mysqlrouter restart
or
    $ systemctl start mysqlrouter
or
    $ mysqlrouter -c /etc/mysqlrouter/mysqlrouter.conf
InnoDB Cluster 'myinnodbcluster' can be reached by connecting to:
## MySQL Classic protocol
- Read/Write Connections: localhost:6446, /tmp/mysql.sock
- Read/Only Connections:  localhost:6447, /tmp/mysqlro.sock
## MySQL X protocol
- Read/Write Connections: localhost:6448, /tmp/mysqlx.sock
- Read/Only Connections:  localhost:6449, /tmp/mysqlxro.sock
[root@INNODBNode1 ~]#
```

This command will create the configuration in */etc/mysqlrouter/mysqlrouter.conf*, as well as new files such as keys and certificates necessary for SSL connections.

3. Start MySQL Router:

```
[root@INNODBNode1 ~]# systemctl start mysqlrouter
[root@INNODBNode1 ~]#
```

a. Check the status of the MySQL Router service:

```
[root@INNODBNode1 ~]# systemctl status mysqlrouter
mysqlrouter.service - MySQL Router
    Loaded: loaded (/usr/lib/systemd/system/mysqlrouter.service;
    disabled;
    preset: disabled)
```

```
       Active: active (running) since Mon 2024-02-19 17:16:41 UTC; 41s ago
     Main PID: 17477 (mysqlrouter)
       Status: "running"
        Tasks: 25 (limit: 22829)
       Memory: 14.9M
          CPU: 3.500s
       CGroup: /system.slice/mysqlrouter.service
               └─17477 /usr/bin/mysqlrouter

Feb 19 17:16:41 INNODBNode1 systemd[1]: Starting MySQL Router...
Feb 19 17:16:41 INNODBNode1 systemd[1]: Started MySQL Router.
[root@INNODBNode1 ~]#
```

b. Enable the automatic startup of the MySQL Router service during system boot by using the systemd init system:

```
[root@INNODBNode1 ~]# systemctl enable mysqlrouter
Created symlink /etc/systemd/system/multi-user.target.wants/
mysqlrouter.service
→ /usr/lib/systemd/system/mysqlrouter.service.
[root@INNODBNode1 ~]#
```

4. Unblock the ports for MySQL Router in the following steps:

a. Open a specific network port (6446 in this case) for TCP traffic in the firewall configuration:

```
firewall-cmd --permanent --zone=public --add-port=6446/tcp
```

b. Add a rule to the firewall on a Linux system, allowing incoming TCP traffic on port 6447:

```
firewall-cmd --permanent --zone=public --add-port=6447/tcp
```

c. Open TCP port 6448 for incoming traffic:

```
firewall-cmd --permanent --zone=public --add-port=6448/tcp
```

d. Open TCP port 6449 for incoming traffic:

```
firewall-cmd --permanent --zone=public --add-port=6449/tcp
```

e. Reload the firewall configuration to apply the recent changes made to the firewall settings without restarting the firewall service:

```
firewall-cmd --reload
```

Be aware that port 6446 is designated for both read/write operations, while port 6447 is exclusively intended for read operations of the traditional MySQL protocol. The remaining two ports are allocated for the MySQL X protocol. Upon implementing the provided firewall rules, all IPs will gain permission to connect to the designated ports. To restrict the IPs authorized to establish contact with the MySQL Router, use this command:

```
firewall-cmd --permanent --add-rich-rule="rule family="ipv4" source
address="192.168.10.0/24" port protocol="tcp" port="6446" accept"
```

This command permits only IPs falling within the range of 192.168.10.0/24 to establish a connection with port 6446. Execute this final step on each server.

Monitoring cluster status

To ensure that your cluster is functioning correctly, it's important to regularly monitor its status. Several tools can help you monitor your cluster's status, including PMM (open source) and MySQL Enterprise Monitoring (a commercial product).

You can use either tool to monitor your cluster's status by following these steps:

1. Install and configure the tool on your server.
2. Configure the tool to monitor your cluster by adding the appropriate data sources.
3. Use the tool to monitor your cluster's status by checking the status of the data sources.

Troubleshooting cluster issues

If you encounter issues with your cluster, troubleshoot them as quickly as possible. You can use tools like PMM and MySQL Enterprise Monitoring to help.

Both provide a range of features that can help troubleshoot your cluster, including real-time monitoring, query analytics, and trend analysis. You can use either to troubleshoot your cluster by following these steps:

1. Use the tool to identify the source of the issue by reviewing the metrics and logs.
2. Determine the appropriate corrective action to resolve the issue.

Conclusion

This chapter equips you with essential knowledge on HA and scalability in MySQL 8. By mastering clustering concepts and tools such as Orchestrator and sysbench, you can effectively manage MySQL environments for optimal performance and reliability.

## CHAPTER 8

MySQL Performance Tuning

MySQL *performance tuning* is the process of optimizing a MySQL database to improve its efficiency, throughput, and scalability. The main objective of MySQL performance tuning is to ensure that the database can handle increasing loads, respond quickly to user requests, and provide consistent and reliable results. Effective performance tuning can result in faster response times, reduced resource consumption, and improved overall system performance.

In today's data-driven world, managing database performance has become critical to the success of businesses. MySQL, one of the most widely used relational databases, requires careful tuning to ensure optimal performance. In this chapter, we explore the key concepts and techniques for MySQL performance tuning. We cover topics ranging from configuring memory usage to optimizing disk I/O.

Considering Hardware Resources

The performance of the underlying hardware, including CPU, memory, and disk I/O, can significantly impact the performance of a MySQL database. Proper hardware selection and configuration are critical for optimal database performance.

When reviewing MySQL performance and considering hardware resources, you should focus on several key areas. Here are some of the most important factors to review:

CPU

The CPU is one of the most critical resources for MySQL performance, especially for workloads that involve heavy processing or complex queries. Review the number of cores, clock speed, and cache size of the CPU to ensure that it can handle the expected workload.

RAM

MySQL uses a lot of memory to cache data and improve performance. Review the amount of RAM available and ensure that it is sufficient to handle the workload. In general, more RAM is better for MySQL performance.

Storage

MySQL performance is highly dependent on the storage system used. Review the type of storage—hard disk drive (HDD), solid-state drive (SSD), or nonvolatile memory express (NVMe). Also review the amount of available storage, and the performance characteristics (e.g., read/write speeds, IOPS) to ensure that they can handle the workload.

Network

If the MySQL server is accessed over a network, review the network performance characteristics (e.g., bandwidth, latency, and packet loss) to ensure that they are sufficient for the expected workload.

Operating system

Review the operating system configuration and ensure that it is optimized for MySQL performance. This includes settings such as filesystem tuning, kernel parameters, and network stack tuning.

Monitoring

Implement a monitoring solution to track the performance of the MySQL server and identify any bottlenecks or performance issues. This can include tools such as PMM, MySQL Enterprise Monitor, Nagios, or Zabbix.

By reviewing these hardware resources, you can identify any potential performance bottlenecks and optimize the MySQL server for optimal performance.

CPU Configuration

The CPU is the most critical component of your hardware, as it directly impacts the speed at which your database can process queries. To enhance your database's performance, opt for a CPU with multiple cores, which MySQL can utilize for faster parallel query execution, and a high clock speed to expedite single query processing.

When it comes to performance tuning for MySQL, several CPU-related variables can have a significant impact on the database's performance. Three key variables to consider are `innodb_buffer_pool_instances`, `innodb_flush_log_at_trx_commit`, and `max_connections`.

The `innodb_buffer_pool_instances` variable controls the number of buffer pool instances that are created for InnoDB. The default value is 8, but increasing this value can help distribute the load across multiple CPUs and improve performance. The optimal value for this variable depends on several factors, including the size of the buffer pool, the number of CPU cores, and the workload characteristics. In general, a good rule of thumb is to set `innodb_buffer_pool_instances` to the number of CPU cores on your system. This can help ensure that each CPU core has its own buffer pool instance to work with, which can improve performance by reducing contention for shared resources.

However, this is not a hard-and-fast rule, and you may need to adjust the value based on your specific workload and hardware configuration. For example, if you have a very large buffer pool, you may need to increase the number of instances to avoid contention for the buffer pool mutex. Conversely, if you have a small buffer pool and a low-concurrency workload, you may be able to get by with fewer instances. Ultimately, the best approach is to test different values of `innodb_buffer_pool_instan ces` under your specific workload and measure the performance impact to find the optimal value for your system.

The `innodb_flush_log_at_trx_commit` variable controls the timing of writing and flushing transaction logs or redo logs to disk in MySQL, impacting data durability. When set to the default value of 1, logs are written and flushed to disk at each transaction commit, ensuring full ACID compliance. With a setting of 0, logs are written and flushed to disk once per second, potentially risking data loss for uncommitted transactions in the event of a crash. A setting of 2 writes logs after each transaction commit and flushes them to disk once per second, presenting a similar risk of data loss for uncommitted transactions. Choosing the appropriate setting depends on your specific data integrity and performance requirements, as lower values (2 or 0) may offer better performance but with reduced durability.

The `max_connections` variable controls the maximum number of concurrent connections to the MySQL server. Increasing this value can improve performance by allowing more clients to connect simultaneously.

It's important to note that these variables are just a few of the many parameters that can impact MySQL performance. The optimal values for these variables will depend on the specific workload and hardware configuration of the database server. Carefully measure the impact of each variable change to ensure that the changes result in improved performance.

Memory Configuration

Memory is another critical component for MySQL performance. The more memory you have, the more data your database can cache, resulting in faster query processing. To optimize your memory configuration, ensure that you allocate enough memory for your MySQL database to avoid swapping to disk, which can significantly slow your queries.

Several MySQL variables are related to memory and can affect performance tuning. Some of the key variables include the following:

`innodb_buffer_pool_size`
Governing the size of the buffer pool utilized by InnoDB, this parameter influences the storage engine default in MySQL. Augmenting this variable can enhance read performance by enabling more data to be cached in memory.

`sort_buffer_size`
Responsible for managing the buffer size in sorting operations, this parameter's enlargement can optimize the performance of unindexed sorting.

`join_buffer_size`
Overseeing the buffer dimensions for join operations, this parameter's increase can refine the performance of queries involving the joining of substantial tables.

`tmp_table_size`
Temporary tables are managed differently in MySQL 8, specifically from version 8.0.28 onward. This parameter defines the maximum size of any individual in-memory internal temporary table created by the TempTable storage engine. Once the `tmp_table_size` limit is reached, MySQL automatically converts the in-memory internal temporary table to an InnoDB on-disk internal temporary table.

Global TempTable resources are governed by the `temptable_max_ram` and `temptable _max_mmap` settings.

Jemalloc and Transparent HugePages

By default, MySQL uses the built-in memory allocator to manage memory allocation and deallocation. However, you can use alternative memory allocators such as jemalloc. *Jemalloc* is a general-purpose memory allocator that is designed to be efficient and scalable. It is known for its ability to reduce memory fragmentation and provide better performance than the default memory allocator used by MySQL.

In addition to using jemalloc, disabling Transparent HugePages (THP) can further improve MySQL performance. THP is a Linux kernel feature that enables the use of large memory pages to reduce memory fragmentation. However, THP can also cause performance issues in some cases, particularly for workloads that involve many small memory allocations. Disabling THP can prevent the Linux kernel from transparently merging non-hugepages to hugepages. During this merge, access to those pages is blocked at the kernel level, which can lead to stalls.

When jemalloc is configured along with the disabled THP, the result is more efficient resource management of available memory. This can lead to better overall performance and scalability of the MySQL database. However, the specific configuration will depend on the workload and hardware environment of the database, and careful tuning may be necessary to achieve optimal performance.

The steps for installing and configuring jemalloc on a CentOS/RHEL system for use with MySQL are as follows:

1. Install jemalloc using the yum package manager. The following command installs the Extra Packages for Enterprise Linux (EPEL) repository on a system using the yum package manager, such as RHEL:

```
[root@mysql8 ~]# wget https://dl.fedoraproject.org/pub/epel/
epel-release-latest-9.noarch.rpm
--2024-02-22 04:38:57--
Saving to: 'epel-release-latest-9.noarch.rpm'
epel-release-latest-9.noarch. 100%[=================>]  18.73K  --.-KB/s
in 0.1s
2024-02-22 04:38:57 (195 KB/s) - 'epel-release-latest-9.noarch.rpm' saved
[19179/19179]
[root@mysql8 ~]#
[root@mysql8 ~]#  yum install epel-release-latest-9.noarch.rpm -y
Last metadata expiration check: 0:08:13 ago on Thu 22 Feb 2024
04:32:12 AM UTC.
  Preparing      :
  Installing     : epel-release-9-7.el9.noarch
  Running scriptlet: epel-release-9-7.el9.noarch
  Verifying      : epel-release-9-7.el9.noarch
Installed products updated.
Installed:
  epel-release-9-7.el9.noarch
Complete!
[root@mysql8 ~]#
```

2. Install the jemalloc library:

```
[root@mysql8 ~]# yum install jemalloc
Last metadata expiration check: 0:00:02 ago on Thu 22 Feb 2024
04:42:24 AM UTC.
Dependencies resolved.
========================================================================
 Package                 Architecture
 Version                         Repository              Size
========================================================================
Installing:
 jemalloc                x86_64                          5.2.1-2.el9
                         epel                    203 k
Transaction Summary
========================================================================
Install  1 Package
Is this ok [y/N]: y
Downloading Packages:
jemalloc-5.2.1-2.el9.x86_64.rpm
2.4 MB/s | 203 kB     00:00
------------------------------------------------------------------------
```

```
Total
415 kB/s | 203 kB     00:00
  Preparing        :
  Installing       : jemalloc-5.2.1-2.el9.x86_64
  Running scriptlet: jemalloc-5.2.1-2.el9.x86_64
  Verifying        : jemalloc-5.2.1-2.el9.x86_64
Installed products updated.
Installed:
  jemalloc-5.2.1-2.el9.x86_64
Complete!
[root@mysql8 ~]#
```

3. Confirm that the *libjemalloc.so.2* file exists post-installation:

```
[root@mysql8 ~]# ls -ltr /usr/lib64/libjemalloc.so.2
-rwxr-xr-x. 1 root root 558840 Dec 27  2021 /usr/lib64/libjemalloc.so.2
[root@mysql8 ~]#
```

4. Edit the *mysqld* service file by using the systemctl command:

```
[root@mysql8 ~]# systemctl edit mysqld
[root@mysql8 ~]#
[root@mysql8 system]# cat /etc/systemd/system/mysqld.service.d/override.conf
[Service]
Environment="LD_PRELOAD=/usr/lib64/libjemalloc.so.2"
[root@mysql8 system]#
```

5. Add the following lines to the file to set the LD_PRELOAD environment variable to load the *libjemalloc.so.2* library before starting the MySQL daemon:

[Service]

Environment="LD_PRELOAD=/usr/lib64/libjemalloc.so.2"

6. Reload the daemon configurations:

```
[root@mysql8 ~]# systemctl daemon-reload
[root@mysql8 ~]#
```

7. Restart the MySQL service to apply the new configuration:

```
[root@mysql8 ~]# sudo systemctl restart mysqld
[root@mysql8 ~]#
```

8. Verify that the *jemalloc* library is being used by MySQL by searching for its presence in the process's memory map:

```
[root@mysql8 system]# sudo grep jem /proc/$(pidof mysqld)/maps
7f7c44e00000-7f7c44e06000 r--p 00000000 ca:04 9357377
/usr/lib64/libjemalloc.so.2
7f7c44e06000-7f7c44e76000 r-xp 00006000 ca:04 9357377
/usr/lib64/libjemalloc.so.2
7f7c44e76000-7f7c44e81000 r--p 00076000 ca:04 9357377
/usr/lib64/libjemalloc.so.2
7f7c44e81000-7f7c44e87000 r--p 00080000 ca:04 9357377
/usr/lib64/libjemalloc.so.2
```

```
7f7c44e87000-7f7c44e88000 rw-p 00086000 ca:04 9357377
/usr/lib64/libjemalloc.so.2
[root@mysql8 system]#
```

The following commands are used to disable the THP feature in the Linux kernel, which can help improve the performance of certain applications such as databases:

1. Check whether THP is enabled on your system:

   ```
   [root@mysql8 ~]# cat /sys/kernel/mm/transparent_hugepage/enabled
   [always] madvise never
   [root@mysql8 ~]#
   ```

2. If THP is enabled, we recommend disabling it. You can disable THP as follows:

   ```
   [root@mysql8 ~]# echo never > /sys/kernel/mm/transparent_hugepage/enabled
   [root@mysql8 ~]#
   ```

3. The next command is used to set the THP defrag setting to never:

   ```
   [root@mysql8 ~]# echo never > /sys/kernel/mm/transparent_hugepage/defrag
   [root@mysql8 ~]
   ```

4. After disabling THP, verify the THP settings, confirming that it is set to never:

   ```
   [root@mysql8 ~]# cat /sys/kernel/mm/transparent_hugepage/enabled
   always madvise [never]
   [root@mysql8 ~]#
   ```

These commands will disable THP both for allocation and defragmentation. Here is what each command does:

echo never > /sys/kernel/mm/transparent_hugepage/enabled

Sets the value of the enabled file in the *transparent_hugepage* directory to never, which disables THP. The enabled file controls whether THP is enabled or disabled on the system. When THP is disabled, the kernel will not use it for memory allocation.

echo never > /sys/kernel/mm/transparent_hugepage/defrag

Sets the value of the defrag file in the *transparent_hugepage* directory to never, which disables THP defragmentation. The defrag file controls whether the kernel will attempt to defragment the memory that has already been allocated using THP. When THP defragmentation is disabled, the kernel will not attempt to rearrange memory to create larger pages.

These commands should be run with administrative privileges (e.g., using sudo), and they should be added to a startup script to ensure that they are applied every time the system is booted. Disabling THP may be necessary for certain applications, but it should be done with caution as it may slow the performance of other workloads.

Disk I/O Configuration

Disk I/O can significantly impact MySQL performance, as disk access is often the slowest operation in a database system. To optimize your disk I/O configuration, consider doing the following:

Use SSDs
> Solid-state drives (SSDs) can significantly improve MySQL performance by providing faster disk access.

Use RAID
> Redundant array of inexpensive disks (RAID) configuration can improve disk I/O performance by spreading data across multiple disks. For optimal performance, consider using RAID 0 or RAID 10.

Tune your filesystem
> Filesystem tuning can improve MySQL performance by reducing the overhead of disk I/O. For optimal performance, consider using the XFS or ext4 filesystem.

Several MySQL variables are related to disk I/O and can affect performance tuning. Some of the key variables include the following:

`innodb_io_capacity`
> Setting the I/O capacity limit for background tasks in InnoDB, this parameter governs the efficiency of InnoDB background operations. Increasing this variable can improve the throughput of I/O operations.

`innodb_io_capacity_max`
> This parameter controls the maximum I/O capacity limit for InnoDB background tasks. Increasing this variable can improve the throughput of I/O operations.
>
> Avoid arbitrary increases in the variables `innodb_io_capacity` and `innodb_io_capacity_max`. Instead, it is crucial to assess the available IOPS and workload through thorough testing and monitoring before adjusting these variables. Setting them to excessively high values can result in performance problems due to overloading.

`innodb_flush_method`
> This determines the manner in which InnoDB flushes data to disk. Changing this variable can affect I/O performance, but note that some options may not be available on all platforms.

`innodb_flush_log_at_trx_commit`

This defines the level of durability for InnoDB transactions. Setting a value of 2 can improve write performance, but it comes at the cost of potentially losing up to 1 second of data in the event of a crash.

`innodb_redo_log_capacity`

The size of the InnoDB redo logfiles is governed by this variable. A larger logfile size can improve performance by reducing the frequency of disk writes. The `innodb_log_file_size` and `innodb_log_files_in_group` are deprecated in MySQL 8.0.30. `innodb_redo_log_capacity` variable takes precedence over the `innodb_log_files_in_group` and `innodb_log_file_size` variables. If you define an `innodb_redo_log_capacity` setting, the `innodb_log_files_in_group` and `innodb_log_file_size` settings are disregarded. In the absence of an `innodb_redo_log_capacity` setting, these variables are employed to calculate the `innodb_redo_log_capacity` setting (`innodb_log_files_in_group` × `innodb_log_file_size` = `innodb_redo_log_capacity`). When none of these variables are configured, the redo log capacity defaults to the `innodb_redo_log_capacity` default value.

`binlog_row_image`

Setting this variable to `minimal` reduces the amount of data written to the binary log during write operations, resulting in lower disk I/O and potentially faster write performance.

`max_allowed_packet`

The MySQL server's maximum packet size for both sending and receiving is regulated by its value. Increasing this variable can improve the performance of bulk data transfers.

`slow_query_log`

This variable controls whether slow queries are logged to a file. Enabling this feature can help identify performance issues but can also increase disk I/O.

Changing these variables can have unintended consequences, so consult with a MySQL expert or thoroughly test any changes before implementing them in a production environment.

The variables mentioned in this chapter aren't a comprehensive list; we covered additional variables in Chapter 3.

Planning the Database Design

Designing a database schema for MySQL 8 requires careful planning and consideration of several factors, including table structure, indexing, and query optimization. Poor database schema design can result in performance issues, such as slow query execution and data inconsistencies.

Table Structure

The table structure is a crucial aspect of a MySQL database schema design. A well-designed table structure can improve database performance and reduce data redundancy. Here are some best practices for table structure:

Normalize the table structure
Break down large tables into smaller ones to reduce data redundancy and improve data consistency.

Use the appropriate data types
Choosing the right data types can improve database performance and reduce storage space. For instance, using the INT data type for small numbers can save storage space and improve query performance.

Avoid using NULL values
Using NULL values can make it difficult to maintain data consistency and query performance. Consider using default values instead of NULL values.

Use meaningful table and column names
Meaningful names can make it easier to understand the database schema and query data.

Primary keys
Review the primary keys being used in the database. Make sure that each table has a primary key, and that it is a unique and stable identifier for the table. Using primary keys can improve performance and help ensure data integrity.

GIPK
In MySQL 8, it is advisable to utilize GIPKs. Starting from MySQL version 8.0.30, the platform introduces support for automatically generated invisible primary keys on InnoDB tables that are created without an explicitly defined primary key. When the sql_generate_invisible_primary_key server system variable is enabled, the MySQL server will autonomously incorporate a GIPK for any relevant table.

Foreign keys
Review the foreign keys being used in the database. Make sure that all relationships between tables are defined using foreign keys and that the foreign keys are

properly indexed. Using foreign keys can improve query performance and help ensure data integrity.

Partitioning

Review the partitioning strategy being used in the database. If the database is very large, consider partitioning it into smaller, more manageable pieces. Partitioning can improve performance by allowing queries to run in parallel and reducing the amount of data that needs to be scanned.

By reviewing these aspects of the database schema, you can identify any potential performance bottlenecks and optimize the MySQL server's performance. It's important to regularly review the database schema to ensure that it is designed in the most efficient and effective way possible.

Indexing

Indexing is a crucial aspect of optimizing database performance, and MySQL offers a range of indexing options. In this section, we discuss the best practices for MySQL indexing and explore the types of indexes available.

Indexing is the process of creating an index on a table column to speed up data retrieval. It works by creating a copy of a table's column data in a separate data structure, which can be sorted and searched much faster than the original table. When a query is executed, the database engine uses the index to quickly find the relevant rows instead of scanning the entire table, resulting in faster query execution times.

MySQL supports several types of indexes, each with its own unique properties and use cases. Let's take a closer look at best practices and the types of indexes in MySQL.

Indexing best practices

Indexing is an essential part of a MySQL database schema design. Indexes can speed up query execution and improve database performance. Here are some best practices for indexing:

Use the appropriate index type

Choosing the right index type depends on the type of data and queries being used. For instance, using a full-text index can improve query performance for text-based searches.

Avoid over-indexing

Over-indexing can slow database performance and increase storage space. Consider indexing only columns that are frequently used in queries.

Use composite indexes

Composite indexes can improve performance for queries that involve multiple columns.

Choose the right index type

Each of the indexes that MySQL offers has its own unique properties and use cases. It's important to choose the right index type for the column being indexed and the type of queries being executed. For example, B-tree indexes are well suited for range-based queries, while hash indexes are better for exact-match queries.

Keep indexes updated

Indexes can become fragmented over time because of insertions, updates, and deletions. Fragmented indexes can harm performance by slowing data retrieval. It's important to regularly optimize and rebuild indexes to keep them updated and running efficiently.

Use EXPLAIN to analyze query performance

The EXPLAIN statement can be used to analyze query performance and determine whether the query is using the proper indexes. It shows how the database engine is executing the query and which indexes are being used. This can help identify performance bottlenecks and optimize query execution times.

B-tree indexes

B-tree indexes are the most commonly used type of index in MySQL. They work by creating a balanced tree structure that allows for fast searching, insertion, and deletion of data. B-tree indexes are well suited for handling range-based queries and are used for indexing both primary and secondary keys. Consider the following example table employees:

```
mysql> CREATE TABLE employees (
    ->     emp_no INT AUTO_INCREMENT PRIMARY KEY,
    ->     birth_date DATE NOT NULL,
    ->     first_name VARCHAR(14) NOT NULL,
    ->     last_name VARCHAR(16) NOT NULL,
    ->     gender ENUM('M','F') NOT NULL,
    ->     hire_date DATE NOT NULL
    -> ) ENGINE=InnoDB;
Query OK, 0 rows affected (0.02 sec)

mysql>

mysql> show create table employees\G
*************************** 1. row ***************************
       Table: employees
Create Table: CREATE TABLE `employees` (
  `emp_no` int NOT NULL AUTO_INCREMENT,
  `birth_date` date NOT NULL,
  `first_name` varchar(14) NOT NULL,
  `last_name` varchar(16) NOT NULL,
  `gender` enum('M','F') NOT NULL,
```

```
  `hire_date` date NOT NULL,
  PRIMARY KEY (`emp_no`)
) ENGINE=InnoDB DEFAULT CHARSET=utf8mb4 COLLATE=utf8mb4_0900_ai_ci
1 row in set (0.00 sec)

mysql>
```

The following SQL query uses the EXPLAIN ANALYZE feature to retrieve specific columns from the employees table, where the first_name is Mohan, providing insight into how the database optimizer executes the query for performance analysis:

```
mysql> explain analyze select emp_no, first_name, last_name,
    -> birth_date, gender from employees where first_name='Mohan';
+----------------------------------------------------------------+
| EXPLAIN                                                        |
+----------------------------------------------------------------+
| -> Filter: (employees.first_name = 'Mohan')  (cost=14.1 rows=13.8)
(actual time=0.268..0.271 rows=1 loops=1)
    -> Table scan on employees  (cost=14.1 rows=138)
    (actual time=0.0521..0.168 rows=138 loops=1)
 |
+----------------------------------------------------------------+
1 row in set (0.00 sec)

mysql>
```

This SQL command creates an index named employees_firstname_inx on the first_name column of the employees table:

```
mysql> CREATE INDEX employees_firstname_inx on employees(first_name);
Query OK, 0 rows affected (0.02 sec)
Records: 0  Duplicates: 0  Warnings: 0

mysql>
```

After adding the index, you can confirm the EXPLAIN ANALYZE output, which should now indicate that the query has shifted to an index lookup on the employees table using the first_name index:

```
mysql> explain analyze select emp_no, first_name, last_name, birth_date, gender
    -> from employees where first_name='Mohan';
+-------------------------------------------------------------------+
| EXPLAIN                                                           |
+-------------------------------------------------------------------+
| -> Index lookup on employees using employees_firstname_inx
(first_name='Mohan')  (cost=0.35 rows=1) (actual time=0.0286..0.0313
rows=1 loops=1)
 |
+-------------------------------------------------------------------+
1 row in set (0.00 sec)

mysql>
```

The table structure, after adding the `first_name` index, appears as follows:

```
mysql> show create table employees\G
*************************** 1. row ***************************
       Table: employees
Create Table: CREATE TABLE `employees` (
  `emp_no` int NOT NULL AUTO_INCREMENT,
  `birth_date` date NOT NULL,
  `first_name` varchar(14) NOT NULL,
  `last_name` varchar(16) NOT NULL,
  `gender` enum('M','F') NOT NULL,
  `hire_date` date NOT NULL,
  PRIMARY KEY (`emp_no`),
  KEY `employees_firstname_inx` (`first_name`)
) ENGINE=InnoDB AUTO_INCREMENT=139 DEFAULT CHARSET=utf8mb4 COLLATE=
utf8mb4_0900_ai_ci
1 row in set (0.00 sec)

mysql>
```

Hash indexes

Hash indexes are designed for fast lookups of exact-match queries. They work by hashing the indexed column value and storing it in a hash table. When a query is executed, the database engine calculates the hash of the search value and looks it up in the hash table. Hash indexes are not well suited for range-based queries and are not used for indexing primary keys.

To create a hash index on a table in MySQL, you can use the `CREATE INDEX` statement with the `USING HASH` option:

```
CREATE INDEX index_name ON table_name(column_name) USING HASH;
```

The `MEMORY` storage engine in MySQL supports both `HASH` and `BTREE` indexes, and you can specify which one to use for a given index by adding a `USING` clause. `MEMORY` tables can have up to 64 indexes per table, 16 columns per index, and a maximum key length of 3,072 bytes.

Here's an example of creating a `MEMORY` table with a hash index:

```
mysql> CREATE TABLE `students` (
    -> `first_name` varchar(32) NOT NULL,
    -> `last_name` varchar(32) NOT NULL,
    -> `mobile_no` varchar(10) DEFAULT NULL,
    -> `age` int DEFAULT NULL,
    -> KEY `hash_index` (`age`)
    -> ) ENGINE=MEMORY DEFAULT CHARSET=utf8mb4 COLLATE=utf8mb4_0900_ai_ci;
Query OK, 0 rows affected (0.00 sec)

mysql>
```

To create a new procedure called `load_data` that will insert 100,000 rows of randomly generated data into the `students` table, take the following steps:

1. Set the delimiter to $$:

```
mysql> DELIMITER $$
mysql>
```

2. Create the procedure and define its behavior by using the BEGIN and END keywords. In this case, the procedure will generate 100,000 random rows and insert them into the `students` table:

```
mysql> DELIMITER $$
mysql>
mysql> CREATE PROCEDURE load_data()
       BEGIN
            DECLARE i INT DEFAULT 0;

            WHILE i < 100000 DO
                INSERT INTO `students` (`first_name`, `last_name`, `age`,
                `mobile_no`)
                VALUES (
                    CONV(FLOOR(RAND() * 99999999999999), 10, 36),
                    CONV(FLOOR(RAND() * 99999999999999), 10, 36),
                    ROUND(RAND() * 100, 2),
                    LPAD(FLOOR(RAND() * 10000000000), 10, '0')
                );
                SET i = i + 1;
            END WHILE;
       END$$
Query OK, 0 rows affected (0.00 sec)

mysql>
```

3. Reset the delimiter to ; to indicate the end of the query:

```
mysql> DELIMITER ;
mysql>
```

4. Now, you should be able to execute the `load_data` procedure to insert 100,000 rows of random data into the `students` table by calling it like this:

```
mysql> CALL load_data();
Query OK, 1 row affected (2 min 37.96 sec)

mysql>
```

5. Run `explain analyze` and check the cost:

```
mysql> explain analyze select first_name, last_name, age, mobile_no
from students where age = 20 or age = 40;
+------------------------------------------------------------------------
------------------------------------------------------------------------
------------------------------------------------------------------
```

```
------------------------------------------------------------------------+
| EXPLAIN                                                                |
+------------------------------------------------------------------------
------------------------------------------------------------------------
------------------------------------------------------------------------
------------------------------------------------------------------------+
| -> Filter: ((students.age = 20) or (students.age = 40))  (cost=421
rows=1980) (actual time=0.0106..4.75 rows=1997 loops=1)
    -> Index range scan on students using hash_index over (age = 20)
    OR (age = 40)  (cost=421 rows=1980) (actual time=0.00596..1.99
    rows=1997 loops=1)
 |
+------------------------------------------------------------------------
------------------------------------------------------------------------
------------------------------------------------------------------------
------------------------------------------------------------------------+
1 row in set (0.00 sec)

mysql>
```

Full-text indexes

Full-text indexes are used for full-text search queries, which allow for searching text data for specific words or phrases. They work by creating an inverted index of the text data, which allows for fast searching of large volumes of text. Full-text indexes are used for indexing text-based columns, such as article content or product descriptions. Consider this example table named products:

```
mysql> show create table products\G
*************************** 1. row ***************************
       Table: products
Create Table: CREATE TABLE `products` (
  `productCode` varchar(15) NOT NULL,
  `productName` varchar(70) NOT NULL,
  `productLine` varchar(50) NOT NULL,
  `productScale` varchar(10) NOT NULL,
  `productVendor` varchar(50) NOT NULL,
  `productDescription` text NOT NULL,
  `quantityInStock` smallint NOT NULL,
  `buyPrice` decimal(10,2) NOT NULL,
  `MSRP` decimal(10,2) NOT NULL,
  PRIMARY KEY (`productCode`)
) ENGINE=InnoDB DEFAULT CHARSET=latin1
1 row in set (0.00 sec)

mysql>
```

You can create a full-text index on the productDescription column by using the CREATE FULLTEXT INDEX command. Name the index idx_prodDesc_inx so you can reference it later:

```
mysql> CREATE FULLTEXT INDEX idx_prodDesc_inx ON products(productDescription);
Query OK, 0 rows affected, 1 warning (0.20 sec)
Records: 0  Duplicates: 0  Warnings: 1

mysql>
```

Once the full-text index has been created, you can use the MATCH and AGAINST operators to search for text within the productDescription column. Here's an example of
how to use these operators to search for the word replica:

```
mysql> explain analyze SELECT * FROM products WHERE
MATCH(productDescription) AGAINST('replica');
+-------------------------------------------------------------------------
-------------------------------------------------------------------------
-------------------------------------------------------------------------
------------------------------------------------------------------------+
| EXPLAIN                                                                |
+-------------------------------------------------------------------------
-------------------------------------------------------------------------
-------------------------------------------------------------------------
------------------------------------------------------------------------+
| -> Filter: (match products.productDescription against ('replica'))
(cost=0.35 rows=1) (actual time=0.0296..0.0368 rows=2 loops=1)
    -> Full-text index search on products using idx_prodDesc_inx
    (productDescription='replica')  (cost=0.35 rows=1)
    (actual time=0.0256..0.0303 rows=2 loops=1)
 |
+-------------------------------------------------------------------------
-------------------------------------------------------------------------
-------------------------------------------------------------------------
------------------------------------------------------------------------+
1 row in set (0.00 sec)

mysql>
```

When employing the LIKE operator in a WHERE clause with a preceding %, the index is
not used:

```
mysql> explain analyze select productCode, productName, productLine from
    -> products where productDescription like '%replica%';
+-------------------------------------------------------------------------
-------------------------------------------------------------------------
------------------------------------------------------------------------+
| EXPLAIN                                                                |
+-------------------------------------------------------------------------
-------------------------------------------------------------------------
------------------------------------------------------------------------+
| -> Filter: (products.productDescription like '%replica%')
(cost=0.45 rows=1) (actual time=0.031..0.0409 rows=2 loops=1)
    -> Table scan on products  (cost=0.45 rows=2)
    (actual time=0.0257..0.0327 rows=2 loops=1)
 |
+-------------------------------------------------------------------------
```

```
--------------------------------------------------------------------------
-------------------------------------------------------------------------+
1 row in set (0.00 sec)

mysql>
```

Covering index

Sometimes when working with MySQL, you may need to use an index in a different way than usual. In such cases, a covering index may be useful. A *covering index* includes all the fields necessary for a query to succeed. When a query is run and a covering index is present, the results can be retrieved directly from the index, rather than having additional access to the disk.

In other words, if you use an index that already contains the values of the columns you want to search, MySQL will not have to access the disk. Instead, it can retrieve the results directly from the index, which can result in a significant performance improvement, especially for large tables with many rows.

Explain the query to analyze it without a covering index:

```
mysql> EXPLAIN Analyze SELECT first_name, last_name, age FROM
students WHERE last_name = 'AIJRFAMF5';
+--------------------------------------------------------------
--------------------------------------------------------------
--------------------------------------------------------------+
| EXPLAIN                                                      |
+--------------------------------------------------------------
--------------------------------------------------------------
--------------------------------------------------------------+
| -> Filter: (students.last_name = 'AIJRFAMF5')  (cost=5589
rows=4965) (actual time=0.0103..72.6 rows=1 loops=1)
    -> Table scan on students  (cost=5589 rows=49654) (actual
    time=0.00363..36.3 rows=49654 loops=1)
  |
+--------------------------------------------------------------
--------------------------------------------------------------
--------------------------------------------------------------+
1 row in set (0.08 sec)

mysql>
```

Let's create a covering index on the students table now:

```
mysql> CREATE INDEX idx_students_covering ON students (age,last_name,first_name);
Query OK, 100000 rows affected (0.10 sec)
Records: 100000  Duplicates: 0  Warnings: 0

mysql>
```

Next, use EXPLAIN to analyze the query after creating the covering index:

```
mysql> EXPLAIN Analyze SELECT first_name, last_name, age FROM students
WHERE last_name = 'AIJRFAMF5';
+----------------------------------------------------------------------
----------------------------------------------------------------------
------------------------------------------------------------------+
| EXPLAIN                                                           |
+----------------------------------------------------------------------
----------------------------------------------------------------------
------------------------------------------------------------------+
| -> Filter: (students.last_name = 'AIJRFAMF5')  (cost=11252 rows=10000)
(actual time=146..146 rows=0 loops=1)
    -> Table scan on students  (cost=11252 rows=100000)
    (actual time=0.00348..72.8 rows=100000 loops=1)
 |
+----------------------------------------------------------------------
----------------------------------------------------------------------
------------------------------------------------------------------+
1 row in set (0.15 sec)

mysql>
```

Composite indexes

Composite indexes cover multiple columns. They can be useful for queries that involve multiple WHERE clauses or for sorting on multiple columns. By creating a composite index, you can avoid creating separate indexes on each column, which can help reduce the overall number of indexes and improve performance. You can create a composite index as follows:

```
CREATE TABLE orders (
  id INT NOT NULL PRIMARY KEY,
  customer_id INT NOT NULL,
  order_date DATE NOT NULL,
  total DECIMAL(10,2) NOT NULL,
  INDEX idx_orders_customer_date (customer_id, order_date)
);
```

Query Optimization

Proper query optimization can significantly improve the performance of MySQL databases. This includes optimizing queries, minimizing the number of queries, and reducing the complexity of queries.

Optimizing queries is one of the most effective ways to improve the performance of a MySQL database. Here are some best practices for optimizing queries:

INDEX
Can significantly speed up the execution of queries by allowing MySQL to quickly locate the relevant data. Make sure to create indexes on columns that are frequently used in queries.

SELECT
> Can lead to slower query execution times, so you should avoid using it. Instead, select only the columns that are needed.

EXPLAIN
> Can be used to analyze the query execution plan and identify potential performance issues.

WHERE
> Can be used to filter out unnecessary data and return only the relevant data.

Consider the following example where we create an index on a specific column and perform an EXPLAIN on the query with a WHERE clause on that column to analyze its execution plan and confirm whether the query is using the index:

```
CREATE INDEX index_name ON table_name (column_name);
EXPLAIN SELECT column_name FROM table_name WHERE column_name = 'value';
```

Minimizing the number of queries can also significantly improve the performance of a MySQL database. Here are some best practices for minimizing the number of queries:

- Use JOINs to combine multiple queries into a single query:

```
SELECT column_name FROM table_name1 JOIN table_name2 ON
table_name1.column_name = table_name2.column_name;
```

- Use Subqueries to retrieve data from multiple tables in a single query.

```
SELECT column_name FROM table_name WHERE column_name IN (SELECT
column_name FROM table_name2);
```

- Use UNION to combine the results of multiple SELECT statements into a single result set.

```
SELECT column_name FROM table_name1 UNION SELECT column_name FROM
```

Reducing the complexity of queries can also improve the performance of a MySQL database. Here are some recommended guidelines for simplifying query complexity:

- Avoid complex JOINs that involve multiple tables or complex conditions.
- Avoid complex subqueries that involve multiple tables or complex conditions.
- Use temporary tables to break complex queries into smaller, more manageable parts.

Network Latency

Network latency refers to the delay that occurs when data travels from one point to another over a network. Network latency can affect the response time of queries

---

issued by the client. The response time measured on the database server side will not include any network latency, except for a few special cases (with group replication or semisync), while measured on the client it will include the time spent on the network. At the end of the day, database performance is determined by the response time that is seen by the client.

Impact of Network Latency on Database Performance

For MySQL, network latency can significantly impact database performance. The following are some of the effects:

Slow query execution
Network latency can cause delays in the transmission of data between the MySQL server and the client, leading to slow execution of queries.

Poor response times
Slow response times can result from network latency, which causes delays in transmitting data between the MySQL server and the client, ultimately leading to poor performance.

Reduced throughput
Network latency can reduce the amount of data that can be transmitted over the network, leading to reduced throughput.

Best Practices for Minimizing Network Latency

To minimize network latency and optimize database performance, consider the following best practices:

Use a reliable network connection
Ensure that you use a reliable network connection with low latency and high bandwidth to help reduce network latency and improve database performance.

Optimize database configuration
Optimize the MySQL database configuration settings to reduce network latency.

Lower the `wait_timeout` *value*
This value determines the amount of time a connection can remain idle before it is closed. It can help keep fewer threads open on the server, which can lead to better response time in some cases.

Use connection pooling
Connection pooling can help reduce network latency by reusing existing connections instead of creating new connections for every request.

Two new features in MySQL 8, SSL session reuse with a timeout setting and the `caching_sha2_password` authentication plug-in, can potentially help improve network latency in different ways:

SSL session reuse with timeout setting
> By supporting SSL session reuse by default and introducing the timeout setting, MySQL 8 can enhance network latency in secure connections. SSL/TLS handshakes are computationally expensive and can introduce latency. With session reuse, a previously established SSL/TLS session can be reused for subsequent connections, reducing the need for full handshakes. This can significantly reduce the overhead associated with SSL/TLS, leading to lower network latency for secure communication.

`caching_sha2_password` *authentication plug-in*
> This plug-in is designed to address latency issues that can occur during authentication. It implements SHA-256 password hashing, similar to the `sha256_password` plug-in, but it incorporates caching. Caching can improve the efficiency of authentication by temporarily storing the results of expensive hashing operations. If a user with the same credentials logs in again during the caching period, the server can avoid recomputing the hash, resulting in faster authentication and lower latency.

Workload

The *workload* of the database system, including the number of concurrent users and the type of queries being executed, can impact performance. The first step in managing the workload of a MySQL database system is to understand the workload. This includes the following:

Number of concurrent users
> The number of users accessing the database system at the same time. This can impact the system's performance.

Types of queries
> Some queries may be more resource-intensive than others, which can also impact performance.

Query frequency
> How often queries are being executed. Frequent execution of resource-intensive queries can put a strain on the system.

Data volume
> The amount of data being queried by each query. Identify any queries that are querying large amounts of data and consider optimizing them to improve performance.

Once you have an understanding of the workload, it is important to monitor it on an ongoing basis. This can be done using various monitoring tools, including these:

PMM
Workload monitoring provides real-time insights into database performance and resource utilization, aiding in the proactive management and optimization of database workloads.

MySQL Enterprise Monitor
This powerful monitoring tool provides real-time visibility into the performance of a MySQL database system.

MySQL performance schema
This MySQL feature provides a way to inspect the performance of the database system.

MySQL Workbench
A visual tool for DBAs to monitor the performance of the database system.

`pt-query-digest`
A powerful tool used to analyze MySQL queries from slow logs, process lists, and `tcpdump` captures on database servers. This open source tool is part of Percona Toolkit and is designed to provide detailed reports and statistics on query performance.

The *slow query log* MySQL feature records all queries that take longer than a certain amount of time to execute. This log can be used to identify queries that are performing poorly and optimize the performance of the database server. However, manually reviewing and analyzing the slow query log can be a time-consuming and difficult task. This is where `pt-query-digest` comes in.

The `pt-query-digest` tool can identify slow queries, group them by type, and provide detailed information on their performance. The tool generates a report that includes the number of queries, the time taken to execute each query, the number of rows examined, and the number of rows returned. This report can be easily used to identify poorly performing queries and optimize their performance.

Here's an example `pt-query-digest` command that will analyze the MySQL slow query log located at */var/log/mysql/slow.log* and output a report with the grouped and sorted query information to */tmp/query_digest.log*:

```
pt-query-digest /var/log/mysql/slow.log > /tmp/query_digest.log
```

One of the most powerful features of `pt-query-digest` is its ability to group similar queries together. This allows you to identify common patterns in the queries and to optimize the performance of the database server by making changes that apply to all queries in a group. For example, if you notice that many queries are performing full table scans, you can optimize the database schema or add indexes to improve perfor-mance across the board.

You can also use the `--group-by` option to specify the level of grouping that you want. For example, to group queries by the digest of the SQL text, use the following command:

```
pt-query-digest --group-by fingerprint /var/log/mysql/slow.log >
/tmp/query_digest.log
```

Grouping similar queries by their SQL text fingerprints can be useful for identifying patterns in the types of queries that are causing performance issues. The `--group-by` option is an array in `pt-query-digest` that specifies the attribute of the events to group by. You can group queries into classes based on any attribute of the query, such as user or database, which will by default show you which users and databases get the most query time. The default attribute is `fingerprint`, which groups similar, abstrac-ted queries into classes.

A report is printed for each `--group-by` value (unless `--no-report` is given). There-fore, if you use `--group-by` *user, db*, it will report on queries with the same user and report on queries with the same database. It does not mean "report on queries with the same user and database" together.

By using this tool as part of your performance review process, you can identify per-formance bottlenecks and optimize the performance of your database server for max-imum efficiency and reliability. To optimize the workload of a MySQL database system, consider the following best practices:

Query optimization
    Optimize the queries being executed to reduce the amount of resources required. This can be done by using indexes, reducing the size of result sets, and using query caching.

Resource allocation
    Ensure that the database system has adequate resources to handle the workload. This includes CPU, memory, and storage.

Connection management
    Optimize the way that connections are managed to reduce overhead and improve performance. This includes using connection pooling and optimizing connection parameters.

By reviewing these aspects of the query workload, you can identify any potential per-formance bottlenecks and optimize the MySQL server for optimal performance. It's important to regularly review the query workload to ensure that the database is run-ning efficiently and effectively.

Understanding the MySQL Query Execution Process

The MySQL query execution process consists of several stages, including parsing, optimization, and execution. Understanding how MySQL processes queries can help identify performance bottlenecks and optimize query performance. The stages are as follows:

Parsing

The parsing stage involves analyzing the SQL statement and validating its syntax. If the syntax is invalid, the parsing stage will return an error.

Optimization

The optimization stage involves generating an execution plan for the SQL statement. MySQL generates the execution plan by analyzing the query, table structure, and indexing. The optimization stage can significantly impact query performance.

Execution

The execution stage involves executing the SQL statement and returning the result set. The execution stage can be impacted by several factors, including network latency, disk I/O, and CPU usage.

Tuning the MySQL InnoDB Buffer Pool

The InnoDB buffer pool is a dedicated memory space in MySQL where frequently accessed data and indexes are stored. The buffer pool caches the data and indexes in memory so that they can be quickly accessed without having to read from disk. This reduces disk I/O and improves database performance. The size of the buffer pool determines the amount of data and indexes that can be cached in memory. Therefore, configuring and monitoring the InnoDB buffer pool is essential for ensuring optimal performance.

Configuring InnoDB Buffer Pool Size

The size of the InnoDB buffer pool is determined by the `innodb_buffer_pool_size` system variable. The default value of this variable is 128 MB. However, the optimal size of the buffer pool depends on the size of the database, the amount of available memory, and the workload on the database. The following are the best practices for configuring the InnoDB buffer pool size:

Determine the available memory

Before configuring the buffer pool size, it is important to determine the amount of memory available on the server, which you can do with this command:

```
[root@mysql8 ~]# free -m
              total        used        free      shared  buff/cache   available
Mem:           3644         717        1899          18        1097        2927
Swap:             0           0           0
[root@mysql8 ~]#
```

Determine the optimal buffer pool size

The optimal buffer pool size is about 70–80% of the available system memory, taking into account the overall size of the database as well. You set this amount with the `innodb_buffer_pool_size` variable.

Configure the buffer pool size

The buffer pool size can be configured by setting the `innodb_buffer_pool_size` variable in the MySQL configuration file (*my.cnf*). For example:

```
[mysqld]
innodb_buffer_pool_size = 4G
```

Test and adjust

Once the buffer pool size has been configured, it is important to test the performance of the database and adjust the size if necessary (for example, if there are a lot of disk reads for the queries).

Monitoring InnoDB Buffer Pool Usage

Monitoring use of the InnoDB buffer pool is important for detecting performance issues and optimizing its size. The following are the best practices for monitoring InnoDB buffer pool usage:

Use the InnoDB buffer pool status

The InnoDB buffer pool status provides information about buffer pool usage, such as the size of the buffer pool, the number of pages in the buffer pool, and the hit rate. The status can be obtained by using tools like PMM and MySQL Enterprise Monitoring, or by using the following command:

```
SHOW ENGINE INNODB STATUS\G
```

Use performance schema

Performance schema provides detailed information about InnoDB buffer pool usage, such as the number of pages read and written, the number of cache hits and misses, and the average read and write time. It can be enabled by setting the `performance_schema` variable to `ON`.

Use monitoring tools

Several monitoring tools are available for monitoring InnoDB buffer pool usage, such as MySQL Enterprise Monitor, PMM, and Nagios.

Tuning InnoDB Thread Concurrency

InnoDB thread concurrency is the ability of MySQL to handle multiple client requests simultaneously. To achieve this, MySQL creates a pool of threads that can be used to serve client connections. The `innodb_thread_concurrency` variable plays a vital role in optimizing the performance of MySQL. In a multithreaded environment, proper configuration of the thread pool can ensure that the database server can handle a large number of requests efficiently. In this section, we discuss the best practices for tuning MySQL thread concurrency to achieve optimal performance.

The variable `innodb_thread_concurrency` sets the limit for the number of simultaneous threads that can access the InnoDB kernel for processing. Essentially, it determines the number of concurrent queries InnoDB can handle at any given time. The default value of this variable is 0, which implies an unlimited number of threads. However, if it is set to a nonzero value, it restricts the number of threads that InnoDB can accommodate. As a result, if the number of threads exceeds this limit, InnoDB will place them in a queue until the previous threads have been processed.

The `innodb_thread_concurrency` variable is primarily designed for optimizing performance on systems with high levels of concurrency. To achieve optimal results, consider setting the value to `2*nproc` (two times the number of CPUs); this is considered a best practice. However, note that this variable is dynamic and therefore requires constant monitoring and adjustment after setting its value.

Using MySQL Performance Schema

MySQL performance schema provides a way for DBAs to obtain detailed information about the performance of the MySQL server. This instrumentation interface collects performance-related information in a structured way, which can then be queried via SQL commands.

The performance schema allows you to monitor the performance of your database by providing insight into query execution, resource usage, and other metrics. It can be used to identify performance issues and optimize database performance.

Configuring the Performance Schema

The performance schema is enabled by default. To configure it, you need to enable it in the MySQL configuration file. You can do this by adding `performance_schema=ON` to *my.cnf*. Once you've enabled the performance schema, you can start to configure it to suit your needs by setting various configuration options in *my.cnf*.

Using the Performance Schema to Identify Performance Issues

The performance schema can be used to identify performance issues in your database by providing detailed information about query execution and resource usage. You can use SQL queries to get information about slow queries, query execution times, and resource usage.

This query will show you the top 10 slowest queries that contain the word SELECT in their text:

```
SELECT * FROM performance_schema.events_statements_summary_by_digest
WHERE digest_text LIKE '%SELECT%'
ORDER BY sum_timer_wait DESC LIMIT 10;
```

This query will show you the top 10 queries with the longest execution times:

```
SELECT * FROM performance_schema.events_statements_history_long
ORDER BY timer_wait DESC LIMIT 10;
```

This query will show you the top 10 resource-intensive events related to mutexes:

```
SELECT * FROM
performance_schema.events_stages_summary_global_by_event_name
WHERE event_name LIKE '%wait/synch/mutex/sql/THD%'
ORDER BY sum_timer_wait DESC LIMIT 10;
```

The rest of this section walks you through how to use the performance schema to identify and optimize a slow query.

First, enable performance schema in your MySQL configuration file by adding the following line:

```
performance_schema=ON
```

Next, create a test database with a large table:

```
mysql> create database test;
Query OK, 1 row affected (0.01 sec)

mysql>
```

The USE statement is used to select a specific database, making it the current or active database for subsequent queries:

```
mysql> USE test;
Reading table information for completion of table and column names
You can turn off this feature to get a quicker startup with -A

Database changed
mysql>
```

Create the table mytable:

```
mysql> CREATE TABLE mytable (
       id INT PRIMARY KEY AUTO_INCREMENT,
```

```
        name VARCHAR(50),
        age INT
    );
Query OK, 0 rows affected (0.03 sec)
```

Insert test records into the table:

```
mysql> DELIMITER $$
mysql> CREATE PROCEDURE insert_random_records()
        BEGIN
            DECLARE i INT DEFAULT 0;
            DECLARE random_name VARCHAR(50);
            DECLARE random_age INT;

            WHILE i < 100000 DO
                SET random_name = CONCAT(Name,
                LPAD(FLOOR(RAND() * 100000), 5, 0));
                SET random_age = FLOOR(RAND() * 100);

                INSERT INTO mytable (name, age) VALUES
                (random_name, random_age);

                SET i = i + 1;
            END WHILE;
        END$$
Query OK, 0 rows affected (0.01 sec)

mysql> DELIMITER ;
mysql>

mysql> CALL insert_random_records();
Query OK, 1 row affected (8 min 50.07 sec)
mysql>
```

Now, run a *slow* query against the table:

```
mysql> SELECT * FROM mytable WHERE name='Name12908' and age > 30;
+-------+-----------+------+
| id    | name      | age  |
+-------+-----------+------+
| 26596 | Name12908 |   47 |
| 27290 | Name12908 |   98 |
| 72075 | Name12908 |   70 |
+-------+-----------+------+
3 rows in set (0.07 sec)
```

Use the performance schema to identify the slow query by running the following SQL query:

```
mysql> SELECT * FROM performance_schema.events_statements_summary_by_digest
        WHERE digest_text LIKE '%mytable%' ORDER BY sum_timer_wait DESC LIMIT 10\G
*************************** 1. row ***************************
            SCHEMA_NAME: test
                 DIGEST: 74c9fd506a1390b451519bbd394a786fbd879ca33d44a7c1
```

```
                       aa76216df72a209f
                DIGEST_TEXT: SELECT * FROM `mytable` WHERE NAME = ?
                AND `age` > ?
                COUNT_STAR: 1
           SUM_TIMER_WAIT: 64452974000
           MIN_TIMER_WAIT: 64452974000
           AVG_TIMER_WAIT: 64452974000
           MAX_TIMER_WAIT: 64452974000
            SUM_LOCK_TIME: 6000000
               SUM_ERRORS: 0
             SUM_WARNINGS: 0
         SUM_ROWS_AFFECTED: 0
            SUM_ROWS_SENT: 3
         SUM_ROWS_EXAMINED: 143137
SUM_CREATED_TMP_DISK_TABLES: 0
    SUM_CREATED_TMP_TABLES: 0
      SUM_SELECT_FULL_JOIN: 0
 SUM_SELECT_FULL_RANGE_JOIN: 0
         SUM_SELECT_RANGE: 0
    SUM_SELECT_RANGE_CHECK: 0
          SUM_SELECT_SCAN: 1
      SUM_SORT_MERGE_PASSES: 0
           SUM_SORT_RANGE: 0
            SUM_SORT_ROWS: 0
            SUM_SORT_SCAN: 0
         SUM_NO_INDEX_USED: 1
    SUM_NO_GOOD_INDEX_USED: 0
             SUM_CPU_TIME: 0
     MAX_CONTROLLED_MEMORY: 67200
          MAX_TOTAL_MEMORY: 892304
          COUNT_SECONDARY: 0
               FIRST_SEEN: 2024-06-17 14:59:49.452104
                LAST_SEEN: 2024-06-17 14:59:49.452104
              QUANTILE_95: 66069344800
              QUANTILE_99: 66069344800
             QUANTILE_999: 66069344800
         QUERY_SAMPLE_TEXT: SELECT * FROM mytable WHERE name='Name12908'
         and age > 30
         QUERY_SAMPLE_SEEN: 2024-06-17 14:59:49.452104
    QUERY_SAMPLE_TIMER_WAIT: 64452974000
```

This will show you the top 10 slowest queries that contain the word SELECT in their text. In this case, you should see the slow query that you just ran.

Use the EXPLAIN statement to analyze the query execution plan and identify any performance bottlenecks:

```
mysql> explain SELECT * FROM mytable WHERE name='Name12908' and age > 30\G
*************************** 1. row ***************************
           id: 1
  select_type: SIMPLE
        table: mytable
   partitions: NULL
```

```
            type: ALL
    possible_keys: NULL
              key: NULL
          key_len: NULL
              ref: NULL
             rows: 139682
         filtered: 3.33
            Extra: Using where
1 row in set, 1 warning (0.00 sec)
```

Based on the EXPLAIN output, identify any indexes that could be added to improve performance:

```
mysql> ALTER TABLE mytable ADD INDEX nameage_index(name,age);
Query OK, 0 rows affected (1.84 sec)
Records: 0  Duplicates: 0  Warnings: 0
```

Rerun the EXPLAIN statement and verify that performance has improved:

```
mysql> explain SELECT * FROM mytable WHERE name='Name12908' and age > 30\G
*************************** 1. row ***************************
           id: 1
  select_type: SIMPLE
        table: mytable
   partitions: NULL
         type: range
possible_keys: nameage_index
          key: nameage_index
      key_len: 208
          ref: NULL
         rows: 3
     filtered: 100.00
        Extra: Using where; Using index
1 row in set, 1 warning (0.00 sec)
```

After rerunning the query, use the performance schema to verify that it is now running faster:

```
mysql> SELECT * FROM mytable WHERE name='Name12908' and age > 30;
+-------+-----------+------+
| id    | name      | age  |
+-------+-----------+------+
| 26596 | Name12908 |   47 |
| 72075 | Name12908 |   70 |
| 27290 | Name12908 |   98 |
+-------+-----------+------+
3 rows in set (0.00 sec)

mysql> SELECT * FROM performance_schema.events_statements_summary_by_digest
    WHERE digest_text LIKE '%mytable%' ORDER BY sum_timer_wait DESC LIMIT 10\G
*************************** 2. row ***************************
            SCHEMA_NAME: test
                 DIGEST: 74c9fd506a1390b451519bbd394a786fbd879ca33d44a7c1
                         aa76216df72a209f
```

```
                DIGEST_TEXT: SELECT * FROM mytable WHERE NAME = ?
                AND age > ?
                 COUNT_STAR: 3
             SUM_TIMER_WAIT: 46249439000
             MIN_TIMER_WAIT: 721772000
             AVG_TIMER_WAIT: 15416479000
             MAX_TIMER_WAIT: 44787707000
              SUM_LOCK_TIME: 23000000
                 SUM_ERRORS: 0
               SUM_WARNINGS: 0
          SUM_ROWS_AFFECTED: 0
              SUM_ROWS_SENT: 9
          SUM_ROWS_EXAMINED: 98830
 SUM_CREATED_TMP_DISK_TABLES: 0
      SUM_CREATED_TMP_TABLES: 0
         SUM_SELECT_FULL_JOIN: 0
  SUM_SELECT_FULL_RANGE_JOIN: 0
            SUM_SELECT_RANGE: 3
       SUM_SELECT_RANGE_CHECK: 0
             SUM_SELECT_SCAN: 0
        SUM_SORT_MERGE_PASSES: 0
              SUM_SORT_RANGE: 0
               SUM_SORT_ROWS: 0
               SUM_SORT_SCAN: 0
            SUM_NO_INDEX_USED: 0
        SUM_NO_GOOD_INDEX_USED: 0
                SUM_CPU_TIME: 0
       MAX_CONTROLLED_MEMORY: 50768
            MAX_TOTAL_MEMORY: 3103478
             COUNT_SECONDARY: 0
                  FIRST_SEEN: 2024-06-17 15:09:52.807844
                   LAST_SEEN: 2024-06-17 15:28:04.788340
                 QUANTILE_95: 45708818961
                 QUANTILE_99: 45708818961
                QUANTILE_999: 45708818961
           QUERY_SAMPLE_TEXT: SELECT * FROM mytable WHERE name='Name12908'
                and age > 30
           QUERY_SAMPLE_SEEN: 2024-06-17 15:28:04.788340
     QUERY_SAMPLE_TIMER_WAIT: 739960000
```

By following this process, you can use the performance schema to identify and optimize slow queries, ultimately improving the performance of your database.

Conclusion

This chapter equips you with essential knowledge and practical techniques to enhance MySQL database performance by addressing hardware- and software-related factors, query optimization, and the effective use of performance-monitoring tools like MySQL performance schema.

## CHAPTER 9

MySQL Monitoring and Management

As your MySQL database grows in size and complexity, monitoring and management become increasingly important tasks. Fortunately, MySQL provides several tools and techniques for monitoring and managing your database effectively. In this chapter, we cover the essential concepts of MySQL monitoring and management and explore the most useful tools and best practices for these tasks.

Understanding Essential Management Concepts

Monitoring and managing MySQL are crucial for ensuring optimal performance, detecting and fixing issues, preventing downtime, and ensuring data security. Effective monitoring and management practices can help organizations in the following ways:

Performance optimization
> Monitoring helps identify and resolve performance bottlenecks and optimize the database for efficient operations.

Security
> Monitoring can detect and prevent security threats, such as SQL injection attacks, unauthorized access, and data breaches.

Compliance
> Monitoring and management can help ensure compliance with regulatory requirements, such as GDPR, HIPAA, and Payment Card Industry Data Security Standard (PCI DSS).

Availability
> Monitoring can help ensure high availability and uptime of the database systems.

Capacity planning
> Monitoring can provide insights into resource usage trends and help plan for capacity upgrades and expansions.

To monitor the performance of MySQL databases, it is essential to track key performance indicators (KPIs). Critical KPIs to monitor include the following:

CPU utilization
> The percentage of CPU resources used by MySQL

Memory usage
> The amount of memory used by the MySQL server and its processes

Disk I/O
> The IOPS and throughput of the disk subsystem

Connection count
> The number of active database connections

Replication lag
> The time difference between the source and replica database servers in a replication setup

Several monitoring tools are available for MySQL, including the following open source options:

Percona Monitoring and Management (PMM)
> Provides real-time performance and security metrics, query analysis, and trend analysis

Nagios
> Supports alerting, reporting, and trend analysis for MySQL databases

Zabbix
> Supports monitoring of MySQL performance and availability

Capacity planning is the process of estimating the future resource requirements of a MySQL database system and planning for capacity upgrades and expansions. Monitoring plays a critical role in capacity planning by providing insights into the resource usage trends and patterns over time. With this information, DBAs can predict future resource requirements and plan for capacity upgrades and expansions accordingly.

MySQL management involves a variety of tasks, including these:

Configuration management
> Configuring and optimizing the MySQL server and its components for optimal performance, security, and availability

Backup and recovery
> Developing and implementing backup and recovery plans to ensure data availability and minimize data loss

Security management
> Implementing security measures, such as user access control, authentication, and encryption, to protect the database from unauthorized access and data breaches

Performance tuning
> Optimizing the database and its components for efficient operations, such as tuning the InnoDB buffer pool, optimizing the table structure, and indexing

Maintenance and patching
> Performing routine maintenance tasks, such as database vacuuming, index optimization, and patching, to ensure that the database systems are running optimally and securely

Percona Monitoring and Management

PMM is an open source platform designed to help database and system administrators monitor and manage their database environments efficiently. It provides a comprehensive set of metrics for monitoring resource usage, system metrics, and query performance. PMM offers real-time monitoring, historical data analysis, query analytics, and alerting to identify and troubleshoot performance issues effectively.

Quick PMM Server Installation

Installing PMM server and client on Docker-compatible Unix-based systems is a streamlined process that brings powerful monitoring and management capabilities to your database infrastructure. With PMM, you can easily deploy a PMM server instance in a Docker container, allowing you to efficiently monitor your database environments. Additionally, you can set up PMM client on your database hosts, enabling data collection and communication with the PMM server. This installation method provides a flexible and containerized solution for database monitoring, making it easier to keep a close eye on your database performance and health.

We've streamlined the installation process with a convenient script that ensures all required software is installed. Run the following command with `sudo` privileges or as root:

```
curl -fsSL https://www.percona.com/get/pmm | /bin/bash
```

Upon completion, the installation will provide details on accessing the interface and default login credentials.

PMM Client Installation

For a client installation, we'll illustrate with a Red Hat example; follow these steps:

1. Download and install the Percona repo package:

   ```
   sudo yum install https://repo.percona.com/yum/
   percona-release-latest.noarch.rpm
   ```

2. Install the PMM Client:

   ```
   sudo yum install pmm2-client
   ```

   To connect the client to the server, you must meet specific requirements. This includes ensuring client-to-server communication occurs on a secure port (assumed as 443) on the PMM server, a step that must be performed on every monitored system. Additionally, you need to register the PMM client with the server.

3. Register the PMM client with the server:

   ```
   sudo pmm-admin config --server-insecure-tls --server-url=https://
   admin:<password>@pmm.example.com
   ```

4. Create a dedicated PMM user for monitoring by using the MySQL CLI:

   ```
   CREATE USER 'pmm'@'localhost' IDENTIFIED BY 'pass' WITH MAX_USER_CONNECTIONS
   10;
   GRANT SELECT, PROCESS, SUPER, REPLICATION CLIENT, RELOAD, BACKUP_ADMIN ON *.*
   TO 'pmm'@'localhost';
   ```

5. Register the server for monitoring:

   ```
   sudo pmm-admin add mysql --username=pmm --password=<password>
   --query-source=perfschema
   ```

MySQL Enterprise Monitor

MySQL Enterprise Monitor is a powerful tool that helps DBAs and developers monitor and manage MySQL databases. It provides a comprehensive view of your MySQL environment, allowing you to identify and resolve performance issues before they impact your applications. This section covers the installation, configuration, and usage of MySQL Enterprise Monitor.

Installing and Configuring MySQL Enterprise Monitor

To use MySQL Enterprise Monitor, you must first install and configure it on your system. The installation process is straightforward and can be completed in a few simple steps. Once it's installed, you can configure it to monitor one or more MySQL instances. You can configure alerts and notifications to receive real-time updates on your database's health.

Understanding MySQL monitoring and management concepts is essential for successful management of MySQL databases. Installing MySQL Enterprise Service Manager is a critical part of this process, as it enables users to monitor and manage their MySQL servers from a central location.

Installing MySQL Enterprise Service Manager

Before installing, ensure that the installer is executable on Unix and Linux platforms. We also recommend installing MySQL Enterprise Service Manager with root privileges. However, it shouldn't be run as the root user. After installing with root access, you must create a dedicated user for MySQL Enterprise Service Manager. If MySQL Enterprise Service Manager is installed without root privileges, it will not automatically initialize on system boot and must be started manually.

To install MySQL Enterprise Service Manager, follow these steps:

1. Execute the installer as per the operating system's requirements.

2. Select a language and then click OK in the Language Selection dialog.

3. Click Forward in the Welcome dialog.

4. Select the installation directory or simply accept the default path in the Installation Directory dialog; then click Forward.

5. Pick the necessary installation size from the options available in the Select Requirements dialog. The installer allows you to select the installation type, which configures parameters appropriate for your chosen installation type:

   Small
   > Monitor one to five MySQL servers using a laptop or a low-end server with a maximum of 4 GB of RAM.

   Medium
   > Monitor as many as one hundred MySQL servers using a medium-sized, shared server with a RAM capacity ranging from 4 to 8 GB.

   Large
   > Monitor over one hundred MySQL servers from a dedicated high-end server exclusively designated for MySQL Enterprise Service Manager, boasting more than 8 GB of RAM.

6. Click Forward.

7. Fill out the Tomcat Server Options dialog as necessary. The default value for the Tomcat Server port is 18080, while the Tomcat SSL port defaults to 18443. This port is essential for communication with Agents, as they are required to use SSL for interaction with MySQL Enterprise Service Manager.

8. In the Service Manager User Account dialog, input the username that MySQL Enterprise Service Manager should operate under. If this user account doesn't already exist, the installer will create it. Afterward, click Forward.

9. Choose one of the following options in the Database Installation dialog:

   - I want to use the bundled MySQL database: Choose this option to install a MySQL server. By selecting this option, the installation procedure will grant full control of the repository to the Service Manager user defined during the installation proccss.

   - I want to use an existing MySQL database: Choose this option to use an existing MySQL server as the repository. If you opt for this choice, ensure that the prerequisites for the MySQL Enterprise Monitor Repository are satisfied prior to installing MySQL Enterprise Service Manager.

10. Click Forward.

11. Fill in the fields in the Repository Configuration dialog as follows:

    Repository username
    Provide the username that MySQL Enterprise Service Manager uses to establish a connection with the repository. If you've opted to utilize an existing database, this user should already exist within the target MySQL instance. The default username is `service_manager`.

    Password/re-enter
    Input the password and confirm it by entering it again in the Re-enter field.

    MySQL hostname or IP address
    (Shown when selecting to utilize an existing MySQL database only.) Input the hostname or IP address of the MySQL instance.

    MySQL database port
    Enter the port number that MySQL Enterprise Service Manager utilizes to connect to the MySQL instance. If you've selected the bundled repository, the default port number is 13306. If you've opted for an existing instance, the default port number is 3306.

    MySQL database name
    Provide the name for the MySQL Enterprise Service Manager repository. Each MySQL Enterprise Service Manager should have a distinct repository name, as sharing a repository among multiple MySQL Enterprise Service Managers is not supported.

12. Click Forward. If you're trying to use a MySQL version earlier than MySQL Server 5.7.9 as an external repository, you will encounter an error, and the

installation won't succeed. The minimum required version is MySQL Server 5.7.9, while MySQL Server 5.7.18 is the recommended version.

13. The Configuration Report dialog appears. Click Forward to proceed with the installation of MySQL Enterprise Service Manager.

Accessing the Installation Logfile for MySQL Enterprise Service Manager

The logfile generated during installation is saved at the root of the installation directory and named *install.log*, following a standard naming convention. This logfile provides a comprehensive record of all files installed and the actions performed by the installer, including starting services, populating database tables, and more.

Similarly, the uninstall process also generates a logfile. In case of an upgrade installation, the existing installation logfile is automatically backed up to the backup directory, and the new logfile for the upgrade replaces the previous one. This ensures that a complete record of the installation is maintained throughout the upgrade process.

Using MySQL Enterprise Monitor

MySQL Enterprise Monitor provides a comprehensive view of your MySQL instances. It monitors your database's key metrics, including CPU usage, memory usage, disk I/O, network traffic, and more. You can view this information in real time or generate historical reports to identify trends and potential issues. With MySQL Enterprise Monitor, you can easily identify performance bottlenecks and optimize your MySQL instances for better performance.

MySQL Enterprise Monitor includes a powerful Query Analyzer tool that allows you to diagnose performance issues quickly. You can analyze your SQL queries, identify slow queries, and optimize them for better performance. You can also analyze your database schema and identify potential schema design issues that may impact performance.

MySQL Enterprise Monitor includes an Enterprise Backup dashboard that allows you to easily manage MySQL backups. You can schedule backups, monitor backup status, and generate reports on backup activity. With MySQL Enterprise Monitor, you can ensure that your database backups are up-to-date and that you can recover your data in case of a disaster.

MySQL Enterprise Monitor includes an upgrade advisor that provides guidance on upgrading your MySQL instances. You can use this tool to analyze your environment and identify potential issues that may impact your upgrade. The upgrade advisor provides recommendations on upgrading your MySQL instances and helps you ensure a smooth and successful upgrade process.

MySQL Workbench

MySQL Workbench serves as a visual tool tailored for database architects, developers, and administrators. It facilitates the design, creation, and management of MySQL databases by offering a user-friendly interface. This interface supports a wide array of database-related functions, such as database modeling, querying, administration, and performance tuning.

Installation and Configuration of MySQL Workbench

The process of installing MySQL Workbench is simple and involves downloading the suitable installer from the MySQL website. Once the installation is complete, you'll need to configure MySQL Workbench to establish a connection with your MySQL server. To achieve this, follow these steps:

1. Open MySQL Workbench.
2. Click the Setup New Connection button.
3. Enter the connection details, such as the hostname, port number, username, and password.
4. Test the connection to make sure it's successful.
5. Save the connection details for future use.

MySQL Workbench Performance Monitoring Tools

MySQL Workbench offers a variety of tools for monitoring MySQL instances and diagnosing performance problems:

Server status dashboard
Presents real-time data concerning the server's condition, encompassing CPU and memory usage, connections, and queries

Performance schema dashboard
Offers detailed insights into server performance, including details on query execution times, table scans, and index usage

SQL performance analyzer
Assesses SQL statements and detects performance bottlenecks

Database Creation and Management with MySQL Workbench

MySQL Workbench offers a range of tools for creating and managing MySQL databases:

Database modeling
> Enables you to design and modify database schema diagrams through a drag-and-drop interface

SQL editor
> Enables you to write and execute SQL statements, including tasks like table creation, data insertion, and data querying

Schema synchronization
> Enables you to synchronize the schema of two databases, whether they are on the same server or different servers

How do you use MySQL Workbench for a common task, such as creating a new database and table? Follow these steps:

1. Launch MySQL Workbench and establish a connection to your MySQL server by clicking the Setup New Connection button and providing your connection information. Once it's connected, access the database modeling tool by clicking the "Create a new schema" button located in the sidebar.

2. Within the database modeling tool, you can initiate a new table creation process. Simply choose the Table tool from the toolbar and then drag it onto the canvas.

3. Give a name to your table and proceed to incorporate the desired columns by clicking the Columns tool and dragging it onto the canvas.

4. For each column, define the column name, data type, and any other pertinent properties, such as length or default value.

5. After creating all your columns, you can select the Index, Constraint, or Relationship tools to define indexes, constraints, or relationships and then drag them onto the canvas.

6. To preserve your database schema, click Save in the toolbar, and provide a name for your schema when prompted.

7. After saving your schema, you can produce the SQL script for building your database and tables by choosing Database > Forward Engineer from the main menu.

8. Within the Forward Engineering wizard, pick your database schema and configure the settings for constructing your database and table. Additionally, you have the option to decide whether to incorporate any data into your table at this stage.

9. Click Next and inspect the SQL script that is about to be generated. If everything appears accurate, click Execute to proceed with creating your database and table.

With these steps, you can effortlessly establish a fresh database and table via MySQL Workbench. This tool boasts a user-friendly interface and robust functionalities, simplifying MySQL database management and facilitating various database-related tasks.

Backup and Recovery Solutions with MySQL Workbench

MySQL Workbench provides a range of tools to perform backup and recovery tasks:

Backup and Restore wizard
Creates and restores backups of databases, including both full and incremental backups.

Point-in-time recovery
Recovers a database to a specific point in time, using binary logfiles.

Data export and import
Exports and imports data between MySQL databases and other file formats, such as CSV and JSON.

Performance Diagnosis Tools in MySQL Workbench

MySQL Workbench offers an array of diagnostic tools designed to identify and address performance-related issues:

Query profiler
Profiles SQL queries and identifies performance bottlenecks, such as slow queries and full table scans

Visual explain plan
Displays a visual representation of the query execution plan, allowing you to identify performance issues

Performance reports
Provides detailed performance reports, including query execution times, buffer pool usage, and lock waits

MySQL Command-Line Tools

MySQL command-line tools enable DBAs and developers to interact with MySQL instances through a terminal or command prompt. These tools can be used to perform a wide range of tasks, including creating and managing databases, executing SQL queries, and managing user accounts:

`mysql`
This is the most commonly used MySQL client tool that allows you to connect to a MySQL instance and execute SQL statements. You can use this tool to perform various tasks such as creating and modifying databases, tables, and users.

`mysqlshell`

> This is a powerful command-line tool and scripting environment provided by MySQL for interacting with MySQL database instances. It is a versatile tool that offers multiple interfaces, including SQL, JavaScript, and Python, allowing DBAs and developers to work with MySQL databases in various ways.

`mysqladmin`

> This tool allows you to perform various administrative tasks such as starting and stopping the MySQL server, checking the status of the server, and managing user accounts.

`mysqlbinlog`

> This tool lets you read and analyze binary log files, which are used to record changes to MySQL databases. You can use this tool to perform various tasks such as recovering data, replicating databases, and troubleshooting issues.

`mysqlimport`

> This tool allows you to import data from external sources into MySQL databases. You can use this tool to import data from CSV files, text files, and other database systems.

`mysqlslap`

> This utility can be used to simulate load on a MySQL server. It is particularly useful for testing the performance of a MySQL instance under multiple scenarios.

Managing MySQL Logs

MySQL logs are an essential component of MySQL database management. They provide a way to track database activity, diagnose errors, and monitor performance. There are several types of MySQL logs, each with a specific purpose. The following are the most commonly used types:

Error log

> Logs all errors experienced by the MySQL server, encompassing startup, shutdown, and runtime errors.

Slow query log

> Captures SQL statements with execution times exceeding a defined threshold, aiding in the identification of performance bottlenecks.

Binary log

> Contains a record of all modifications made to the database, including `INSERT`, `UPDATE`, and `DELETE` statements. It is used for replication and PITR.

General query log

 Records every SQL statement executed by the MySQL server, including those executed by users, applications, and scripts.

Configuring MySQL logs involves modifying the MySQL configuration file to specify the log type, location, and verbosity level. The following is an example configuration for each type of MySQL log:

1. To configure the error log, add the following to the MySQL configuration file:

   ```
   [mysqld]
   log_error=/var/log/mysql/error.log
   ```

   This specifies the location of the error logfile.

2. To configure the general query log, add the following to the MySQL configuration file:

   ```
   [mysqld]
   general_log=1
   general_log_file=/var/log/mysql/query.log
   ```

   This enables the general query log and specifies the location of the logfile.

3. To configure the binary log, add the following to the MySQL configuration file:

   ```
   [mysqld]
   log_bin=/var/log/mysql/bin.log
   ```

   This enables the binary log and specifies the location of the logfile.

4. To configure the slow query log, add this to the MySQL configuration file:

   ```
   [mysqld]
   slow_query_log=1
   slow_query_log_file=/var/log/mysql/slow_query.log
   long_query_time=5
   ```

   This enables the slow query log, specifies the location of the logfile, and sets the minimum execution time for a query to be considered slow to 5 seconds.

Conclusion

This chapter comprehensively explored MySQL database monitoring and management. It underscored the importance of these practices in ensuring performance and security, introducing KPIs and best practices for enhancing database performance. This chapter has given you a well-rounded understanding of MySQL monitoring and management principles and tools.

## CHAPTER 10

How to Facilitate Major MySQL Upgrades

This chapter explores the critical process of facilitating major MySQL upgrades. It covers server-side testing using MySQL Shell upgrade checker and application-side query testing with the `pt-upgrade` tool. The chapter outlines the requirements and steps for testing application queries, including a high-level plan. It delves into read-only and read/write testing using `pt-upgrade`. The chapter also discusses production upgrade strategies, including in-place upgrades and setting up a new environment with cutover.

The Significance of Upgrading MySQL Major Versions

Upgrading the major version of MySQL is an important process that can provide many benefits to your database. The upgrade installs a new version of MySQL and migrates your data from the old version to the new one. In this process, the database structure and configuration may also need to be changed, so it's important to plan and test the upgrade process carefully before making any changes to production systems.

One of the main reasons to upgrade the major version of MySQL is security. Major version upgrades often include important security updates and patches that can protect your database from vulnerabilities and exploits. As hackers and attackers continue to find new ways to exploit databases, it's important to keep your database up-to-date with the latest security patches and upgrades.

Another reason to upgrade the major version of MySQL is performance. New versions of MySQL may include optimizations that can improve database performance and speed up queries. These optimizations may include improvements to indexing, caching, and other performance-related features that can make your database faster and more efficient.

Upgrading to a new major version can also give you access to new features and functionality that may not be available in previous versions. For example, MySQL 8 introduced new JSON features, improved performance and scalability, and added support for new data types. These features can be very useful for developers and DBAs who need to work with complex data structures and large data sets.

As MySQL continues to evolve, older versions may no longer be supported. This can leave your database vulnerable to bugs and security issues that may not be fixed. Upgrading to a supported version can ensure that you have access to bug fixes and technical support if needed.

Finally, upgrading to a new major version can help ensure compatibility with other applications and tools that may require a specific version of MySQL to function properly. For example, if you're using a third-party application that requires MySQL 8 or later, upgrading to that version can help ensure that the application continues to work as intended.

In summary, upgrading the major version of MySQL is an important process that can provide many benefits to your database. However, it's important to plan and test the upgrade process carefully to ensure that your database remains stable and functional during and after the upgrade.

Server-Side Testing (MySQL Shell Upgrade Checker)

MySQL Shell upgrade checker is a useful utility that assists in compatibility testing between MySQL 5.7 instances and MySQL 8 upgrades. It is included in the *mysql-shell-utilities* package, which provides various tools and utilities for database administrators to manage their MySQL environment.

The util.checkForServerUpgrade() function is a crucial component of the MySQL Shell upgrade checker. This function performs checks to determine whether the MySQL 5.7 instance is ready for the MySQL 8 upgrade and generates a report that includes warnings, errors, and notices for preparing the current MySQL 5.7 setup for upgrading to MySQL 8.

To generate the report, we recommend running the upgrade checker utility in the current MySQL 5.7 environment. It is advisable to run it on one of the replica instances that have the same configuration as the production environment. This way, the results obtained are more representative of what would be expected in the production environment.

Note that the user account used to execute the upgrade checker tool must have *all* rights up to MySQL Shell 8.0.20. As of MySQL Shell 8.0.21, the user account requires additional capabilities such as RELOAD, PROCESS, and SELECT. Therefore, it is crucial to ensure that the user account used to execute the upgrade checker tool has the required permissions to avoid any issues during the upgrade process.

To generate a report by using the upgrade checker utility, two options are available. The first option is to log in to the shell prompt, while the second is to execute the utility directly from the command prompt:

```
$ mysqlsh

MySQL JS > util.checkForServerUpgrade('mysquser@localhost:3306', \{
"targetVersion":"8.0.32", "configPath":"/etc/my.cnf"})
Please provide the password for 'mysqluser@localhost:3306':
To exit the mysqlsh command prompt, simply enter the command "\exit".
MySQL JS > \exit

Bye!
```

You have the flexibility to choose between two options for running the upgrade check by using mysqlsh. You can either run it interactively using the mysqlsh command and provide the password within the session as shown previously, or you can run it directly with command-line parameters for convenience. Both options (the preceding block and the following one) serve the same purpose, allowing you to check for a server upgrade. You can opt for the one that suits your workflow or preferences—this one involves running directly with command-line parameters:

```
mysqlsh -- util checkForServerUpgrade 'mysquser@localhost:3306'
--target-version=8.0.32 --config-path=/etc/my.cnf >
CheckForServerUpgrade_Report.txt
Please provide the password for 'mysquser@localhost:3306':
```

This is an example of running the tool directly with command-line parameters:

```
# mysqlsh -- util checkForServerUpgrade 'root@localhost:3306'
--target-version=8.0.32 --config-path=/etc/my.cnf | grep -B 6 -i
"query_cache"

15) Removed system variables
Error: Following system variables that were detected as being used will be
removed. Please update your system to not rely on them before the upgrade.
More information:
https://dev.mysql.com/doc/refman/8.0/en/added-deprecated-removed.html
#optvars-removed
query_cache_size - is set and will be removed
ERROR: 1 errors were found. Please correct these issues before upgrading
to avoid compatibility issues.
```

To get the report in JSON format, use --output-format=JSON:

```
# mysqlsh -- util checkForServerUpgrade 'root@localhost:3306'
--target-version=8.0.32 --config-path=/etc/my.cnf --output-format=JSON
```

Application-Side Query Testing

Databases running on outdated versions are at risk of missing new features, performance improvements, and bug fixes. However, upgrading to a major version can pose challenges if not properly tested with the application. The upgrade process may cause the application to break, fail to function correctly, or lead to performance issues.

Percona Toolkit offers three tools to aid in the upgrade process. First, there's `pt-upgrade`, which is a tool that allows you to execute application `SELECT` queries and generate reports on how each query pattern performs on different versions of MySQL that have been tested.

Then, there's `pt-query-digest`, which helps you gather all application queries by enabling the slow log for a period of time. However, the slow log can become quite extensive, and applying it can be time-consuming. This is where the `pt-querydigest` tool comes in handy, as it can assist in query digest preparation for upgrade testing.

Finally, there's `pt-config-diff`, a tool that can help you identify the differences in MySQL settings between files and server variables. This tool allows you to compare the upgraded version with the previous version and validate the configuration differences. For example, you can use `pt-config-diff` as follows:

```
pt-config-diff h=<Testnode1> h=<Testnode2>
```

This command instructs `pt-config-diff` to compare the MySQL configurations on two specified nodes, helping you pinpoint any variations in their settings.

Testing Application Queries Using pt-upgrade

You should have two servers that meet production specifications and are connected to the same network for testing purposes. For instance, if you wish to test MySQL 5.7 and MySQL 8, you'll need two instances—one with MySQL 5.7 and the other with MySQL 8, both from a recent production backup.

You must set up replication for both test nodes for a day, replicating from the production primary to see if the replication works from the lower current production version to the newer version (i.e., covering the actual application workload). Before you begin `pt-upgrade` testing, you need to stop replication on both test nodes at the same binary log position to ensure the data in both nodes are identical.

To ensure a smooth `pt-upgrade` testing process, follow these high-level steps:

1. Install MySQL on both test nodes, with the current version on one node and the target version on the other.
2. Restore the production data to the test nodes using Percona XtraBackup.

3. Set up replication for both test nodes for a day, covering the actual workload, replicating from the production primary.

4. Use the slow log to collect all queries from the production nodes by using `long_query_time = 0` and `log_slow_rate_limit = 1`. You need to activate the slow log for a day or a few hours, covering most of the application queries. However, in most cases, the slow log will be massive, and applying queries in it using the `pt-upgrade` tool will take time, so you can use the `pt-query-digest` tool to prepare a query digest for `pt-upgrade` testing.

5. In the query digest, for example, you can take a maximum of 50 samples per query:

```
pt-query-digest --sample 50 --no-report --output slowlog <slow_log_file>
> <digest>.out
```

If any of the following session variables are detected in the digested slow log, they should be reviewed and possibly removed to ensure that queries can continue to run smoothly:

```
MAX_JOIN_SIZE=....,SET SQL_SAFE_UPDATES=...,SQL_SELECT_LIMIT=...
```

To ensure that the data on both test nodes is consistent before conducting `pt-upgrade` tests, replication on both nodes must be stopped at the same binary log position.

Read-only Testing Using pt-upgrade

After ensuring that the data is identical, use the `pt-upgrade` tool play back all queries in read-only mode two times on the test nodes, with the results logged. You can ignore the results of the first run because it's simply warming up the InnoDB Buffer pool. Execute the same `pt-upgrade` command again to obtain accurate results:

```
$ pt-upgrade h=TestNode1_V5.7 h=TestNode2_V8.0 --max-examples=1
<digest>.out 1> pt-upgrade_results.out 2> pt-upgrade_results.err
```

Read/Write Testing Using pt-upgrade

Execute the queries in read/write mode on the test nodes while enabling the `--no-read-only` option, and log the results:

```
$ pt-upgrade h=TestNode1_V5.7 h=TesNodet2_V8.0 --no-read-only
--max-examples=1 <digest>.out 1> pt-upgrade_results_RW.out 2>
pt-upgrade_results_RW.err
```

After completing the read-only and read/write tests, you can analyze the reports to identify queries that are slower, return more/fewer rows, or produce different results than expected, as well as any errors or warnings. Based on the findings of the `pt-upgrade` testing, you can make improvements to address the issues. This may involve changes to the MySQL setup, query optimization, query rewriting, schema modifications, index additions or revisions, and other actions to improve performance and functionality. By addressing the issues highlighted by pt-upgrade, you can ensure a smooth upgrade process and minimize the risk of problems arising when you upgrade to a new version of MySQL.

Here's one example of how a failed query is reported by the tool:

```
####################################################################
# Query class B14316CG59AD6215
####################################################################
Reporting class because there are 1 query errors.
Total queries 1
Unique queries 1
Discarded queries 0
insert into mytable (emp_id, date) values(?+)
##
## Query errors diffs: 1
##
-- 1.
No error
vs.
DBD::mysql::st execute failed: Column 'date' cannot be null [for
Statement "INSERT INTO mytable (emp_id, date VALUES (20, NULL)"]
INSERT INTO mytable (emp_id, date) VALUES (20, NULL)
```

Let's attempt to manually create the test table and insert records to identify why it was flagged by the pt-upgrade tool. Review the example carefully:

```
MySQL 5.7:

mysql> CREATE TABLE `mytable` (
 -> `id` bigint(20) NOT NULL AUTO_INCREMENT,
 -> `emp_id` int(11) DEFAULT NULL,
 -> `date` timestamp *NOT NULL* DEFAULT CURRENT_TIMESTAMP,
 -> PRIMARY KEY (`id`),
 -> KEY `index1` (`emp_id`)
 -> ) ENGINE=InnoDB AUTO_INCREMENT=247416795 DEFAULT CHARSET=utf8
ROW_FORMAT=COMPRESSED ENCRYPTION='Y';
Query OK, 0 rows affected (0.08 sec)

mysql> INSERT INTO mytable (emp_id,date) VALUES (10, NULL);
Query OK, 1 row affected (0.01 sec)

MySQL 8.0.15:

mysql> CREATE TABLE `mytable` (
 -> `id` bigint(20) NOT NULL AUTO_INCREMENT,
 -> `emp_id` int(11) DEFAULT NULL,
 -> `date` timestamp *NOT NULL* DEFAULT CURRENT_TIMESTAMP,
 -> PRIMARY KEY (`id`),
 -> KEY `index1` (`emp_id`)
```

```
-> ) ENGINE=InnoDB AUTO_INCREMENT=247416795 DEFAULT CHARSET=utf8
ROW_FORMAT=COMPRESSED ENCRYPTION='Y';

Query OK, 0 rows affected, 1 warning (0.08 sec)

mysql> INSERT INTO mytable (emp_id,date) VALUES (10, *NULL*);

ERROR 1048 (23000): Column 'date' cannot be null

mysql> INSERT INTO mytable (emp_id,date) VALUES (10,*'2022-03-07
03:38:04'*);

Query OK, 1 row affected (0.01 sec)

mysql> CREATE TABLE `mytable` (
-> `id` bigint(20) NOT NULL AUTO_INCREMENT,
-> `emp_id` int(11) DEFAULT NULL,
-> *`date` timestamp DEFAULT CURRENT_TIMESTAMP,*
-> PRIMARY KEY (`id`),
-> KEY `index1` (`emp_id`)
-> ) ENGINE=InnoDB AUTO_INCREMENT=247416795 DEFAULT CHARSET=utf8
ROW_FORMAT=COMPRESSED ENCRYPTION='Y';

Query OK, 0 rows affected, 1 warning (0.05 sec)

mysql> INSERT INTO mytable (emp_id,date) VALUES (10, *NULL*);

Query OK, 1 row affected (0.00 sec)
```

Our upgrade project will be divided into two phases: testing and actual production upgrade. In the testing phase, we will use tools to assess the upgrade and based on the findings, we will plan the actual upgrade for the production phase. The testing phase will require a significant amount of time and planning prior to the actual upgrade to minimize potential issues and troubleshooting in the eleventh hour during production upgrade. This approach will help reduce the actual production upgrade time and ensure a smoother transition.

Production Upgrade Strategy

You have two main options for performing a MySQL upgrade: in-place or stand-up a new environment and cutover. The in-place upgrade option has the advantage of requiring less additional infrastructure cost since it requires only the test nodes. However, this type of upgrade can take some time to complete with cooldown periods between reader node upgrades. Additionally, failing over production traffic may be necessary, and in order to achieve zero downtime, good HA tools are required.

On the other hand, the stand-up a new environment and cutover option may have additional infrastructure costs since both the operating system and the database management system (DBMS) need to be upgraded at the same time. However, this approach allows for the concurrent upgrade of hardware, which can be advantageous. Only one cutover window is required for this option.

in-place Upgrade (Async)

To perform an in-place major version upgrade of MySQL, follow these steps:

1. Set the `innodb_fast_shutdown` to 0. When the InnoDB shutdown mode is set to 0, it triggers a gradual shutdown process: InnoDB performs a complete purge and change buffer merge before finally shutting down.

2. Stop the MySQL server and make a backup of the configuration file.

3. Remove the old binaries to install the targeted version of MySQL.

4. Update the configuration file (*my.cnf*) with any necessary changes for the new version.

5. Start the MySQL server by using the new binaries.

6. Run the `mysql_upgrade` command to perform any necessary upgrade tasks. Note that as of MySQL 8.0.16, the MySQL server performs these tasks automatically during startup.

7. Restart the MySQL server to ensure that any changes to the configuration file take effect.

To perform an in-place upgrade, the MySQL server must be shut down and its binaries or packages replaced with the new ones. After that, MySQL should be restarted using the existing data directory, and `mysql_upgrade` should be run. Starting from MySQL 8.0.16, the MySQL server automatically carries out the `mysql_upgrade` tasks during the startup process:

1. Before stopping MySQL, set `innodb_fast_shutdown` to 0 in InnoDB to initiate a slow shutdown, performing a full purge and change buffer merge before the shutdown process completes:

```
mysql> SET GLOBAL innodb_fast_shutdown=0;
Query OK, 0 rows affected (0.00 sec)
mysql>
```

2. To upgrade MySQL, stop the instance gracefully:

```
[root@mysql8 ~]# systemctl stop mysqld
[root@mysql8 ~]#
```

3. Ensure that MySQL has been cleanly stopped by verifying the log:

```
[root@mysql8 ~]# tail -10 /var/log/mysqld.log
2024-02-22T05:41:03.033560Z 0 [Note] InnoDB: Buffer pool(s) dump
completed at 240222  5:41:03
2024-02-22T05:41:04.142262Z 0 [Note] InnoDB: Shutdown completed;
log sequence number 2769150
2024-02-22T05:41:04.143376Z 0 [Note] InnoDB: Removed temporary tablespace
data file: "ibtmp1"
2024-02-22T05:41:04.143405Z 0 [Note] Shutting down plugin 'MEMORY'
2024-02-22T05:41:04.143414Z 0 [Note] Shutting down plugin 'CSV'
2024-02-22T05:41:04.143419Z 0 [Note] Shutting down plugin 'sha256_password'
2024-02-22T05:41:04.143422Z 0 [Note] Shutting down plugin
'mysql_native_password'
2024-02-22T05:41:04.143646Z 0 [Note] Shutting down plugin 'binlog'
2024-02-22T05:41:04.144105Z 0 [Note] /usr/sbin/mysqld: Shutdown complete
```

4. Create a backup of the *my.cnf* file and then make the necessary updates to the configuration:

```
[root@mysql8 ~]# cp /etc/my.cnf /etc/my.cnf_bkp22Feb2024
[root@mysql8 ~]#
```

During the testing phase in this example, the MySQL Shell upgrade checker utility flagged the query_cache_size as a problem that needs to be removed from the *my.cnf* configuration file. The following code is just one example of the server-side testing report and pt-upgrade report, which highlights the need to update any deprecated, removed, or recommended changes in the configuration file:

```
vi /etc/my.cnf
….
query_cache_size=128M
query_cache_type=1
--> Based on the aforesaid example report, the variable needs to be removed.
….
esc :wq (Save the configuration file)
```

5. Generate a list of packages related to MySQL 5.7 and uninstall them:

```
[root@mysql8 ~]# yum list installed | grep mysql
mysql-community-client.x86_64
5.7.44-1.el7                            @mysql57-community
mysql-community-common.x86_64
5.7.44-1.el7                            @mysql57-community
mysql-community-libs.x86_64
5.7.44-1.el7                            @mysql57-community
mysql-community-server.x86_64
5.7.44-1.el7                            @mysql57-community
mysql57-community-release.noarch
el7-9                                   @System
[root@mysql8 ~]#
```

6. Remove the MySQL Community Edition server package with version 5.7.41-1.el7.x86_64 on a system using the yum package manager:

```
[root@mysql8 ~]# rpm -qa | grep -i mysql
mysql-community-libs-5.7.44-1.el7.x86_64
mysql57-community-release-el7-9.noarch
mysql-community-common-5.7.44-1.el7.x86_64
mysql-community-server-5.7.44-1.el7.x86_64
mysql-community-client-5.7.44-1.el7.x86_64
```

```
[root@mysql8 ~]# sudo yum remove mysql-community-server-5.7.44-1.el7.x86_64
-y
Dependencies resolved.
=========================================================================
 Package                    Architecture       Version
 Repository                         Size
=========================================================================
Removing:
 mysql-community-server     x86_64             5.7.44-1.el7
 @mysql57-community                 796 M
Removing unused dependencies:
 libaio                     x86_64             0.3.112-1.el8
 @rhel-8-baseos-rhui-rpms           93 k
 mysql-community-client     x86_64             5.7.44-1.el7
 @mysql57-community                 120 M
 mysql-community-common     x86_64             5.7.44-1.el7
 @mysql57-community                 2.8 M
 mysql-community-libs       x86_64             5.7.44-1.el7
 @mysql57-community                 11 M
Removed:
  libaio-0.3.112-1.el8.x86_64
  mysql-community-client-5.7.44-1.el7.x86_64
  mysql-community-common-5.7.44-1.el7.x86_64
  mysql-community-libs-5.7.44-1.el7.x86_64
  mysql-community-server-5.7.44-1.el7.x86_64
Complete!
[root@mysql8 ~]#
```

```
[root@mysql8 ~]# yum remove mysql57-community-release-el7-9.noarch
Dependencies resolved.
Running transaction
  Preparing        :
  Erasing          : mysql57-community-release-el7-9.noarch
  Verifying        : mysql57-community-release-el7-9.noarch
Removed:
  mysql57-community-release-el7-9.noarch
Complete!
[root@mysql8 ~]#
```

7. Download and add the MySQL yum repository with the following command. You can find the exact MySQL version and the required repository based on the Linux distribution (*https://repo.mysql.com*). Keep in mind that you should always

download software from official, trusted sources to ensure its integrity and security:

```
[root@mysql8 ~]# wget https://repo.mysql.com/
mysql80-community-release-el8-1.noarch.rpm
--2024-02-22 06:02:02--  https://repo.mysql.com/
mysql80-community-release-el8-1.noarch.rpm
Resolving repo.mysql.com (repo.mysql.com)... 104.104.9.203,
2600:1409:9800:15a1::1d68, 2600:1409:9800:1582::1d68
Connecting to repo.mysql.com (repo.mysql.com)|104.104.9.203|:443...
connected.
HTTP request sent, awaiting response... 200 OK
Length: 30388 (30K) [application/x-redhat-package-manager]
Saving to: 'mysql80-community-release-el8-1.noarch.rpm'
mysql80-community-release-el8-1.noarch.rpm    100%
[========================================>]  29.68K  --.-KB/s    in 0.04s
2024-02-22 06:02:02 (735 KB/s) - 'mysql80-community-release-el8-1.noarch.rpm'
saved [30388/30388]
[root@mysql8 ~]#

[root@mysql8 ~]# yum localinstall mysql80-community-release-el8-1.noarch.rpm
Last metadata expiration check: 0:16:33 ago on Thu 22 Feb 2024
05:45:50 AM UTC.
Dependencies resolved.
================================================================================
Package                         Architecture     Version
Repository              Size
================================================================================
Installing:
 mysql80-community-release                        noarch
 el8-1            @commandline          30 k
Transaction Summary
================================================================================
Install  1 Package
Total size: 30 k
Installed size: 29 k
Is this ok [y/N]: y
Downloading Packages:
Running transaction check
Transaction check succeeded.
Running transaction test
Transaction test succeeded.
Running transaction
  Preparing        :
  Installing       : mysql80-community-release-el8-1.noarch
  Verifying        : mysql80-community-release-el8-1.noarch
Installed:
  mysql80-community-release-el8-1.noarch
Complete!
[root@mysql8 ~]#
```

8. Confirm the successful addition of the MySQL yum repository:

```
[root@mysql8 ~]# yum repolist enabled | grep "mysql.-community."
mysql-connectors-community    MySQL Connectors Community
mysql-tools-community         MySQL Tools Community
mysql80-community             MySQL 8.0 Community Server
[root@mysql8 ~]#
```

9. Install the latest MySQL 8.0 version by executing this command:

```
[root@mysql8 ~]# sudo yum install mysql-community-server
Last metadata expiration check: 0:08:40 ago on Thu 22 Feb 2024
06:03:06 AM UTC.
Dependencies resolved.
================================================================================
 Package                      Architecture    Version
 Repository             Size
================================================================================
Installing:
 mysql-community-server         x86_64          8.0.36-1.el8
 mysql80-community      64 M
Installing dependencies:
 mysql-community-client         x86_64          8.0.36-1.el8
 mysql80-community      16 M
 mysql-community-client-plugins x86_64          8.0.36-1.el8
 mysql80-community      3.6 M
 mysql-community-common         x86_64          8.0.36-1.el8
 mysql80-community      668 k
 mysql-community-icu-data-files x86_64          8.0.36-1.el8
 mysql80-community      2.2 M
 mysql-community-libs           x86_64          8.0.36-1.el8
 mysql80-community      1.5 M
Installed:
  libaio-0.3.112-1.el8.x86_64
  mysql-community-client-8.0.36-1.el8.x86_64
  mysql-community-client-plugins-8.0.36-1.el8.x86_64
  mysql-community-common-8.0.36-1.el8.x86_64
  mysql-community-icu-data-files-8.0.36-1.el8.x86_64
  mysql-community-libs-8.0.36-1.el8.x86_64
  mysql-community-server-8.0.36-1.el8.x86_64
  net-tools-2.0-0.52.20160912git.el8.x86_64
  perl-Carp-1.42-396.el8.noarch
Complete!
[root@mysql8 ~]#
```

10. Verify the packages that have been installed:

```
[root@mysql8 ~]# yum list installed | grep mysql
mysql-community-client.x86_64              8.0.36-1.el8
@mysql80-community
mysql-community-client-plugins.x86_64      8.0.36-1.el8
@mysql80-community
mysql-community-common.x86_64              8.0.36-1.el8
@mysql80-community
```

```
mysql-community-icu-data-files.x86_64          8.0.36-1.el8
@mysql80-community
mysql-community-libs.x86_64                    8.0.36-1.el8
@mysql80-community
mysql-community-server.x86_64                  8.0.36-1.el8
@mysql80-community
mysql80-community-release.noarch               el8-9
@mysql80-community
[root@mysql8 ~]#
```

11. Start the MySQL service and check the logfile to ensure that the upgrade process was completed successfully without any issues:

```
[root@mysql8 ~]# systemctl start mysqld
[root@mysql8 ~]#

[root@mysql8 ~]# tail -f /var/log/mysqld.log
2024-02-22T06:26:47.525092Z 1 [System] [MY-013576] [InnoDB]
InnoDB initialization has started.
2024-02-22T06:26:48.121045Z 1 [System] [MY-013577] [InnoDB]
InnoDB initialization has ended.
2024-02-22T06:26:50.735124Z 2 [System] [MY-011003] [Server]
Finished populating Data Dictionary tables with data.
2024-02-22T06:26:52.409864Z 5 [System] [MY-013381] [Server]
Server upgrade from '50700' to '80036' started.
2024-02-22T06:27:00.129986Z 5 [System] [MY-013381] [Server]
Server upgrade from '50700' to '80036' completed.
2024-02-22T06:27:00.230424Z 0 [Warning] [MY-010068] [Server]
CA certificate ca.pem is self signed.
2024-02-22T06:27:00.230469Z 0 [System] [MY-013602] [Server]
Channel mysql_main configured to support TLS. Encrypted connections are
now supported for this channel.
2024-02-22T06:27:00.250554Z 0 [System] [MY-011323] [Server]
X Plugin ready for connections. Bind-address: '::' port: 33060, socket:
/var/run/mysqld/mysqlx.sock
2024-02-22T06:27:00.250607Z 0 [System] [MY-010931] [Server]
/usr/sbin/mysqld: ready for connections. Version: '8.0.36'  socket:
'/var/lib/mysql/mysql.sock'  port: 3306  MySQL Community Server - GPL.
```

Users of eXtended Architecture (XA) transactions with InnoDB should run XA RECOVER before upgrading to check for any uncommitted XA transactions. If there are any, they should be either committed or rolled back by issuing XA COMMIT or XA ROLLBACK statements.

It's also important to configure MySQL to perform a slow shutdown by setting innodb_fast_shutdown to 0. In an in-place upgrade scenario, the replication instances should be upgraded first before failing over to the current master, using tools like Orchestrator.

After upgrading the replicas, you can use Orchestrator for failover and tools like ProxySQL or a virtual IP (VIP) controller for redirecting application connections.

Orchestrator is a powerful tool designed to manage the replication topology of MySQL databases. It can automatically identify and monitor the topology and status of the replication tree, and users can interact with it through a GUI, CLI, or API to perform tasks such as failovers.

As you learned in Chapter 7, ProxySQL is an open source, high-performance MySQL protocol proxy designed to reduce database administration overheads and improve application performance. It sits between the database client and server, providing a set of advanced features, including load balancing, query routing, query filtering, and query caching. ProxySQL is a popular tool used in MySQL environments to improve the scalability, reliability, and manageability of the database tier. It is commonly used in conjunction with HA solutions like Orchestrator and Keepalived to ensure maximum uptime and failover handling in MySQL clusters.

ProxySQL uses the `read only` variables of the MySQL servers to determine which server should be the new master. It does not have knowledge of the topology, which is a critical piece of information. The server with the `read only` variable set to `off` will receive the writes. If the old master fails and the topology changes, the `read only` variables on the new master must be adjusted accordingly. Tools like MHA or Orchestrator can be used to assist with this process.

In contrast, a VIP controller is a custom IP controller script responsible for managing the primary and replica databases. It handles the writer VIP and (optionally) the reader VIP. The script identifies the master by checking for a read/write (RW) state to add the writer VIP and identifies the replica by checking for a read-only (RO) state to add the reader VIP.

After upgrading the replicas to MySQL 8.0, behold the refined architecture of MySQL source-replica Orchestrator with ProxySQL (Figure 10-1):

1. Once the replicas have been upgraded to MySQL 8, you can leverage Orchestrator to move them to any of the MySQL 8.0 replicas, which will subsequently become the new primary instance following failover. The former primary node running MySQL 5.7 will then be upgraded to MySQL 8 and resume replication from the new MySQL 8 primary instance.

2. Redirecting read queries from the application in advance via ProxySQL to the upgraded replicas is done to verify the functionality of all modules and to detect any potential issues.

3. Before falling over, it is important to upgrade the replication instances first in an in-place upgrade scenario.

To upgrade the system from MySQL 5.7 to MySQL 8.0, follow these steps:

1. Upgrade all replicas to MySQL 8.0.

2. Use Orchestrator to move the MySQL3 Replica and MySQL4 Replica nodes under MySQL2 Replica.

3. Perform a switchover of the MySQL2 Replica to make it the new primary node.

4. Upgrade the former primary node, MySQL 5.7, to MySQL 8.0.

5. Resume replication on the upgraded node, replicating from the new MySQL 8.0 primary instance.

Following the upgrade, the architecture appears as shown in Figure 10-2.

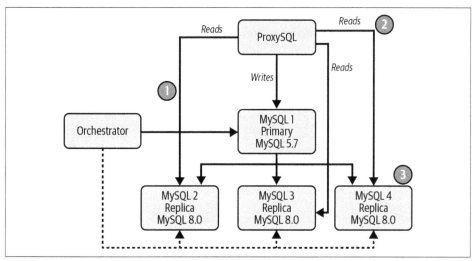

Figure 10-1. MySQL source-replica Orchestrator with ProxySQL architecture

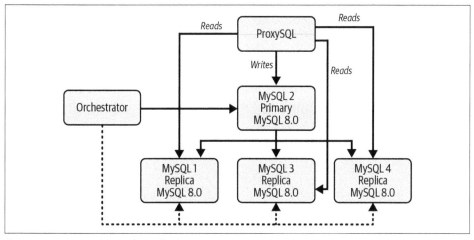

Figure 10-2. Post-upgrade architecture

Stand Up New Environment and Cutover

To prepare for a version upgrade, you need to provision a duplicate environment with the same number of servers and hardware specifications as the production environment. You'll install the target version of MySQL on the new hardware, and set up the new environment by recovering the production data onto it. Verify the MySQL configurations using `pt-config-diff`.

Replication will then be established from the current production source to the newly built environment. During the cutover time, all writes on the current source will be halted, the replication from the old version environment to the new version will stop, and the application traffic will be redirected to the new source. This cutover can be done manually, updating ProxySQL configuration or by using a VIP to redirect the application. Finally, the old environment will be decommissioned (Figure 10-3).

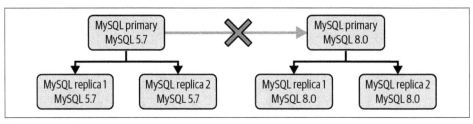

Figure 10-3. Cutover

 In the Cutover approach, the new servers with the latest version of MySQL are being set up. The installation steps are covered in Chapter 2.

Conclusion

This chapter offered valuable insights and practical guidance on successfully managing significant MySQL version upgrades. You now have the tools and knowledge you need to smoothly navigate major MySQL version upgrades, ensuring the continuity and reliability of your database systems.

## CHAPTER 11

MySQL on the Cloud: Amazon RDS

This chapter presents the numerous benefits of using Amazon Relational Database for MySQL (RDS), including simplified management, enhanced scalability, and robust security measures. We'll start with an overview of RDS for MySQL architecture, storage options, and replication. Then we'll guide you through the process of creating an RDS for MySQL instance, helping you select the right instance class and storage type, and configure essential settings like Amazon Virtual Private Cloud (VPC), security groups, and backup retention.

The chapter also covers connecting to the instance, user management, performance optimization, and security measures, both through the AWS Management Console and AWS CLI. You'll gain insights into data encryption, automated backups, restoring from backups, and parameter group and security group considerations. Scaling options such as storage scaling and adding read replicas are explored, along with Amazon CloudWatch metrics and alarms for monitoring. The chapter concludes with cost-optimization best practices for RDS for MySQL, emphasizing right-sizing database instances, utilizing reserved instances, reserved capacity, and efficient database backups.

Exploring RDS for MySQL Architecture

In the realm of cloud-based databases, four core components are pivotal: database instances, database subnet groups, security groups, and parameter groups. These components collectively define your database environment, from isolation and network configuration to security and fine-tuning:

Database instance
> An isolated database environment in the cloud, which includes compute, storage, and networking resources

Database subnet group
> A collection of subnets used to specify the VPC in which an Amazon RDS instance is created

Security groups
> Control access to a database instance by allowing or denying incoming traffic based on IP address and port number

Parameter groups
> Manage configuration settings for your database instance

Now, let's explore the storage options available for RDS for MySQL instances.

RDS for MySQL provides various types of storage to cater to different performance and capacity requirements. The following types of storage are available:

General purpose
> Also known as *gp3*, this is the default storage type for RDS MySQL. It provides a balance of performance and cost-effectiveness and is suitable for most workloads. It uses SSDs for storage.

Provisioned IOPS
> This storage type, known as *io1*, is designed for applications with high I/O requirements. It allows you to provision a specific number of IOPS based on your workload's needs. This type also uses SSDs.

Magnetic
> This is an older and less commonly used storage type in RDS and is also called *standard*. It offers lower performance compared to SSD-based storage, making it suitable for workloads with lower I/O demands.

Replication is a crucial aspect of database management, offering various methods to enhance performance, availability, and data protection. Some methods of replication are as follows:

Read replicas
Offload read traffic from the primary database

Multi-AZ deployments
Automatically replicate data to a standby instance in a different availability zone (AZ)

Parameter groups
Customize database settings by using parameter groups, which store configuration settings for your instances

Snapshots
Create and manage backups of your instances using snapshots

Understanding the Benefits of Using RDS for MySQL

RDS for MySQL offers several advantages that make it a powerful choice for database management. Table 11-1 breaks down some of its key benefits.

Table 11-1. Advantages of using RDS for MySQL

Benefit	Description
Simplified management	Automatic backups, monitoring, and maintenance. No need to worry about infrastructure provisioning and management.
Scalability	Scale up or down resources to accommodate workloads. Vertical scaling (instance size) and horizontal scaling (read replicas).
Security	Data encrypted at rest and in transit. Integrates with AWS Identity and Access Management (IAM) for access.
Pay-as-you-go pricing model	No up-front costs or long-term commitments required. You only pay for the resources you use.
High availability and durability	Multi-AZ deployments ensure fault tolerance and automated failover, enhancing the availability and durability of your database.
Backups stored in multiple locations	Data backups are stored redundantly across multiple physical facilities, ensuring data durability and availability in case of failures.
Monitoring and performance tuning	Comprehensive performance metrics and insights, simplifying the process of optimizing your database for better performance.
Managed service	Handles routine database tasks such as maintenance, backups, and patching, freeing you to focus on developing and running your applications.

Creating an RDS for MySQL Instance

When setting up a database instance on the AWS Management Console, you have the option to enable or disable "Easy create." If this option is enabled, you need to specify only the database engine type, instance size, and instance identifier. "Easy create" will then use default settings for other configuration options. If "Easy create" is not enabled, you'll have the flexibility to specify additional configuration options, such as availability, security, backups, and maintenance, when creating the database.

Use "Easy create" to set up a MySQL database instance with the db.t3.micro database instance class by following these steps:

1. Log in to access the Amazon RDS console (*https://console.aws.amazon.com/rds*):

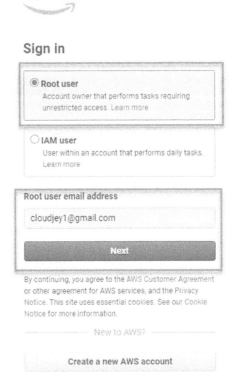

2. Choose RDS from the AWS console page:

3. Select the desired AWS Region from the upper-right corner of the Amazon RDS console to create the DB instance:

4. In the navigation pane on the left, choose Databases and click the "Create data-base" button:

5. On the "Create database" page, ensure that "Easy create" is selected:

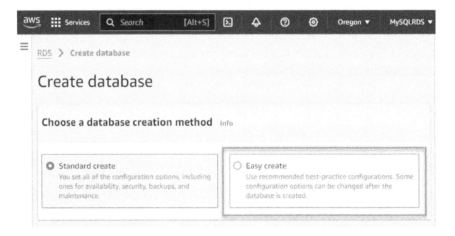

6. In Configuration, choose MySQL, which will automatically select the MySQL Community Edition:

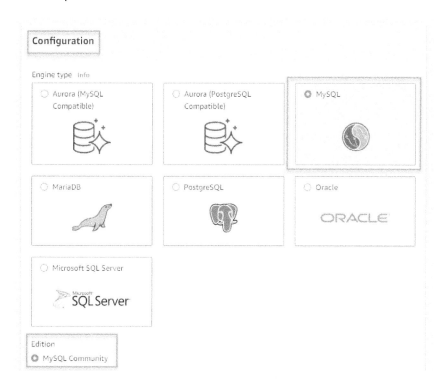

7. Select the "Free tier" option for the database instance size:

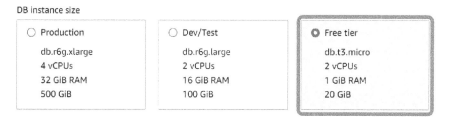

8. Enter **database-1** as the database instance identifier:

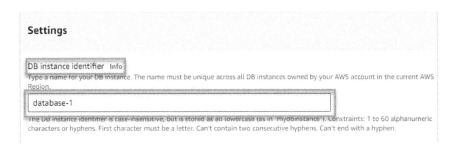

9. Enter a name for the master user in the "Master username" field, or keep the default name:

10. To set the master password for the DB instance, either select "Auto generate password" to use an automatically generated master password, or clear "Auto generate password" to enter your own. In the latter case, input your desired password in both the "Master password" and "Confirm password" fields:

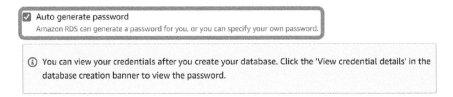

11. You have several options regarding the default settings used with "Easy create." First, examine the "Editable after database is created" column to see which settings can be changed after creation. If a setting is marked "No," opt for "Standard create." If marked "Yes," you can either choose "Standard create" or modify the database instance:

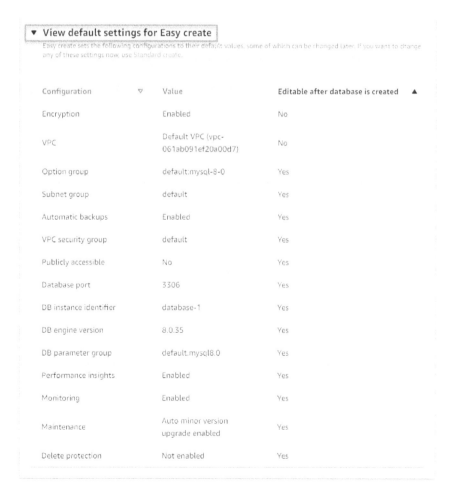

▼ View default settings for Easy create

Easy create sets the following configurations to their default values, some of which can be changed later. If you want to change any of these settings now, use Standard create.

Configuration	Value	Editable after database is created
Encryption	Enabled	No
VPC	Default VPC (vpc-061ab091ef20a00d7)	No
Option group	default:mysql-8-0	Yes
Subnet group	default	Yes
Automatic backups	Enabled	Yes
VPC security group	default	Yes
Publicly accessible	No	Yes
Database port	3306	Yes
DB instance identifier	database-1	Yes
DB engine version	8.0.35	Yes
DB parameter group	default.mysql8.0	Yes
Performance insights	Enabled	Yes
Monitoring	Enabled	Yes
Maintenance	Auto minor version upgrade enabled	Yes
Delete protection	Not enabled	Yes

12. Click the "Create database" button.

13. In the Databases list, choose the new MySQL database instance's name to show its details. The database instance has a status of Creating until it is ready to use:

14. Wait for the Region & AZ value to appear and make a note of the value because you will need it later. In the following image, the Region & AZ value is us-west-2a:

15. When the status changes to Available, you can connect to the database instance. Depending on the database instance class and the amount of storage, it can take up to a few minutes before the new instance is available. While the database instance is being created, you can move on to the next step:

Creating RDS Instance Using the AWS CLI

Creating an RDS instance using AWS CLI involves a series of commands executed within the CLI provided by AWS. This process typically includes specifying parameters such as instance type, storage capacity, database engine, and authentication details. By leveraging the AWS CLI, you can automate the deployment of RDS instances, streamlining setup and ensuring consistency across environments. Additionally, using the CLI allows for easy integration with scripts and other automation tools, facilitating efficient management of RDS resources within the AWS ecosystem.

In this example, AWS CLI creates an RDS for MySQL instance with 20 GB of storage, a `db.t3.micro` instance class:

```
aws rds create-db-instance \
--db-instance-identifier mysqldbistance \
--db-instance-class db.t3.micro \
--engine mysql \
--engine-version 8.0.32 \
--master-username mysqladmin \
--master-user-password Pass21word$$ \
--allocated-storage 20 \
--storage-type gp2 \
--publicly-accessible
```

Choosing the Right Instance Class and Storage Type

When setting up an RDS for MySQL, selecting the appropriate instance class and storage type is crucial to optimize performance, cost, and resource utilization. Consider the following best practices for selecting the right options for your use case:

Memory requirements
Evaluate the memory demands of your application to ensure the chosen instance has enough RAM.

CPU requirements
Choose an instance class with adequate processing power to support your application's workload.

Network performance
Ensure that the instance class has sufficient network bandwidth for your application's data transfer needs.

Performance
Consider the performance requirements of your application, such as the number of transactions per second and response times.

Cost

> Balance your budget constraints with the required resources and performance. Balance your performance requirements with your budget constraints.

RDS for MySQL offers several instance classes to choose from, such as standard classes (`db.m6g`), memory optimized (`db.r6g`, `db.x1`), and burst capable (`db.t3`). It also provides different storage types to suit various application requirements. Take the following considerations into account when choosing a storage type:

IOPS requirements

> Determine the IOPS based on your application's performance needs.

Storage capacity

> Estimate the required storage space for your database.

Backup and snapshot requirements

> Understand your data protection needs for backups and snapshots.

Budget

> Consider the cost implications of various storage types.

Setting Up VPC and Security Groups

A VPC provides a secure, isolated environment for your RDS for MySQL instance. Security groups act as virtual firewalls, controlling inbound and outbound traffic. Follow these best practices for setting up VPC and security groups:

Create a dedicated VPC

> Set up a separate VPC for your RDS instance to isolate it from other resources.

Configure subnets

> Create at least two subnets in different AZs for HA.

Set up security groups

> Create security groups with appropriate rules to control access to your RDS instance.

Configuring Advanced Settings: Backup Retention and Maintenance Window

Fine-tune your RDS for MySQL configuration with precision by focusing on two critical settings:

Backup retention

> Set an appropriate backup retention period based on your data recovery requirements. RDS for MySQL allows retention of 1 to 35 days.

Maintenance window

Select a maintenance window during which any required updates or patches will be applied. Choose a time with minimal impact on your application's users.

These two settings help optimize your backup strategy and minimize disruptions during maintenance updates. Once you have configured the appropriate settings, launch the RDS for MySQL instance. You can then connect to it by using a MySQL client or application.

Connecting to RDS for MySQL by Using MySQL Clients

To effectively manage and interact with your RDS for MySQL databases, it is important to follow best practices when using MySQL clients to connect. In this section, we explore various methods and configurations to ensure secure and efficient connections.

Several MySQL clients are available for connecting to RDS for MySQL. Some popular choices include MySQL Workbench, HeidiSQL (Windows only), DBeaver (cross-platform), and the command-line `mysql` client.

To connect using the command-line `mysql` client, use the following command:

```
[root@ip-172-31-37-254 ~]# mysql -h database-1.cgbvu6nloqfx.us-west-2.rds.
amazonaws.com -u admin -p -P 3306
Enter password:
Welcome to the MySQL monitor. Commands end with ; or \g.
Your MySQL connection id is 234
Server version: 8.0.32 Source distribution

Copyright (c) 2000, 2022, Oracle and/or its affiliates.

Oracle is a registered trademark of Oracle Corporation and/or its
affiliates. Other names may be trademarks of their respective owners.

Type 'help;' or '\h' for help. Type '\c' to clear the current input statement.
mysql>
```

Creating Users and Managing Permissions

Empower your RDS for MySQL database security and access control with confidence by mastering the art of creating users and effectively managing permissions. Let's dive into the essential steps to secure your data and ensure controlled data access.

Enabling and disabling IAM database authentication for RDS for MySQL

Enabling and disabling IAM database authentication for RDS for MySQL involves modifying the database settings to allow or disallow users to authenticate using their

IAM credentials. This ensures secure access to the database and better control over user permissions.

To enable IAM database authentication for an existing RDS for MySQL database instance, follow these steps:

1. Open the Amazon RDS console:

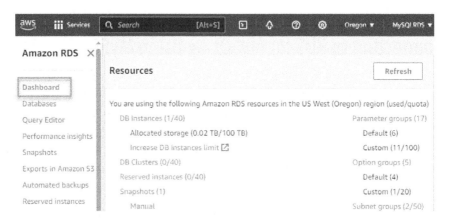

2. In the navigation pane, choose Databases:

3. Choose the database instance you want to modify and then click Modify:

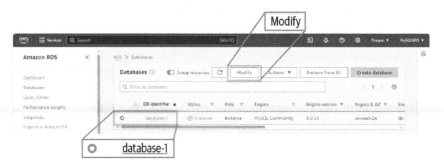

4. To enable IAM database authentication, select "Password and IAM database authentication" in the "Database authentication" section and click Continue:

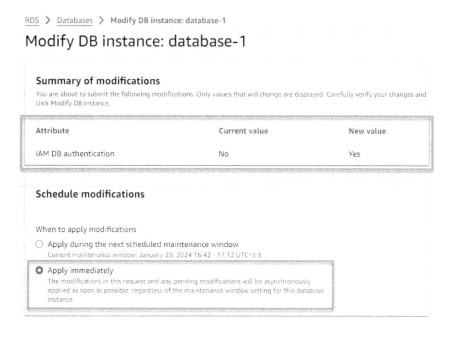

Database authentication

Database authentication options Info

○ Password authentication
   Authenticates using database passwords.

● Password and IAM database authentication
   Authenticates using the database password and user credentials through AWS IAM users and roles.

○ Password and Kerberos authentication
   Choose a directory in which you want to allow authorized users to authenticate with this DB instance using Kerberos Authentication.

5. To apply the changes immediately, select "Apply immediately" in the "Schedule modifications" section. Then click the "Modify DB instance" button:

RDS > Databases > Modify DB instance: database-1

Modify DB instance: database-1

Summary of modifications
You are about to submit the following modifications. Only values that will change are displayed. Carefully verify your changes and click Modify DB Instance.

Attribute	Current value	New value
IAM DB authentication	No	Yes

Schedule modifications

When to apply modifications

○ Apply during the next scheduled maintenance window
   Current maintenance window: January 29, 2024 16:42 - 17:12 UTC+5.5

● Apply immediately
   The modifications in this request and any pending modifications will be asynchronously applied as soon as possible, regardless of the maintenance window setting for this database instance.

Using IAM authentication with MySQL

When using IAM authentication with MySQL, authentication is managed by AWSAu thenticationPlugin, which is provided by AWS and works seamlessly with IAM to authenticate your users. To use IAM authentication, follow these steps:

1. Connect to the database instance as the master user or another user who can create users and grant privileges. Then issue the CREATE USER statement, as shown here:

```
mysql>
mysql> CREATE USER app_user IDENTIFIED WITH AWSAuthenticationPlugin AS 'RDS';
Query OK, 0 rows affected (0.23 sec)
```

2. Download the root certificate and set appropriate permissions:

```
[root@ip-172-31-37-254 mysql]#
[root@ip-172-31-37-254 mysql]# wget https://s3.amazonaws.com/
rds-downloads/rds-ca-2019-root.pem
--2023-04-25 05:44:31-- https://s3.amazonaws.com/rds-downloads/
rds-ca-2019-root.pem
Resolving s3.amazonaws.com (s3.amazonaws.com)... 52.216.108.5,
52.216.108.157, 52.216.114.173, ...
Connecting to s3.amazonaws.com (s3.amazonaws.com)|52.216.108.5|:443...
connected.
HTTP request sent, awaiting response... 200 OK
Length: 1456 (1.4K) [binary/octet-stream]
Saving to: 'rds-ca-2019-root.pem'

rds-ca-2019-root.pem        100%[============================================>]
1.42K --.-KB/s in 0s
2023-04-25 05:44:31 (63.0MB/s) - 'rds-ca-2019-root.pem' saved [1456/1456]

[root@ip-172-31-37-254 mysql]#
```

3. Once the certificate is downloaded, you need to grant read and write permissions for the owner (user), and no permissions for group and others. Use the command chmod 600 to modify the permissions for the *rds-ca-2019-root.pem* file accordingly:

```
[root@ip-172-31-37-254 mysql]#
[root@ip-172-31-37-254 mysql]# chmod 600 rds-ca-2019-root.pem
[root@ip-172-31-37-254 mysql]#
[root@ip-172-31-37-254 mysql]# ll
total 4
-r--------. 1 root root 1456 Sep 4 2019 rds-ca-2019-root.pem
[root@ip-172-31-37-254 mysql]#
```

4. Set the environment variable RDSHOST as follows:

```
[root@ip-172-31-37-254 mysql]#
[root@ip-172-31-37-254 mysql]#  RDSHOST=
```

```
"database-1.cgbvu6nloqfx.us-west-2.rds.amazonaws.com"
[root@ip-172-31-37-254 mysql]#
```

5. Set the environment variable TOKEN with a command to generates an auth token for an AWS RDS instance using the specified hostname, port, region, and username. The token can then be used to securely connect to the RDS instance:

```
[root@ip-172-31-37-254 mysql]#
[root@ip-172-31-37-254 mysql]# TOKEN="$(aws rds generate-db-auth-token
--hostname $RDSHOST --port 3306 --region us-west-2 --username app_user)"
[root@ip-172-31-37-254 mysql]#
```

6. Use the following command to establish a secure connection to the specified RDS instance:

```
[root@ip-172-31-37-254 mysql]#
[root@ip-172-31-37-254 mysql]#  mysql --host=$RDSHOST --port=3306
--ssl-ca=/root/mysql/rds-ca-2019-root.pem --enable-cleartext-plugin
--user=app_user --password=$TOKEN
mysql: [Warning] Using a password on the command line interface can be insecure.
Welcome to the MySQL monitor. Commands end with ; or \g.
Your MySQL connection id is 23
Server version: 8.0.32 Source distribution

Copyright (c) 2000, 2022, Oracle and/or its affiliates.

Oracle is a registered trademark of Oracle Corporation and/or its
affiliates. Other names may be trademarks of their respective owners.

Type 'help;' or '\h' for help. Type '\c' to clear the current input statement.
```

By following these best practices, you can effectively enable and disable IAM database authentication for RDS for MySQL, ensuring secure and controlled access to your database resources.

Configuring RDS for MySQL for Optimal Performance

Unlock the full potential of your RDS for MySQL database by configuring it for optimal performance. Here are some key strategies to ensure that your database delivers peak performance and reliability:

Choose the right instance class

Select an RDS for MySQL instance class that meets your performance requirements.

Configure storage

Opt for either general-purpose SSD (recommended) or provisioned IOPS SSD for improved storage performance.

Enable multi-AZ deployments
> For HA, enable multi-AZ deployments, which automatically creates a standby instance in another availability zone.

Configure read replicas
> To offload read traffic, create read replicas and configure your application to direct read queries to the replica instances.

Monitor performance
> Use Amazon RDS Performance Insights and Amazon CloudWatch to monitor your instance's performance and identify potential bottlenecks.

Optimize queries and indexes
> Regularly analyze your application's queries and optimize them as needed. Use the MySQL EXPLAIN statement to identify slow or inefficient queries, and create appropriate indexes to improve query performance.

Implement connection pooling
> To efficiently manage database connections, use connection pooling techniques in your application. This reduces the overhead of creating and closing connections, ultimately improving performance.

Schedule regular backups and maintenance
> Set up automatic backups and maintenance tasks, such as vacuuming and reindexing, to ensure the health and integrity of your database. Also, test your backup and recovery process periodically to ensure data durability and minimize downtime in case of any failures.

By following these best practices, you can effectively connect to and manage your RDS for MySQL instances by using MySQL clients. These measures ensure that your connections are secure, your databases are optimized for performance, and your data is protected.

Configuring Parameter Groups for Optimal Performance

When managing an RDS for MySQL instance, it's crucial to configure parameter groups properly to ensure optimal performance. In RDS for MySQL, *parameter groups* are collections of database engine configuration settings that can be applied to one or more database instances, enabling you to fine-tune your database's performance, security, and maintenance settings. While default parameter groups come with preconfigured settings, you also have the flexibility to create custom parameter groups tailored to your specific requirements.

Here's how to create a database parameter group in the AWS Management Console:

1. Sign in to the AWS Management Console and go to the Amazon RDS console (*https://console.aws.amazon.com/rds*):

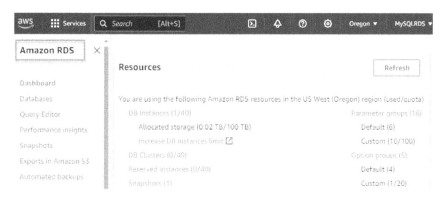

2. In the navigation pane, click the "Parameter groups" option:

3. Click the "Create parameter group" button:

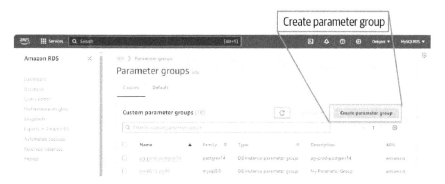

4. On the "Create parameter group" page, select a database parameter group family from the "Parameter group family" list:

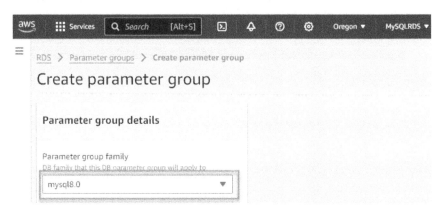

5. In the Type list, select DB Parameter Group:

6. Enter a name for the new database parameter group in the Group Name box:

7. Enter a description for the new database parameter group in the Description box and then click Create:

Description
Description for the DB parameter group

database-1-mysql80 creating for testing

Modifying Parameter Settings

To modify a database parameter group, follow these steps:

1. Sign in to the AWS Management Console and go to the Amazon RDS console:

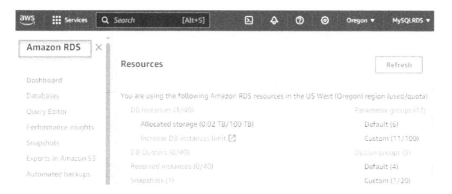

2. In the navigation pane, select "Parameter groups":

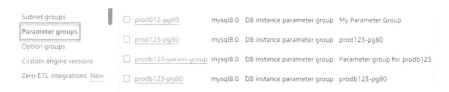

3. Choose the parameter group that you want to modify from the list:

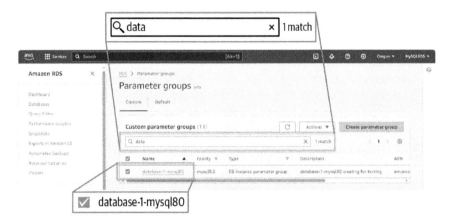

4. Click the Edit button to change the parameters:

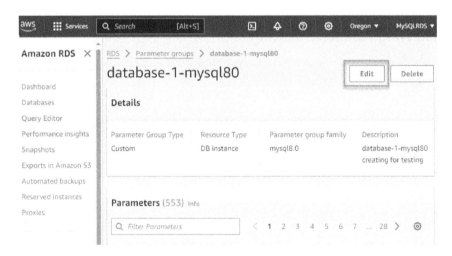

5. Modify the values of the parameters that you want to change. You can navigate through the parameters by using the arrow keys located at the top right:

6. You can't change values in a default parameter group. After making the necessary modifications, click the Save Changes button to save the new settings:

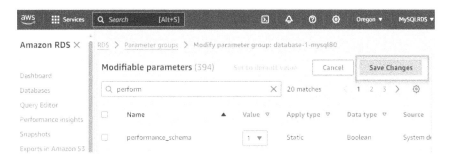

By following these steps, you can successfully modify your parameter groups.

Here are some important parameters to consider modifying for optimal performance:

innodb_buffer_pool_size
    Adjust this to optimize memory usage for your database instance.

innodb_redo_log_capacity
    Change this to control the size of the redo logfiles.

innodb_flush_log_at_trx_commit
    Modify this to control the balance between performance and data durability.

Modifying Database Parameter Values with AWS CLI

Streamline your database management with AWS CLI by effortlessly adjusting parameter values. Enhance performance and efficiency while maintaining control over your AWS database configurations. Run the `aws rds modify-db-parameter-group`.

This command displays the `'max_connections'` configuration variable in a MySQL database:

```
mysql> SHOW VARIABLES LIKE 'max_connections';
+-------------------------+
| Variable_name | Value   |
+-------------------------+
|max_connections | 60      |
+-------------------------+
1 row in set (0.02 sec)

mysql>
```

This AWS CLI command is used to modify a database parameter group in RDS for MySQL:

```
[root@ip-172-31-37-254 mysql]# aws rds modify-db-parameter-group \
        --db-parameter-group-name mysqlrdstest \
        --parameters "ParameterName=max_connections, ParameterValue=100,
  ApplyMethod-immediate"
{
        "DBParameterGroupName": "mysqlrdstest"
}
[root@ip-172-31-37-254 mysql]#
```

Then, run the `aws rds modify-db-parameter-group`:

```
mysql> SHOW VARIABLES LIKE 'max_connections';
+-------------------------+
| Variable_name   | Value |
+-------------------------+
| max_connections | 100   |
+-------------------------+
1 row in set (0.01 sec)

mysql>
```

Properly configuring parameter groups is essential for achieving optimal performance in an RDS for MySQL environment. By creating custom parameter groups, modifying key parameter settings, and assigning them to your database instances, you can fine-tune your database's performance, security, and maintenance settings to best suit your specific needs. Always monitor performance and test changes in a development environment before applying them to production.

Securing Access to RDS for MySQL

To ensure a secure environment for your RDS for MySQL, it is crucial to follow network security best practices. These include the following:

- Restricting access to specific IP addresses or IP ranges
- Using Amazon VPC for isolation
- Implementing security groups to control inbound and outbound traffic

Modifying Security Settings via the AWS Management Console

To modify the security settings for your RDS MySQL instance on AWS, follow these steps:

1. Log in to your AWS account and navigate to the RDS console. In the navigation pane, choose Databases then select the RDS MySQL instance that you want to modify:

2. On the "Connectivity & security" tab, click the sampledb link under "VPC security groups":

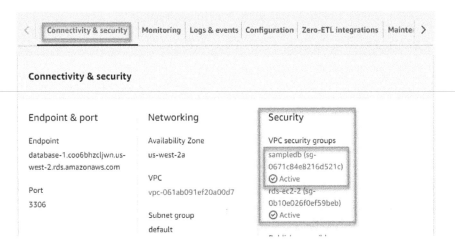

3. From here, you can modify the inbound and outbound rules to allow only specific IP addresses or IP ranges to access your RDS MySQL instance. To do this, click the "Edit inbound rules" button:

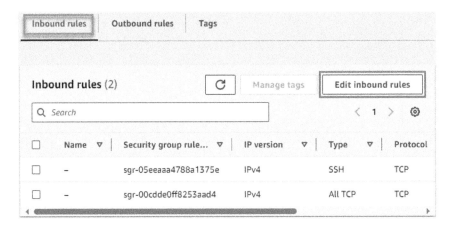

4. To add a rule, click "Add rule" and specify the desired IP addresses or ranges. To modify an existing rule, select the rule and adjust the allowed traffic accordingly. Once you have made the necessary changes, click Save to update the security group settings:

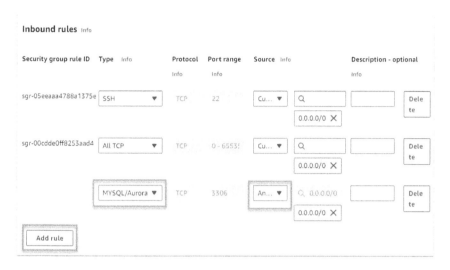

This will ensure that only authorized IP addresses or IP ranges can access your RDS for MySQL instance, thereby enhancing the security of your database.

Modifying Security Settings via the AWS CLI

Use the `aws ec2 authorize-security-group-ingress` and `aws ec2 authorize-security-group-egress` commands to configure the security group rules for your RDS for MySQL instance:

```
[root@ip-172-31-37-254 mysql]#
[root@ip-172-31-37-254 mysql]# aws ec2 authorize-security-group-ingress
--group-id sg-051f997aa495db56d --protocol tcp --port 3306
--cidr 203.0.113.1/32
{
"Return": true,
"SecurityGroupRules": [
{
"SecurityGroupRuleId": "sgr-08fd92de178f40e6c",
"GroupId": "sg-051f997aa495db56d",
"GroupOwnerId": "953274801226",
"IsEgress": false,
"IpProtocol": "tcp",
"FromPort": 3306,
"ToPort": 3306,
```

```
    "CidrIpv4": "203.0.113.1/32"
    }
    1
    }
[root@ip-172-31-37-254 mysql]"
```

To protect sensitive data in RDS for MySQL, it is essential to enable encryption both at rest and in transit. Ensuring encryption is up-to-date requires periodic updates to the Key Management Service (KMS) key used for encryption.

Updating the KMS Key via the AWS Management Console

Updating the KMS key in RDS for MySQL enhances security and compliance measures and helps maintain data integrity and meet regulatory requirements, as well. Ultimately the steps in this section will help you safeguard sensitive information stored in your database.

To update the KMS key in RDS for MySQL, follow these steps:

1. Open the Amazon RDS console and select the RDS instance for which you want to update the KMS key. Then click Modify to modify the RDS instance setting:

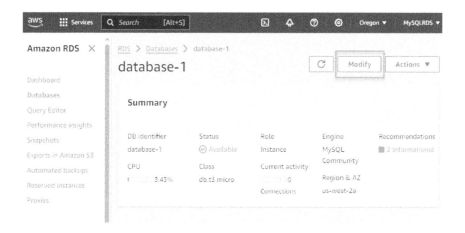

2. In the Settings section, check the "Manage master credentials in AWS Secrets Manager" box and select the encryption key. Then, click the Continue button:

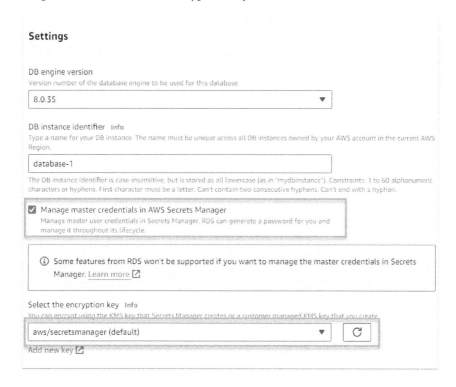

3. Review the changes and click the "Apply immediately" option. Then click the "Modify DB instance" button to apply the changes:

Modify the Encryption Key via the AWS CLI

To change the encryption key for an RDS for MySQL database instance through the AWS CLI, use the following steps:

1. Open the AWS CLI on your local machine or EC2 instance and then run the following command to create a new AWS KMS key alias:

   ```
   aws kms create-alias --alias-name alias/<new_key_alias> --target-key-id
   <new_key_id>
   ```

2. Replace *new_key_alias* with the new alias you want to use for the key and *new_key_id* with the ID of the new AWS KMS key.

---

3. Run the following command to modify the database instance to use the new key:

```
aws rds modify-db-instance --db-instance-identifier
<db_instance_identifier> --kms-key-id <new_key_alias>
```

4. Replace *db_instance_identifier* with the identifier of the RDS instance you want to modify and *new_key_alias* with the alias of the new AWS KMS key you created previously.

5. Wait for the modification to complete. You can use the following command to check the status of the modification:

```
aws rds describe-db-instances --db-instance-identifier
<db_instance_identifier> | grep KmsKeyId
```

This command will return the new AWS KMS key alias that is being used by the RDS instance.

That's it! You have successfully changed the encryption key for your Amazon RDS database instance through AWS CLI.

Enabling Automatic Backups

Automated backups are an essential aspect of database management, as they ensure that you always have a copy of your data in case of any failures or accidents. Let's dive into the best practices for enabling automated backups for RDS for MySQL.

To enable automated backups for your RDS for MySQL instance, you need to follow these steps:

1. Sign in to the AWS Management Console and open the Amazon RDS console. In the navigation pane, choose Databases, and then select the database instance:

2. Click the Modify option:

3. For the backup retention period, choose a positive nonzero value (for example, three days). Then click the Continue button:

If you manage your backups in AWS Backup, you can't enable automated backups.

4. Click the "Apply immediately" option. Then click the "Modify DB instance" or "Modify cluster" to save your changes and enable automated backups:

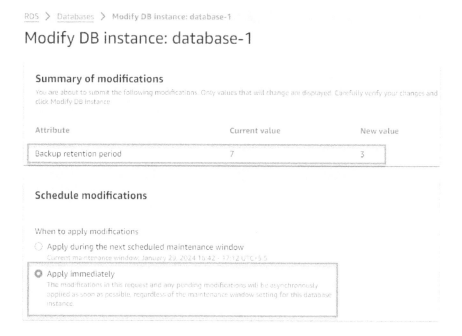

Restoring from Automated Backups

PITR allows you to restore your RDS for MySQL database to a specific point in time. This helps you recover from accidental data loss or corruption. You can use either the AWS Management Console or the AWS CLI to perform PITR. To perform PITR, follow these steps:

1. Sign in to the AWS Management Console and navigate to the RDS console. Select the Databases tab and click the database instance you want to restore:

2. Click Actions and choose "Restore to point in time":

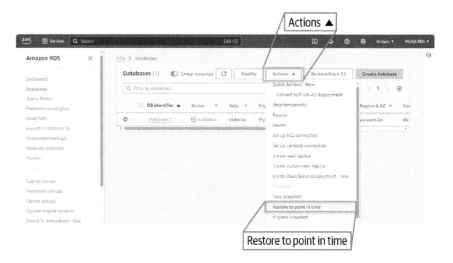

3. Choose the desired point in time by specifying the date and time:

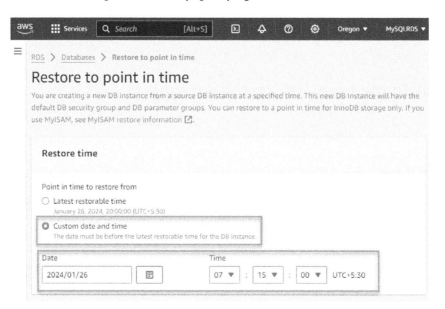

4. Provide the necessary details for the new database instance, such as the instance name, instance class, and VPC, and click Restore DB Instance:

5. In the "Instance configuration" section, choose the database instance class:

Instance configuration

The DB instance configuration options below are limited to those supported by the engine that you selected above.

DB instance class   Info

▼ Hide filters

⬤ Include previous generation classes

○ Standard classes (includes m classes)

○ Memory optimized classes (includes r and x classes)

◉ Burstable classes (includes t classes)

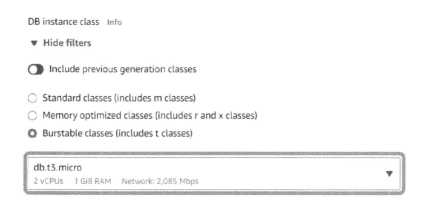

6. In the Connectivity section, choose the VPC. Then click the "Restore to point in time" button:

7. In the "Additional configuration" section, choose the database name:

Restoring Databases via the AWS CLI

You can use the AWS CLI to restore an RDS for MySQL database instance to a specific point in time. You'll then want to execute the following command, replacing the placeholders with appropriate values:

```
[root@ip-172-31-37-254 ~]# aws rds restore-db-instance-to-point-in-time \
[root@ip-172-31-37-254 ~]# --source-db-instance-identifier database-1 \
--target-db-instance-identifier testdbcli \
--restore-time 2023-04-25T15:30:00Z
"DBInstance": {
"DBInstanceIdentifier": "testdbcli", "DBInstanceClass": "db.t3.micro",
"Engine": "mysql",
"DBInstanceStatus": "creating",
"MasterUsername": "admin",
"AllocatedStorage": 20,
"PreferredBackupWindow": "12:10-12:40",
"BackupRetentionPeriod": 7,
"DBSecurityGroups": [],
"VpcSecurityGroups": [
{
"VpcSecurityGroupId": "sg-eb20d2c7d334b6acd",
"Status": "active"
}
```

The command requires specifying the identifier of the source database instance that will be used as the source for the restore operation, as well as the identifier of the new database instance that will be created. Additionally, you need to specify the time to which the database will be restored.

Creating a Database Snapshot in RDS for MySQL

Amazon RDS provides an easy way to create backups of your database instance through database snapshots. This feature allows you to create a point-in-time backup of your entire database instance, including all databases, settings, and configurations.

When you create a database snapshot, RDS for MySQL backs up the entire database instance, which can result in a brief I/O suspension. For single-AZ instances, this suspension can last seconds or minutes, depending on the size and class of your instance. However, for multi-AZ deployments, I/O activity is not suspended on your primary during backup because the backup is taken from the standby.

To create a DB snapshot using the AWS Management Console, sign in (*https://console.aws.amazon.com/rds*) and follow these steps:

1. In the navigation pane, choose Databases. Then, in the list of database instances, choose the database instance for which you want to take a snapshot:

2. From the Actions menu, choose "Take snapshot":

3. On the Take DB snapshot page, enter the name of the snapshot in the Snapshot Name box. Then click "Take snapshot" to create the database snapshot:

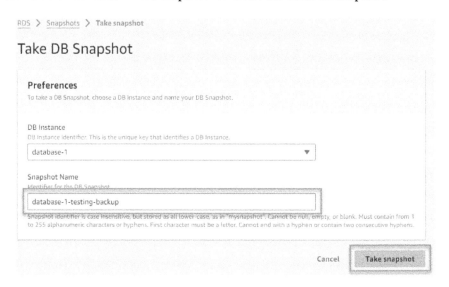

4. The Snapshots page appears with the new database snapshot's status shown as Creating. Wait for the status to change to Available, and you can then see its creation time:

Restoring Backups and Snapshots

You can restore your RDS for MySQL database from a backup or snapshot by using either the AWS Management Console or the AWS CLI. Restoring from a database snapshot can be a simple process, but you should keep some best practices in mind. Here are some factors to consider regarding parameter groups:

- Ensure that you preserve the DB parameter group when generating DB snapshots. This ensures that your restored DB instance is linked with the accurate parameter group.

- The restored instance is linked with the default DB parameter group unless an alternative is selected.

- There are no customized parameter configurations accessible within the default parameter group.

For security groups, consider the following factors:

- Upon restoring a DB instance, the default VPC, DB subnet group, and VPC security group are automatically linked with the restored instance, unless alternative selections are made.

- You have the option to designate a customized VPC security group for association with the instance or to generate a new VPC security group.

To Restore a Database Instance from a Database Snapshot

When it comes to database recovery, knowing how to effectively restore a database instance from an RDS for MySQL database snapshot is paramount. Follow these steps to bring your data back to life and ensure business continuity:

1. Sign in to the AWS Management Console and open the Amazon RDS console. In the navigation pane, choose Snapshots:

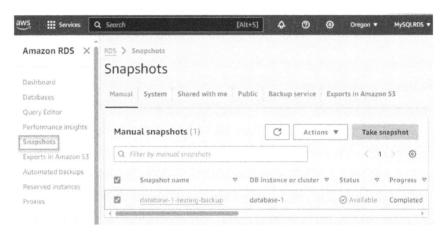

2. Choose the database snapshot that you want to restore from:

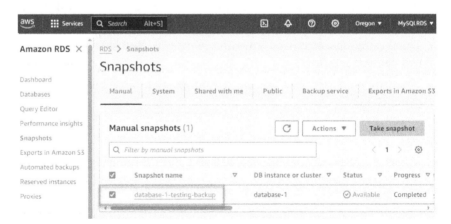

3. From the Actions menu, choose "Restore snapshot":

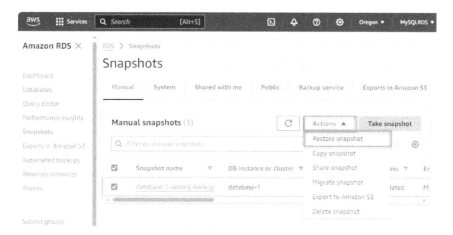

4. On the "Restore snapshot" page, enter the name for your restored database instance in the "DB instance identifier" field:

5. Specify other settings, such as database instance class, VPC security group, and parameter group:

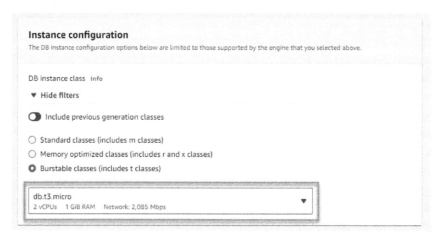

6. In the "Instance configuration" section, select the "Choose existing" option and then choose your VPC security group:

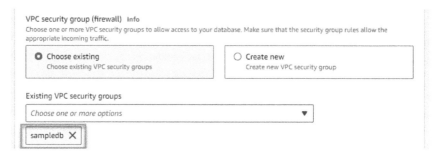

7. In the "Additional configuration" section, choose the DB parameter group. Then click "Restore DB instance":

Restore Snapshot Backup Using the AWS CLI

You can use the AWS CLI to restore an RDS for MySQL database instance from a specific database snapshot. Execute the following command, replacing the placeholders with appropriate values:

```
[root@ip-172-31-37-254 ~]#
[root@ip-172-31-37-254 ~]# aws rds restore-db-instance-from-db-snapshot \
--db-instance-identifier testdbsnapcli\
--db-snapshot-identifier database-1-testing-backup
"DBInstance": {
"DBInstanceIdentifier": "testdbsnapcli",
"DBInstanceClass": "db.t3.micro",
"Engine": "mysql",
"DBInstanceStatus": "creating",
"MasterUsername": "admin",
"AllocatedStorage": 20,
"PreferredBackupWindow": "12:10-12:40",
"BackupRetentionPeriod": 7,
"DBSecurityGroups": [],
"VpcSecurityGroups": [
{
"VpcSecurityGroupId": "sg-0b20d2c7d334b6acd",
"Status": "active"
```

Testing and Validating Backups and Restores

You must test and validate backups and restores to ensure data integrity and recovery, which you can do using either the AWS Management Console or the AWS CLI.

1. Sign in to the AWS Management Console and navigate to the RDS console. Select the restored database instance and connect using your preferred MySQL client:

2. Run queries to verify data consistency and integrity:

```
[root@ip-172-31-37-254 ~]# mysql -h devdb.cgbvu6nloqfx.us-west-2.
rds.amazonaws.com
Enter password:
Welcome to the MySQL monitor. Commands end with ; or \g.
Your MySQL connection id is 10
Server version: 8.0.32 Source distribution

Copyright (c) 2000, 2022, Oracle and/or its affiliates.

Oracle is a registered trademark of Oracle Corporation and/or its
affiliates. Other names may be trademarks of their respective
owners.

Type 'help;' or '\h' for help. Type '\c' to clear the current input
statement.

mysql>
```

Scaling RDS for MySQL

You can scale your RDS for MySQL instances to meet the changing demands of your application by using either the AWS Management Console or the AWS CLI.

Scaling your database instance and storage is an important aspect of optimizing the performance and cost efficiency of your database infrastructure. Let's explore the best practices for scaling up and down your instance size and storage, as well as adding read replicas.

Before you scale up or down your database instance size and storage, it's important to evaluate your current workload. This will help you determine the optimal instance size and storage for your workload. Here are some factors to consider:

- Current CPU usage
- Memory usage
- Storage usage

- Network usage
- Number of active connections
- Application requirements

RDS for MySQL offers various instance types to meet your performance and cost requirements. It's important to choose the right instance type for your workload. Instance types to consider include the following:

General purpose (M class)
  For small to medium workloads

Memory optimized (R class)
  For memory-intensive workloads

Compute optimized (C class)
  For CPU-intensive workloads

Storage optimized (I class)
  For high storage capacity and I/O performance

Scaling Up the Storage

RDS for MySQL also supports scaling up the storage capacity of your database instance. This can be done using the AWS Management Console or the AWS CLI. When you scale up the storage, you are increasing the amount of storage available for your database.

To scale up or down the storage of your database using the AWS Management Console, follow these steps:

1. From the AWS Management Console, navigate to the RDS console. Select the database instance you want to scale:

2. Click the Modify button:

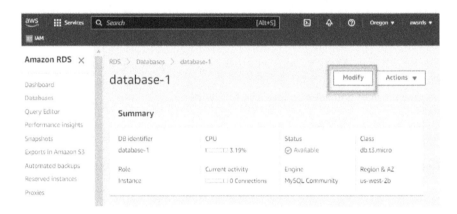

3. Adjust the instance class or storage size as needed and click Continue:

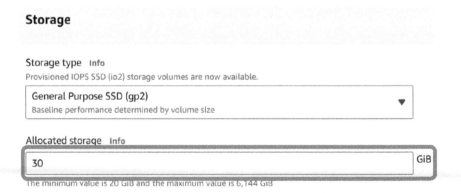

4. Review your changes and then click "Modify DB instance":

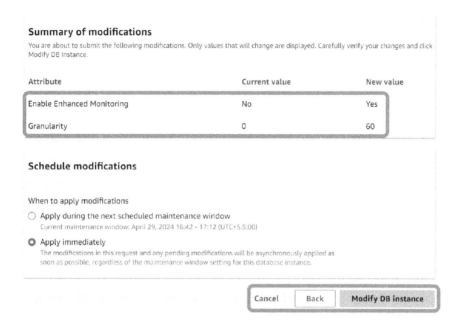

Adding Read Replicas for Improved Scalability

RDS for MySQL enables you to create a special type of database instance, called a *read replica*, from a source database instance. The source database instance becomes the primary database instance, and any updates made to the primary database instance are asynchronously copied to the read replica.

Setting up one or multiple read replicas for a specific source database instance can be advantageous in different situations, such as:

- When surpassing the computing or input/output capabilities of a single DB instance due to heavy read workloads, you can route the excess read traffic to one or more read replicas to scale effectively.

- Providing read traffic access during unavailability of the source DB instance. There are instances where the source DB instance cannot handle I/O requests, such as during I/O suspension for backups or scheduled maintenance. During these times, directing read traffic to read replicas is an option. However, it's important to note that in this scenario, the data on the read replica may be outdated ("stale") due to the unavailability of the source DB instance.

- In business reporting or data warehousing situations, you may prefer running business reporting queries against a read replica instead of your production DB instance.

- Setting up disaster recovery involves promoting a read replica to a standalone instance in case the primary DB instance encounters a failure.

Follow these steps to create a read replica from a source database instance:

1. Open the Amazon RDS console. In the navigation pane, choose Databases and select the database instance that you want to use as the source for a read replica:

2. From the Actions menu, choose "Create read replica":

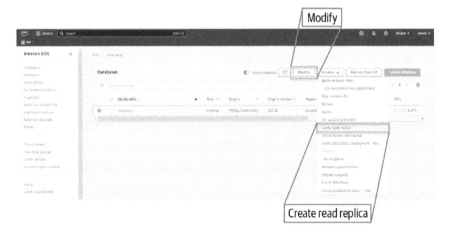

3. For the database instance identifier, enter a name for the read replica:

4. Choose your instance specifications. We recommend that you use the same or larger database instance class and storage type as the source database instance for the read replica:

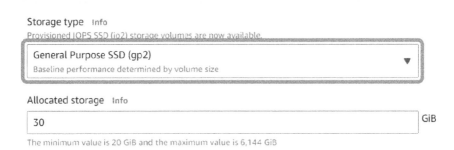

5. Choose "Multi-AZ DB instance" to create a standby replica in another zone, allowing automatic failover in case of an outage in the primary zone:

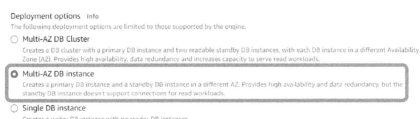

You can create your read replica with multi-AZ functionality regardless of whether the source database is multi-AZ.

6. To create an encrypted read replica, select the "Enable encryption" checkbox. For the AWS KMS key, choose RDS KMS. Note that the source database instance must be encrypted:

Encryption

☑ Enable encryption
Choose to encrypt the given instance. Master key IDs and aliases appear in the list after they have been created using the AWS Key Management Service console. **Info**

AWS KMS key   Info

(default) aws/rds   ▼

7. Specify other settings, such as allocated storage size and whether you want to use storage autoscaling. Then click the "Create read replica" button:

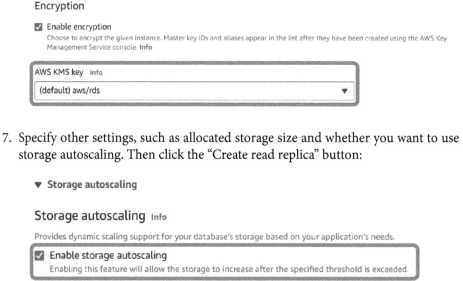

▼ **Storage autoscaling**

Storage autoscaling Info

Provides dynamic scaling support for your database's storage based on your application's needs.

☑ **Enable storage autoscaling**
Enabling this feature will allow the storage to increase after the specified threshold is exceeded.

Maximum storage threshold Info

Charges will apply when your database autoscales to the specified threshold

100   GiB

The minimum value is 33 GiB and the maximum value is 6,144 GiB

8. Once your read replica is ready, you'll find it listed on the Databases page in the RDS console. Look for "Replica" in the Role column to identify it:

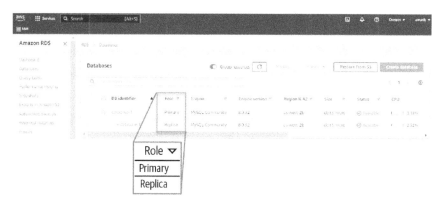

Adding Read Replica Using the AWS CLI

With the following AWS CLI command, you can seamlessly add a read replica to its database instance:

```
[root@ip-172-31-37-254 ~]#
[root@ip-172-31-37-254 ~]# aws rds create-db-instance-read-replica
--db-instance-identifier rr-database-1 -source-db-instance-identifier
databa se-1 --db-instance-class db.t3.micro-allocated-storage 30
"DBInstance": {
"DBInstanceIdentifier": "rr-database-1",
"DBInstanceClass": "db.t3.micro",
"Engine": "mysql",
"DBInstanceStatus": "creating",
"MasterUsername": "admin",
"AllocatedStorage" : 30,
"PreferredBackupWindow": "12:10-12:40",
"BackupRetentionPeriod": 0,
"DBSecurityGroups": [],
"VpcSecurityGroups": [
{
"VpcSecurityGroupId": "sg-051f997aa495db56d", "Status": "active"
},
}
"VpcSecurityGroupId": "sg-027300d30db0aa0fc", "Status": "active"
```

Scaling up and down the instance size and storage of your RDS for MySQL database is an important task for managing its performance and capacity. By following the best practices and using the AWS Management Console or the AWS CLI, you can easily scale your database instance and avoid downtime.

 You can create RDS read replicas either in the same AWS Region as the source database instance or in a separate AWS Region.

Configuring CloudWatch Metrics and Alarms

One of the critical aspects of managing an RDS instance is monitoring its performance and setting up alarms to get timely notifications about potential issues. Amazon CloudWatch is a powerful monitoring tool that you can use to track various metrics and set up alarms for your RDS MySQL instances.

Understanding Key CloudWatch Metrics for RDS MySQL

Before you can configure CloudWatch alarms, it's essential to understand the key metrics that are available for RDS for MySQL instances. The following are some critical metrics you should monitor:

CPU utilization
    The percentage of CPU resources used by your RDS instance

Freeable memory
    The amount of available memory in your RDS instance

Database connections
    The number of current connections to your RDS instance

Read and write IOPS
    The number of input/output operations per second for read and write operations

Read and write latency
    The average time taken for read and write operations

Creating CloudWatch Alarms

CloudWatch alarms can notify you when certain thresholds are met or exceeded. For example, you can create an alarm to notify you when the CPU utilization of your RDS instance exceeds a certain threshold.

To create an alarm for monitoring RDS for MySQL, follow these steps:

1. From the AWS Management console, access the CloudWatch console (*https://oreil.ly/AyLuo*):

2. From the navigation pane, Alarms > All alarms will display all existing alarms:

3. Click the "Create alarm" button. This action launches the alarm creation wizard:

4. Click the "Select metric" button. This allows you to choose the metric for triggering the alarm:

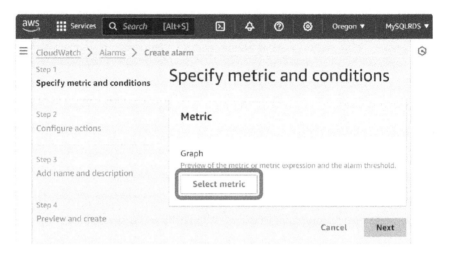

5. Browse and choose RDS. Then in the Browse section, choose RDS to display available Amazon RDS metrics:

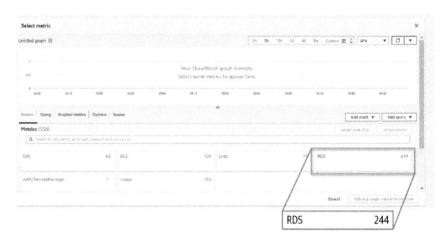

6. Search for the desired metric. For example, search for **CPUUtilization** to monitor CPU usage. To display only Amazon RDS metrics, search for the identifier of your resource:

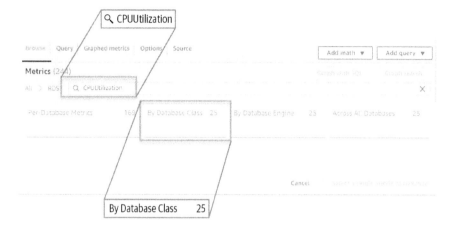

7. Choose the metric name CPUUtilization and then click "Select metric":

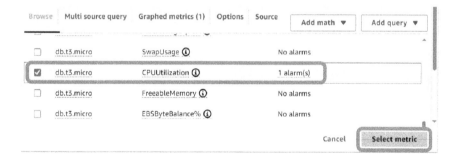

8. In the Conditions section, specify the alarm condition (e.g., when CPU utilization is over 80%). Then click the Next button:

Conditions

Threshold type

◉ Static
Use a value as a threshold

○ Anomaly detection
Use a band as a threshold

Whenever CPUUtilization is...
Define the alarm condition.

○ Greater
\> threshold

◉ Greater/Equal
\>= threshold

○ Lower/Equal
<= threshold

○ Lower
< threshold

than...
Define the threshold value.

80

Must be a number

▶ Additional configuration

Cancel   **Next**

9. In the "Specify metric and conditions" section, verify the metric name (such as CPUUtilization) and other details:

Specify metric and conditions

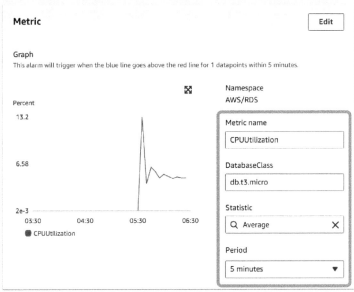

10. Configure how you want to be notified when the alarm state is reached, and then click Next. To receive an email notification, follow these steps:

a. Choose "In alarm" and click the "Create new topic" option:

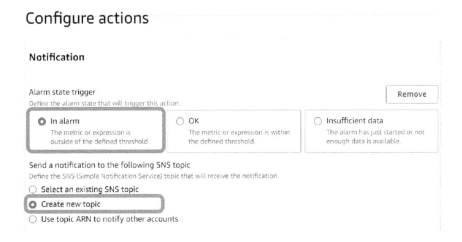

b. Enter a topic name:

Create a new topic...
The topic name must be unique.

> DBA_RDS_Team

SNS topic names can contain only alphanumeric characters, hyphens (-) and underscores (_).

c. Enter the email endpoints, click the "Create topic" button, and then click the "Add notification" button. Note that email addresses must be verified before they can receive notifications:

Email endpoints that will receive the notification...
Add a comma-separated list of email addresses. Each address will be added as a subscription to the topic above.

> jramcloud1@gmail.com

user1@example.com, user2@example.com

d. Select the OK radio button:

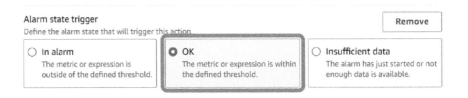

e. Choose the "Select an existing SNS topic" option. Then click Next:

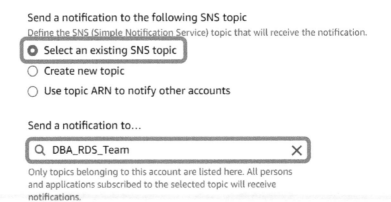

f. Enter a name and description for the alarm: The name must contain only ASCII characters. Then click Next:

Name and description

Alarm name

database-1-CPUUtilization-RDS

Alarm description - *optional* View formatting guidelines

Edit   Preview

This is an H1
double asterisks will produce strong character
This is [an example](https://example.com/) inline link.

Up to 1024 characters (0/1024)

ⓘ Markdown formatting is only applied when viewing your alarm in the console. The description will remain in plain text in the alarm notifications.

Cancel   Previous   Next

g. Review the alarm configuration and then click the "Create alarm" button:

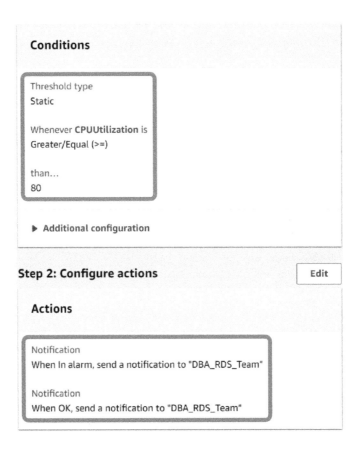

Conditions

Threshold type
Static

Whenever **CPUUtilization** is Greater/Equal (>=)

than...
80

▶ Additional configuration

Step 2: Configure actions   Edit

Actions

Notification
When In alarm, send a notification to "DBA_RDS_Team"

Notification
When OK, send a notification to "DBA_RDS_Team"

By following these steps, you can create a CloudWatch alarm for your RDS for MySQL instance, which will notify you when specific conditions are met. This helps ensure the health and performance of your database, enabling you to take proactive actions when necessary.

Enabling Enhanced Monitoring

Enhanced Monitoring is a feature of RDS for MySQL that enables the collection of additional metrics beyond the standard CloudWatch metrics. By default, RDS collects metrics every five minutes, but with Enhanced Monitoring, you can collect metrics as frequently as every second.

To enable Enhanced Monitoring, log in to the AWS Management Console, go to the RDS Dashboard, and follow these steps:

1. Select the database instance you want to scale:

2. Click the Modify button:

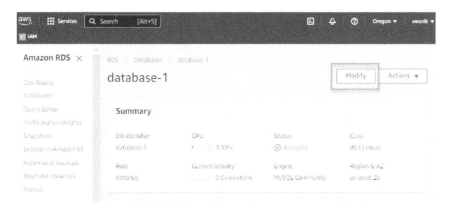

3. Scroll down to Monitoring and select Enable Enhanced Monitoring. Click the Continue button:

Monitoring

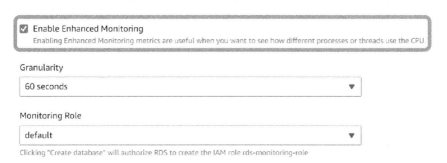

Granularity

| 60 seconds | ▼ |

Monitoring Role

| default | ▼ |

Clicking "Create database" will authorize RDS to create the IAM role rds-monitoring-role

4. Review the changes and then click the "Modify DB instance" button:

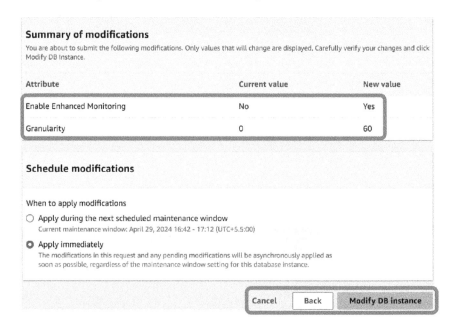

Analyzing Database Logs for Troubleshooting

Database logs can provide valuable insights into the health and performance of your database. RDS for MySQL generates several types of logs, including error logs, slow query logs, and general logs, which can be accessed via the Amazon RDS console or command-line tools like MySQL Workbench:

Error logs
Information about errors encountered by the MySQL server. This helps diagnose and troubleshoot issues with the server.

Slow query logs
Logs are generated for information about queries that exceed a predefined execution time. These logs help identify and optimize slow queries, ultimately enhancing overall performance.

General logs
Information about the server's activity, such as connections and queries. You can use these logs to diagnose issues with the database and optimize performance.

Accessing the Logs, Events, and Streams for Your Database Instance

To view logs, events, and streams for your database instance in the RDS console, follow these steps:

1. From the AWS Management Console, access the Amazon RDS console. In the navigation pane, choose Databases:

2. Choose the name of the DB instance that you want to monitor. This example shows a MySQL database named database-1:

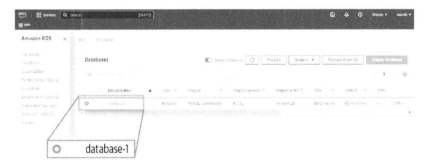

3. In the database page, choose the tab called "Logs & events":

4. When you choose the logs and events, you will be able to find recent events such as instance start, stop, restart, backup status, etc. in the events section. Additionally, in the log section, you will find different logs like MySQL errors, upgrades, etc.:

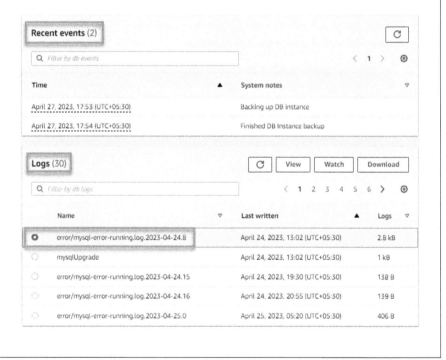

Using Performance Insights to Identify Bottlenecks

Performance Insights is a feature in RDS for MySQL that provides a real-time view of database performance. It can help you identify and troubleshoot performance issues, such as high CPU utilization, slow queries, and database load.

To use Performance Insights to identify bottlenecks, follow these steps:

1. Go to the Amazon RDS console and log in with your credentials:

2. Select your MySQL database instance from the list of instances:

3. In the left navigation pane, select "Performance insights" and then select the DB instance for which you want to view the performance metrics:

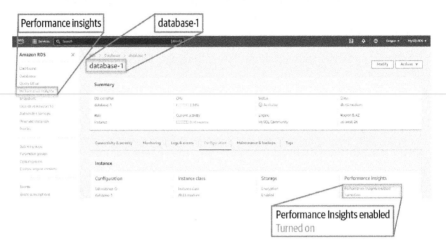

4. Select the time range for the performance data and click the Apply button:

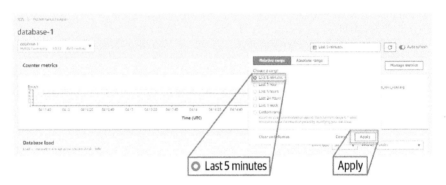

5. The RDS Performance Insights dashboard will load, displaying high-level performance indicator metrics. You can drill down to individual queries, waits, users, and hosts generating the load:

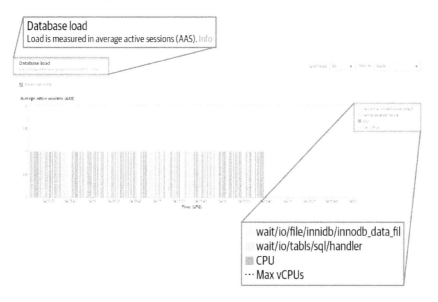

6. Analyze the data by using the various tabs such as "Top SQL," "Top hosts," and "Top users":

Troubleshooting Network Connectivity Issues

Network connectivity issues can prevent your application from accessing the MySQL database instance. To troubleshoot issues in Amazon RDS, follow these steps:

1. Check the security group settings to ensure that the inbound rules allow traffic from your application.

2. Check the routing and firewall settings on your local machine and any intermediate network devices.

3. Check the database instance status in the RDS console to ensure it is available and running.

4. Use the `telnet` command to test connectivity to the database endpoint.

Cost Optimization Best Practices for RDS for MySQL

RDS for MySQL is a fully managed database service that simplifies the process of setting up, operating, and scaling a MySQL database in the cloud. However, running a MySQL database on RDS can be expensive if not optimized properly. Let's cover cost optimization best practices for RDS for MySQL, including ways to reduce costs without compromising database performance.

Right-Sizing Database Instances

Choosing the right instance size for your database is crucial to optimizing cost. Consider your workload requirements, such as CPU usage and IOPS, to determine the appropriate instance size. Avoid using an overprovisioned instance that leads to unused resources and high costs.

You can configure your instance size as follows:

1. From the Amazon RDS console, select the MySQL database instance:

2. Click the Modify button to change the instance type:

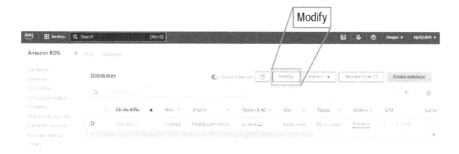

3. Select an instance type that fits your workload requirements and then click Continue:

Instance configuration

The DB instance configuration options below are limited to those supported by the engine that you selected above.

DB instance class Info

▼ Hide filters

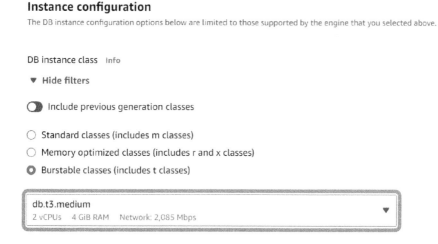

4. Review the changes and then click the "Apply immediately" option and the "Modify DB instance" button to apply them:

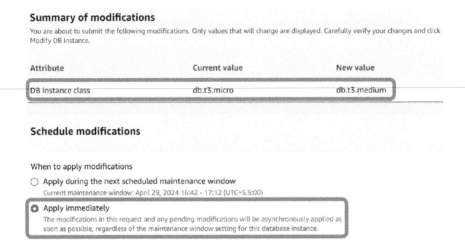

Summary of modifications

You are about to submit the following modifications. Only values that will change are displayed. Carefully verify your changes and click Modify DB Instance.

Attribute	Current value	New value
DB instance class	db.t3.micro	db.t3.medium

Schedule modifications

When to apply modifications

○ Apply during the next scheduled maintenance window
  Current maintenance window: April 29, 2024 16:42 - 17:12 (UTC+5.5:00)

◉ Apply immediately
  The modifications in this request and any pending modifications will be asynchronously applied as soon as possible, regardless of the maintenance window setting for this database instance.

Optimizing Amazon RDS Database Backup Costs Efficiently

Reserved instances offer a significant cost savings compared to on-demand instances. They allow you to commit to a specific instance size for a period of one to three years, which can result in savings of up to 75%.

Amazon RDS Reserved Capacity provides additional flexibility and cost savings by allowing you to reserve capacity for multiple instance groups and sizes within a region. This means you can choose the most cost-effective instance type for your workload while still benefiting from reserved instance pricing.

Database backups are crucial for disaster recovery and data protection. However, creating frequent backups can increase costs. To optimize costs, consider using the automated backup feature, which allows you to schedule backups based on your specific requirements. Here's an example configuration using the console:

1. Go to the Amazon RDS console and select the MySQL database instance:

2. Click the Modify option to change the backup settings:

3. Choose the backup retention period, set the backup window, and click Continue:

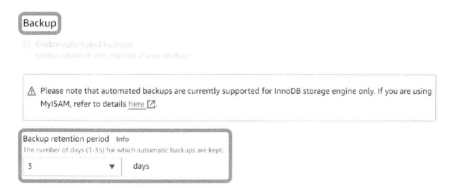

4. Review the changes. Click "Apply immediately" and "Modify DB instance":

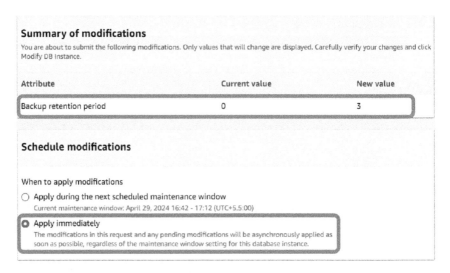

Conclusion

This chapter provided a comprehensive introduction to RDS for MySQL, covering its benefits, architecture, setup, management, performance optimization, and monitoring capabilities.

## CHAPTER 12

MySQL on the Cloud: Amazon Aurora

Amazon Aurora is a fully managed, high-performance, and highly available relational database service built for the cloud. It is compatible with the MySQL database engine, providing seamless integration with existing applications and tools. This chapter focuses on the *Amazon Aurora MySQL* variant.

You will gain insights into MySQL deployment on Aurora, covering key features, Aurora's storage architecture, use cases, and cluster setup. The chapter addresses configuration, backup, monitoring, troubleshooting, and performance optimization, including read replicas and autoscaling. High-availability, replication, and failover strategies are detailed, as well as backup, recovery, and security best practices. Cost optimization and resource management are discussed, along with integration with AWS.

Let's delve into the prominent features and advantages of Aurora MySQL as we explore its capabilities:

High performance
> Aurora MySQL is designed to deliver up to five times the throughput of standard MySQL databases. This performance gain is achieved through optimizations at the storage and engine levels, providing low-latency read and write operations.

Scalability
> Aurora MySQL automatically scales storage capacity without any downtime, allowing the database to grow with your application's needs. Additionally, Aurora supports read replicas for horizontal scaling of read-heavy workloads.

High availability
> Aurora MySQL is designed with built-in fault tolerance and automatic failover to provide a highly available database service. It automatically replicates data across

multiple availability zones and supports up to 15 read replicas for further redundancy.

Security

Aurora MySQL provides multiple layers of security, including network isolation using Amazon VPC, encryption at rest and in transit, and integration with AWS IAM.

The storage architecture of Aurora MySQL is designed to deliver high performance, durability, and availability. Key aspects of this architecture include the following:

Distributed and shared storage

Data is automatically distributed across multiple storage nodes, allowing for parallel processing and increased performance.

Automatic replication

Aurora replicates data across multiple availability zones, ensuring data durability and fault tolerance.

Backups and PITR

Aurora automatically takes continuous backups of your database and supports PITR to restore data in case of accidental deletion or corruption.

Aurora MySQL is well-suited for a variety of applications, including these:

Web and mobile applications

Its high performance and scalability make Aurora MySQL an excellent choice for powering web and mobile applications with high traffic and demanding workloads.

Ecommerce platforms

Aurora MySQL can handle the complex transactions, inventory management, and analytics required by modern ecommerce platforms.

Gaming

The low-latency and high throughput of Aurora MySQL are ideal for supporting real-time gaming experiences with large numbers of concurrent users.

Data warehousing and analytics

Aurora MySQL's powerful query processing capabilities and compatibility with existing MySQL tools make it a strong choice for data warehousing and analytics workloads.

Creating an Aurora MySQL DB Cluster

In this section, we walk through the process of creating an Aurora MySQL DB cluster by using the "Easy create" option. The example will demonstrate the creation of an Aurora MySQL DB cluster with a `db.r6g.large` DB instance class. Follow these steps:

1. Navigate to the AWS Management Console and open the Amazon RDS console (*https://console.aws.amazon.com/rds*):

2. In the upper-right corner of the RDS console, select the AWS Region where you want to create the DB cluster:

3. In the navigation pane, click Databases:

4. Click "Create database," which will lead you to a screen where you need to select "Easy create." After that, you will be directed to the "Engine options" screen:

5. In the Configuration section, choose Aurora (MySQL Compatible) as the engine type:

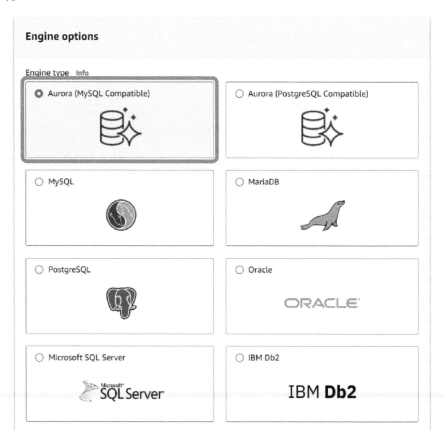

6. For the DB instance size, select Dev/Test:

7. For the DB cluster identifier, input **database-1**:

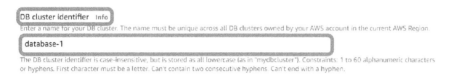

8. For the "Master username" option, input a name for the master user or maintain the default name:

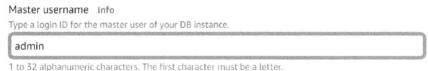

9. To use an automatically generated master password for the DB cluster, select the "Auto generate password" checkbox:

If you wish to input your master password manually, uncheck "Auto generate password" and enter the same password in both the "Master password" and "Confirm master password" fields:

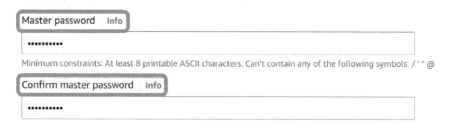

10. To establish a connection with the EC2 instance created earlier, expand the "Set up EC2 connection - optional" section:

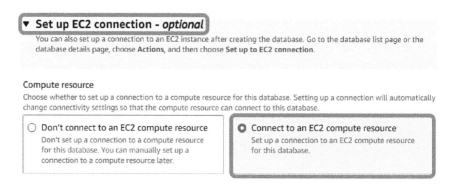

11. Select "Connect to an EC2 compute resource" and choose the EC2 instance you previously created:

12. Click "View default settings for Easy create" to examine the default settings:

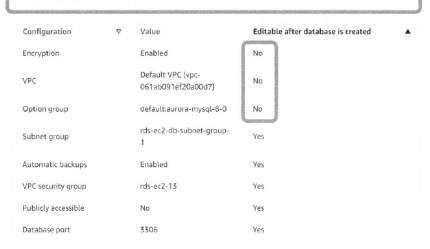

▼ View default settings for Easy create

Easy create sets the following configurations to their default values, some of which can be changed later. If you want to change any of these settings now, use Standard create.

Configuration ▽	Value	Editable after database is created ▲
Encryption	Enabled	No
VPC	Default VPC (vpc-061ab091ef20a00d7)	No
Option group	default:aurora-mysql-8-0	No
Subnet group	rds-ec2-db-subnet-group-1	Yes
Automatic backups	Enabled	Yes
VPC security group	rds-ec2-13	Yes
Publicly accessible	No	Yes
Database port	3306	Yes

13. If a setting displays No in the "Editable after database is created" column and you desire a different setting, click "Standard create" to create the DB cluster:

▼ View default settings for Easy create

Easy create sets the following configurations to their default values, some of which can be changed later. If you want to change any of these settings now, use Standard create.

Configuration ▽	Value	Editable after database is created ▲
Encryption	Enabled	No
VPC	Default VPC (vpc-061ab091ef20a00d7)	No
Option group	default:aurora-mysql-8-0	No
Subnet group	rds-ec2-db-subnet-group-1	Yes
Automatic backups	Enabled	Yes
VPC security group	rds-ec2-13	Yes
Publicly accessible	No	Yes
Database port	3306	Yes

If a setting displays Yes in that column and you desire a different setting, either use "Standard create" to create the DB cluster or modify the DB cluster after its creation to change the setting. Then click the "Create database" button:

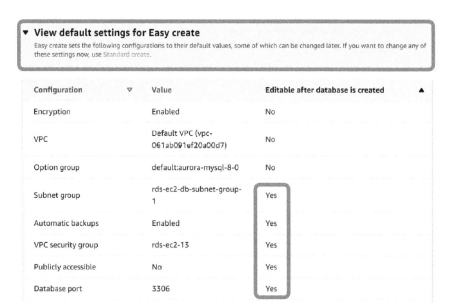

▼ View default settings for Easy create

Easy create sets the following configurations to their default values, some of which can be changed later. If you want to change any of these settings now, use Standard create.

Configuration ▽	Value	Editable after database is created ▲
Encryption	Enabled	No
VPC	Default VPC (vpc-061ab091ef20a00d7)	No
Option group	default:aurora-mysql-8-0	No
Subnet group	rds-ec2-db-subnet-group-1	Yes
Automatic backups	Enabled	Yes
VPC security group	rds-ec2-13	Yes
Publicly accessible	No	Yes
Database port	3306	Yes

14. In the Databases list, select the name of the new Aurora MySQL DB cluster to view its details:

15. Once the main database instance shows an Available status, you can connect to your new DB cluster. This process might take up to 20 minutes, depending on the chosen instance class and storage size:

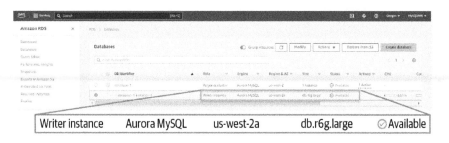

16. The following connection detail belongs to the database writer instance on the Aurora cluster:

```
PS C:\Users\Administrator> mysql -h database-1.cluster-cgbvu6nloqfx.us-west-2
.rds.amazonaws.com -P 3306 -u admin -p
Enter password: ************
Welcome to the MySQL monitor. Commands end with; or \g.
Your MySQL connection id is 592
Server version: 8.0.26 Source distribution

Copyright (c) 2000, 2023, Oracle and/or its affiliates.

Oracle is a registered trademark of Oracle Corporation and/or its
affiliates. Other names may be trademarks of their respective owners.

Type 'help;' or '\h' for help. Type '\c' to clear the current input
statement.

mysql>
```

Configuring DB Instance Settings

The following list describes the important configurations you need to consider when creating the Aurora MySQL DB instance:

Instance identifier
Set a unique name for your instance (e.g., `aurora-mysql-instance`).

Master username and password
Provide credentials for the database administrator.

DB instance class
Choose the appropriate size based on your needs (e.g., `db.t3.medium`).

Availability zone
Select an appropriate zone to ensure high availability and fault tolerance.

Virtual Private Cloud
Choose an existing VPC or create a new one for your DB instance, setting up security groups and IAM roles.

Security groups
Create a new security group or select an existing one to control inbound and outbound traffic to your DB instance. Add rules to allow specific IP addresses or Classless Inter-Domain Routing (CIDR) ranges to access the database.

Example rule
Allow inbound traffic on port 3306 from a specific IP address (e.g., `1.2.3.4/32`).

Set up IAM roles

To enable your DB instance to access other AWS services—such as backups, monitoring, or logging—you need to create an IAM role. This role will serve as a conduit for granting necessary permissions. Attach the required policies to the IAM role (e.g., "AmazonRDSFullAccess" or "AmazonRDSEnhancedMonitoring-Role") to ensure that your DB instance can seamlessly interact with these services, enhancing its functionality and operational capabilities.

Enable automatic backups

In the "Backup" section of the DB instance settings, choose a backup retention period (e.g., seven days). Optionally, enable cross-region backups for disaster recovery.

Set up monitoring

You can enhance your system with advanced insights and performance tracking through the seamless integration of Enable Enhanced Monitoring. Elevate your monitoring capabilities to create a more resilient and efficient operational environment:

- Enable Enhanced Monitoring to collect detailed metrics on your DB instance.
- Configure alarms for specific metrics (e.g., CPU usage, storage space) to receive notifications when thresholds are crossed.

Connecting to the Aurora MySQL Database

You can effortlessly access the potential of Aurora MySQL database with the MySQL client connection. To connect to the Aurora MySQL DB instance, first, retrieve the endpoint and port number from the "Connectivity & Security" section of the RDS console. These details are essential for configuring the connection settings. Once obtained, use a MySQL client or application to establish the connection. Input the provided endpoint, port number, and credentials into the client or application settings. This straightforward process allows for seamless connectivity to the Aurora MySQL DB instance, facilitating efficient management and interaction with the database resources:

```
PS C:\Users\Administrator> mysql -h database-1.cluster-cgbvu6nloqfx.us-west-2.
rds.amazonaws.com -P 3306 -u admin -p
Enter password: ************
Welcome to the MySQL monitor. Commands end with; or \g.
Your MySQL connection id is 592
Server version: 8.0.26 Source distribution

Copyright (c) 2000, 2023, Oracle and/or its affiliates.

Oracle is a registered trademark of Oracle Corporation and/or its
```

```
affiliates. Other names may be trademarks of their respective owners.

Type 'help;' or '\h' for help. Type '\c' to clear the current input
statement.

mysql>
```

By following these guidelines, you can ensure a secure, scalable, and high-performance Aurora MySQL environment for your applications.

Configuring Performance and Memory Settings

To ensure optimal performance and scalability for your database, it's important to properly configure the performance and memory settings. Here are some key points to consider:

Adjusting the instance class
Choose the right instance class based on your workload requirements. Larger instance classes offer more memory and processing power.

Configuring the IOPS
Increase the IOPS value for better read and write performance.

Optimizing the buffer pool size
Configure the buffer pool size to fit the majority of your database's working set in memory.

Modifying an Amazon Aurora DB Cluster

When it comes to managing your Amazon Aurora DB cluster, making modifications is a crucial aspect of ensuring that it meets your specific needs. But before making any changes to your cluster, evaluate the impact of the changes on your application's performance and availability. You should also determine the best time to perform the modifications, ideally during a maintenance window or a period of low traffic.

To ensure data safety, create a manual snapshot of your DB cluster before making any modifications. This will enable you to restore the cluster to its previous state in case of any issues. In the Amazon RDS console, you can easily initiate backups for your selected DB cluster by choosing a cluster to back up, accessing the Actions menu, and creating a snapshot with a specified name for data preservation.

Once you initiate the modification process, monitor its progress in the Amazon RDS console. This will help you track any issues that arise and take appropriate action. To ensure smooth management of your DB cluster in Amazon RDS, it's essential to monitor its status for ongoing modifications and completion. Additionally, keeping an eye on the Events tab allows you to promptly address any crucial notifications or errors that may arise during the process.

After the modification is complete, test your application to ensure that it is functioning correctly with the new configuration:

- Perform end-to-end tests to verify the application is working as expected.
- Monitor the application's performance and adjust the configuration if necessary.

Here's how to modify the instance class of an Amazon Aurora DB cluster step by step:

1. Sign in to the AWS Management Console and open the Amazon RDS console:

2. In the navigation pane, choose Databases, and then select the DB cluster that you want to modify:

3. Click Modify. The Modify DB cluster page appears:

4. In the "Instance configuration" section, select a new instance class (https://oreil.ly/FH_o6) from the DB instance class drop-down menu:

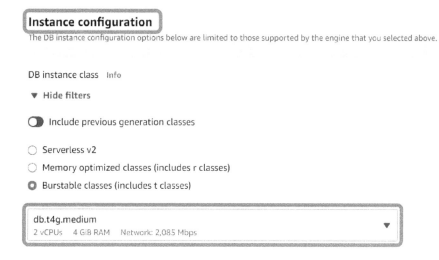

5. Click the Continue button and review the summary of modifications:

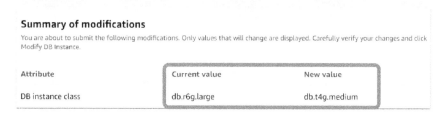

6. To apply the changes immediately, select "Apply immediately," and then click the "Modify DB instance" button:

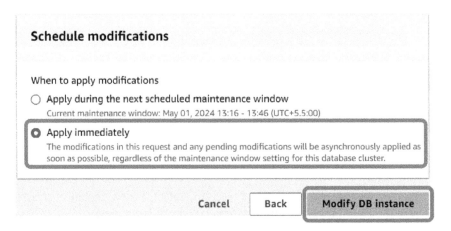

7. Monitor the progress of the modification and test your application once the changes are complete:

After the modification is completed, it displays the Available status:

Optimizing Queries and Indexes

Optimizing queries and indexes can greatly improve the performance and scalability of your database. Consider the following best practices:

Analyze slow queries
Use tools like the slow query log to identify and optimize poorly performing queries.

Use EXPLAIN
Use the EXPLAIN statement to understand how queries are executed and identify potential optimizations.

Create indexes
Indexes can significantly speed up query execution. Make sure to create the appropriate indexes for frequently accessed columns.

Optimize indexes
Regularly review and update your indexes to ensure that they remain efficient.

Using Amazon RDS Performance Insights

Amazon RDS Performance Insights helps you monitor your database's performance and identify potential issues. The following are key capabilities of this feature:

Monitoring the database load
Use the Performance Insights dashboard to monitor the overall load on your database.

Identifying performance bottlenecks
Analyze the top SQL statements and wait events to find queries causing high load or latency.

Setting up alarms
Configure alarms to alert you when specific performance metrics exceed a threshold.

Autoscaling Amazon Aurora Read Replicas

Amazon Aurora Auto Scaling is a feature that automatically adjusts the number of Aurora replicas in your Aurora DB cluster based on the specified target metric and target value. This helps maintain consistent performance and efficiently manage resources in response to changes in workload.

Autoscaling Amazon Aurora read replicas helps balance read-heavy workloads and improve scalability. Key considerations include the following:

Enabling read replica autoscaling
Activate the autoscaling feature to automatically add or remove read replicas based on demand.

Configuring scaling policies
Define target tracking policies to ensure that the read replicas maintain a specific performance level.

To configure an autoscaling policy for your Aurora DB cluster, follow these steps:

1. From the AWS Management Console, open the Amazon RDS console. In the navigation pane, click Databases:

2. Select the Aurora DB cluster to assign a policy to:

3. View the log and event data in the "Logs & events" tab:

4. Add a new policy via the "Auto scaling policies" section. Click the "Add auto scaling policy" button to access the "Add Auto Scaling policy" dialog box:

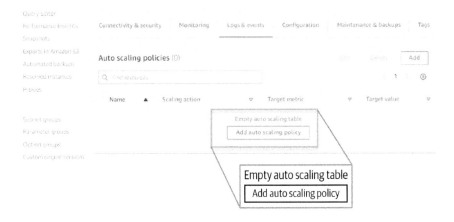

5. In the "Policy name" field, enter a descriptive name for your policy:

Policy details

Policy name

A name for the policy used to identify it in the console, CLI, API, notifications, and events.

Policy name must be 1 to 256 characters.

6. From the following options, select the metric that will be used to decide when to automatically scale your resources:

   a. Select "Average CPU utilization of Aurora Replicas" to create a policy based on the average CPU utilization

   b. Select "Average connections of Aurora Replicas" to create a policy based on the average number of connections to Aurora replicas

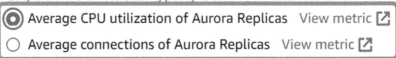

7. Enter a number in the "Target value" field to establish when automatic scaling occurs:

   a. If you selected "Average CPU utilization of Aurora Replicas" in the previous step, enter the desired average CPU usage percentage for your replicas. This value will be used to automatically scale replicas to maintain optimal performance.

   b. If you selected "Average connections of Aurora Replicas" in the previous step, enter the desired number of connections you want your replicas to handle. This will trigger scaling when that number is exceeded:

Automatic scaling keeps things balanced: when the chosen metric (like CPU usage or connections) gets close to the value you set, Aurora will automatically add or remove replicas to keep things running smoothly.

8. For more control over scaling behavior, consider Additional Configuration options. Here, you can set a cooldown period to prevent excessive scaling actions:

9. Set a minimum number of replicas with the "Minimum capacity" option. Enter the lowest number of Aurora Replicas you want this policy to maintain. This ensures your database always has enough resources available:

10. Set a limit on replica scaling with the "Maximum capacity" option. Enter the highest number of Aurora Replicas you want this policy to allow. This prevents excessive resource usage during peak traffic. Then click the "Add policy" button:

Cluster capacity details

Configure the minimum and maximum number of Aurora Replicas you want Aurora Auto Scaling to maintain.

Minimum capacity

Specify the minimum number of Aurora Replicas to maintain.

| 1 | Aurora Replicas |

Maximum capacity

Specify the maximum number of Aurora Replicas to maintain. Up to 15 Aurora Replicas are supported.

| 14 | Aurora Replicas |

11. Head to the Databases page to confirm the new instance was added successfully. This will ensure you have the connection details you need:

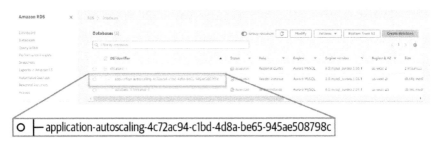

application-autoscaling-4c72ac94-c1bd-4d8a-be65-945ae508798c

Implementing Caching Strategies

Caching can significantly improve the performance and scalability of your database. Here are some best practices:

Use in-memory caching
Store frequently accessed data in memory to reduce read operations on the database.

Implement query caching
Cache the results of frequently executed queries to avoid redundant computations.

Use Amazon ElastiCache
Integrate your database with Amazon ElastiCache to improve performance by offloading read operations to the cache.

Monitoring and Troubleshooting

Let's now discuss best practices for monitoring and troubleshooting Aurora. We'll cover monitoring key performance metrics, setting up Amazon CloudWatch alarms, analyzing slow query logs, detecting and resolving performance bottlenecks, and troubleshooting common issues.

Monitoring Key Performance Metrics

Monitoring key performance metrics is crucial for maintaining the health and performance of your Aurora database. Some important metrics to monitor include:

CPU utilization
> The percentage of CPU capacity used by the database instance. High CPU utilization may indicate a need for a more powerful instance or query optimization.

Database connections
> The number of active database connections. A sudden increase in connections can indicate a potential issue with the application or the need to scale your database.

Read and write latency
> The average time taken for read and write operations. High latency may indicate performance issues or the need for query optimization.

To monitor these metrics, you can use the Amazon RDS console or the CloudWatch console. In the RDS console, navigate to the Databases section and select your Amazon Aurora database. In the Monitoring tab, you can view graphs and data for the key performance metrics.

Setting Up Amazon CloudWatch Alarms

Amazon CloudWatch alarms play a critical role in maintaining the health and performance of your AWS resources. These alarms act as proactive guardians, providing real-time notifications and triggering automated actions when predefined thresholds are breached. By monitoring metrics and responding swiftly to anomalies, CloudWatch alarms contribute to the reliability, scalability, and cost-effectiveness of your cloud infrastructure, helping you address issues promptly and ensure a seamless user experience.

To learn more about setting Amazon CloudWatch alarms, see "Configuring CloudWatch Metrics and Alarms" on page 476.

Analyzing Slow Query Logs

Slow query logs provide valuable insights into the performance of your database by logging queries that take longer than a specified time to execute. To enable and analyze slow query logs, follow these steps:

1. In the RDS console, navigate to the "Parameter groups" section.
2. Create a new parameter group for your Amazon Aurora database or modify an existing one.
3. Set the `slow_query_log` parameter to 1 and the `long_query_time` parameter to your desired threshold value.
4. Apply the parameter group to your Aurora database and reboot the instance for the changes to take effect.

To analyze the slow query logs, you can use Amazon RDS Performance Insights or a third-party tool such as Percona Toolkit.

Detecting and Resolving Performance Bottlenecks

Detecting and resolving performance bottlenecks is essential for maintaining optimal performance of your Amazon Aurora database. To detect performance bottlenecks:

- Monitor key performance metrics and set CloudWatch alarms.
- Analyze slow query logs and optimize queries as needed.
- Use the Performance Insights feature in the RDS console to identify resource-intensive queries and take appropriate action.

To resolve performance bottlenecks, you can do the following:

- Optimize queries to reduce resource consumption.
- Add or modify indexes to improve query performance.
- Scale your Amazon Aurora database by increasing the instance size or adding read replicas.

Troubleshooting Common Issues

When troubleshooting common issues with your Amazon Aurora database, consider the following:

Connection issues
Ensure that the security group rules allow traffic from the necessary IP addresses or CIDR blocks, and verify the endpoint and port configuration.

High CPU utilization
Check for long-running queries, optimize queries, or consider upgrading to a larger instance size.

Insufficient storage
Regularly monitor storage usage, and if needed, increase the allocated storage or enable autoscaling.

Slow query performance
Analyze the slow query logs to identify poorly performing queries. Optimize these queries by rewriting them, adding appropriate indexes, or considering the use of partitioning for large tables.

Backup and restore issues
Ensure that automated backups are enabled, and regularly perform manual snapshots to create restore points. In case of data loss or corruption, you can restore the database from a snapshot or point-in-time backup.

Scaling issues
If your database is experiencing performance issues due to increased load, consider vertical scaling (upgrading to a larger instance size) or horizontal scaling (adding read replicas or partitioning data) to accommodate the growth.

By following these best practices for monitoring and troubleshooting your Aurora database, you can maintain high performance and availability while minimizing downtime and potential issues. Regularly assess the health of your database, optimize queries and resources, and ensure that your database is properly scaled and configured to handle the demands of your application.

High-Availability and Failover Strategies

When it comes to ensuring the uninterrupted operation of critical systems, understanding HA and failover strategies is paramount.

Understanding Amazon Aurora Replication

Amazon Aurora employs a unique approach to replication, which is designed to improve both availability and fault tolerance. Key features of Aurora MySQL replication include the following:

Shared storage architecture
Stores multiple copies of the database across AZs to ensure data durability.

Fast, asynchronous replication
Helps reduce the replication lag between the primary and replica instances.

Automatic failover
> Promotes a replica to take over the primary role in the event of a primary instance failure, ensuring minimal downtime.

Configuring Multi-AZ Deployments

Multi-AZ deployments in Amazon Aurora provide an additional layer of redundancy and fault tolerance. To configure a multi-AZ deployment, follow these steps:

1. In the AWS Management Console, navigate to the RDS section.
2. Select "Create database" and choose Amazon Aurora as the engine type.
3. Enable the "Multi-AZ deployment" option.
4. Configure other required settings, such as instance size, storage, and network.
5. Create the database, and AWS will automatically provision a primary and a standby instance in separate AZs.

Implementing Aurora Global Database

Aurora Global Database enables you to create a single, globally distributed database across multiple AWS Regions. This feature helps improve read latency, provides disaster recovery, and allows for low-latency failover. To implement Aurora Global Database, follow these steps:

1. Create an Amazon Aurora DB cluster in your primary AWS Region.
2. In the RDS console, select the primary DB cluster and choose "Add region" to create a secondary cluster in another AWS Region.
3. Configure the replication between the primary and secondary clusters.
4. Update your application's connection string to use the appropriate Aurora Global Database endpoints.

Testing and Monitoring Failover Scenarios

Regularly testing and monitoring your failover scenarios is essential to ensure the reliability and effectiveness of your high-availability and failover strategies. Best practices include the following:

- Use the Failover option in the RDS console or the `aws rds failover-db-cluster` CLI command to simulate failover events.
- Monitor key performance metrics such as replica lag, read and write latencies, and CPU utilization.

- Set up CloudWatch alarms to receive notifications in case of any issues or performance degradation.

Designing for Fault Tolerance

A well-designed fault-tolerant system should be able to withstand failures without impacting application performance or availability. Here are some best practices to consider when designing your Amazon Aurora deployment for fault tolerance:

- Deploy your Amazon Aurora instances across multiple AZs and, if possible, use Aurora Global Database to distribute your instances across multiple AWS Regions.
- Use read replicas to offload read traffic and improve the performance of your primary instance.
- Employ Amazon RDS Proxy to help manage connections and improve the scalability of your Amazon Aurora deployment.
- Implement application-level retries and back-off strategies to handle transient errors and failovers gracefully.

By following these best practices, you can ensure that your Aurora deployment is highly available, fault-tolerant, and capable of handling various failover scenarios.

Backup, Recovery, and Point-in-Time Restore

Backup, recovery, and point-in-time restore are crucial topics in discussions about managing data and maintaining business operations continuity due to their pivotal roles in safeguarding data integrity and enabling swift recovery in case of data loss or system failures.

Creating and Managing Amazon Aurora Backups

Aurora automatically creates backups of your database instances. These backups include snapshots of the entire database as well as transaction logs. To manage these backups effectively, follow these best practices:

Enable automated backups
 Ensure that automated backups are enabled for your Aurora instance. This will create daily backups and maintain them for a specified retention period.

Choose an appropriate backup window
 Select a time when the database load is low to minimize the impact of backup operations on performance.

Monitor backup status

Regularly monitor the status of your backups by using the AWS Management Console, AWS CLI, or Amazon RDS APIs.

Aurora offers automated backups, enabling the creation and management of backups without manual intervention. To set up automated backups, refer to "Enabling Automatic Backups" on page 455.

 Backups are automatically created during the maintenance window, and you can also create manual backups called *snapshots* anytime.

Restoring from Backups and Snapshots

You can restore your Aurora database from an automated backup or a manual snapshot. To restore from an automated backup, use the "Restore to Point in Time" feature to revert your database instance to a specific time within the backup retention period. For manual snapshot restoration, access the "DB Snapshots" section in the AWS Management Console, select the desired snapshot, and opt for the "Restore Snapshot" option.

To learn more about restoring from backups and snapshots, see "Restoring Backups and Snapshots" on page 463.

Implementing Point-in-Time Recovery

Point-in-time recovery (PITR) allows you to restore your database to a specific point in time. To implement PITR, follow these steps:

1. Enable binary logging in your Aurora instance to capture transaction logs required for PITR.

2. Select a recovery point within the backup retention period using the AWS Management Console, AWS CLI, or Amazon RDS APIs.

3. Execute the PITR operation by specifying the target recovery point.

To learn more about point-in-time recovery on MySQL, see "Restoring from Automated Backups" on page 457.

Best Practices for Backup Retention and Scheduling

To optimize backup retention and scheduling, follow these guidelines:

Set an appropriate retention period
> Determine the optimal retention period for your business requirements, taking into account regulatory compliance, disaster recovery, and data retention needs.

Schedule regular backups
> Schedule daily backups during periods of low database activity to minimize performance impact.

Monitor and manage backup storage
> Regularly monitor backup storage usage to ensure that you stay within allocated limits and to identify opportunities for optimizing storage consumption.

Disaster Recovery Planning

To ensure the availability of your Aurora database in the event of a disaster, implement the following best practices:

Create multiregion replicas
> Configure multiregion read replicas to provide redundancy and improve performance in the event of a regional outage.

Monitor replica lag
> Regularly monitor the replication lag between your primary and replica instances to ensure that data is synchronized and up-to-date.

Test your disaster-recovery plan
> Periodically test your disaster-recovery plan by simulating a failure and verifying that your recovery procedures are effective.

Document your disaster-recovery plan
> Maintain a comprehensive and up-to-date disaster-recovery plan that includes detailed procedures for backup, recovery, and point-in-time restore operations.

By following these best practices for backup, recovery, and point-in-time restore in Aurora, you can ensure that your database remains secure, available, and recoverable in the event of a disaster or data loss.

Security and Compliance Best Practices

Within the scope of Amazon Aurora, prioritizing the security and compliance of your database is of utmost importance. Let's delve into the fundamental best practices to aid in protecting your data and ensuring adherence to regulatory requirements.

Implementing Encryption at Rest and in Transit

Encryption is a vital security measure for protecting sensitive data from unauthorized access. In Aurora, you can implement encryption both at rest and in transit. Amazon Aurora uses AWS Key Management Service (KMS) for encryption at rest. You can either use the default AWS managed key or create a custom customer managed key.

To encrypt data in transit, you can use SSL or TLS. Connect to the Amazon Aurora instance using your preferred client and then execute the following SQL command to require SSL/TLS connections:

```
ALTER INSTANCE SET rds.force_ssl=1;
```

Restart the instance for the changes to take effect.

Configuring Network Security and Firewall Rules

To enhance the security of Aurora, it's crucial to configure network security and firewall rules. Deploy your Aurora instance within a VPC for enhanced security and isolation. Use security groups to restrict database access to specific IP addresses, and configure network access control lists (NACLs) for additional traffic control within your subnet.

Managing Users, Roles, and Permissions

Effective management of users, roles, and permissions is essential for database security. Follow these best practices for Aurora:

Create separate users
> Avoid using the root account. Instead, create separate users with specific permissions for different tasks.

Implement least privilege
> Grant users the minimum permissions required to perform their tasks. This limits the potential for unauthorized access or data manipulation.

Use roles
> Create roles to group permissions and assign them to users. This streamlines permission management and simplifies audits.

Auditing and Logging Database Activity

Auditing and logging are essential for monitoring database activity, detecting anomalies, and ensuring compliance. In Aurora, you can enable the following login options for monitoring and troubleshooting Aurora databases:

Aurora database activity streams
Capture all database activity, including DDL, DML, and data control language statements. Use AWS Management Console to enable and configure activity streams.

Aurora slow query logs
Identify performance issues by logging slow queries. Enable slow query logs by modifying the parameter group associated with your Amazon Aurora instance.

Aurora error logs
Monitor and troubleshoot issues by reviewing error logs. Access error logs through the AWS Management Console, Amazon RDS APIs, or Amazon CloudWatch logs.

To ensure compliance with data protection regulations like GDPR and HIPAA, consider the following best practices for your Amazon Aurora MySQL instance:

Data protection regulations
Understand the data protection regulations applicable to your business (e.g., GDPR, HIPAA) and implement necessary controls.

Data classification
Classify your data based on sensitivity and risk, and apply appropriate controls for each category.

Data retention and deletion
Establish and enforce data retention and deletion policies to comply with regulations.

Incident response plan
Develop an incident response plan to handle data breaches and security incidents.

Regular audits
Conduct regular audits of your security and compliance measures to ensure ongoing effectiveness and adherence to regulations.

By following these best practices, you can ensure that your Aurora database remains secure and compliant with data protection regulations.

Cost Optimization and Resource Management

To optimize costs and manage resources effectively in Aurora, it is essential to understand its pricing structure. Aurora pricing consists of the following components:

Instance hours
> The cost of running the DB instances for a certain number of hours.

Storage
> The cost of storing data in Amazon Aurora, which includes the amount of storage used and the number of I/O operations performed.

Backup storage
> The cost of storing backups in Amazon S3.

Data transfer
> The cost of transferring data in and out of Amazon Aurora.

Choosing the Right Instance Types and Storage Options

Selecting the appropriate instance types and storage options can help you optimize costs and manage resources efficiently. Consider the following factors when making your decision:

Performance requirements
> Choose an instance type that meets your performance needs in terms of CPU, memory, and network capacity.

Storage requirements
> Determine your storage needs based on your application's requirements and select the appropriate storage type (e.g., General Purpose SSD or Provisioned IOPS SSD).

I/O requirements
> Evaluate the I/O capacity required by your application and select a storage option that meets those needs.

Implementing Cost-Saving Strategies

Implement the following cost-saving strategies to optimize your Aurora costs:

Use reserved instances
> Purchase reserved instances to save on instance costs compared to on-demand pricing.

Leverage Aurora Serverless
> Utilize Aurora Serverless for workloads with variable or unpredictable workloads, as it automatically scales the compute capacity based on actual usage.

Implement multi-AZ deployments
> Use multi-AZ deployments to reduce costs by distributing workloads across multiple availability zones.

Enable auto-pause
> Enable the auto-pause feature to automatically stop your Aurora instance when it is idle, reducing costs.

Monitoring and Controlling Resource Usage

Monitor and control resource usage in Aurora by following these best practices:

Enable Enhanced Monitoring
> Use Enhanced Monitoring to gain insights into your instance's performance and resource utilization.

Set up Amazon CloudWatch alarms
> Configure CloudWatch alarms to monitor key metrics and receive notifications when specific thresholds are exceeded.

Use Performance Insights
> Leverage Performance Insights to identify and resolve performance issues in your Amazon Aurora database.

Using AWS Cost Explorer and Budgets

AWS provides several tools to help you manage and monitor costs effectively. With AWS Cost Explorer, you can analyze your spending patterns, identify cost drivers, and uncover opportunities for cost optimization. With AWS Budgets, you can set up budgets to track your costs and usage, enabling you to receive alerts when your spending exceeds predefined limits. These tools empower you to maintain control over your AWS expenditures and optimize your resource allocation for maximum efficiency.

To use AWS Budgets, navigate to the Amazon RDS console to create an Amazon Aurora MySQL instance, selecting the appropriate instance type and storage options. Enable features like Enhanced Monitoring and set up CloudWatch alarms for efficient monitoring, while leveraging AWS Cost Explorer and Budgets for cost analysis and alerts.

Integrating Amazon Aurora with Other AWS Services

Let's explore the benefits of AWS services and how they can be used in conjunction with Amazon Aurora. We'll set up example configurations by using the AWS Management Console.

Connecting to AWS Lambda for Serverless Computing

AWS Lambda is a serverless compute service that allows you to run your code without provisioning or managing servers. It can be easily integrated with Aurora to execute functions in response to events such as data changes or triggers. Benefits of using Lambda with Amazon Aurora include the following:

- Automatic scaling of compute resources
- No server management required
- Cost-effective execution based on usage

To connect Lambda to your Aurora instance, follow these steps:

1. Create an AWS Lambda function in the AWS Management Console.
2. In the Lambda function configuration, set the environment variables for database connection information, such as DB_HOST, DB_USER, DB_PASSWORD, and DB_NAME.
3. Modify your Lambda function code to import the necessary MySQL libraries and establish a connection to your Aurora database.
4. Create a trigger in your Aurora instance that invokes the Lambda function when specific events occur.

Integrating with Amazon S3 for Storage and Data Transfer

Amazon S3 is a highly scalable, durable, and low-latency object storage service. Integrating S3 with Aurora allows you to store and retrieve data such as backups, logs, and binary large objects (BLOBs). Benefits of using S3 with Amazon Aurora include the following:

- Cost-effective storage for large amounts of data
- Easy data transfer between Amazon Aurora and other AWS services
- Simplified data backup and restoration

Use these steps to integrate S3 with your Aurora instance:

1. Create an Amazon S3 bucket in the AWS Management Console.

2. Grant the necessary permissions for your Amazon Aurora instance to access the S3 bucket.

3. Use the `LOAD DATA FROM S3` and `SELECT INTO OUTFILE S3` SQL statements in your Amazon Aurora instance to transfer data between the database and the S3 bucket.

Using AWS App Runner for Containerized Applications

AWS App Runner is a fully managed service that makes it easy to build, deploy, and scale containerized applications quickly. Integrating App Runner with Aurora allows you to build and deploy applications that interact with your database without managing the underlying infrastructure. Benefits of using App Runner with Aurora MySQL include the following:

- Simplified deployment and scaling of applications
- Integration with your existing development workflow
- Support for custom runtime environments

Follow these steps to use App Runner with your Aurora instance:

1. Create a container image for your application, including the necessary libraries and environment variables to connect to your Amazon Aurora database.

2. Create an AWS App Runner service in the AWS Management Console.

3. Configure the App Runner service to use the container image and provide the necessary environment variables to connect to your Amazon Aurora instance.

4. Deploy and scale your application by using App Runner.

Implementing Amazon API Gateway for RESTful APIs

Amazon API Gateway is a fully managed service that makes it easy to create, publish, maintain, monitor, and secure APIs at any scale. By implementing API Gateway with Amazon Aurora, you can expose your database as a RESTful API, allowing external applications and services to interact with your data. Using API Gateway with Amazon Aurora has the following benefits:

- Simplified API management and deployment
- Built-in security features, such as authentication and authorization
- Integration with other AWS services, such as Lambda

To implement API Gateway with your Aurora instance follow these steps:

1. Create an AWS Lambda function to handle API requests and interact with your Amazon Aurora database.

2. In the Lambda function configuration, set the environment variables for database connection information, such as DB_HOST, DB_USER, DB_PASSWORD, and DB_NAME.

3. Modify your Lambda function code to import the necessary MySQL libraries, establish a connection to your Amazon Aurora database, and handle API requests.

4. Create an Amazon API Gateway in the AWS Management Console.

5. Define your API resources and methods, and configure the integration between API Gateway and your Lambda function.

6. Deploy your API and configure the necessary security features, such as API keys, authentication, and authorization.

Leveraging Amazon Kinesis for Real-Time Data Streaming

Amazon Kinesis is a platform for data streaming, allowing you to collect, process, and analyze large volumes of data in real time. By integrating Kinesis with Aurora, you can ingest and analyze data from your database in real time, enabling use cases such as analytics, monitoring, and machine learning. Benefits of using Kinesis with Amazon Aurora include the following:

- Scalable data ingestion and processing
- Real-time data analysis and visualization
- Integration with other AWS services, such as Lambda and S3

To leverage Kinesis with your Aurora instance, follow these steps:

1. Create an Amazon Kinesis Data Stream in the AWS Management Console.

2. Configure your Amazon Aurora instance to write data changes to the Kinesis Data Stream by using the aws_kinesis_streams plug-in and AFTER INSERT, AFTER UPDATE, or AFTER DELETE triggers.

3. Create an AWS Lambda function or a Kinesis Data Analytics application to process and analyze the data from the Kinesis Data Stream.

4. Optionally, configure the Lambda function or Kinesis Data Analytics application to store the processed data in another AWS service, such as Amazon S3 or Redshift.

By following these best practices and integrating Aurora with other AWS services, you can build robust, scalable, and cost-effective applications that take full advantage of the AWS ecosystem.

Conclusion

We've covered a wide array of Aurora topics, spanning its features, benefits, storage architecture, use cases, setup, and configuration. With this knowledge, you're well equipped to harness the full potential of Aurora and ensure the reliability of your database systems.

## CHAPTER 13

MySQL on the Cloud: Azure Database for MySQL

Azure Database for MySQL is a fully managed, globally available database service that enables organizations to easily deploy, manage, and scale MySQL databases in the cloud. As more organizations move their applications and databases to the cloud, it's essential to understand the best practices for optimizing performance, security, and reliability. This chapter covers the recommended best practices for configuring and managing MySQL on Microsoft Azure, providing you with guidance, example configuration code, and answers to common questions.

Getting Started with Azure Database for MySQL

Beginning your adventure with Azure Database for MySQL unveils numerous opportunities for streamlining data management and application development. Let's delve into the crucial steps and factors to launch your journey successfully. Azure Database for MySQL offers three tiers. You must choose the appropriate tier for your application requirements, budget, and expected growth to ensure optimal performance:

Basic tier
> Suitable for small-scale applications with light workloads, low concurrent connections, and modest storage requirements. It offers up to 2 vCores, 2 GB of RAM, and 1 TB of storage.

General-purpose tier
> Designed for applications with moderate workloads, higher concurrent connections, and larger storage needs. It provides up to 64 vCores, 512 GB of RAM, and 8 TB of storage.

Memory-optimized tier

Suitable for applications with memory-intensive workloads or high-performance requirements. It offers up to 32 vCores, 1 TB of RAM, and 8 TB of storage.

Azure Database for MySQL supports several versions of MySQL, including MySQL 5.7 and MySQL 8. Choose the appropriate version based on your application's compatibility and requirements. We recommend using the latest supported version for better performance and security features. To get started with Azure Database for MySQL, you need to create a free Azure account. Follow these steps to create an account and set up a MySQL instance:

1. Go to the Azure free account sign-up page (*https://oreil.ly/mjNFz*).

2. Click the "Start free" button.

3. Sign in with your Microsoft account or create a new one.

4. Fill in the required information, including your name, email, phone number, and payment information. Note that you won't be charged unless you decide to upgrade your account.

5. Verify your account with a phone number and credit card.

6. Once your account is set up, navigate to the Azure portal.

To connect to your Azure Database for MySQL instance, you can use various tools and programming languages. Some common methods are as follows:

MySQL Workbench

A popular GUI-based tool that allows you to manage your MySQL databases. To connect, use the connection details provided in the Azure portal, such as the server name, administrator username, and password.

CLI

You can use the MySQL command-line client to interact with your Azure Database for MySQL instance. Install the MySQL client on your local machine and use the following command to connect:

```
mysql -h server_name -u admin_username -p
```

Replace *server_name* and *admin_username* with the corresponding information from the Azure portal.

Programming languages

You can connect to your Azure Database for MySQL instance by using various programming languages, such as Python, PHP, and Java. Ensure that you have the appropriate MySQL connector library installed for your chosen language and use the provided connection details to establish a connection.

Securing Your MySQL Instance

To ensure the security of your data, follow these best practices when using Azure Database for MySQL:

Enable SSL connections
> Azure Database for MySQL provides SSL support to encrypt data in transit. Ensure that SSL connections are enabled and properly configured for your applications.

Restrict access
> Use firewall rules and virtual network service endpoints to control access to your MySQL instance. Allow connections only from trusted IP addresses and networks.

Monitor and audit
> Regularly monitor and audit database activity to detect and respond to security incidents. Azure Database for MySQL provides built-in monitoring and auditing features that can be easily integrated with Azure Monitor and Azure Security Center.

Use strong passwords
> Always use strong, unique passwords for the administrator and database users. Avoid using default or easily guessable passwords.

Keep software up-to-date
> Regularly update your applications and MySQL connectors to ensure compatibility with the latest security patches and features.

By following these best practices, you can ensure the security and reliability of your Azure Database for MySQL instance while building and deploying scalable applications.

Using Flexible Server

Flexible Server is a versatile solution designed to empower your database management with flexibility and scalability. It is a managed database service that's fully equipped to handle production workloads. It's designed to provide users with more control over database management functions and configuration settings. With its flexible server architecture, you can choose HA options, including single or multiple AZs.

This service comes with improved cost-optimization controls, such as the ability to stop/start the server and access burstable compute tiers, which are perfect for workloads that don't require continuous full-compute capacity. It also supports reserved instances, which can save you up to 63% on costs, making it an ideal choice for production workloads with predictable compute capacity requirements.

Flexible Server supports the community versions of MySQL 5.7 and 8 and is widely available in various Azure regions. To optimize your database infrastructure, it's crucial to understand where flexible servers shine brightest. Let's explore the scenarios and use cases where flexible servers are best suited, unlocking their full potential:

- Simplify deployments, streamline scaling, and minimize database management overhead for tasks such as backups, HA, security, and monitoring.

- Build applications using the community version of MySQL, which offers enhanced control and customization options.

- Ensure HA for production workloads within the same zone or across zones, with managed maintenance windows.

- Create a simplified development experience for improved usability.

- Implement enterprise-level security, compliance, and privacy measures.

Enhanced Restore Experience

The Restore experience, a Flexible Server feature (*https://oreil.ly/h8Hfg*), offers additional flexibility to adjust the compute and storage settings during the provision of a restored server. At the time of provisioning, the restored server can be configured to have a higher compute tier, compute size, and storage capacity than the source server. Additionally, you can modify settings such as "Storage auto-grow," "Backup retention days," and "Geo-redundancy" to specify different values from those of the source server.

To create an Azure Database for MySQL - Flexible Server, follow these steps using the Azure portal:

1. Sign in to the Azure portal using your credentials. You will be directed to your service dashboard by default:

2. Search for Azure Database for MySQL servers in the portal and select it. Then click the Create button:

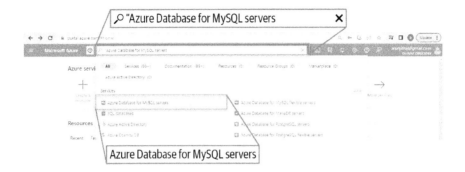

3. On the "Azure Database for MySQL servers" page, choose Create:

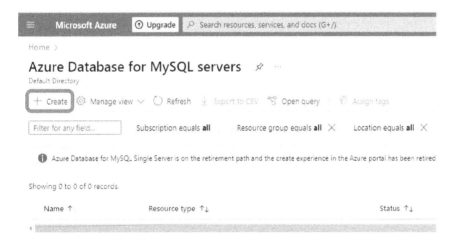

4. On the "Select Azure Database for MySQL deployment option" page, choose "Flexible server" as the deployment option:

5. On the Basics tab, provide the following information:

a. Add the name of the Azure subscription you want to use for your server. If you have multiple subscriptions, choose the one you want to be billed for this resource:

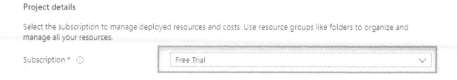

b. Include a new resource group name or an existing one from your subscription:

c. Use a unique name to identify your flexible server. The domain name *mysql.database.azure.com* will be appended to this name. The server name can contain only lowercase letters, numbers, and hyphens (-). It must have 3 to 63 characters:

d. Add the location closest to your users and choose 8.0 as the MySQL major version:

e. Select "For development or hobby projects" as the "Workload type":

f. Set the compute, storage, IOPS, and backup configurations for your new server. The default values are Burstable, Standard_B1ms, 10 GiB, 100 IOPS, and 7 days for Compute tier, Compute size, Storage size, IOPS, and backup retention period. You can adjust these values as needed:

g. Select "No preference" unless your application client is provisioned in a specific AZ:

h. Uncheck the box for nonproduction servers, or choose between zone-redundant HA and same-zone high availability for production servers:

i. Include your own sign-in account to use when you connect to the server. The admin username can't be `azure_superuser`, `admin`, `administrator`, `root`, `guest`, `sa`, or `public`:

j. Add a new password for the server admin account. It must have 8 to 128 characters and contain characters from at least three of the following categories: English uppercase letters, English lowercase letters, numbers (0 through 9), and nonalphanumeric characters (!, $, #, %, and so on):

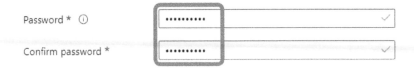

k. Click the "Next: Networking >" button.

6. Configure networking options on the Networking tab, where you can choose how your server is reachable by using public access (allowed IP addresses) or private access (VNet Integration):

7. Configure network access control for Azure resources with "Firewall rules." Ensure secure connectivity and adherence to your organization's security policies:

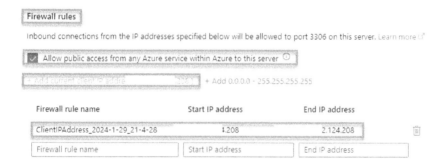

8. Click the "Review + create" button, and then click the Create button. This process may take a few minutes.

Monitor the deployment process by selecting Notifications on the toolbar. Once the deployment is complete, select "Pin to dashboard" to create a tile for the flexible server on your Azure portal dashboard. This tile provides a shortcut to the server's Overview page. When you select "Go to resource," the server's Overview page opens:

Monitor the "Deployment succeeded" status by selecting Notifications on the toolbar:

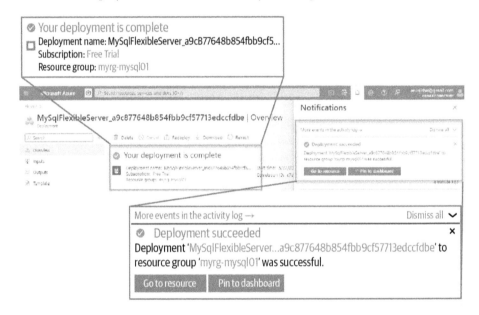

Managing Read Replicas in Azure Database for MySQL - Flexible Server via Azure Portal

This section will guide you through creating and managing read replicas in Azure Database for MySQL - Flexible Server by using the Azure portal. Before proceeding with the creation of a read replica, ensure that you have an Azure Database for MySQL - Flexible Server that will be used as the source server.

To create a read replica server, sign in to the Azure portal (*https://portal.azure.com/#home*) and follow these steps:

1. Select the existing Azure Database for MySQL - Flexible Server that you want to use as a source from the Overview page:

2. From the Settings menu, choose Replication:

3. Click the "Add replica" option:

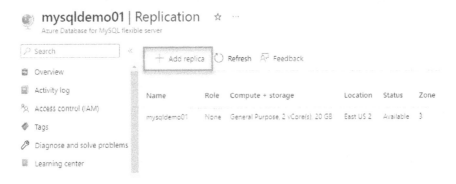

4. Enter a name for the replica server, and if your region supports AZs, select the AZ of your choice. Then click the "Review + create" button:

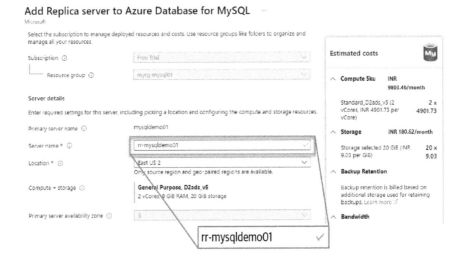

Azure Database for MySQL server must be created in the General Purpose or Memory Optimized pricing tiers, as data-in replication is supported only in these tiers. GTID is supported on versions 5.7 and 8.0 and only on servers that support storage up to 16 TB (general-purpose storage v2).

5. To create the replica, click the Create button:

Note that when you create a replica for a source that has no existing replicas, the source will restart to prepare itself for replication. Therefore, we recommend you perform these operations during an off-peak period.

When creating a read replica, keep in mind that read replicas are created with the same server configuration as the source. The replica server configuration can be changed after it has been created. The replica server is always created in the same resource group, same location, and same subscription as the source server. If you want to create a replica server in a different resource group or subscription, you can move the replica server after creation. To ensure that the replica is able to keep up with the source, we recommend that the replica server's configuration should be kept at equal or greater values than the source.

Once the replica server has been created, you can view it from the *Replication blade*. Note that the replica server is read-only and cannot be used for write operations. However, it can be used for read-heavy workloads to offload the read traffic from the source server.

In summary, creating and managing read replicas in Azure Database for MySQL - Flexible Server is a straightforward process that can help improve the performance and scalability of your database. With the Azure portal, you can easily create and manage read replicas to support your workload requirements.

Creating Azure Database for MySQL Server Using Portal and CLI

When it comes to setting up an Azure Database for MySQL server, you have the flexibility to choose between using the user-friendly Azure portal or the powerful Azure command-line interface. Let's explore both methods, so you can create your MySQL server with ease and efficiency.

Azure Cloud Shell is a powerful tool that provides an interactive command-line environment for managing Azure resources. It supports both bash and PowerShell, allowing you to choose the command-line experience that suits your needs. To make the most out of Azure Cloud Shell, it is important to follow some best practices for its configuration. Next, you will find detailed information and example configuration code for each topic.

Launching Azure Cloud Shell

To launch Cloud Shell, open the Azure portal and navigate to the top navigation bar. Click the Cloud Shell button to launch it:

The first time you start Cloud Shell, you will be prompted to create an Azure Storage account for the Azure file share. This storage account is used to persist your Cloud Shell settings and files. When you create the account and file share, you'll need to select the subscription you want to use and click the "Create storage" option to initiate the process.

In Cloud Shell, you have the option to use either bash or PowerShell as your command-line environment. You can opt for the one that you are most comfortable with or the one that best aligns with your specific requirements. In this instance, we use PowerShell:

In order for Azure Cloud Shell to manage resources within your subscription, you need to register the `Microsoft.CloudShell` namespace:

```
PowerShell
Bash


Cloud Shell.Succeeded.
erminal...

Welcome to Azure Cloud Shell
```

```
Type "az" to use Azure CLI
Type "help" to learn about Cloud Shell

MOTD: Azure Cloud Shell now includes Predictive IntelliSense!
Learn more: https://aka.ms/CloudShell/IntelliSense

VERBOSE: Authenticating to Azure
VERBOSE: Building your Azure drive
PS /home/arunjith>
```

To list all the subscriptions associated with your Azure account, you can use the following command:

```
az account list --query '[].name'
```

Set a specific subscription as active with the following command:

```
az account set --subscription my-subscription-name
```

Replace *my-subscription-name* with the actual name of the subscription you want to set as active:

```
az account set --subscription "Free Trial"
```

Register the Microsoft.CloudShell namespace:

```
az provider register --namespace Microsoft.CloudShell
```

Check the status of the Microsoft.CloudShell namespace:

```
PS /home/arunjith> az provider show -n Microsoft.CloudShell
{
  "authorizations": [
      {
              "applicationId": "2233b157-f44d-4812-b777-036cdaf9a96e",
              "roleDefinitionId": "b0ddbf2d-f082-4fa8-97b2-3a069c305e47"
      }
  ],
  "id": "/subscriptions/c3db2d4f-1160-4d4a-8679-92b10d60b4f6/providers/
  Microsoft.CloudShell",
  "namespace": "Microsoft.CloudShell",
  "providerAuthorizationConsentState": null,
  "registrationPolicy": "RegistrationRequired",
  "registrationState": "Registered",
  "resourceTypes": [
      {
        "aliases": null,
        "apiProfiles": null,
        "apiVersions": [
          "2023-02-01-preview",
          "2020-04-01-preview",
          "2018-10-01",
          "2017-12-01-preview",
          "2017-08-01-preview",
```

```
          "2017-01-01-preview"
    ],
```

To display all subscriptions linked to your Azure account, use the command `az account list`:

```
PS /home/arunjith> az account list
[
    {
        "cloudName": "AzureCloud",
        "homeTenantId": "424ca6f0-5122-449b-9da4-299d63df47ed",
        "id": "c3db2d4f-1160-4d4a-8679-92b10d60b4f6",
        "isDefault": true,
        "managedByTenants": []
        "name": "Free Trial",
        "state" "Enabled",
        "tenantId": "424ca6f0-5122-449b-9da4-299d63df47ed",
        "user": {
            "cloudShellID": true,
        "name": "live.com#arunjitha@gmail.com",
        "type": "user"
    }
  }
]
PS /home/arunjith>
```

By default, Azure Cloud Shell displays output in the language specified by your browser settings. However, you can explicitly set the output language to English by using the following command:

```
az configure --defaults cli_output=english
```

Following these best practices for configuring Azure Cloud Shell will help you optimize your experience and make the most of this powerful command-line tool.

Creating a Server by Using the CLI

Azure Database for MySQL - Flexible Server provides a fully managed database service for MySQL with flexible server parameters, including the ability to customize server configurations and version upgrades.

1. Create a new resource group by running the following command in the terminal:

```
PS /home/arunjith> az group create --name mysql-rg01 --location eastus2
{
  "id":"/subscriptions/c3db2d4f-1160-4d4a-8679-92b10d60b4f6/resourceGroups/
  mysql-rg01",
  "location": "eastus2",
  "managedBy": null,
  "name": "mysql-rg01",
  "properties": {
     "provisioningState": "Succeeded"
```

```
        },
        "tags": null,
        "type": "Microsoft.Resources/resourceGroups"
    }
    PS/home/arunjith>
```

2. Create a new Azure Database for MySQL - Flexible Server instance:

```
PS /home/arunjith> az mysql flexible-server create --location eastus2
--resource-group mysql-rg01 --name mysqltestsvr01 --admin-user testdbuser
--admin-password Pass21word --sku-name Standard_D2ads_v5
--tier GeneralPurpose --public-access 0.0.0.0 --storage-size 32
--tags "key=value" --version 8.0.21 --storage-auto-grow Enabled --iops 500

Checking the existence of the resource group 'mysql-rg01'..
Resource group 'mysql-rg01' exists? : False
Creating Resource Group 'mysql-rg01'...
IOPS is 500 which is either your input or free(maximum) IOPS supported
for your storage size and SKU.
Creating MySQL Server 'mysqltestsvr01' in group 'mysql-rg01'...
Your server 'mysqltestsvre1' is using sku 'Standard_D2ads_v5' (Paid Tier).
Please refer to https://aka.ms/mysql-pricing for pricing details
Configuring server firewall rule, 'azure-access', to accept connections from
all Azure resources...
Creating MySQL database 'flexibleserverdb'.
Make a note of your password. If you forget, you would have to reset your
password with az mysql flexible-server update -n mysqltestsvre1
-g mysql-rg01 -p <new-password >'.
Try using az 'mysql flexible-server connect' command to test out connection.
{
"connectionString": "mysql flexibleserverdb --host mysqltestsvr01.mysql
.database.azure.com --user testdbuser --password=Pass21word",
'databaseName': "flexibleserverdb",
"firewallName":"AllowAllAzureServicesAndResourcesWithinAzureIps_
2023-5-31_9-8-35",
"host": "mysqltestsvr81.mysql.database.azure.com",
"id": "/subscriptions/c3db2d4f-1160-4d4a-8679-92b18d6b4f6/resourceGroups/
mysql-rg01/providers/Microsoft.DBforMySQL/flexibleServers/mysqltestsvr01",
"location": "East US 2",
"password": "Pass21word",
"resourceGroup": "mysql-rg01",
"skuname": "Standard_D2ads_v5",
"username": "testdbuser",
"version": "8.0.21"
}
```

3. After creating the Flexible Server instance, create a new database:

```
PS /home/arunjith> az mysql flexible-server db create --resource-group
mysql-rg01 --server-name mysqltestsvr01 --database-name newdatabase
Creating database with utty charset and utf8 general_ci collation
{
    "charset":"utf8mb3",
    "collation": "utf8mb3_general_ci",
```

```
    "id": "/subscriptions/c3db2d4f-1160-4d4a-8679-92b10d60b4f6/resourceGroups/
    mysql-rg01/providers/Microsoft.DBforMySQL/flexibleServers/mysqltestsvr01/
    databases/newdatabase",
    "name": "newdatabase",
    "resourceGroup": "mysql-rg01",
    "systemData": null,
    "type": "Microsoft.DBforMySQL/flexibleServers/databases"
}
PS /home/arunjith>
```

4. To view the server details, run the following command in the terminal:

```
PS /home/arunjith> az mysql flexible-server show --resource-group mysql-rg01
--name mysqltestsvr01
{
  "administratorLogin": "testdbuser",
  "administratorLoginPassword": null,
  "availabilityZone": "3",
  "backup": {
    "backupRetentionDays": 7,
    "earliestRestoreDate": "2023-05-31T07:57:18.136328+00:00",
    "geoRedundantBackup": "Disabled"
  },
  "createMode": null,
  "dataEncryption": null,
  "fullyQualifiedDomainName": "mysqltestsvr01.mysql.database.azure.com
  "highAvailability": {
        "mode": "Disabled",
        "standbyAvailabilityZone":
        "state": "NotEnabled"
  },
  "id": "/subscriptions/c3db2d4f-1160-4d4a-8679-92b10d60b4f6/resourceGroups/
  mysql-rg01/providers/Microsoft.DBforMySQL/flexibleServers/mysqltestsvr01",
  "identity": null,
  "location": "East US 2",
  "maintenanceWindow": {
    "customWindow": "Disabled",
    "dayOfWeek": 0,
```

5. Connect to the server:

```
az mysql flexible-server connect -n <servername> -u <username> -p
<password> -d <databasename>
```

For example, if the server is mysqltestsvr01, the user testdbuser, the password Pass21word, and the database flexibleserverdb, your command would look like this:

```
PS/home/arunjith> az mysql flexible-server connect -n mysqltestsvr01
-u testdbuser -p "Pass21word" -d flexibleserverdb --interactive
Password:
MySQL
mycli 1.26.1
Home: http://mycli.net
Bug tracker: https://github.com/dbcli/mycli/issues
Thanks to the contributor - Colin Caine
flexibleserverdb>
flexibleserverdb>
flexibleserverdb> show databases;
+------------------------+
| ☐ Database             |
+------------------------+
| flexibleserverdb       |
| information_schema     |
| mysql                  |
| performance_schema     |
| sys                    |
+------------------------+
5 rows in set
Time: 0.211s
flexibleserverdb>
```

6. To run a query on the server, run the following command in the terminal:

```
az mysql flexible-server connect -n <server-name> -u <username> -p
"<password>" -d <database-name> --querytext "<query text>"
```

For example, to run the query select * from table1; on the server mysql testsvr01 with the user testdbuser and password Pass21word and database flexibleserverdb, your command would look like this:

```
az mysql flexible-server connect -n mysqltestsvr01 -u testdbuser -p
"Pass21word" -d flexibleserverdb --interactive
```

Migrations

Azure Database Migration Service (DMS) for MySQL is a fully managed service that enables seamless migration of MySQL databases to Azure with minimal downtime (see Table 13-1).

Table 13-1. Migration scenario, tools, details, and more information for migrating MySQL databases to Azure Database for MySQL

Migration scenario	Tool(s)	Details	More information
Single to Flexible Server (Azure CLI)	Custom shell script	Migrate from Azure Database for MySQL - Single Server to Flexible Server in five easy steps!	The script also moves other server components such as security settings and server parameter configurations.
MySQL databases (>= 1 TB) to Azure Database for MySQL	Dump and Restore using mydumper + High Compute VM	Migrate large databases to Azure Database for MySQL using mydumper	Best practices for migrating large databases to Azure Database for MySQL
MySQL databases (< 1 TB) to Azure Database for MySQL	Database Migration Service (classic) and the Azure portal	Migrate MySQL databases to Azure Database for MySQL using DMS (classic)	If network bandwidth between source and target is good (e.g., high-speed express route), use Azure DMS
Amazon RDS for MySQL databases (< 1 TB) to Azure Database for MySQL	MySQL Workbench	Migrate Amazon RDS for MySQL databases (< 1 TB) to Azure Database for MySQL using MySQL Workbench	If you have low network bandwidth between source and Azure, use mydumper + High compute VM to take advantage of compression settings to efficiently move data over low-speed networks.
Import and export MySQL databases (< 1 TB) in Azure Database for MySQL	mysqldump or MySQL Workbench Import/Export utility	Import and export - Azure Database for MySQL	Use the mysqldump and MySQL Workbench Export/Import utility tool to perform offline migrations for smaller databases.

Azure Database for MySQL Migration Guide

Migrating an instance of Azure Database for MySQL – Single Server to Azure Database for MySQL – Flexible Server can be achieved by using Azure DMS, a fully managed service designed to enable seamless migrations from multiple database sources to Azure data platforms. In this tutorial, we'll walk you through the process of an offline migration of a sample database from an Azure Database for MySQL single server to a MySQL Flexible Server (both running version 5.7) using a DMS migration activity.

When migrating to a Flexible Server, we recommend implementing the following best practices to ensure faster data loads:

- Use General Purpose or Memory Optimized tiers for your Flexible Server.
- Enable binary logging for your target Flexible Server.
- Enable GTIDs for your target Flexible Server.

Create and Configure a Target Flexible Server

Before setting up DMS to migrate your single server to a flexible server, you need to deploy and configure your target Flexible Server. This can be done by performing the following steps:

1. Sign in to the Azure portal and then click "Create a resource."
2. Search for the term `Azure Database for MySQL`, and then select Azure Database for MySQL from the drop-down list.
3. On the Basics tab, provide a name for your Flexible Server, select the appropriate subscription and resource group, and then select a region.
4. Under "Server admin login," specify a unique login name and a strong password.
5. Under "Compute + storage," select the General Purpose or Memory Optimized tier based on your needs.
6. Under Networking, select the Virtual Network (VNet) and subnet that you want to use for your Flexible Server.
7. Review the configurations, view the terms, and then click Create.

Create a DMS Instance

To use DMS to migrate your single server to a Flexible Server, you first need to create a DMS instance by performing the following steps:

1. Sign in to the Azure portal, and then search for and select `Subscriptions`:

2. Select the subscription that you want to use to create the DMS instance:

3. Choose "Resource providers" in the settings:

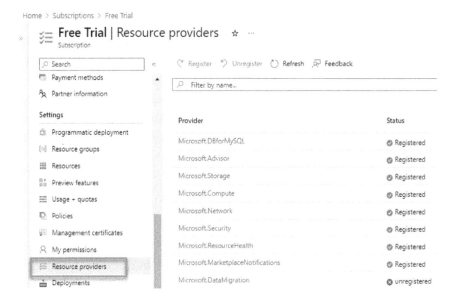

4. Search for the term **Migration**, and then, for Microsoft.DataMigration, click Register:

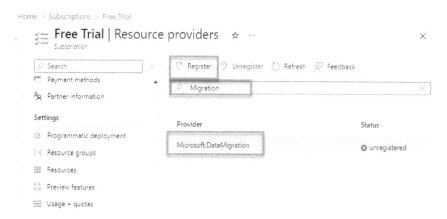

5. Click "+ Create a resource," search for the term **Azure Database Migration Service**, and then select Azure DMS from the drop-down list:

6. On the "Create a resource" page, choose Azure DMS:

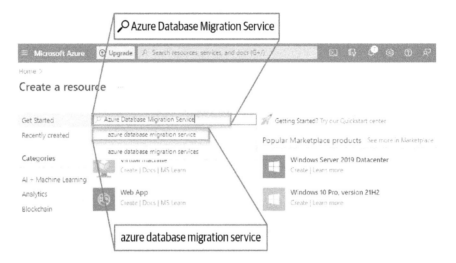

7. On the Azure DMS screen, click the Create button:

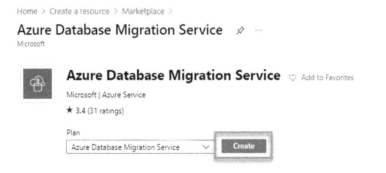

8. In the "Migration scenario" section, select MySQL as the source server type, and then select Azure Database for MySQL as target server type. Then click Select:

Select migration scenario and Database Migration Service   ...

Migration scenario

Tell us about your migration scenario, the source database type and target database type, and based on that we will recommend the best Database Migration Service.

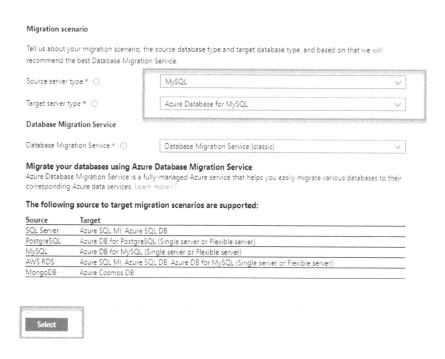

Source server type *   ○   [MySQL   ⌄]

Target server type *   ○   [Azure Database for MySQL   ⌄]

Database Migration Service

Database Migration Service *   ○   [Database Migration Service (classic)   ⌄]

Migrate your databases using Azure Database Migration Service
Azure Database Migration Service is a fully-managed Azure service that helps you easily migrate various databases to their corresponding Azure data services. Learn more ⬈

The following source to target migration scenarios are supported:

Source	Target
SQL Server	Azure SQL MI, Azure SQL DB
PostgreSQL	Azure DB for PostgreSQL (Single server or Flexible server)
MySQL	Azure DB for MySQL (Single server or Flexible server)
AWS RDS	Azure SQL MI, Azure SQL DB, Azure DB for MySQL (Single server or Flexible server)
MongoDB	Azure Cosmos DB

[Select]

9. On the Basics tab, in the "Project details" section, select the appropriate subscription, and then select an existing resource group or create a new one:

| **Basics** | Networking | Tags | Review + create |

Azure Database Migration Service is designed to streamline the process of migrating on-premises databases to Azure. Learn more ⬈

Project details

Select the subscription to manage deployed resources and costs. Use resource groups as you would use folders, to organize and manage all of your resources.

Subscription *   ⓘ   [Free Trial   ⌄]

    Resource group *   ⓘ   [mygr-mysql01   ⌄]
                             Create new

10. In the "Instance details" section, specify a name for the service, select a region, and then verify that Azure is selected as the service mode:

11. Select the Premium pricing tier with 4 vCores for your DMS instance on the Configure page, and then click Apply:

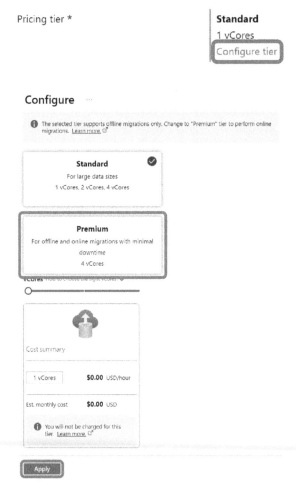

12. Select an existing VNet from the list or provide the name of new VNet to create on the Networking tab, and then click "Review + create":

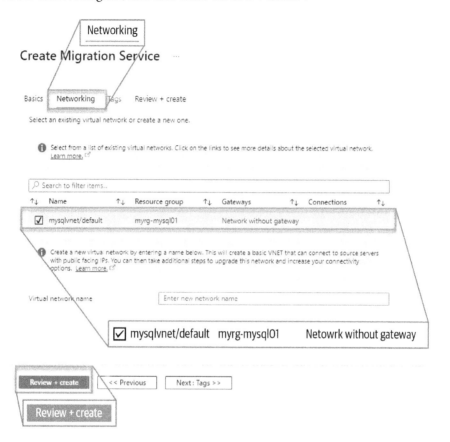

13. Review the configurations, view the terms, and then click the Create button:

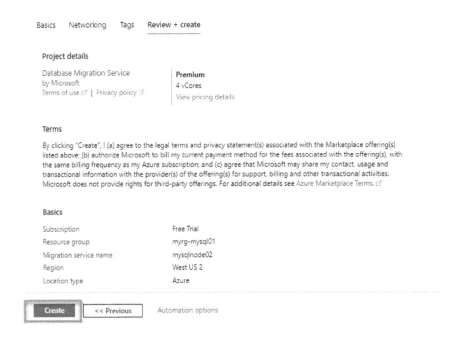

Create Migration Service ...

Basics   Networking   Tags   Review + create

Project details

Database Migration Service | **Premium**
by Microsoft | 4 vCores
Terms of use ☑ | Privacy policy ☑ | View pricing details

Terms

By clicking "Create", I (a) agree to the legal terms and privacy statement(s) associated with the Marketplace offering(s) listed above; (b) authorize Microsoft to bill my current payment method for the fees associated with the offering(s), with the same billing frequency as my Azure subscription; and (c) agree that Microsoft may share my contact, usage and transactional information with the provider(s) of the offering(s) for support, billing and other transactional activities. Microsoft does not provide rights for third-party offerings. For additional details see Azure Marketplace Terms. ☑

Basics

Subscription   Free Trial
Resource group   myrg-mysql01
Migration service name   mysqlnode02
Region   West US 2
Location type   Azure

Create   << Previous   Automation options

Create a MySQL Migration Project in DMS

After creating the DMS instance, the next step is to create a MySQL migration project by performing the following steps:

1. Select the DMS instance from the Azure portal:

2. On the DMS instance page, click "+ New Migration Project":

3. Specify a name for the project:

New migration project   ···

A database migration project is a group of database activities that you can migrate together.

Migration project name

Project name * ⓘ

4. Under Source, select MySQL as the source database engine, and then provide the required information, such as the server name, port number, and login credentials:

Choose your source and target server type.

Source server type * ⓘ

Target server type * ⓘ

5. Under Target, select Azure Database for MySQL as the target database engine, and then provide the required information, such as the server name, port number, and login credentials:

Choose your source and target server type.

Source server type * ⓘ

Target server type * ⓘ

6. Set the migration type to online migration, and then select the version of MySQL that is running on the source and target servers:

Choose your migration activity type.

Migration activity type * ⓘ

7. Review the project settings, and then click the "Create and run activity" button.

Configure the Migration Project

To configure your DMS migration project, follow these steps:

Select source settings

On the "Select source" screen, you need to provide the necessary information about your source server, as shown here:

1. Enter source server name or IP address for data migration, ensuring necessary access permissions and network connectivity.

2. Specify the port number of the source server to facilitate DMS connection establishment.

3. Input the username associated with the source server, ensuring it has required privileges for database access and migration.

4. Provide the corresponding password for the specified username, ensuring accuracy for successful connection establishment.

Select target settings

On the "Select target" screen, you need to provide the necessary information for your migration project:

1. Choose the Azure subscription for the migration project, determining billing and access rights.

2. Select the geographical location for deploying the migration service and associated resources, considering data sovereignty and proximity.

3. Specify the Azure resource group for provisioning the migration service and related resources, serving as a logical container.

4. Pick the target database platform, Azure Database for MySQL - Flexible, as the migration destination.

5. Enter the username for the target Azure Database for MySQL - Flexible instance, used for authentication and management.

6. Provide a secure password for the target Azure Database for MySQL - Flexible instance, meeting security requirements and best practices.

Select databases

Click "Next: Select databases" and on the "Select databases" tab, choose the appropriate server migration option. You can either select "Migrate all applicable databases" or manually select the server objects you want to migrate:

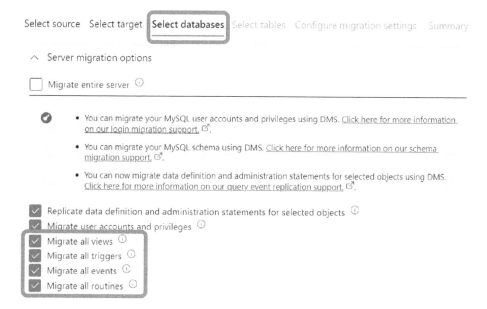

When selecting the "Migrate all applicable databases" checkbox, all user-created databases and tables will be migrated. However, be aware that Azure Database for MySQL - Flexible Server does not support mixed-case databases, so mixed-case databases on the source won't be included in the online migration.

Select source databases

In the "Select databases" section, under Source Database, choose the specific database(s) that you want to migrate:

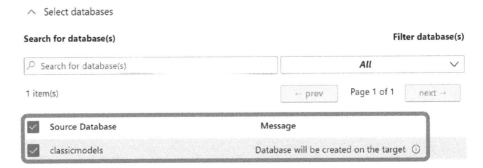

The migration process will migrate all nontable objects in the specified database(s) while skipping the items you didn't select. Note that you can select only source and target databases with matching names on both servers. If you choose a database on the source server that doesn't exist on the target server, it will be created on the target server.

Select tables

Click "Next: Select tables" to navigate to the "Select tables" tab. Before the tab populates, the DMS fetches the tables from the selected database(s) on the source and target servers and determines whether the tables exist and contain data. Choose the tables that you want to migrate:

If the selected source table doesn't exist on the target server, the online migration process will ensure that the table schema and data are migrated to the target server. DMS validates your inputs, and if the validation passes, you will be able to start the migration.

After configuring the schema migration and selecting the desired tables, click the "Review and start migration" button:

 You need to navigate to the "Configure migration settings" tab only if you are troubleshooting failing migrations.

On the Summary tab, name the migration activity in the "Activity name" text box. Review the summary to ensure that the source and target details match your previous specifications. Then select "Start migration." The migration activity window will appear, and the status of the activity will be "Initializing." The status will change to "Running" when the table migrations start:

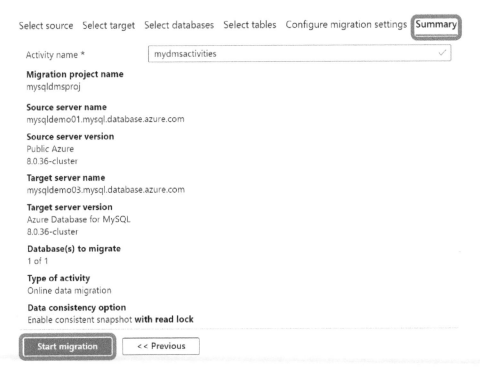

Monitor the Migration

During the migration process, you need to monitor the progress. After the initial load activity is completed, navigate to the "Initial Load" tab. Here, you can view the completion status and the number of tables that have been successfully migrated:

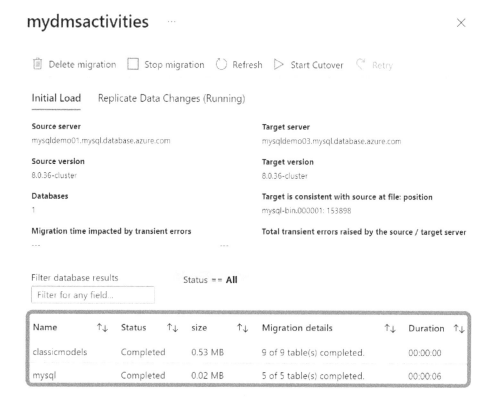

You will be automatically redirected to the Replicate Data Changes tab. The migration progress will be continuously updated on this screen, refreshing every 30 seconds:

🗑 Delete migration   ☐ Stop migration   ⟳ Refresh   ▷ Start Cutover   ⟲ Retry

Initial Load | Replicate Data Changes (Running) |

Source server
mysqldemo01.mysql.database.azure.com

Target server
mysqldemo03.mysql.database.azure.com

Source version
8.0.36-cluster

Target version
8.0.36-cluster

Activity status
Running

Starting binlog file: position
mysql-bin.000001: 153898

Migration details

Replication start time   4/29/2024, 23:49:17

Duration   00:04:54

Selected databases

classicmodels

Migration progress

Timestamp of last committed binlog event   4/29/2024, 23:53:47

Position of last committed binlog event   mysql-bin.000001: 153898

Seconds behind source ⓘ   0

Number of rows inserted   0

Number of rows updated   0

Number of rows deleted   0

Number of query events processed ⓘ   0

Number of write row events processed ⓘ   0

Number of update row events processed ⓘ   0

Number of delete row events processed ⓘ   0

Migration health information

Warnings encountered   0

Is currently retrying   No

Migration time impacted by transient errors   00:00:00

Source retries   0

Target retries   0

Other retries   0

Then, click Refresh to update the display and view the replication data changes:

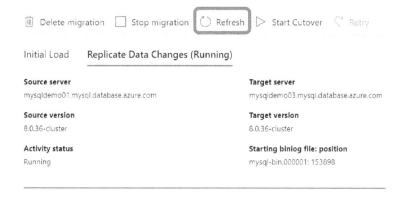

Navigate to the Start Cutover tab located at the top of the migration activity screen:

Follow the steps in the cutover window before you perform the cutover:

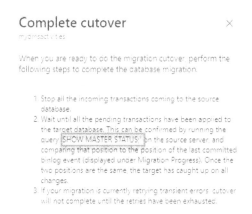

After completing all the necessary steps, click Confirm and then Apply. Check the status of the cutover. It will indicate 100% when finished:

Cutover progress: Completed

100%

Perform Post-Migration Activities

Once the migration has finished, it is essential to complete the following post-migration activities:

Sanity testing
> Perform sanity testing of the application against the target database to ensure a successful migration.

Update connection string
> Update the connection string to point to the new flexible server.

Delete the source server
> After ensuring application continuity, delete the source single server.

Scale back the target server
> If you scaled up the target flexible server for faster migration, scale it back by selecting the appropriate compute size and compute tier based on the source single server's pricing tier and vCores, as indicated in Table 13-2.

Table 13-2. Server pricing tier

Single server pricing tier	Single server vCores	Flexible server compute size	Flexible server compute tier
Basic	1	Burstable	Standard_B1s
Basic	2	Burstable	Standard_B2s
General Purpose	4	General Purpose	Standard_D4ds_v4
General Purpose	8	General Purpose	Standard_D8ds_v4

Implement Best Practices for Performing a Migration

To ensure a successful migration, we recommend implementing the following best practices:

1. Test the migration in a non-production environment before migrating your production database.

2. Back up your source database before starting the migration process.

3. Monitor the migration closely to identify and address any issues that arise.

---

4. Use the latest version of DMS and ensure that your source and target servers are running a supported version of MySQL.

5. Implement performance optimizations, such as using the General Purpose or Memory Optimized tiers for your flexible server, and enabling binary logging and GTID.

Migrate Large Databases to Azure Database for MySQL

When it comes to migrating sizable databases to Azure Database for MySQL, employing tools like `mydumper` and `myloader` can be a game-changer. Let's delve into the process of seamlessly transferring your extensive data sets by using these efficient tools.

When migrating MySQL databases exceeding 1 TB in size to Azure Database for MySQL, we advise you use community tools like `mydumper`. These tools offer several advantages, including:

- To reduce migration time, parallelism is used.

- Expensive character set conversion routines are avoided for better performance.

- The output format separates tables, metadata, etc. into separate files, making it easy to view and parse data. Consistency is maintained across all threads by keeping a snapshot.

- Accurate primary and replica log positions are ensured.

- Perl Compatible Regular Expressions (PCRE) are supported for specifying database and table inclusions and exclusions, making management easy.

- Unlike other logical migration tools, schema and data are handled together, eliminating the need for separate handling.

Before initiating the migration process for your MySQL database, it's essential you first set up an Azure Database for MySQL server via the Azure portal. Additionally, you'll need to create an Azure Virtual Machine running Linux through the Azure portal.

 If your source is on premises and has a high-bandwidth connection to Azure (using ExpressRoute), consider installing the tool on an Azure VM.

If there are challenges in the bandwidth between the source and target, consider installing `mydumper` near the source and `myloader` near the target server. Use tools like AzCopy to move the data from on premises or other cloud solutions to Azure.

To install the MySQL client, follow these steps:

Update the package index on the Azure VM running Linux as follows:

```
$ sudo apt update
```

Install the MySQL client package:

```
$ sudo apt install mysql-client
```

To install mydumper/myloader, follow these steps:

Download the appropriate package for mydumper/myloader based on your OS distribution. To do this, run the following command:

```
$ wget
https://github.com/maxbube/mydumper/releases/download/v0.10.1/
mydumper_0.10.1-2.$(lsb_release
-cs)_amd64.deb
```

> The $(lsb_release -cs) command can help to identify your distribution.

Install the downloaded *.deb* package by running the following command:

```
$ dpkg -i mydumper_0.10.1-2.$(lsb_release -cs)_amd64.deb
```

> The command used to install the package will vary depending on your Linux distribution, as different installers are used. mydumper/myloader is available for the following distributions: Fedora, Red-Hat, Ubuntu, Debian, CentOS, openSUSE, and macOS.

Create a Backup

To create a backup using mydumper, run the following command, replacing *server name*, *username*, *Password*, and *Db_name* with the appropriate values for your database:

```
$ mydumper --host=<servername> --user=<username> --password=<Password>
--outputdir=./backup --rows=100000 --compress --build-empty-files
--threads=16 --compress-protocol --trx-consistency-only --ssl --regex
'^(<Db_name>\.)' -L mydumper-logs.txt
```

You can find more information on other options available with `mydumper` by running the command `mydumper --help`. For further details, refer to the `mydumper/myloader` documentation.

To dump multiple databases in parallel, modify the regex variable in the command above as follows: regex `'^(DbName1\.|DbName2\.)'`.

Restore Your Database

To restore a database that was previously backed up using `mydumper`, use the following command:

```
$ myloader --host=<servername> --user=<username> --password=<Password>
--directory=./backup --queries-per-transaction=500 --threads=16
--compress-protocol --ssl --verbose=3 -e 2>myloader-logs.txt
```

To learn about other options available for myloader, run this command: `myloader --help`.

After restoring the database, it's important to verify the data consistency between the original and restored databases.

Conclusion

This chapter provided a comprehensive guide to kickstarting Microsoft Azure Database for MySQL, covering crucial aspects like choosing the right MySQL option, securing instances, and managing read replicas. We included practical steps using Cloud Shell and CLI, enhancing Azure navigation. The chapter also detailed database migrations through the DMS, including insights into configuring settings, monitoring, and best practices.

This chapter has equipped you with the knowledge you need for a seamless transition to Azure Database for MySQL, whether you're a beginner or experienced cloud user.

Wrapping Up

In navigating the comprehensive landscape of MySQL 8, this book offers extensive coverage of topics essential for database administrators, developers, and anyone seeking a deep understanding of MySQL's intricacies. From the fundamental installation and configuration processes to advanced topics such as transaction data dictionary, InnoDB architecture, backup and recovery strategies, security considerations, and performance tuning, each chapter has contributed to a holistic comprehension of MySQL.

The journey takes us through the cloud, exploring MySQL on AWS RDS and Aurora, as well as Microsoft Azure MySQL, shedding light on the intricacies of cloud-based database management. The book provides insights into HA and scalability concepts and monitoring and management tools, and offers practical advice on facilitating major MySQL upgrades.

As we conclude this exploration, we hope that our blend of knowledge and practical, hands-on guidance has made this book a valuable resource for both beginners and experienced professionals in the realm of MySQL. Whether you are a database administrator aiming to optimize performance, a developer seeking to implement robust security measures, or a cloud enthusiast navigating MySQL in cloud environments, the wealth of information in this book equips you with the tools and understanding needed to master MySQL 8.

Index

About the Authors

Arunjith Aravindan is a highly experienced professional with over 14 years of open source and MySQL consulting expertise. Holding a master's of computer application (MCA) postgraduate degree, he joined Percona in 2014 as a consultant, where he collaborates with managed services customers to establish and maintain robust MySQL infrastructures. Arunjith specializes in performance analysis and optimization of MySQL, RDS, Aurora, and Azure, query optimization, troubleshooting, as well as high availability and scalability. His dedication to following industry developments is reflected in his blogs and speaking engagements. Arunjith's exceptional technical communication skills, coupled with his passion for open source and MySQL technologies, distinguish him in his field.

Jeyaram Ayyalusamy is a seasoned professional with over 18 years of expertise in open source and Oracle database technologies. His proficiency spans MySQL, PostgreSQL, MSSQL, and cloud platforms such as AWS, Oracle Cloud OCI, and Azure, with a focus on performance tuning and high availability. As a project manager at Doyensys since 2014, he oversees enterprise application projects, ensuring that clients leverage innovation for success. Jeyaram holds certifications in Oracle, MySQL, AWS, and ITIL, and is committed to continuous learning. His passion for open source and diverse technologies, as well as his master's degree in information technology, makes him a valuable asset in managing complex IT projects. Jeyaram's extensive experience and dedication make him a knowledgeable and indispensable professional.

Colophon

The animal on the cover of *Hands-On MySQL Administration* is a common kingfisher (*Alcedo atthis*), a small kingfisher with seven subspecies across Eurasia and North America. It lives on the shores of lakes, ponds, and streams, as well as in wetlands.

The bird's most noticeable trait is its bright blue and orange coloring. Its wings, back, and head are blue, and it has small red feet. The male's beak is jet black; the female's is black on top and brown on bottom. The common kingfisher flutters its wings quickly when hunting for prey in the water. It eats about 60% of its body weight in small fish, crustacea, and crabs each day. The common kingfisher is sensitive to river pollution and has an IUCN Red List conservation status of Least Concern. Many of the animals on O'Reilly covers are endangered; all of them are important to the world.

The cover illustration is by Karen Montgomery, based on an antique line engraving from *British Birds*. The series design is by Edie Freedman, Ellie Volckhausen, and Karen Montgomery. The cover fonts are Gilroy Semibold and Guardian Sans. The text font is Adobe Minion Pro; the heading font is Adobe Myriad Condensed; and the code font is Dalton Maag's Ubuntu Mono.